American Egyptologist

American
Egyptologist

The Life of James Henry Breasted
and the Creation of His Oriental Institute

Jeffrey Abt

University of Chicago Press
Chicago and London

JEFFREY ABT is associate professor of art and art history at Wayne State University and the author of *A Museum on the Verge: A Socioeconomic History of the Detroit Institute of Arts, 1882–2000*.

The University of Chicago Press, Chicago 60637
The University of Chicago Press, Ltd., London
© 2011 by The University of Chicago
All rights reserved. Published 2011.
Printed in the United States of America

20 19 18 17 16 15 14 13 12   2 3 4 5

ISBN-13: 978-0-226-00110-4   (cloth)
ISBN-10: 0-226-00110-5   (cloth)

Material in chapter 7 was first published in Jeffrey Abt, "Drawing over Photographs: James H. Breasted and the Scientizing of Egyptian Epigraphy, 1895–1928," *Visual Resources* 14, no. 1 (1998): 19–69. Material in chapter 8 was first published in Jeffrey Abt, "The Breasted-Rockefeller Egyptian Museum Project: Philanthropy, Cultural Imperialism, and National Resistance," *Art History* 19, no. 4 (December 1996): 551–72; and Jeffrey Abt, "Toward a Historian's Laboratory: The Breasted-Rockefeller Museum Projects in Egypt, Palestine, and America," *Journal of the American Research Center in Egypt* 33 (1996): 173–94 (now available through JSTOR). The author is grateful to the journals' editors for permission to use these materials here.

Library of Congress Cataloging-in-Publication Data

Abt, Jeffrey.
    American Egyptologist : the life of James Henry Breasted and the creation of his Oriental Institute / Jeffrey Abt.
        p.   cm.
    Includes bibliographical references and index.
    ISBN-13: 978-0-226-00110-4 (cloth : alk. paper)
    ISBN-10: 0-226-00110-5 (cloth : alk. paper) 1. Breasted, James Henry, 1865–1935.
2. University of Chicago. Oriental Institute—History 3. Archaeology—Egypt—
History. I. Title.
    D15.B67A26 2011
    932.0072'02—dc22
    [B]
            2011012848

♾ This paper meets the requirements of ANSI/NISO Z39.48-1992
(Permanence of Paper).

To my parents

Arthur Abt and Lottie W. Abt

for introducing me to the wonders of museums

and travel to distant places

Contents

Maps

Epigraph

Among the stately and polished grave markers in Greenwood Cemetery is a stone that looks out of place. At a distance it seems to be unfinished and abandoned, but as one approaches, it turns out to be roughly hewn from a mottled gray granite. The cemetery is near the center of Rockford, Illinois, a modest American town nestled among the gently rolling hills of the nation's heartland. Like cemeteries in many older communities, Greenwood is on a high place, a rounded bluff above the river that shaped it and the verdant land beyond. Rockford was settled during the country's westward expansion when early-nineteenth-century pioneers migrated along the most easily traversed land and water routes. The town's name is a prosaic acknowledgment of its location. It's alongside a readily forded bend in the Rock River, a crossing point that made it an ideal junction for the era's growing commerce.

Rockford's leaders plotted out Greenwood Cemetery on land where mourners could console themselves with a lovely vista over their homes and the neighboring hills. As the town expanded, however, the cemetery's once-comforting views were obstructed by residential neighborhoods and business districts that surrounded and extended beyond Greenwood's arbors. Rockford became a manufacturing center for furniture and farm equipment and grew into a tran-

Fig. E.1 Greenwood Cemetery, Rockford, Illinois. Photograph by author, June 2009.

sit hub when railroad lines linked it with surrounding cities, including Chicago about eighty miles southeast. Visitors to Greenwood Cemetery can glean traces of this history from tantalizingly cryptic gravestone inscriptions memorializing the lives of those buried there.

If one walks around the out-of-place stone, it reveals a smoothed and engraved face with details about another of Rockford's one-time residents:

UNDER THIS GRANITE BLOCK FROM
ASSUAN EGYPT LIE THE ASHES OF
JAMES HENRY BREASTED
HISTORIAN
ARCHEOLOGIST
BORN IN ROCKFORD ILLINOIS
AUGUST 27 1865
DIED IN NEW YORK CITY
DECEMBER 2 1935

The stone is not only hewn in an uncommon fashion, it's foreign to American soil as well. Yet the differences separating this stone from its neighbors end there. It still marks a burial place and bears witness to a person's life, and its inscription follows the conventions typical of gravestones in this part of the world. Like legends on most grave markers, it offers little more than the barest facts. There are birth and death locations, the dates of each, and a few words hinting at the person's life. When the inscription is considered alongside the unusual origins of the stone, however, it invites closer scrutiny.

To make sense of an object like this requires something akin to the skills of an epigrapher, a scholar who specializes in the study of inscriptions. At minimum one ought to know the inscription's language and the nuances of its use. A sense of the historical context in which it was engraved and the cultural import of its physical expression are important too. At its best, epigraphy is sensitive to the complex interplay of text, context, and material that gives rise to a meaning greater than mere words alone. In this case, the inscription's opening lines tell us the stone was transported over 6,500 miles from Egypt. For those conversant with the ancient history of Egypt, the reference to Assuan—usually spelled Aswan today—hints at more. A relatively small town along the Nile River about 425 miles south of Cairo, Aswan is home to a number of ancient sites dating to as early as 3000 BCE. Among the oldest are quarries from which granite was hewn for towering obelisks and statuary found among ancient temples hundreds of miles north of Aswan. To Egyptologists, scholars who study ancient Egypt, the granite used for this tombstone is a vivid reference to the grandeur of ancient Egyptian art and architecture and to the engineering genius behind the quarrying and transport of this exceedingly hard and heavy stone. The selection of Aswan granite for an American grave marker signifies that Breasted's historical and archaeological studies were pursued in Egypt.

The duration of Breasted's seventy-year life was long for his time. Only about 10 percent of his fellow citizens born in 1865 would have lived until 1935. He would have been among a relative handful of Americans whose lives spanned the extraordinary changes that reshaped the country between the middle of the nineteenth century and the first few decades of the twentieth century. Breasted grew up surrounded by adults who had just lived through a civil war that very nearly destroyed the United States. He lived long enough to experience the industrialization and urbanization of his country, a world war, and a worldwide economic collapse. He witnessed the modernization of daily life with the advent of electric lighting and appliances, telephones and radios, and automobile and airplane travel. As remarkable as these changes were, equally dramatic would have been the differences he encountered between the lush midwestern landscape of his youth and the barren expanses of Egypt, between churches in towns like Rockford and ancient temples in Luxor. More startling yet would have been Breasted's crossing from the relentless, secularizing modernism of his nation as it entered the "American century" to the remnants of a civilization whose

Fig E.2 Cover, *Time* magazine, 14 December 1931. ©1931 Time Inc. Used under license.

language and religion could hardly be more ancient. The odd stone with its terse inscription conveys only so much.

For local-history enthusiasts in Rockford today, the stone might seem an insufficient memorial to one of the town's most accomplished sons. Its papers followed the high points of Breasted's career during his lifetime, prompted in part by marks of distinction rendered from afar—like a *Time* magazine cover story—that brought to local news desks and mailboxes word of his rising national and international fame. Citizens were no doubt intrigued by stories of Breasted's association with John D. Rockefeller Jr., one of the great philanthropists of the era, or Teddy Roosevelt, or government officials from Washington to London to Cairo. Students in Rockford schools, like their peers across America, were likely introduced to ancient Near Eastern history through textbooks filled with vivid illustrations he selected and felicitous expressions he coined, such as "Fertile Crescent," to render ancient and distant cultures more accessible.[1]

For others, the comparatively small gravestone might suggest the extent to which Breasted's renown has faded with the passage of time. Just a few of his scholarly works remain useful to Egyptologists today, and only a handful of his insights continue to circulate through the more enduring writings of figures like Sigmund Freud or less well-known authors. Breasted's most lasting contribution to the field of his endeavors may be similarly indirect. He established the Oriental Institute at the University of Chicago—a museum and research center that has become one the world's most prominent and productive institutions for ancient Near Eastern exploration, research, publishing, and teaching. Although Breasted's name has all but disappeared from collective memory, the institute's continuing accomplishments have connected the university with the ancient Near East in the public mind. Near the beginning of the 1981 blockbuster *Raiders of the Lost Ark*, the main character, Indiana Jones, mentions studying archaeology at the University of Chicago. When the film's creator, George Lucas, was asked about the reference, he replied that he selected Chicago because he believed it was "one of the best universities for archaeological study."[2]

Whether or not the somewhat misshapen, coarsely chiseled stone in Greenwood Cemetery is a fitting memorial to Breasted, it conveys the challenges posed by the ancient Egyptian inscriptions he devoted his life to deciphering. It's not enough to read the legend engraved on this stone. One has to consider the context in which it was written, the modern society in which Breasted dwelled, the ancient civilization that occupied his intellectual life, and the scholarly disciplines through which he articulated his findings. Much like the hieroglyphic inscriptions Breasted studied throughout his life, the text engraved on this stone poses many questions.

Note to the Reader

There are some unavoidable spelling and usage inconsistencies in *American Egyptologist*. Breasted usually spelled *archaeology* as "archeology." I follow the former, more current version except when quoting Breasted or his peers using the latter. They also designated ancient dates as "BC" ("before Christ") and "AD" (*anno Domini*, "in the year of the Lord"). Unless quoting them, I designate comparable dates as "BCE" ("before the Common Era") or "CE" ("of the Common Era"). Although Breasted and his contemporaries referred to the geographical area of their work as the "Orient" or "ancient Orient," when I write about the region in modern times, I refer to it as the "Middle East," and when discussing it as the subject of Breasted's and others' research, I refer to it as the "ancient Near East" or "Near East." My approach is guided by the practice of scholars such as Susan Pollock and Reinhard Bernbeck, as explained in their introduction to *Archaeologies of the Middle East: Critical Perspectives*, edited by Pollock and Bernbeck (Oxford: Blackwell Publishing, 2005), 3.

The transliteration of pharaohs' names and dating of dynasties are more settled today than in Breasted's time. When quoting him, I leave his names and dates as they are, and when I write about them directly, I follow usually the modern standards in John Baines and Jaromir Malek, *Cultural Atlas of Ancient Egypt*, revised edition (Oxford: Checkmark Books, 2000) with one exception: In Breasted's era scholars transliterated Amenhotep IV's renamed self as "Ikhnaton," which is rendered "Akhenaten" today. Because of the frequency with which I quote and discuss Breasted's and others' considerations of the pharaoh, I employ their transliteration to avoid confusion. In all instances, pharaohs' dates are for their reigns only and are approximate until the Ptolemaic period.

The rendering of place names in the Middle East has also changed since Breasted's time. If his transliterations are reasonably close to current versions, I use them. But if modern transliterations are noticeably different, I turn for guidance to two sources: *Merriam-Webster's Geographical Dictionary*, 3rd edition (Springfield, MA: Merriam-Webster, 2001), and *The Times Atlas of the World*, 6th comprehensive edition (London: Times Books, 1981).

Money figures prominently in Breasted's story, and the question often arises, What would these sums be in today's terms? In most instances I utilize an excellent website-based conversion tool—cited at "CPI" in the abbreviations list at the beginning of the endnotes—to provide modern equivalents in the notes. For example, in 1907 Breasted proposed a plan costing between $354,450 and $434,450. The endnote includes the statement "$354,450 and $434,450 = $8.35 and $10.20 million CPI 2009," indicating the equivalents in today's economy. "CPI," the Consumer Price Index, was used as the conversion basis because it is the most relevant for this book, and 2009 is the most recent year for which I could obtain modern equivalents. Please note, however, that these numbers are rough approximations only and should be regarded with caution.

The Oriental Institute Publications Office is reissuing Breasted's and the institute's works as free digital-file downloads. If downloadable versions of works I cite are available, I provide links in the endnotes. The institute's list of digitally converted and printed books is vast and steadily growing, and readers are encouraged to peruse it at http://oi.uchicago.edu/research/pubs/catalog/ (accessed August 2010).

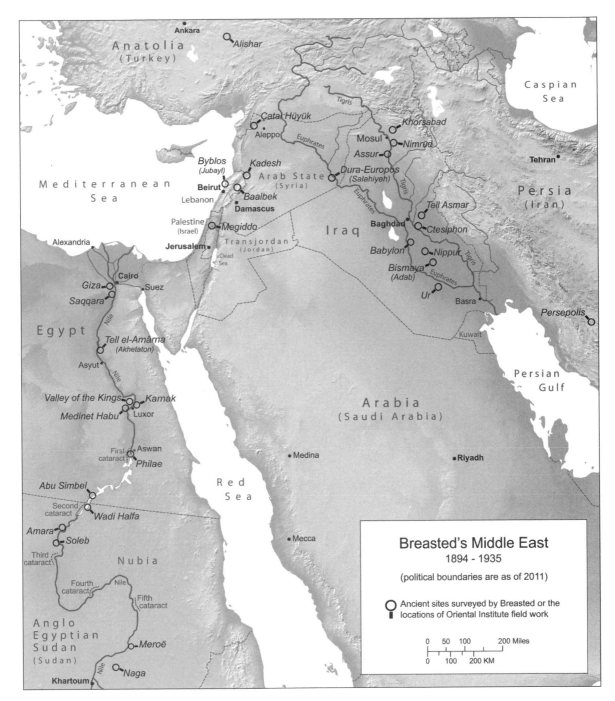

Map 1

1

Equipment for a Great Work

Pharmacist, Minister, Egyptologist

The third of Charles and Harriet Breasted's four children, James Henry was an active and inquisitive youngster. He grew up fishing and camping, and he played sports, including baseball, with abandon. His "catching pitched balls without a mask" resulted in his nose being broken in two places, injuries that remained faintly evident for the rest of his life. Around the age of five he somehow learned of a nearby school he wanted to attend. Overcoming his mother's objections that he was too young, Breasted began at "Mrs. Squire's School—a single room in a stone house above the Rock River," named for the elderly woman who ran it. He remembered Rockford as a "very pious town," an impression reinforced by his religious upbringing. Sunday school was "one of the greatest things" of Breasted's life, and many years later he recalled "so well the stories—they were really history—of the Bible lands" to which he owed "an immeasurable amount of inspiration."

Charles Breasted, who began his work life as an apprentice to a "master tinsmith," became a successful merchant in Rockford and then established a large hardware store in downtown Chicago. He was poised for considerable prosperity when he lost the store in the

1871 Chicago fire. The devastation reduced him to the station of a traveling sales-
man for the Michigan Stove Company, a loss of independence, stature, and income that deeply affected his outlook and health. In 1873 he moved the family
to Downers Grove, Illinois, then a small town just over twenty miles southwest
of Chicago, to be closer to the train network that connected him to his territories
in Illinois and Wisconsin. He built a home on a seven-acre property the family
called "The Pines," from which many of "Jimmy" Breasted's earliest memories
derived: raising asparagus to market in Chicago; milking cows; collecting birds'
eggs, butterflies, and coins; and handcrafting furniture. He also took up drawing
around this time, apparently with the intent of augmenting his collections with
drawings of "animals and objects." He drew a variety of subjects from about his
twelfth year on, launching a lifelong interest in developing his observation skills
as well as his lettering and rendering ability. A nearby train station, where an
engineer invited Breasted to ride in a locomotive cab, inspired his first ambition,
to become a railroad engineer.[1]

For many summers, from his childhood through his midtwenties, Breasted
returned to Rockford, where he stayed with a close family friend of both his
father's and mother's families, Theodocia Backus, or "Aunt Theodocia." By then
a widow of modest means, she nonetheless devoted herself to his success. The
summers he spent with her were filled with "grooming Dobbin, her carriage
horse, mowing lawns, running errands, pumping the church organ, singing in
the choir, and [assisting her] in a multitude of other thoughtful ways."

But Breasted was also mischievous. He could "throw snowballs with fiendish
accuracy, especially at top hats on Sundays"; he had a "genius for inflicting enrag-
ing penalties upon mean or unkind neighbors"; and during his teenage years he
staged a prank that entered the family annals. He and a friend found a section
of wooden conduit that they persuaded a local blacksmith to cap at one end and
reinforce with metal straps every few inches. They outfitted it with a mount
and wheels, transforming the thing into a formidable-looking toy cannon that
became genuinely dangerous when they discovered that wooden croquet balls fit
the barrel perfectly. They saved their pennies, purchased containers of gunpow-
der and fuses, and introduced their ordnance early on the Fourth of July in Rockford's courthouse square. They set off a few harmless blasts, rousing neighbors,
before a final shot blew out a window in a nearby house and the cannon recoiled,
scattering an angry crowd that was gathering. Breasted confessed his part in the
mayhem to Backus, who, though a deeply moral woman, usually found his antics
humorous. She soothed Rockford's peeved citizens, paid for damage wreaked by
the fusiliers, and attempted to sternly admonish her playful charge.

At a young age Breasted acquired a passion for books, nurtured by his father,
who read aloud to him such works as Dickens's *Pickwick Papers* and *Master Hum-
phrey's Clock*. Though not formally educated, Charles Breasted assembled a mod-

Fig. 1.1 Layard, *Discoveries in the Ruins of Nineveh and Babylon* (1859), 113. Public domain, reproduction by author.

est library, where his son discovered such childhood classics as *Robinson Crusoe* and *The Swiss Family Robinson*. The boy became a voracious reader, silently moving his lips as he read—a habit he never lost—and grew into more challenging works by Plutarch, Shakespeare, and Vasari. Particular favorites included James Fenimore Cooper's *The Last of the Mohicans* and Richard F. Burton's multivolume *Arabian Nights*, though he must have read the latter in his twenties because it was first published between 1885 and 1888.

Among the readings of Breasted's youth was his father's copy of Austen Henry Layard's *Discoveries in the Ruins of Nineveh and Babylon*. Published in 1859, it recounts Layard's expeditions and finds, including the monumental winged bulls now displayed in the British Museum. The hefty, nearly seven-hundred-page book, written expressly for popular consumption, is richly illustrated with maps, the plans of ancient temples, engravings of everything from pottery to bas-reliefs, and tables of cuneiform inscriptions (figure 1.1). But among the Breasteds' books, the Bible was far and away their favorite and most frequently read text. It was also the preeminent source of ideas and values that each of them, including James, quoted as they navigated the challenges of modern life.[2]

Breasted felt his "early 'education' was wholly haphazard and without pattern." After Mrs. Squire's School in Rockford, he attended a "two-room red brick" school near his family's home in Downers Grove until September 1880, shortly after he turned fifteen. About that time, having graduated from high school, he became interested in North-Western College, located in Naperville, Illinois, about seven miles west of his home. The college's appeal was due to a "scientific exhibition" mounted by a professor of natural sciences that made a "profound impression . . . upon [Breasted's] youthful but highly receptive mind." He enrolled in the college and flourished. Years later a classmate recalled that Breasted

> soon won his way into the hearts of his fellow students and won the confidence of the faculty who looked upon him as an ideal student looking forward to a brilliant career. He had a wiry makeup always bubbling over with energy, he was always neat in appearance and profoundly impressed us with the loftiness of his . . . ideals. Although he was one of the youngest members of the class he taught us the art of studying. He was interested in the deeper aspects of Nature as revealed by science and mathematics. He never regarded an assignment met until he had thoroughly mastered it. In mathematics he often wrote out . . . full demonstrations which staggered the other members of his class. While some . . . were content to give an approximate translation of a passage in the ancient classics he never passed it by until he had rendered it into immaculate English. Even we neophytes listened with intense pleasure to his recitations.

Despite his apparent robustness, Breasted was "troubled by a serious illness" in early spring 1881 and dropped out of school for a brief time. Instead of returning to North-Western after his recovery, however, he pursued an "apprenticeship in pharmacy" that he thought might advance his longer-term "ambitions in chemistry or botany." During 1882–83 he enrolled at the Chicago College of Pharmacy and did some pharmacy clerking on the side, first in his brother-in-law's business in Rochelle, Illinois, about six miles south of his family's earlier home in Rockford, and then back in Downers Grove.

By fall 1883, he returned to North-Western, picking up where he'd left off in the "Latin & Scientific Course," now with the notion of specializing "solely in literature." He remained there until spring 1885, shifting at some point to the "Classical" department with a concentration in Latin. Breasted took more courses in mathematics, the natural sciences, and philosophy, as well as one in "Surveying" and another intriguingly titled "Comics." He spent his summers working in a "small country bank," where he acquired bookkeeping skills as his responsibilities grew from back-room clerking to window teller.

He also found time in the summer of 1884 to visit family on the East Coast, a trip that took him through Washington, DC. His letters home, teeming with descriptions of scenic vistas and stimulating conversations, reveal his growing observational skills and ability to write vivid narratives rich with detail and nu-

Fig. 1.2 Breasted's pencil drawing, "My Reading Corner," 26 September 1887. Courtesy of the Oriental Institute, University of Chicago.

ance. While in Washington, Breasted made the usual tourist stops. Among them, the US Patent Office building's extensive "model rooms" filled with miniatures of inventions impressed him the most. After describing their size and number and the cases in them, he continued: "Every shelf is filled with models. It would take a lifetime to see them all. All models of the same kind are placed together, that is reapers with reapers & scales with scales. Being curious I counted the number of different models of patent fruit jar-covers, with which one shelf was full, & found there were 246."[3]

In fall 1885 Breasted had another change of heart, returned to the Chicago College of Pharmacy, and completed his pharmacy degree the following spring. His brother-in-law, who now had a business in Omaha, Nebraska, invited Breasted to work there as a pharmacist. He settled into the new job by fall but lasted only through early spring 1887, when he returned to Downers Grove at his family's behest. Perhaps his brother-in-law's religious laxity, such as selling cigars on Sunday, contributed to Breasted's return. He looked for work around Downers Grove without success, began exploring the purchase—with his father's assistance—of a pharmacy in a nearby town, and was about to acquire a drug store in Chicago when he suddenly fell ill again. Breasted convalesced the following summer and early fall in Rockford with Theodocia Backus, whiling away his time drawing and reading (figure 1.2). Her care included the spiritual as well as physical, and when

Breasted returned home in October 1887, it was with an entirely new vocation in mind.[4]

Aunt Theodocia and her husband were Seventh-Day Adventists, but after he died, she became a Congregationalist, the denomination in which Breasted was raised. The Congregationalist Church was among the more liberal American Protestant denominations, deeply engaged in social action by the 1880s and striving to become a "non-sectarian" community, "a union of Christians who are not asked to renounce their previous denominational teachings but . . . to join in a simple covenant pledging cooperation and fellowship." Yet Backus remained faithful to the more conservative values of the Seventh-Day Adventists, and she had the zeal of a proselytizer, too, seizing the opportunity of Breasted's care to steer him toward what she believed was his true calling: a Christian ministry. She counseled him on questions of personal morality and faith and encouraged his attendance at church and at least one tent-revival gathering—then a popular means of rallying the faithful. Backus's attentions were effective and even show up in Breasted's drawings from the time (figures 1.3 and 1.4). Thus primed, Breasted attended a life-changing meeting at the Downers Grove Congregational Church, where, Breasted wrote, "President Fiske of [Andover] Theological Seminary . . . forcefully said something about striving for high goals, about relentlessly making one's ambition go 'up—*up*—UP.' . . . The way in which he separately emphasized those three words impressed me more than anything else had." Around this time, Breasted recalled, "it suddenly flashed into my mind as if conveyed by an electric spark, that I ought to preach the gospel." But the decision did not settle easily: "I fought all this for nearly two weeks . . . with every power and faculty within me, but . . . finally I gave up. . . . Then came a struggle such as I have never dreamed of; . . . to tear out selfish ambition and ride down worldly desires. I was in a wild tumult, . . . like a tree bending to the ground before a mighty wind. But the calm came; and now . . . what have been my dearest hopes are dead ashes and out of them has sprung a new, a holier ambition."

In late October 1887, and now just over twenty-two years old, Breasted began taking classes in Hebrew and Greek, probably on a part-time, nonmatriculated basis, at the Chicago Theological Seminary, then located by Union Park on Chicago's near west side. It was affiliated with the Congregationalists and often referred to as the "Congregational Institute" or "Union Park Theological Seminary." Breasted was proud he could attend at no cost to his parents, but even so, they sold their property in Downers Grove and took an apartment near the seminary to remain near him. Meanwhile, Breasted had yet to complete his baccalaureate work at North-Western. He apparently tied up the loose ends during 1887–88 while also taking classes at the seminary. For some reason, however, he did not receive the North-Western degree until 1890.[5]

Of Breasted's seminary professors, one, Samuel Ives Curtiss, was especially

Fig. 1.3 Breasted's pencil drawing, "Some Rockford Steeples," 23 September 1887. Courtesy of the Oriental Institute, University of Chicago.

Fig. 1.4 Breasted's pencil drawing, "Tabernacle Tent, Cherry Valley," 24 August 1887. Cherry Valley, a hamlet a few miles southeast of Rockford, is now part of the larger town's metropolitan area. Courtesy of the Oriental Institute, University of Chicago.

influential. Curtiss was among the many Americans who, lured by the high intellectual standards and scholarly accomplishments of German universities earlier in the nineteenth century, crossed the Atlantic to pursue advanced training, earning a doctorate at the University of Leipzig in 1876. He studied with Franz Delitzsch, a Lutheran theologian and expert Hebraist of Jewish descent who is credited with helping develop the Higher Criticism in Old Testament studies. Some trace the origins of the Higher Criticism to the comparative, "literary-historical"—as distinguished from canonical or devotional—studies of the New Testament introduced by Erasmus. With the refinement and increasingly systematic application of these methods in the late eighteenth and early nineteenth centuries, the stage was set for scholars of Delitzsch's generation to begin using the techniques to disentangle the sources and chronological sequence of the most ancient of Old Testament writings: the Pentateuch.

Curtiss began teaching at the Chicago Theological Seminary in 1878. He introduced Old Testament literature and Hebrew into the seminary's curriculum, thus leading a handful of scholars working to transform American seminary education. At his formal installation in 1879 he pleaded "for a more thorough study of Semitic Languages," by 1882 he created a "prize division" in Hebrew to encourage students to master it, and he offered a correspondence course in Hebrew for prospective students. Curtiss taught "Hebrew as one would teach a modern language, where the effort should be not only to read but also speak the language," and he claimed to have been "one of the first, if not the first, to introduce the custom of sight reading." Under Curtiss's leadership, rigorous Hebrew training enabling students to study the Old Testament in its original language became one of the seminary's compulsory requirements. This emphasis on Old Testament studies found adherents among many within and outside American divinity schools, and Curtiss's efforts were yet more evidence that "Hebrew Scriptures had never been far from the consciousness of Americans who . . . interpreted their reality with Old Testament images." Curtiss's advocacy of Hebrew studies was certainly not without precedent in America: "God's Sacred Tongue" had been taught in non-Jewish circles from colonial times.[6]

Although Breasted had studied Latin at North-Western, his particular genius for acquiring languages became especially evident during 1887–88 when he learned Hebrew for the seminary's admission exam. He created hundreds of small flip cards with a Hebrew word on one side and its translation on the other to speed memorization, developing such mastery that he could recite entire passages from the Hebrew Old Testament, discuss their topics and historical contexts, and "think in Hebrew." Breasted's command of the language, after just a year's study, earned him one of Curtiss's Hebrew-exam prizes in fall 1888. Breasted caught the professor's attention for other reasons as well, for he called Breasted to a meeting and urged him to consider a career in ancient Near Eastern studies, perhaps Egyptology (the study of ancient Egyptian language and history), "a vacant field" in America. As Breasted recalled their conversation many years later, Curtiss correctly sensed his student was "wavering away from the ministry," telling him: "You are torn . . . because the pulpit appeals emotionally to your imaginative and somewhat dramatic temperament. But intellectually, it confounds you with doubts which will only grow. . . . You have the passion for truth which belongs to the scholar." In time Breasted came to agree. He later found a quote from the Orientalist and journal editor William Hayes Ward that captured Breasted's dawning realization: "I would rather devote my life to research and the pursuit of truth than to anything else."

The passion for truth Curtiss sensed in Breasted, and the unsettling doubts left in truth's wake, surfaced in a conversation around this time with his mother. He could not help but notice a pattern of differences between the King James rendition of Old Testament passages and their Hebrew sources. Noting the "scores and scores of such mistakes," Breasted said, "I could never be satisfied to preach on the basis of texts I know to be full of mistranslations. It's my nature to seek the sources of everything I study. The Hebrew writers fascinate me, I shall never be satisfied until I know their entire history and what forces created them."[7]

The methodology underlying Breasted's disquieting observations—comparison of texts, deference to sources in their original languages, concern for historical context—reveals that Curtiss had been introducing him to the Higher Criticism as well. Curtiss acknowledged the "highest ideals of study and literary activity" that he'd acquired in Germany, and he drew on them "to make contributions of importance to critical questions which were beginning to agitate the church in America." Those "critical questions" included what some Americans perceived as the Higher Criticism's frontal assault on the verity of Judeo-Christian sacred texts. The issues were aired in debates such as one provoked in 1888 by William Rainey Harper, then a young professor of Semitic languages and biblical literature at Yale University, over the "multiple authorial sources in the Book of Genesis and . . . the role of an unknown Redactor who edited the divergent sources into a uniform narrative."

Harper and like-minded scholars were refining "what became and remains the classical documentary paradigm for the authorship of Genesis." It was the result of efforts to answer such questions as why Genesis contains two distinct creation stories. Based on close linguistic analyses of Genesis, scholars showed that two different "authorial sources" were responsible for the competing stories as well as other passages and that a third source redacted the various strands into what is now the book of Genesis. The "documentary paradigm" supplanted theological interpretations of the Bible with linguistic analyses and in so doing threatened to transform it from sacred writ to secular text. Devotees of the Higher Criticism like Delitzsch and Harper, and no doubt Curtiss too, did not intend to undermine believers' faith in sacred scripture. Rather, they wished to expand knowledge of the Old and New Testaments with the new tools of modern philology and historical scholarship. As Harper wrote of Delitzsch, they were attempting to provide a rigorous introduction to the Old Testament "without denying the essential truth of the history, and without surrendering the reverence [owed] to the Holy Scriptures." They wanted to lead their coreligionists from "an unthinking to a rational faith." Harper's observation might have been shaped by his own concern that, as Breasted later commented, "this altered appreciation of Hebrew literature should be widely understood by all intelligent people without any disturbance of faith, and without any of the painful and trying destructive criticism which we ourselves had been obliged to confront."

It was into this arena of philological science and theological modernization that Breasted unwittingly stepped when he applied his skills to comparing the King James Bible with its Hebrew source. Curtiss found in Breasted's probing mind and linguistic abilities a combination of gifts well suited to the cause of Higher Criticism, and he thus urged Breasted to study with Harper. Curtiss almost certainly met Harper a few years earlier when the latter was teaching at the Baptist Union Theological Seminary in Morgan Park, Illinois, about thirteen miles south of Chicago.[8]

Harper the Great

William Rainey Harper, like Breasted, hailed from rural America, was the son of a merchant of modest success, and was raised in the Christian faith. But Harper was also a child prodigy, entering a local college at the age of ten, where he was introduced to Hebrew, mastered it, and graduated at fourteen. His parents, concerned that he was too young to depart for more advanced studies, kept him at home, where he assisted with the family business, studied languages at the college, and by the age of sixteen began teaching Hebrew there as well. When he reached seventeen, his parents and teachers agreed the time was right for Harper to move on, and he entered Yale. He completed his doctorate in just two years with a dissertation titled "A Comparative Study of the Prepositions in Latin, Greek, Sanskrit, and Gothic."

At Yale, Harper worked most closely with William Dwight Whitney, a Sanskritist and linguist interested in comparative philology, who received his formal training in Germany a generation before Delitzsch. Whitney pursued a wide range of interests, wrote an astonishing number of publications, and was a leading presence in the American scholarly community, helping establish the American Philological Association in 1869 and contributing mightily to the activities and journal of the American Oriental Society, which was founded in 1842–43. Through Whitney, Harper was introduced to the ideas and methods of German scholarship and more generally "a concern to get at all the facts, the desire to make study a life work, and the use of an ancient language as a means of coming to terms with the modern world." From Whitney's example Harper also learned how scholarly organizations center professional communities and how their publications accelerate the dissemination of new knowledge. After completing his degree at Yale in 1875, Harper moved quickly through three teaching positions—at Macon College in Tennessee, Denison University in Ohio, and the Baptist Union Theological Seminary—before being called back to Yale in 1886.[9]

During his seminary tenure, Harper's interest in promoting "historico-grammatical" studies of the Old Testament narrowed to focus on Hebrew studies and pedagogy. In 1880 he started a Hebrew correspondence school for ministers and students, in 1881 a summer school, and in 1882 he established the American Institute of Hebrew "to unite teachers in his Hebrew movement into an organization." During the next few years, he established over thirty more summer schools in the East and Midwest providing instruction for over three hundred students each summer, his correspondence-study program serving hundreds and later thousands more with the help of grading assistants.

In 1882 he began publishing *The Hebrew Student*, a journal for educated readers and scholars alike that became "an important vehicle for bringing the Higher Criticism to America." Within a few years it evolved into *The Old and New Testament Student* and by 1893, *The Biblical World*, a popular-interest magazine that grew beyond its initial philological specialization to include biblical literature and ancient Near Eastern studies as well. With articles written for a general audience by scholars in biblical studies, Semitic languages, and archaeology, *The Biblical World* became one of America's most popular platforms for the Higher Criticism. By 1884, the scholarly content of *The Hebrew Student* was separated and published in a new journal, *Hebraica*, which became *The American Journal of Semitic Languages and Literatures* in 1895. *The Biblical World* became Harper's main platform for promoting the Higher Criticism among ordinary Americans, and *Hebraica* became a leading outlet for American scholars investigating the ancient Near East.[10]

Were his summer-school, correspondence-school, and editorial duties not enough, in 1883 Harper began teaching for the Chautauqua movement too. Named for the location of its origin, a town on the northwestern shore of Lake Chautauqua in western New York State, the movement combined the trappings of an academic festival with spiritual revivalism in a summer-retreat setting. At the time, it focused on adult education and the training of Sunday school teachers and church workers in a nondenominational if predominantly Protestant environment. Then headquartered amid a campus of companionable summer-camp-like buildings along the lake, the movement was physically as well as spiritually refreshing.

The variety of teachers, attendees, and visiting luminaries—the latter including Woodrow Wilson, Theodore Roosevelt, Frances Willard, Alonzo Stagg, and Booker T. Washington—suited Harper's vision of a community of learners united in pursuing the higher life through biblical studies. By all accounts, Harper was among the most captivating speakers. "No man ever lived," recalled a fellow teacher, "who could inspire a class with the enthusiasm that he could awaken over the study of Hebrew, could lead his students so far in the language in a six weeks' course, or could impart such broad and sane views of the Biblical literature." He became a major presence at Chautauqua and with the encouragement of its leaders had, by 1890, established its "comprehensive structure" of Schools of Sacred Literature that included six separate programs, among them the School of Hebrew and the Old Testament and the School of Semitic Languages and Ancient Versions.

Harper managed his many enterprises by driving "himself relentlessly." He was often "up at his desk by 4:00 a.m. [and] extended his working day until 10:30 or 11:00 at night." His most urgent priority was to bring a deeper and more critical understanding of scripture to as many Americans as possible. Complicating Harper's task, however, was his conviction that the Bible was "both the voice of God and the work of men." More than any other scholar of his time, in "his commanding messianic vision and his ambitious educational scheme Harper was a figurative embodiment of an era when modernist, ecumenical Protestantism sought to determine the values of the whole of American culture through education."[11]

Following Curtiss's recommendation, Breasted sought out Harper in 1889 while the professor was teaching at one of his summer schools in Evanston, Illinois. Curtiss had already told Harper of Breasted's gifts, and he encouraged Breasted to attend Yale that fall. Harper breezily offered to "arrange something" in the way of financial assistance, saying Breasted should "jot [Harper] a line of reminder a fortnight before the term opens." Yet this step was not to be lightly taken. Changing direction once again, moreover to pursue a career in scholarship and teaching in a field that was foreign to his experience, gave Breasted pause: "The richness and fullness of life as I saw it [then], were very much embittered by anxieties and complete unfamiliarity with the road I was attempting to travel. A single friend who knew the road, and could have put a reassuring hand on my shoulder from time to time, would have saved me years of suffering."

Then there was the question of money. Breasted sensed Harper's offer would not cover his expenses, and he looked to his parents for help. He had financed his seminary studies by forming a musical quartet—he had a "fine tenor voice" and played the flute—that earned an average of ten to fifteen dollars an evening for its frequent performances. In his second year Breasted earned additional income by substituting for pastors in Naperville and the Chicago area. But he feared that, lacking connections in New Haven, he could not rely on such schemes and would need even more money to pay living as well as tuition expenses. Breasted struggled with the formidable task of explaining yet a new career plan *and* enlisting his family's aid, all for a field that offered uncertain job prospects. Though he was approaching only his twenty-fourth birthday, by late-nineteenth-century standards he should have been well on his way toward financial independence.[12] Another concern may have been the nation's economic mood in 1889. A depression still lingered from the winter of 1887, when a horrific blizzard that killed thousands of cattle was followed by drought, widespread crop failures, and an ensuing crash of land values. In the midst of these travails the Breasted family was struck by a profound and shocking tragedy.

Breasted had two surviving siblings: his older sister May, born five years before James in 1860, and a younger brother, Charles Jr., born thirteen years after James in 1878. A typical, boisterous child of eleven years, Charles Jr. was playing outside in the summer of 1889 when he accidentally inhaled the dried seed head of a stalk of "Timothy," a perennial grass widely cultivated for hay. As he coughed and gasped for breath, the seeds separated and penetrated ever deeper into his lungs, causing such intense irritation and pain that he lost his appetite. Lacking a cure, doctors could only ease the boy's pain while his distraught family kept helpless watch over his steady decline until he died that August. Breasted's grief-stricken mother cried for weeks, and his father's gray hair turned "snowy white." Heartbroken, Breasted set aside future plans, spending the remainder of 1889 in Chicago comforting his parents, compiling a notebook of Hebrew synonyms (figure 1.5), and taking additional seminary classes on a part-time basis in the winter and spring of 1890.[13]

He eventually resumed conversations with his parents about Yale, and they, with some help from Theodocia Backus, scraped together enough money for a year's worth of study. At Curtiss's suggestion, Breasted attended classes that summer with Harper at Chautauqua, where professor and prospective student could take each other's measure while Breasted also prepared for the rigors of Yale. Breasted enrolled in Chautauqua's School of Hebrew and the Old Testament, studying Assyrian too, which he learned so quickly that by midsummer he could report, "I shall be able to enter the second year class in Assyrian next fall Harper says."

Chautauqua's lecture program included speakers known to inspire Christian faith. One, John Wanamaker, founder of the Philadelphia department-store chain that bore his name and—at the time—postmaster general of the United States, particularly impressed Breasted. Wanamaker was active in Philadelphia's Presbyterian community, the national and international branches of the Sunday School movement, and founding of the Bethany Sunday School, which at the time was the nation's largest. Breasted saw in Wanamaker a "simplicity and a

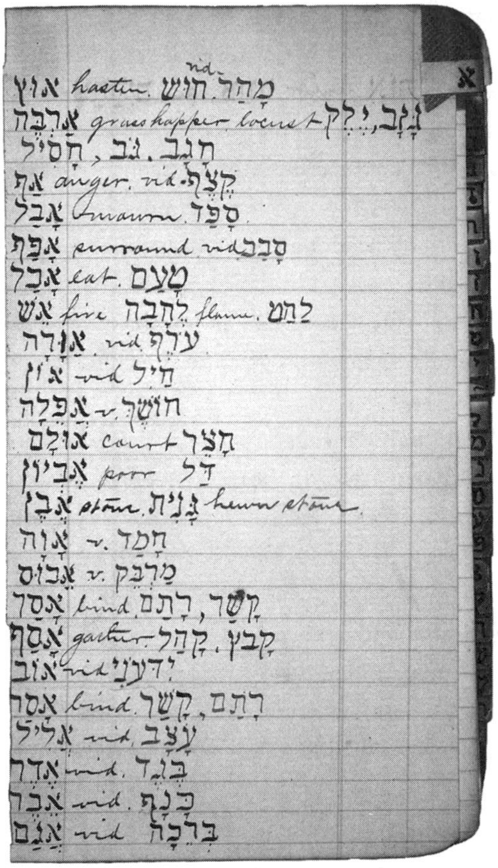

Fig. 1.5 First page of Breasted's "Hebrew Synonyms," October 1889. Courtesy of the Oriental Institute, University of Chicago.

certain kindliness leading those 3000 young hearts in the worship of God,—presenting in his own personality a warm incentive to lead a life of Christian manhood & usefulness—& a beautiful demonstration that Christian principles can be carried out & exemplified . . . the longer a man's influence, & reach of power become." Breasted's citing of Wanamaker's translation of accomplishments and prominence into Christian good works suggests his thinking remained unsettled about how he might sustain a commitment to service, which he associated with the ministry, into a career in scholarship. He personified the experiences of others of his generation for whom "the problems of vocation" were "those of a world in which the ministry was unattractive and the university a place of fabled possibilities, long dreamed of but as yet untried."

Breasted's sojourn at Chautauqua was not, however, wholly occupied with solemn study and pious reflection. He also found time to letter a Hebrew sign with "ladies' shoe polish," which he hung over the balcony of a cottage he occupied with fellow students, mocking their sagacity and virtue (figure 1.6).[14]

Before arriving at Yale in September 1890, Breasted wrote to Harper that

בית נביאים
ראשית חכמה קנה חכמה

House of prophets
Wisdom is the principle thing, get wisdom.

Fig. 1.6 Hebrew text and translation of a sign Breasted made for the Chautauqua cottage he shared with fellow students, ca. July 1890. Courtesy of the Oriental Institute, University of Chicago.

although he had decided to pursue the "doctorate course," he had since "been obliged to modify that resolution," because "my good father seems so much opposed to my abandoning . . . the divinity course that I find myself unwilling to withstand his wishes." However, Breasted concluded, "The Divinity Course once finished, I am at liberty to study as I will. I hope to be able to take five hours a week with you in the doctorate course & will put my main strength in that work." When Harper learned of these plans, just prior to the beginning of classes, he called Breasted in to tell him they were "all right" but asked Breasted to rearrange the sequence. Harper disclosed that the current academic year might be his last at Yale because the trustees of the new University of Chicago, being established with a gift from John D. Rockefeller, had just elected Harper to be the university's first president. Harper had some time to decide whether or not to accept the offer, a decision complicated by an earlier offer from Yale that required him to make a long-term commitment there in exchange for a generous salary increase, support for his extracurricular teaching and publications programs, and leave with pay for an extended European trip.

Despite this news, Harper encouraged Breasted to pursue a doctorate, saying he could "do a work which not one man in a hundred can do" and observing that Breasted "had now enough Hebrew for a doctorate" and that he "could take Aramaic this year—get enough to pass the doctor's examination" and be nearly through by spring. Breasted, ever mindful of his limited finances, pointed out the doctorate would require a second year's commitment he could not then make.

Harper responded by offering money for correcting proof for *Hebraica*. Breasted concluded he should accept Harper's proposal, mainly because he could "see by what Harper offers that he wants me." Breasted trimmed his expenses further, worked out the finances with his parents, and set to work. Yet he reserved the possibility of finishing a seminary degree at either Yale or the Chicago Theological Seminary. Plainly, he was retaining as many options as possible with a view toward his studies' practical applications in teaching Hebrew or preaching the Old Testament.[15]

In addition to reading proof for *Hebraica*, Breasted worked as Harper's grading assistant, paid by the hour, reading and marking as many as 120 essays per assignment by Yale juniors and seniors. The job added to an already hefty load. Breasted discovered his academic work was "much heavier than divinity school work would be,—for the theologues have loads of time for tennis and loafing & never seem very much pressed." Then, too, he felt his college training left him ill-prepared for the rigorous courses now confronting him:

Firstly, In Assyrian
>   The inscription of Tiglath-Pileser I, 1120 B.C. with W. R. Harper, or Harper the great. The inscription of Esarhaddon (son of Sennacherib) 675 B.C. with R. F. Harper, or Harper the less [Robert Francis Harper, William Rainey Harper's younger brother who was also teaching at Yale, was just a year older than Breasted, and had earned his doctorate in Assyriology at Leipzig with Franz Delitzsch's son, Friedrich].

Secondly, In Arabic
>   The Quran for the theology of Mohammed with . . . a tutor. The Quran for its syntax with W. R. H.

Thirdly, In Hebrew
>   Isaiah with W. R. H. The legal literature of the Old Testament or Jewish law with W. R. H. The Pentateuch according to the latest critical theories in the Hebrew Club.

Fourthly, Miscellaneous
>   Assyro-Babylonian History with R. F. H. Lectures on exilic & post-exilic Jewish History with . . . a tutor. Comparative Philology with W. R. H.

The course selection, no doubt made with Harper's advice, laid a broad foundation for advanced studies in Semitic languages and literatures. Breasted's training in Assyrian through primary texts, the instruction in Islamic theology along with Arabic syntax, and a course in comparative philology reflect Harper's developing ideas about preparation for work in the Higher Criticism beyond Hebrew language and literatures. The underlying methodological assumption was that one ought to study Judeo-Christian sacred texts in the context of the ancient Near Eastern linguistic and historical traditions from which they emerged. Breasted embraced this approach, quickly and enthusiastically imbibing the ancient texts in their original languages:

> [Robert F.] Harper has . . . inaugurated a new scheme . . . for writing a syntax of the Assyrian language,—each man who is reading with him is to take a branch of it. . . . This has never been done by any one,—the language['s] decipherment is so recent there has not been time for it. It is a stupendous task as it is to cover an examination of all the historical inscriptions which we possess,—but by dividing the work among eight or nine men & simply doing the work in connection with each day's reading, it is rendered very systematic & not at all burdensome. I am taking the verb,—you can well imagine how intensely interesting it is to compare the manner of speech of a king who lived a thousand years before Christ,—with that of one 400 or 500 yrs. later.[16]

Despite Breasted's linguistic acumen, the direction of his future studies remained unresolved because, paradoxically, of Harper's deepening appreciation of Breasted's extraordinary promise and Breasted's growing regard for his teacher. Just as Breasted became ever more enamored of continuing under Harper, and Harper more invested in his student's success, the professor was torn about his own future. Though rumors of Harper's selection for the Chicago presidency had begun to circulate, he confided to Breasted that he had "not settled the question yet, —but . . . wanted to have a talk" about the following year as soon as he made a decision. Harper was dragging his feet over concern about doctrinal differences with some of his fellow Baptists that arose two years earlier. The issue weighed on him because the University of Chicago was being created by the American Baptist community. The major donor, John D. Rockefeller, was a Baptist, as were all the key organizers including Harper, and Rockefeller's $600,000 founding gift was matched by $400,000 in contributions from churches, other groups, and individuals from throughout the United States solicited by the American Baptist Education Society. Further, the university was to absorb the Baptist Union Theological Seminary as its divinity school.

The doctrinal issue arose from a series of Bible lectures Harper delivered at Vassar College that were reported privately to Rockefeller by one of Harper's critics in December 1888. At issue was his advocacy of the Higher Criticism and the challenges it posed to Baptists who were biblical literalists. Although Harper successfully fended off the attack at the time, he worried it might come up again once he was president of the university, had responsibility for its divinity school, and sought to introduce the same ideas there. Seeking Rockefeller's assurance,

Harper wrote, "I . . . believe, from the results connected with my teaching of the Bible, that it is the will of God that I should teach it . . . the way . . . I have been teaching it. I cannot, therefore . . . accept a position in which that privilege will be denied me. On the other hand, I do not wish to . . . bring upon the institution the distrust of the denomination." After a flurry of correspondence and consultations, Harper's concerns were allayed, and he accepted the presidency in mid-February 1891.[17]

While Harper was struggling with the Chicago decision, Breasted's studies were questioned at home. In early November his father wrote, "The world at large measures things so naturally by their power to contribute to . . . worldly desires and 'vice versa.' Now the question is what has old senackarib [sic] got to do with my raising the money to pay the rent." Breasted's reply does not survive, but his father's concerns were apparently assuaged, and the latter wrote on Christmas Eve, "I wish the University was built just to Harper's notion and that you hold down a chair in said varsity that afforded a good satisfactory salary. . . . But we will hope for the best and go ahead." In February, the same week Harper decided the Chicago matter, he called Breasted in to discuss the latter's future. There were, Breasted wrote, "three possibilities now open,—1st, If Harper goes abroad I want to go with him, & he wants me to go; 2nd, If he does not go he might offer me something to do in the New university and I would study until the position was open, or;—3rd, If he does not go abroad & does not offer me anything to do . . . I will go to Leipzig or Berlin as quickly as I can get there."

Harper was still planning to visit Europe, now to recruit faculty and purchase library collections for Chicago, and he may have been encouraging Breasted to assist him with travel logistics and to meet scholars at major universities there. In early March they discussed three other alternatives: Breasted would continue studies, presumably in Hebrew, at the universities of Leipzig or Berlin; if this was not affordable, he would teach for a while to earn some money and then study in Germany; or he would go to a seminary, probably at Yale, complete a "B.D." degree, and then return to Chicago, though in what capacity remained unclear. Breasted was clearly lost and searching for guidance. Then, in mid-March, during a "chance conversation" with Harper, Breasted broached the possibility of pursuing Egyptology. Harper's initial response was reserved, but he warmed to the idea. According to Breasted, Harper "said he had been looking for a man for some time who would go into it. . . . 'Well' said he, 'Breasted, perhaps you are just the man.' . . . Harper remarked that he would stand by a man thro' thick and thin who would go into it. It would take four or five years. . . . He had even tho't of going into it himself."[18]

Although Egyptology had lingered in Breasted's mind since Curtiss first mentioned it two years earlier, he did not appreciate that it would require even more years of study. He wanted to explore the matter with his parents but couldn't because his father had become quite ill. He had already persuaded them that the lower costs of living and study in Germany meant he could take his second year of classes there rather than at Yale for no additional money, and Theodocia Backus offered help "in going over the water." But three or four additional years of study were another matter. Then, near the end of April, Breasted learned secondhand that Harper assumed he was "'going to Berlin to study in Egyptology and that [Harper] was going to give him the place [in Egyptology] in the New university. . . .' Well, if he had hit me between the eyes with a saw-dust pudding," Breasted wrote, "I could not have been more astonished." About a week later Breasted "had a midnight interview with Harper. . . . He was as kind and friendly as if he were a brother. The conclusion . . . is this: I go to Berlin to study Egyptology for two years—come back and teach in Chicago University—at first only as 'docent.' That means between Instructor and Professor, but as fast as money and circumstances will permit 'we will push you right along' said he." Harper's plan alleviated Breasted's financial concerns about studying in Germany with the promise of work upon his return.[19]

Harper's belief that Breasted ought to seek advanced training in Germany was consistent with widely held views in America about the superiority of German science and scholarship in the nineteenth century. The "lure of the German university" was particularly strong for Americans aspiring to careers in "the higher learning," and the structures and rigorous standards of German universities inspired the creation of new research universities in America, especially Johns Hopkins in 1876, Clark University in 1887, and—under Harper's leadership—the University of Chicago, which would open in 1892. German universities began attracting Americans earlier in the century as word of their strides crossed the Atlantic. After the Civil War increasing numbers of Americans, like Samuel Ives Curtiss and Robert Francis Harper, began traveling to Germany to experience firsthand the seminars and laboratories of leading German professors and later to obtain advanced degrees. Americans were especially smitten with the positivist ethos of German research and its ideology of "science" that came to stand for exactitude and verifiability in all spheres of learning. For those eager to supplant amateur puttering with professional rigor, the German university was the ideal training ground for learning how to collect and marshal "hard facts" into disciplinary structures, approaches, and outcomes that accorded well with American pragmatism of the era.

Americans seeking training in Semitic languages and literatures found Germany's leadership in the critical study of primary texts and philology particularly appealing. Led by scholars such as Leopold von Ranke and Julius Wellhausen, the community of German researchers investigating ancient texts modeled scrupulous and dispassionate research. By the late 1880s the study of Near Eastern languages had become a well-established province of German scholarship, with

Egyptology emerging as an area of particular strength owing to the pioneering contributions of Richard Lepsius at the University of Berlin and Heinrich Brugsch, who taught briefly at the University of Göttingen and subsequently divided his time between Germany and Egypt. Lepsius, who died in 1884, left in Berlin a teaching program rich with scholarly talent, major collections in the New (Neues) Museum, and publications in the Royal Library, all of which he developed and supervised. By Breasted's time, the University of Berlin's faculty and resources in Egyptology were peerless.[20]

Though preoccupied with the coming year's uncertainties, Breasted forged ahead with his studies at Yale. Adept at creating his own language-learning aids, he fashioned clever tools for historical studies, too. One is a chronological chart for sorting out the intricacies of Old Testament history from the time of Saul to the Babylonian Exile (figure 1.7). The period is difficult to comprehend because of the division, after Solomon's death, of the once great land David formed by uniting the northern kingdom of Israel with the southern kingdom of Judah. Solomon's son, Rehoboam, could not hold the union together, and a group of dissidents from the kingdom of Israel, led by Jeroboam ("Jereboam I" on the chart), splintered off. This resulted in a pair of parallel, intertwining histories that Breasted's chart, which reads chronologically from top to bottom, attempts to illustrate.

The left-hand column represents the kingdom of Israel, the right-hand column the kingdom of Judah. The top third shows the two kingdoms as united under the rule of the successive monarchies, the middle third shows the period of the divided monarchy, and the bottom third the different endings of the two kingdoms. Israel was annexed by Assyria about 721 BCE and ceased to exist (thus the left side is blank), while Judah continued as a vassal state under Assyrian rule. The chart ends in 586 BCE, when the remnants of the kingdom of David were conquered and dispersed in the Babylonian Exile. But the chart graphs other stories, too. The sideways "L"-forms in the center of the left-hand column denote the life spans of Old Testament prophets, beginning with Elijah and descending to Hosea. Micah and Isaiah are barely visible in the right-hand column toward the bottom center section adjacent to the labels for Jotham as "regent" and as "king."

Also noteworthy are Breasted's choices of graphic conventions. The vertical bars of elongated, alternating black and white rectangles separated by a descending column of numbers are adapted from mapmaking, where they are typically used in legends to indicate scale or along margins to highlight the precise location of longitude and latitude markings. Perhaps picked up during his North-Western College class in surveying, this graphic convention is used by Breasted to clarify the relative duration of monarchs' reigns, the tiny numbers to the left and right of the bars indicating the precise dates of changes (the "8" below "David" show-

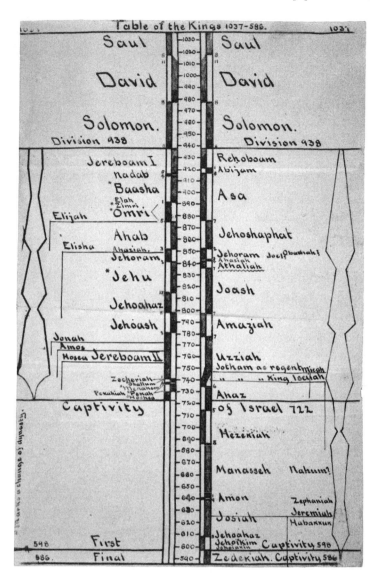

Fig. 1.7 Breasted's "Table of the Kings, 1037–586 [BCE]." Created ca. April 1891. Courtesy of the Oriental Institute, University of Chicago.

ing his rule ended about 978 BCE). The descending column of numbers shows the passage of years in decadal increments like the ticks of a metronome.

Less clear, but far more innovative, are the swelling and tapering geometric columns on the left edge of the left-hand column's center section and the right edge of the right-hand column's center and bottom sections. The relative width of each column denotes the comparative power and prosperity of the successive monarchies. When the distance between the lines is greater, the monarchies are stronger; when the lines narrow things have gotten worse. Accordingly, the lines come to a point when the kingdom of Israel is conquered by the Assyrians (left-hand column) and when the kingdom of Judah disappears with the Babylonian Exile (right-hand column).

Breasted's integration of multiple types of information makes the chart what scholars today might call an "information graphic." He was hardly a forerunner in this regard, however. By the late eighteenth and early nineteenth centuries, the Scottish engineer and author William Playfair had pioneered bar charts and histograms, and the French engineer Charles Joseph Minard designed graphs containing up to four sets of variables in a single image. Their efforts led to a flourishing visual culture of charts and graphs, or schemata, by the end of the nineteenth century. Although the dates in Breasted's chart would be considered a bit inaccurate today, it nonetheless offers an intelligible summation of Old Testament chronologies within a single temporal framework. It also signals Breasted's dawning awareness of visual aids as a means for digesting and communicating the tangled stuff of history. Breasted showed the chart to Harper, who "was pleased with it" and later printed about a hundred copies so he could "have them . . . for the men in [his] classes some day."[21]

Breasted continued to progress rapidly in his studies, delivering his first conference paper at a meeting of the American Oriental Society in late spring 1891. The paper, which became the basis for his Yale master's thesis as well as his first publication, was on using the evolution of Hebrew syntax to date the Old Testament book of Daniel. The cautiously argued eight-page study shows the speed with which Breasted was assimilating his knowledge of Hebrew, Aramaic, Assyrian, and Arabic. Contrary to prior opinion that "the Hebrew of Daniel offers too scanty material . . . to . . . date its composition," Breasted used comparative philology and statistics, as well as close syntactical analysis to suggest "the late date of Daniel." A concise and clearly presented analysis, the article shows an emerging scholar learning to apply his knowledge of the Semitic languages and philological techniques in exemplary fashion. Because he was writing for scholars accustomed to the uses of comparative philology and criticism in Old Testament studies, Breasted could take the notion of linguistic evolution—the development, maturation, and decay of ancient languages—as a given, even though he was addressing a sacred text. Breasted was drinking the cool waters of Higher Criticism and they were good.[22]

By late spring, Charles Breasted's health had improved, and he and Harriet mulled over their son's new plans. With much reluctance over the prospect of a long separation while he was in Europe, they gave their blessing and financial help. Breasted came home briefly before he set off for Germany, and Harriet marked his forthcoming adventure with the gift of a simple gold ring, advising him, "You are going out into a world filled with temptation. If you are ever tempted to do evil, let this ring give you the strength to resist it." He wore the ring on the little finger of his left hand for the rest of his life.

Breasted returned to Yale and "passed the doctor's examination with honors." Although he completed enough of Yale's course-work requirements for a doctorate, he had not fulfilled a two-year residency requirement before leaving for Europe. He settled for a master's degree that he received in absentia a year later. Breasted traveled to New York, where he joined Harper, the professor's family, and a handful of other students for the ocean voyage to Hamburg. They departed at the end of July 1891, about a month before Breasted's twenty-sixth birthday.[23]

From Kandidat to Professor

Breasted arrived in Germany uncertain of a university admission and without a firm sense of his objectives beyond two years' study of Egyptology, vagaries compounded by the strangeness of a foreign culture. Germany in the fall of 1891 was experiencing a moment of relative economic stability after a disastrous depression in the 1870s. The astonishing industrial growth that would transform Germany into a major economic and military power was just gaining momentum. Yet one could still see primitive dog-drawn milk carts slowly rolling through the streets of its major cities.

It was also a time of political change and anxiety following the resignation of the German Empire's founder and first chancellor, Otto von Bismarck, about a year earlier. Friedrich Wilhelm II, who requested Bismarck's resignation, was young and had been kaiser for only two years. Breasted's introduction to German politics included a massive military parade, prominently attended by the kaiser, that commemorated the twenty-first anniversary of Germany's triumph over France at the Battle of Sedan. Essentially concluding the Franco-German War, the battle had all but ended French hegemony in Europe and laid the foundation for a unified Germany. The scale of this display of German military might deeply impressed Breasted, but it also left him with a sense of disquiet.

There were less momentous experiences of everyday life in a different culture, including one that caused a stir at home. Breasted learned that drinking water was rarely if ever served with meals and one had to adjust to beer as the default potable—a notion his teetotaler family found more difficult to swallow than he.[24]

Shortly after their arrival in Germany, Harper began introducing Breasted to scholars, hoping to ease his admission into a major university. In early September, Breasted wrote home, "Dr. H. says he will pull [the University of] Berlin all he can for my degree as he would like me to take it there if possible,—but if not, at Leipzig." In the interim, because Harper by his own admission "hadn't the slightest ear for spoken language," Breasted was called upon to help his teacher navigate German society. Breasted was sufficiently fluent in German, which he probably learned at the Chicago Theological Seminary, to serve as Harper's translator, tutor, and aide-de-camp in business negotiations. He helped find accommodations for the Harper family in Berlin and accompanied Harper on trips around Germany as the latter promoted the new University of Chicago, recruited faculty members, and sought book collections for its as-yet-unbuilt library.

In return, Breasted could look on as Harper worked out his vision for Chicago and discussed it with leading scholars at universities in Leipzig, Dresden, Göttingen, Munich, and Berlin. Harper succeeded in attracting Hermann von Holst, a prominent historian from the University of Freiburg, and he found a major antiquarian book collection to form the core of what, by 1896, would make Chicago's the second-largest university library in the United States. Breasted took part in the "Berlin Collection" acquisition, details of which remained to be settled after Harper returned to America. The experience of negotiating the difference between asking price and actual worth, as well as verifying the collection's true contents, was invaluable for Breasted. No doubt Harper's confidence in Breasted's judgment strengthened the relationship between mentor and former student, a regard cemented by Breasted's looking after Harper's wife and children, who remained in Berlin after he returned to America. Breasted tutored Harper's children in Latin and other subjects and traveled a bit more with the professor's family in Germany acting as their translator.[25]

During this time Breasted, along with Yale classmates Lester Bradner and Charles Foster Kent, were accepted by the University of Berlin, and the three found an apartment to share (figures 1.8 and 1.9). In October 1891 Breasted matriculated and, as was then the tradition, received the august title of Herr Kandidat der Philosophie Breasted, Hochwohlgeborner—"high- and well-born," much to Breasted's amusement. Then formally called Friedrich Wilhelm University, the University of Berlin was founded in 1809–10 by the Prussian minister of education, Wilhelm von Humboldt, and named after the king at the time. Humboldt, an educational reformer, as well as philologist, poet, and philosopher, designed the university as a constellation of loosely affiliated units run by professors who were accorded considerable autonomy. By the 1890s, the university was world renowned for its advanced scientific institutes, wide-ranging and modern curriculum, spirit of impartial and probing inquiry, and most especially for its distinguished faculty. Some, including several of Breasted's professors, were at the forefront of their disciplines. "In studies like my own," Breasted wrote, "the professor is often the sole textbook to be had. . . . To secure his degree the student *must* attend the lectures. . . . [There is] no other way of acquiring knowledge:

Fig. 1.8 Breasted (center) with Charles Kent (left) and Lester Bradner (right), ca. 1890–91. Courtesy of the Oriental Institute, University of Chicago.

Fig. 1.9 Breasted in the Berlin apartment he shared with Charles Kent and Lester Bradner, winter term, 1891–92. Courtesy of the Oriental Institute, University of Chicago.

[students] are simply jugs into which the professors are continually pouring information at a stupendous rate."[26]

Breasted commenced a program of rigorous studies under Adolf Erman, arguably the foremost Egyptologist of the day. Erman had studied with Lepsius, becoming the latter's assistant at the New Museum and Royal Library, and Erman began teaching at the university in 1881. After Lepsius's death in 1884, Erman succeeded his teacher as director of the Egyptian and Assyrian departments at the museum and as professor of Egyptology at the university. A man of many accomplishments, Erman was the first "to recognize fully the early relationship between Egyptian and ancient Semitic languages, the first to divide the language into three periods—Old, Middle, and Late Egyptian, and the first to establish . . . scientific and accurate philology [for Egyptian] including Coptic." By the time Breasted enrolled, Erman's work had elevated the "Berlin school" to a position of influence "felt all over the world so that all [subsequent] students of Egyptian language . . . are in a sense his pupils." Beyond Erman's expertise in philology, it was the breadth of his interests—archaeology, history, religion, and art—that inspired Breasted to look beyond texts and study the material remains of Egyptian daily life in everything from humble pots to majestic monuments.

Before all else, however, Breasted had to pass the doctoral program's linguistic boot camp, "and so the hieroglyphic war is on," he wrote. "Besides the work in Egyptian I have Coptic, Hebrew, and Arabic. One is obliged to offer for his degree *three* languages and philosophy. I will present Egyptian, Hebrew, and Arabic." In his first term, in the fall of 1891, he formally declared his major in Egyptology, which included "hieroglyphic, Coptic, [and] history"—all studied with Erman—and minors in Arabic, Hebrew, and philosophy under other professors. He originally planned to study Assyrian, but Erman urged him to take Arabic instead to better prepare for fieldwork in Egypt. Breasted attacked the work with now characteristic alacrity such that, after about six weeks in school, he could send his parents a handwritten Arabic text and translation to convey "an idea of the Moslem notions of creation" (figure 1.10). He continued to practice the language later in life, once startling fellow pedestrians on a Chicago street corner while absorbed in practicing Arabic guttural sounds aloud. Breasted mastered "colloquial Arabic—in striking contrast to many of his colleagues" in ancient Near Eastern studies.[27]

Seeing that his student was "anxious to get on," Erman doubled the pace of the hieroglyphic class that fall so Breasted could start reading Egyptian texts before the approaching winter holidays. Breasted complained there was no Egyptian grammar of the "slightest use whatever" and he could "go no faster than [Erman] lectured," relying entirely on lecture notes to progress (figure 1.11). Breasted's greatest concern, however, was Erman's declaration that Breasted "must stay . . . three years,—that one can get no more than a superficial knowledge of the sub-

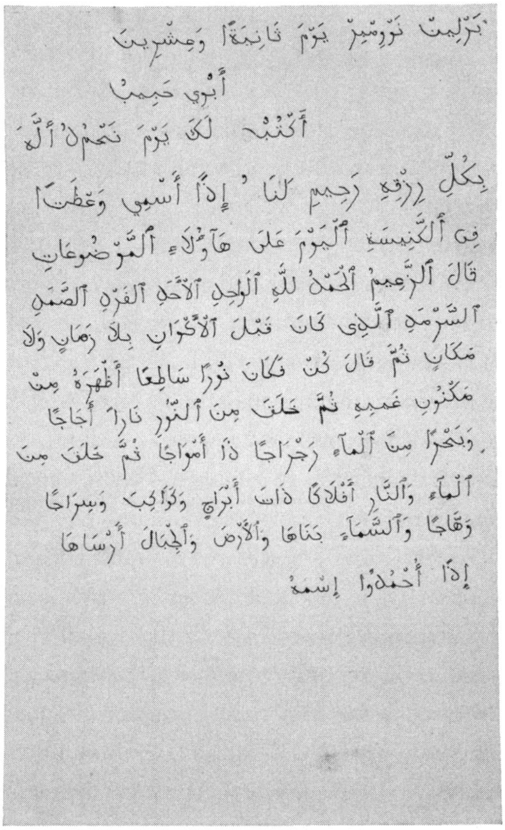

Fig. 1.10 Breasted's transcription of an Arabic text, 22 November 1891. Courtesy of the Oriental Institute, University of Chicago.

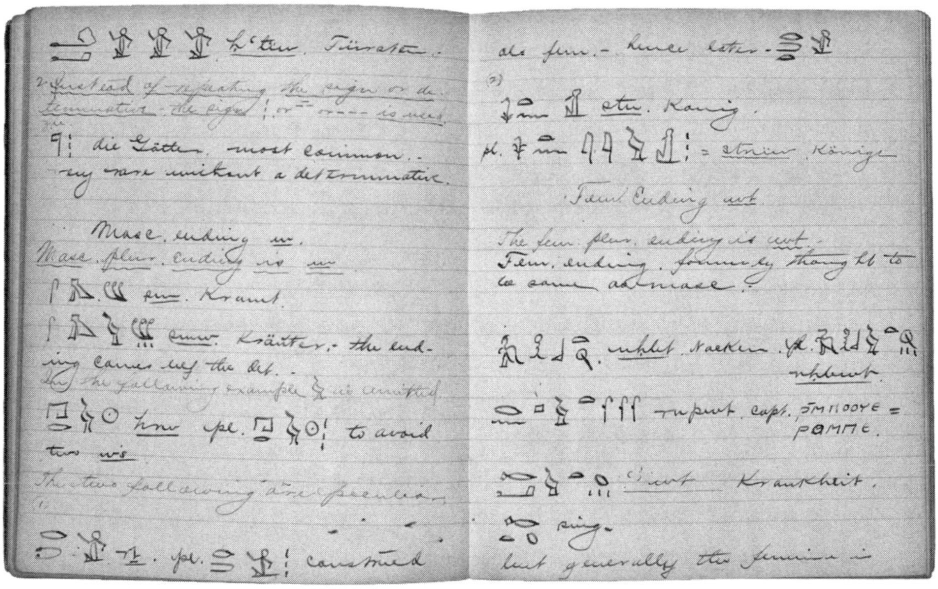

Fig. 1.11 Breasted's notebook for "Hieroglyphische Grammatik, Prof. Dr. Erman, Winter Sem., [18]91–92." Courtesy of the Oriental Institute, University of Chicago.

ject in less time." Because this was a year more of study than he and Harper had originally discussed, Breasted sought Harper's advice, wondering "if the plan of staying three years rather than two . . . is in accordance with your ideas." Shortly thereafter Breasted's father questioned whether Harper's offer was contingent on a doctorate. Breasted confided, "Dr. H. did not really know how much work this undertaking involved. He did not mean that I was necessarily to take my degree here but that after two years he would give me a position any way." But doing two years' work and departing without a degree made no sense. Now that completing a doctorate in two years was out of the question, the long-term value of Harper's offer seemed far less practical. Nonetheless, Breasted made the most of his remaining time in Berlin by increasing his course load the following semester to "1. Ancient Hieroglyphics (reading), two hours (weekly); 2. Grammar of Late Hieroglyphic, two hours; 3. Coptic—reading, two hours; 4. Coptic (syntax), one hour; 5. Archeology (in Museum), two hours; 6. Egyptian History, two hours; 7. Arabic (Koran), two hours; 8. Arabic Legends (Philosophy), two hours; 9. 1001 Nights, two hours; 10. Philosophy, two hours."[28]

Breasted worked incessantly after the term ended in March and into the summer. Early in August Erman, perhaps sensing his student's worry, invited Breasted to join him, some German colleagues, and another of Erman's brilliant students, Kurt Sethe, in the Harz Mountains for what had become an annual sojourn of like-minded scholars and students. The cost, about eighty-eight cents a day, seemed a bit extravagant to Breasted. But with careful budgeting he found the money and set out with Sethe for the mountains, about 125 miles west-southwest of Berlin. They enjoyed two weeks of fellowship and play, mountain hiking to the tunes of German students' songs and American popular ditties like "Shoo Fly," and pursuing occasional forays into scholarly questions—all the while housed and well fed in the cottage of a forest ranger. Breasted found the trip restorative and more. Erman had become Breasted's mentor and friend, and by including his student in this gathering of German intellectuals, he was validating Breasted's promise, a gesture that encouraged him as he entered his second year.[29]

Breasted's work continued to progress quickly, attributable in part to his growing German fluency, "which to the amazement of his professors he learned to speak and write like a native." His command of hieroglyphs was also improving, and in October 1892 he could report, "Just one short year ago, I was painfully committing signs to memory through tedious, endless hours. *Now* I can read pages in a day—*then* things seemed somewhat dark and uncertain, *now* the reins are in my hands." Breasted was also forging a scholarly identity, albeit one influenced by the nature of his training: "I begin to see that it is not so much the comprehensiveness of a man's *learning*, as his rational and careful method, which will bring reliable results, and I am very sure I *have* such a method." That being said,

Breasted continued to believe his studies ought to have a higher purpose, vowing to "make my own field of work like a sublime service for which the world will be my cathedral." But what, precisely, that work would be remained unsettled.

Meanwhile Breasted had to clarify an apparent misunderstanding with his parents about when he would join the University of Chicago's payroll. "As for the matter of a paying fellowship," he wrote, "I do not anticipate I will receive anything for the coming year, but when I see Dr. H. (if I come home next year) I intend asking boldly for . . . some definite statement or written contract stating my position in the university when I return." Harper did arrange for Breasted's appointment at the University of Chicago as a "Non-Resident Fellow" in Egyptology for the 1892–93 academic year, though the amount of his compensation must have been quite modest. Mindful of Breasted's financial needs, Harper also invited submissions for *The Biblical World*—"some Oriental notes" and "also to report regularly on the 25th of every month items of general and Oriental interest from Germany"—for which, Breasted ruefully observed, "I will be paid,—not much I suppose." Apparently emboldened by the appointment, Breasted decided to remain in Berlin and pursue a doctorate. His parents concurred, even though they longed for his return, a frequent topic in their letters.[30]

In December 1892 Breasted settled on a dissertation topic, Egyptian "sun-hymns," and by the following April he was immersed in collecting evidence, "finding such a tremendous lot of texts for my thesis that I am thinking I should . . . divide the subject & treat the hymns of only one period." He initially planned a comprehensive study of the hymns, which began to appear among Old Kingdom inscriptions about 2600–2500 BCE but evolved and proliferated over time with changes in Egyptian cosmology, relocations of priestly centers, and pharaonic succession. His original plan was also affected by the quality of his sources, as he discovered numerous errors in translations made by French scholars, noting in particular "places . . . where [Urbain] Bouriant of the [Egyptian] Museum . . . utterly failed to find the true sense. These fellows are experienced Egyptologists too."

As his knowledge grew, Breasted became increasingly wary of other Egyptologists' translations, turning instead to reproductions of the original inscriptions when available. This preference resulted from Breasted's training in the Egyptian collections of the New Museum, a pedagogical approach that involved a close relationship between scholarship and museology fostered by Erman and his predecessor, Lepsius. Erman's dual roles as university professor and museum curator allowed him to acquire museum objects of intellectual significance, thereby furnishing his students with fresh, previously unknown inscriptions and artifacts, the publication of which would help advance their careers. Breasted found his studies in the museum particularly fascinating and wrote of them often. He cut his philological teeth on inscribed objects and papyri in the museum and developed a heightened appreciation for ancient Egypt's material culture as well, which whetted his appetite for a journey to its source.[31]

The pace of Breasted's work quickened through the end of the academic year and summer of 1893. That July he published his second article, a ten-page comparison of priesthoods in ancient Israel and Egypt for Harper's *Biblical World*. By then well versed in the Higher Criticism and the documentary paradigm for the Pentateuch, Breasted cited the "J document in Genesis"—the "J" referring to one of the groups to whom scholars attributed the authorship of certain passages in the Pentateuch. Mindful of the journal's popular audience, he carefully concluded that "the message which Israel brought to the world is not less divine though it was written with 'the pen of a man.'" The same month he was at work on a new project, translating Erman's recently published hieroglyphic grammar into English. Breasted's translation, issued in London later that year, assured Erman's pathbreaking discoveries in hieroglyphic philology would be far more widely disseminated than if they had remained in German alone.

Meanwhile, Breasted's family found money to bring him home for August and September, after which he returned to Berlin refreshed and determined to complete his doctorate in 1894. If possible, he wanted to cap off his training with a trip to Egypt, but that would delay his arrival at Chicago by a few months, and Breasted sought Harper's assurance the delay would not jeopardize his appointment. The question led to other terms-of-employment issues—his salary, academic rank, Egypt travel assistance, and a small purchase fund for teaching materials such as photographs and casts of inscriptions and reliefs. Harper supported the Egypt plan in principle but was vague about delaying Breasted's teaching or providing travel and acquisition funds. Worried but undaunted, Breasted pressed on with his dissertation, reporting in February 1894 that he had written its first paragraph. The work was both difficult and rewarding: "After long months of toiling drudgery, there come times when the consciousness of growing intellectual power, of irresistible grasp, is so uplifting that a day of the intensest effort is gone like a moment. Such is coming to be my feeling as I work—a keenness of enjoyment that is inexpressible."[32]

Strapped for money as usual, Breasted continued to earn modest amounts writing for *Biblical World* and was pleased to receive ten dollars doing the same for the *New York Post*. Around this time, he received a feeler for a position in "Hartford" that interested him, probably at the Congregationalists' Hartford Theological Seminary. But in April he learned from Harper that he had "been elected to an 'Assistantship' in Egyptology by the Trustees of Chicago University at [an annual] salary of $800 [and] that the position would enable [him] to make as much more in [off-campus] University extension lectures." Having "received nothing definite from Hartford," Breasted cabled his acceptance to Harper, but with mixed feelings. Although delighted the job would reunite him with family, he estimated the salary level would compel him to pursue Harper's extension-lecture offer, not only to make ends meet but to repay his parents' support. The extra work meant his plan to "within a year . . . get out a book on the religion of Egypt in the New Empire," a project requiring "four or five hours a day," was no longer possible. On the other hand, Breasted observed, the extension lectures "will bring me 'popular' reputation and that seems to be the chief thing in American scholarship and the only requisite to success, judging from Harper's case."

The University Extension was Chicago's program of off-campus, evening, and correspondence courses for the general public. It was one of three major divisions designed by Harper, the others being the University Proper—its academic colleges and departments—and University Publication Work, for the production of official university records, teaching materials, and scholarly books and journals written or edited by faculty. This "tripartite design . . . plainly bore the personal stamp of a teaching investigator, an educator of the public at large, and a writing editor," that is, William Rainey Harper. "For its enthusiasts, University Extension was the secular counterpart of evangelism" in its mission to disseminate the university's work to the public. "The higher learning was to be carried across the land by the University as the Bible had been taken to the frontier by an earlier generation of itinerant preachers," the modern-day preachers being Chicago faculty members. Harper's ideas for the extension were partly based on a British model for educational outreach, but in practice the extension's design carried all the earmarks of his Bible-study programs—including summer schools and popular magazines. Breasted had personally experienced Harper's approaches to public education at Chautauqua. Although Breasted appreciated the value of popularizing research, his time in Berlin had tempered this view with the realization that an academic career was built with scholarly publications, not popular lectures. From his new perspective, public outreach seemed to be an unwelcome if necessary burden.[33]

Notwithstanding the Chicago appointment, Breasted was "every moment conscious of being still on the home stretch with the goal unattained," and he dared "not relax an instant." By early April, Breasted had nearly completed the dissertation and, because it was written in German, started polishing the final text. A few weeks later he began transcribing the manuscript on his first "machine," a typewriter he had just acquired, laboriously inserting by hand hieroglyphs and relevant images (figure 1.12). Once it was nearly done, Breasted mused:

> It has cost me an enormous amount of work, but in the end I have been able to achieve some hitherto unattained results in the history of Egyptian religion. It is with a strange feeling that I look upon them and think . . . these thoughts . . . were living in hearts now still, these four thousand years,—since then they were lost to the world till my months of toil have brought them forth again.

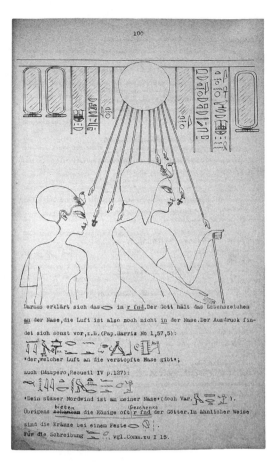

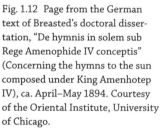

Fig. 1.12 Page from the German text of Breasted's doctoral dissertation, "De hymnis in solem sub Rege Amenophide IV conceptis" (Concerning the hymns to the sun composed under King Amenhotep IV), ca. April–May 1894. Courtesy of the Oriental Institute, University of Chicago.

They are old friends. I almost love them,—but as if some patriarch had stepped forth from the silent temples where these thoughts once lived and moved, and had whispered them to me, so I look upon them with reverence, because they are one more phase of that never ceasing struggle in the life of man.—The struggle for the truth. And because too, that they have taught me that <u>history</u> is only the story of that struggle and that therefore the history of all men is <u>one</u>. He who can raise up out of the dust, the forgotten story of one battle in the conquest, can enrich the common life of man . . . and show his fellows how we stand between the past and future indissolubly linked with both; and under the solemn responsibility of giving to all coming time the impulse that may inspire to the best.[34]

Breasted was beginning to distinguish himself from his fellow Egyptologists in his approach to the materials and aims of his discipline. For him the texts were living things that communicated the beliefs of people who, he imagined, faced difficulties like those of his own time, challenges that tested one's faith and inspired in every generation attempts to reconcile the impediments of earthly existence with lofty ideals. He was starting to look beyond the linguistic nuances and mechanics of translation, beyond Egyptology's philological theories and methods, to consider the ancient texts' relevance to modern life.

The other hurdle in Breasted's doctoral program was an oral examination. Its topics were Arabic, Hebrew, philosophy, and of course Egyptology. The examining committee consisted of Erman, Karl Eduard Sachau (Arabic, also prominent in Syriac studies), Eberhard Schrader (Hebrew, best known as an Assyriologist), and Eduard Zeller (philosophy, by then internationally known for his expertise on ancient Greece). By custom, when the date was set, Breasted called on each professor to formally invite him to the examination. He did not have any classes with Zeller, and the professor suggested Breasted prepare to "give an account of the Stoic School." He returned home and promptly "crammed night and day on the Stoics. It was uphill business, but I learned *by heart* all that . . . Zeller ever had said about the Stoics, till I could grind it out with swing and rhythm, paragraph after paragraph, page after page, chapter after chapter." Evidently feeling better prepared for his other subjects, Breasted mentioned reviewing only for Hebrew.

The examination, though surrounded with formalities, was itself a rather casual, private gathering with each of the professors entering the room for his share in the proceedings and then departing. Only Erman remained for the entire affair. Meanwhile, chatting amiably in the background with another colleague was one of the university's most famous scholars, Theodor Mommsen, historian and archaeologist of ancient Rome. Erman led off the examination by having Breasted translate a pyramid text—"the most difficult of all hieroglyphics," a passage from the Papyrus Harris, and an unidentified Coptic text. Zeller followed, and, much to the professor's satisfaction, Breasted contrasted Plato, Aristotle, and the Stoics in his response, shrewdly citing one of Zeller's key contributions to the field. For Schrader, Breasted had to discuss Hebrew philology and Old Testament criticism. In addition to reading and translating a pair of texts, he was asked to situate Hebrew in the context of other Semitic languages, to analyze the Pentateuch, and "divide Isaiah, chapter by chapter." Sachau had Breasted read and translate an Arabic text and all went well, so much so that he was "exulting" in anticipation of completing the examination. Then Sachau posed a question for which Breasted was unprepared, summarizing "the critical history of the Koran." Breasted was stumped. The examination concluded, and he retired to another room to await the professors' decision. After a short while he was called back and learned he had passed cum laude, a distinction earned previously by just one other American and—of particular gratification for him and his mentor—Erman many years earlier.[35]

Only the dissertation's formal publication and defense now remained. Breasted submitted it for approval prior to his oral examination, and it passed with one of the university's highest rankings. In accordance with the university's requirements, he translated the German text into a condensed Latin version that would be published. To make it publishable, however, he had to hand-letter virtually the entire text—hieroglyphs and Roman letters alike—with a special pencil so it could be "autographed," or reproduced by a lithographic process. Those pages were then bound together with a typeset cover, title page, dedication ("parentibus carissimis," to his beloved parents), "sententiae controversae"(a list of four controversial assertions challenged during his defense), and a one-page vita.

The dissertation, titled "De hymnis in solem sub Rege Amenophide IV conceptis" (Concerning the Hymns to the Sun Composed under King Amenhotep IV), is far more narrowly focused than Breasted initially planned. It begins with a critical overview of only those hymns composed during the reign of Amenhotep IV (1353–1336 BCE) and then proceeds to a thematic analysis that divides a total of 101 hieroglyphic lines into eight sections. Each section consists of a hieroglyphic transcription, a line-by-line Latin translation immediately below it, and an extended line-by-line critical analysis following that (figure 1.13).

Amenhotep IV is recalled as the "heretic pharaoh" because he supplanted the existing religion with a new, rigorously monotheistic creed that was most prominently articulated in the sun hymns. The new religion, which possessed certain aesthetic and intellectual qualities bearing a rough semblance to Judaic theology, lasted less than two decades before a successor began restoring the previous religion. The sun hymns are essential to understanding Amenhotep's new doctrine because they capture the essence of the pharaoh's radical act: the elevation of Aten the sun god (abstracted into a solar disk emitting rays terminating in human hands; see figure 1.12) as the solitary god over all other gods, including Amon-Re (represented in human form, often with a ram's head) who was previously regarded as the most powerful in a pantheon of more local deities. Amon-Re combined attributes of Amon, venerated as king of the gods and patron of pharaohs in the ancient city of Thebes, with Re, *also* worshiped as a sun god in ancient Heliopolis.

The demotion of Amon-Re resulted in a humiliating loss of status for the priesthood dedicated to the god's worship. But Amenhotep went further, changing his name to Akhenaten (spelled by Breasted as Ikhnaton), meaning "One Useful to Aton," and the pharaoh ordered the name "Amon" be chiseled off inscriptions throughout ancient Egypt. This form of state-sponsored vandalism was reciprocated a generation later when the Amon cult was restored by Akhenaten's successors and nearly all vestiges of his rule were similarly erased. The radical nature of the pharaoh's reforms, and the reactions to them evident in the violent excisions and recuttings of ancient inscriptions, captured Breasted's imagination and provided rich material for his growing fascination with the interrelations of civil society and religion in ancient Egypt.[36]

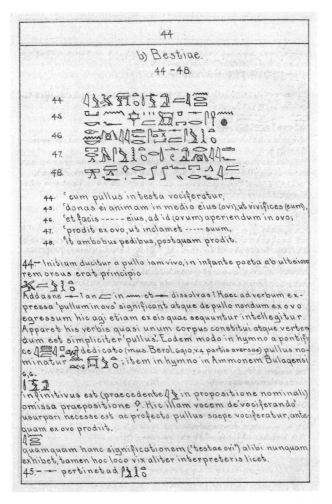

Fig. 1.13 Page from the published Latin text of Breasted's doctoral dissertation, "De hymnis in solem sub Rege Amenophide IV conceptis," August 1894. Courtesy of the Oriental Institute, University of Chicago.

He defended his dissertation in a pro forma ceremony in mid-August. It was conducted in Latin, and Breasted had to respond to the prearranged objections of three fellow students. Each of Breasted's interrogators would later make significant contributions to Egyptology: Ludwig Borchardt, Carl Schmidt, and Kurt Sethe. By tradition, following his defense Breasted declared his allegiance to the university and to learning, swearing "To be a pure man, to serve the highest ends of scholarship, and to pursue and ever to declare the truth," whereupon he was proclaimed a master of arts and doctor of philosophy.

This final step behind him, Breasted turned attention to a now much hoped-for trip to Egypt with return stopovers to study Egyptian collections in Paris and London. Hoping to do it all, he would nonetheless settle for the European trip only, using the time and resources there for preparing classes, especially extension lectures. Breasted's father objected to yet another postponement of his return home, to which Breasted replied, "You see I have done no work here that is fitted for popular presentation—the pills must all be sugar-coated—they must be put into a vehicle which popular taste is capable of appreciation." Breasted was also anxious about his preparation to teach regular university classes, confiding to his father: "Night before last I dreamed that I was teaching at the university & who do you think were in my class,—you, and Dr. Harper and Charley Kent and Prof. Goodspeed! You behaved very badly and told funny stories all the time & kept the rest all laughing so that they couldn't pay any attention. When you were not telling yours Goodspeed was gravely telling all he knew about the subject so that I couldn't get a word in edgewise,—Charley Kent grinned and Dr. Harper sat grim and silent and only remarked that I must begin pretty soon or I wouldn't get through in time."

"Prof. Goodspeed," was George Stephen Goodspeed, then an associate professor of comparative religion at Chicago. A former student of Harper's at the Baptist Union Theological Seminary, where the two struck up a relationship "far closer than that of teacher and pupil," Goodspeed later followed Harper to Yale, earned a doctorate there, became an "Assistant in the Semitic Department," and worked in Harper's American Institute of Sacred Literature before following him to Chicago. Breasted would have met Goodspeed at Yale when their attendance overlapped during the 1890–91 academic year.[37]

Still determined to visit Egypt, Breasted tried prying loose some travel money from Harper. Breasted offered a variety of justifications. One was the opportunity it afforded to acquire photographs and plaster casts of statuary and reliefs for "our new museum," referring to recently announced plans for the Haskell Oriental Museum. It was the second in a constellation of departmental museums and libraries Harper intended to create for the specialized research and teaching needs of the university's proliferating disciplines. The Walker Museum, opened about a year earlier for the natural sciences, was the first. Breasted was already acquiring books in Berlin to support the university's research and teaching needs, so the photographs and casts would merely enlarge the scope of these resources. Furthermore, Breasted argued, "The practical knowledge I should obtain ought to be of considerable advantage to the museum . . . in its arrangement and development." He also thought, judging by his work with Erman at the New Museum, that, like Erman, he might persuade archaeologists and the Egyptian Antiquities Service to send Chicago duplicate objects out of professional courtesy: "As our new museum is the first university museum of the kind in the world, the officials in Egypt ought to grant us a good many favors and concessions."

The Haskell Oriental Museum would indeed be the first *university* museum devoted exclusively to ancient Near Eastern studies, and Breasted was correct that archaeologists and the Antiquities Service were sharing finds then. But Harper was still unwilling to fund the trip, and Breasted's parents along with Theodocia Backus once more came to his aid. Their support was not entirely adequate, so he wrote to Harper again, this time seeking a paid leave through the beginning of the spring quarter beginning in April 1895. It was necessary, Breasted argued, because "a great deal of time will be taken from my studies" during the trip to "give all possible attention to acquisitions and donations for the new museum." Finally, in early October Breasted could report that "the little Dr. has not at all deserted me" and that Harper had authorized a paid leave of absence at full salary ($400 for six months) and $500 to acquire photographs and casts. Breasted's determination to obtain museum accessions was also bound up in career ambitions that he confided to his parents: "If I can obtain any gifts of value or . . . donations for the Museum, it will be a long step toward the directorship of the institution." All was set but for one wrinkle remaining to be smoothed, his wedding plans.[38]

With his large brown-gray eyes, curly dark hair, angular features, and compact athletic build—he stood about five feet eight inches—Breasted readily attracted the attention of young women (figure 1.14). He just as readily reciprocated their interest. But he was capricious, too, at one point ardently pursuing a love interest and at the next abruptly abandoning her. Breasted's family and friends recalled at least five girlfriends during his college years. His fickleness alarmed his parents and especially Theodocia Backus, who, after his visits to Rockford, was left to "rehabilitate . . . stricken hearts" there. This inconstancy surely contributed to his parents' skepticism about Breasted's changing career ambitions, but they were especially fearful he might impulsively enter into a marriage he'd later regret. Indeed, he was engaged to a "Rockford girl" when he left for Germany and began seeing another young lady after arriving in Berlin. The family also viewed him as an "idealist" in his dealings with people of both sexes, a quality Breasted's son later attributed to his intellectual intensity and "innate detachment." Breasted's "industry left him little time for the normal . . . give-and-take which most . . . took for granted." Whether he was overly optimistic about others' motivations or incapable of the social banter useful for gauging others, Breasted possessed what his family regarded as a penchant for miscalculating relationships.

Breasted dutifully reported all his involvements to his parents and did so again in December 1891 when he met a "Miss Hart" from San Francisco. Frances Hart was then nineteen and the oldest of four daughters brought to Berlin by her widowed mother, who wanted to introduce them to the cultural and social refinements of a European capital. A "dark-haired, dark-eyed beauty," Hart was characterized as "intelligent, a good listener, eager to learn, intuitive, . . . conscientious, and proper to the point of prudery." Also a talented pianist, she was

Fig. 1.14 Breasted, May 1896. Courtesy of the Oriental Institute, University of Chicago.

preparing for a concert career, likely another reason for the family's Berlin sojourn. Breasted met her at the Home School for American Girls, established just
a few years earlier by another American widow to provide a level of education
still inaccessible to young women in America. The school's clientele obviously
attracted Berlin's eligible bachelors, its appeal cultivated by the proprietress with
activities including regular Friday receptions honoring a "visiting American lu-
minary." Of the weekly gatherings Breasted wrote, "They are simply delightful,
and I go in order to keep 'alive.' . . . The other evening Mark Twain was there,
and I had an exceedingly pleasant talk with him—and with his daughter, who is
quite a pretty girl."

Active in the American expatriate community, Breasted shared in its various
social gatherings (figure 1.15), and was sufficiently well regarded to be honored
with delivering a toast to "The Ladies" at the American ambassador's Thanksgiving Day dinner in 1893. He was especially drawn to the Home School, and soon
he along with his apartment mates began teaching Bible classes there. According
to Breasted, "We three are awakening an interest in Bible studies. . . . The young

Fig. 1.15 Group photograph of students in Berlin, n.d. Breasted is second from the left, bottom row, and Lester Bradner is second from the right, back row. Courtesy of the Oriental Institute, University of Chicago.

ladies are quite industrious in preparation. . . . It is an excellent thing for us, too. We are kept in contact with people and life and popular thought, and most of all, *popular need*, and thus from the danger of drifting into dry scholasticism." Plausibly there was another kind of awakening as well.[39]

Over the year following their first meeting, Breasted's acquaintance with Hart grew into a courtship that included concerts by the Berlin Philharmonic and the Royal Opera. Around December 1892 he wrote that she was "as kind and thoughtful as if I were her own brother. She listens patiently to endless tales of my work and ambitions. You know, it is true of all souls: like the 'Ancient Mariner,' they reach a state when repression is no longer possible, they must recite their tale of hope and longing . . . , and will not be stilled until they have found someone who will listen." In November 1893, shortly after his visit home, they became engaged. He most assuredly told his parents of his affection for Hart and obtained their approval of his pending proposal. By the following April she was adding to Breasted's letters home notes about which his father commented, "I . . . admire her practical way of putting things and I discover much that leads me to think she is just the person to bring back the absent minded student when he is wandering away from this world unconscious of his surroundings."[40]

All the while, Breasted continued planning the Egypt trip, now in the company of Carl Schmidt so the two could share expenses. The original plan was for

Hart to return to America to spend "at least a year in study at some women's college" while Breasted went to Egypt and then Chicago, the idea being that the separation would be good for their marriage's long-term health. Among Breasted's preparations, he thought to borrow Lester Bradner's "pocket camera"—a "tupenny," "tiny Kodak hand camera," which the latter sent from New York. In late August, however, Schmidt dropped out, and Hart expressed interest in the trip. Since their traveling together out of wedlock would be inconceivable, however, they quickly arranged to marry. Breasted wrote to his parents for a document certifying their approval for the German authorities, adding the unromantic assurance that "Erman made the Nile voyage in the same way with his bride, and did not consider it any hindrance to his practical work."

Yet the cost of Hart's joining the trip posed an obstacle. She paid her own way during their courtship, as was the custom at the Home School, and knew Breasted could not afford her expenses. Hart planned to sell some jewels to raise the needed cash but then got cold feet. By the beginning of October, Schmidt was temporarily back in the picture, and Hart decided to return to America. A snafu with her luggage on the train out to the ship, however, forced her to miss its departure, and she resolved to join Breasted on the Egyptian trip after all. They hurriedly set a wedding date of 22 October, arranged the necessary documents, and in the company of Hart's family and their mutual friends—including George A. Reisner, another midwest-American Egyptologist-to-be, and his wife—trooped through two weddings: a civil ceremony required by their foreign status and a church service. Outwardly unperturbed by his fiancée's vacillations, Breasted completed preparations for what was now to be an Egyptian honeymoon as well. At some point he broke off his engagement to the "Rockford girl," and his family picked up the pieces.[41]

Discovering Egyptology's Egypt

Newlywed, newly minted Egyptologist, and just-appointed University of Chicago emissary in search of teaching materials, Breasted landed in Egypt barely prepared for the experiences that lay ahead. As he had just completed his dissertation, his longer-term scholarly goals were unformed. He would be visiting ancient sites with little more purpose than a desire to see as much as possible in the allowable time. However, Erman invited Breasted to collect information for an Egyptian dictionary he had in mind, a project that required Breasted to accurately copy hieroglyphic inscriptions in various locations. The Breasteds' visit would thus embrace the worlds of tourism and scholarship at a time when both enterprises in Egypt were still relatively young and changing.

Egypt was then entering a period of political and economic change. Beginning in the late eighteenth century, while still part of the Ottoman Empire, it was the site of intensifying imperialist rivalries between France and Britain, high-lighted by Napoleon's ill-fated invasion in 1798. A succession of Egyptian rulers under the scrutiny of, and with occasional assistance from, European powers presided over nearly a century of military ventures along Egypt's borders while political and economic instability within the country began to rise. Things came to a head in 1882 when government disarray and financial collapse threatened to engulf Egypt, setting the stage for European intervention to protect its strategic interests. The British stepped in, establishing military and political hegemony that was eventually recognized by France as part of the Anglo-French Entente Cordiale in 1904, an agreement that sorted out their respective spheres of interest there and beyond.

As part of the deal, however, the French retained and consolidated their oversight of the Egyptian Antiquities Service, a role that began in 1858 when they "re-founded" a program begun under Egyptian auspices in 1835. The Egypt visited by the Breasteds in fall 1894 was securely under British control, offering at least the appearance of a relatively stable country with an increasingly robust economy. Because most of its government bureaus were staffed or shadowed by British officials, it behooved visitors with any ambitions in Egypt—whether scholarly or commercial—to befriend them. The situation drew outsiders into a vortex of political intrigues involving Egyptian and British officials and, when it came to antiquities, the French, providing an endless source of gossip and, for Egyptians, humiliation.[42]

It was Breasted the tourist who, on the train from Alexandria—Egypt's main port—to Cairo, "discovered the [Giza] Pyramids . . . with such a shout that . . . native fellow voyagers started from their seats in astonishment" (maps 1 and 2). The Breasteds settled into a hotel well past its prime near Cairo's "great bazaar," Khan al-Kahlili. But then, to save money, they moved to even more modest accommodations in a pension converted from an "old Turkish palace." They were planning on just a brief stopover as Breasted made arrangements to visit ancient sites, deferring a longer visit in Cairo to just before they returned home.

The most cost-efficient way to visit the ancient sites was via a *dahabiyya* (houseboat) on the Nile. Breasted hired one for them to board in Asyut, located about 235 miles south of Cairo and reachable by train. Depending on how well they were constructed and outfitted, *dahabiyyas* could vary from primitive, leaky affairs to lavish yachts. On a visit to the eminent and well-heeled Assyriologist Archibald Henry Sayce, who wintered in Egypt and did some research there, too, the Breasteds saw one of the finer versions of *dahabiyya*, Sayce's being "the broadest boat on the river, a perfect little palace." With their limited resources, however, they had to settle for less. Even at that, theirs was an elaborate enterprise "with bedding, linen, kitchen equipment, a crew of four sailors, captain and second captain, dragoman, cook and boy." The total cost for the couple, "in-

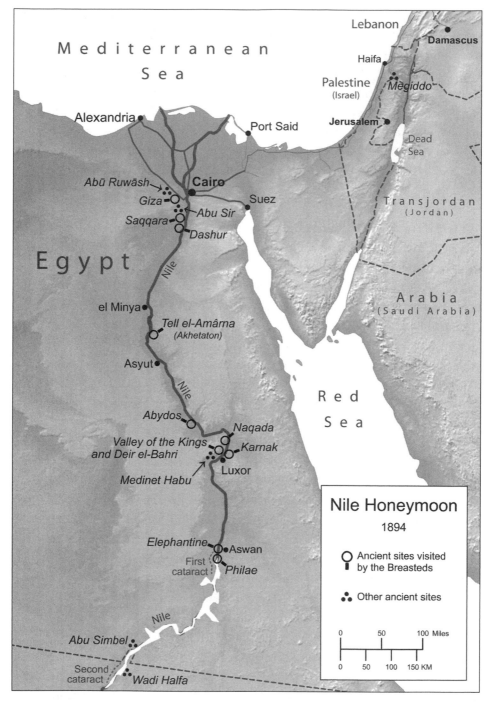

Mediterranean Sea

Lebanon

Damascus

Haifa

Palestine
(Israel)

Megiddo

Jerusalem

Dead
Sea

Alexandria

Port Said

Cairo

Suez

Transjordan
(Jordan)

Abū Ruwāsh

Giza

Abu Sir

Saqqara

Dashur

Egypt

Nile

Arabia
(Saudi Arabia)

el Minya

Tell el-Amârna
(Akhetaton)

Asyut

Nile

Red
Sea

Abydos

Naqada

Valley of the Kings
and Deir el-Bahri

Karnak

Luxor

Medinet Habu

Elephantine

Aswan

First
cataract

Philae

Nile

Abu Simbel

Nile

Second
cataract

Wadi Halfa

Nile Honeymoon

1894

Ancient sites visited
by the Breasteds

Other ancient sites

0   50   100 Miles

0   50   100   150 KM

Map 2

cluding all table and household expenses and hire of donkeys at all stops" would come to almost ten dollars a day. Breasted considered the expense worthwhile, for it would enable him to pursue his work without interruption. Never mind, as his son drily observed many years later, that the honeymoon itself might have justified some of the cost.

The Egyptological necessity of a *dahabiyya* is explained by the Nile's prominent role throughout Egypt's history. As the country's principal source for drinking water and irrigation and its once primary avenue of transportation, the Nile has been the life-giving artery of Egyptian civilization since humans first gathered along the bluffs and fertile valley formed by the river's annual floods in ancient times. Prehistoric settlements along the river's length grew into the civilization of ancient Egypt, which in turn erected nearly all its major monuments along the Nile as well. Some are close by the river, others a couple of miles to the east or west, where alluvial plains, formed from sediment deposited over thousands of years of Nile inundations, give way to deserts and mountains.

The Nile originates in what is now the Sudan where the Blue Nile and White Nile join, their headwaters rising respectively in modern-day Ethiopia and Rwanda. The river flows northward, the "upper Nile" being in Sudan and southern Egypt and the "lower Nile" being the stretch from mid-Egypt to where the river empties through the Nile delta into the Mediterranean. As Egypt modernized in response to foreign trade, especially in cotton and sugarcane, its population grew around the Nile delta, an inverted triangle marked by Alexandria to the west, Port Said to the east—alongside the entrance to the Suez Canal, which was completed in 1869—and Cairo to the south. Because of changes in topography, climate, and abundance of arable land, Egypt's population thins as one travels south, or up the Nile. In 1894, train service went only as far as Asyut, and it would not be extended to the city of Aswan near Egypt's southern border until 1898. To reach ancient Egyptian sites along the upper Nile beyond Asyut, travel by water was not just the best option, it was the only option.[43]

Breasted used the brief layover in Cairo to study in the Egyptian Museum, then located in Giza about three miles from the Breasteds' pension, a trip made by donkey. There Breasted copied inscriptions for Erman, researched the collections, and introduced himself to the museum staff, including its French director, Jacques de Morgan, who, by tradition and for reasons of administrative expediency, also headed the Egyptian Antiquities Service. Established to protect Egypt's ancient patrimony from looting and illicit trade, the Antiquities Service, along with the Egyptian Museum, was a central institution in the management of all matters pertaining to the excavation, sale, and export of antiquities. The Antiquities Service annually authorized who could excavate where, it automatically received 50 percent of all finds, it had right of first refusal over all remaining finds, and it controlled the export of objects purchased by institutions or individuals. All excavated or seized objects went to the museum.

Breasted's hopes that Antiquities Service staff would release duplicates for the Haskell Oriental Museum were quickly dashed: "I find the administration of the antiquities . . . by the French, corrupt to the core. Nothing is done in the name of truth or science, but all is a mere scramble for good things to sell & the money goes into private pockets. The only German official at the Museum, Emil Brugsch, brother of the great Brugsch, is even worse than the French. . . . Of course with such a spirit prevailing it is impossible to secure any donations." This corruption and the generally decrepit condition of the museum, "housed in an old tinder-box" adapted from a former palace, alarmed Breasted.[44]

The Breasteds took the train to Asyut on 21 November and boarded their *dahabiyya*, the *Olga*, the next day. "She had an overall length of about fifty-five feet and a nine-foot beam. The galley was forward of the mainmast and the crew's deck. The higher, after portion of the boat contained a dining room, a dragoman's cabin, two minute 'master' cabins each with one narrow berth, a bathroom with a much-dented home-made zinc tub, a toilet consisting of an orthodox seat over a removable box of sand, a dressing room and tiny after deck pierced by a rudder-shaft. The roof was a deck covered with an awning and furnished with easy chairs. Above the water line the *Olga* appeared staunch enough, but . . . the condition of her hull was problematical. There was little about her to remind one of Professor Sayce's trim and patrician vessel." *Dahabiyyas* were powered by sails or, if the air was still, by oars or even tow ropes lugged by the crew.

Breasted decided to head directly for Aswan, about 350 miles further up the Nile, and then drift with the river's current from site to site back to Asyut. Sailing up the Nile was easy when the prevailing north wind was strong but quite arduous when it died. Towing a boat against the Nile current is difficult when the river is high or forced through narrow channels. But the hard work fell to the crew, and Breasted could write that he had never dreamed "of making the journey in such enchanting conditions. Here I am with my dear wife, monarch of all I survey on this boat—I walk the deck and feel like a naval officer in one of [James Fenimore] Cooper's sea tales, for I have only to raise my hand and [the crew is] ready to obey my slightest word!" Along the way, Breasted drew on his classical Arabic to learn the contemporary spoken version through "diligent practice," mostly with the crew. The trip was Frances Breasted's "first venture into housekeeping—for before her marriage she had never so much as boiled the proverbial egg."

They reached Luxor in early December. Located on the east bank of the Nile, about 185 miles from Asyut, it is the modern embarkation point for Thebes, one of antiquity's most fabled cities and a capital of the Egyptian empire. Numerous surviving monuments are distributed over an area of approximately eight square miles on both sides of the Nile, with the Luxor temple and the sprawling Karnak temple complex on the east bank, and on the west side—just beyond the tillable lands—a string of great mortuary temples, royal tombs, and, over the crest of a ridge, the Valley of the Kings. Despite his plan of sailing straight for Aswan, Breasted could not resist Thebes's allure. "For three days, from dawn till dark, I never lost a moment copying inscriptions—and on one night at Karnak I copied by moonlight. The silver light streamed down through the broken roof of the vast colonnaded hall, splashing with bright patches the dusky outlines of the enormous columns. . . . Imagine a forest of 134 columns, the middle two rows sixty-nine feet high and twelve feet thick, with capitals eleven feet high." The Breasteds then continued southward, observing "mile after mile of palm-grown banks, with mauve and yellow mountains sometimes low in the distance, again rising bold and dazzling from the water's edge, often honeycombed with rock tombs, long since plundered, silent, empty."[45]

The landscape changed little until they approached Aswan, where the distant hills bordering the Nile valley abruptly narrow into jagged granite cliffs and the Nile's eroding power is mightily resisted and channeled into dangerous boulder-filled rapids. It is the first of six cataracts along the upper Nile between Aswan and Khartoum, where the White Nile and Blue Nile converge, the numbering going from north to south, each cataract serving like a watery milepost for those traversing the seemingly endless Nubian desert of northern Sudan. Breasted saw in Aswan's dramatic scenery the dry records of history suddenly come to life. It was there that "the granite for all the obelisks of Egypt was quarried and transported downriver. For thousands of years this place has marked the southern frontier of Egypt proper. The country beyond was inhabited by black people over whom Egypt usually ruled. On the rocks you will find the names of Twelfth Dynasty Pharaohs [1938–1755 BCE] or the rude scratchings of the Roman soldiers who for centuries were garrisoned here on this distant frontier of the Empire."

Breasted found innumerable inscriptions on the ancient ruins of Elephantine, one of the largest islands along Aswan, and on the nearly perfectly preserved Ptolemaic-era structures (305–30 BCE) of Philae, another island south of Aswan. Of yet another island he wrote, "over 200 [inscriptions] are cut into the rocks of a valley. I traced the high priesthood of the cataract god Anek through three generations of priests who had recorded themselves there. With a little search, this could undoubtedly be carried much further. Oh, for the time to copy and publish these inscriptions!"

Having reached the southernmost point of their journey, the Breasteds turned and began drifting northward with the Nile's current, visiting ancient sites along the way. In late December they returned to Luxor for a brief visit. The day before resuming their journey, Breasted went to what some call the "Tomb of the Royal Cache," the site of a sensational discovery located on the west side of the Nile on a steep slope near the mortuary temples of Deir el-Bahri. The tomb, at the base of a deep vertical shaft, was the source of precious objects that began appearing on the market in the 1870s. Antiquities Service officials suspected a tomb had been plundered by thieves and finally, in 1881, identified them. The thieves led officials to the site, where they found over thirty mummies, including those of several pharaohs, although most of the valuable funerary objects had long since been looted. The mass burial vault was created about 1100 BCE, after the pharaohs' original tombs had been disturbed, when ancient guardians wanted to relocate their contents to a more secure location. Breasted wanted to enter the difficult-to-reach tomb, and, although his Egyptian crew members begged him not to, he

> ignored their nonsense and stripped myself of all superfluous clothing. . . . I stationed them behind some projecting rocks, made them . . . brace their feet as in a college "tug of war" and hold fast to the rope. With a candle and some matches in my pocket, I swung over the edge and, hand over hand, let myself down [the thirty-eight foot shaft] to the bottom.
>
> I lighted my candle and began crawling along a very low passage [that] led 195 feet into the mountain. The air . . . was suffocatingly hot, and the perspiration poured from me. Behind and before me was inky darkness, and a silence so deep that even the burning of the candle flame became loudly audible.
>
> Suddenly there was a rushing sound, the candle went out, and . . . something struck me full in the face. It was only a bat, but match after match failed to strike, and though there was nothing to be afraid of, it seemed an eternity in that horrible blackness till the candle flickered again.
>
> The passage ended in a chamber about twenty feet square. . . . Huge blocks had fallen from the ceiling till it was difficult to move about in the chamber (a small piece came down while I was there). . . . I . . . sat down for a few minutes [and] tried to envisage the strange scene which took place here 3000 years ago—first when the workmen cut . . . into the limestone mountain, next when the most trusted men of the priesthood secretly brought the mummies (which to them already seemed very old) to this hiding place.

Breasted climbed out to the "heavenly brightness and relative coolness" above and returned by nightfall to the boat, which, in the meantime, the crew had festooned with lanterns, palm fronds, and tamarisk branches. It was the first Christmas of the Breasteds' marriage.[46]

They continued downriver about fifteen miles to Naqada, where Flinders Petrie, a British archaeologist, was excavating a predynastic cemetery of about 4800–3100 BCE. He pioneered a number of modern archaeological techniques, including sequence dating based on the comparative study of pottery shards.

Petrie's advances grew out of meticulous and systematic methods of excavation, documentation, and analysis of *all* materials found at a given site, thereby setting a new standard of accuracy and thoroughness in Middle Eastern archaeology. Breasted was eager to meet Petrie, hoping in part that he might obtain some finds for Chicago. He remained several days to learn about Petrie's excavation techniques as well as the costs and challenges of fielding a large archaeological operation. They got along well, and Petrie, having a couple of years earlier broken off relations with his funding source, proposed Breasted partner with him on future projects, perhaps hoping his university affiliation could bring much-needed cash to the enterprise. Breasted was flattered but declined. He was trained to transcribe, translate, and interpret texts, not dig. Petrie was refining archaeological practices that Breasted would have appreciated not only for their increasing exactitude and reliability but for the additional training required to master them. Rather than engage in yet more schooling, he was eager to apply the knowledge he already possessed on inscriptions that, he was just beginning to appreciate, were vast and endangered.

Moreover, he was beginning to formulate a plan of his own: "I have tried of late to find some short phrase or fitting idea to sum up the work I want or can do. And it has finally condensed itself to this; to study and read to my fellow men the oldest chapter in the story of human progress. This of course includes a thousand themes that touch the history of the people of redemption and the story of how they brought a higher life to man." By "read . . . the story," Breasted meant that he wanted to approach the texts as *historical* rather than philological evidence, and his reference to "progress" signaled his inclination to view human history as ipso facto one of steady improvement. Unbeknownst to Breasted, his declaration allied him with other American scholars who were just then laying the foundations for American Progressive History, a movement among American historians that would become more fully articulated about a decade later. Rooted in an intermingling of "scientific history," based on scrupulous methodological practices, with the conceptual model of evolution as one of endless improvement in human development, American Progressive History drew on scholarly innovations Breasted had personally observed in Germany. Having arrived at his historical perspective through studies in Hamito-Semitic philology, Breasted was groping for his own distinctive contribution to the story of human evolution. His references to the "history of the people of redemption" and the "higher life" of man mark steps in this direction as he began to narrow his focus on the *pre*history of Jewish thought, that is, the sources of Judaic ethical teachings in the religious texts of ancient Egypt.[47]

The Breasteds concluded their Nile journey in late January 1895 at el-Minya, but not before stopping at Tell el-Amârna, site of Akhenaten's short-lived, newly created capital, Akhetaton. The rambling complex of temples, tomb chapels, and

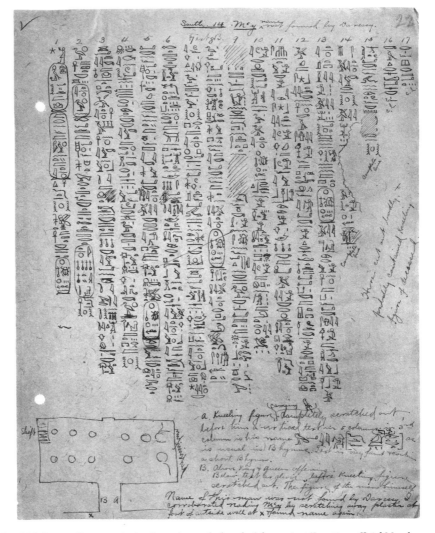

Fig. 1.16 Breasted's transcription from the tomb chapel of the ancient Egyptian official May, located among the southern Tombs of the Nobles (no. 14) at Tell el-Amârna, Egypt, ca. 26 January 1895. Courtesy of the Oriental Institute, University of Chicago.

other structures were of special interest to Breasted because his dissertation research suggested the site might contain more evidence of the pharaoh's radical theology. Breasted had worked from other scholars' transcriptions made at Akhetaton, and he was eager to study the originals. He was shocked to find, however, that one of the inscriptions treated in his dissertation had recently been vandalized. The sight of the now irreparably damaged inscription, as well as his discovery that previously published inscriptions had been incorrectly transcribed (figure 1.16), impressed on him the value of accurately recording such sources before they were permanently lost to vandalism or natural erosion. But

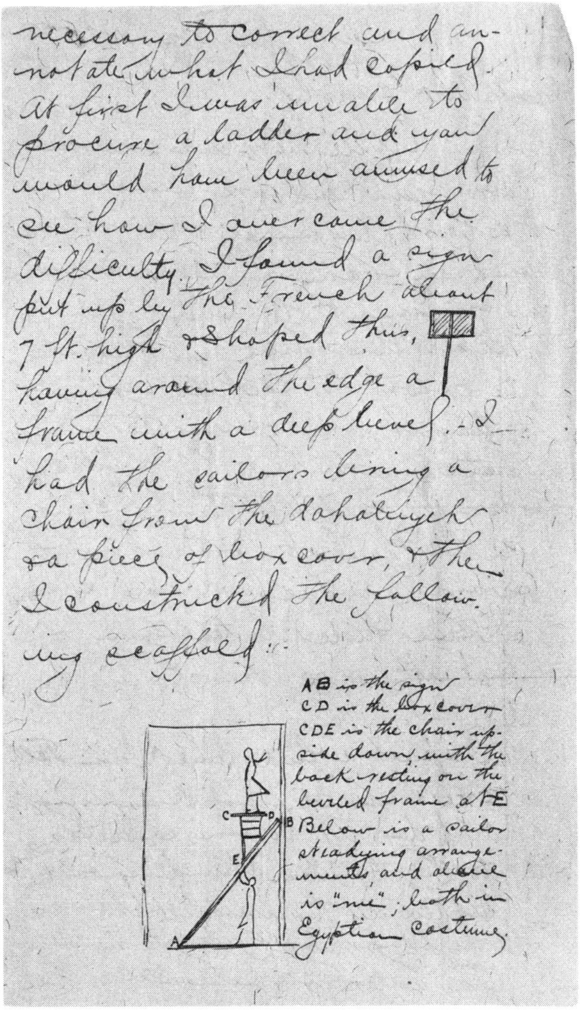

necessary to correct and an-
notate what I had copied.
At first I was unable to
procure a ladder and you
would have been amused to
see how I overcame the
difficulty. I found a sign
put up by the French about
7 ft. high & shaped thus,
having around the edge a
frame with a deep bevel. I
had the sailors bring a
chair from the dahabiyeh
& a piece of box cover, & then
I constructed the follow-
ing scaffold:

AB is the sign
CD is the box cover
CDE is the chair up-
side down with the
back resting on the
beveled frame at E
Below is a sailor
steadying arrange-
ments and above
is "me"; both in
Egyptian costume

Fig. 1.17 Breasted's account and Egyptian-style illustration of an improvised scaffold erected at Tell el-Amârna, Egypt, from a letter to his parents, 24 January 1895. Courtesy of the Oriental Institute, University of Chicago.

the trip also taught Breasted that copying inscriptions was no easy matter. At el-Amârna the task entailed improvising a scaffolding, which Breasted humorously depicted hieroglyph-style in a letter home (figure 1.17). From el-Minya they traveled the remaining 150 miles north by train to Cairo, where they remained for a few more weeks.

By 1895 Cairo had become a cosmopolitan crossroads of trade, culture, and international politics. On its streets one could encounter not only the diverse religious groups native to the city—Moslems, Copts, and Jews—but a variety of foreign populations as well, especially those still rivaling for imperial control over Egypt's destiny: Ottoman Turks, British, French. The growth in international tourism brought flocks of Westerners to its most famous sites, from the pyramids and sphinx on the Giza plateau, just beyond the western fringes of the city, to the great Islamic enclave dominated by the Citadel built on a rise on

Cairo's east. Begun in the 1100s and enlarged by subsequent rulers including the Ottomans, the Citadel was the seat of power until the late nineteenth century. Within its precincts and beyond, the area is crowded with Islamic Cairo's oldest buildings, including a number of mosques dating to the Middle Ages. Among the earliest is the al-Azhar Mosque, begun in 970, which is also home to the world's oldest continuously functioning university. The nearby "great bazaar" added to that sense of exoticism and mystery so attractive to foreigners. But Cairo was also the capital, and anyone needing to transact business in Egypt, including Egyptologists seeking permission for research, had to learn to navigate the country's layered bureaucracies, all of which were headquartered there.

The Breasteds toured Islamic Cairo and took day trips to nearby locations such as the very ancient pyramid complexes of Dashur and Saqqara. Breasted also sought photographs, casts, and antiquities for the university, working from a methodically compiled checklist. Striving to achieve a full chronological representation of ancient Egypt's material culture, Breasted hoped to lay the foundation of a teaching collection at minimum cost. He soon learned it was a task that required not only his improving Arabic skills but a "poker face" too, the artful use of disinterest to haggle with those possessing important objects. Antiquities prices were already high in Cairo, and he avoided dealers there, going instead "up into the country" to find things among the "natives." Despite his limited budget, Breasted acquired several cases of materials. He was less successful with donated objects and began contemplating an alternative: fund-raising to buy them. "I think the way is now prepared for diverting to . . . Chicago . . . a larger share of the remarkable finds which are to be made in Egypt during the next ten years. I have worked and planned . . . with that end in view and I am sure a fair presentation of the matter in America will bring the necessary funds."[48]

The Breasteds set sail for Marseilles on 10 February on their way to a wintry Paris. Cold and dreary, *la Ville Lumière* seemed anything but, absent the "genial sun of Egypt." Conserving what little cash they still had, they lodged in "a cramped room under the eaves of a melancholy hotel . . . crouched over a tiny grate in which a feeble flame fluttered hopelessly against the freezing night air." Breasted went to the Louvre, where he met Paul Pierret, curator of the museum's Egyptian collections, and received permission to enter early and work "a solid week from morning till evening." He later regretted that he spent only an hour "among the Asiatic collections, and ten minutes among the Greek marbles, to see the Venus de Milo," adding that he saw "nothing" of Paris, instead shuttling "like a mole . . . between a shabby little hotel and the Louvre. This was obviously not the way to broaden one's horizon or enrich one's cultural experience. It was, in fact, reprehensible and stupid. But I was trying desperately to make myself an Egyptologist according to a concept I had evolved alone and could not find words to impart to those around me."

He also met Gaston Maspero, the leading French Egyptologist of his generation. A prolific scholar, Maspero published numerous books, essays, and reviews, and he supervised several important field projects in Egypt as director of the Egyptian Antiquities Service from 1881 to 1886 and again from 1899 to 1914. During their conversation Breasted asked Maspero about a recent publication Breasted had been asked to review. Maspero replied "that ever since he had begun it, when he was only eighteen years old, he had worked at almost no other subject," prompting Breasted to "wonder at my brashness in having consented to review it." Yet Breasted was heir to a rivalry between French and German Egyptologists in which he fell very much on the German side. Of the French he wrote, "Their methods are inclined to be slipshod. . . . The most obvious details escape them, and they hide their distaste for the drudgery of solid research behind a facade of facile, sometimes brilliant, but too often inaccurate generalization." Breasted's review of Maspero's book was unstinting in his enumeration of its errors albeit tempered with an appreciation of the scholar's many accomplishments.[49]

From Paris the Breasteds continued to London, where the British Museum's major collection of Egyptian antiquities was the main destination, followed by a side trip to Oxford University and the Ashmolean Museum's collection. Breasted was astonished by labeling errors in the British Museum, which he had been taught was "the standard of solid reliability, a sort of scholastic Bank of England." He introduced himself to E. A. T. Wallis Budge, the museum's then recently appointed "Keeper of Egyptian and Assyrian Antiquities" and one of England's leading Egyptologists. A prodigious author of scholarly and popular books, Budge was frequently criticized for his error-filled publications, a habitual carelessness Breasted felt was evident in the British Museum's galleries as well. He undiplomatically pointed out error after error among the Egyptian gallery labels, and Budge readily acknowledged them, explaining that many of the labels were old and citing the distractions of more pressing concerns. Whether for reasons of youth and inexperience, the hardening of German training, or the temerity of a brilliant and quick intellect, Breasted was outspoken in the presence of greater lights and fiercely determined to improve on the work of his predecessors.

The Breasteds sailed for America on 13 March 1895. Summing up his sojourn abroad, he wrote, "It has cost almost inhuman effort . . . to accomplish all I set out to do. . . . Now at last it is finished. I have not yet gained financially, though we shall all have enough. But I have acquired the equipment for a great work."[50]

2

What the Monuments Say

F.A.M.E. and Family

The University of Chicago opened its doors in 1892 in Hyde Park, a neighborhood about seven miles south of Chicago that was annexed by the city in 1889. It was built over a patchy expanse of low prairies, sandy ridges, and wetlands whose filling and draining leveled the area into a Euclidean plain upon which the university's ambitious campus plan was mapped. The "Gray City" of the university and the "White City" of its neighbor, the 1893 World's Columbian Exposition, were erected almost simultaneously and with amazing speed. By the time of Breasted's return, however, the fair's mostly temporary structures had all but disappeared, while the "Gray City" of the university was still expanding. The trustees' selection of a Gothic architectural style, uniformly realized in blue Bedford limestone on a quadrangular campus plan, imposed a sense of order and permanence on the university's dizzying growth. For its inaugural class the university offered a multipurpose building—Cobb Hall (figure 2.1)—initially housing classrooms, faculty and administration offices, an assembly room, three men's dormitories, and a temporary gymnasium and library building. By the time Breasted arrived in 1895, the university had added four women's dormitories, a pair

Fig. 2.1 Cobb Hall (nearest the camera) and men's dormitories, viewed from the northeast, ca. 1890s. Archival Photofiles, apf2-01788, Special Collections Research Center, University of Chicago Library.

of laboratory buildings for physics and chemistry, the Walker Museum—erected for the natural sciences—and the president's house. From the beginning, however, the influx of faculty, students, books, laboratory equipment, and the many other accouterments of university research and teaching outpaced the buildings' capacities to house them. Space was tight as well for Breasted's home department, Semitic Languages and Literatures, which was crammed into two rooms on Cobb Hall's top floor, where he was "assigned to a small office." Upon moving in he was frustrated to discover that there "was no room for filing even the photographs" Breasted had purchased or taken with his "tupenny camera." The antiquities he acquired had to be stored in the Walker Museum basement.[1]

The university's academic program was "in the most elemental and essential ways, Harper writ large." He expected it to be "broad and Christian in the fullest sense," contributing not only to the betterment of society through its research and teaching, but also "to nurtur[ing] a religion for modernity, a religion that could unite all the dimensions of life which modernity separated." Harper "strenuously sought to keep the critically interpreted scriptures integrally related to modern scholarship" while also addressing the more specialized research needs of a "new generation of academic professionals returning from Germany and emerging from the new graduate programs . . . in American universities." In striving to integrate the sacred teachings of scripture with the secular ethos of modern research, Harper envisioned the university's leading society to a better life in which material needs and those of the spirit would be brought into greater harmony.[2]

The practical realization of Harper's ideas was based partially on his limited knowledge of precedents in Europe and America and primarily on his teaching experiences in the seminary, university, and Chautauqua, as well as his correspondence-study programs and publishing ventures. Accordingly, in composing Chicago with the three divisions of the University Proper, the University Extension, and University Publication Work, Harper created an institution "in which the generation of knowledge would be intimately linked to teaching and publication, and in which the authority of scholarship would derive in great degree from the extent of its penetration of the social fabric."

The design of the academic calendar regularly freed professors to alternate teaching duties and research. The academic year was divided into four quarters of twelve weeks separated by one-week interims, with courses scheduled to allow a wide array of major and minor degrees. Faculty members were required to teach three quarters in each calendar year for up to twelve hours a week. Harper's plan permitted an extra degree of flexibility in that a "professor would be permitted to be out of residence any one of the four quarters in a year, or to take two vacations of six weeks in different quarters by teaching two quarters at half time in place of one quarter at full time. The professor could also teach beyond the required three quarters a year and thus accumulate credit toward extra pay or extra vacation time," the "vacation time" becoming in effect paid leaves for research.

In "merging . . . undergraduate education, graduate research, and extension courses within a single institution," Harper's plan offered "a fresh and appealing idealism in the conception of an academic setting that would permit faculty to move easily from regular classroom teaching to other spheres of activity—extension lectures, travel, research, writing—all permitted, in fact expected, within the cycle of the new unending academic year." Imbedded in this plan was Harper's "ideal of the university scholar" who "would be an instructor in the classroom, on the lecture platform, in the graduate seminar, through correspondence courses, and on the printed page, both in the popular press and periodical literature and in the more rigorous forums of professional monographs and journals. The scholar would be an administrator as well as teacher, organizing a varied program of instruction given by himself and others and directing the course of research projects."

Harper's plan also reflected his own work ethic. What he viewed as its inestimable advantages for the university community were due to "his urgent, almost fanatical, desire to help students and faculty to maximize time and to achieve efficiency, discipline, and economy. Harper's ideal world was one in which every minute was accounted for, and no day properly concluded without a bounty of productive work." By his example, as well as his plans, Harper cultivated a sense of urgency about productivity: "the University was to be a meritocracy of accomplishment, not credentials. 'What are you doing?' was to be a more important question than 'What have you done?'"[3]

With his advanced German training in Egyptology, a new field to America, Breasted fit Harper's goal of building the university into one of the world's leading centers for, as he put it, "pure" scholarship and science. Among the university's areas of special strength were religious and ancient Near Eastern studies to be pursued in the university's Divinity School and a purposefully separate Department of Semitic Languages and Literatures. Harper appointed himself head of the latter department and regularly taught courses in it and the Divinity School. The composition of the two faculties corresponded to specializations represented in Harper's scholarly and popular journals, from biblical studies and the Higher Criticism to ancient Near Eastern languages and literatures. The Department of Comparative Religion, housed in the Divinity School, was the nation's first, and, accompanied by "ancillary disciplines" in the Semitic languages department—Assyriology, Egyptology, Hebrew, Aramaic, Old Testament studies, Arabic, and Islamic studies—it helped fulfill Harper's objective that the university "not only be religious in a new way" but also enrich "the scientific study of religion as a way of enhancing the role of professional theology in urban, mass society." Yet by separating religious studies, housed in the Divinity School, from Old Testament studies, housed in the Semitic languages department, Harper shielded the Divinity School from attacks by religious conservatives upset over the Higher Criticism.

When Breasted began teaching in late spring 1895, about a half year shy of thirty, he began at the level of "Assistant" in Egyptology but within a year was promoted to "Instructor." In addition to his home-department appointment in Semitic Languages and Literatures, he had joint appointments in the Divinity School—in Old Testament Literature and Interpretation, the Department of Archaeology, and the University Extension. Breasted was also named assistant director and curator of Egyptology of the Haskell Oriental Museum, which was under construction that spring. While his appointment helped fill out the array of scholarly fields Harper wanted to staff, Breasted's position was unusual because of his comparative youth and inexperience.

The president strove to open the university with an all-star academic staff and was largely successful, recruiting accomplished scholars and scientists from throughout the United States and abroad, among whom were university presidents he lured back into scholarship from institutions such as Brown, Wellesley, and the University of Wisconsin. A large percentage of the 120 faculty members on hand when the university opened had been recruited from the leading universities of the day, including, in order of representation, Yale, Johns Hopkins,

Clark, and Harvard. More than a third of Chicago's staff had trained in German universities, and about half of the faculty had doctorates, medical degrees, or—among the contingent being absorbed from the Baptist Union Theological Seminary—doctor-of-divinity degrees. As a whole, the university's first faculty reflected "a distinctive amalgam of liberal democratic Baptist idealism and German-based investigative rigor."[4]

Breasted's workload was not confined to teaching and museum duties. With a starting salary of $800 per year, at the time respectable though not sufficient to support him, his wife, and his parents, he immediately began accepting off-campus speaking engagements. While Breasted was in Europe, his parents had moved again, this time to Englewood, a small community southwest of downtown Chicago that was annexed by the city in 1889. The newlyweds moved into his parents' twelve-room wood-frame home for reasons of convenience as well as economy: he could bicycle to campus about three miles east. His father had retired by this point, his mother had never been employed, and Breasted was determined to repay their financial support by providing comfortable, worry-free care in their old age. Public speaking thus brought extra income needed to meet his obligations, and it was advantageous to Breasted's career development as well. Alongside extension classes, public appearances furthered the university's outreach to the community, a high priority in Harper's institutional mission. And by the last quarter of the nineteenth century in America, giving "popular lectures" had become an oft-traveled path for establishing a professional career by cultivating public renown and respectability, contributing to society's well-being, and promulgating new ideas.

There were plenty of speaking opportunities, but they were not individually very remunerative, so Breasted had to take as many as possible to satisfy his family's needs. From the moment he began in April 1895 until four years later, he listed every talk he gave including locations and subjects in a "Pastor's Pocket Record." The first was titled "Recent Archaeology Work in Egypt," hosted by Harper at the president's house within days of Breasted's return. In the following months and years his travels gradually expanded from the Chicago area to the Midwest and the East Coast. He gave individual lectures on such topics as the "Old Empire," "Egyptian Art," and "Egyptian Folklore," and he gave three-to-six-session lecture series, usually thematically related, such as one called "The First Reformer."

Breasted also learned the art of composing engaging titles, and after about a year certain key words and concepts—pharaoh, pyramid, afterlife—began to appear: "Land of the Pharaohs," "Life after Death among the Egyptians," and "Origins and History of the Pyramids." He spoke at churches and at least one synagogue, student club meetings, private clubs, museums, high schools, and colleges; he addressed professional associations of teachers and college endowment administrators, amateur folklore associations, Bible and Semitics students, and devotees of archaeology. Years later he recalled, "Often I traveled several hundred miles to earn twenty-five dollars and expenses, and only after years of barnstorming was this gradually increased to what was known among University Extension lecturers as 'F.A.M.E.'—'fifty and my expenses'!"[5]

Because of the popular interest in all things Egyptian, Breasted had little difficulty attracting large and enthusiastic audiences. The material culture and texts of ancient Egypt have captivated other civilizations since as early as the Macedonian supremacy in ancient Greece. But public curiosity in late-nineteenth-century Europe and America was surging thanks to the wide exposure to Egyptian-style architecture and related displays at world's fairs beginning with England's 1851 Crystal Palace exposition and continuing with increasing regularity through the turn of the century. The World's Columbian Exposition introduced its visitors to Egypt in a tawdry commercial exhibit titled "Streets of Cairo," complete with exotic dance performances that lodged in cultural memory as the artistry of a woman known as "Little Egypt." When Breasted embarked on the lecture circuit, he learned that "Egyptology was . . . commonly regarded by the public and the press as something bizarre, an oddity at a county fair, a fakir's imposition upon the general credulity." Many in his audiences came because they associated ancient Egypt with the occult—necromancy, astrology, palmistry, spells, curses. Breasted tried to set people straight by undercutting superstition with scholarship, a task that forced him to begin articulating Egyptology's methodology and findings in language accessible to the general public.[6]

His most succinct statement came in an address titled "Looking Eastward," delivered to the Chicago Women's Club in summer 1896. Based on an amalgam of outline, notes, and more fully developed text—a reflection of his increasing confidence in speaking extemporaneously—"Looking Eastward" begins with a comparison between "Theosophy" and "History & Archaeology." "Theosophy" was Breasted's shorthand for popular superstitions associated with ancient Egypt. He chose the term because of the notoriety surrounding the Theosophical Society, founded in 1875 by Helena Blavatsky, and in particular the success of Blavatsky's book *Isis Unveiled*, published two years later, in which she denounced traditional Western religions and modern science, arguing that mystical disciplines and teachings offered the only true path to enlightenment. The "Isis" of the title is Greek for a goddess of ancient Egypt. In the first part of her book Blavatsky concocted out of what little was known at the time about Isis worship a fantasy of Egyptian occultism centered on the goddess.

Breasted then offered examples of people "looking east": Abraham, who in old age "turned back from the land of his adoption, to his eastern home that there . . . he might choose a helpmeet for his only son"; men who, "when the best thought of Greece was shattered . . . before the problem of matter and of spirit, . . . turned to the east and the mysteries of Isis and the infernal deity Anubis . . . ; [and when] all eyes were turned to the east again, as the Christ arose." "Little wonder," Breasted continued, "that we of today should be looking earnestly eastward." But he distinguished between those "looking in a sober, historical and critical spirit" and those "looking for the mysterious, the hidden, the inexplicable, the symbolical." He and his fellow "Orientalists," working in the "historical and critical spirit" and following a "purely & coldly scientific" method, were studying "the childhood of the race, . . . man achieving the first elements of human culture." That type of study is useful, Breasted argued, because it produces an "added prospect of human experience, the added link to our evolution." By way of contrast, Breasted characterized "much of modern enthusiasm for the east in this country, like theosophy, symbolism, or astrology" as having "only a perverted utilitarian purpose . . . to resuscitate its beliefs and adopt them today."[7]

Imbedded in his attack on these superstitions is an indication of Breasted's expanding scholarly affinities. He was signaling his partiality toward history as a methodological path he wanted to pursue, and closely related to it was an emerging interest in situating ancient origins, via the theoretical model of evolution, as a foundation of modern society. Equally important is his self-identification as an "Orientalist," as opposed to the narrower designation "Egyptologist." "Orientalist" might seem an odd usage today, but in Breasted's time "Orient" was the most commonly accepted term among Europeans and Americans for the lands extending from northern Africa and the Middle East to South and East Asia, and even the South Pacific. Thus, when a university official suggested some years later that Breasted's department change its name from "Semitic Languages and Literatures" to "Oriental Languages and Literatures," he was drawing upon then conventional usage to represent the department's expansion beyond its areas of expertise in ancient Near Eastern languages to include Chinese and Japanese studies as well.

While the "Orient" was not quite the geographical opposite of the "Occident," in some ways it did serve as an umbrella term for the West's cultural others. Yet the extent to which this nomenclature also represented a widely shared intellectual position—for example, "Orientalism" as cultural imperialism in Middle Eastern studies—is much less clear. While there were traces of cultural hegemony in the scholarship of Breasted's peers and eventually his own, the nuts and bolts of their work concentrated on deciphering ancient languages and ever more rigorous archaeological investigations. For most of them their interactions with the contemporary Middle East were incidental to a project that bypassed it on the way to understanding a distant past. This is not to excuse unacceptable attitudes and behavior. Rather, it's to point out that, to a large extent, were it possible to put the Orientalists and their critics—who came along a few generations later—in the same room, they would find themselves talking about very different concerns. As one scholar observed, "Rather than demonstrating the bankruptcy of Western attempts to understand the human world around it, Orientalism supplied . . . the tools even its harshest censurers need to argue against it."

Ironically, the most lasting damage wreaked by scholars of Breasted's generation was not on the Middle East or Islam but on the founding stories and ethical underpinnings of Judaism and Christianity. As the Orientalists' discoveries worked their way into the Higher Criticism and ancient historiography, it was the theological origins and intellectual primacy of Western civilization that would have to be fundamentally rethought.[8]

Breasted's lectures were popular because of his growing skill in presenting complex ideas in a lucid and colorful manner and in selecting vivid photographs to illustrate them. One reviewer wrote: "Pilgrim Congregational Church is to be congratulated upon the successful and interesting University Extension course by Dr. James Henry Breasted, upon 'Egypt and the Nile Dwellers,' now being there. Dr. Breasted is an adept in the handling of his subjects, holding his listeners with unabated interest throughout the lectures. The many views are exceptionally clear and many are pictures which will never be lost from memory. The analysis of the rosette [sic] stone, the poetic treatment of the trip up the Nile, the different tribes found in the country . . . and the placing of the dynasties, life on the estates, pyramid builders and pyramids themselves were some of the very interesting subjects" (figure 2.2).

The presentations were illustrated with various types of lantern-slide projections. An 1896 prospectus for Breasted's six-lecture series titled "Egypt—Its History and Civilization" declares it would be "fully illustrated by Stereopticon Views, some 500 in all." The stereopticon, invented in 1863, showed two or three images side by side, and some instruments were equipped to overlap images, allowing the projectionist to dissolve from one to the next. Breasted used lantern slides to draw audiences into the settings of ancient Egypt by showing views of contemporary as well as ancient Nile-valley "scenes." For a subsequent University Extension "Lecture-Study" series, he explained "Prehistoric Egyptians" with images of "pottery, stone vessels, flint, wood carving, stone sculpture"; Egyptian ideas about life, death, and the afterlife with views of tomb architecture and furnishings; and ancient "social and industrial life" with views of bas-reliefs depicting "a hunt in the swamp, fish spearing, bird snaring, . . . a banquet, . . . carpenters, woodcutters, boat-builders, . . . a pleasure sail, moving a colossus."[9]

Breasted's lectures also focused on the aesthetic qualities of ancient Egypt's visual culture. In an 1898 University Extension lecture on Old Empire "graphic art," by which he meant bas-reliefs as opposed to architecture or statuary, he addressed such issues as the

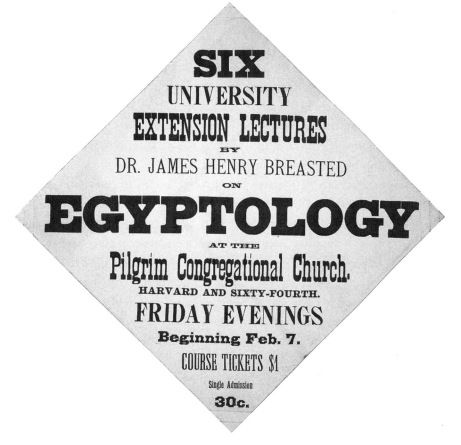

Fig. 2.2 Poster, ca. January–February 1896. Courtesy of the Oriental Institute, University of Chicago.

problem of putting an object possessing thickness and roundness on a flat surface. . . . The unconscious effort of the Egyptian, like that of the child at the present day, drawing not what he sees but what he knows. Laws of Egyptian drawing: first, all objects must be represented with the characteristic dimension . . . across the line of vision . . . ; second, no nearer part may intervene to completely hide a further part . . . ; third, all figures must, if possible . . . face toward the observer's right, due to the influence of hieroglyphic [writing] which also faces the right. . . . Composition: the single group, with each figure thrust out from behind any intervening figure, usually before or above the latter; groups in different fields, with each distant field pushed up above the intervening fields.

For a scholar trained in ancient languages and philology, Breasted showed a remarkable capacity for perceiving and explaining Egyptian pictorial techniques.

Perhaps he acquired this ability while learning to detect the slight differences in the composition of individual hieroglyphs and their sequences in lines of text so necessary for understanding the shades of meaning they convey. Eye training is essential in Egyptology, and Breasted readily used his skill to open others' eyes to the rich material culture of ancient Egypt.[10]

The stress of teaching regular classes, conducting University Extension courses, and attending to out-of-town speaking engagements, as well as pursuing his scholarly objectives, began to affect Breasted's health. He started experiencing "chronic enteric trouble" that would recur in subsequent years. Life at home was no easier. His father's health began to fail in the year following Breasted's return, and he died at home in spring 1896. The family's grief was alleviated somewhat by news of Frances Breasted's pregnancy with her first child, due the following September. They rallied over the summer in anticipation of the new arrival only to be cast down again when a drunk doctor bungled the delivery and the baby died. Breasted, his wife, and mother all felt the loss acutely. But for Frances Breasted in particular, it "aggravated . . . a tendency to extreme nervousness, to moodiness, and to unpredictable outbursts of querulous condemnation of those about her, followed always by fits of abject self-deprecation and remorse." Then Theodocia Backus began to decline that fall and died in January 1897 at her home in Rockford. She had become by then a regular family visitor in Englewood, her close relationship with the Breasteds having grown to include Frances, and her passing deepened the gloom.

Without Charles Breasted, "who had always had a knack of keeping the family peace" during his son's lengthening absences for work and travel, Frances Breasted's "black moods seized her more frequently and fiercely, until they affected the whole household, and James would come home to find the air tense with anger, Frances locked in her room, and no one speaking to anyone." So, despite their limited means, the couple moved out of the Englewood home to a rental apartment converted from the top floor of a house near the university. About that time she became pregnant again, and to their great relief and joy, in September 1897, a year to the day after the death of their first child, they welcomed a healthy son into their family. They named him Charles.[11]

Museum Work

Unlike many university colleagues whose ambitions exceeded the young institution's still inadequate facilities, Breasted could look forward to completion of the Haskell Oriental Museum. The Gothic-style building, designed by Henry Ives Cobb in accordance with the university's campus plan, opened in summer 1896 with speeches and celebratory conferences on archaeology, comparative religions, and the Bible (figure 2.3). Speaking on behalf of the donor, Caroline

Fig. 2.3 Haskell Oriental Museum, viewed from the east, ca. 1890s. Archival Photofiles, apf2-03433, Special Collections Research Center, University of Chicago Library.

Haskell, who could not attend the ceremony, George S. Goodspeed conveyed the donor's intentions:

> It is a long step from the brilliant, modern, and intensely practical work of physics to what . . . may seem the much more remote, scholastic, theoretical, and less immediately useful department of oriental study. But [to our] bene- factor . . . , the "light from the East" shines still with undiminished brightness upon our western science. . . . In providing this building it is [her] thought . . . that oriental studies . . . should find their center and their greatest utility in their contributions to the better knowledge of the divine revelation contained in the Jewish and Christian Scriptures. . . . The Bible is a new book in the light of our new studies in oriental life, oriental philology, oriental history, oriental archaeology, and oriental religion. And who can deny that what contributes to our better understanding of the divine truth of the Holy Scriptures contributes in the most immediate and practical way to the progress of the world?

Oddly, Harper—who spoke next—only briefly acknowledged the occasion and the building's function. The reason was soon clear. He had to explain that the museum's intended purpose would, with the donor's permission, be compro- mised from the outset. Of the museum's four flours, only the first floor and part of the second were allocated for an "Egyptological museum," an "Assyriological museum," and "material which shall specially illustrate the writings of sacred

Scriptures, in other words, a Palestinian museum." The remainder of the building was designated for general classrooms, faculty offices, and, on the third floor, the Divinity School library and a "museum of Comparative Religion." There was far less space for the Egyptian materials than Breasted expected, but it was a start.[12]

The disciplinary specializations of the Haskell and Walker museums, and the fact they were among the university's earliest buildings, fit the university's "theory of education," which "demanded, not only departmental libraries, but also departmental museums." Within a year of Chicago's opening, Harper added an administrative division of University Libraries, Laboratories, and Museums, signifying his belief that the "museum is as essential an element in educational work as is the library. It is these two factors which have revolutionized educational methods in the last quarter of a century." But the speed of faculty and student-body growth during the first few years soon overwhelmed the university's ability to provide facilities for general instructional needs. The reallocation of space in Haskell to classrooms and offices echoed the Walker Museum's uses when it opened in 1893. Designated for natural history exhibits, it, too, had to accommodate other instructional demands, as well as storage of "Semitic Archaeology and Comparative Religions" collections until Haskell opened, and those in "Botany, Osteology, and vertebrate Paleontology" until the Hull Biological Laboratories opened in 1897. Six years later "a large part of the space" in Walker was still used for classrooms and laboratories, and the creation and support of museums remained a priority and problem at the conclusion of the university's first decade.

In 1903 Harper reported, "The progress . . . in establishing Museums has not been very considerable. With the exception of the Oriental Museum, which is fairly well developed in the Archaeology of Egypt, and the various paleontological collections . . . , little has been accomplished." He hoped to create a "Historical Museum," "Botanical Museum," "Zoölogical Museum," "Commercial Museum," and "a museum for the education of the public." At this point, Harper admitted, "The whole policy of the museum work requires to be definitely considered and decided." His initial plan called for bringing "together the material of all Departments, and to have what would be called a General Museum." Harper realized, however, that "each group of Departments desires to establish a museum and to have it located in the closest possible relationship to the lecture work of these Departments. In other words, the Departmental Museum seems to commend itself, after the fashion of the Departmental Library. . . . Yet it is these same two factors in the University equipment which are least fully developed. . . . The libraries are only half way developed; the museums have hardly begun." Lacking a ready solution to these problems, Harper asked the Board of Libraries, Laboratories, and Museums, "What is to be the future policy of the University regarding Museums?"[13]

The board appointed a subcommittee of interested faculty to address the matter. Unsurprisingly, the committee concluded that museums were an "urgent necessity" and "absolutely essential to the proper development of several of the departments." It recommended that "the museums should be developed with primary reference to <u>investigation</u> and <u>instruction</u>, and only subordinately for purposes of exhibition. . . . In so far as the latter purpose finds a place, the exhibition should have primary reference to the <u>University public</u> rather than the general public." The committee then proposed a two-part approach, one being creation of a "general composite museum," the other a network of existing and new departmental museums. The composite museum would, first, "bring together into a single collection, or systematic series of collections, a typical synoptical representation of all those phases of inquiry that admit of successful museum representation" in its "exhibit portion" and, second, "bring together in drawers and other suitable modes of accessible storage, collections for advanced study and investigation"—the second function being "regarded by the Committee as the more important." The committee's proposal regarding departmental museums affirmed existing practices, the main purpose being "to furnish to the departments to which a museum is necessary . . . their own special illustrative and investigative material, within their own buildings, so as to be immediately accessible and completely under departmental control." But above all else, space was the "imperative physical factor."[14]

The committee's recommendations concerning a general museum along with departmental museums echoed discussions about the future of the university's library system. In his second *Official Bulletin*, one of a series in which he mapped out his plans for Chicago, Harper wrote: "In addition to the General Library . . . , a special library and reading-room will be established in connection with each department." Soon after the university opened, however, questions arose over the purview of the general library versus that of the departmental branches. While there were obvious concerns about administrative efficiency and needless duplication, a deeper issue was the cohesion of knowledge represented by the *university* as opposed to the deepening specialization of the disciplines which populated it. For some, addressing these questions was tantamount to addressing the nature and purpose of the university itself. As faculty members grappled with the issues,

> Two distinct positions emerged. If library books and journals were seen as an embodiment of the sum of human learning, then the unity of the University would require that they be consolidated into a single, centralized collection

available to all faculty and students on a uniform basis. If, on the contrary, books and journals were viewed as the products of . . . individual disciplines and the resources for further work in [them], then they ought properly to remain under the control of individual . . . departments and be housed in close proximity to seminar rooms and laboratories. . . .

The university ideal thus promoted two incompatible modernisms, one tending toward a greater procedural uniformity and central programmatic control, and the other promoting the fullest development of scholarly . . . knowledge in accordance with the . . . individual academic disciplines. One modernism could not be substantially enhanced without diminishing the strength of the other.

In response to the museum subcommittee's recommendations, a separate "Board of Museums" was created to discuss its building proposals with the university Trustees' Committee on Buildings and Grounds. Then planning stalled. Nearly a year later, replying to a query from Harper, a Board of Museums member replied that "nothing definite . . . can be accomplished . . . without considerable financial aid. . . . This is, perhaps, not so much a matter for the Board of Museums as for the Trustees." The board's meetings became less and less frequent as funding constraints rendered the prospect of new construction increasingly unlikely.[15]

While the effort to solve the Haskell and Walker space problems did not yield any immediate results, it did force an articulation of the university community's interests in museums. Serving its research and teaching needs was essential, but serving the general public was not—a stance that ran counter to Harper's initial vision of the university's museums' helping to bring the higher learning to the public. Harper's views were certainly in keeping with the time's civic spirit. The collective philanthropic effort that created the university, albeit sparked by John D. Rockefeller's offer, was one among many of the era's comparable endeavors in Chicago and other American cities. A host of major public museums were established in the 1870s and 1880s: the American Museum of Natural History and the Metropolitan Museum of Art (New York, 1869 and 1870 respectively), the Boston Museum of Fine Arts (1870), the predecessor institution to the Philadelphia Museum of Art (1876), the Art Institute of Chicago (1879), and the Detroit Institute of Arts (1885), to name a few. Their founders—like those who supported Chicago's founding—established museums out of a philanthropic consensus that related these "engines of culture" to civic improvement.

Harper's efforts to satisfy the university's museum needs may ultimately have foundered on his leading trustees' other museum interests in Chicago. Two key members of the Trustees' Committee on Building and Grounds were Martin A. Ryerson, who had been president of the university's board of trustees since

1892, and Charles L. Hutchinson, the board's treasurer since 1891. Both were also deeply involved in the city's museums. Ryerson was a trustee of the Art Institute of Chicago and vice president of its board during this period, as well as a founder and board vice president of the Field Columbian Museum of Natural History since 1893. Hutchinson was a founder of the Art Institute in 1879 and became president of its board of trustees in 1882, a post he held until his death. They, like other Chicago philanthropists and opinion leaders, were eager to support institutions that increased the city's cultural opportunities and civic amenities but not initiatives that needlessly duplicated those of others already in Chicago.[16]

Breasted assumed his Haskell Museum responsibilities without formal training in museum work. Associations of museum professionals were just forming about this time, and the formulation of standards of practice and museum studies programs were still off in the future. If scholars of Breasted's and previous generations who found themselves in museum positions had any museum experience at all, it was usually acquired while they did research in museum collections. From Erman and the New Museum Breasted learned the importance of building up a great collection as a stimulant for teaching and research, and he was eager to assemble one in Haskell. But whereas the New Museum was backed by a king and government, Haskell was merely a unit within a large university that—in addition to having other priorities—was itself competing with other institutions for the support of private donors.

Breasted's first encounter with this problem came during the Egyptian trip when he crossed paths with Edward E. Ayer, a Chicago lumberman, collector, and philanthropist. Ayer, also one of the Field Museum's founders and president of its board of trustees at the time, was in Egypt along with "other wealthy Chicagoans" to acquire casts and antiquities for the museum. Breasted wondered to Harper whether he should "try and divert the money of these men to a university collection." Breasted thought he might enlist Ayer's support for another kind of initiative, a notion he pursued a few years later when—in view of Ayer's backing the Field Museum's Egyptian acquisitions—he requested a donation for an annual purchase fund for Haskell's "working collection." Ayer resisted, writing in part that it was not "at all fair for the University to make any efforts toward an Egyptian Collection" because the Field Museum was already doing so and there was one at the Art Institute as well. He suggested, however, that he *would* contribute if the university's and the Art Institute's Egyptian collections were consolidated at the Field Museum.

Breasted persisted in order to correct what he regarded as Ayer's "false impression" about the Haskell Museum: that it performed the same functions as the Field Museum and the Art Institute. To the contrary, Breasted argued, students studying archaeology needed a "body of working materials which can be unlocked and handed out . . . to be used for hours or days at a time, in properly equipped work rooms [each] containing as its equipment a complete library of the subject studied." He implied this was impossible at the city's other museums and that it would be very costly to change them, adding that he only wanted to "push the study" of ancient Egypt on a par with work in Paris, London, and Berlin. Ayer acknowledged Breasted's argument but declined again. Though Breasted failed, he was learning to compete for donors' support in an environment with many worthy causes.[17]

The full extent of Breasted's museum responsibilities was left largely undefined for much of his first year, probably because Harper was uncertain about the extent of Haskell's availability for collections display and storage. Harper originally planned for Breasted to direct it, discussed the matter with him, and then had second thoughts. In April 1896 he wrote to Breasted, "It has been thought best that I should assume the directorship . . . ; that you take the assistant directorship as well as the curatorship [for Egyptology]. This will relieve any anxiety on your side, and . . . give you freedom of action." In addition to Egyptology, the museum's other curatorial departments were Assyriology, biblical archaeology, and comparative religions, each supervised by other faculty members. Breasted's concern, which is not recorded, was probably his reluctance to supervise other faculty members with curatorial assignments, all of whom held more senior appointments.

As assistant director, Breasted was chiefly responsible for overseeing the museum's operations, including the collections catalog, displays, acquisitions, and loans as well as a host of periodic tasks such as preparing updated descriptions of the museum for the university's *Annual Register*. Breasted was also the most enterprising of the curators, taking the lead in arranging displays for other fields when colleagues were unavailable, for example, and in pursuing funds for Egyptian acquisitions. He successfully lobbied the Chicago Women's Club to support Flinders Petrie's excavation work in exchange for a share of the finds, and he persuaded the head of a center where he taught an extension course to contribute its share of the proceeds for Petrie's work too.

His most ambitious effort was establishment of the Chicago Society of Egyptian Research, which held its first annual meeting in December 1897 and by 1898 had eighty-eight members paying annual dues of five dollars each. The income also went to Petrie, and his finds soon began enlarging Haskell's fledgling collection (figure 2.4). Breasted also courted donors supporting other Egyptologists and institutions, such as American businessman Theodore M. Davis, who sponsored excavations and collected antiquities, later giving works to the Boston Museum of Fine Arts and the Metropolitan Museum of Art, and who rewarded Breasted's attentions with a few gifts.

Breasted's museum skills led Harper, burdened with more urgent matters, to

Fig. 2.4 Antiquities excavated by Petrie during 1895–96 and on display in Haskell, ca. 1897. Courtesy of the Oriental Institute, University of Chicago.

press Breasted into becoming Haskell's director despite the latter's objections. In addition to his reservations about staff seniority, Breasted also found the museum work increasingly burdensome. Exhibit space for the Egyptian collections became ever more congested, and he had to frequently reinstall the displays to accommodate a steady flow of acquisitions as he worked them into "a visualization of [his Egyptian history] courses . . . , as well as an embodiment of the life of the east" (figure 2.5). Hence the routine work of record keeping lagged. In 1905 Breasted reported that cataloging of the Egyptian collection had counted nearly 4,700 items, with the inventory "probably two-thirds finished. . . . We have not yet been able to begin the numbering of objects in the other collections." The space problem was exacerbated within a few years of Haskell's opening when exhibits were confined to the second floor. Expecting some relief in 1902, Breasted proposed a reallocation of the collections to the first and third floors, with the "Egyptian Museum" taking over the entire second floor—the redistribution justified by the Egyptian holdings' growth. But the expansion was not to happen, and the congestion remained until 1925–26 when the Divinity School acquired its own building and moved out, taking the Far Eastern and comparative religion collections with it.[18]

Reorganization schemes were not confined to space, however. In July 1905 Harper asked his brother, Robert Francis Harper, whom he had brought to Chicago in 1892 as an associate professor in Assyriology, and Breasted to reorganize the Haskell Oriental Museum's administration. Breasted had recently been elevated to the museum's directorship, replacing W. R. Harper in that capacity, so

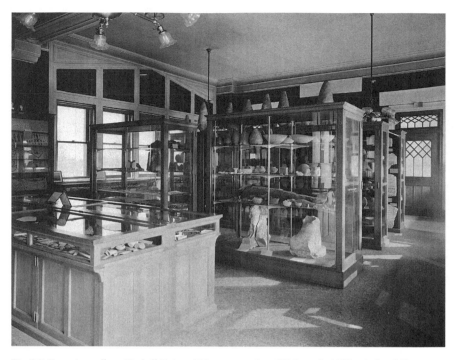

Fig. 2.5 Egyptian gallery, Haskell Oriental Museum, ca. late 1890s–early 1900s. Archival Photo-files, apf2-03432, Special Collections Research Center, University of Chicago Library.

his advice was crucial. But it's unclear why R. F. Harper was included in the task, because he was not especially active in the museum up to that point, in an official capacity at least, and after he had served only a few years as Assyriology curator, another faculty member replaced him. After exploring the organizational question, R. F. Harper and Breasted found they could not agree on a proposal, and Breasted sought W. R. Harper's intervention.

There were two issues. First, R. F. Harper wanted to departmentalize the museum, meaning he believed the museum ought to expel collections not associated with the research and teaching program of Semitic Languages and Literatures: holdings of the Department of Archaeology, which consisted of some Hellenistic objects; those of the Department of Comparative Religion, primarily Far Eastern objects; and what were likely some early Christian objects obtained by the Department of Biblical Archaeology. Second, R. F. Harper proposed his brother resume directorship of the museum and Breasted be demoted to assistant director, later modifying the proposal by suggesting the director position be changed to "Secretary," presumably comparable to the title of the Smithsonian Institution's head. Breasted opposed ejecting the other collections because it was out of keeping with the spirit of the museum's representation of "the whole Orient," not just the Near East, and he was infuriated at the suggestion of changing his position and title because, aside from the "serious professional injury and injustice" to him personally—over an office that he reminded W. R. Harper he was never eager to occupy—the change was "out of harmony with the present . . . organization of the museums of the University."

As an alternative, Breasted proposed reconfiguring the museum staff by promoting the faculty member then overseeing the Assyriology collection to assistant director and R. F. Harper to curator of Assyriology. Breasted's other changes included adding two more curatorial sections, papyrology and Islamic, and appointing an acting curator for the comparative religion collection to replace George S. Goodspeed, who had died earlier that year. Nothing came of the dustup, however, which was doubtless precipitated by a convergence of three issues: the university-wide review of museums that W. R. Harper had set underway the previous year, Goodspeed's death, and R. F. Harper's dissatisfaction with Breasted's museum leadership.

There's no evidence to show whether discontent with Breasted resided with R. F. Harper alone or was shared by others. On one hand, Breasted and R. F. Harper had begun to clash a few years earlier over relatively minor matters in which both were at fault, generating a mutual wariness despite outward displays of collegiality. On the other hand, there were faculty members outside the museum and Semitic Languages and Literatures who spoke disapprovingly of Breasted. In one instance he privately admitted "that perhaps a momentary ascendancy of pride over humility earned me this rebuke." With regard to R. F. Harper, one of his biographers characterized him as possessing "a happy combination of the qualities of a devoted and accurate scholar and a genial and companionable man."[19]

The Photograph as *Zettel*

Teaching, popular lectures, museum work, family. Breasted found scant time for new research, and it showed in his publication record. During his first few years at Chicago he mainly wrote for Harper's *Biblical World*, and he squeezed out a pair of scholarly book reviews and two short articles for other journals. The *Biblical World* pieces included a sequence of historical "sketches" on Egypt, excavation news reports, and Haskell acquisitions notes. Befitting the *Biblical World*'s audience, Breasted's articles were written for popular consumption, and he endeavored to strike the right balance between scholarship and simplification. Despite his best efforts, he tended to err on the side of the former, beginning one essay with that immortal scholarly disclaimer "The limited space to which this article must be confined will permit no more than the meagerest outline." Breasted

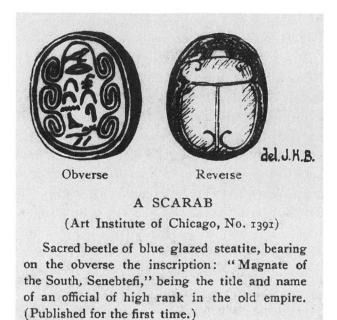

Fig. 2.6 Breasted's drawing of a scarab for "A Sketch of Egyptian History with Special Reference to Palestine Down to about 950 B.C.," *Biblical World* 7, no. 6 (June 1896): 443. Public domain, reproduction by author.

had a better feel for illustrations, however, and with the exception of book reviews, his publications were all accompanied by generous numbers of interesting photographs and quite a few of his own drawings (figure 2.6).

The book reviews are far more surefooted—rigorous and yet respectful. A review of Gaston Maspero's second in a three-volume history of the ancient Near East is at turns deeply appreciative and highly critical. Breasted saluted Maspero's "picturesque and interesting style," "the vast quantity of scattered material . . . brought together," his "sober and judicial . . . interpretation," and Maspero's generous acknowledgment of opinions differing from his own. But Breasted also found numerous problems: "The main outlines of the picture . . . are sometimes lost," and "the work contains more errors than it should." He then itemized a long list of problems ranging from the Egyptological to Maspero's reading of Old Testament texts and criticism. Even so, Breasted concluded, such errors "do not mar the impression of the author's great critical insight and marvelous *arbeitskraft* [work ethic], which the reader feels as he lays down a volume representing so many years of self-denying toil."

The other review, of the second in a multivolume history of Egypt by Flinders Petrie, is generally very complimentary but with reservations. Breasted noted Petrie's work depended on "monumental sources," meaning archaeological finds, the documentation, description, and interpretation of which form the bedrock of Egyptological scholarship. "Such materials Mr. Petrie is rarely endowed to sift and investigate, and if these materials occupy so prominent a position in his history the fact is to be attributed to the above considerations." Yet, Breasted lamented, "It cannot be denied that this method mars the symmetry and the architectural effect of the whole; the general impression [being] obscured by the prominence . . . of often irrelevant archaeological detail." It was, however, Petrie's analysis of Amenhotep IV's religious reforms—Breasted's area of greatest expertise—that drew his heaviest critical barrage. Petrie attributed the changes "to external influences introduced chiefly through the foreign marriages of . . . later eighteenth-dynasty kings, especially Amenhotep IV's alien mother, Tey." Breasted swiftly undercut it, pointing out there was a "tendency toward solar monotheism" in prior Egyptian dynasties, and there was no evidence of monotheistic beliefs in adjacent cultures. But far more noteworthy is Breasted's characterization of Amenhotep as "that remarkable idealist, the world's first reformer," an early indication of his interest in the larger ramifications of the pharaoh's religious innovations.[20]

The coin of Egyptology's realm in those days was the close study of inscriptions and reliefs. There was much about the language, religion, and history of ancient Egypt that was either unknown or subject to lively scholarly dispute, and what one Egyptologist considered settled fact another would call into question, including such basics as the order and dates of pharaonic succession. Breasted dived into the fray starting in 1899 as he addressed a range of topics from the fine points of hieroglyphic grammar and transliteration to questions of chronology and religious philosophy. One of his articles challenged previous interpretations of a passage in a major relief and accompanying inscriptions located in the Karnak temple complex north of modern Luxor on the Nile's east bank (figure 2.7). The relief depicts a major battle led by Seti I (1290–1279 BCE; some write "Sety" today) showing the pharaoh vanquishing his enemies. Toward the bottom or foreground of one scene is a prince then conventionally identified as Ramses II (1279–1213 BCE; many write "Ramesses" today) accompanying his father into battle. The placement of Ramses II alongside his father was confusing, however, because he would have been too young to take part in the battle. When Breasted examined photographs of the scene, he noticed alterations made after the main relief and accompanying hieroglyphs had been cut. Breasted discovered evidence of a partially erased profile over which the figure of Ramses II had been carved (figure 2.8a) and traces of a personage whose image was incompletely effaced (figure 2.8b). After carefully analyzing all the evidence, Breasted concluded that Ramses II probably had two elder brothers, one of whom stood in the way of his regal accession and had his profile added to their father's relief as a visual assertion of his priority in the succession following Seti's death. After Ramses II came

Fig. 2.7 The subjects of Breasted's study are located within the outlines superimposed over this relief at Karnak (drawings of the outlined areas are in figures 2.8a [left] and 2.8b [right]). This photograph of the relief, as it appears today, is from The Epigraphic Survey, *Reliefs and Inscriptions at Karnak*, vol. 4, *The Battle Reliefs of King Sety I*, Oriental Institute Publications, no. 107 (Chicago: Oriental Institute, University of Chicago, 1986). Courtesy of the Oriental Institute, University of Chicago.

to power, Breasted conjectured, he ordered images of his older brother replaced by his own, but only one was fully completed.

The article's illustrations show Breasted employing schematic line-drawing techniques to compare prior renderings of the relief with his photographic evidence in order to clarify reworkings of the relief. This is especially evident in figure 2.8a, where he used a dashed line for the faint outline of the first personage—the one that was added and then effaced—and a dotted line to show where the second person and accompanying hieroglyphs are placed. The solid lines indicate the original relief and hieroglyphs, and the parallel hatching shows lacunae in the relief, in this instance surface damage and seams between the limestone blocks—rendering conventions that had become more or less standard practice among professionally trained and more rigorous amateur Egyptologists of the day. Despite the considerable amount of information Breasted extracted from the photographs, he regretted not studying the reliefs when he was at Karnak. "There is no doubt," Breasted wrote, "that a careful examination of Seti's reliefs in the original stone would throw much more light on the relation of the . . .

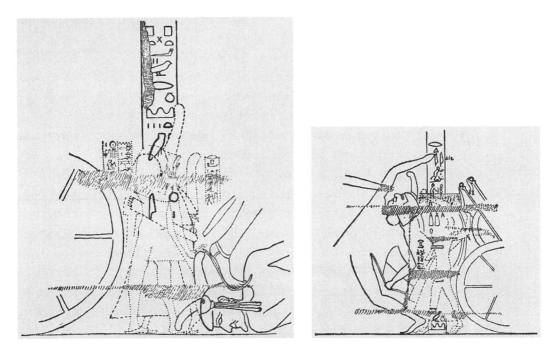

Figs. 2.8a (left) and b (right) Hand-drawn illustrations by Breasted for "Ramses II and the Princes in the Karnak Reliefs of Seti I," *Zeitschrift für ägyptische Sprache und Alterthumskunde* 37 (1899): 131. Public domain, reproduction by author.

princes." The next best thing would be a detailed drawing of the relief that combined the mechanical accuracy of photography, the human eye's ability to discern differences between aging and deliberately carved marks, and an Egyptologist's knowledge. "Unfortunately," Breasted closed, "a carefully collated publication of these reliefs does not exist."[21]

The inaccurate or incomplete reproductions of hieroglyphs and reliefs compounded an even larger problem: the small percentage of inscriptions in Egypt or major Western collections that had been published. Breasted felt this problem acutely because of a scholarly project he began in 1896 of "collecting all the historical sources of ancient Egypt, from earliest times to the Persian conquest [and creating] a solid foundation of documentary source material for the production of a modern history of ancient Egypt." Pursuing this project from a base in America was difficult, however, because nearly all the sources resided in Egypt or in European museums. In September 1898, after compiling materials for about eighteen months, Breasted requested Harper's permission for a year's unpaid leave commencing in fall 1899, noting that he had banked the time during the previous three vacation quarters. Breasted wanted to spend the year recording inscriptions in major European collections. Harper approved the leave, including a fractional salary, and Breasted covered his travel expenses with earnings from "barnstorming among the women's clubs and University extension lecture centers."

Breasted departed for Europe in fall 1899 with his wife, two-year-old Charles, a trunk containing "his working library of scientific books," and a "gray canvas-covered telescopic case filled with his growing manuscripts" for books he was writing. The work of collecting and translating sources would occupy him for the next five years and would entail at least eleven transatlantic crossings and dozens of trips within Europe as he crisscrossed the continent going from one repository to another in search of hieroglyphs of historical interest. He would "copy all the . . . inscriptions in the museums of Europe (except St. Petersburg and Athens)" before he was done. Berlin served as the family's home base, and occasionally Frances and Charles came along on forays to other cities. Although the work was arduous, Breasted acquired a personally validated repository of raw material for his "documentary sources" project.[22]

Recording the sources would be difficult and time consuming because so much of it had to be done on the road and in museums with limited public hours. Anticipating these impediments, Breasted planned to expedite the work by photographing inscriptions rather than transcribing them by hand. He acquired a 5″ × 7″–view camera in America and a shutter board and lenses at the "Goerz works" in Berlin, and he purchased chemicals as well as film in Germany so he could develop his negatives while away from Berlin to make sure photographs he took in other cities' museums were satisfactory before leaving them. The prints needed for translating the inscriptions could be made later in Berlin. He initially planned to work with glass-plate negatives but "found there was a duty on plates in Italy (by weight) and . . . my 20 doz. glass plates weigh over 60 lb. So I gave up the idea of using glass plates. . . . But film rolls cost twice as much as glass plates, so I experimented with German cut films each weighing no more than a sheet of paper 5 × 7 inches. I find they work well,—I developed them myself and have not had a failure. I had to get my bookbinder to make a lot of little frames to fit into my plate holders so that they would hold the films. Then I had to get the films cut at the factory, the special [American camera] size I use, as it is not found in Germany."

The itinerary for Breasted's first excursion indicates the speed with which he hoped to work: "Vienna, Sept. 19–23; Venice, Sept. 24–26; Rome, Sept. 27–Oct. 15; Naples, Oct. 15–22; Florence, Oct. 23–30; Pisa, Oct. 30–31; Turin, Oct. 31–Nov. 10; Nuremberg, Nov. 11–12; Munich, Nov. 13–15; Berlin, Nov. 16." He spent nearly each day exclusively on photography and each evening developing negatives. Breasted described an average day's work and its impediments while in Florence to study Egyptian collections in the Museo Archeologico: "It is only open from 10–4 and taking a lunch hour, I can't get more than 20 pictures a day,—that is the extent of my plate holders. Before I can get back to the hotel

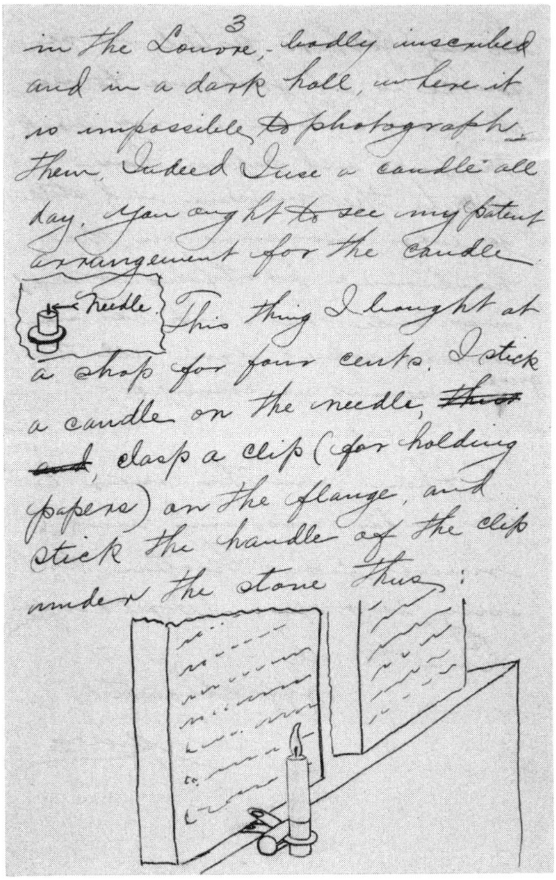

3

in the Louvre,—badly inscribed
and in a dark hall, where it
is impossible to photograph
them. Indeed I use a candle all
day. You ought to see my patent
arrangement for the candle

Needle

This thing I bought at
a shop for four cents. I stick
a candle on the needle, ~~thus~~
~~and~~, clasp a clip (for holding
papers) on the flange, and
stick the handle of the clip
under the stone thus:

Fig. 2.9 Breasted's explanation and sketches of his museum candle holder, from a letter to Harriet Breasted, 27 January 1901. Courtesy of the Oriental Institute, University of Chicago.

and load them again it is too late to resume work. . . . I spend the whole evening unloading and reloading my plate holders."

It took him a while to learn to photograph large numbers of inscriptions efficiently and reliably. After a year, he could report: "I am taking now a list of nearly 60 large stones . . . , clearly inscribed and in a well lighted hall. It would take me at least two and probably 3 weeks to copy those by hand. With the camera I can do them in 3 forenoons and the copies contain no mistakes!" But even then he ran into unforeseen problems: "There are 434 tablets from the Serapeum alone in the Louvre,—badly inscribed and in a dark hall, where it is impossible to photograph them. Indeed I use a candle all day" (figure 2.9). While Breasted's photographs were intended to serve as little more than a relatively quick and clinical form of documentation, the dim lighting often lent to them a haunting beauty as well (figure 2.10).

The speed of photography enabled Breasted to return to Berlin after short survey trips, print his negatives, and use them to compile his translations. This method allowed him to research unusual hieroglyphs and translation problems

Fig. 2.10 One of Breasted's photographs taken in the Museo Archeologico, Florence, in October 1899 and probably printed in Berlin shortly thereafter. The subject is a tomb stela, and Breasted's translation of the text, later published in his *A History of Egypt* (1905), is in note 23 to the present chapter. Courtesy of the Oriental Institute, University of Chicago.

in Berlin's library and museum collections or discuss them with his colleagues. It soon yielded some publications too. Within a year he wrote a brief article confirming the identity of a figure in a fragment in Vienna, his insight made possible by cutting out the fragment's shape from his photograph and placing it alongside the reproduction of another fragment in Leiden to complete the image.[23]

Halfway through the year, Adolf Erman, impressed by the speed and quality of Breasted's research, invited him to officially assist with compilation of the *Wörterbuch der aegyptischen Sprache*, or Egyptian dictionary. The project was overseen by Erman through the Royal Academy of Sciences in Berlin with the participation of scholars associated with academies in Leipzig, Munich, and Göttingen. Breasted had already been providing a bit of assistance with texts in Berlin, but Erman hoped he could remain in Europe for another year, ideally on paid leave from Chicago because the academy could not afford to support him. Representatives of the academies wrote directly to Harper requesting Breasted's assistance, and he was granted an additional year's leave at two-thirds salary. The academies made up the difference and also covered Breasted's travel expenses. His assignment entailed returning to major European and British collections to record their hieroglyphic inscriptions, it being understood that he would use his photographic method to accelerate the work. Breasted hoped the research would contribute to his own projects as well.[24]

In describing the Egyptian dictionary project, Breasted liked to compare it to the ten-volume *New English Dictionary on Historical Principles*, which was published in parts between 1884 and 1928. The latter was conceived and its preparation begun in 1857 under the aegis of England's Philological Society, and the effort required the voluntary labors of dozens of contributors, "sub-editors," and others. (A corrected, updated, and expanded version was published in 1933 as *The Oxford English Dictionary*, the title retained by subsequent editions.) Breasted's comparison was based on the English dictionary's "historical principles," the method by which it was compiled: searching out the usage of every word in the English language, in each variant of the word's use, in context, from its first appearance to the present time. This information was collected by examining all known English texts, isolating words of interest, and recording each word in the upper left-hand corner of a paper slip and the citation of its source—date, author, title of work, page, etc., and a quotation of sufficient length to illustrate its usage—below. By its completion, "some five millions of excerpts" had been collected, from which about 1.8 million quotations were printed. Each word's entry in the dictionary therefore contains, in addition to the usual information, a sequence of brief quotes, in chronological order, demonstrating the word's usage through time.

Erman's model for the Egyptian dictionary, however, was probably an earlier lexicon: the *Deutsches Wörterbuch*, begun by the Brothers Grimm and intended to be the first German dictionary based on "scientific" standards, including provision of each word's etymology demonstrated with historical quotations. The first volume was published in 1854, and with "its plan and methods . . . the direct product of the then new scientific philology," it certainly would have been familiar to Erman. Although Erman formally proposed the Egyptian dictionary to the Royal Academy in 1897 and it was approved in 1899, he was considering its development at least as early as 1894 when he asked Breasted to copy inscriptions for it while on the honeymoon trip.[25]

The Egyptian dictionary project was an international effort involving more than eighty collaborators from ten nations, including Germany. Breasted was America's only contributor. The first of the dictionary's initial five volumes was published in 1926 and the last in 1931, but supplements and indexes continued to be issued through 1963, bringing the total to thirteen. Like the *Deutsches Wörterbuch* and *New English Dictionary*, it was compiled from individual records, or *zettel* (note cards), containing inscription excerpts. But it was at this point that the Egyptian dictionary's method parted company with the other lexicons.

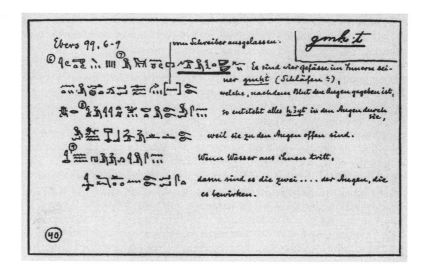

Fig. 2.11 *Zettel*, for Egyptian dictionary project, after editorial markup, reproduced from Breasted's *The Oriental Institute* (1933), 385. Courtesy of the Oriental Institute, University of Chicago.

Here the editors' goal was to transcribe each source text in its entirety, but in segments of about thirty words each. These would be transcribed in single-line clauses in a column on the left side of the card with line-by-line translations into German on the right side. The recording and translation was done in lithographic ink so the information on the original *zettel* could be transferred directly to a printing matrix and copies made, a minimum of one per word, the number of copies depending on the number of different words transcribed on the card. For example, for a thirty-two-word excerpt at least thirty-two copies would be made. An editor would take the first copy, underline the first word in red, transliterate it into Latin letters in the upper-right-hand box, and file it alphabetically by the transliteration (figure 2.11). This procedure would be repeated for the second word in the excerpt, the third, and so forth. The collaborators produced over one and a half million of these before the dictionary was completed.

The number of *zettel* Breasted contributed to the project is unknown because none of the participants regularly signed their work. He retained copies of some cards for his own research, a handful of which he translated into English rather than German, a sure sign they were destined for his documentary sources project.[26]

Living in Berlin was inexpensive in comparison to Chicago at the time, so the Breasteds could afford a modest apartment in the city—although without a bathroom because those were still a bit too pricey. Later they found a place in Gross-Lichterfelde, a small community just outside Berlin. Money still had to be managed carefully because of the frequency with which they "crossed and recrossed the Atlantic" or had to pull up stakes for Breasted's work in places like London or Paris. When they were in Berlin for sufficiently long durations, Frances would rent a piano and practice as much as six hours a day. She was as fluent in German as her husband and used her skill to translate into English a collection of contemporary Egyptian folk songs one of her husband's fellow Egyptologists had compiled in Egypt and translated from Arabic into German. Breasted found time for occasional flute lessons, and the two would play duets for evening relaxation. They visited often with the families of Breasted's colleagues, forming new friendships and renewing old ones, especially with the Ermans, whom young Charles, growing up speaking German, called "Onkle" and "Tante."

While the family's nomadic existence could be stressful, it also had its comic moments. During their travels Frances purchased an inflatable tub, similar to modern toddlers' pools, for sponge baths. After washing up one evening Breasted lifted the tub to pour out its contents. The sides buckled, water sloshed out, and he slipped, falling headfirst into the watery mess. Observing the scene, Frances intoned a psalm: "Save me, O God, . . . for the waters are come in unto my soul. I sink in deep mire, where there is no standing . . . where the floods overflow me."

Charles recalls his father as attentive and playful when he wasn't working. He enjoyed "spur-of-the-moment games" with Charles's toys and "romps which left [Charles] weak from . . . laughter." To calm him, Breasted drew on his "inexhaustible fund of stories about the Tailor Who Hadn't Enough Money to Buy Cloth . . . , and the Adventures which befell him when he closed his Shop, and with a bundle and stick over his shoulder went forth into the World." Toward the end of a letter to his parents, Breasted described Charles "sitting on the floor playing with a clockwork seadog. The thing is really half alive. [It] makes a rush to get away, wildly waving both . . . flippers. . . . The boy, hardly able to stand for laughter, makes a dive for it, when the creature flits its tail and shoots off on a new tack. He finally captures it and comes back . . . , and pokes the beast under my nose with: 'Noch einmal auf ziehen, Papa.' (Wind it up again, Papa),—and that is what papa has been doing every 10 lines of this contribution." Although Breasted spent time with his family when not traveling, he limited play with Charles to an hour or so on weekday evenings and a few hours on Sundays (figure 2.12). While in college Breasted "determined to put to good use every moment of his time," and its management remained a concern for the rest of his life. Whatever remained after meeting Egyptian dictionary responsibilities was reserved for his book manuscripts, a working regimen that "dictated the whole pattern" of the Breasteds' lives.

In addition to Breasted's "documentary sources" project, the other manuscript occupying his attention was a general-interest history of Egypt he'd agreed to write for Charles Scribner's Sons. He signed the contract in 1898 and hoped

Fig. 2.12 Breasted and son Charles, ca. 1901, in either London or Berlin. Courtesy of the Oriental Institute, University of Chicago.

to complete the book by October 1899. But the nature and number of his discoveries in Europe changed his plans. Breasted felt these findings "had to be published and demonstrated fully and technically," something not possible in a book written for popular consumption. Yet that type of work would be "too long for the scientific journals." At the invitation of Kurt Sethe, who by then was teaching at the University of Göttingen and editing a book series on ancient Egypt, Breasted decided to publish some of his material in a short scholarly book. This would expedite publication of some of his findings and add to his scholarly record but without rushing completion of the documentary sources project. As his documents accumulated and he checked them against previous publications, he found ever more errors in other scholars' work. This knowledge only hardened Breasted's determination to take "nothing second hand from any middleman" for his own work: "Before I write a history based on the original monuments . . . , I propose to <u>find out what the monuments say</u>."[27]

3

Two Years, Three Books, Seven Volumes

Guiding the Home-Tourist

Between 1895 and 1907, Breasted transformed himself from a freshly minted scholar to a rising star in Egyptology on an international scale. A dizzying amount of research, much of it conducted in Europe, came to fruition in a wide range of books that were published within two years of each other, between 1905 and 1907. Breasted set the stage in 1898 when he began to clarify and flesh out his research agenda, concluding in 1900 that he would emphasize "historical work" in the form of three projects:

1. Reproduction of certain original inscriptions (with hieroglyphic type) and detailed discussion (1st book, next winter, published in Leipzig)
2. Translation of all inscriptions (in English, no hieroglyphic type) with explanatory introduction to each (2 possibly 3 volumes for University Press Chicago; my present book of the last 3 years)
3. Digestion of all the facts and data of the inscriptions into a readable narrative of good literary form, referring continually to [item] 2 for proofs (History of Egypt for Scribner).

You will see how I gradually move from the inscriptions to the non-technical reader.

He was about to enter what promised to be a period of remarkable scholarly productivity when a decidedly nonacademic opportunity suddenly arose. In 1901 he was invited to write the guide for a stereograph "home tour" of Egypt.[1]

The request came from Underwood & Underwood, an American stereograph company that began with a modest Ottawa, Kansas, office in 1882 and by 1901 had established itself as the nation's leader, "publishing twenty-five thousand stereographs a day and [manufacturing] three hundred thousand stereoscopes a year . . . far outstripping any previous or contemporary company." Stereographs consist of pairs of photographs taken with special cameras employing two lenses set a few inches apart, similar to the distance between one's eyes. The resulting photographs are mounted side by side on a single card and, when viewed through a stereoscope—a binocular viewing device—they appear optically merged, giving the illusion of a three-dimensional image. The phenomenon of stereoscopy was being explored during the same period as the rudiments of photography, and not long after the latter's practical introduction in 1839, it was adapted for the production of stereographs.

Around 1900 Underwood inaugurated a new marketing strategy, a "travel system" consisting of a boxed set of one hundred views, an accompanying guidebook with special maps to which the views and guide were keyed, and a stereoscope to view the images. Customers could buy the stereographs separately or in smaller thematically related groups. The travel sets, however, provided the additional experience of a "tour" obtained by reading the guidebook while viewing the images, all without leaving the comfort of one's home. Crucial to a set's success was the guidebook's quality.

Underwood & Underwood likely approached Breasted for several reasons. First, there was his area of expertise. Starting in the 1850s, photographs of distant lands became a lucrative and ever more readily available commodity in Europe and America. By the late nineteenth century, conventional and stereograph views of the Middle East and Egypt were especially popular, and publishers eagerly expanded such offerings to satisfy that demand. Breasted became known to Underwood & Underwood a couple of years prior when he reviewed their "Oriental photographs" and permitted the company to publish his endorsement in an 1899 catalog of its stereograph sets. Then there was Breasted's gift for conveying knowledge of ancient Egypt to general audiences in colorful and compelling lectures. In approaching Breasted, Underwood sought a writer who could "put what he has to say in the first person much as he would talk if he could stand with a person in the presence of the actual places. . . . The aim should be to write more for the general reader than the specialist and yet, since these 'parts' of Egypt are

Fig. 3.1 Stereograph card 21, "Second Pyramid S. W. from summit of Great Pyramid," from Breasted's *Egypt through the Stereoscope* (1905). Public domain, reproduction by author.

to be in a man's home for years, there should be more solid information than would be given in talks for a transient visit."

Breasted accepted the Underwood proposal in July 1901 and by the following October had sent a list of "many hundred" sites to be photographed, a travel book for Egypt, and "marked . . . maps and plans, with detailed instructions" to direct an Underwood & Underwood photographer sent to Egypt to take the views. "From the thousand or more views" taken by the photographer and other images already in Underwood & Underwood's stock, Breasted selected one hundred and wrote a text for each view or "Position," completing that part of the manuscript in August 1903. More than a year later, however, the project was still unpublished because the guide lacked an introduction. In February 1905 an editor urged Breasted to complete it, offering suggestions to help speed things along. Among the editor's ideas were extolling the virtues of "Stay-at-home travel" and "the practical good that can come [from] a first-hand acquaintance with the Nile valley, with even a short survey of its vast history." Breasted complied in early April, and the set was issued later that spring.

As was Underwood & Underwood's usual practice at the time, the mounting cards for the hundred views were printed on the front, or stereograph side, with brief captions and numbers keyed to the guide and accompanying maps (figure 3.1) and on the back with related excerpts from Breasted's guide and somewhat longer versions of the captions in six languages: English, French, Spanish, German, Swedish, and Russian. The guide was published as *Egypt through the Ste-*

reoscope: A Journey through the Land of the Pharaohs "conducted by James Henry Breasted, Ph.D."[2]

The plain cloth book came with a pocket on the outside of the back cover to hold a booklet of twenty folded maps, the largest of which—a map of the Nile valley from the delta to Khartoum—opens out to twenty-five inches long. The text starts with an introduction, followed by a brief "Story of Egypt" summarizing its topography, climate, and history; a chronological table; and "The Itinerary." The back matter includes, in addition to an index to the book and stereographs, a publisher's note suggesting eight shorter tours "if for any reason it seems impracticable to take this entire tour of Egypt," one being "the 12 positions about and within the Pyramids."

The introduction begins with an endorsement of the Underwood stay-at-home travel system that Breasted wrote for an earlier Underwood promotional brochure. He validates this approval by citing his experience "making a public wider than that of the university lecture-room, acquainted with the . . . ancient Egyptians." Because of his belief in sharing his knowledge with that wider public, Breasted continues, "I have undertaken, in the midst of a heavy burden of numerous other duties, the task of standing with the traveler at every point of view, to be his cicerone, and to furnish him with the indispensable wealth of associations, of historical incident, or archaeological detail suggested by the prospect . . . before him." There is an almost boyish quality to Breasted's disclosure that, "In the preparation of the following pages, I have constantly had my eyes within the hood of the stereoscope, and I cannot forebear to express here the growing surprise and delight, with which . . . it became more and more easy to speak of the prospect revealed in the instrument, as one actually spread out before me." In an aside, addressed to fellow academics as though his general audience were no longer reading, he avers: "Should this book fall into the hands of an oriental scholar, let him be assured that the orthography of the Arabic proper names is as unsatisfying to the author as to him." Breasted explains this state of affairs by reminding his peers that the book "is intended for . . . readers who know nothing about and care less for the intricacies of Arabic orthography,—readers to whom the complications of a . . . system of transliteration . . . would . . . cause only vexation and confusion."[3]

The guide's front matter concludes with "The Itinerary," which serves as a kind of guide to the guide, highlighting themes that will recur throughout: "Locality" (the nature and precise locations of the settings discussed), "History," "Art," and "Mechanics" (ancient Egyptians' technical achievements and the processes used to realize them). The itinerary itself follows the route of a typical turn-of-the-century Egyptian tour. It begins in Alexandria, where actual visitors arrived by ship, stops for a few days of excursions in Cairo and to nearby sites, such as the pyramids at Giza, and then proceeds up the Nile with stops at the major points of interest including Asyut, Abydos, Thebes (Luxor), Aswan, and Abu Simbel, with the tour concluding at Khartoum.

The best way to appreciate the set is by reading one of the tour-stop talks with stereograph and map in hand. "Position 21," among the Giza pyramids, is a good example (figure 3.1). To follow Breasted's references to "Map 5" (figure 3.2), look for the inverted "V" with the apex at the center of the "Great Pyramid," each arm terminating in "21," one toward the lower left side and the other at the bottom of the map. The apex marks the viewer's "position" or "stand-point," and the spreading arms of the "V" designate the field of view. The other "Vs" are for other views, and the circled numerals near their apexes and matching numerals at the arms' ends are keyed to other images and discussions. Because the collection includes three views from the top of the "Great Pyramid," there is an oval just to the left of the pyramid's center with the numerals "20–22," designating all three views that originate from that point.

It is the superimposition of these sight lines, in red, over otherwise fairly conventional maps and plans that constituted Underwood & Underwood's "Patented Key Map" system. Breasted selected the underlying map, complete with the "Comparative Table of Heights," from one prepared for a Baedeker guide to Egypt. It was originally created by Richard Lepsius and updated by an Egyptologist of Breasted's generation, Georg Steindorff. Breasted employed the map without any changes save one: he wisely had the map rotated by ninety degrees so north was at the top. Now for Breasted's talk:

> We stand looking southwestward toward the heart of Africa, with Cairo almost behind us. . . . Before us looms the second pyramid, completely hiding the third and smallest, which lies behind it. . . . That yonder cap of casing masonry which still crowns it, extends for 150 feet down its sides, this may serve as a scale by which to measure the rest. . . . How splendidly it rises against that background of billowy desert, which stretches away southward.
>
> Here . . . is the northern extremity of a line of pyramids distributed in groups extending some sixty miles in length, from the pyramid of Illahun in the south, to the ruinous group of Abu Roâsh just behind us here on the north of the Gizeh group. This sixty-mile line of pyramids represents a line of Pharaohs, who reigned over a thousand years. . . .
>
> Peeping out from behind the second pyramid you see one of those small ones, which stand at the base of the third pyramid. . . . Further east (left), but nearer to us, you observe three low sand-covered walls, two extending eastward, and one at right angles to these. The nearer of the two parallel walls is part of the enclosure wall surrounding the second pyramid; that at right angles to it, is part of a similar wall enclosing the third pyramid; while the further of the two parallel walls is really not a wall at all, but the upper end of the cause-

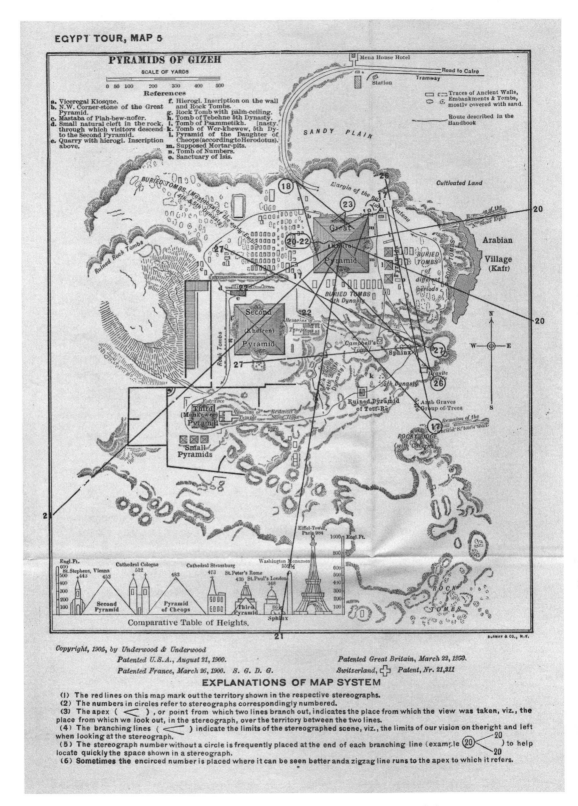

Fig. 3.2 "Egypt Tour, Map 5: Pyramids of Gizeh," from Breasted's *Egypt through the Stereoscope* (1905). Public domain, reproduction by author.

way leading from the plain to the desert plateau and the third pyramid, up which the material for it was transported, and by means of which, after the king's death, access was gained to the temple of the pyramid, where his mortuary ritual was regularly carried on by an endowed priesthood. . . .

Follow that causeway . . . westward (to the right), and as your eye approaches the second pyramid, you notice just on this side of the tiny pyramid, a small heap of ruins. Those ruins are all that remains of . . . a temple, detached from the [third] pyramid. . . . Look at the ruins here at the extreme left . . . , over this standing native's head. These are the remains of the temple of the second pyramid. . . . There in that desolated sand-covered ruin, once a splendid sanctuary, an endowed priesthood carried on the ritual and worship of the dead Khafre, who lay in the pyramid; and there . . . he daily received the offerings of food and drink, which were to maintain him in the hereafter. . . .

The pyramid before us lacked nine feet of being as high as that . . . on which we stand; . . . but as it has lost but a trifle at its summit, while [this one] has lost thirty feet, and as [the other] also stands upon higher ground, we look up to its peak even from the top of the great pyramid. . . . When Belzoni opened it on March 2nd, 1818, he found that it had been robbed in antiquity and the body had disappeared. The futility of all this enormous expense of human labor and . . . skill in the vain attempt to preserve the body and thus secure immortality for the spirit, is as depressing as that illimitable sweep of the barren desert, that stretches away from the pyramid at our feet till it is lost on the distant horizon. It forms a fitting background for the silent pyramid in which both the body and the hope of Khafre were entombed.[4]

Throughout the hundred views, as here, Breasted is attentive to virtually every aspect of each except one: the human subjects. Usually included in the views to establish scale and distance, the figures often pass unremarked. The inclusion of figures to show the monuments' relative size was a common feature of photography in Egypt from its advent in the mid-nineteenth century. The photographer who took most of the views for Breasted's guide was more clever than most, often using several figures for especially deep vistas, placing them in the foreground, middle distance, and far distance to heighten a scene's depth. All are Egyptians in typical native dress except for four views that contained Westerners.[5]

A few of the hundred views were published by Underwood & Underwood between 1897 and 1900, before Breasted's guide was prepared. In most instances Breasted selected them to illustrate aspects of contemporary Egyptian life, but there are a few that were chosen for their background information. One, dated 1897, shows a relatively famous scene on an exterior wall of Medinet Habu, a mortuary temple complex built by Ramses III (1187–1156 BCE, figure 3.3). Af-

Fig. 3.3 Detail, stereograph card 78, "The hunting of the wild bull depicted on temple wall of Ramses III, Medinet Habu, Thebes," from Breasted's *Egypt through the Stereoscope* (1905). Public domain, reproduction by author.

ter discussing its subject—the pharaoh hunting bulls—and its artistic qualities, Breasted finds a way to briefly acknowledge the people in the foreground: "Upon the common people of that remote day, when the Pharaohs flourished, such temple scenes as this must have exerted a marked influence; and we can imagine the multitude of ancient Thebes standing in awed admiration before these exploits of the Pharaoh, as do these modern descendants . . . who insistently offer us the dubious privilege of a drink from their gullehs, or water bottles, always expecting a return in coin for their trouble."

As with comparable views elsewhere in the set, Breasted's comments about contemporary Egyptian life are neither especially instructive nor wholly uninformative, and sometimes similarly rueful. When he does more fully discuss current subjects such as Moslem prayer, the lives and dress of Moslem women, or agricultural work like threshing grain and raising water, his tone is respectful and explanations reasonably complete. In general, Breasted tended to overlook Egyptian society at the time, in much the same way he looked past those populating the foreground of the Medinet Habu stereograph, as being of marginal interest and then treated only in passing. Breasted neither pandered to contemporary Western taste for the Orient's apparent exoticisms nor raised the subject of contemporary Egypt to the level of more sober and probing inquiry. Because he was professionally focused on Egypt's distant past, his choices masked the fact that he followed a well-established pattern that insisted on dramatic views of ancient monuments and "rejected the Egypt of its current inhabitants . . . except as a source of piquant details."[6]

The Egypt travel set was one of Underwood & Underwood's most popular, along with those for China, Japan, Ceylon, and India. The price? In 1908 the stereographs, book, and a case to hold them cost nineteen dollars.[7]

Ancient Records

Work on *Egypt through the Stereoscope* came in the midst of collecting, collating, and translating inscriptions for Breasted's "documentary sources" project, which ordinarily took precedence over all else when he wasn't busy completing *zettel* for the Egyptian dictionary or teaching at Chicago. He completed most of his dictionary work in summer 1901 and returned to regular teaching that fall, all but bringing his research to a halt. Harper provided a timely boost when, in May 1902, he allowed Breasted to fulfill his teaching load in two quarters instead of three, albeit at five/sixths his regular salary, enabling Breasted's return to Europe for a half year's worth of research and writing, the new schedule's duration being left open. The partial leave was financially manageable because Breasted was also promoted to associate professor with a salary increase to $2,500 a year, a sum that the leave reduced to $2,083, a bit more than his pay before the promotion. This type of arrangement was not at all unusual at Chicago thanks to Harper's support of faculty research. Some years earlier he extended the same terms to R. F. Harper so he could spend six months each year on cuneiform research in the British Museum.[8]

Breasted was well aware of his project's ambitious scale when he set it under way, but he seems to have underestimated the years required to achieve the degree of comprehensiveness and editorial precision he envisioned. To expedite the work and still maintain an active scholarly presence, Breasted concentrated all his academic publications from about 1899 to 1904 on texts later to be included among the documentary sources. One example is the first "book" he listed in his long-term work program. Published in 1900 as *A New Chapter in the Life*

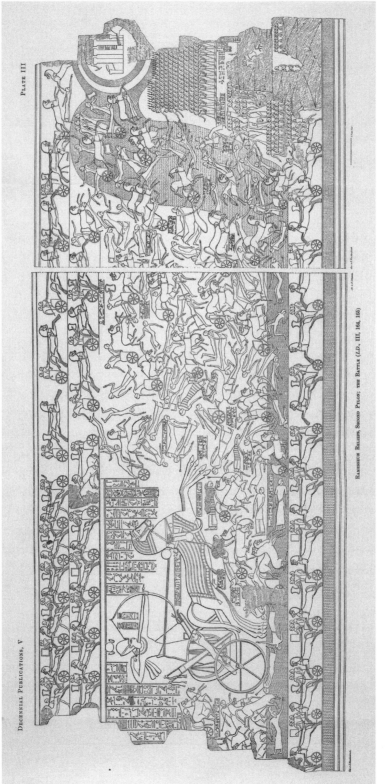

Fig. 3.4 "The Battle," plate III from Breasted's "The Battle of Kadesh" (1904), image copied from Richard Lepsius, *Denkmäler aus Aegypten und Aethiopien*, 12 vols. (Berlin: Nico-laische Buchhandlung, 1849–59), 3:164–65.

of Thutmose III, the thirty-one-page study is closer to an article in ambition as well as length insofar as it consists of a close analysis of several texts that were transcribed into hieroglyphic type and accompanied by English translations and critical commentary.

A more complex and engaging piece is his article "The Battle of Kadesh," which appeared in a 1904 volume, one among a series marking the University of Chicago's tenth anniversary. The battle was between the army of Ramses II and a force of Hittites near the ancient city of Kadesh on the western edge of modern-day Syria, about 1300 BCE. "The young king's [Ramses's] supreme effort to save himself and his army from destruction is so often depicted and in such graphic pictures upon the walls of the great temples, that no visitor, not even the most blasé 'globe-trotter' can ever forget it," Breasted wrote (figure 3.4). Because the various versions had never been subjected to "exhaustive study," Breasted compared them to establish a comprehensive and accurate account. It is based on three sets of inscriptions, seven sets of reliefs, and a hieratic papyrus. The result—complete with topographical maps, Breasted's hand-drawn maps showing military formations, typeset transcriptions of the hieroglyphic narratives, and borrowed and original renderings of the reliefs—is a masterful walk through evidentiary minutiae that nonetheless captures the conflict's drama and pageantry.[9]

When, in October 1904, Breasted called a halt to gathering more materials for his documentary-sources project, his manuscript was over ten thousand pages long. By the time he completed his preface and five months' proofreading in September 1905, he had spent nearly nine years on the project. The results were published by the University of Chicago Press as *Ancient Records of Egypt: Historical Documents from the Earliest Times to the Persian Conquest*. It was issued in four volumes, totaling nearly seventeen hundred pages, between February and July 1906. A fifth, two-hundred-page volume of indexes compiled by one of Breasted's students was published separately in 1907. The sources and commentary are organized chronologically, with the translations in each arranged by era or pharaonic succession, and thematically within each pharaoh's reign. The number of sources Breasted collected for *Ancient Records* is so impressive that a quantitative assessment alone overshadows his methodological contributions to Egyptology, which are contained in the preface and two introductory essays: "Documentary Sources of Egyptian History" and "Chronology."[10]

Breasted begins the preface by observing, "In no particular have modern historical studies made greater progress than in the reproduction and publication of documentary sources from which our knowledge of the most varied peoples and periods is drawn." Among the most important sources are texts "from the early epochs of the world's history." However, reading them requires "either a knowledge of ancient languages . . . or a complete rendition of the documents into English." The publication of *Ancient Records* was thus necessary because "no attempt has ever been made to collect and present all the sources of Egyptian history in a modern language."

Breasted's reason for translating the texts into English, rather than German, for example, is not given. One would think German to have been the better choice, given the German dictionary resources to which he was privy, his access to the latest German work on Egyptian grammar, his decision to employ the Berlin school's system of transliteration, and his familiarity with German as a modern language of translation for hieroglyphs. Ten years earlier, in his translator's preface for Erman's *Egyptian Grammar*, he framed the difficulties he encountered then by applauding German leadership in the field, observing that "the fact that the new science of Egyptian Grammar, as it has been created by the German grammatical school in the last fifteen years, does not yet exist in English." The deciding factor in favor of English must have been his now concurrent project, a history of Egypt written with materials from *Ancient Records*. As the last in his publication program leading "from the inscriptions to the non-technical reader," the history of Egypt was intended from the beginning for an American audience, and its reliance on English translations in turn colored Breasted's approach to *Ancient Records*.[11]

He hoped to translate the sources "as literally as possible without wrenching the English idiom." When not entirely successful, he "deliberately preferred this evil to a glib rendering which reads well and may be a long distance from the sense of the original." One quandary was the "gulf due to the total difference between the semitropical northern Nile valley of millenniums ago, and the English-speaking world of this twentieth century!" Breasted found the problem comparable to a translation of the New Testament recently published "for the tribes of Alaska," and the task of rendering "the term 'Good Shepherd,' for the reason that many of these people never saw a sheep and never heard of a shepherd." Another impediment was the relative youth of Egyptology and its "lack of those indispensable helps, the legion of concordances, glossaries, handbooks, and compilations for ready reference" available for scholars working in Greek or Hebrew: "The exhaustive study of syntax and of verbal forms which has been in progress for generations in the classic languages, or even in the Semitic group, has been going on for only a little over a quarter of a century in Egyptian." Indeed, Breasted found "a good many distinctions in the meanings of words" only became evident "in the course of the work." As a result, for example, "the common word *sr* is usually translated 'prince,' and this is undoubtedly sometimes the meaning of the word; but it very frequently means 'official,' a fact which I did not observe until far along in the . . . work. . . . We have as yet no history of titles— one of the most needed works in the entire range of Egyptian studies."[12]

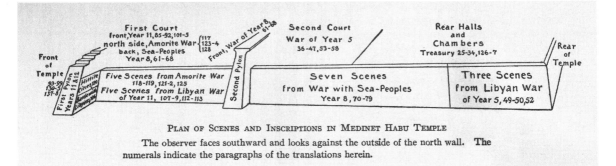

The observer faces southward and looks against the outside of the north wall. The numerals indicate the paragraphs of the translations herein.

Fig. 3.5 Illustration from Breasted's *Ancient Records of Egypt* (1906–7), 3:61. Public domain, reproduction by author.

Another fundamental issue was defining "what should and what should not be included in the term 'historical document.'" Breasted decided that "all purely religious compositions, as well as all exclusively literary documents (*belles-lettres*), all science, like mathematics and medicine, and in most cases all business documents" would be excluded. "In all cases, however, where the other classes of documents were of vital historical importance—that is, bore directly on events and conditions closely touching the career of the Egyptian state—they have been included." Breasted also ruled out "the products of the artist and the craftsman . . . , the domain of the archaeologist," by which he meant bas-reliefs, statuary, vessels, and other objects through which the "general course and the gradual development of Egyptian civilization are . . . roughly traceable." What appears to be a clear distinction made between Egypt's material culture—the stuff of archaeology and its texts—and the raw material of philology and history, is not so sensible when it comes to bas-reliefs, which seem to fall somewhere between archaeology and philology. The meanings produced by the juxtaposition of bas-relief scenes and inscriptions are nearly always greater than those in just the texts or the images alone.

Breasted was unable to entirely exclude images from *Ancient Records*, and though it has very few illustrations, it does have some, including his drawings for the Seti I relief article (figures 2.8a and b) and a few diagrams to show the progression of texts and scenes in especially large narrative sequences like one on Medinet Habu, the temple complex of Ramses III (figure 3.5). Despite his policy of avoiding images as a source of historical evidence, *Ancient Records* introduces texts with verbal descriptions of surrounding reliefs throughout. A section of inscriptions at Medinet Habu is a good example (this typographical layout follows Breasted's):

2. RELIEF SCENES OUTSIDE NORTH WALL AND IN SECOND COURT, YEAR 8

69. These scenes depict the war against the invading sea-rovers of Asia Minor with unusual interest. We see the equipment of the troops, the march to Syria, even possibly a lion hunt on the march, the great battle, both on land and sea, furnishing the earliest known representation of a naval battle, and the final triumphs.

Scene

70. Ramses III stands on a balcony, with two sunshade-bearers of the army, who kneel in salute, followed by a trumpeter. Beside these appear lines of the new recruits levied for the coming war, to whom the officers are distributing bows and quivers of arrows. Spears, quivers, bows, and swords lie piled up beside them.

71. The inscriptions are these:

Behind the King

All the gods are the protection of his limbs, to give to him might against every country.

Before the King

————king; he saith——to the princes, every leader of the infantry and chariotry, who are before his majesty: "Bring out the weapons."

Not unlike a film script that sets scenes with visual descriptions, *Ancient Records* is actually an intermingling of translated inscriptions and verbal descriptions of the images surrounding them.[13]

Next Breasted addresses the book's scholarly apparatus, the structure of introductory comments, notes, and editorial conventions that help explain each text, its origins, issues related to translation and nomenclature, and prior scholarly treatments. Because he intended *Ancient Records* to be a comprehensive resource, he used footnotes to describe the physical makeup and size of each source, its "state of preservation" when known, all the "publications in which the text of the monument has appeared," and "the comparative value of the more important publications," and when he considered any of the latter "inaccurate and untrustworthy," he reported the deficiency.

Each text is "supplied with a usually short introduction, setting forth the historical significance of the document, its character, and where necessary, a résumé of its content." Breasted refers readers to his history of Egypt, where "much of the historical background, and literary value of the more important documents" are "set forth more fully" (the history went to press about the same time as the first volume of *Ancient Records*). Leaving little to chance, Breasted marshaled the tools of design and typography to improve the book's utility. As illustrated in the example above, each document was "divided into logical paragraphs, each with a subtitle." And each paragraph was numbered, "thus furnishing a . . . system of reference to all the monuments, by means of the volume number (Roman) followed by the paragraph number (Arabic)." Other typographic tools included italics to set off section headings, short horizontal lines in texts to indicate from one to five missing words—the number of lines indicating the number missing, and long lines to indicate more than five missing words, as in the excerpt above. All in all, the scholarly apparatus of a work like *Ancient Records* is not dissimilar to household plumbing, never pretty but always necessary.[14]

Breasted's essay "The Documentary Sources of Egyptian History" surveys the extent and character of surviving inscriptions. His discussion proceeds chronologically by kingdom and dynasty, with the text swelling for periods when there was more evidence and shrinking when there was less. Unfortunately, he observes, only "accident has preserved . . . the merest scrap of the vast mass of written records which the incessant political, legal, administrative, religious, industrial, commercial, and literary activities filling the life of this ancient people, were constantly putting forth." With the exception of a pair of pharaohs' annals, scholars were "dependent upon a miscellaneous mass of documents of the most varied character and value." Worse yet, these sources "have reached us, with very few exceptions, in a state of sad mutilation. This mutilation and gradual destruction are a ceaseless process, which, if not as rapid as formerly, nevertheless proceeds without cessation at the present day." While the degradation was most pronounced in Egypt, even "stone monuments . . . in the museums of Europe suffer . . . ; and I have seen valuable stelae so attacked by the moist air of northern Europe that whole layers might be blown from the inscribed surface by a whiff of the breath."[15]

Errors in published transcriptions, mostly of sources in remote parts of Egypt that Breasted did not study, added more problems. The difficulty was partly due to copies' being made before scholars realized that what appeared to be random variations in the delineation and placement of hieroglyphs represented, in fact, differences in meaning. Further, Breasted observes, "To copy an inscription of any kind with accuracy is not easy. So close and fine an observer of material documents as [John] Ruskin, could copy a short Latin inscription with surprising inaccuracy. In his incomparable *Mornings in Florence* he reproduces" a brief text "in the church of Santa Croce; and in his copy of these eight short lines, which I compared with the original, he misspells one word, and omits two entire words." After a short historiography of bad hieroglyphic copying in the work of French, German, and English scholars from the 1870s to his present, Breasted laments that the advent of hieroglyphic type only exacerbated the problems by lending an air of definitiveness to texts set from inaccurate transcriptions.

Consequently, "he who wishes to know exactly what the original documents of ancient Egypt state cannot work exclusively in his library, but must go behind the publications and turn back to the originals themselves, in Egypt and the museums of Europe."[16]

Breasted attacked these problems by making and continually revising "his own copies of practically all the historical monuments in Europe, before the originals themselves. In the few cases where the original was not accessible, good squeezes [thick paper or papier-mâché impressions made directly from inscriptions on site in Egypt] and photographs supplied the deficiency, or professional colleagues furnished from the originals specially collated readings of doubtful passages." He also collated previously published texts with original sources whenever possible to assure their accuracy. While in Germany, Breasted could study the extensive collection of "squeezes" in the New Museum that were made by Lepsius during his pioneering 1840s expedition to Egypt. In instances where none of these approaches yielded a desired transcription, Breasted could turn to "the extensive collations made for the Berlin Egyptian Dictionary; and where these failed, he was able, in all important cases, to secure large-scale photographs of the originals."

Despite these efforts, Breasted still had to depend on transcriptions that couldn't be verified against the original inscriptions because they had either "perished entirely . . . [or] have lost more or less important portions of the text" since the transcriptions were published. In those instances, Breasted established a method based on comparing all the surviving copies that entailed taking "the best copy as a basis and collat[ing] with it all the other publications, noting in parallel columns all the variant readings. By this laborious means, . . . all that is now available, whether in publications or in the original, was thus incorporated in the final composite copy, from which the translation was made."[17]

Breasted's "Chronology" essay commences with a heavily annotated explanation of how he arrived at his own, new chronology, which is followed by the table itself, so densely footnoted that it spans seven pages. Egyptian dating systems are in fact a matter of daunting complexity, one that remains the source of occasional dustups among Egyptologists to this day because ancient Egyptians' annals rarely extended beyond the reigns of individual pharaohs. To ascertain the durations of dynasties and empires, scholars compiled the life spans of successive pharaohs and then correlated those dates with Egyptians' other calendrical aids: a civil calendar based on a 365-day year inaugurated in the third millennium BCE; one of two religious calendars based on months of twenty-nine or thirty days with intercalated months every three or four years; and a handful of ancient texts containing references to astronomical or other events linking the Egyptian calendar to externally verifiable dates. A chronology might seem a needless digression, but the scope of *Ancient Records*—from the "Earliest Times," around 4200 BCE, to the "Persian Conquest" in 525 BCE—required a framework that would undergird Breasted's organization of the sources, a necessity that compelled him to stake out his position on this crucial historical problem.[18]

Ancient Records was highly regarded from the outset and garnered praise from Egyptologists and nonspecialists alike. Among the former was Francis Llewellyn Griffith, a member of Breasted's generation, one of the leading British Egyptologists of the time, and later a professor at Oxford. Griffith reviewed the first volume shortly after publication and the remaining volumes in a subsequent piece. His first review placed *Ancient Records* in the context of other recent compendia, including a collection abridged from previously published sources by Kurt Sethe, a history of Egypt by W. M. Flinders Petrie that Griffith characterizes as "less a history than a *catalogue raisonné* of kings and their monuments," and a book on Egyptian chronology published by University of Berlin scholar Eduard Meyer in 1904. While acknowledging their respective strengths, Griffith notes that

> they are useless for any one but the specialist, and even he demands something more. The specialist in this slippery subject urgently needs a standard translation which he can both learn from and tinker at; and further, the command of the material given by the compactness and clearness of the European alphabet in collected translations, once seen, is recognised to be indispensable. Dr. Breasted has realised all this. . . . Besides being a useful instrument in the hands of the researcher this translated *corpus* . . . is a notable contribution to the understanding of the texts.

Griffith's subsequent review of the remaining four volumes briefly summarizes their contents and concludes that the "work as a whole is a very remarkable contribution to Egyptology" despite "certain omissions . . . explained by the author's [closing the manuscript] to additions in October 1904." Griffith did find a few minor problems here and there, but when his reviews are read in the context of Egyptology's take-no-prisoners discourse of the era, they constitute high praise.[19]

Typical of the nonspecialist reviews is one by Assyriologist Christopher Johnston that was written after all five volumes had been published. Also of Breasted's generation, Johnston was a widely published professor at Johns Hopkins, who specialized in cuneiform lexicography. He begins his review by considering *Ancient Records* in the context of the "historical records of Babylonia and Assyria," observing that while they "have long been accessible, . . . it is somewhat remarkable that up to the present time there has been no similar provision for . . . the records of ancient Egypt." Accordingly, for scholars "without a competent knowledge of the Egyptian language" who wish to "consult the sources of Egyptian history . . . the difficulties have been well-nigh insuperable."

Johnston therefore lauds Breasted for having "made the conditions as favorable as possible." Although he finds that in "the selection of his material . . . Breasted has shown excellent judgment," Johnston questions why some items were considered to be of historical importance while others were omitted. As one might expect, Johnston's examples are from his own area of expertise: "Except for the Abydos inscription of the reign of Khenzer (Vol. I, §781), Professor Breasted does not give any monuments of the Hyksos period." A group of mixed Semitic-Asiatics who migrated into northern Egypt during the eighteenth century BCE, the Hyksos were for Johnston an important cultural bridge linking the region of his own research, Mesopotamia, with ancient Egypt.

In all other respects, Johnston was unstinting in his praise. He admired the front matter of the first volume for its "valuable discussion of the documentary sources . . . and a very clear exposition of the complicated subject of Egyptian chronology." With regard to the translations, Johnston applauds Breasted's careful notations of "lacunae, restorations, variant readings, and words of doubtful import" and the "employment of headings, indicating the contents of respective paragraphs, . . . a useful device." "While the most advanced Egyptologist may consult it with profit," Johnston concludes, "to the less experienced scholar it will prove an invaluable boon. . . . Professor Breasted's *Ancient Records* takes high rank."[20]

It also became one of Breasted's most durable contributions to scholarship, being reprinted four times—in 1923, 1962, 1988, and 2001—and in 1990 an abridged Arabic version was published. In his introduction to the 2001 reprint, Egyptologist Peter Piccione observes, "At the time of publication, the *Ancient Records of Egypt* represented the pinnacle of Egyptological achievement and the highest standard of philological research. It was the most complete translation . . . of historical texts according to the most modern understanding of Egyptian grammar. It even employed a modification of the new Berlin system of transliteration, . . . the most highly evolved of the contemporary systems for rendering Egyptian hieroglyphs into Roman letters and which ultimately became the international standard." The longevity of *Ancient Records* should not be surprising because, as Piccione notes, "publications of purely archaeological data or inscriptions have a longer scholastic lifetime than do wholly interpretive and synthetical studies," which often depend on contemporary intellectual fashions that are "always in flux." Egyptology has continued to advance in the hundred years since *Ancient Records* was published, and Breasted's work has gradually become less useful for his successors. More sources have been discovered, scholars have improved their knowledge of Egyptian grammar, and research has shown Breasted's chronology and broader interpretations of the texts' meanings "can no longer be relied upon to any great extent." Nonetheless, the scope of the texts included in *Ancient Records* has yet to be superseded by any other single publication, and it contains "texts and inscriptions that have not been retranslated into English" since its publication. Taken in light of these strengths and weaknesses, *Ancient Records* "can be used reliably by the general reader and student as a comprehensive introduction to Egyptian historical inscriptions."[21]

A Definitive History of Egypt

The idea of writing a history of Egypt based on original sources came to Breasted sometime after he began the *Ancient Records* project, and it probably grew out of an invitation from his fellow Yale student and Berlin apartment mate, Charles Foster Kent. After a year in Berlin, Kent left for a position at the University of Chicago, where he taught from 1892 to 1895, visiting often with Breasted's parents, before moving to Brown University. During this period Kent proposed that Breasted write a compact history of Egypt for "The Historical Series for Bible Students," a textbook series published under Kent's editorship by Charles Scribner's Sons. In July 1898 Breasted signed a contract with Scribner's for a book titled "The Egyptians," intending to complete it by October 1900. Apparently he hoped to base "The Egyptians" on a combination of secondary sources and materials he'd already begun to collect for the documentary sources project, assuming the latter would be mostly done before 1900. As it stretched out and his contractual deadline for "The Egyptians" loomed, Breasted's ideas began to shift. Discussions with Erman about joining the Egyptian dictionary project may have provided the impetus for Breasted to change course. Instead of completing the documentary sources project first and then beginning the history, in January 1900 Breasted decided to "try the experiment" of writing the history "hand in hand with the inscriptions" work. The experiment not only succeeded, it prompted him to expand the scope of both.[22]

By July 1900 he had settled on the new work plan outlined above, hardening the documentary sources project into what would become *Ancient Records* and resolving that his history would primarily be "based on [those] original monuments." Breasted avowed, "This is what the other fellows have not yet done; it's taking me years, but before I am forty, I propose to make myself the leading authority on Egyptian history. . . . If I had been willing to compile a history out of the books of Germans, as Kent has done, I could have finished it in six months. . . . But I went back of the Germans to the monuments and I find they have not picked the bones clean."

Realizing the history he now had in mind would be longer than a standard textbook and fashioned for educated adults and scholars rather than students, Breasted proposed a "New Plan for a History of Egypt" to Scribner's in 1903. He argued the textbook format of the series was too confining, did not allow a sufficient number of illustrations, and would not reach the scholarly and popular audiences he wanted to address. The publisher's response was cool because the "probable cost and quality of the larger work makes us reluctant to embark upon so considerable an enterprise." Furthermore, Scribner's continued, "It seems to us . . . you are disposed to underestimate the importance of the smaller [textbook] in comparison with the larger volume," arguing "the textbook would be addressed primarily to scholars . . . as a measure of your knowledge in this special field." Scribner's proposed instead that Breasted complete the textbook "in accordance with our original agreement" and submit a more detailed proposal for a separate book to be considered de novo, the proposal to include a sample chapter and "careful estimate of the number, size, and character of the illustrations likely to be required." Breasted was offended by Scribner's remark concerning the "quality of the larger work," shot off a clarification, and threatened to take his work elsewhere. Scribner's accepted Breasted's point but gave no ground, suggesting only "if both [books] are to be published, it is desirable . . . [they] be issued by the same house." Breasted cooled off and asked the publisher to maintain the contract and await the larger history for prior review. Scribner's agreed. Writing to his mother, Breasted confided, "I can only hope [Scribner's] does not expect a definitive history of Egypt to prove as fascinating as the latest summer novel! After doing purely scientific work for so long, I have found it hard to strike the right style for such a book. I believe I have it now."[23]

Breasted completed the manuscript for his larger, adult-audience history first. He delivered it personally to Scribner's in New York in September 1904, on the way home from what he expected would be his last research leave in Europe, his work on the Egyptian dictionary and book projects now completed. The publisher responded about two months later, apologizing for the delay and hinting at the manuscript's length as the reason: "We have given the book a very careful reading, which was no inconsiderable task in itself, and have found it as interesting as we think it will prove valuable, both to scholars and to the general public."

Aiming to have the book in stores by the following fall, author and publisher soon cleared away various stylistic details. Scribner's accepted Breasted's large number of images and planned to distribute them evenly throughout the book, some printed on glossy paper and others on the "softer" text paper, "reducing very materially the weight of the volume." Breasted hoped for small "head-" and "tail-piece" images to open and close each chapter, a notion Scribner's found unworkable, countering that its design would appear more "sumptuously and richly illustrated." By March 1905 the first set of galleys was ready and most production issues settled save one, the placement of figure captions, which Breasted was to write after receiving the galley and illustration proofs. Breasted wanted ample space for sometimes lengthy discussions of the images, while Scribner's wanted less obtrusive captions. They compromised on single-line titles set in small caps with no more than two additional lines of lowercase descriptive text. If Breasted needed more space, he could footnote the figure reference in the text and place an extended discussion in the note. Although Scribner's was amenable to a generous illustration budget, the publisher did not understand why Breasted wanted so much space to discuss the images, much less to place the captions in close proximity to them—a scheme Scribner's thought was inelegant and ugly. For Breasted, who had learned the benefits of verbally guiding readers through the views of *Egypt through the Stereoscope*, captions were an integral part of his history's illustration scheme.

Once the caption matter was settled, Breasted was soon immersed in proof-reading. *Ancient Records* was also being typeset at this time, and the finishing touches for *Egypt through the Stereoscope* were under way too. From April through September 1905, "proofs bulged from his pockets, distended his briefcase. He read proofs wherever he went—at mealtimes, or walking to and from his classes, or in crowded [train] day-coaches." Assisted by Frances, her younger sister Imo-gen Hart who was visiting with them that summer, and his brother-in-law, Breasted completed proofreading and the preface for his history in early Sep-tember, and it was published before year's end under the title *A History of Egypt: From the Earliest Times to the Persian Conquest*.[24]

Weighing in at over two pounds and with more than 700 pages of text, 187 illustrations, and 13 maps, it is a hefty book. *A History of Egypt* is almost a large-format volume, too, measuring nine and a half inches tall by seven inches wide, its ample size allowing spacious margins and a fairly large typeface, as well as generous space for illustrations. Fashioned to attract a popular audience, the book is bound in a deep blue book cloth stamped on the spine and front cover with elegant gold- and red-foil designs based on ancient Egyptian motifs com-posed in a proto–art deco style (figure 3.6). Flattened forms that occur in Egyp-tian architectural ornamentation such as papyrus stalks, papyrus weavings, and lotus-flower, bud, and leaf patterns are worked into the side and bottom panels of the front cover. They are surmounted by outstretched vulture wings, often associated with Nekhbet, the goddess of Upper Egypt, and a dung beetle, which, as placed here, would have represented Khepri, a god who the Egyptians believed rolled the sun from horizon to horizon each day. The vertical left- and right-hand panels are reminiscent of Egyptian column decorations, while the top panel is similar to the long, narrow designs found on the faces of gorge cornices or the undersides of lintels leading into Egyptian temples. Produced before the advent of eye-catching book jackets, the book's richly colored binding, including gold-leaf finishing on the top edges of the text block, was intended to make *A History of Egypt* especially attractive. The high quality of the book's production added to

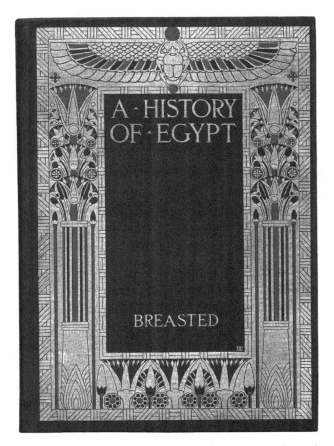

Fig. 3.6 Cover of Breasted's *A History of Egypt* (1905). Public domain, reproduction by author.

its cost, but Scribner's may have justified the expense as necessary to counterbalance its fearsome bulk, which, the publisher feared, might otherwise daunt a popular readership. It sold for five dollars.[25]

A History of Egypt's chronological scope, "from ancient times to the Persian conquest," precisely matches that of *Ancient Records*. Its structure is quite similar too. Following the preface is a ten-page introduction to Egyptian geography and climate—"The Land," a twelve-page chapter titled "Preliminary Survey, Chronology and Documentary Sources" condensed from *Ancient Records*, and then the main narrative. An explanation of footnotes and abbreviations as well as lists of illustrations and maps are grouped with the book's front matter. A "Chronological Table of Kings," extracted from *Ancient Records*, and two indexes close the book, one a proper-name and subject index, the other an index to Old Testament passages. A fold-out map of the Nile valley from the delta to Khartoum is bound into the back.

Breasted begins his preface by pitching the book to three audiences: first, the "ever-increasing number of those who visit the Nile Valley with every recurring winter"; next, the "growing circle of those who . . . realize the significance of the early East in the history of man," especially those "who are in civilization the children of early Europe"; last, "and possibly the most numerous . . . students of the Old Testament." Breasted introduces "the plan" of his book by drawing heavily on prefatory material from *Ancient Records*, sometimes quoting himself verbatim, to show how the "combined results of the revised copies from the originals and the new grammatical study" of them published in *Ancient Records* form the basis of this new history. "Therefore," he writes, "it may be fairly claimed that [this history] rests upon the . . . original documents themselves." Breasted then explains the citation method by which he links the book to *Ancient Records*—roman numerals for the *Ancient Records* volumes followed by arabic numerals for the numbered paragraphs. "It is hoped," Breasted continues, "by this means of keeping all technical discussion of sources in [*Ancient Records*], the author has succeeded in unburdening this history of the workshop *debris* . . . while at the same time the advantage of close contact with the sources for every fact adduced is not sacrificed."

As in *Ancient Records*, Breasted distinguishes between "*written* documents" and the "*material* documents" of archaeology, "the vast sources" of which he did not examine. This time he argues that "Egyptian archaeology is in its infancy" and it has made "but few of the fundamental studies and researches already completed in classical archaeology." His assertion must have startled colleagues such as W. M. Flinders Petrie who had already made important contributions along these lines. However, Breasted was trying to articulate a specific methodological point. He certainly had noticed that inscriptions on objects can clarify the meaning of archaeological finds and vice versa. The problem was that there was not a sufficient amount of Egyptological research that integrated the results of epigraphy and archaeology. Thus the scholar "with the enviable combination of archaeological and philological capacity," Breasted writes, "would find a rich field to cultivate, in working for the production of an Egyptological Overbeck." Johannes Overbeck, a nineteenth-century German scholar specializing in ancient Greek statuary, was particularly interested in sculptural representations of Greek mythology. One of his methodological innovations was the use of ancient writings to investigate the symbolic functions of statuary in ancient Greece, thereby uniting interpretation and aesthetics in studies of those works.[26]

In a departure from *Ancient Records*, Breasted *does* include religion, but with the qualification that "the mere quantity alone of the materials make any attempt at an exhaustive" study impossible. There was one exception, however: "the Amarna period and the solar faith," which received "the author's special attention." Being the subject of his dissertation, Breasted could hardly resist it, and thus "all the documents on the unparalleled religious revolution of Ikhnaton, and all the known hymns to the Sun, throughout Egyptian history, were collected and examined." For "Egyptian religion, as a whole," he acknowledges drawing on Erman's work. Further expressions of gratitude follow for access to museums and those who supplied him with drawings and photographs, not least "Messrs. Underwood & Underwood" for "their superb stereographs of Egyptian monuments in situ." Plugging *Egypt through the Stereoscope*, Breasted adds that for "those to whom a journey through the Nile Valley is an impossibility, . . . the system of travel represented in these beautiful stereographs makes possible to every one a voyage up the Nile which falls little short of the actual experience."[27]

The narrative arc of *A History of Egypt* is majestic. Breasted sweeps through the civilization's four millennia with clear, often vivid prose that beckons the reader along. Moving gracefully from broad vistas of entire empires to the minutiae of daily life, he shows a fine ability for articulating expansive themes and, when the narrative begins to flag, leavening them with entertaining historical nuance. The text all but pulses with the enthusiasm of a passionate teacher who "believed . . . the subject could be presented more significantly than as a mere catalogue of facts. With the eye of his imagination Breasted could reconstruct the ancient Egyptian scene." One experiences Breasted's fervor in the text, just as one of his former students recalled, "with a thrill, standing with him above Deir el-Bahri on the great cliff overlooking the Theban plain while he re-created the teeming life of the Egyptian capital."[28]

Breasted conscientiously tells the story of Egypt's monarchs and great officials, its conquests and defeats, and the ebb and flow of its imperial realm. Yet he is at his scholarly best when attending to the day-to-day texture of Egyptian administration, law, and commerce, the particulars of social history assembled from the margins of inscriptions and the backgrounds of reliefs. Here, for example, are excerpts from the beginning of chapter 13, "The New State: Society and Religion," the first in book 5 addressing what Breasted called the first period of "The Empire," or the beginning of the eighteenth dynasty (about 1539 BCE), which leads off the era known more familiarly as the New Kingdom. The chapter opens with the reign of Nebpehtire Ahmose (1539–1514 BCE), to whom Breasted refers as Ahmose I:

> [The Pharaoh] was accustomed every morning to meet the vizier, still the main spring of the administration, to consult with him on all the interests of the country and all the current business which necessarily came under his eye. . . . The Pharaoh's office . . . was the central organ of the whole government where all its lines converged. All other reports to government were likewise handed in here. . . . Even in the limited number of such documents preserved to us, we discern the vast array of detailed questions in practical administration which the busy monarch decided. The punishment of condemned criminals was de-

termined by him. . . . Besides frequent campaigns in Nubia and Asia, he visited the quarries and mines in the desert or inspected the desert routes, seeking suitable locations for wells and stations. Likewise the internal administration required frequent journeys to examine new buildings and check all sorts of official abuses.

[T]he officers of administration are incidentally the dispensers of justice. . . . The vizier is no exception. All petitioners for legal redress applied first to him in his audience hall; if possible in person, but in any case in writing. For this purpose he held a daily audience or "sitting" as the Egyptian called it. Every morning the people crowded into the "hall of the vizier," where the ushers and bailiffs jostled them into line that they might "be heard," in order of arrival, one after another. In cases concerning land located in Thebes he was obliged by law to render a decision in three days, but if the land lay in the "South or North" he required two months. . . . All crimes in the capital city were denounced and tried before him, and he maintained a criminal docket of prisoners awaiting trial or punishment. . . . All this, and especially the land cases, demanded rapid and convenient access to the archives of the land. They were therefore all filed in his offices. No one might make a will without filing it in the "vizier's hall." Copies of all nome archives, boundary records and all contracts were deposited with him. . . . Every petitioner to the king was obliged to hand in his petition in writing at the same office.

The . . . vizier was the motive power behind the organization and operation of this ancient state. [Other than the Pharaoh] the only other check upon his untrammeled control of the state was a law constraining him to report the condition of his office to the chief treasurer. Every morning as he came forth from his interview with the king he found the chief treasurer standing by . . . the palace front, and there they exchanged reports. The vizier then unsealed the doors of the court and of the offices of the royal estate so that the day's business might begin; and during the day all ingress and egress at these doors was reported to him, whether of person or of property of any sort. His office was the means of communication with the local authorities, who reported to him in writing on the first day of each season, that is, three times a year. It is in his office that we discern with unmistakable clearness the complete centralization of all local government in all its functions. This supervision of the local administration required frequent journeys and there was therefore an official barge . . . on the river in which he passed from place to place. It was he who detailed the king's bodyguard for service as well as the garrison of the residence city; general army orders proceeded from his office; the forts . . . were under his control; and the officials of the navy all reported to him. . . . He had legal control of the temples throughout the country . . . , so that he was minister of ecclesiastical affairs. He had economic oversight of many important resources of the country; no timber could be cut without his permission, and the administration of irrigation and water supply was also under his charge. In order to establish the calendar for state business, the rising of [the star] Sirius was reported to him. He exercised advisory functions in all the offices of the state. . . . He was a veritable Joseph and it must have been this office which the Hebrew narrator had in mind as that to which Joseph was appointed.[29]

In the original, this excerpt contains twenty-six footnotes for an equal number of sources—all but two referencing translations in *Ancient Records*. They are like the fine cracks running across the surface of a skillfully restored vessel. Here the shards are the numerous scattered and fragmentary texts Breasted carefully assembled into coherent narrative.

Breasted's mention of Joseph typifies his use of figures and events likely known to his readership as a way of rendering ancient Egypt accessible by linking it to neighboring civilizations. He was particularly fond of showing connections between Egypt and ancient Greece and the events of the Old Testament, often to conjecture about Egypt's influence on the formation of Greek philosophy and Old Testament theology. Breasted similarly alludes to Christian theology, and the histories of Europe and America. He was especially interested in Egypt's ostensible role in supplying ideas critical to the development of Greek thought and Judeo-Christian religion. A theme that had arisen in earlier work, it finds more complete expression here in the context of his chapter on the "religious revolution" promulgated by Amenhotep IV:

Amenhotep IV immersed himself heart and soul in the thought of the time, and the philosophizing theology of the priests was of more importance to him than all the provinces of Asia. In such contemplations he gradually developed ideals and purposes which make him the most remarkable of all the Pharaohs, and the first *individual* in human history.

The profound influence of Egypt's imperial position had not been limited to the externals of life . . . , but had extended likewise to the thought of the age. Such thought was chiefly theological. . . . The priests had made great progress in the interpretation of the gods, and they had now reached a stage in which, like the later Greeks, they were importing semi-philosophical significance into the myths. . . . Thus Ptah, the artificer-god of Memphis, furnished the priesthood there with a fruitful line of thought, . . . guiding the thinker, in . . . a language without terminology for such processes. . . . Ptah had been from the remotest ages the god of the architect and craftsman. . . . Contemplating this god, the Memphite priest, little used as his mind was to abstractions, found a tangible channel, moving along which he gradually gained a rational and . . . a philosophical conception of the world. The workshop of the Memphite temple, where, under Ptah's guidance, were wrought the splendid statues, utensils and offerings for the temple, expands into a world, and Ptah, its lord, grows into the master-workman of the universal workshop. As he furnishes all designs to the architect and craftsman, so now he does the same for all men in all that they do; he becomes the supreme mind. . . . The world and all that is in it existed as thought in his mind; and his thoughts, like his plans for buildings and works of art, needed but to be expressed in spoken words to take concrete form as material realities. Gods and men alike proceeded from mind, all that they do is but the mind of the god working in them. . . .

The Egyptian had thus gained the idea of a single controlling intelligence, behind and above all sentient beings, including the gods. The efficient force by which this intelligence put his designs into execution was his spoken "word," and this primitive "logos" is undoubtedly the incipient germ of the later logos-doctrine which found its origin in Egypt. Early Greek philosophy may also have drawn upon it.[30]

At this point Breasted argues that with the expansion of the Egyptian empire in the period leading up to Amenhotep IV's reign, the conception of the gods' dominions expanded as well: "Living now under the Pharaohs who ruled a world-empire, the priest of the imperial age had before him in tangible form a world-dominion and a world-concept, the prerequisite of the notion of the world-god." The stage was thus set for a universalizing theology:

We have thus far given this god no name. Had you asked the Memphite priests they would have said his name was Ptah . . . ; the priests . . . at Thebes would have claimed the honour for Amon, the state god, . . . while the High Priest . . . at Heliopolis would have pointed out the fact that the Pharaoh was the son of Re and the heir to his kingdom, and hence Re must be the supreme god of all the empire. . . . Already under Amenhotep III [Amenhotep IV's father] an old name for the material sun, "Aton," had come into prominent use. . . . [This] sun-god, too, was now and again designated as the "sole god" by Amenhotep III's contemporaries.

The already existent conflict with traditional tendencies into which [Amenhotep IV] had been forced, contained . . . difficulties enough to tax the resources of any statesman without the introduction of a departure involving . . . dangerous conflicts with the powerful priesthoods and touching religious tradition, the strongest conservative force of the time. It was just this rash step which the young king now had no hesitation in taking. Under the name of Aton, then, Amenhotep IV introduced the worship of the supreme god.

He would break with the priesthoods and make Aton the sole god. . . . It was no "Götterdämmerung" which the king contemplated, but an immediate annihilation of the [other] gods. . . . The priesthoods . . . were dispossessed, the official temple-worship of the various gods throughout the land ceased, and their names were erased wherever they could be found upon the monuments. The persecution of Amon was especially severe. . . . Even the royal statues of his ancestors, including the king's father, were not respected; and, what was worse, as the name of that father, Amenhotep, contained the name of Amon, the young king was placed in the unpleasant predicament of being obliged to cut out his own father's name . . . on all the temples of Thebes. . . . And then there was the embarrassment of the king's own name, likewise Amenhotep, "Amon rests," which could not be spoken or placed on a monument. It was of necessity also banished and the king assumed in its place the name "Ikhnaton," which means "Spirit of Aton."

Thebes was now compromised by too many old associations to be a congenial place of residence for so radical a revolutionist [as Ikhnaton]. As he looked across the city he saw stretching along the western plain that imposing line of mortuary temples of his fathers which he had violated. They now stood silent and empty. The towering pylons and obelisks of Karnak and Luxor were not a welcome reminder of all that his fathers had contributed to the glory of Amon.[31]

Thus Ikhnaton built an entirely new city located along the Nile about two hundred miles downriver from Thebes (Luxor), which he called Akhetaton (Tell el-Amârna). In discussing the context of the city's creation, Breasted focuses on two surviving hymns to Aton, which Breasted conjectures were composed by Ikhnaton. "Of all the monuments left by this unparalleled revolution," Breasted declares, "these hymns are by far the most remarkable; and from them we may gather an intimation of the doctrines which the speculative young Pharaoh had sacrificed so much to disseminate." Further, Breasted suggests, "the hundred and fourth Psalm of the Hebrews shows a notable similarity" to the longer of the two hymns "in the thought and the sequence." To prove his point, Breasted offers "the most noticeably parallel passages side by side." Here are two of the pairings:

The barques sail up-stream and down-stream alike.	Yonder is the sea, great and wide, Wherein are things creeping innumerable
Every highway is open because thou hast dawned.	Both small and great beasts.
The fish in the river leap up before thee,	There go the ships; There is leviathan, whom thou has formed to sport with him.
And thy rays are in the midst of the great sea.	(Ps. 104:25–26)

How manifold are all thy works!	O lord, how manifold are thy
They are hidden from before us,	works!
O thou sole god, whose powers no	In wisdom hast thou made
other possesseth.	them all;
Thou didst create the earth	The earth is full of thy creatures.
according to thy desire.	(Ps. 104:24)

Although Breasted claims that in his translation of the Aton hymn "no attempt has been made to do more than to furnish an accurate rendering," he nonetheless presents it in a manner that echoes the scriptural flavor of the Psalms. Perhaps he is trying to make his comparison of the Aton hymn and Psalms less jarring in order to focus the reader's attention on their contents, a stylistic decision that might well have been appropriate for an early-twentieth-century, Bible-reading audience. The language of the Psalms is close but not identical to that in the King James Bible. Breasted does not indicate his source for the Psalms, and it's possible he translated them from a Hebrew text. He does not note the source for the Aton hymn either, but its translation is based on the critical edition in his dissertation.

Breasted may have passed over the details because he wanted to emphasize that Ikhnaton's ideas "are not thoughts which we have been accustomed to attribute to the men of some fourteen hundred years before Christ." "A new spirit has breathed upon the dry bones of traditionalism in Egypt," Breasted argues, and "he who reads these lines for the first time must be moved with involuntary admiration for the young king who in such an age found such thoughts in his heart."[32]

As Breasted spent more time on Ikhnaton, he found more reasons to admire him: "He grasped the idea of a world-dominator, as the creator of nature, . . . which . . . revealed the creator's beneficent purpose for all his creatures." The pharaoh "based the universal sway of God upon his fatherly care of all men alike, irrespective of race or nationality, and to the proud and exclusive Egyptian he pointed to the all-embracing bounty of the common father of humanity, even placing [the subjected peoples of] Syria and Nubia" among the beneficiaries of Aton's protection. "It is this aspect of Ikhnaton's mind," Breasted continues, "which is especially remarkable; he is the first prophet of history. While to the traditional Pharaoh the state god was only the triumphant conqueror, . . . Ikhnaton saw in him the beneficent father of all men. It is the first time in history that a discerning eye has caught this universal truth."

Lest the reader think too highly of Ikhnaton, Breasted notes that his theology does not include "a very spiritual conception of the deity nor any attribution to him of ethical qualities. . . . The king has not perceptibly risen from . . .

Fig. 3.7 "Ikhnaton and His Queen Decorate the Priest Eye and His Wife," figure 139 from Breasted's *A History of Egypt* (1905). "Leaning upon the cushioned balustrade of the palace balcony with his queen and infant daughters by his side, the king throws down golden collars, vessels, rings and ornaments to his favourites. . . . The servants . . . of Eye dance with joy or bow ceremoniously. Above . . . are the waiting chariots of Eye and his wife, while . . . below these his scribes make record of the event." From p. 370: The king and queen are shown "together standing under the disk of Aton, whose rays, terminating in hands, descend and embrace" the royal family. Public domain, reproduction by author.

beneficence to . . . righteousness . . . , nor to his demand for this in the character of men." Instead, Breasted finds "a constant emphasis upon 'truth' such as is not found before nor since. The king always attaches to his name the phrase 'living in truth,' and that this phrase was not meaningless is evident in his daily life. . . . Thus his family life was open and unconcealed before the people. He took the greatest delight in his children and appeared with them and the queen, their mother, on all possible occasions. . . . He had himself depicted on the monuments while enjoying the most familiar and unaffected intercourse with his family," which Breasted cites as evidence also of the increased naturalism in art encouraged by Ikhnaton (figure 3.7). Ikhnaton's reforms were short lived, however. Foreign pressures toward the end of his life and internal turmoil in the years following his death made way for a revival of old traditions. "To his own nation he was afterward known as 'the criminal of Akhetaton.'"[33]

Breasted's history is not without flaws. Beyond a handful of interpretive mistakes, grammatically flawed readings, and conclusions now rendered obsolete by subsequent discoveries, there are injudicious asides made in the course of larger arguments. Readers sensitized by a generation of critical writings on Orientalism, for example, would notice instances of Western bias. In one instance Breasted shrugs off a "gross laxity in the oversight of . . . local administration" as "abuses which always arise under such conditions in the orient"; in another, he explains that after a decline in central power led to anarchy and the rise of "local nobles, chiefs and rulers of towns . . . the common people" were victimized in a way that "only the orient ever experiences."

But these lapses are rare. Instead, one comes away from the book recalling lively descriptions and memorable turns of phrase. As the book draws to a close, Breasted begins his summation with a brief account of Egypt's deliquescence under the sway of the Persian empire: "And if a feeble burst of national feeling enabled this or that Egyptian to thrust off the Persian yoke for a brief period, the movement may be likened to the convulsive contractions which sometimes lend momentary motion to limbs from which conscious life has long departed."[34]

The critical response to *A History of Egypt* was mixed among Egyptologists. Francis Llewellyn Griffith expressed the enthusiasm of some when he described it as "the fullest as well as the most vivid and interesting that has ever been written." Others qualified their praise, even while recognizing Breasted was not writing for a scholarly audience alone. Max Müller, one of Breasted's generation of Egyptologists, who trained in Germany and taught at the University of Pennsylvania, begins his review: "This book fills a great want. Hitherto there has been no history of Egypt in the English language at once sufficiently reliable, full, and popular. . . . His book is lucidly and elegantly written, and I have heard that it reads like a novel to the non-orientalist. The illustrations, among which there are some good, new photographs, contribute considerably to the attractive nature of the book." Müller finds that for specialists there are "many recent discoveries and researches incorporated in the volume and several original observations."

Yet, Müller adds, the "book is not addressed to the student of historical science who is himself no Egyptologist. It lacks the apparatus of references which the scientific worker cannot do without. There are, indeed, some footnotes, but with rare exceptions the author refers only to his own publications." Müller's biggest complaint is that Breasted "does not emphasize the many uncertainties and problems of Egyptian history the historian would like. A popular work, of course, must smooth over such difficulties. The writer has done this . . . and has filled out gaps, often with some poetic license." By "poetic license," he means Breasted's "overrating of the small military achievements of the Egyptians," such as at the Battle of Kadesh. Müller believes that Breasted "concentrates his interest so strongly on this period of Syrian conquests . . . that he treats the period after . . . rather slightly." Yet "that later period . . . offers so many points of contact with the history of other nations that it may seem to very many people the most interesting epoch."

More generally, Müller feels Breasted views "Egypt too often not as a critic but as an over-enthusiastic lover and admirer, a fault rather general with the older school Egyptologists. In face of the one-sidedness of historians who knew only Greece and Rome, orientalists found it necessary to paint the Orient and its importance sometimes with very thick coloring." Even so, Müller concedes, "it would rob the book of its most attractive features, if its warm enthusiasm should be reduced everywhere to meager, cool, cautious statements accompanied by the heavy apparatus of the historian."[35]

Nonspecialists were very keen on the book. Columbia University professor Franklin Giddings, a founding father of sociology in America and the first appointed to a faculty position in the field, was typical of several in his spirited review: "For the first time we have in one volume a history of Egypt worthy of the name; a history based on the latest results of archaeological research, written by a man whose knowledge is wide and accurate, whose conceptions of human society are a product of comparative study and the scientific spirit and who has, withal, the literary gift." It might seem odd for a sociologist to review an ancient history, but Giddings's career at Columbia began with responsibilities in the history of civilization as well as sociology, reflecting his wide-ranging interests, which in his earlier years included "consciousness of kind," or "collective feelings of similarity and belonging," in earlier as well as contemporary societies.

Giddings thus focused on *A History of Egypt* as a resource for the social sciences, finding that it "presents a remarkably complete picture of the social evolution of one great people . . . from the moment of its emergence from the tribal life of barbarism, through every stage of its religious, economic and political development. . . . Acquainted with this history, the student has a basis for comparative study." Another of Giddings's observations must have deeply gratified Breasted: "So long as Egyptian civilization awakened in the . . . student a feeling of something apart and strange, we knew that we were not yet in close touch with the vital facts. As depicted in Professor Breasted's pages, Egyptian life has ceased to be queer. It is like the human life that we know. Social conditions, industry and politics present familiar aspects."[36] Breasted had found a way to overcome popular assumptions about Egypt and the occult—he told a far more compelling story.

The book sold well. Scribner's reprinted the first edition after three years and issued a revised edition in 1909. That version was reissued a dozen times, the last in 1959, before other publishers picked it up, producing at least four more printings, the most recent being in 2003. *A History of Egypt* was reprinted a dozen times in the United Kingdom, and it has been translated into French, German, Russian, Arabic, Hebrew, and Braille. Surprisingly, *A History of Egypt* has also remained of interest to Egyptologists. Peter Piccione reports:

Breasted's rigorous methodology gave his history a longevity unsurpassed by any other general Egyptian history book. Indeed, the first cracks in the historical narrative did not begin to appear until more than thirty years after its publication. Even so, much of the book was still considered professionally useful for at least another twenty years. . . . Its popular reputation was so great that as late as the 1960s and 1970s, it remained the first serious reading on ancient Egypt for most fledgling ancient historians and amateur Egyptologists. To this day [2001], no other general history of Egypt has had a useful lifetime as extensive as . . . *History of Egypt*. . . . Breasted's scholarship, although dated, is still highly regarded, and as late as 1995, *Who Was Who in Egyptology* cited it as "probably the best general history of Pharaonic Egypt ever published." [It] and . . . *Ancient Records* . . . mark a milestone in the history of Egyptology, so precise and well-considered was Breasted's methodology.[37]

Breasted dedicated *A History of Egypt* to his mother, and one cannot help but wonder if, as he wrote the book, he had her in mind as an ideal reader. Harriet Breasted was a woman of modest education who, "even in her younger days . . . had only vaguely understood the nature of his work." As Breasted's career advanced, "with inexhaustible patience he had in his gratitude tried to tell her about" his work, using "the same simple words with which he used to tell" stories to young Charles. Breasted's letters to her in those "latter years" are laced with careful explanations of his research and occasional reflections on his ability to write effectively for popular consumption. Shortly after completing *A History of Egypt*, Breasted wrote to her: "I have been too long and too deeply submerged in writing it to judge whether it makes good reading or bad. . . . It is my own work, based throughout on my own study of the original sources . . . so whatever its undoubted faults, they too are mine alone." In the end, he had "only one *great* regret—that I could not have copied *all* the extant inscriptions along the entire Nile valley before completing both the *History* and the *Ancient Records*."[38] Returning to Egypt remained an unrealized dream.

4

Expeditions to Nubia

Grant Applications and the Rhetoric of Research

"What I could do!" Breasted wrote in April 1900, "if I could only find some fellow ready to put in a few thousand a year for scientific work. I shall find him some day." Shortly after he began collecting materials for what would become *Ancient Records*, Breasted confronted the limitations of his sources. Eager and restless, he imagined the possibilities of enlarging his project beyond those preserved in European museums and previous publications to include monuments along the Nile. Thought led to action. "I am now laying plans to copy all the inscriptions of Egypt and publish them," he wrote. "The plan will require $25,000 a year for 15 or 20 years, and I expect to begin, as soon as I have finished the year's [Egyptian dictionary work]; the only possible thing which can upset the plan is the lack of the money."

Breasted's knowledge of patronage came from two experiences. First was the underwriting of the University of Chicago's founding and early years of development by John D. Rockefeller, Chicago-area philanthropists, and less affluent donors solicited by the American Baptist Education Society. The other was the Egyptian dictionary's sponsorship by Kaiser Friedrich Wilhelm II. Differences between the two types of patrons spoke volumes about the sponsorship of research in the Old World and the New and about the concentration and distribution of wealth as well as the institutions by which wealth might be dispersed in those two worlds. There were no American government agencies funding research then, and the nearest candidate, the National Academy of Sciences—established by act of Congress in 1863—was a rather quiescent organization at the turn of the century that neither sponsored research nor was regarded by Congress as a conduit for scholarly support. Instead, there was the accumulation of vast, well-publicized fortunes by Gilded Age industrialists, merchants, and financiers, accompanied by the belief among some, such as Andrew Carnegie and John D. Rockefeller, that they should share their wealth with charitable causes. This set the stage for what would become a philanthropic free-for-all that found legions of worthy individual and institutional supplicants besieging donors for support. Breasted was about to step into that fray.

There were also smaller fortunes being personally dispersed by America's moneyed elites, Chicago's among them, and several of the city's leaders contributed to the University of Chicago's founding and expansion. It made sense for Breasted to begin with them, and in early 1901 he presented his "plans for work in Egypt" to Edward E. Ayer, the Field Museum backer and Egyptian antiquities collector Breasted had approached before while both were in London. Ayer was uninterested but recommended Breasted "tackle" Charles T. Yerkes. He was a Chicago transportation financier of doubtful reputation, whose 1892 gift built the university's then world-leading astronomical observatory, and he had just moved to London, where he was investing in that city's rail system expansions. Nothing came of Breasted's appeal, and he began looking elsewhere.[1]

The only sources of information then about prospective donors were either word of mouth or newspaper accounts of significant contributions. None of the era's benefactions were so widely publicized as those of Carnegie and Rockefeller, the scale of whose acquisition and dispersal of wealth held Americans in continual thrall. News of Andrew Carnegie's $10 million gift establishing the Carnegie Institution of Washington swept the nation in December 1901. It was intended to promote original research and the advancement of science in America by identifying the "exceptional man," regardless of discipline or institutional affiliation, and provide the means for investigations free of financial worry or other obligations. The news moved more swiftly than the institution's trustees, and before they convened for their first meeting, eager researchers were readying proposals. Breasted was among them.[2]

His proposal is a model of concision and organization. It opens with an introductory discussion of the problem, segues into the methodology for solving it, presents a budget and justification, and closes with assurances of qualifications and ability to complete the work. Breasted begins by stating that the "great field of Egypt" has been "hitherto entirely neglected" by American philanthropy and that American scholars have "therefore been unable to make any contribution to the preservation and publication of the vast body of monuments in the Nile Valley." He then contrasts America's "great opportunity" with the current Egyptological activities of the "larger governments of Europe" sponsoring French, Italian, and German investigators. By distinguishing between America and Europe, Breasted was appealing to Carnegie's goals of promoting American research while also advancing an argument for America's technical and methodological superiority. Breasted noted that the European expeditions were "before the days of the practical application of modern methods of photography and epigraphy" and before "exhaustive accuracy in epigraphy and archaeology." By "epigraphy" Breasted meant not only the study and deciphering of ancient inscriptions, but their accurate copying or transcription—a fundamental prerequisite to further research and publication. Thus the "inaccuracy and incompleteness" of transcriptions published in prior decades rendered them inadequate for the more rigorous demands of modern research like the Egyptian dictionary project.

Furthermore, Breasted argued, the "monuments of Egypt are rapidly perishing. Weather, the [annual] inundation [of the Nile], other causes of natural decay, and modern vandalism are rapidly obliterating" them. This observation was hardly new. Jean-François Champollion, who began decoding the meaning of hieroglyphs in 1822, noted the monuments' accelerating decay after visiting Egypt in 1829, and an American student of ancient Egypt, George Gliddon, published a discussion of the monuments' deterioration in 1841. Breasted's reference to the problem in this context *is* novel in the sense that he was positioning the accurate recording and publication of inscriptions as a form of historic preservation: "In this age of photography and highly developed mechanical methods in epigraphy, it is now possible for America to step in and rescue these precious records of the past."[3]

Breasted's project, "the recopying and republication of all Egypt" seemed extravagant. It "is not a mere dream," Breasted insisted, as "the writer copied . . . practically all the Egyptian inscriptions in Europe, outside of Germany" for the Egyptian dictionary. "If this can be done by one man, the attempt to copy and save ancient Egypt is entirely feasible." The plan combined staff and equipment to achieve the necessary efficiency and precision: "an expedition of six men, consisting of a director, two assistants, a photographer . . . , and two unpaid student assistants, with all modern equipment for photographing and surveying." Breasted calculated that, working nine months a year, the expedition could complete the project in ten to twelve years. Breasted's time estimate underscores the key role of photography in the plan, confirmed by his allocation of $1,500 out of a total $2,500 total equipment and supply outlay for photographic equipment and supplies. However, his justification highlights not only the speed but the accuracy of photography as well.

The per annum budget, including salaries, per diem costs, transportation, photography and drawing supplies, "Native Help," and incidentals came to $10,000, a sum based on figures that Breasted confidently states "are based upon actual experience . . . in Egypt." Breasted also validated his approach by citing his appointment to the Egyptian dictionary project by the German academies, and he assured Chicago's endorsement in the form of Harper's commitment to publish the expedition's findings at the University of Chicago Press and to grant Breasted "sufficient leave of absence" for the project. Breasted closed the proposal by observing "there is no enterprise in Archaeology more needed or which if well done, could be more creditable to American scholarship."[4]

The proposal was addressed to Daniel Coit Gilman, the Carnegie Institution's founding president, in February 1902, less than two months after the institution was created and Gilman assumed his duties. He was then preoccupied with interpreting Carnegie's aims and arranging the institution's day-to-day operations—all matters that remained very much unresolved when Breasted's proposal arrived. His proposal was not funded, in part because he had jumped the gun. By not waiting until the institution's goals and priorities were fully articulated, he miscalculated in emphasizing the preservation of inscriptions. The institution decided to focus on the production of new knowledge through fundamental research. Breasted had not shown how an epigraphic survey of known sources, no matter how exacting, constituted new learning. The closest he came was a reference to "scientific discoveries" that would come as by-products rather than being the central purpose of his project.[5]

A little over a year later, in May 1903, Breasted tried again, this time appealing to John D. Rockefeller Jr., now on behalf of Chicago's Department of Semitic Languages and Literatures for a program of expeditions in the Middle East. Rockefeller senior had by this time begun handing off aspects of his business empire and philanthropies to his only son and namesake, assisted by a trusted advisor, Frederick T. Gates. The elder Rockefeller first met Gates, a clergyman and later organizer and fund-raiser for the Baptist Church, when Gates helped lay the groundwork for the University of Chicago's founding. Impressed by his business and analytical skills, Rockefeller invited Gates to New York as an advisor and troubleshooter for Rockefeller's business and philanthropic interests. After the turn of the century the junior Rockefeller and Gates became closely involved in the University of Chicago's affairs as members of the university's board of trustees and representatives of the Rockefeller family. Rockefeller senior remained an active contributor to the university until 1910, when he concluded his support with a final $10 million gift. Harper was the university's representative to Rockefeller regarding major matters, but given the relatively small sum Breasted and his colleagues were seeking, and in view of the junior Rockefeller's increasingly active role, Harper undoubtedly steered the initiative to him. Although the proposal was presented on behalf of the Semitic Languages and Literatures faculty, Breasted "made the suggestion, devised the plan," and wrote the text.[6]

In contrast to his Carnegie submission, this one emphasizes the biblical associations of ancient Near Eastern studies rather than America's leadership or advanced research. In particular, Breasted references the "Bible Lands" and the Old Testament to contextualize proposed exploration sites. Thus, in a passage regarding an Egyptian example, he writes of an inscription on "the great wall of Shishak who captured Jerusalem in the days of Solomon's son." Breasted's shift in context and tone was calibrated for a different audience. Instead of fellow academics, he was addressing Baptists known for their support of Christian causes. Both Rockefellers, father and son, were devout Baptists, and the younger's religious beliefs were illuminated about this time in press coverage of a Bible class he regularly taught in New York. By arguing for the Semitic department's "attempt to rescue . . . the fast vanishing civilization of Bible Lands," Breasted was using a language of biblical teaching and salvation familiar to the younger Rockefeller and Gates in order to link ancient Near Eastern research with Christian charity.

The proposal focuses on three regions—"Syria-Palestine," "Assyro-Babylonia" (Mesopotamia), and Egypt—and it calls for the establishment of "a permanent archaeological mission or institute at Beyrut, and another at Cairo: the first to work in Syria-Palestine and the Tigro-Euphrates valley; the other to work in Egypt." These would serve as bases for "a series of annual journeys for survey and exploration" followed later by "exhaustive excavations and surveys of all important remains thus found. . . . By this method," Breasted explains, "these scientific missions would gradually but steadily rescue the vanishing remnants of the early East." Equally important, the findings of preliminary explorations would be published in annual or semiannual bulletins, and excavation results would be published annually in "an elaborate volume." The cost of all of this would be kept to a "moderate sum" by staffing the project with members of the Semitic faculty "serving on the half-year basis, but receiving no salary" and the "unpaid service of experienced students and interested visitors under careful superintendence." To begin the work, the faculty would need an annual grant of $10,000, it being "necessary, of course, to supplement this income by other contributions."[7]

After receiving the proposal, the younger Rockefeller forwarded it to Gates for his advice, and Gates in turn asked to meet with Breasted. The proposal was submitted without budget details, and Gates wanted them. Breasted complied, sending a ten-page estimate to Harper, who approved and forwarded it to Gates in June 1903 with a cover note endorsing the "accuracy of [Breasted's] figures" and commenting that Breasted "has had experience." The estimate differentiated between initial equipment outlays for each of the expeditions and their annual operating costs in the field, which would vary because each one would last from six to eight months depending on the local climate. Breasted also pointed out that the sequence of work in Syria-Palestine and Egypt would begin with "exhaustive photographing and copying of inscriptions on a large scale to preserve them" and then they would turn to excavations. "Hence . . . [for] Syria-Palestine and Egypt, estimates for the annual maintenance of <u>both</u> . . . kinds of work are presented, but both would not be conducted at the same time." But the annual expenses for Syria-Palestine and Egypt would be lower than for Babylonia, "owing to increased distance and difficulties." The annual cost of all three expeditions came to $17,000–$18,000.[8]

The budget lists equipment outlays for each expedition, and unsurprisingly the Egyptian estimates are the most specific and revealing. Breasted recast the budget from his Carnegie proposal, adding new items such as a "Portable darkroom and equipment for same." In place of the "photographic apparatus" line in his Carnegie estimate, Breasted now specified "2 large cameras, 30 × 40 cm. [just shy of 12″ × 16″] and 18 × 24 cm. [just short of 7″ × 9½″]." These large-format cameras would have to be loaded with glass-plate negatives rather than roll film, which did not come in such large sizes. When taking his museum photographs Breasted would have preferred a roll-film camera for reasons of speed and efficiency, a notion that he now set aside in favor of much larger photographs. Perhaps he was thinking of the far larger subjects he would be photographing, entire walls as opposed to fragments and individual stelae. The portable darkroom would be for processing negatives daily in the field for the same reason he did so in Europe. Breasted also itemized photographic supplies as a separate category, listing quantities and costs by photograph size—500 30 × 40 cm images, 250 18 × 24 cm images, etc.—and within each category, figures for negative plates, chemicals, and photographic print paper. Photography's potential as a research method was growing in Breasted's planning as a result of his *Ancient Records* and Egyptian dictionary work, which was still ongoing when he authored this proposal.

After Gates received Breasted's estimate and discussed it with Rockefeller, the latter wrote to his father reporting "a request made by . . . Chicago through its professor of Oriental History . . . for excavations in the Bible Lands." Rockefeller distilled from the proposal the argument that "each year . . . indications of earlier civilizations are being rapidly destroyed" and the two-stage plan to first photograph "the various inscriptions found in old ruins in Bible Lands" and next "excavate ruins and rescue inscriptions, works of art and other valuable historical data." Noting the overall budget of about $17,000 per year, Rockefeller added that "Professor Braisted" believed "that arrangements should be made to conduct the work for at least five years. This same professor thinks that if you would give $10,000 a year for five years he can secure the balance from other friends." The younger Rockefeller concluded that, "being thoroughly pleased with the careful, systematic and economical manner in which this professor has laid his plans, Mr. Gates and I heartily recommend" a pledge of $10,000 a year for five years. His father concurred, and Rockefeller notified the university, stipulating, however, that the pledge was conditional "upon the understanding . . . that Professor Braisted and others will make every effort to secure the remaining $7,000 or $8,000 a year, or so much thereof as is possible."[9]

The funding was administered by a new university-based Oriental Exploration Fund with William Rainey Harper as director and Robert Francis Harper, Breasted, and James Richard Jewett (professor of Arabic language and literature) directors respectively for "Assyro-Babylonia," Egypt, and Syria and Palestine; Ira M. Price, professor of Semitic languages and literatures, was secretary for financial affairs; George S. Goodspeed was secretary for editorial work; and university trustee Charles L. Hutchinson was treasurer. Breasted had every reason to believe his would be among the first explorations to embark. William Rainey Harper thought so, too, because in requesting university trustees' approval of the proposal, he added that "if a decision could be reached . . . during the summer, at least a portion of the work could be initiated upon Mr. Breasted's return to Europe in September [1903]." The determination of which expedition should be dispatched first remained unsettled, however, and Breasted departed for a quarter's research leave in Europe, telling Price and Goodspeed before he left that he was unprepared to begin work in Egypt that year. Based on that remark and an immediate opportunity to excavate in Mesopotamia, Harper authorized two years of work there, writing to Breasted that if $10,000 could be raised to match Rockefeller's grant in the meantime, Breasted could commence his Egyptian expedition in fall 1904.

Well aware of the grant-matching commitment, on the eve of his departure for Europe in late August Breasted sent a proposal to Hutchinson to be forwarded to the Carnegie Institution, of which he was now a trustee. Breasted requested $5,000 a year for just the Egyptian portion of the Oriental Exploration Fund plan and provided additional details about his intentions. He wanted to launch a photographic survey of temples along the Nile between the fourth and first cataracts, or the stretch in Nubia (now northern Sudan) between Aswan in the north and a point roughly midway between it and Khartoum. With the additional funding, Breasted argued, he could "rescue and preserve <u>all the inscriptional material in Nubia</u>" and, once that was done, extend the work down the Nile to "undertake <u>all the temples in Egypt</u>," giving as a particular example Medinet Habu. Absent are any biblical references, and instead Breasted returned to the twin themes of patriotism and research invoked in his first Carnegie proposal: "What a grand piece of work for America to have accomplished! I assure you that we could in a very few years put out a series of splendid volumes which would reflect the greatest credit upon the Carnegie Institute, and form an inestimable contribution to Science." The proposal was declined.[10]

Seeds for the Mesopotamian expedition were sown in 1888–89 when Robert Francis Harper was associated with an ill-fated first season of work at the ancient site of Nippur sponsored by the American-based Babylonian Exploration Fund. He soon resigned, never to return to fieldwork, but he remained interested in the possibilities, as did his older brother. Then, in 1900 Edgar James Banks wrote to William Rainey Harper asking him to serve as "Honorary President" of a committee Banks had formed to underwrite an excavation at "Biblical Ur of the Chaldees." Banks had studied at Harvard and then, like Robert Francis Harper, trained with Friedrich Delitzsch, specializing in Assyriology, before earning a doctorate at the University of Breslau in 1897. He found work in the American consulate in Baghdad, dealt in antiquities on the side, and published an article in Harper's *Hebraica* before returning to America.

Harper accepted Banks's invitation and endorsed a third-party request for John D. Rockefeller's assistance, which Banks received provided he could obtain others' backing and an excavation permit. These were issued by Ottoman officials in Constantinople, where Banks sought and failed to receive one. He remained in touch with Harper, who offered him some income writing articles for *The Biblical World*. Banks continued to deal in antiquities purchased in Baghdad but developed a reputation for bad "business methods resulting in loss of public confidence," word of which found its way back to Harper. After a few more tries Banks applied for an excavation permit for a different location, Bismaya—located south of Nippur and about a hundred miles south-southeast of Baghdad—when, in July 1903, the "Ur Committee" decided to dissolve and return its remaining assets to their donors. Shortly thereafter Harper, who was in Europe, made a side trip to Constantinople to obtain an Oriental Exploration Fund permit for yet another site. Despite questions about Banks's character, Harper seized upon his availability and asked Banks to head the Oriental Exploration Fund's explorations in Mesopotamia for three years. They agreed to commence work at the first available site, and Banks was appointed to a three-year research position in Turkish and Semitic languages at Chicago. In October his Bismaya request was approved, and he went to work under R. F. Harper's direct, if far-removed supervision.[11]

Breasted was annoyed by Harper's decision to put work in Mesopotamia ahead of Egypt, especially in light of the commitment to three years of funding Breasted had raised. The matter "still rankled" in summer 1904, when Harper continued to support Banks's expedition despite problems including rumors he was illegally exporting antiquities. Irritated by what he felt was a flagrant injustice, Breasted questioned whether anyone "in America, least of all the University of Chicago," valued his work. The Breasteds were in Germany at the time, and while they were visiting Eduard Meyer and his family, Meyer startled Breasted with a question about his future. Meyer was a highly regarded professor specializing in ancient Near Eastern and Egyptian history. Although Breasted had not worked closely with Meyer during his doctoral studies, they became quite friendly in subsequent years. At the behest of Erman and others, Meyer approached Breasted about a professorship at one of Germany's research universities, perhaps Berlin, Göttingen, Leipzig, or Heidelberg. None had openings at the moment, but the Egyptological community there was contemplating future appointments, Breasted was high on its list, and they were looking into Breasted's availability and salary requirements. The inquiry came as a great honor because of the high esteem in which Breasted held German scholarship and as a balm because of lingering doubts about his American prospects. A comparable query arrived from the University of Vienna shortly thereafter, making the possibility of a European move seem all the more real.

Over the next two months the Breasteds weighed the alternatives, fretting especially about income and the cost of living in Germany versus that in America, his mother's welfare, and relations with Chicago and other American colleagues. Breasted found himself "returning to the same simple conclusion. 'Putting everything else aside, . . . we are, above all, Americans!'" Breasted gratefully declined the Germans' invitation. They understood his position, and Erman added, "I am glad that you now know the feeling about you here." Breasted's half-year leaves for work in Europe concluded with the 1903–4 academic year, and he expected his return to Chicago to mark the beginning of a long hiatus in his research abroad.[12]

Meanwhile Banks's troubles continued, and the Ottoman government canceled his permission for further work in spring 1904. His Oriental Exploration Fund funding was cut off in June 1904, and expenditures for further fieldwork in Mesopotamia were suspended as the Harper brothers coped with the fallout, including rumors of legal proceedings against Chicago by the Ottoman government. Robert Francis Harper traveled to Constantinople in January 1905 to reassure the authorities, but to no avail. In April 1905 Banks certified that the antiquities sent to Chicago from Bismaya were removed legally, and, in return, the Harpers entered into a severance agreement that permitted Banks to publish his Bismaya findings.

Breasted observed the calamity from arm's length as he spent fall 1904 teaching and completing the manuscripts for *Egypt through the Stereoscope*, *Ancient Records*, and *A History of Egypt*, with all three going into typesetting in early 1905. Just as Breasted began proofreading galleys that spring, Harper surprised him by announcing that the following autumn seemed "a propitious time" for Breasted to launch the Egyptian survey and that he would be granted a leave of absence to do so. They agreed on an Oriental Exploration Fund allocation of $7,000 a year for three years' work. At the age of forty and a decade after first setting foot in Egypt, Breasted was about to return.[13]

The First Season: Writing on Photographs

Breasted scrambled to finish proofreading while preparing for what he expected to be a six-month expedition. He soon realized the equipment costs for all three seasons' work would be incurred in the first. Breasted sought an advance on the second season's budget to spread the expenses for more costly items, like cameras and lenses, more evenly across two seasons' budgets. The request was denied, forcing Breasted to budget for a shortened first expedition. He initially hoped to spend the first season surveying all the monuments along the upper Nile in Nubia but had to limit his goal to "Lower Nubia," or the area between Wadi Halfa and Aswan (maps 1 and 3).

In October, just days after completing the galleys and preface for *Ancient Records*—*History of Egypt* had been finished a few weeks earlier—the Breasteds set sail for Germany. Frances and eight-year-old Charles were to remain in Berlin while Breasted continued to Egypt. However, he became "gravely ill" with an unspecified ailment. He recovered enough to resume preparations but "an eminent bacteriologist at Berlin university 'forbade [Breasted] to undertake a journey in tropical Africa without either a physician or at least [his] wife.'" So the entire family sailed to Egypt in November. After arriving Breasted made the rounds of British officialdom, obtaining approvals of and assistance with his travel plans, and he visited the director of the Egyptian antiquities service for permission to copy monuments. The director was Breasted's "old friend" Gaston Maspero, the French Egyptologist he had first met in Paris ten years prior.

Breasted spent much of November and December assembling equipment and provisions, selecting a *dahabiyya*, and attending to the innumerable details of planning a long expedition into a distant region. Most of the supplies and equipment came from America, England, Denmark, France, Switzerland, and Germany. They included everything from biscuits, butter, milk, bottled water, and chocolate to standard camping equipment, binoculars, and "a few revolvers and rifles." "There was equipment against every emergency—tools, medical supplies, even dental instruments and gutta-percha [a natural semiflexible material] for temporary fillings." Breasted also packed along "some Ingersoll [inexpensive] watches, cheap candy, wool sweaters, and jackknives, to give as baksheesh [a tip or bribe] or to use for occasional trading with natives for chickens and sheep" to be consumed along the way.[14]

The photography equipment was somewhat different than originally planned. A "large mahogany camera with a great bellows," designed for 27 × 21 cm glass

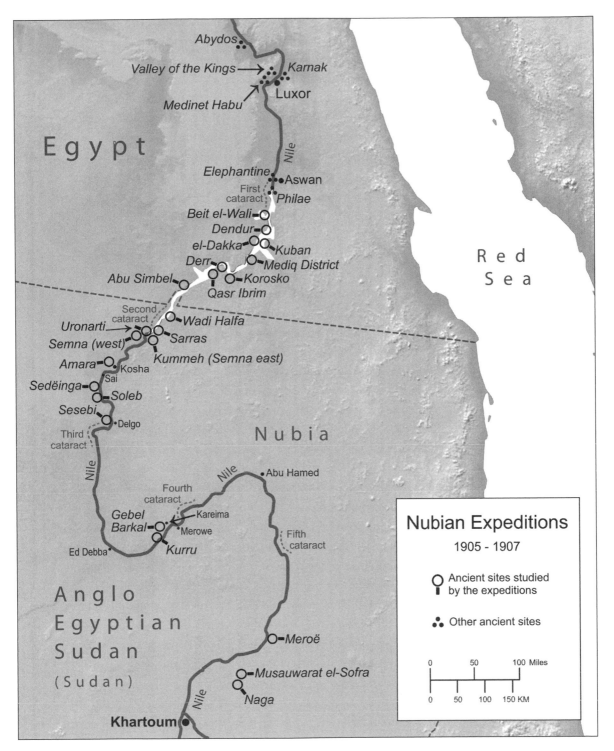

Abydos

Valley of the Kings →
Medinet Habu →

Egypt

Nile

Karnak

Luxor

Elephantine
First
cataract
Beit el-Wali
Dendur
el-Dakka
Derr
Abu Simbel
Qasr Ibrim

Aswan
Philae

Kuban
Mediq District

Korosko

Second
cataract
Uronarti →
Semna (west)
Amara
Sedëinga
Sesebi

Wadi Halfa
Sarras
Kummeh (Semna east)
Kosha
Sai
Soleb
Delgo

Third
cataract

Nile

Nubia

Abu Hamed

Nile

Fourth
cataract
Gebel
Barkal
Ed Debba

Kareima
Merowe
Kurru

Fifth
cataract

Red
Sea

Anglo
Egyptian
Sudan
(Sudan)

Nile

Meroë

Musauwarat el-Sofra

Naga

Khartoum

Nile

Nubian Expeditions

1905 - 1907

○ Ancient sites studied
by the expeditions

∴ Other ancient sites

0   50   100 Miles

0   50   100   150 KM

Map 3

plates (ca. 10½″ × 8¼″), was specially constructed to "withstand the heat of the tropics without warping" by camera maker Kurt Bentzin in Görlitz, Germany, and a kit of lenses was supplied by Carl Zeiss of Jena, Germany. The camera's size, falling about halfway between the larger and smaller formats specified in Breasted's Rockefeller proposal, was chosen because of its relative portability while still being big enough to yield large-format prints. The large photographs were crucial for a new method Breasted had devised that he hoped would address problems intrinsic to recording inscriptions and reliefs.

Noting that the inscriptions "are plastic in character; and a method of . . . reproducing them, such as outline-drawing, which neglects their plastic character is an insufficient record," Breasted believed "that the solution of the problem is to be found in the . . . camera, which, besides being far more speedy and more accurate than the draughtsman, at the same time also furnishes a record more nearly complete, in that it fully preserves the plastic character of each sculptured figure or sign on the wall." However, from his experiences photographing museum objects, Breasted knew that the camera's ability to fully capture a given subject was limited: "A photograph . . . represents but one illumination of the wall; whereas it may be illuminated from many different directions successively, each different illumination bringing out lines not visible before. Furthermore, the eye of the trained epigrapher, who can read the inscription . . . , can discover more in the lacunae than the lense of the camera can ever carry to the plate. These facts demand some field process by which the speed, accuracy, and plastic character of the photograph may be combined with the reading ability, epigraphic skill, and varied illumination at the command of the Egyptologist."

Breasted's new "field process" was simplicity itself: "As soon as a given section of the wall had been photographed, the negative was immediately developed on the spot. This was in order to employ the same scaffolding [erected to hold the camera] in making another negative, should the first prove to be unsatisfactory. If the negative was good, a print was made at once. This I took to the wall and collated from a ladder, entering on the print in red ink any readings or details which the camera had failed to record." Thus the prints had to be sufficiently large to allow for hand-drawn clarifications and annotations. By shooting large-format negatives, they could be proofed as "contact" prints, meaning they could be made by placing the negative directly on the photographic paper, exposing it to light, and then developing it. This eliminated the need for enlarging required for smaller negatives; though it was theoretically possible to work with smaller negatives, it would have been wholly impractical in the field because of the weight and special power requirements of enlargers.[15]

Lighting was another problem Breasted anticipated because "many portions of a temple, inside and out, are never properly lighted for a good photograph. The difficulties [are] of two kinds: inside walls [are] insufficiently lighted; outside walls [receive] so much reflected light from so many different directions that there [are] no shadows," and the outlines of reliefs and inscriptions become all but invisible. Breasted's solution was to acquire "artificial illumination." "Long study of the conditions" led Breasted to settle on two sources. One was based on "a French lamp on the Nadar system." It was designed by Frenchman Paul Nadar, son of Félix Nadar, a late-nineteenth-century caricaturist, writer, photographer, and inventor who pioneered the use of artificial lighting in photography, most famously in Parisian catacombs. Paul Nadar designed a lamp that slowly released pressurized air into a chamber containing granulated magnesium, the air carrying the magnesium through a tube past an alcohol-fed flame, resulting in a bright, steady light. Magnesium powder had been used for photography since at least the 1860s, but usually in open trays that, when ignited, produced a brilliant but explosive flash. Despite its hazards, magnesium-based lighting was preferred because of its intense brightness, but flashes would not work because the glass-plate negatives Breasted employed required long exposures—photographs taken with the shutter open for several seconds or more. Moreover, open-tray flashes would be concussive in the enclosed spaces of ancient monuments. However, the alcohol-diluted magnesium light was not always practical because on "windy nights out of doors . . . the Nadar lamp does not resist the draught." As an alternative, Breasted also stocked up on "composition time-cartridges (*Zeitlichtpatronen*)," slow-burning disposable lights similar to flares that are suitable only for outdoor use because of their excessive smoke.[16]

As these and the other expedition supplies arrived, Breasted checked and re-checked them against his planning lists because an "oversight might mean weeks or months of time lost upriver, awaiting for forgotten equipment." Altogether the provisions, photography supplies, and equipment filled over "one hundred wooden cases." Breasted's final preparations were assisted by the expedition's two staff members who joined him in Cairo, Victor S. Persons, an American with training in civil engineering and field experience on the Bismaya expedition, and photographer Friedrich Koch, who came from Berlin. Together they and the Breasteds departed for Upper Egypt in late December. They obtained a *dahabiyya* above the first cataract near Aswan, outfitted it, and from there set sail under an American flag for Wadi Halfa, just below the second cataract, on Christmas Day 1905. Because of Breasted's health problems and shipment delays, this was a substantially later start than he initially planned.

Breasted was not the first American to explore ancient Egypt. Already in the seventeenth and early eighteenth centuries a handful of colonists toured Egypt to examine and collect its antiquities. By the mid- to late eighteenth century there were a few explorers who contributed to the emerging international scholarly discourse about the translation of hieroglyphs and the contours of ancient Egyptian history. For the most part, however, the Americans were collectors or patrons

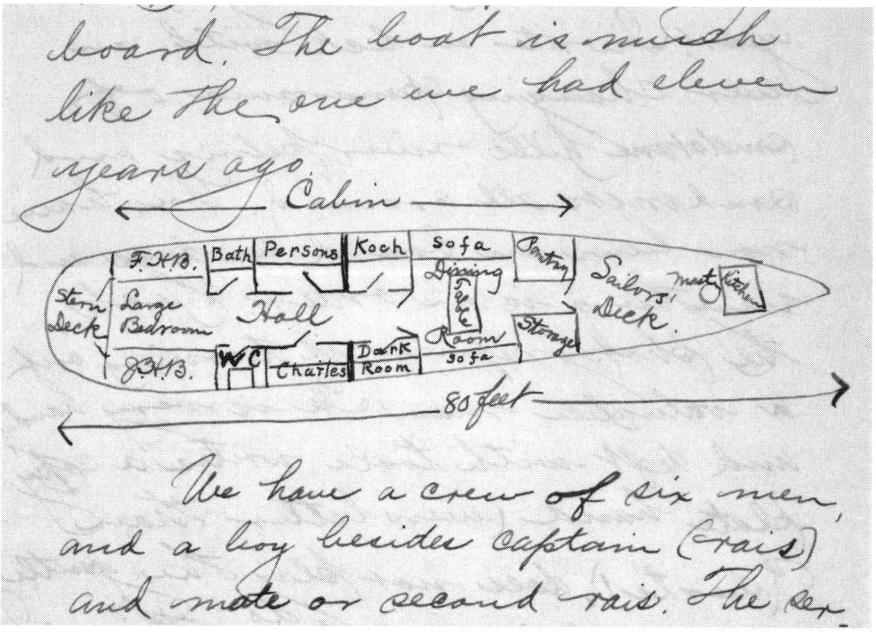

Fig. 4.1 Breasted's sketch of the expedition *dahabiyya*'s deck plan, from a letter to Harriet Breasted, 30 December 1905. Courtesy of the Oriental Institute, University of Chicago.

of others who scoured Egypt for collectible objects. As America's first formally trained Egyptologist, Breasted stood apart from his contemporaries by virtue of his ability to read and translate hieroglyphs. Further, in his focus on systematically studying and recording hieroglyphic inscriptions for scholarly purposes, he separated himself from peers concentrating on excavations that were sponsored by individuals or museums mostly interested in developing collections.[17]

Their *dahabiyya*, the *Mary Louise*, was eighty feet long and sufficiently large to provide below-deck cabins for the Breasteds, their son, Persons, and Koch, along with a dining room, bathroom, darkroom, and living space for the crew (figure 4.1). The main deck, covered over with a large awning, served as an all-purpose work area and living room. The boat's crew included a captain (*reis* in Arabic), first mate, cook, household servant, and two "boys" to help with everything from washing dishes to going "ashore for . . . milk, eggs, chickens and vegetables." All six helped sail the *Mary Louise* whenever it was under way. Everyone promptly went to work, Breasted wrote:

Frances and Persons run the kitchen and commissary end of things. . . . Koch . . . is very handy and deft with tools, . . . does not play the gentleman, and is ready to do anything I set him at. He . . . can put through anything . . . in the way of odd jobs, like setting window panes or mending cupboards.

I selected a good chest of tools . . . in Berlin, and they are now in constant use. Saw and hammer are common sounds, Koch is now engaged in fixing up his darkroom. . . .

Persons is . . . of sunny disposition, anxious to learn and equally anxious to please. Of course he knows nothing of the country or its history and can only assist in mechanical matters. The entire scientific work of the expedition rests upon me alone, and as soon as we reach the site of work, I shall have all I can do, and more. . . . Of course I have much writing to do, and <u>endless</u> accounts. I expect to turn these over to Persons very soon.

The group had about ten days to prepare for the first site as it sailed through "an ever changing panorama of sandstone hills, river palms, and sand drifts all around." The weather was typically wonderful for that time of year: "At 6 a.m., the temperature is 50° . . . ; by three o'clock it runs up as high [as] 78°, and drops again to 70° at sundown." For Breasted the climate and calm was a much-welcomed interlude: "I have never experienced anything so quieting and restful to the nerves, as the afternoon hours on the cushioned divans under the awning of our upper deck."[18]

The expedition arrived at Wadi Halfa, the site of two ancient temples, on 7 January 1906, and Breasted and the others set to work the next day. "I went through the temple every morning and laid out Koch's . . . work," Breasted wrote in his field notes, "and then went on collating & copying. As fast as he can furnish me the blueprints I collate them with the wall and add what readings I can make out (beyond the record of the camera), inserting them directly on the blueprint."

The "blueprints" were cyanotypes, blue-toned prints made with a process invented in 1842 that was adapted later in the century for copying engineering and architectural drawings. Photographs printed by this method were still called "blueprints" at the turn of the century. The papers were relatively easy to prepare and develop, and images could be made with the "contact-print" method by exposing them to sunlight. Their only drawback was a relatively low level of contrast and definition. It was for this reason that Breasted abandoned the cyanotype process, apparently within the first week or so of the expedition, switching instead to silver-gelatin papers, which could also be contact-printed, though developing them was more complicated. The only collated images that survive from Breasted's first expedition are silver-gelatin prints, with annotations made in vivid red ink (figure 4.2).[19]

Breasted had every intention of making the survey's documentation fully comprehensive. Once confronted with the vast, seemingly endless number of inscriptions and reliefs lining virtually every surface of Egypt's monuments, however, Breasted was forced to limit his ambitions. Falling back on distinctions

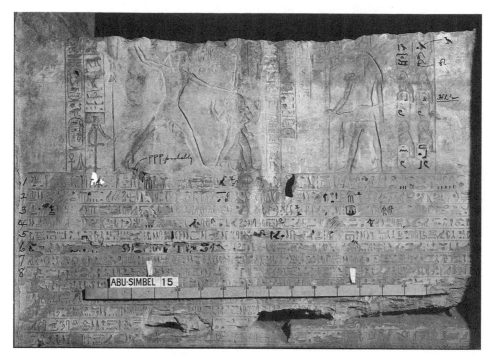

Fig. 4.2 Breasted's annotations on photograph, Great Hypostyle Hall, Temple of Ramses II, Abu Simbel, late January–early February 1906. Courtesy of the Oriental Institute, University of Chicago.

he drew in compiling *Ancient Records*, Breasted determined "that all reliefs and inscriptions of *historical* import should be included. As for those of *religious* character, there are in most temples such a host of purely conventional scenes that it would be of slight use and involve a prohibitive size and price for the publication, to include all these." Breasted decided "the innumerable small offerings and other religious scenes which cover the columns, pillars, pilasters, and door-thicknesses" of temples should only be cataloged along with relevant details about the ritual act, names, titles, and utterances. Similarly, "it seemed wise not to burden the enterprise with responsibility for a detailed architectural survey; but rather to make the main object of the expedition an *epigraphic* survey."

The comparatively short duration of the season forced another limitation too. "It was further determined to confine our efforts to the pre-Ptolemaic temples of the region in question, as the most important monuments existing there." This meant bypassing a handful of temples, including those on one of Egypt's most famous and enchanting sites, the Ptolemaic complex on the island of Philae. Once exceptionally well preserved, the monuments were being damaged by annual flooding resulting from the "old" Aswan Dam's completion in 1902. The temples were reinforced and documented in 1895–96 in anticipation of the flooding, but the records were not up to Breasted's standards.[20]

Fig. 4.3 General view of Abu Simbel, late January–early February 1906. In the foreground, from left to right, Victor Persons, Frances Breasted, Charles Breasted, Breasted, and Friedrich Koch; in the distance, the temples of Ramses II on the left and Nefertari on the right. Courtesy of the Oriental Institute, University of Chicago.

The expedition concluded its work at Wadi Halfa on 13 January, having taken sixty 21 × 27 cm plates on the large camera and forty 13 × 18 cm (ca. 5″ × 7″) plates on a smaller camera Breasted had brought for more general, nonepigraphic purposes. After stopping at a couple of other sites, the group arrived at Abu Simbel, the majestic rock-cut temple complex created by Ramses II in the mid- to late 1200s BCE (figure 4.3). It was there that unforeseen problems began arising that demanded continual improvisation. One was processing negatives in "the turbid Nile water." Although Breasted hoped "in some future report to return to this side of the enterprise," he never did explain how the crew filtered the water needed for developing negatives and prints.

Also challenging were the tasks of photographing subjects in hard-to-reach locations, lighting walls in very high or narrow chambers, and controlling light in overly bright settings. A particular difficulty was placing the Nadar lamp so it didn't shine into the camera lens, especially "in interiors, where columns, pillars, or end walls were in the way." The problem's solution, "a complicated matter of many hands," was almost comical:

> This obliged us to erect a large black screen between the lamp and the camera, so placed that it did not intervene between the lense and the portion of wall to be photographed. This screen has sometimes to be elevated thirty feet above the floor, the lamp in such case necessarily being equally high. . . . The photographer stood on his scaffolding with the [camera ready] and the shutter at his hand [figure 4.4]; two men with two long poles held the black screen stretched taut . . . , while the photographer, sighting across the lense . . . , kept them from cutting into the picture with the screen. At the same time he was also watching lest they should sway the screen too far back and expose the lense to the light. The lamp was likewise mounted on the end of a long pole, held erect by a man standing below, while another, standing at the top of a ladder beside the lamp, was ready at the word to pump . . . granulated magnesium into the . . . lamp, already lighted for the purpose. Exposures as long as twenty-five seconds were made in this way with complete success.

Initially a problem, the intense daylight became a useful resource once it was controlled and channeled: "Occasionally it was possible to illuminate a large expanse of wall by throwing daylight upon it from large reflectors at a sharply acute angle with the wall." The reflectors were made from "new and very bright sheet-tin" Breasted had brought, and the crew tacked in "overlapping sheets upon a wooden frame" that could be readily positioned as needed. Ultimately, the reflectors "proved much more useful in another class of work, in which the camera could not be employed." This was the occasional inscription that was "too badly weathered to be photographed," having become a "blur of rough sandstone in the abundance of light which falls upon it." In such cases Breasted made a "hand facsimile":

> I had a scaffold built before it, and inclosed the whole scaffold, except the lowest portion, in canvas, thus darkening the whole monument. . . . At the left end, close to the surface of the stone, the canvas was then drawn back. At the same side, fifty feet away a reflector was set up, and through the opening . . . it shot a broad beam of sunshine at an acute angle upon the darkened surface of the stone. . . . This furnished the sharply oblique light necessary to the reading of such an inscribed surface. Nevertheless no half-illegible monument can be exhausted if the light come[s] from one direction only. It is surprising how seemingly illegible signs will suddenly come out clearly if the direction of the light can be widely varied. To accomplish this the word under examination could be covered with the left hand, thus cutting off the [reflected] sunshine from the

Fig. 4.4 Friedrich Koch, with unidentified Egyptian assistant, photographing inscriptions illuminated with a Nadar lamp concealed by columns to the right, Great Hypostyle Hall, Temple of Ramses II, Abu Simbel, late January–early February 1906. Courtesy of the Oriental Institute, University of Chicago.

left. At the same time I held at the proper angle on the right side of the word
a hand-mirror, which caught the sunshine coming from the large reflector and
threw it upon the word from the right . . . [figure 4.5]. This method brought out
many new readings.[21]

Photographing some inscriptions required acrobatic feats. In one case, a stela
high up on a cliff had to be photographed from the masthead of a neighboring
dahabiyya (figure 4.6). To copy another stela partly buried in sand drifts, a trench
was dug along its face so that Breasted could lower himself into it headfirst,
"alternately holding a kerosene lamp at various angles to secure a reading, then
entering the latter in his transcription." Recording the main "sun-temple" was a
particularly "slow and arduous task" because of the height of the interior chambers. "Day by day the tall scaffolding rose and fell, as we passed slowly across the
walls, the camera recording for us a thousand data." The deepest chambers were
the most forbidding: "The men would have to work for days at a stretch in the
suffocating blackness . . . where the air which had never been changed was not
merely hot but stank unspeakably from untold generations of bats hanging in
regiments from the fouled ceilings. Here all photographic adjustments had to be
made by candlelight. . . . The bats would beat out the candle flame or fly into a
burning magnesium [light] during an exposure."[22]

There were other hindrances. Prevailing northerly winds kicked up sand-
storms that clouded the horizon "in a deep . . . twilight," and fine airborne sand
could get into the most tightly sealed spaces and gear. "Besides such storms,
other annoyances seemed unimportant. Sometimes, with a high, shrill hum of
almost deafening volume, . . . clouds of gnats would engulf us, as thick as tar
smoke and so tiny no screens could exclude them. Occasional scorpions and ta-
rantulas would drop on to the deck from overhanging trees; and when we . . .
[were] moored near native cargo fleets, roving swarms of ugly, vicious rats . . .
would overrun our boat."

These ordeals afflicted the local population as well, and whenever the expedition "moored near a village, all the halt and the blind, the sick and the injured
who could be carried or led, would gather on the river bank . . . and beg to be
cured—for the impression persisted among them that every white person was a
doctor." Young Charles would later recall, "My mother was indefatigable in doing
what she could for these sufferers, and in extreme cases my father would inter-
rupt his work to draw upon his pharmaceutical knowledge for such remedies as
our modest medical supplies would allow. . . . All this set my mother to dreaming
of one day equipping and staffing several hospital boats which would minister
to the ills of every village in the Nile valley beyond the reach of the few existing
missionary infirmaries—a dream she was never to realize even in part."[23]

Fig. 4.5 Breasted, in the background, reading an inscription by the light of a reflector in the foreground, manipulated by an unidentified Egyptian assistant, January 1906. Breasted is using his left hand to block some of the light from the reflector and a small mirror in his right hand to bounce the remaining light across the inscription from the right side. Exterior, Temple of Ramses II, Abu Simbel. Courtesy of the Oriental Institute, University of Chicago.

Fig. 4.6 Photography of rock-cut stelae from *dahabiyya* masthead, cliff face just south of Abu Simbel, January 1906. Photograph by Victor Persons. Breasted is on the left, Friedrich Koch on the right, and unidentified Egyptian assistants below. Courtesy of the Oriental Institute, University of Chicago.

Toward the end of January, word reached Breasted of William Rainey Harper's death earlier that month. Breasted wrote in his journal, "I have put the flag at half-mast with my own hands, and it will remain so during the rest of the voyage." He had lost a mentor of seventeen years, whose profound influence is obscured by the exceedingly restrained nature of their correspondence. Balanced and polite, they were not given to expressing strong emotions even when they sharply disagreed or were disappointed in one another. Lowering the *dahabiyya*'s flag was as powerful a public display of grief as Breasted would make. Though quaint, Breasted's gesture expressed the loss of a valued shipmate on a voyage the two had shared from rural childhoods to the frontiers of modern research. Breasted owed to Harper not only his position at Chicago but an introduction to the ethos of advanced scholarship. In ways that became clear only later in life,

Breasted also learned from Harper a larger lesson: the opportunities open to charismatic intellectuals possessing the drive and entrepreneurial skill to weave scholarship, teaching, and philanthropy into constructive social change. About two years earlier, after Harper had undergone surgery for appendicitis, Breasted wrote to him wishing a speedy recovery. Breasted also confessed his fear of Harper's dying and added, "It has for years been a habit of mind with me to think as I work: 'What will President Harper think of this or that piece of work that I am doing?'"[24]

On 24 February, after five weeks, the recording at Abu Simbel was completed. Of the labors there Breasted wrote: "None of our party will ever lose the impressions gained . . . under the shadow of the marvelous sun-temple. In storm and sunshine, by moonlight and in golden dawn, in twilight and in midnight darkness, the vast colossi of Ramses had looked out across the river, with the same impassive gaze and the same inscrutable smile. . . . What are the privations of travel, and prolonged separation from home and friends" if they allow the creation of records preserving "for another thousand years, such matchless works!"

Over the next several weeks the expedition worked its way northward, stopping at a number of sites, including Qasr Ibrim, Derr, Korosko, the "Mediq District," el-Dakka, and Dendur (figure 4.7). On 4 April, after finishing work at Beit el-Wali, the north wind had once again "risen to a gale which made any progress northward hopeless." The party waited a few days for the storm to abate "while busily arranging and indexing . . . records." The winds persisted, so Breasted decided to cast off and drift with the wind southward to survey a site at Kuban and then work northward searching for inscriptions among the eastern cliffs. However, Breasted found that "the wind had now strengthened to the heaviest gale we had yet met. . . . Across the Nile vast clouds of sand were driving along the horizon, the palms, dimly visible through the murky atmosphere, bowed and heaved, and tossed wild tops, while the yellow river was a mass of white-capped waves."[25]

Soon after the storm subsided, Persons, "whose health had been bad throughout the trip, was completely incapacitated." They rushed to Aswan, about twenty-five miles away, "where on physician's advice he was sent to Cairo, and sailed immediately for America." Having originally intended to conclude the expedition at Beit el-Wali, Breasted could call it a success. They had surveyed eighteen major temples, chapels, and tombs, as well as a large number of stelae and ancient "graffiti" of historical interest. "Thus *all* the pre-Ptolemaic monuments of Lower Nubia are included and completed in this winter's work." It took until 22 April for Breasted to complete "the filing of materials and the packing of the outfit," which he stored in Aswan for the next season's expedition.

The Breasteds returned to America via Italy, where they spent part of May

Fig. 4.7 Temple of Dendur with unidentified Egyptian assistants, March 1906. The temple was dismantled in 1963 to preserve it from the rising waters formed after completion of the Aswan High Dam and was given to the United States by Egypt in 1965. The gift, in gratitude for American assistance with the preservation of other similarly endangered monuments, was awarded to the Metropolitan Museum of Art, New York, and reassembled there for permanent display in 1978. Courtesy of the Oriental Institute, University of Chicago.

on a brief visit to Sicily and ancient mainland sites including Pompeii. Vesuvius erupted violently in April, lowering the volcano's height and destroying a funicular that ran up to the old crater. Despite the volcano's continuing activity, Breasted arranged for the family to visit the new crater's edge on 28 May. They made it to the crest just as the simmering mass began heaving again, and they hastily retreated just before another eruption later that day that forced the evacuation of nearby Torre del Greco.[26]

The Second Season: Ancient Egypt's Remotest Frontiers

With Harper's death, Breasted had no assurance his expedition's funding would continue. Harry Pratt Judson, the university's dean of the faculties of arts, literature, and science, was appointed acting president after Harper passed. He was a professor of history, academic administrator, and loyal servant of the university since its opening, becoming Harper's second in command as well. Judson's elevation, placing him in line for the presidency once a search was launched, was greeted with faculty disquiet about "his ability to lead the institution in a forthright and independent way." He was not familiar with the Oriental Exploration Fund, so Breasted had to submit his budget anew. While awaiting Judson's decision, Breasted prepared a detailed and richly illustrated article on the previous season's work, "First Preliminary Report of the Egyptian Expedition," in which he outlined his epigraphic method, discussed the sites surveyed, and offered initial conjectures on his findings' meanings, such as an Egyptian word he believed meant "snow." Judson approved the expedition's continuation "for at least another two seasons of work," and Breasted immediately prepared for a survey starting at a more remote point up the Nile, deeper in Sudan.[27]

By early October Breasted and his family were back in Cairo, where he met up with a new staff. The photographer was Horst Schliephack, a tall, "happy-go-lucky, good-natured, inordinately boastful, tawny-haired and bearded Russo-German" in his midthirties. The other addition was Norman de Garis Davies, a "short, wiry, *pince-nez-ed* English Egyptologist of about the same age . . . with a quick temper and militant sense" of British superiority. Davies was an experienced copyist who had been recording inscriptions and reliefs in Egypt since arriving there in 1898. He was chosen to help Breasted transcribe inscriptions in settings where photography alone was inadequate. The three spent about two weeks selecting and packing supplies for a planned expedition of nearly six months' duration. Their needs for this "campaign" were "more complex: large sums of money in gold, silver, and small change (the gold [carried] in leather belts worn under . . . clothes, the silver and small change . . . packed in a special 'treasure chest'); endless supplies . . . ; a felucca [small river boat]; and a cargo boat fitted with temporary living quarters." Breasted planned on hiring camels locally "wherever we cannot travel by boat." Because of the length of their journey—from the vicinity of Khartoum to just below the second cataract (Wadi Halfa, where the previous season's work began), about a thousand miles—and the remoteness of the sites to be visited, supplies had to be prepositioned at four points along the route. The currency in precious metals was necessary to hire boats and workers and acquire supplies in distant places where banknotes and lines of credit were meaningless.[28]

Breasted "firmly decreed" that his wife and Charles remain in Cairo while the expedition passed through the more dangerous and remote regions of the upper Nile, planning to send for them when it reached "easier country." The decision did not sit well with Frances, but she accepted it, and Charles was enrolled in a Lutheran German-language school in Cairo. The expedition departed Cairo 20 October 1906 for Aswan, where Breasted hired "two native assistants, besides the cook and camp servants," picked up the previous season's equipment, and—with thirty crates of supplies and equipment in tow—continued on to Wadi Halfa and then to a "little wayside" train station near Meroë, an ancient capital

Fig. 4.8 Northern group of pyramids at Meroë, November 1906. Courtesy of the Oriental Institute, University of Chicago.

of the Nubian kingdom of Cush. Breasted did not originally plan to begin this far up the Nile. But he changed his mind because the "later independent Nubian kingdom . . . left important hybrid Egyptian monuments much farther south at the classical Meroë, and at other points still farther up the river." The decision was risky. Extending the expedition's work at the beginning of the season jeopardized the group's ability to pass through the Nile's lower cataracts toward the end of the season when the river's level begins to fall, its highest levels being during the winter months.[29]

To reach Meroë, which is about 150 miles northeast of Khartoum, Breasted hired fourteen camels to transport the crew and supplies for the "two hours' march" into the desert where they would spend the next two weeks. The most prominent of the remaining monuments are a series of about ninety pyramids stretching in three groups from east to west (figure 4.8). The expedition began documenting the pyramids and soon encountered a host of annoyances.

> Our first problem . . . has been sterilized water. One drinks perpetually in this scorching sun, in which the thermometer goes up to 130° or 140°! Luckily the air is so dry that a felt-covered flask kept wet on the outside furnishes a really cool drink in the worst heat. . . . One of our camel drivers spends every hour of daylight going to and from the river carrying four sheepskins of water each trip. . . . But such water! Even when strained, it is so full of mud as to be almost

Fig. 4.9 Portable darkroom at expedition campsite near Kummeh (Semna east) with unidentified staff member, in shadow, and Egyptian assistant, late February–early March 1907. Courtesy of the Oriental Institute, University of Chicago.

> unusable for photography. We filter and . . . boil it for drinking, but after it has
> sizzled and . . . churned all day in a vile sheepskin . . . on a camel's back between
> the river and our camp the taste is disgusting. We put in lime juice . . . and
> make tea . . . to disguise the flavor of ancient mutton, but it still comes through
> very distinctly.

Further, the black "iron-stone" of the monuments absorbed so much of the sun's radiant energy that "it made trouble with instruments, producing such heat that the bubble in the level on one's camera disappeared . . . owing to the expansion of the liquid in the glass tube. It was impossible to level a camera . . . near mid-day." The scarcity of water also made "development of negatives on a large scale quite impossible; nor was our excellent portable dark room [figure 4.9] . . . large enough to permit . . . a great quantity of work" and Breasted was forced to "sus-pend [the] otherwise unvarying rule of developing, and . . . on the spot" collation until the expedition returned to the Nile. Breasted and Davies copied inscrip-tions by hand, employing photography only in exceptional cases.

A final insult was the pyramids' devastation by looters, including some working for museums, between the mid-nineteenth century and just a few years before Breasted's arrival. "The conscientious scientist of today knows that an exhaustive record of *everything* stationary or movable found on the spot is the supremely important thing. . . . The search for fine museum pieces is mere commercial treasure-hunting."[30]

Keeping an entire expedition's crew working efficiently took Breasted away from his own assignments, though his irritation with managerial distractions periodically melted into humor:

> Hassan [the head servant] wants to know where to put the men next. Schliephack wants another list of negatives to be made. . . . Davies wants soft pencils & having forgotten to pack his ink bottle, wants to borrow my fountain pen bottle; the cook wants to know what we shall have for dinner, some native clamors for his pay, or Hassan needs money for eggs, or the camel drivers strike! Yesterday Schliephack exposed negatives all day, using the wide-angle objective, without computing that the . . . lens demands five or six times the exposure of the ordinary objective. So a day's work was lost, and a lot of plates were spoiled. . . . Our provisions are also low. In Cairo Davies packed one vegetable box full of celery, thinking it was peas, and also gave us an excess of jam. So we lunch on jam and celery and dine on celery and jam!

The expedition's work was not all drudgery, however, and its travels from one site to another were filled with intriguing experiences. One came after work was completed at Meroë and the group made its way fifty miles southward toward the ancient site of Naga. Along the way it encountered an encampment of Bishārin, one of the larger nomadic tribes in the region.

> The men were all away, and an impressive, aged woman came out to meet me, doing a solemn reverence as she advanced. I gave her my gun to hold and took several pictures of the curious skin tepees in which they lived [figure 4.10].
>
> The women, clothed only from the waist down, were handsome and well-proportioned. They generally drew up a loose end of their garments and threw it about their shoulders as I approached. Their children, brown and chubby, were clean and fine looking. I offered several of the women money to let me photograph them with their babies, but they refused, perhaps because they did not understand Arabic. I tried to enlist the old woman in my favor, for she spoke a little Arabic; but she finally waved me away with a face so solemn and with such commanding gestures that I felt hypnotized and compelled to obey.

This combination of touristic curiosity, attention to ethnological detail, and respect in Breasted's account is characteristic of his other encounters with "native" peoples in the Sudan. He tended to be less dispassionate about Egyptians, especially those with whom he had to do business, leaving the impression that as

Fig. 4.10 Bishārin women and children between Naga and Musauwarat el-Sofra, November 1906. Courtesy of the Oriental Institute, University of Chicago.

he became more familiar with others, he formed stronger opinions about them, especially when business transactions went awry.[31]

After a few days' work at Naga the expedition mounted its camels and continued to Musauwarat el-Sofra, about fifteen miles northeast, for a couple of days' surveying (figure 4.11). At Abu Hamed, on the Nile, they exchanged the camels for boats. Abu Hamed lies above the fourth cataract, a nearly 140-mile-long region of islands, turbulent rapids, and calm waters. In an ancient quarry near Cairo, Breasted had seen an inscription suggesting there were markers designating the southernmost boundaries of ancient Egypt in the fourth cataract. They had never been found, and Breasted hoped to discover them. He hired a boat "about twenty feet long and eight feet wide, heavily built of acacia wood, [that] can carry between four and five tons and is very steady." The expedition cast off, drifting with the fast-moving Nile current from broad, smooth passages into narrow, tumbling rapids and then back into more tranquil waters, stopping at night in sheltered coves. Of one Breasted wrote: "We shall sleep ashore in a little natural garden hedged in with thorn bushes, . . . overlooking the broad moonlit river. . . . There is a cool, lambent softness in the air, as if one were enveloped in a magic element not of this earth but derived from some new and youthful world. The stars come twinkling out so subtly that before one is aware they are all blazing with tropical brilliancy. The silver sheen of the moon floods all the

Fig. 4.11 Expedition caravan between Naga and Musauwarat el-Sofra, November 1906. The vertical streaking resulted from silty water used to develop the negative. Courtesy of the Oriental Institute, University of Chicago.

palms and the wide river from which floats up the faint roar of heavy rapids in the distance."

The sailing was not without mishaps, including one rocky encounter sufficient to cause a "bad leak." Despite the dangers, "words cannot convey the blood-tingling exhilaration of such splendid moments when the boat darts with a bird's swiftness down the tumbling, surging river." Unfortunately, the river's flow was so precipitous and the many islands and boulders so jagged that it was all but impossible for the expedition to stop at promising sites, and Breasted's "search finally resolved itself into careful observation of all smooth rocks facing the river, with a glass." When the group emerged from the fourth cataract on 30 November, it had only a goose—which Breasted had shot—to show for its efforts.[32]

The expedition landed at Kareima, where Breasted hired two additional boats to take on more supplies. The larger one, a two-masted *giyassah*, "was about fifty feet long and twelve feet wide, and bore forward of the cabin a convenient dark-room"; the smaller boat was a felucca to carry supplies (figure 4.12). With the additional living space and hoping for less hazardous conditions ahead, Breasted sent for his wife and son. The three Breasteds "slept in what by day was the mess room." Charles's bed "was a camp cot suspended by wires from the ceiling beams" over his mother's cot. Frances assumed head-housekeeper duties, much to the displeasure of Davies and Schliephack, who "were militantly independent bach-

Fig. 4.12 Detail, expedition boats at Kareima, December 1906. Courtesy of the Oriental Institute, University of Chicago.

elors." As Charles later recalled, "Gradually the nervous tension bred by sand-storms, personal idiosyncrasies and the unpredictable minor crises of expedition life increased until it flared and crackled—as my father . . . put it—'like an over-charged Leyden jar.' . . . But such was my father's patience and forbearance that the personal equation seldom impeded the expedition's scientific work."

Somehow the kinds of vermin afflicting the expedition's first season were not a problem when the group was above the fourth cataract, but below was another story. Breasted recalled nighttime on the boat as a "carnival of riotous rats. . . . They danced and galloped across the roof in a constant tattoo, they dropped through a window onto my bed so that I would be awakened by one sitting on my face! They invaded the kitchen, rattled about among tins and frying pans, even managed to gnaw holes in theoretically unattainable bags of dried beans suspended from the ceiling, so that their contents poured onto the floor with the sound of heavy rain!"[33]

The expedition recorded temples and pyramids in the vicinity of Gebel (Mount) Barkal, a tall plateau that afforded opportunities for high-angle photo-graphs, which suggested to Breasted the possibilities of aerial surveys with tele-photo lenses (figure 4.13). On 20 December, the expedition pushed on to the "so-called pyramids" of Kurru and Tangassi, which Breasted described as "little more than burial tumuli." Breasted continued his search for inscriptions along

Fig. 4.13 Detail, view of the "Great" Temple of Amun from the top of Gebel (Mount) Barkal, December 1906. Courtesy of the Oriental Institute, University of Chicago.

both banks of the Nile but sometimes found himself too close to one side to scan the other, especially in shallow passages where the river widened to nearly two miles. He would ask local residents if there were ruins on the far shore, drawing on their amazing

> ability to converse with one another across great stretches of water. . . . We would watch a man address a friend so far away on the opposite bank as to be a mere speck wholly out of earshot. He would stand at the very edge of the river perhaps ten feet above its surface, and cupping his hands some four inches in front of his lips, would talk into the water at an angle of about 45°, in a loud voice but without shouting. At intervals he would stop to listen. . . . But we who stood close by heard no sound. Presently the exchange would end, and he would tell us in a matter-of-fact way what he had learned.

By Christmas Eve the expedition had reached Ed Debba, where its progress was halted by a strong northern headwind. Between Abu Hamed and Ed Debba, the Nile flows in a southwesterly direction, and the boats were sailing not only with the river current but with the prevailing northerly winds behind them as well. In the vicinity of Ed Debba, however, the river turns almost due north so that the swift current and strong winds were in opposing directions. These conditions turned out to be very helpful in the hands of a skillful sailor negotiating the third cataract's treacherous rapids, which lay just ahead. After a few days' work on the island of Argo and near Tumbos, on 11 January 1907, Breasted hired a local *reis* to guide the boats through the Kagbar rapids of the third cataract:

> At only one place have the waters been able to force through it a passage of any navigable depth—a narrow sluice-like channel . . . which the natives call a "bab" or "gate." The gates in the successive granite ridges are not opposite each other but are staggered; so that in shooting through one, there is great danger of being wrecked on the next ridge below.
>
> The method used by these Nubian reises in navigating such difficult waters is most interesting. They wait for a strong wind against the current. . . . They then drift with the current to the head of the cataract where they hoist all sail. With the wind directly astern, their craft now begins to move slowly upstream; whereupon the reis loosens the sheets, spilling enough wind so that [the boat] moves slowly downstream [with the current], until [it] reaches the first rocks. Since [it] moves down much more slowly than the current, [it] still has plenty of steerage way. If [the *reis*] is opposite a "bab," he lets the boat slowly down stern-on till [it] passes safely through the gate. But the instant he has dropped through it he must haul his sheets tight again to prevent crashing into the next line of rocks.

The expedition passed through the first set of rapids without mishap but was not so fortunate with others as the headwinds turned into a gale, ripping the sails and tossing the boats against rocky crags. The worst incident came five days into the descent through the rapids (figure 4.14), when the main boat took on water and nearly capsized, the crew having to quickly evacuate all the season's photographs and records, as well as supplies and equipment. Luckily, word of the expedition's predicament reached a British survey team working ashore. With its assistance, the boat was repaired, and by 21 January the expedition had emerged from the third cataract and sailed toward Delgo, where, across the river, lay the ruins of Sesebi, site of a well-known temple "heretofore attributed to Seti I," where Breasted made one of his most important discoveries (figure 4.15).[34]

Among the inscriptions and reliefs on the three surviving columns, Breasted discerned traces of figures that had not been previously noticed. These partially effaced but still visible reliefs were created during the reign of "the great revolutionary Ikhnaton. His reliefs show every characteristic of his monotheistic period, and it cannot be doubted that the building was a sun temple built by him, the only one from this remarkable man's reign of which any portion is still standing." During subsequent research Breasted noticed in "the itinerary of

Fig. 4.14 Expedition boats navigating the Kagbar rapids of the Nile's third cataract, January 1907. The view is toward the east, and the boats traveled from right to left, or northward, with the Nile current but against the prevailing winds. Courtesy of the Oriental Institute, University of Chicago.

king Nastesen . . . dating not long after 525 B.C., a town called Gm-Ytn [Gem-Aton]. . . . [Heinrich] Schaefer had located this town in the vicinity of the Third Cataract, on the basis of the references to it by Nastesen." Breasted also recalled that "the sun-temple of Ikhnaton at Thebes bears the name Gm-Ytn." Using this evidence, Breasted confirmed "that our newly found sun-temple of Sesebi is the ancient Gm-Ytn."[35]

After completing work at Sesebi, the group had begun traveling toward Soleb when its progress was halted as northerly winds turned into a howling gale for sixteen days "with but one day's moderation, and for eleven days it had raged night and day." At one point

> it quickened into a furious tempest burying us in vast clouds of flying dust and sand. Even in the [boat's] cabin it fell on one's papers in appreciable thickness, like snow, within an hour. . . . There was a pungent odor of dust in the air, it grated between one's teeth, one's ears were full, one's eye-brows and lashes were laden like the dusty miller, it sifted into all boxes and cupboards, photographs and papers, . . . and it settled on the chemical trays in the dark-room in such quantities that it destroyed disquieting amounts of our precious supplies and sadly injured the plates.

Finally the winds abated and the expedition reached Soleb, site of a major temple erected by Amenhotep III (1390–1353 BCE), where Breasted made another significant find. The ruins include a pylon that was left bare by the pharaoh and subsequently completed with reliefs by his son, Ikhnaton, forming "the only extensive series of temple reliefs surviving" from the latter's reign. They show an important transitional phase in Ikhnaton's theological thinking "because they date from the earliest years of his reign," before his "antipathy for [the god] Amon had begun." Accordingly, "the name and figure of Amon in [Ikhnaton's] own reliefs and also" those created by his father "were expunged. But here a remarkable fact arises: the figure of Ikhnaton's father as god of the temple of Soleb" were left undisturbed.

The expedition was unable to transport its longest and most sturdy ladders into "this inaccessible wilderness," and staff could not reach the highest inscriptions at Soleb. Breasted borrowed "four tall palm trunks forming the roofing timbers of a native's house, who obligingly consented to dispense with the roof of his dwelling for a week, and with these as uprights . . . we succeeded in building a scaffolding, for the floor of which we had only the two gang-planks from the [boats]. One of these was badly fractured in the middle, making . . . its ability to sustain us a piquant element in our . . . efforts to secure a complete record. . . .

Fig. 4.15 Ruins of the temple of Seti I at Sesebi, with unidentified Egyptian assistant, late January 1907. Courtesy of the Oriental Institute, University of Chicago.

During our entire work . . . we were exposed to a violent north wind which . . . at times threatened to shake down the scaffold" (figure 4.16).[36]

The expedition completed work at Soleb and cast off, drifting northward for thirteen miles to Sedëinga, then to the long island of Sai, and finally to Amara. On 15 February the river portion of the journey ended, and the expedition transferred to a thirty-three-camel caravan to bypass the second cataract. The group trekked to Kosha and then through deep gorges on narrow, "precipitous" trails, reaching the twin fortress-and-temple complexes of "Kummeh on the east and Semneh on the west bank" (now Semna east and west) on 21 February. Work on the east temple took place among its current occupants. "The wind, whirling in furious eddies through the roofless halls, buried us in the foul residue of generations of native life. We look and feel like coals miners, but much dirtier—for coal is *clean* by comparison. . . . Goats run about . . . baa-ing at us, and babies with fly-ridden eyes cry in our ears as we work."

High up on cliffs near the fortresses the expedition noticed mysterious, smooth "pot-holes," which Breasted and Davies correlated to nearby twelfth-dynasty inscriptions (about 1938–1755 BCE) marking the Nile's level as once being at that height. The "holes" were carved by the Nile's eddying waters. "Some great barrier below Kummeh and Semneh has since been removed by the river. Four thousand years is probably enough lapse of time to account for such a

Fig. 4.16 Photography in the Temple of Soleb, late January–early February 1907. Courtesy of the Oriental Institute, University of Chicago.

change." The northerly winds began intensifying again, and the "largest camera was overthrown and too seriously damaged by the wind to be used again." While completing a collation of inscriptions on a granite ledge above the camp, begun by de Garis Davies (figure 4.17), Breasted "slipped, lost his balance in the terrific wind, and pitched headforemost more than twenty feet down onto some rocks below." He miraculously survived, and after the patient's "ugly lacerations" were bandaged and his pain soothed with some brandy, he resumed work.

The expedition completed its survey at Semna on 3 March and continued northward to an ancient fortress at Uronarti, then Sarras and Gemai, just days from Wadi Halfa, the previous year's starting point. Its work done, the group took a steamer to Aswan and spent two weeks "closing up the season's work, packing away equipment and apparatus, [and] cataloguing the materials collected" in preparation for a third expedition the following season.[37]

A Magnificent Plan, a Backward Swing

The previous October, just as Breasted was departing for Egypt, he received a thank-you note from Frederick Gates for a copy of *History of Egypt* Breasted had

Fig. 4.17 Norman de Garis Davies copying Nile-level records on a cliff at Kummeh (Semna east), the cliff from which Breasted fell the next day, early March 1907. Courtesy of the Oriental Institute, University of Chicago.

sent. It impressed Gates's children and their teachers, and he had "already dipped into it deeply enough to see that [it is] a rare treasure." Gates wondered if "some slight part" of the book was due to the Rockefeller gift he had "secured . . . for exploration in Oriental Lands." Breasted replied that the results of his Egyptian explorations would surely have been used in it but that his share of funding was not allocated until after the book was done. Breasted promised to send a report on the 1905–6 expedition and his goals for the 1906–7 season that was about to begin.

Breasted then transformed Gates's query into an opening for a new proposal. He previewed plans for a third expedition: making a start on the remaining sites located between the first cataract (above Aswan) and the Mediterranean, cautioning that in "this last stretch the monuments are much more numerous and the task will consume years." But, he continued, if "we can go on and 'march to the sea,' we shall be able to issue in permanent form <u>all the monuments of Egypt</u>, in a splendid series of volumes. . . . It would be the standard edition in all the libraries and universities of the world for all time." Breasted added that the "present efficiency of our work would be much increased if I could organize it on a more permanent basis than is at present possible. After you have looked over my first report, I should be very grateful, if you could give me your opinion as to the probable continuance of the enterprise."

Gates replied in late December, writing that before answering Breasted's letter he had "a few preliminary inquiries": "How many years? . . . Will the organization on a more permanent basis mean more than [the currently budgeted] $7,000 a year? Will you not kindly send me an estimate of annual expenses with the main elements itemized? This should include also a publication in permanent form." Noting he had not yet discussed the subject with Rockefeller, Gates wondered if the publication could be dedicated to the donor and then encouraged Breasted to take his time assembling the information so his reply would "contain as little margin of doubt as to cost as possible." Gates confessed, "The idea of perpetuation of all the monuments of Egypt for all time in this way, is to me an alluring thought. . . . This much I will say as between us. How far, however, it may attract Mr. Rockefeller we can only learn when we can place before him, in a reliable and final way, the financial estimates."[38]

Gates's letter reached Breasted above the third cataract, around early January 1907. He began collecting estimates after reaching Cairo in late March and completed a proposal by mid-April. It concentrated on the most efficient way to complete and publish the records. Explaining that "of the magnificent temples on the Nile . . . , just one alone has been published in fairly accurate and modern form" and others are "falling to ruin," Breasted argued the situation was thus a "great opportunity for a compactly organized, efficient expedition, reenforced by the best modern mechanical equipment available." By "modern mechanical equipment," he meant the photography-based methods he was "applying in the field during the past two seasons" as described in the first season's report he sent to Gates. The field testing of his new approach, Breasted claimed, "has demonstrated the rate at which such work can now be done. Despite the vast size and great number" of the remaining monuments, it was "perfectly feasible" for "a properly equipped expedition to . . . record and publish them all within a reasonable period."[39]

Breasted planned to speed up the epigraphy process by acquiring a "stereopticon and acetylene outfit, for drawing enlargements of inscriptions from lantern-slides [based] on a new system of mine" using a "diapositive camera and outfit for making slides" and a pantograph. The stereopticon was a projector and the "acetylene outfit" its very bright gas-fed lamp; the diapositive camera produced positive images on glass plates or film, and the pantograph was a hand-operated device that enabled its operator to enlarge or reduce an image by tracing its contours with a stylus attached to one arm while a pen or pencil attached to another arm rendered the scaled version. Breasted's "new system" was designed to translate expedition photographs into line drawings for publication by projecting diapositive lantern slides—made from expedition negatives—onto blank drawing paper, outlining the projected inscriptions, and then scaling the outlines up or down with the pantograph to fit a uniform publication size.

In addition to the technologies, Breasted budgeted for an "annual library fund for current technical [i.e., Egyptology] publications" necessary for "the work conducted in Egypt of editing and preparing volumes for publication." Breasted expected that Egyptologists would contribute to the recording process at two junctures. The first would be when they collated the tracings of photographs against the inscriptions and reliefs, a task that required an Egyptologist's knowledge of hieroglyphs and figural conventions. The second would be in relating recorded sites with earlier studies of the same sites or comparable texts and reliefs elsewhere, work that necessitated access to an up-to-date Egyptology library. Breasted's "new system" thus combined the rapid translation of photography into publishable line drawings under the supervision of Egyptologists—all in proximity to the original hieroglyphs and reliefs against which the drawings' accuracy could be checked. Speed, efficiency, and "scientific" verification were being integrated by Breasted into a higher standard for Egyptian epigraphy.

To record the remaining temples, which are much taller, the "equipment will be considerably increased in bulk." Because the current expedition's "equipment (exclusive of provisions and supplies) now fills over fifty boxes and bales, besides seventeen ladders and much timber for scaffolds," a larger conveyance would be needed to transport it from site to site. The most efficient way to move this material, Breasted explained, was by boat. However, renting and specially outfitting a boat each season would be costly in time and money. Accordingly, he looked into building a custom-designed boat that would serve as a "floating headquarters and working laboratory planned and arranged especially for the permanent installment of . . . equipment" and found that one could be constructed and furnished in Cairo for $14,000. In addition to the estimate, Breasted prepared a drawing showing the layout of a boat that would be eighty feet long, twenty-two feet wide, and constructed with a steel hull and wooden "deck house" but without a built-in propulsion system because he envisioned it being towed from site to site (figure 6.1).[40]

The "floating laboratory" would also be equipped to prepare materials for publication so that work could be "carried on parallel" with recording sites in the field. However, this would "necessitate increasing the staff by two men: one on the scaffold to replace the director [Breasted], who must now give much of his time to publication; and the other a draughtsman." The full staff would include director, assistant, photographer, student assistant, draftsman, and two fellows. Given Egypt's fieldwork season of October to April, Breasted would use the remainder of the year to concentrate on readying publications. "This organization . . . should not, like other organizations out here, lie idle during the entire five summer months. . . . It should be transferred to a European headquarters, with work-rooms and filing rooms, where all will go on as before, close to the presses where the publication is appearing," that is, in Germany. Excluding publication costs, the annual price of all this would be $15,000 per year.

With regard to publication, the "monuments above the First Cataract will fill about twenty folio volumes. The eight hundred miles below it . . . will make about eighty volumes more." "Organized in this manner," Breasted estimated, the "entire one hundred volumes could . . . be issued in fifteen or sixteen years." Each volume would consist almost exclusively of images, approximately one hundred plates in each one, intended primarily for scholars rather than "some dilettante and a few other interested persons of wealth." Such text as necessary would be confined to a standard scholarly apparatus—statement on methods, notes, and relevant bibliography. Breasted recommended the hundred-volume set be wholly subsidized in an edition of three hundred copies distributed to "every important library and . . . responsible Egyptologist," but he provided a budget estimate based on sales as well. His proposal included a few images "roughly made up as plates" to convey the scale and look of a completed volume's pages. Breasted believed the "first volume bearing the dedication to Mr. Rockefeller, could be issued within a year." "One can hardly imagine," Breasted declared, "a more impressive or a more enduring monument than these one hundred stately volumes, perpetuating for all time both the fast perishing monuments of Egypt, and the memory of the man whose liberality should have given their records permanent form and made them accessible to all the civilized world forever."

Breasted summarized his estimates in two tables, one if the publication were to be sold, the other if distributed for free. The total cost for the entire project's fifteen-year duration, including fieldwork and publication, would be $354,450 for the first option, $434,450 for the second. The budget included a portion of his salary, and he felt "obliged" to discuss it "however reluctantly." He was then earning $3,000 per year, and while he was leading the expedition about 25 percent was paid from the expedition's budget. He assumed the university would continue to pay part of his salary if Rockefeller approved the proposal. Because of higher living costs in Cairo and expenses for travel between Egypt, Europe, and America, however, Breasted budgeted an increase, to $4,000 per year, with the university paying half and the balance coming from the proposed grant. In divulging his financial needs, Breasted wrote:

> I need hardly say that I should devote to [the project's] completion every energy and all the ardor I possess. . . . Yet to speak frankly, the prospect of . . . the quiet academic life of research at home . . . is not less enticing than the long exile, the loss of a home for my family, and the heavy responsibilities involved in the great plan. I have put it before you from a profound conviction that it was my duty to neglect no opportunity for possibly saving . . . the monuments of this

ancient land from rapid destruction. In the same spirit my wife, who is my constant support in all this work, is ready to undertake the sacrifice involved.

Because of the potential hardships, Breasted continued, "Whatever the decision, I shall not be disappointed." Breasted mailed the proposal from Cairo, remarking to son Charles, "Well . . . whatever comes of it, I may as well hang for a goose as a gander!"[41]

Gates received the proposal in early May, showed it to others in the Rockefeller offices, and then contacted Robert Francis Harper. Harper was appointed acting head of Semitic Languages and Literatures after his brother's death and became head of the Oriental Exploration Fund as well. Gates sought his comment because there were still two years of the Rockefeller pledges to be paid on the fund. Not having seen the proposal, Harper thought Breasted's total estimate too low on the basis of Gates's description and suggested the sum should be increased by 50 percent. There was some uncertainty on both sides, however, and Gates forwarded the proposal for Harper's review. In his cover note Gates expressed great admiration for the "model pages" and remarked that it would be "folly" for him, given his limited knowledge of Egyptology, to say "the $400,000 or $500,000 or anything like [it], might not be a justifiable expenditure." That said, Gates continued, "I know of nothing at all which would . . . justify so vast an expenditure for [what] Professor Breasted wishes to do." Gates concluded that, although "none of our Committee" could recommend the project to Rockefeller, perhaps Harper could persuade them otherwise.

After receiving the proposal and asking for time "to give it careful consideration," Harper remarked, "I was not prepared for such enlarged plans." As an alternative, he suggested "it might be well for us to take up the whole subject of excavations again," referring to Mesopotamian explorations. But Harper preferred to meet Gates face to face, closing: "I regard Dr. Breasted's plan as magnificent, as ideal. I know of no one who could carry it to completion better than he. With me, and I suppose with you, the whole question is one of relativity." Before a meeting could be arranged, however, Gates wrote to Breasted: "After considerable thought and conference . . . , we are not prepared to recommend to Mr. Rockefeller the taking up of this monumental work involving such great expense and covering so many years. We recognize in you the one man in the world who is qualified to do this work." Picking up on the concluding comments in Breasted's letter, Gates continued, "I fear this letter will be a disappointment to you and yet I . . . hope that you may welcome it. It releases you perhaps from fifteen years of arduous and self-defeating labor; it gives to you, let me hope, fifteen years of home with its delights, and quite possibly . . . of fruitfulness in study or teaching which prove of as great, or even greater, importance."

Breasted responded with a combination of feigned resignation and almost manic desperation. "I cannot say that I personally have any feeling of disappointment. My sole regret is for the sake of the monuments now hopelessly lost. My plan would have saved them for another thousand years." Breasted then advanced another plan, completion of "Nubia entire, including also the eastern desert, and the many records there on the ancient roads leading from the Nile to the Red Sea and the land of Ophir of the Hebrews." It would take two years to record inscriptions and three years for excavations; the total cost—including publication of findings—would be $92,000. Alternately, they could drop the excavations, survey inscriptions for two more seasons only, and then publish all four seasons' findings for a total of $56,000.

Not quite two weeks later, however, Breasted began confusing matters when he wrote to Harper that he was reviewing the records already collected and wondered if he would "ever be able to edit and publish such a mass if we go on at this rate every season. There is a bad congestion already." He asked Harper what he thought of "accumulating our [Rockefeller] funds" for a year while Breasted stayed in Berlin to "issue a few volumes and get the material in better shape before it becomes hopelessly bulky?" Breasted was unenthusiastic about the idea because he wanted to "finish Nubia as soon as possible." On the other hand, he confided, "As I grow older, I find the desire very strong to settle down among friends and colleagues at the university. I am sick and tired of this wandering life, but I am ready to do whatever is wise for our work in the Orient."

Rather than wait for replies from either Gates or Harper, Breasted wrote to Gates again, this time suggesting "a sweeping modification" of the second proposal. He dropped the Nubian plan altogether and returned to the original plan, now eliminating the publication and summer work in Europe, reducing the original budget to $195,000. "The negatives, prints & c. could be filed for all time as a complete series of Egyptian archives in Haskell Museum. Each year we could issue with the annual report, a complete negative list of all the documents collected during the year." The original plan's appeal for Gates, a sumptuous and important publication dedicated to Rockefeller, got lost in the shuffle.[42]

Gates met in late July with Harper, who recommended on behalf of the Oriental Exploration Fund's faculty committee that Breasted's work in Egypt "be continued during the next year, and that [he] be given an extra year." However, Breasted's rapid-fire proposals, rather than restoring Gates's interest, had the opposite effect. He rejected the committee's recommendation, countering that Breasted's work in Egypt should be terminated with the season just completed. In its place he would authorize use of the coming year's pledge for "excavations in Palestine, the Hittite country, Assyria, or Babylonia," provided a permit could be obtained. Gates also said that if work continued in Egypt, using up next year's allocation without pursuing excavations elsewhere, the remainder of the pledges would not be paid.

Harper carried the news back to Chicago and "after long deliberation and with the unanimous vote of the members of the Oriental Exploration Fund," Harper informed Breasted his funding for the coming year was terminated effective immediately. As a concession, they recommended to Judson, who had become university president earlier that year, that Breasted be given a year's research leave. Harper cabled to Breasted, "Make no arrangements for coming season. Await letter." Two days later Breasted cabled back, "Too late, staff engaged, boat engaged, orders in, funds needed immediately." Thereupon a flurry of letters and cables between Harper and Breasted and between Harper and Gates ensued. Breasted did not understand why, at this late date and with a budget already approved, his preparations were being canceled. In late August, after meeting with Gates, Judson cabled to Breasted, "Final instructions. All Egypt work necessarily stopped. Cancel obligations . . . least possible loss. Leave of absence extended if desired April first next." By this time Breasted had contracted for Friedrich Koch, the photographer from the first expedition, and a former student, Harold H. Nelson, who was teaching at the American University of Beirut, to work on the third expedition, and he had ordered several pieces of equipment and many supplies as well. Accordingly Breasted replied, "Began preparations for third year's work on basis of three years appropriation signed by Pres. Harper. Original document here. Is it revoked. Need $2500 to close up." Judson replied, "All former arrangements for three years revoked. Twenty five hundred remitted."[43]

Breasted was furious. He was humiliated by having to cancel agreements with colleagues and trusted suppliers, and Gates's sharp reversal caused him to suspect Harper of manipulating things behind the scenes to further his own expedition plans. But Harper's letters to Breasted leading up to the Gates proposal are consistently supportive, even enthusiastic, to the extent that Harper covered a $500 shortfall for the current season out of departmental funds. After learning that Gates had turned down Breasted's proposal, Harper sought without success to replace the money for Breasted's third expedition with university funds and Rockefeller support to publish the findings accumulated thus far.

Meanwhile, by his own admission, Breasted was sending mixed signals. After reporting to Harper the details of his first proposal, Breasted wrote, "The conviction has deepened in my mind, that it would be a great relief, if I were not called upon to take up such a grave responsibility." Accompanying a copy of his hasty, third proposal to Gates, sent just after his "wandering life" confession, Breasted admitted to Harper, "I expect after my last letter, you will think the enclosed letter which I am sending Mr. Gates, is an amazing inconsistency. . . . I shall not be sending in any more unexpected schemes. This is the last." And after receiving Harper's cable suspending Breasted's third expedition, he replied, "I am very sorry if my letter [proposing a year's suspension of work and containing the "wandering life" comment] has caused a tangle in our plans, for which I fear I am largely responsible." The long distances separating them added a further measure of confusion as questions and answers crossed in the mails.

When word of Breasted's anger got back to Harper, he made several overtures to smooth over their differences. Early on he wrote, "I wish to tell you for myself and for the other members of the Department that we were very sorry about this discontinuance. . . . I hope that you will not form any final opinion about it until, (a) you have been able to discuss it with the President, myself and other members of the Committee and (b) until you have seen the original papers and documents on the subject." Later he suggested, "When you return . . . we must take up all these matters in the friendliest way and attempt to unravel them."[44]

Breasted learned that Harper alone was not responsible for the outcome, and he started questioning the attitudes of other faculty members. He regarded the absence of their backing as "a vote of 'no confidence'" and a signal that he ought to look for a position elsewhere, perhaps reconsidering his European options. Out of despair, Breasted wrote to his friend Ernest DeWitt Burton, a professor of New Testament and early Christian literature in the university's Divinity School and a member of the faculty since its opening. Breasted summarized the story and questioned whether he should pursue another position, wondering about his colleagues: "Are they trying to drive me out?" In closing, he wrote that he would be "deeply grateful for any light, or any advice, which will help me to a course consistent with self-respect." Burton replied that "Mr. Gates is a man of wide reading, of decided opinions and of strong will." In recent years, even William Rainey Harper had struggled with "increasing difficulty" to obtain Rockefeller support. Therefore Judson and Robert Francis Harper would have had far less success in advancing Breasted's cause. Indeed, Burton wrote, Harper "has been sorely perplexed himself over the matter. . . . Had you been on the ground continuously for the last few years," Burton added, "you would appreciate this point."

The "increasing difficulty" Harper faced, of which Breasted may well have been unaware, was a sharp reduction of Rockefeller's previously generous support. During Chicago's first decade Harper had been astonishingly successful in persuading Rockefeller, and many other donors, to underwrite the university's remarkable growth in faculty, students, academic programs, and physical plant. After the turn of the century, however, the university began to run steady and increasing deficits, which Rockefeller covered, but not without mounting alarm. A stringent financial plan was imposed by Rockefeller, and monitored by his son and Gates in the last few years of Harper's presidency, that sharply curtailed Harper's freedom to continue growing the university. With regard to Gates's sudden reversal on Egypt, Burton observed:

> Mr. Gates has . . . read books on Egypt and books on Assyria and Babylonia, and has come to the conclusion that Egypt's contribution to the civilization of which we are heirs is much less important [than] that of Assyria or Babylon. . . . Could you have seen him face to face . . . , you might have convinced him that he was wrong. . . . Did those who stood back of you do their best to represent you? I think so. . . . I am disposed to think that the large figures which you sent to Mr. Gates staggered even him. Perhaps when he contemplated a ten years' work at an expense of a half a million he underwent a reaction, in the backward swing of which he concluded that it was best to stop work in Egypt at once.

As for Breasted's colleagues:

> The course of action at this end, which [was] seen by you only thru the medium of cablegrams has seemed to you . . . hostile.
>
> Is it hostile? I believe not. Are they trying to get rid of you? No. . . . I will not affirm that there has not been some irritation at this end because of your very large suggestions respecting future work in Egypt or because you "died so hard." Just as you have been greatly hurt and disturbed because they did not understand your point of view, so they perhaps have felt that you were slow in seeing the situation at this end. . . .
>
> I understand that you may perhaps find it difficult to escape the suspicion that some other influences have been at work. . . . But Mr. Harper has talked with me about the matter at every stage, and I have seen the letters that have passed both ways. I know that at one time Mr. Harper expected Mr. Gates to favor doing large things in Egypt and was pleased thereat.

Burton was eager for his old friend to return to Chicago and set things straight with their colleagues: "If there is any trace of feeling against you here it is only that you have been so interested and absorbed in your own special work that you have not thought a great deal of the department or the University. If this _has_ been so, it has been natural if not inevitable. But the feeling, if it exists, you can easily overcome by personal presence and a period of working with the team."[45] Breasted settled accounts with suppliers as well as Koch and Nelson. As for the expedition equipment left in Aswan, the "Berlin Academy . . . purchased [it] entire, adopted our field methods, took over our personnel as far as available, and completed the work to the Temple of Philae inclusive, just above the Aswan Dam . . . completing the record of the inscribed Nile monuments from their southern limit northward to Philae." Breasted continued to harbor ill feelings toward Harper until the latter's untimely death at the age of fifty in 1914. Breasted also doubted Burton's estimation of their colleagues' attitudes, and he explored a position at Harvard in the following months, an effort that proved futile. The

Oriental Exploration Fund never received an excavation permit for Mesopotamia, Rockefeller ceased his pledge payments, and the money remaining from Breasted's aborted third season was gradually spent on other needs.

Breasted's two expeditions traveled about twelve hundred miles and produced more than twelve hundred records in the form of unmarked and hand-corrected photographic prints, hand-rendered transcriptions, and Breasted's field notes. The "notebooks and negatives produced by the expedition's two campaigns when published" would, Breasted calculated, fill "about sixteen folio volumes." The publication he envisioned never appeared, however, possibly because even the annotated photographs were not—despite his best efforts—quite detailed enough to serve the increasingly rigorous needs of modern Egyptian epigraphy. Fortunately the documents all survive, and the photographs in particular are now valued as better records than none at all of inscriptions that were, as Breasted feared, damaged over the intervening years. Despite his goal of returning to the Sudan and "completing Nubia entire," Breasted never again traveled south of Wadi Halfa.[46]

5

Spreading Wings

Teaching, Curriculum Design, and Disciplinary Boundaries

Amid the turmoil surrounding Breasted's expedition funding, in June 1907, he was elected a corresponding member of the Berlin Royal Academy. It was a rare honor for an American; there were just five others at the time, and just one in the "philosophical-historical" class to which he was elected—the eminent philosopher and psychologist William James. As Breasted commented, the honor resulted from his choosing at the very beginning of his career "to cut out [a] big piece of work . . . about which nobody knew anything till it suddenly all appeared within a year, and was therefore likely to make an impression." The scholarly acclaim for *Ancient Records* and *History of Egypt* brought Breasted "for the first time . . . a feeling of quiet confidence in the future, of freedom from being always on the scientific defensive." Although mentally bolstered, Breasted was physically exhausted by the second Nubian expedition and in fall 1907 came down with bronchial pneumonia while visiting in Lucerne, Switzerland, where he remained a few months recuperating before returning to Berlin in November 1907. His health remained weak, however, and his doctors urged him to move to a more congenial climate for rest. Chicago extended his leave into the winter quarter, and the family moved to Italy, where he convalesced and caught up on unfinished work, completing a report on the second Nubian expedition and a condensed version of *History of Egypt*.[1]

The condensed version of *History of Egypt* fulfilled Breasted's promise to prepare a textbook edition for Scribner's. It was published in late 1908 as *A History of the Ancient Egyptians*, the fifth volume in a "Historical Series for Bible Students." Works in the series were intended as textbooks for "college, seminary, and university classes"; "handbooks for the use of Bible classes, clubs, and guilds"; "guides for individual study"; and books for "general reference." The series was coedited by Charles Kent and one of Kent's Yale colleagues, Frank K. Sanders, who also studied with William Rainey Harper and succeeded him at Yale when Harper left for Chicago. They sought works based on "thoroughly critical scholarship" that emphasized "assured and positive rather than transitional positions" and that, taken as a whole, presented "a complete and connected picture of the social, political, and religious life of the men and peoples who figure most prominently in the biblical records." In referring to "critical scholarship," the editors signaled their fidelity to the Higher Criticism, but the distinction drawn between "positive" and "transitional" positions is far less clear. It may have been made to ally themselves with a taste among late-nineteenth-century American historians for a positivist methodology that aspired to the certainty of "scientific" objectivity.[2]

Breasted prefaced the book by arguing its value to students of the Old Testament, expressing "the hope that [this] little book may contribute somewhat toward a wider recognition of the fact, that the rise and development, the culture and career, of the Hebrew nation were . . . vitally conditioned and . . . deeply influenced by surrounding civilizations." He adjusted the book to the "design" of the series by making it "as far as possible a history of the Egyptian *people*." However, in abridging *History of Egypt* he made few changes in organization or emphasis. The two books' tables of contents are virtually identical, and a comparison of passages shows Breasted condensed the text by eliminating paragraphs and sentences where cuts could be made without disrupting the narrative. Breasted concluded the text with "Notes on Recent Discoveries" subsequent to *History of Egypt*'s publication and an index to Old Testament references. One reviewer represented the views of many in applauding it as "a model of its kind. The narrative is lucid, simply told, yet crowded with incident and rich with description." *A History of the Ancient Egyptians* was nearly as popular as its predecessor, being reprinted eight times in the United States, most recently in 1990, and seven times in the United Kingdom.[3]

When Breasted and his family returned to Chicago in fall 1908, he was fearful of his reception after the previous year's problems. He was welcomed back into the fold, however, and soon immersed himself in the routines of teaching and committee work. Breasted was promoted to full professor in 1905 and his title expanded beyond Egyptology to include "Oriental History." In addition to his home appointments in the Department of Semitic Languages and Literatures and the University Extension, he was also appointed to the Divinity School, the Department of Archaeology, the Department of the History of Art, the Department of General Literature, and the Department of History. Breasted's course offerings grew correspondingly diverse. Along with classes in hieroglyphs, ancient Egyptian literature and history, Coptic literature, and Arabic language and literature, he also offered courses on "Egyptian Archaeology," "Egyptian Archaeology and the Old Testament," and "Egyptian Life and Antiquities" for the Department of Archaeology (established in 1894) and a course on the "History of Oriental Art from the Earliest Times to the Conquests of Alexander" for the Department of the History of Art (established in 1902).[4]

When Robert Francis Harper died in 1914, Semitic Languages and Literatures was opened to new leadership for the first time in nearly a decade and to changes that might allow Breasted to flesh out his vision of Egyptology as a separate discipline. Previous efforts to revitalize the department had been unsuccessful. In 1911, for example, Harry Pratt Judson, had suggested renaming it the "Department of Oriental Languages and Literatures," anticipating the addition of courses in Japanese and Chinese at some point in the future. The name change was not made until April 1915, however, and then only to add Russian studies. Lip service was paid to adding "the larger Asiatic or Far Orient . . . , and also the languages of Eastern Europe where it merges in the Near Orient." The leadership transition culminated in Breasted's elevation to department chair, his term commencing with the implementation of the department's new name and configuration in July 1915.[5]

In his first year as chair, Breasted led his colleagues in making further changes to the department's organization and curriculum that suggest the multiplying specializations within ancient Near Eastern studies and the growing prominence of his own teaching agenda. The curriculum was divided into three "sub-departments": "Semitic Languages and Literatures," "Egyptology," and "Russian Language and Institutions." The Semitics program was further subdivided into "Hebrew Philology, Literature, and History," "General Philology and History," "Rabbinical Language and Literature," "Aramaic Philology, Literature, and History," "Babylonian-Assyrian Philology, Literature, and History," and "Arabic Philology, Literature, and History." Although, strictly speaking, Breasted was not a member of the Semitics section faculty, he taught all the courses under the "General Philology and History" heading. He also began offering what became immensely popular ancient history surveys: a two-semester "History of Antiquity" that went from "Prehistoric Times" to Alexander the Great and a one-semester condensed version of the same topic. Breasted's other courses included "The Literature of the Early Orient" and "The Sources of Early Oriental History"—a methods course on the physical "form, paleography, field-methods of recording, processes of publication . . . character, classification . . . , historical value, and . . . use of the monumental and documentary" materials of ancient Near Eastern history.

This expanding emphasis on historical methodology was inspired by his association with John M. P. Smith, a Hebrew scholar specializing in Old Testament literature. Smith received his doctorate at Chicago, and he was hired to help fill gaps left by the deaths of the two Harper brothers and Goodspeed. Smith and Breasted became good friends during these years of transition as they discussed their "common responsibility for oriental science" at Chicago. Smith tended to contextualize his work in historical terms and drew Breasted in that direction. "As the years passed," Breasted wrote, "we saw . . . that our ultimate task was historical interpretation. . . . In mutual encouragement and stimulation we two together transformed the once so largely linguistic and philological Department of Oriental Languages into a primarily *historical* department."

Breasted also began to follow American research on ancient history. In 1910 a group of "youthful practitioners of the new discipline" organized an ancient history session at the American Historical Association's annual conference in Indianapolis. One of them later recalled that, after the session, when they were "wondering whether they had put ancient history across, a handsome man with a magnificent crest of white hair walked over and said: 'Boys, that was a fine program. I heard you were having an ancient history session and I came down from Chicago. I'm Breasted.' Already recognized as one of America's outstanding historians, he would have been welcomed by his ranking colleagues. Instead, he dined . . . with us, discussed our problems, praised our work, made tactful suggestions."[6]

Before long, Breasted's Egyptology course offerings began to subdivide into ever more specialized topics and methodologies. He split his curriculum into four sections: group 1, "Language and History Courses, Including Coptic," which included a four-course sequence that ran from "Beginner's Hieroglyphic" to "Historical Inscriptions of the Late Period, Including Persian and Ptolemaic" as well as "Beginner's Coptic," "Coptic Version of the Old Testament," and an Egyptian history seminar based on his *Ancient Records*; group 2, "Egyptian Literature, Including the Acquisition of Hieratic," consisting of two courses, one on hieratic and the other on "Egyptian Literature of Entertainment," which explored "narratives and tales (the forerunners of the *Arabian Nights*) and love poetry"; group 3, "Egyptian Religion and Thought," comprising four chronologically arranged courses, "The Pyramid Texts," "The Social Prophets and the Coffin Texts," "The Monotheistic Revolution," and the "Book of the Dead"; and group 4, "Egyptian Art, Archaeology, and Epigraphy," which included a one-course conflation of his art and archaeology classes mentioned above, a course titled "The Inscriptions and the Monuments" based on "descriptions of their buildings and monuments by the Egyptians themselves," and a course on "Egyptian Epigraphy" organized around "a study of original inscriptions in Haskell Museum and Field Museum [wherein students'] facsimile copies are compared with the originals, and corrected, and field methods of epigraphic work are taught."

The evolution of Breasted's course offerings between 1908 and 1915 reveal two lines of fresh work. The classes grouped under "Egyptian Religion and Thought" mark an intensifying interest in theological and moral issues. His Semitics-area history-survey classes show an expansion of Breasted's teaching beyond Egypt and a new focus on "the cultural connection between the Orient and the earliest civilization of Europe." Breasted's other Semitics-group courses fleshed out the widening range of his interests, especially his ancient Near Eastern literature class, which explored in translation "the rise of literary forms and . . . earliest development of literary art[: the] . . . literature of entertainment, tales, romances, poetry, epics, drama, wisdom, mortuary and religious compositions, scientific treatises, business and legal documents."[7]

Breasted was known as an inspiring and doting teacher who "always gave special time and attention to students." The labor of learning ancient languages, especially hieroglyphs, could be daunting, and Breasted found ways to inject into such classes "an inspirational excitement. For him grammar and syntax were not merely structure: they offered insights into the psychology of men living thousands of years ago. Verb forms were inventions of the human mind to give greater freedom and precision of expression." Breasted approached "the grinding routine of grammatical and philological teaching" as a "means to an end." One student recalled "even after forty years and more, the pauses in the course of his own faltering translation of some Egyptian inscription while the teacher interrupted the philological exercise by skillful questions or pregnant remarks which opened up to the younger mind fascinating vistas of a remote past, giving life and reality to the text and vitalizing the whole subject." As the field grew increasingly cautious and scholars worked in "a pedestrian way through the material and emerge[d] with a cautiously balanced conclusion," Breasted's students could "remember the days when the story was made straightforward and exciting" as he "went right down the middle of the story, brushing aside complexities and uncertainties in order to give us the sweep of mortal triumph and tragedy." Breasted was "generous to younger scholars" who were the products of other programs as well as his own, "always ready to help and to give from his store of knowledge and accumulated notes and observations."[8]

Despite Breasted's renewal of old friendships, return to teaching, and assumption of greater administrative responsibilities, he seems to have been at loose ends. Breasted's restiveness found an outlet in a brief dalliance with literary writing he entertained in 1909. That October he started a new "commonplace book"—a notebook that he titled "Children of the Sun, A Romance of the Early World." It was to be a fiction work, perhaps a play, on "Ikhnaton's . . . unparalleled life and labors." The notebook begins with a long journal-like entry in which he wrote: "For good or ill I am taking the leap. I who have labored only in science am venturing into literature." Breasted admitted, "I have no plan or structure in view; but I will jot down the 'materials' as they come to me. . . . Thus far I have no confidence in my own power to discern or portray the varied characters involved in such a drama; or to rough out the great lines of the dramatic structure." He confided that he would know if the effort fell short, and if so, he would "suppress it." Despite his reservations, Breasted exalted, "What infinite possibilities in such an art-form as this!"

The work was never completed, and the notebook contains just three more additions in subsequent months, each consisting of more or less developed sketches outlining imagined moments during the pharaoh's life. They are all written like scenes from a play in which the principal figures and settings are named and only dialogues or actions are fleshed out. The episodic construction of these "materials," each written during idle moments in various duly noted locations, corresponds to an observation Breasted made when he started the project: "There have been illuminated moments when I have seen the amazing character of Ikhnaton blazing forth like a great beacon in the far off darkness of the early world, and I have felt the appalling blackness when that light went out forever." Breasted regretted not having recorded these flashes of inspiration before and feared they might not return. His "romance" was recuperative, but not only in a historical sense. It suggests the depth and intensity of Breasted's affinity for the pharaoh's religious revolution. Breasted was far from becoming an adherent, but his much less passionate feelings for the religion of his birth are evident in the location where he wrote at least two of these literary passages: church.[9]

That Needful Something

Breasted's turn from the ministry to scholarship two decades earlier was motivated by contradictions in the Bible that seeded, as his seminary professor Samuel Ives Curtiss put it, "doubts that would only grow." Near the end of his life Breasted confirmed those doubts, adding telling details:

> Like most lads . . . I learned the Ten Commandments. . . . I remember that whenever I fibbed I found consolation in the fact that there was no commandment, "Thou shalt not lie." . . . In later years . . . , I began to be troubled by the fact that a code of morals which did not forbid lying seemed imperfect; but it

was a long time before I raised the interesting question: How has my own realization of this imperfection arisen? . . . When that experience began, it was
a dark day for my inherited respect for the theological dogma of "revelation." I
had more disquieting experiences . . . when as a young orientalist I found that
the Egyptians had possessed a standard of morals far superior to that of the
Decalogue over a thousand years before the Decalogue was written.

The evolution of Breasted's beliefs in the decade following his seminary departure was gradual and intertwined with his studies. While he trained at Yale and
Berlin and then launched his career, he periodically spoke to questions of faith,
organized religion, and biblical doctrine. Whether addressing these issues in relation to family matters, his research, or more abstractly, Breasted struggled to
balance skepticism about the truth of biblical teachings with a deepening interest in the origins of what he perceived as humanity's universal, inherent hunger
for justice.

His correspondence throughout this period shows Breasted searching for
social values in his research as though to replace what would have been a life
of good works in the ministry. Like a pastor, Breasted scanned his sources for
enduring truths applicable to contemporary life. In 1891, about two years after
leaving the seminary, Breasted wrote to his sister, "do not forget that the religious nature in one is not a mere phantasm, but a deep and infinite reality. It is
as truly of us & and our own. . . . Human experience is one—hearts are buried
under the same sorrows through all the years of time, and they are lifted out of
darkness by the same inspiration." After quoting from the Old and New Testaments, Breasted concluded, "This has been the witness of all humanity and you
can make it yours." About the same time, Breasted proposed a master's degree
thesis to Harper on "prayer as regarded & practiced in Old Testament history . . .
as it is in many ways so radically different from the New Testament conception of
it and so dependent on Old Testament notions of morality and personal responsibility and especially the Old Testament idea of God. . . . Would it be well also to
touch prayer among the Semitic peoples as a whole, e.g. as among the Assyrians
in the penitential psalms?" A couple of years later Breasted wrote to his family:

> It's a grand thing to have an enthusiasm to know things as they are. That is
> what the science of this age is striving to do. I reverence the Bible,—I use it—
> it's the grandest book that was ever written, but I am sorry for people who
> must believe a thing because it's in the Bible. Why, things were, a million, mil-
> lion years before the Bible . . . , and the same divinity that finally sent the Bible
> into the world also ordered things as they are. To study things as they are and
> have been is to study the output of a great intelligence,—for things are intelli-
> gible. Hence no study of things need be materialistic. . . .

The universe is a big thing, but man is the most tremendous thing in it . . . , and I am working away trying to restore a lost chapter in his astounding biography.[10]

Breasted began to articulate these views more systematically in addresses he gave between 1909 and 1912. None, however, were written for scholarly peers. To the contrary, they were presented to student and lay audiences, the pattern of topics suggesting Breasted regarded them as opportunities to present the spiritual encouragement for contemporary society he was gleaning from his research. One is a chapel address, apparently delivered to University of Chicago Divinity School students in February 1909, titled "A Neglected Source of Moral and Religious Enthusiasm." Breasted began with observations about the "decline of belief in . . . spiritual forces, due to the insistent invasion & extension of material forces in science & economics." This had led to a "furtive & uncomfortable apprehension that Darwinism & evolution are undeniable, and that while they leave us without the old bases, they furnish us with no new foundations." As a consequence, "Men ask, Is life worth living? Are men growing better or worse?" Noting that such questions "neglect [the] inspirational value of the idea of evolution in the life of man," Breasted offered examples of contemporary ignorance of history, ranging from prehistoric times to the Renaissance, selected to show the ancient origins of everything from buttons to democratic ideals. "Whatever category we take up, down whatever vista of human activity we look into the remote past, the continual unfolding of man's capacities from the beginning is observable." Of particular importance is the "rise of [mankind's] capacity spiritually to interpret nature & god [in the] capacity to enjoy landscape [and to] discern and believe in [the] spiritual power controlling material forces for moral & righteous ends."

But, Breasted asked, "How make all of this practically effective?" He advised that the "minister of today should know what man now is, what he has been & what he has achieved. [The minister] must study Psychology & Sociology [and] History in the larger sense" in order to unfold "the great panorama of man." Breasted suggested his audience "Be very specific, tangible & concrete [by citing such examples as the erection of the] Great Pyr[amids just] 100 years [after] the earliest stone masonry; Laws of Hamm[urabi]; Idea of Life after death in Egypt & in N[ew] T[estament; and the] Discernment of beauty of nature as earliest found & as in Ital[ian] renaissance." Reciting brief quotations from Goethe and Tennyson, especially the first line of the latter's "De Profundis" ("Out of the deep, my child, out of the deep"), Breasted concluded, "Man has indeed come out of the deeps, but by a divine fatalism he is inevitably decreed to rise & ever to rise."[11]

Breasted's core idea, the substitution of the inspirational story of humanity's evolutionary "rise" for the old "belief in spiritual forces," was refined in a subsequent talk on the nature of inspiration per se. Delivered in a 1910 university chapel address titled "The Study of History and the Idea of Inspiration," it began with the observation that many believed the "old idea" that "Providence [was] limited to the [ancient] Hebrews"—a notion Breasted set out to challenge. Breasted went on to cite science's superiority in verifying its conclusions because "in the study of history we cannot set historical forces at work in a laboratory, watch the result, and repeat the experiment." Nonetheless, history is like science in that "every where in time and place the same forces operate, the same laws govern." Accordingly, it is possible to "apply the same principles to the study and reconstruction of history in Palestine which we apply to Bab[ylonia] or Egypt."

Observing that "prophecy [also] existed in Egypt," and that the "great souls of Israel [just] pushed a little higher up the spiritual steep," Breasted argued that the "method of the prophets [of Israel] was to face the conditions and interpret them in the light of a belief in the god of Israel. . . . We call their words under these circumstances inspired, yet they spoke them in a world governed by the same hist[orical] forces that operate today. . . . The moral indignation that leaps into flame at the contemplation of some great political or social wrong is inspiration. . . . It is the response of the divine capacity within us to our environment, whether in the heart of Isaiah or in yours and mine." Accordingly, Breasted continued, "The study of the early history of the East is proving two things: 1. Man of Israel and the man of today are the same. 2. The world and the forces controlling it, as they operate about man, are the same."

There are three steps in Breasted's theory: first, he equates ancient "man" with "the man of today"; next, he holds that the social "processes" or "forces" affecting human experience are, like the laws of physics, universal and unchanging; and last, he believes these find expression when individuals encounter discrepancies in human affairs between how things are and how they ought to be—insights once thought of as "divine" inspiration, "revelation," or "prophecy." Breasted seems to have been adopting a "presentist" approach, that is, studying "the past for the sake of the present." To a large extent he was, although that outcome was incidental to his much deeper interest in the evolutionary origins and development of moral consciousness. This concern is evident in his interest in "social prophecy" as an indicator of evolving human morality.[12]

The importance of social prophecy was crystallized for Breasted by *The Admonitions of an Egyptian Sage*, an edition of an ancient papyrus published in 1909 by British scholar Alan H. Gardiner. The text contains the ruminations of a wise man named Ipuwer who, in the presence of a pharaoh, laments the social and economic decay of the kingdom and then, criticizing the pharaoh for these problems, wonders if there is a higher power who can set things right. Although Gardiner cautiously summarized the text's content as a sage's reflections on "social and political well-being," Breasted saw in it connotations of far greater importance. In a review of *Admonitions* titled "The Earliest Social Prophet," he observed:

> The Hebrew prophets have always been supposed to have been the first men
> who possessed the detachment and the insight to contemplate the moral,
> social, and political wrongs of a people and contrast these with an ideal state
> in which they passionately believed. . . . The existence of such a tractate [as
> this] . . . , centuries before the rise of social prophets [in Palestine], is very
> significant. . . . There are passages in Ipuwer which strongly remind one of
> the first chapter of Isaiah or similar descriptions in Amos, Hosea, and Micah.
> The . . . sudden rise of . . . prophets in Palestine in the latter half of the eighth
> century B. C. receives a flood of light from the . . . *Admonitions of Ipuwer*.

Breasted supported his assertion by relating it to archaeological finds showing the transmission of Egyptian culture into Palestine. "Such things [as] the
pots and kettles of a Canaanitish kitchen or the foreign amulets and charms
worn by Hebrew women; these and similar *material* documents . . . found in
Palestine . . . can be unmistakably traced back to Egypt." Would not, Breasted
argued, the "elusive elements of an intellectual and religious life" just as easily
be transported from Egypt to Palestine? By demonstrating that Egyptian ideas
informed Old Testament prophecy, Breasted established a developmental model,
based on evolutionary theory, that linked the origins of modern social thought
with ancient Egypt. It was a model that dislodged ancient Israel from being a
place of origins to a site through which more ancient ideas were transmitted to
the modern world. But for Breasted, it was the identification of factors surrounding the origins and transmission of social prophecy as signs of moral evolution
that was most important.[13]

Alongside these ideas Breasted was also articulating his convictions about
the aims and practices of historical research. In a 1911 address to the Chicago Society of Biblical Research, titled "The Old Historical Method," Breasted criticized
as outdated approaches that he identified with the "political structure" method
of Theodor Mommsen and the "economic structure" method of Guglielmo Ferrero. Mommsen, the scholar chatting in the background of Breasted's doctoral
examination, was one of the towering figures of nineteenth-century German
scholarship and author of several seminal works on ancient Roman history. Ferrero, an Italian author whose interests ranged over history, contemporary politics, and literature, had published a popular multivolume history of Rome some
years earlier that was issued in English translation starting in 1907.

Breasted believed Mommsen and Ferrero exemplified "traditional" historians
who hewed too narrowly to the "gospel" of Leopold von Ranke's "wie es eigentlich
gewessen," reducing history "as it actually happened" into lifeless compilations

of historical data. Ranke, who is regarded by many as one of the founding fathers of modern historical scholarship, is remembered for his zealous search for, and rigorous adherence to, primary sources in the historical archives of Europe. As an heir to the research tradition Ranke helped establish, Breasted certainly did not reject the importance of primary sources in establishing historical facts. Rather, instead of pursuing historical knowledge for its own sake, Breasted argued for its application to contemporary problems.

He wrote that the best way to accomplish this was by broadening the sources and methodologies of historical research, an approach he identified with the "New Hist[orical] Method." It encompassed "the career of man in the largest sense, . . . the development of those capacities individ[ual] & social," and it was now realized in an "enlargement of the field in all directions: Anthropology, Psychology, Comp[arative] Rel[igions], Sociology, Political Economy, and even the later periods of geology." Breasted's reference to geology was temporal: "we discern not only that civ[ilization], like man's physical form, is the result of a slow development; but also that the first steps in civ[ilization] . . . were only made possible by an enormously long development preceding them." However, Breasted was especially intrigued by geological *processes* that have existed for thousands of years and which can still be observed today, his favorite example being the action of glaciers.[14]

The reason for this interest became clear in a subsequent address he delivered to the graduating class of the University of Chicago's School of Education in 1912. Titled "Revelation a Historical Process," the address began with a wide-ranging discussion of "intellectual youth and how to maintain it" for prospective teachers seeking to overcome dull teaching methods and textbooks. As a remedy, Breasted focused on "the conscious and deliberate cultivation of an attitude of receptivity." He believed "this can . . . be best accomplished, by the recognition that we live in the course of an unfinished process, in which we are involved,— a process which has produced us, and of which we ourselves represent but a single stage." Breasted proposed that this heightened awareness could be "greatly furthered by the right study of history. Not the study of a mere succession of dynasties and peoples" but one that shows "the career of man, as an imposing vista down which we . . . watch his expanding life as it rises from age to age to the attainment of ever higher capacities."

The "right study of history" is based on a conception of historical time as deep and continuous: "there is no beginning of one period and the conclusion of another, but each age is inextricably rooted in that which has gone before." Through it we can "watch slowly growing a noble fabric of civilization in which the golden threads of man's higher nature multiply from age to age." This approach allows us to "contemplate the gradual emergence of moral distinctions, the slow triumph of the good, the gradual unfettering of conscience as man first discerns that evil must bring inevitable consequences." "Such a vista of man's development will impress upon us the reality" of that "process" which, Breasted argued, continues: "It is the order of the universe that man should <u>rise</u>. . . . Coral islands rise from dark depths, so man." The "right study of history" thus reveals the ages-long process of humanity's evolving standards of personal morality and social justice—a process as inevitable and enduring as the geological forces studied by science.[15]

Breasted realized that in aligning history with science and evolution with progress, he was inviting objections to the "destructiveness of the new position" for those adhering to literal interpretations of the Bible. In a coda to his earlier address on historical method, Breasted countered that "the <u>normal</u> processes of human life & history produced Jesus. . . . That the aeons of man's development could culminate in a personality of such supreme grandeur is the greatest fact in human history and the most encouraging fact that we can hold up before the mind of the modern man."[16]

These explorations of ancient history, moral development, and historical method enabled Breasted to revisit interests that first drew him to the ministry while also pointing a way out of the thicket of doubts fostered by biblical criticism and modern science. They were only loosely connected with his research, however, and it was a timely lecture-series invitation that encouraged him to bring his ideas to bear on Egyptology. The invitation came in January 1911 from the Union Theological Seminary in New York. Founded in 1836 as a Presbyterian seminary, it began loosening its ties following an 1892 heresy trial conducted by the Presbyterian Church against a seminary faculty member over his teaching of biblical criticism. In 1910 the seminary moved to upper Manhattan to be near Columbia University and other institutions as it broadened its mission to serve a wider range of Protestant denominations.

Breasted was invited to deliver a series of eight lectures "on some subject connected with Egyptology or its relation to the Bible or to any portion of the history of Israel." The topic could be construed "in a very broad sense, so that any exposition of the material of Egyptology in scientific form," even "a treatment of Egyptian religion," would fit the bill. The invitation was for the 1911–12 academic year and included a subsequent publication of the lectures by Scribner's. Breasted accepted the invitation, commenting that he saw "great possibilities" for a "presentation of Egyptian religion as a development of intellectual life, a thing which has not yet been done." The lectures were delivered in March and April 1912 under the title "Religion and Thought in Ancient Egypt." For the book he expanded the material into ten chapters and changed the title to *Development of Religion and Thought in Ancient Egypt*.[17]

As early as 1894, while winding up work on his dissertation, Breasted thought of writing a book on "the religion of Egypt in the New Empire." The New Empire was the approximately five-hundred-year period leading up to and including the reign of Amenhotep IV. To him it represented a "phase of that never ceasing struggle in the life of man—the struggle for the truth." It taught him "that <u>history</u> is only the story of that struggle and that therefore the history of all men is <u>one</u>." The scholar who can "raise up out of the dust" that story "can enrich the common life of man" by showing "his fellows how we stand between the past and the future indissolubly linked with both." Writing nearly two decades later in his preface to *Development of Religion and Thought*, Breasted picked up that line of thought: "May I . . . express the hope that this exposition of religion in the making, during a period of three thousand years, may serve not only as a general survey of the development in the higher life of a great people . . . , but also to emphasize the truth that the process of religion-making has never ceased and that the same forces which shaped religion in ancient Egypt are still operative in our own midst and continue to mould our own religion to-day?"[18]

Breasted tailored the lectures for a "popular audience" by avoiding lengthy "technical" discussions of the material. Nonetheless, according to a former student, seminarians and "the general public attending these lectures were disappointed. They had heard that Breasted was a brilliant lecturer and lucid expositor. They found the lectures slow, apparently repetitious, and heavily documented. They were unaware that Breasted was doing an exciting piece of pioneering. . . . It was necessary for him to emphasize and document every step of his argument." The book embodies that cautiousness. Breasted declined to relate "the phenomena adduced with those of other religions," and rather than attempt a broad survey of his topic, he concentrated on those features of Egyptian religion and thought that could be traced with greatest certainty. Further, Breasted noted, "contrary to the popular and current impression, the most important body of sacred literature in Egypt is not the Book of the Dead" but rather the "Pyramid Texts," so called because they were found in pyramids and associated sites. Although they were less well known, he would focus on them because of their greater antiquity and interest. As it happened, Breasted's fellow doctoral student, Kurt Sethe, had a few years earlier begun publishing a comprehensive edition of the Pyramid Texts. Breasted translated and studied them with his students, discovering insights about "the religious and intellectual forces which have left their traces" in them, leading him to claim that they were "to the study of Egyptian language and civilization what the Vedas have been in the study of early East Indian and Aryan culture."[19]

Breasted began the heart of his discussion with a rare reference to personal experience. Pointing out the centrality of "the idea of life beyond the grave . . . among the ancient Egyptians," he attributed this belief to "conditions of soil and climate," which allowed a "remarkable preservation of the [deceased] human body." Breasted then recalled that "going up to the daily task [of recording a] . . .

temple in Nubia, I was . . . obliged to pass through the corner of a cemetery, where the feet of a dead man, buried in a shallow grave, were now uncovered and extended directly across my path. . . . This must have been a frequent experience of the ancient Egyptian, and like Hamlet with the skull of Yorick in his hands, he must often have pondered deeply as he contemplated these silent witnesses." The Pyramid Texts revealed Egyptians' earliest responses to the mysteries of life before and after death. Breasted cautioned, however, that studies of the texts are highly speculative because they are very difficult sources:

> These archaic texts . . . form together almost a *terra incognita*. As one endeav-
> ors to penetrate it, his feeling is like that of entering a vast primeval forest, a
> twilight jungle filled with strange forms and elusive shadows peopling a wilder-
> ness through which there is no path. An archaic orthography veils and obscures
> words. . . . Besides these disguised friends, there is a host of utter strangers,
> a great company of archaic words which have lived a long and active life in a
> world now completely lost. . . . Hoary with age they totter into sight . . . [and]
> vaguely disclose to us a vanished world of thought and speech, . . . [yet they]
> often remain strangers . . . , and no art of lexicography can force them to yield
> up their secrets.

Nonetheless, Breasted felt he could detect in the Pyramid Texts the origins of a distinction between the sun god, Re—later identified as Amon—and the Nile god, Osiris. He believed they show the solar beliefs associated with Re becoming a "state" religion of the monarchy and priesthood and Osirian beliefs becoming those of the people.[20]

Breasted also gleaned what he considered to be the origins of "moral discern-ment," specifically "the origin of good and evil." But he felt it was not until the end of the "Pyramid Age," around 2000 BCE, that a turning point was reached in the formation of personal morality. Breasted conjectured it was born of ques-tions over previous generations' extravagant mortuary practices "impressively embodied" in the sixty-mile string of pyramids along the desert edge lining the fertile plains west of the Nile. "There they stretched like a line of silent outposts on the frontiers of death . . . [in] desolation, deeply encumbered with sand half hiding the ruins of massive architecture . . . , a solitary waste where only the slinking figure of the vanishing jackal suggested the futile protection of the old mortuary gods." If already in the Pyramid Texts the conviction was ebbing "that by sheer material force man might make conquest of immortality, the spectacle of these colossal ruins now quickened such doubts into open skepticism." That skepticism was a catalyst for further changes including "a conscious recognition of personal power to believe or disbelieve, and thus a distinct step forward in the development of self consciousness and personal initiative."[21]

Breasted found the relationship between personal awareness and moral action emerging in two ways. First was the "tragedy of the individual unjustly afflicted," and second was a broader "social misfortune . . . which afflicts men as a body"—both resulting in a "crusade of social righteousness." For evidence of individual troubles, Breasted offered a papyrus dating from about 2000–1650 BCE, "The Dialogue of a Misanthrope with His Own Soul," which he characterized as "our earliest Book of Job, written some fifteen hundred years before [that] similar book among the Hebrews." For evidence of communal suffering, Breasted cited the social criticisms of Ipuwer, the variously described "sage" and "prophet" discussed above. While the "Misanthrope" tale is "a distinct mark in the long development of self-consciousness, the slow process which culminated in the emergence of the individual as a social force," the Ipuwer story reveals "the necessary detachment and the capacity to contemplate society" as a whole, resulting in a "vision of the possible redemption of society."[22]

The next major step in Egyptian social thought was during the 1400s BCE when, under the reign of Thutmose III, Egypt became an imperial power as the pharaoh's military campaigns enlarged it to the far reaches of Mesopotamia to the east and Nubia to the south. This expansion drew Egypt "out of the immemorial isolation of her narrow valley into world-relations, with which the theology of the time must reckon." The first intimation of this change was Thutmose III's merging of all of the disparate priesthoods scattered throughout Egypt into "one great sacerdotal organization" dedicated to Amon, "the earliest national priesthood as yet known in the East, and the first *pontifex maximus*." Just as the many kings of the conquered lands in Egypt's political dominion now bowed in fealty to the pharaoh, so too Egypt's many gods were now subjects of a supreme god. Because the priesthood continued to maintain its ancient "polytheistic tradition," however, it "constituted a powerful political obstacle" to the elevation of Amon over Egypt's theological pantheon. Not until Amenhotep IV, who, as Breasted described in *History of Egypt*, swept away this obstruction by establishing Aton as the centerpiece of a monotheistic "new faith," were Egypt's religious structures unified. "Monotheism," Breasted remarkably observed, "is but imperialism in religion."[23]

All of this was a prelude to Breasted's consideration of Amenhotep IV-cum-Ikhnaton's sun hymns, his dissertation topic now revisited to tease out the threads of two other themes: "universalism" and "the presence of God in nature." Because the newly conceived god is represented in the hymns as "the universal creator who brought forth all the races of man," Breasted sees Ikhnaton as "projecting a world religion" designed to "displace . . . the nationalism" of the old religious theology. Not only is the new god's power universal, but "all men acknowledge his dominion," rendering devotion to Aton universal as well. But Breasted is also intrigued by the hymns' "appeal to nature," an "admonition to 'consider the lilies of the field.'" The hymns disclose "an appreciation of the revelation of God in the visible world such as we find a thousand years later in the Hebrew psalms, and in our poets of nature since Wordsworth." Similar to the assertion he made in "Revelation a Historical Process," Breasted regards religion-as-process as an aspect of "Ikhnaton's movement" in its "gospel of the beauty and beneficence of the natural order, a recognition of the message of nature to the soul of man." Of Ikhnaton's short-lived reforms, Breasted concluded, "All that we have . . . is the wreck of his city, a lonely outpost of idealism, not to be overtaken and passed till six centuries later when those Bedouin hordes . . . had coalesced into a nation of social, moral, and religious aspirations, and had thus brought forth the Hebrew prophets."[24]

Breasted compressed the remaining millennium or so of history into a concluding chapter on personal reverence, which he found emerging in the wake of Ikhnaton's failure, as a "confidence of the worshiper in the solicitude of the Sun-god for all, even the least of his creatures . . . developed into a devotional spirit, and a consciousness of personal relations with the god." "An age of personal piety and inner aspiration to God now dawned among the masses" and was accompanied by a dawning awareness of wrongdoing and its consequences: "Rich and poor alike may suffer the displeasure of the god aroused by sin." Yet "relief may be obtained . . . if repentance follows and the offender humbly seeks the favor of his god." These advances soon gave way to stagnation, however, and by 700 BCE, "the creative age of inner development was forever past," and what remained were the vestiges of a sumptuous but, in Breasted's view, empty "sacerdotal state."

As he brought the book to a close, he returned to the inspiration of the *process* of religious development illuminated by ancient Egypt. As before, Breasted offered the analogy of geological forces, this time explaining his full meaning:

> Louis Agassiz . . . , after studying the resistless action of the Swiss glaciers . . . at length realized that this glacial action had been going on for ages, and the imposing truth burst upon him that the geological processes of past aeons . . . are still going on at the present day, that they have never ceased, that they will never cease.
>
> We have been tracing in broad lines the development of the religion of a great people, unfolding in the course of over three thousand years as the forces within and . . . around this ancient man wrought and fashioned his conception of the divine powers. . . . The ancient ideas of God are but the expression of the best that man has felt and thought embodied in a supreme character of which he dreamed. What was intended by Ingersoll, I suppose, as a biting gibe, "An honest god is the noblest work of man," is nevertheless profoundly true. We

have seen the Egyptian slowly gaining his honest god. We gained ours by the
same process, beginning among the Hebrews.

Robert Green Ingersoll was a late-nineteenth-century lawyer, orator, and cel-
ebrated agnostic, and the quotation is from an 1872 speech titled "The Gods" in
which Ingersoll argued that sacred texts, far from conveying divine teachings,
represented instead humanity's aspirations. For Breasted the quote validated
his interpretation of religious texts, whether those of ancient Egypt, Judaism,
or Christianity, as evidence—analogous to traces of geological change—of religious evolution. Accordingly, Breasted concluded: "It would be well if we of the
modern world as we look back over these ages lying behind us might realize with
Agassiz in the geological world, that religion is still in the making, that the processes which brought forth inherited religion have never ceased, that they are
going on around us every day, and that they will continue as long as the great and
complex fabric of man's life endures."[25]

Development of Religion and Thought in Ancient Egypt was enthusiastically received. Nathaniel Schmidt, professor of Semitic languages and history at Cornell
University, compared it favorably to other works on Egyptian religion by the
leading lights of Breasted's generation. Schmidt, an expert in biblical criticism,
detected in Breasted's treatment "a manner made familiar by similar efforts in the
field of Hebrew religion," referring specifically to "the same principles of textual,
literary, and historical criticism." Schmidt wrote that "it may be doubted whether
the criticism has ever been so searching and radical, and the reconstruction so
comprehensive . . . , so ingenious, logically consistent, and amply supported by
documentary proofs. It is natural that the result should resemble . . . biblical
criticism." Schmidt doubted some claims, including Breasted's "tendency to trace
back to Egyptian influence all sorts of religious ideas." On the other hand, Breasted's apology for presenting the material in a "popular style" notwithstanding,
Schmidt found the book "popular in the best sense. Always dignified and worthy
of the subject, it sometimes rises to a beauty and eloquence rarely met with in
the treatment of Egyptian life and thought by scholars." Although Breasted's
"boundless enthusiasm and his extraordinary gift of vivid presentation lead him
to make statements that may seem venturesome to more cautious students" and
the book's coverage is less than ideally complete, Schmidt concluded that "what
it gives is so instructive and thought-provoking that no student of Egyptian history can afford not to read it."

A reviewer for *The Nation* found the "section of the book which shows in
the clearest way the appreciation of Egyptian religious aspiration is found in
the chapters [on] the religious reforms of . . . Amenhotep IV. . . . The story as
told by Professor Breasted is vital and pulses with the throb of religious emo-

tion." Breasted's old friend Flinders Petrie characterized *Development* as "the most important book that has appeared for many years past upon the religion of Egypt. . . . Breasted has done what every scholar ought to do with his knowledge, applied it to restore the past to our imaginations." Petrie, who had published extensively on Egyptian religion himself, concluded that *Development* "shows throughout the first qualification for writing on the religion—a sympathy with the different beliefs on religion and ethics—a requirement which . . . has been lamentably absent from some other works on the subject. Scholastic precision may translate business documents, but something much larger is needful when we come to human faiths and feelings. Dr. Breasted has that needful something."[26] That "needful something" was a longing to supplant doubts seeded by the Higher Criticism with a new kind of faith that preserved the social value of sacred writ without demanding a belief in God to understand it.

Visualizing the Fertile Crescent

As a result of Breasted's mounting accomplishments, his salary grew from $2,500 a year, which he began receiving in 1903, to $4,500 a year by 1913. Even so, he felt the income was insufficient to support his family. Breasted continued looking after his mother, and he now had a second son, James Henry Jr., born in 1908, and his last child, Astrid, would arrive in 1914. A couple of years earlier Breasted commented that since starting work at Chicago, he had "earned between a third and half my income outside the University." Despite "incessant application and some measure of success," he found that he was "still obliged to do what I had done for 17 yrs., viz.: lecture outside whenever I find opportunity." Breasted relied increasingly on "stereoscopic material," including lantern slides made from stereographs prepared for *Egypt through the Stereoscope* as well as photographs taken during his expeditions. Similar materials were also used to illustrate a series of nine essays he wrote for the monthly *Chautauquan*. Intended as a "travel course," apparently to prepare Americans traveling to Egypt, they were published between November 1909 and May 1910 under the group title "A Reading Journey through Egypt." The essays were written in a conversational style, richly illustrated with photographs and maps, and proceed—much like *Egypt through the Stereoscope*—from Alexandria up the Nile. Initial response to the series must have been good because three months before the final essay appeared, Charles Scribner's Sons offered Breasted a contract to rework the series into a book to be called "Two Thousand Miles up the Nile." Breasted worked on it through 1912, when he set it aside, never to be completed, for an unexpected project.[27]

Breasted's popularizing gifts were evident in his teaching, and one of his most successful courses was a survey of ancient Near Eastern history for "more advanced undergraduates" that attracted graduate students too. Word of the course's following spread off campus to one of Breasted's neighbors, Henry Hoyt Hilton, who was a senior partner of a major textbook publisher at the time, Ginn and Company. Hilton urged him to write a high school–level ancient history textbook for Ginn, a notion Breasted repeatedly declined. In early 1911, familiar with Breasted's extensive lecturing, "from Chicago to Pittsburgh, . . . [Hilton] seized upon this to argue: 'Two nights on the train, a thousand listeners! If you will make us a book, we promise you a daily audience of twenty-five to fifty thousand.'" In the end, however, it was the allure of generous textbook royalties—perhaps as much as $5,000 a year—that won Breasted over: "Under these circumstances," he wrote, "how can I better rid myself of these outside lecture-trips, from which I return completely exhausted. . . ?" Ginn offered an advance of $1,200, a stenographer, and a commitment to illustrate the book "sumptuously."[28]

Another deciding factor was an ambition it reawakened, one Breasted first expressed in 1904 while working on *History of Egypt* and *Ancient Records*. After visiting Eduard Meyer, Breasted wrote, "He sweeps the whole field of the orient down into Greek and Roman times. . . . I sometimes long to stretch my wings over such a field as that! . . . As it is, I only get [ancient man] started with all the material arts and a long experience in government, organization and law. . . . That is, I can only study his early progress . . . ; I cannot follow him into the age of the development of the individual, when he discovers the worth of himself as a soul. This leaves unused in myself capabilities of comprehension and sympathy which I long to employ."

Breasted was also intrigued by the intellectual challenges of working in a different arena and reaching new audiences. To a British Egyptologist, Breasted commented, "American historians are doing more and more to drag me into the historical field. I am becoming more . . . interested in it. Our interests as Egyptologists . . . have been altogether too narrow,—too philological. . . . I am working and reading far afield in historic lines, and already the Egyptians look very different to me." Here, Breasted realized, was an opportunity to draw on those untapped "capabilities," because "long years of work in Hebrew, Arabic, Assyrian, Aramaic, and so forth will now be of great value if I extend my work into a larger historic field." And although his book would require a considerable amount of work, "the best thing about it is, that I should give myself an invaluable course in history." Breasted was also excited by the possibilities of translating his research for even larger and younger audiences: "I recall [Thomas Henry] Huxley's lectures to working-men, his interest in the education of English youth and the serious amount of time he devoted to educational textbooks. . . . Do you not find it very clarifying to be obliged to put your results in form for a general audience?"[29]

After accepting Ginn's offer, Breasted began preparing himself by reading one of the company's college-level textbooks, *An Introduction to the History of Western Europe*, written by James Harvey Robinson. Robinson was a professor of European history at Columbia University who by then was also a leading proponent of the "New History" in America. The two met in 1910 at an American Historical Association conference where Robinson delivered a paper titled "The Relation of History to the Newer Sciences of Man." It reflected his belief that too many historians remained faithful to a now outmoded but still "ruling 'scientific' school of history: its devotion to 'facts,' its ideal of perfect objectivity, and its enthronement of political history as the leading thread in the historical process." Instead, Robinson urged historians to learn from the "newer sciences" and "evolutionary-minded scholars" who led them: "from biologists about the link of humans to primates; . . . from archaeologists about the true length of human history, as opposed to . . . Bible-oriented early history; . . . and from comparative religion about the relativity of Christianity." Breasted heard the paper, was smitten with it, and began incorporating and citing some of Robinson's ideas in his own work, for example, the January 1911 "Old Historical Method" address discussed above. But Breasted did not think so highly of Robinson's treatment of ancient history in his Ginn textbook, dismissing it as "almost all . . . pastepot and shears," being "condensed and edited almost entirely from other men's work." He felt he could do just as well on ancient Greece and Rome and "for the Orient better than any of them."[30]

Not long after Breasted signed with Ginn, Robinson, aware the publisher was courting Breasted, asked him if he would be willing to help write the first of a two-volume, two-year general history textbook for high schools to be published by Ginn. The first volume, if coauthored by Breasted and Robinson, would run from the prehistoric era through the eighteenth century. Robinson had been reading *History of Egypt* and felt "it would be a real pleasure" to work with Breasted, given his "vivid, first-hand knowledge" and that the two had "a good deal in common." As a token of professional regard, Robinson sent a copy of his latest book, an essay collection on contemporary historiography titled *The New History*. Among the experiences they shared in common were a midwestern upbringing, doctoral training in Germany, and a critical attitude toward sacred scripture, although Robinson was a far more ardent "secularist, . . . agnostic, [and] freethinker," his religious "temperament and ideas [coming] from the French: anticlerical."

They also shared a common vision of history's uses, which Robinson articulated in his work on historiography and teaching, but which Breasted had just begun to express. As he explained to Robinson, "I was trained [as] a philologist. I never pursued even so much as one historical course in a university." Many of Robinson's historiographical views are summed up in *The New History*, which includes his Indianapolis address and, like that address, resonated with Breasted, as is evident in an enthusiastic review he had published a month earlier. The perspective offered by Robinson in *The New History* is "fundamentally evolutionary, rationalistic, and optimistic. . . . Progressive social change or betterment is the law of history. The historian can help to establish the direction of change by the study of its roots in the past, and should teach men to cooperate with and control the forces of change in a process of conscious social readjustment." Key here is the word "progressive."[31]

Robinson was one of a handful of scholars referred to as the "Progressive historians" for their application of history to constructive social change. They "were not bent on modernizing the American understanding of history primarily to bring historical scholarship up to date but to persuade American citizens to reform their republic." They opposed histories confined to the lives and political machinations of kings, aristocrats, and other elites because that emphasis is inappropriate to the egalitarian ethos of American democracy. Robinson and his allies "attuned . . . history to the Progressive Era" in order to challenge "dominant thoughts and institutions" they regarded as "the results of outdated orthodoxies, kept in place by self-interests of groups and individuals."

Robinson further believed that the human sciences, like archaeology, "were akin to Progressive history in their aim to bring rational analysis to bear on the problems of the day" and to "see matters in terms of universal structures and processes"; Progressive historians also made common cause with the sciences in their conflicts with organized religion over scientific versus biblical explanations of the world. But for Robinson and other Progressive historians, while their predecessors' Protestant theology had to be fought "as the foremost source of outdated ideas," its "redemptive features were secularized" as part of their scholarly mission. Accordingly they "translated their originally Protestant moral and social ideals into secular reform programs," an effort that found them pursuing a "civic religion that combined secularized Christian ethics with scientific knowledge."

Finally, Robinson and his peers refused to accept the epistemological premise of "scientific historians" that a useful historical synthesis could only be achieved at some future point when the "data would be plentiful enough . . . to form an accurate picture of the past with an absolute minimum of interpretive interference." The amelioration of urgent social problems could not wait for the attainment of a nearly impossible scholarly ideal. Moreover, the "pattern of progress" in history "was already discernible with certainty from the available facts." And since "the pattern of progress derived its authority from facts, and these in turn depended on progress for their meaning, Progressive history . . . established a seamless unity between the facts and interpretation."

There is nothing to suggest that Breasted was familiar with the "New" or "Progressive" history before he learned about Robinson's work. Rather, several of Breasted's publications and addresses show him to have been following much the same trajectory as he attempted to render the products of his scholarship socially meaningful.[32]

Breasted agreed to collaborate with Robinson on what would be the former's second Ginn textbook, the first volume of *Outlines of European History*. Breasted would write on the period from prehistory through the dissolution of the Roman Empire, and Robinson would pick up the narrative from there. They agreed on a deadline of spring 1914 although Breasted was exhausted and ill from lecture trips of the previous year. In June 1913 Chicago president Judson urged Breasted to take a six-week vacation and came up with $500 "for special purposes" to cover travel costs and alleviate income losses from not teaching or accepting speaking engagements. Breasted gratefully accepted, and the family headed to Wyoming. Despite the trip's avowed purpose, he spent some of the time finishing the first three chapters of the larger ancient history textbook he first promised to Ginn, referring to it as "Story of Ancient Man." Anticipating the heavy workload of completing his share of *Outlines* while also writing "Story," Breasted arranged to use accumulated vacation time for a leave from teaching in fall 1913. He began work on *Outlines* in September with a 150-page budget in view, plus about 50 pages of illustrations, and by January 1914 had all but four chapters done.

Breasted and Robinson readily agreed on most matters, though Breasted objected to the book's title. He wondered how "Outlines of European History" "fit a survey including several thousand years of the Orient before Europe woke up?" Robinson accepted Breasted's point but countered that the second volume of the set was already in print and offered to revisit Breasted's concerns for subsequent editions. For his part, Robinson was concerned about Breasted's verbosity and sensitivity to a high school audience's reading level. He reminded Breasted that the book was "to be read by boys and girls of 15 and that it is necessary to have short paragraphs and very clear statements." Breasted tried to come around with regard to wording, but not length. His part of the final version was over three hundred pages long.[33]

It also ran long because of his unusually generous use of illustrations. Staff involved in *Outlines*' production urged Breasted to plan ahead for his ancient history's illustration scheme for economic reasons—images prepared for *Outlines* could also be used in the later book. But the production staff didn't realize what it was inviting. Breasted's liberal use of lantern slides shaped his approach to teaching, and he therefore expected "as a foundation principle" for *Outlines* "to bring before the student more carefully arranged illustrative material than has ever before been available." Breasted repeatedly argued for more images in his share of the text because it is necessary when writing about antiquity to illustrate "material documents," meaning objects and architecture: "From the earlier ages few or no written documents have survived. These ages however left us a great monumental record, and this record can tell its story only in illustrations." To press his point, Breasted noted that the "writers of the existent text-books have taken no account of this self-evident fact because they have been trained only in the use of <u>written</u> records and are unfamiliar with the processes of making monumental remains tell their story." Their textbooks are dull because "the chief difficulty in bringing [antiquity] before modern students . . . is the unreality of it all."[34]

For Breasted, making the ancient world "real" through illustrations meant immersing himself in the minutiae of printing production. Drawing on his "wide experience in photography, and a good deal of experience . . . in careful reproduction of photographs for artistic and archaeological purposes," he began showering the Ginn production staff with detailed illustration instructions. For example, he wanted to have numerous photographs reproduced as "halftones," or photoengravings that translate subtle light and dark images into fine dot-pattern plates suitable for commercial-scale printing. When the *Outlines* production manager countered that plates from handmade line drawings of the photographs would print more effectively, Breasted objected. "When you put a draftsman between your reader and the original," Breasted wrote, "you destroy the realism which the school-boy feels only in the presence of the photograph. . . . If we want to convey the impression . . . that the ancient world . . . actually existed, and that [its] monuments may be touched and examined at the present day, it cannot be done by so large a use of pen-drawings." They compromised, and Breasted was allotted a generous number of halftones.

His "foundation principle" regarding illustrations was that they should be related to the text as clearly as possible. "Hence the text of a book should be written with constant consideration of the illustrations . . . till both interfuse into a symmetrical whole. This <u>inner</u> unity of text and illustration should be enhanced by every possible <u>outward</u> means; not only must the text constantly refer to the figures by number, but every [image] must bear the number of the paragraph to which it belongs." Robinson, initially taken aback by the space required for Breasted's illustrations and captions, eventually adopted this approach for his share of the book, concluding, "This will give [it] double effectiveness. We shall have our text,—and this text will be backed up by a pictorial story which will constantly supplement and enrich the text. I do not know why the plan has not been adopted before." Looking ahead to his ancient history, Breasted wrote, "You will see that I am trying to do a thing totally different from the current [books] now in use. I am treating the ancient world as if it were alive, and I am trying to make my readers see and feel it live."[35]

Robinson finished his part before Breasted, who, upon delivering the manuscript in March 1914, learned "it was found to be much too mature for its infantile users. I then <u>for the first time</u> learned that it was to be used for <u>first year</u> high school children!" Breasted had to rewrite a majority of the chapters, applying the finishing touches over the summer. This included adding study questions, which high school teachers found very useful but which Breasted "dashed . . . off in a few minutes after each chapter was written, not thinking them of much value." The completed volume was in print by September, with at least twenty thousand copies issued by October.

As the first of a two-volume set, it was issued with the title *Outlines of European History, Part I*. Breasted's half was subtitled "Earliest Man, The Orient, Greece, and Rome," and Robinson's was subtitled "Europe from the Break-Up of the Roman Empire to the Opening of the Eighteenth Century." Breasted's portion came to twenty-one chapters subdivided into fifty topical sections numbered to ease their correlation with the end-of-chapter questions. Paragraphs were accompanied by brief, one- to ten-word topic headings in the margins, and cross-references were to page numbers, much to Breasted's annoyance because it added to the work of proofreading. His section has 130 illustrations not counting images he selected for chapter openings and endings, as well as five color plates and eight maps.

Breasted called attention to his illustration-and-captions scheme in the jointly authored preface, noting that it gives "a sort of parallel narrative and [furnishes] a helpful supplement and corrective to the text itself." Most of Robinson's figures were Ginn stock images, while Breasted's came from his Egyptian expeditions, European colleagues, and Underwood & Underwood, the publisher of *Egypt through the Stereoscope*. In exchange for the company's permission to use over twenty of its images, he plugged its offerings at the preface's conclusion by recommending that teachers "who make the Underwood stereographs . . . part of their equipment will find that their teaching gains enormously in effectiveness." Breasted expanded on the instructional use of images in the book's back matter, commenting that although the book is "plentifully" illustrated, merely having the images is insufficient. "The fact cannot be too strongly emphasized that *a careful study of the illustrations belongs to every lesson*. . . . The explanatory matter under each figure should be thoroughly studied . . . with the accompanying text, and full discussion of every illustration and its description should regularly be required of the class."[36]

Teachers noticed that Breasted apportioned more space to the ancient Near East, relative to ancient Greece and Rome, than theretofore seen in comparable textbooks. Hilton asked him to explain why, and Breasted replied:

> Progress is most easily discerned . . . by the young student, as he surveys a series of things which were . . . achieved by early man for the <u>first time</u>. . . . The ability . . . to kindle a fire, to extract metal from ore, . . . to cultivate the wild grasses . . . ; to build a wall of stone masonry; to build and launch a sea-going ship; these and many other things done by man for the first time . . . mark for the young student the slow but steady advance of man. . . . Among these con-

quests . . . which are so instructive, the Orient has far more to tell us than early Europe.

If we turn to . . . man's conquests in the spiritual world, we have to note at once that the dominating religion of civilized Europe and America today is an <u>Oriental</u> religion. It was in the East that man discerned for the first time that <u>right</u> is higher than the will of the gods; that men are to be morally accountable in the hereafter.

This was not to suggest, however, that ancient Greece and Rome should be given less attention than before. Rather, Breasted wrote, "I am interested in the whole human career and do not propose to overemphasize <u>any</u> epoch or <u>any</u> civilization, but to estimate all civilizations on the basis of what they achieved and what they bequeathed to later men."[37]

Within *Outlines'* overall structure, Breasted concentrated on tracing the ancient Near East's influences on Mediterranean culture and society. He assimilated a great deal of information to make this point, as is evident in his *Outlines* bibliography. But one book was particularly helpful, Harry Reginald Hall's *The Ancient History of the Near East* (1913), which Breasted reviewed and reread. A scholarly rather than school text, it struck Breasted because before Hall no one had yet "presented the vast and complicated interaction of Oriental and Mediterranean civilizations." Hall provided a central organizing principle for Breasted's treatment of the ancient Near East and its role in shaping European, and by extension, American civilization. He communicated the idea of cultural transmission with topics that could easily be demonstrated with images as well as prose. Breasted tried out his approach in lantern-slide lectures given to such groups as the Wisconsin State Teachers' Association during the time he was writing *Outlines*. Among the topics that found their way into the book were the clerestory as first found in ancient Egypt, then Greece, and finally in the basilica church of early Christianity or the great arch as first articulated on the Assyrian palace facade and then the Roman triumphal arch.[38]

Orchestrating the narrative, illustrations, and captions to propel the story forward, Breasted adhered to his and Robinson's goal of departing from the "older historical manuals [that] were . . . accounts of past *events*," concentrating instead on "past *conditions* and past *institutions* that are best worth knowing about." Breasted's illustrations include dramatic vistas, several never before published, as Breasted was quick to note (figure 5.1), as well as more conventional views selected to inform rather than inspire. His selection of figures revealing the day-to-day conditions of ancient life, along with their captions, are the most compelling. A relief illustrates woodworking methods and tools during Egypt's fourth dynasty, around 2575–2450 BCE (figure 5.2); ceramic pipes reveal the

Fig. 5.1 "Colossal Portrait Figure of Ramses II at Abu Simbel in Egyptian Nubia," figure 30 from Breasted and Robinson's *Outlines of European History, Part I* (1914). "Four such statues, seventy-five feet high, adorn the front of this temple. . . . Grand view of the Nubian Nile, on which the statues have looked down for thirty-two hundred years. . . . View taken from the top of the crown of one of the statues and never before published. (Photograph by The University of Chicago [1905–6] Expedition)." Public domain, reproduction by author.

Fig. 5.2 "Cabinetmakers in the Pyramid Age," figure 20 from Breasted and Robinson's *Outlines of European History, Part I* (1914). "At the left, a man is cutting with a chisel which he taps with a mallet; next, a man 'rips' a board with a copper saw; next, two men are finishing off a couch, and at the right a man is drilling a hole with a bow-drill." Public domain, reproduction by author.

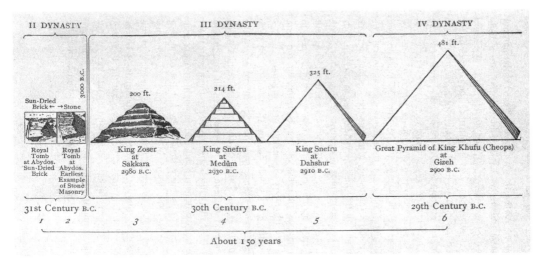

Fig. 5.3 "Diagram Illustrating the Rise of Architecture in Stone within a Century and a Half," figure 13 from Breasted and Robinson's *Outlines of European History, Part I* (1914). Public domain, reproduction by author.

plumbing advances of Cretan civilization about 1600 BCE, the caption comparing them to copper plumbing in Egypt about a millennium earlier; and a practice alphabet on a clay tablet of about 200 CE speaks to schooling itself, as well as the transmission of Greek into Sicily.

Breasted also used diagrams to assemble complex arrays of information. One on the pace with which stonemasonry developed in ancient Egypt correlates its chronological development from left to right with the rising heights of structures from bottom to top (figure 5.3). Another arranges the names of "parent peoples" and cultural descendents, along with directional arrows, to schematically map their dispersion along a broad front ranging from the westernmost reaches of the Mediterranean on the left to south Asia on the right (figure 5.4). Recognizing that the complexity of ideas being presented in certain diagrams was too great for the narrative or caption, Breasted added instructional footnotes for the teacher. At the beginning of the chapter to which figure 5.4 first applies, he explained that the following text addresses a series of "movements which anticipate a large part of ancient history. They are at first not easy for a young student to visualize. . . . The diagram [figure 5.4] should be put on the blackboard and explained in detail by the teacher. . . . This should be done again when the study of the Greeks is begun, and a third time when Italy and the Romans are taken up."[39]

Breasted's narrative bears the heaviest burden, and he drove it forward by knitting the dry facts of history into vivid and memorable scenes. In the chapter

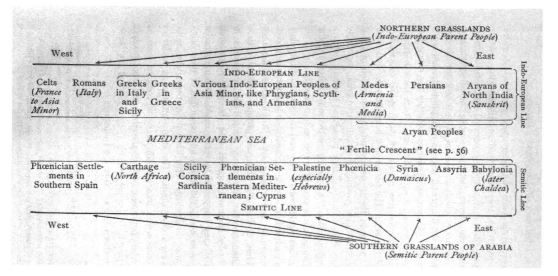

Fig. 5.4 "Diagram Suggesting the Two Lines of Semitic and Indo-European Dispersion," figure 49 from Breasted and Robinson's *Outlines of European History, Part I* (1914). "The actual lines along which these peoples lie are of course not straight. The lines sometimes overlie each other, as in Sicily, mentioned in both lines. Egypt, which geographically belongs in the southern line, has been omitted because it is not purely Semitic, although closely related to the Semites. . . . Notice also that in the west the two races face each other for the most part across the Mediterranean; in the east they confront each other along the 'fertile crescent.'" Public domain, reproduction by author.

on the golden age of Athens, the reader accompanies a citizen of the city-state through its center:

> Wandering into the market place, the citizen found an imposing colonnaded porch along one side . . . : the wall behind the columns bore a series of paintings . . . depicting [the Athenians'] glorious victory at Marathon. . . . He could . . . hear some old man tell how the brother of Aeschylus seized and tried to stop one of the Persian boats drawn up on the beach. . . . Perhaps among the group of eager listeners he might notice one questioning the veteran carefully and making full notes of all that he can learn from the graybeard. The questioner is Herodotus, the "father of history," the first great prose writer to devote himself to the story of the past. He is collecting from survivors the tale of the Persian wars for a history he is writing. . . .
>
> Above him towers the height of the Acropolis crowned with the Parthenon, a noble temple to Athena, whose protecting arm is always stretched out over her beloved Athens. . . . The tinkle of many distant hammers from the height above tells where the stone cutters are shaping the marble blocks for the still unfinished Parthenon; and there . . . the people often see Pericles intently inspecting the work, as Phidias the sculptor and Ictinus the architect of the

building pace up and down the inclosure, explaining to him the progress of the work. . . .

Phidias is the greatest of the sculptors at Athens. In a long band of carved marble extending entirely around the . . . Parthenon, Phidias and his pupils have portrayed . . . the sovereign people of Athens moving in the stately procession of the Pan-Athenaic festival. . . .

When the Athenian citizen turns homeward . . . , he and his neighbor [discuss] how they shall educate their sons. There are the old subjects which have always been taught: reading and writing, the study of the old poets, music and dancing, and the athletic exercises at the gymnasium. But their sons [want] to hear . . . a class of new and clever-witted lecturers, who wander from city to city, and whom the people call "Sophists." The Sophists . . . doubt everything, and make all conclusions impossible. Yes, . . . they are wonderful speakers. . . . And they teach a young man such readiness in speech that he can carry the people with him in the Assembly. They have indeed created a new art, the art of oratory and of writing prose, and no young man can do without it.

[It] is a pity they are such an impious crew . . . ; but when one of them actually writes a book which begins with a statement doubting the existence of the gods, what is a citizen to do but vote that the book be burned? And the worst of it is that there are several bookshops in the city and people read such books. Why, even the sausage-peddler who delivers meat to the citizen's door can read!

Breasted's stroll through Athens knits the lessons of Greek history, historiography, architecture, art, education, philosophy, and literacy into a lively tableau that his young readers could indeed "see and feel it live."[40]

The book's most memorable expression came almost as an afterthought in mid-June 1914 as *Outlines* was being typeset. The illustrations and captions, including maps, were mostly done, and he was concentrating on simplifying wording. At the beginning of chapter 3, on Babylonia, Assyria, and Chaldea, he has a brief description of the area's geography and the arc of land where these ancient civilizations first arose. He initially characterized it as a "borderland between desert and mountains—a kind of cultivatable fringe of the desert." Perhaps recalling an observation in an ancient history survey by his late colleague and friend George S. Goodspeed that "Looking at the whole region . . . , we observe that it has somewhat the character of a crescent," Breasted revised his text, summing up the area's nature and shape as a "fertile crescent." Uncertain about the expression's utility, Breasted had it inserted on a map of the region in tiny type below "cultivatable fringe," an inelegant solution to be cleaned up in his forthcoming ancient history's map (figure 5.5). Breasted realized he was coining a new expression but did not anticipate its rapid dissemination. An indication of the popularity of "Fertile Crescent" as a shorthand is the ire it soon attracted

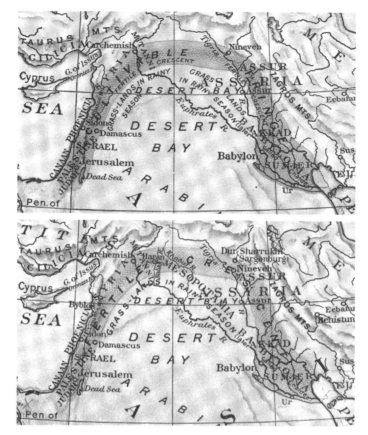

Fig. 5.5 Top, detail of map "The Ancient Orient" from Breasted and Robinson's *Outlines of European History, Part I* (1914), insert between pp. 56–57; bottom, detail of map "The Ancient Oriental World" from Breasted's *Ancient Times* (1916), insert between pp. 102–3. Public domain, reproductions by author.

from scholars who took issue with its accuracy. Whether or not the expression is sufficiently precise, it epitomizes Breasted's genius for translating arcane research into popular, easy-to-grasp language.[41]

Outlines sold well from the outset, thirteen thousand copies in the first half year, and Breasted's share of the royalties, 4 percent, amounted to about $655. His section of *Outlines* was issued as a separate volume in 1915 as *A Short Ancient History*, apparently to mollify the publisher, who was keen on issuing a separate ancient history survey, even if abbreviated, rather than await Breasted's fuller treatment. Revised and enlarged, as well as abridged, editions of *Outlines* were published in subsequent years under a dizzying variety of titles. One estimate places the cumulative sales for the textbook's many versions at over a million copies by the mid-1940s. *Outlines* was not widely reviewed and then only in education journals. Its handful of reviewers held it in high regard, especially for Breasted's illustration scheme. One applauded the images as "well chosen, distinctly reproduced, and accompanied by an explanatory statement. No student needs to miss the significance of a single picture."

There were complaints, however. A Ginn sales representative reported that "people are kicking about the difficulty" of Breasted's writing. "They say the language is often so figurative that the ninth grade kids don't get the point at all. A case in point is the paragraph about Horace. . . . These literal-minded youngsters think that he actually fell into the river." The offending passage tells how Horace "had been caught in the dangerous current of his time, and, as he was swept along in the violent stream of civil war, he had with difficulty struggled ashore and at last found secure footing in the general peace." Hilton forwarded the criticism, commenting, "It may be that you will need to make your ancient history even simpler than your part of the Outlines."[42]

A Proper Knowledge of the Past, a Better Understanding of the Future

To prepare for his ancient history, Breasted surveyed almost forty other textbooks, not "for the sake of their content, but in order to observe the method of treatment" and thereby profit from their "virtues and mistakes." Hilton brought up one volume in particular as exemplary of the competition, Hutton Webster's *Ancient History*, issued in 1913 by one of Ginn's main competitors, D. C. Heath and Company. Hilton said teachers particularly liked the study guides at the end of each chapter, and he called to Breasted's attention Heath's promotional pitch that "Teachers of ancient history have been looking for a text which would portray the life of the people—the industrial, the commercial, the social, the religious life; the school and the home life as well as the military and the political life. Such a text is Webster's." Breasted had read it earlier and found not only an abundance of egregious errors and "ineffective and insufficient" illustrations, but a confusing structure as well. As an example he cited Webster's treatment of Greek art in a section separate from the period in which it was created. Breasted remarked, "I must confess . . . in view of your report that the Webster book is proving a strong competitor, my blood is up."[43]

The content of Breasted's ancient history was determined largely by his share of *Outlines*, although he extended its scope to the rise and spread of Islam in the middle of the eighth century. The narrative grew in depth, and the number of illustrations, including diagrams and maps, expanded. Having now had even more experience with the translation of photographs into line drawings and halftones, he was far more specific about desired results. This knowledge turned problematic, however, as he requested ever finer modifications, often regarding details that were barely visible to the naked eye. He also wanted to systematically incorporate chapter heading and tailpieces in his illustration scheme by numbering and captioning each. At the time, head- and tailpieces were typically used only as

CHAPTER XV

ATHENS IN THE AGE OF PERICLES

SECTION 54. SOCIETY, THE HOME, EDUCATION AND
TRAINING OF YOUNG CITIZENS

546. Athenian society: the wealthy classes   As we have seen, the population of Attica was made up of citizens, foreigners, and slaves. In a mixed crowd there would usually be among every ten people about four slaves, one or two foreigners, and the rest free Athenians (see § 536). A large group of wealthy citizens lived at Athens upon the income from their lands. They continued to be the aristocracy of the nation, for land was still the most respectable form of wealth. The wealthy manufacturer hastened to buy land and join the landed aristocracy. The social position of his family might thus become an influential one, but it could not compare with that of a noble.

NOTE. The above headpiece gives us a glimpse into the house of a bride the day after the wedding. At the right, leaning against a couch, is the bride. Before her are two young friends, one sitting, the other standing, both playing with a tame bird. Another friend approaches carrying a tall and beautiful painted vase as a wedding gift. At the left a visitor arranges flowers in two painted vases, while another lady, adjusting her garment, is looking on. The walls are hung with festive wreaths. The furniture of such a house was usually of wood, but if the owner's wealth permitted, it was adorned with ivory, silver, and gold. It consisted chiefly of beds, like the couch above, chairs (see also Fig. 170), footstools (as at foot of couch above), small individual tables, and clothing chests which took the place of closets.

350

Fig. 5.6 Chapter opening from Breasted's *Ancient Times* (1916). Note the boldface numeral leading the paragraph topic statement in the left margin, the use of the § symbol in the fourth line signaling a cross-reference to paragraph 536, and the caption for the headpiece at the bottom of the page. Public domain, reproduction by author.

ornaments. They sporadically appeared in *Outlines*, and Breasted used them like illustrations, but without numbers or captions, instead explaining them in the text. By assuring there were head- and tailpieces for each of his projected chapters, all included in the illustration plan, Breasted could increase his budget by about sixty images. Ginn met him halfway, allowing headpieces for each chapter, tailpieces where feasible, and captions in the form of footnotes, but they were not to be assigned illustration numbers (figure 5.6).[44]

All initially assumed the new book's design had to follow that for *Outlines*. Such was not the case, however, and Breasted grabbed the opportunity to propose an alternative to cross-referencing with page numbers, an approach he found too imprecise. Instead, he suggested numbering paragraphs—as he did in *Ancient Records*. Ginn tried out Breasted's idea by typesetting a few "dummy" pages but disliked the results on aesthetic grounds and recommended sticking with the *Outlines* design. Breasted sent an intemperate reply, quoting Shakespeare to the effect that the Ginn staff was a bunch of "dotards." This did not go down well at Ginn, and one of the executives sarcastically proposed relying on the index instead. Breasted, not getting the quip, regarded the notion as akin to a

Fig. 5.7 "An Ancient Hittite and His Modern Armenian Descendant," figure 146 from Breasted's *Ancient Times* (1916). "At the left is the head of an ancient Hittite as carved by an Egyptian sculptor . . . over three thousand years ago. It strikingly resembles the profile of the Armenians still living in the Hittite country, as shown in the modern portrait on the right. The strongly aquiline and prominent nose of the Hittites was also acquired by the neighboring Semites along the eastern end of the Mediterranean." Public domain, reproduction by author.

"human body dispossessed of its nervous system." In the end he prevailed, using numbers prefaced with the paragraph symbol (§) for his cross-references.[45]

There were other dustups. One concerned an image comparing an Egyptian relief depicting a Hittite with a profile of a modern Armenian (figure 5.7). Breasted had asked Ginn's artist to "bring out the Jewish type of features, with the prominent aquiline nose," to illustrate an assertion regarding the Hittites' leaving "their mark upon their neighbors": "We recall the prominent aquiline nose of the Hittite people. The same feature among the Hebrews shows how the Hittites drifted down the west end of the Fertile Crescent, until they reached Palestine in sufficient numbers to affect the Hebrew type of face." A Ginn editor objected, regarding the statement as anti-Semitic, and Breasted was asked to delete it. He replied that he was willing to do so but countered by referring the editor to the book's seventh chapter ("The Hebrews and the Decline of the Orient"), where "they are given about as high a place as it is possible to accord a people in human history."

There is some truth in Breasted's statement, though in that chapter he treats their contributions as transitional. The Old Testament, he writes, "tells the story of how a rude shepherd folk issued from the wilds of the Arabian desert, to live in Palestine and to go through experiences there which made them the religious teachers of the civilized world. And . . . crowning all their history, there came forth from them in due time the founder of the Christian religion." In further defense of his Hittite-Hebrew comparison, Breasted argued, "Probably profane Gentile boys would enjoy annoying their Hebrew neighbors as you suggest, but I believe your editor is misinformed about the feeling of intelligent Hebrews. I taught Hebrew for years,—I have had much to do with them, and the best Hebrews are proud of their race, and not ashamed of their noses. I have heard a well-known rabbi refer to their noses in the pulpit. There is a small minority who would conceal their race and reduce their noses if they could." Yet, Breasted allowed, "With some members of this minority you may some time come into conflict, and I am ready to do anything within reason to avoid offending even these few." Despite his concession the text remained unchanged.[46]

Ginn hoped to publish the book early enough in 1915 for it to be adopted by the beginning of the 1915–16 academic year. Breasted was lagging behind schedule, however, and arranged for a leave from teaching during Chicago's spring quarter to speed up work. By March they agreed that the book, which was ballooning to a projected seven hundred pages, would not be done in time, and they aimed for the following year. Most of the production and editorial problems were cleared away in the following months save one: the book's title.

Breasted originally wanted to title it "The Story of Early Man," but Hilton insisted the words "ancient history" be somewhere in the title, so Breasted changed it to "Sketch of Ancient History." An editor shot back that "it does not seem appropriate to call a 700-page book a sketch" and the title was scrapped. Hoping to market Breasted's book alongside an expanded survey by Robinson tentatively titled "Mediaeval and Modern Times," the editor suggested Breasted call his "Ancient Times." Breasted found this "most uneuphonius" and believed "everybody will pronounce it 'Ancientimes.'" He nonetheless agreed—for about a month. Breasted fretted about the absence of "history" from the title and proposed "A History of the Early World" as an appendage to the main title, followed by an already agreed-upon subtitle. After some haggling they settled on the cumbersome "Ancient Times/A History of the Early World/An Introduction to the Study of Ancient History and the Career of Early Man."[47]

Meanwhile, Hilton continued to worry about the text's readability for high school students and proposed having the manuscript "read and criticized by a number of secondary school men" before it was set to type. "We want this book absolutely bullet-proof," Hilton wrote, "and the only way we can be sure of this is to subject it to a bombardment from several directions." Breasted accepted Hilton's suggestion but replied, "I have at last got next to the ordinary first-year high school boy, and I think I have learned the art of simplification to the uttermost. This art takes more time and attention than any style of presentation I have ever before attempted."

The readers' comments were generally approving. One reader who gave the manuscript high marks noted specifically its "remarkable literary style" and commented approvingly on Breasted's handling of large questions including the emphasis "everywhere on man and his progress and civilization. Man and not the organization of history is the theme. . . . Splendid treatment of ethnology and migrations in the ancient world. . . . No other history for secondary schools has accomplished this." Further, the reader found, it possessed "a sincere devotion to history as it is revealed by documentary evidence. . . . Concrete facts of great informational interest. For example . . . writing . . . metals . . . horses . . . castles . . . alphabet . . . paper." Breasted's handling of illustrations, captions, and cross-references were also lauded. On the other hand, he was criticized for the "priority of Egyptian culture and civilization" and for his tendency to argue "the non-existence of things from the absence of historical evidence to the contrary." Robinson, who read the galleys, was enthusiastic: "Gosh, you're a wonder, man! Very delightfully & marvelously fresh & interesting."[48]

Not long after the book had been typeset and Breasted approved the galleys, he learned that another, earlier survey, *Ancient History* (1906) by Philip Van Ness Myers, had been revised and was to be published in time to compete with his own—by Ginn. Breasted felt that "herein lay the fatality of having . . . published my sketch of ancient hist. in Outlines I. On the basis of that Myers has been able to revamp his own antiquated book!" Whether true or not, this news caused Breasted to cut "20% of my illustrative scheme, so that the unusual size of my book would not shut it out in competition with Myers," a change that necessitated over five thousand revisions.

The rivalry and Ginn's role in fostering it speaks to the era's growing commercial opportunities in textbook publishing. Between 1880 and 1910 the number of students attending high school rose from 110,300, less than 3 percent of high school–age children, to 915,000, or over 15 percent of the same age group. By 1915 high school enrollment had risen to 1.3 million, and the upward trend continued to accelerate in subsequent years as the population grew and an increasing percentage was expected to complete high school. Moreover, by 1914–15 about half the students were taking classes in European history, which included separate courses in ancient history.

Between the 1880s and the second decade of the twentieth century, history "was seen as an appropriate vehicle for implementing the cultural and political socialization task of the high school. . . . As perceptions of what this socialization should consist of changed, so did the history curriculum. For example, ancient history, when it was offered in the classical high school complemented the political socialization task of producing students imbued in classical values of government and culture." When education policy leaders and school boards around the nation began to place greater emphasis on history, the number of history-course offerings rose dramatically. The percentage of schools offering ancient history courses increased from about 30 percent on average in the 1880s and 1890s to 100 percent by 1916 and continued at about that level through the 1920s. By 1915 over 50 percent of schools required students to take ancient history courses. Textbook publishers responded with an outpouring of ancient history books, issuing thirty-six titles between 1880 and 1930. Of these about eight enjoyed some measure of popularity, with Myers's *Ancient History* far and away dominating the field from its first appearance in 1888 until well into the first quarter of the twentieth century. Both *Outlines* and *Ancient Times* entered a field of stiff competition. Of all this Breasted wondered, "Will the schools buy Myers's second hand stuff, or show discernment enough to prefer an authoritative treatment?"[49]

Ancient Times was issued in August 1916, in time for the 1916–17 school year. It was long, amounting to over 740 pages, whereas Myers's *Ancient History*, issued the previous spring, came to just under 600 pages. In his preface, Breasted explained that the greater length was due in part to his "symmetrical presentation" of the "origins of civilization and the history of the Orient," in comparison with ancient Greece and Rome, because of recent Near Eastern excavations and discoveries that had yet to be "surveyed and briefly presented in a form intelligible to younger students." Taking a swipe at the competition, Breasted continued, "A textbook which devotes a brief fifty- or sixty-page introduction to the Orient and begins 'real history' with the Greeks is not proportioned in accordance with modern knowledge of the ancient world." In acknowledging that *Ancient Times* was "somewhat larger than the current textbooks on ancient history," he also attributed the "excess . . . to the series of illustrations. The book actually contains a text of about five hundred pages, with a 'picture book' of about two hundred and fifteen pages." He then urged teachers to "make the illustrations and accompanying descriptive matter a part of each lesson" because these "if noted and used, will be found to merge text and illustrations into a unified whole."[50]

The "picture book" quality of *Ancient Times* is evident in many features, including "sequence maps," an expression Breasted coined for groups of maps arranged to present "successive epochs of history . . . in terms of geography." They are based on the creation of two or more maps from the same underlying plate to illustrate the spread or decline of civilizations and other sociocultural changes in chronological steps (figure 5.8). Breasted felt his sequence maps would "prove a powerful aid to the teacher" and included seven sets, along with more than forty individual maps, most printed in elaborate color schemes. A selection was issued as classroom wall maps in 1916, followed by a teacher's manual in 1918 and several subsequent editions that adorned schools throughout the country. Reductions of the wall maps were issued as textbook-size student atlases starting in 1920.

Breasted's illustrations for *Ancient Times* furthered his efforts to make "con-

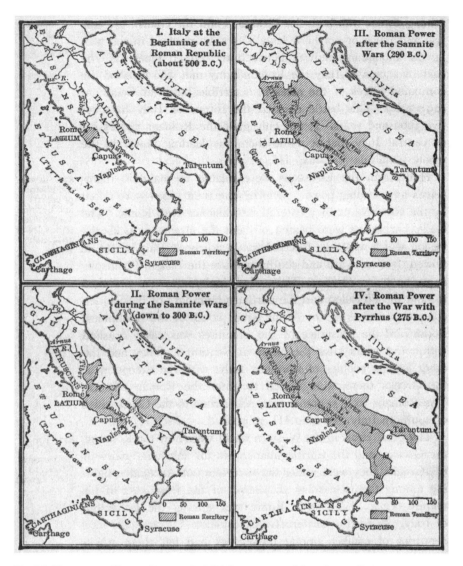

Fig. 5.8 "Expansion of Roman Power in Italy." A "sequence map" from Breasted's *Ancient Times* (1916), 516. Public domain, reproduction by author.

crete" the material reality of famous objects, such as the entire Code of Hammurabi, of which other authors depicted only the relief at the stela's head (figure 5.9). Some are significant revisions of images first presented in *Outlines*, a striking example being a diagram on the evolution of mortuary architecture in Egypt that was augmented with additional images and text, dramatically scaled typography—the "Barbarism-Civilization" sequence likely based on a theory of the pioneering evolutionary anthropologist Lewis Morgan—and an expanded caption the length of a short essay (figure 5.10; compare with figure 5.3).[51]

Fig. 5.9 Left, "Monument Containing the Code of Hammurabi," figure from Webster's *Ancient History* (1913), 37; right, "The Laws of Hammurapi, the Oldest Surviving Code of Laws (2100 B.C.)," figure 93 from Breasted's *Ancient Times* (1916). Public domain, reproductions by author.

Ancient Times was reviewed in more than thirty periodicals published in the United States and, surprisingly for a textbook, abroad. The variety of journals reviewing it strongly suggest Breasted had a hand in the publicity campaign. British, French, and German reviews, many in periodicals related to Breasted's fields of expertise, stand in sharp contrast to those in American education-profession outlets—the former almost certainly suggested by Breasted, the latter from Ginn's marketing list. All the reviews are favorable and the majority unstinting in their praise, even among those who might find reason for complaints. The scholar who read it for the *Jewish Quarterly Review* noted Breasted's "aquiline nose" theory and, finding a precedent for it in another researcher's work, seemed to take comfort in the notion that it "was really a feature belonging to the (non-Semitic) Hittites, who intermarried with the people of Palestine."

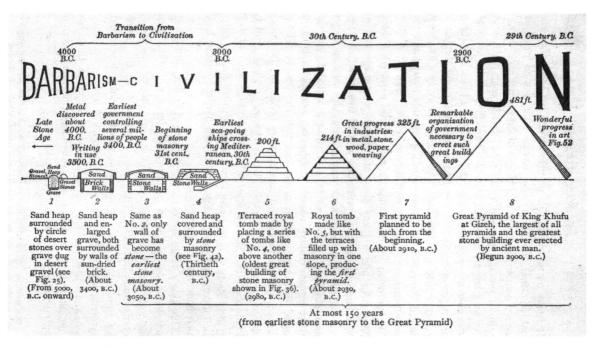

Fig. 5.10 "The Evolution from the Sand Heap to the Pyramid in Two Thousand Years, and the Rise of Stone Architecture in One Hundred and Fifty Years," figure 38 from Breasted's *Ancient Times* (1916). Public domain, reproduction by author.

Scholars writing for ancient history journals were more probing. A reviewer in *Ancient Egypt* questioned the diagram on pyramids (figure 5.10) over the validity of the progression Breasted conjectured from "deep graves" to "discovery of metals" and their relation to the origins of step pyramids. Another, in *Classical Weekly*, wryly observed that those "working in the Greek and Roman fields may think that the latter pages of the history are rather too plentifully sprinkled with libations of Nile water." Nonetheless, he considered *Ancient Times* "the best book on ancient history for Schools that we have. . . . It has better illustrations and better maps than any other book . . . , and the descriptive matter under the illustrations is full, and interesting, and has set a pattern which must be followed."

While the influence of Breasted's illustration scheme on subsequent textbooks is unclear, his views on the importance of the ancient Near East in European history clearly did influence others. There soon emerged a "trend among historians of the ancient world . . . away from an exclusive concern with the European cultures of the Greeks and Romans." Even in Europe "American professor James Henry Breasted . . . won wide acceptance for the thesis that modern civilization—that is, European civilization—had its beginnings not in Greece and Rome, but in the Middle East." Those "roots" of civilization were "seen to have culminated in the global supremacy of the European peoples, their ideals, and their way of life," a perspective that bolstered the interests of European leaders in "creating the modern Middle East" in the wake of the First World War.

For education journals' reviewers, Breasted's scholarly background and growing renown were significant validations. One wrote, "We do not see how any man could be better qualified to write an ancient history than . . . Breasted, a scholar of international reputation, who has spent much time among the actual records. . . . He has . . . been responsible for many important discoveries." Many, whether academics writing for scholarly peers or educators writing for secondary-school teachers, struck a similar theme: "Breasted's Ancient History will be as eagerly welcomed by the advanced scholar as by the high school teacher and pupil." *Ancient Times* found a far greater audience, however, when it was vaulted into the realm of popular reading by the enthusiastic review of a nationally known opinion leader: Teddy Roosevelt.[52]

A published writer and "freelance historian" before he entered politics, Roosevelt returned to these vocations after leaving the presidency in 1909. His devotion to history prompted his election as first vice president of the American Historical Association in 1910 and as its president a year later. Breasted may have met Roosevelt at the association's 1910 conference in Indianapolis, where Breasted also met Robinson. That Roosevelt was acquainted with Breasted's work seems evident from the former's valedictory address as the association's outgoing president in 1912. Titled "History as Literature," it called for historians to transcend the increasing specialization of their discipline in order to embrace not only the empirical tenets of science but the poetic power of literature as well. Roosevelt displayed his historical bona fides, citing Robinson's *New History* for example, but he did so only to argue that history, "taught for a directly and immediately useful purpose to pupils and the teachers of pupils, is one of the necessary features of a sound education in democratic citizenship." Thus the "historian should . . . be a great moralist," "be able to paint for us the life of the . . . ordinary men and women of the time of which he writes," and "bring the past before our eyes as if it were the present." Roosevelt cites examples from many periods, including antiquity, the historians of which have "the genius to reconstruct for us the immense panorama of the past . . . whether it be Egypt, or Mesopotamia" as exemplified by "men like Maspero, Breasted, and Weigall."

Roosevelt's regard for Breasted was based on *History of Egypt. Outlines* and *Ancient Times* were still a few years in the future. When *Ancient Times* was issued, Breasted sent a copy to Roosevelt, who, as he was passing through Chicago in October 1916, invited Breasted to a hotel-room meeting. Roosevelt was traveling across the country rallying support for America's entry into the First World War or, barring that, authorization to raise a division of troops to lead in a flanking operation through the Middle East against Germany. Roosevelt was interested in Breasted's opinion of the latter plan in terms of the terrain Roosevelt hoped to capture and geopolitical interests in the region. Of course nothing came of Roosevelt's plan, but a friendship between the two ensued. At some point during this period Roosevelt offered to review *Ancient Times*, first in *National Geographic*, which turned down his offer. When Roosevelt sought Breasted's advice, confessing "I have not much experience in review writing," he suggested *Outlook* magazine, with which Roosevelt was already associated.[53]

Prior to leaving the White House, Roosevelt was courted by several periodicals including *Outlook*, which pursued him as a "special contributing editor," an assignment he formally took up in June 1910. *Outlook* began in the mid-1860s as a family-oriented Protestant magazine that was subsequently transformed into an independent, nondenominational Christian weekly. By the 1910s *Outlook* "stood for a liberal religion, progressive politics, and a love of letters," and as its editorial philosophy broadened, its circulation rose, from about 30,000 in the early 1890s to over 100,000 by the late 1890s. Its circulation spiked after Roosevelt signed on, and *Outlook* became a widely read source for his views on domestic politics and international affairs, as well as personal accounts of his travels and ruminations on American society and culture.

In February 1917, shortly after Breasted's visit and just six months after *Ancient Times* was issued, Roosevelt reviewed it for *Outlook*. Titled "The Dawn and Sunrise of History," Roosevelt's review is a long, detailed, and approving synopsis. It begins by observing the advances in ancient Near Eastern research during the previous two generations that "until recently the Frenchman Maspero . . . had done most to popularize, without fictionizing." That is, until "one of our own men," Breasted, "produced the best book of its kind that has ever been written on the subject." Noting that it was written for high schools, Roosevelt continues, "perhaps for that very reason—inasmuch as the very best book for intelligent and well-grown boys is usually an uncommonly good book for grown-up men and women—his work is absorbingly interesting for everyone." "If the study of man is to be taken seriously," Roosevelt concludes, then *Ancient Times* "should occupy the foremost place in the curriculum of our schools and colleges, and in the recreative study which hard-working, well-informed, cultivated men and women find essential in after life."[54]

Ancient Times's host of adulatory reviews boosted sales, which reached an average of 100,000 copies a year by 1920. Though it never overtook Myers's *Ancient History* as a "staple of Ancient History teaching" in America, the large adult readership of *Ancient Times* established Breasted's reputation as one of the nation's leading experts in the field and the figure most commonly associated with ancient Near Eastern archaeology for many Americans. The wide acclaim also helped secure Breasted's authority among those in powerful places. One was Rockefeller advisor Frederick T. Gates, who responded effusively: "Your book meets my want, answers innumerable questions on my lips for years, is written in a fascinating style, and for the first time gives me some measure of the debt we owe to ancient times. . . . This is a book . . . to commend to every lover of books . . . & of the story of human progress." Another was Abby Rockefeller, wife of John D. Rockefeller Jr., who, after reading *Ancient Times*, wrote that "Mr. Rockefeller has promised to read it to our daughter of thirteen and myself this summer." She closed by thanking Breasted "with sincere appreciation of what you have done in giving a proper knowledge of the past, which should give us a better understanding of the future."[55]

6

The Near East as a Whole

Grant Applications and Disciplinarity

Breasted was a "lonely man, who, though he possessed an enormous number of acquaintances who were very fond of him, . . . throughout his life numbered only two or three friends for whom he cherished an unreservedly whole-hearted regard and affection. Of these, his friendship for Dr. Hale was by far the greatest." The friend of whom Breasted's son wrote was the world-renowned astronomer and scientific impresario George Ellery Hale. Though three years younger than Breasted, Hale identified his life's work early and achieved a prominent career more quickly thanks to the unstinting support of wealthy parents. He grew up on Chicago's south side in a neighborhood near the future home of the University of Chicago. Hale built instruments for analyzing solar spectra in a workshop adjacent to his parents' home *prior* to formal training at the Massachusetts Institute of Technology. After returning from Cambridge, he designed and equipped a comparatively advanced observatory, also on his parents' property, and began contributing findings to scientific journals. By his twenty-third birthday he had invented a valuable new instrument for solar spectography, cofounded a scientific journal, and been elected a fellow of Great Britain's Royal Astronomical Society.

William Rainey Harper recruited Hale at the rank of associate professor and as director of his observatory, which Hale's father donated to the university. Hale worked without salary, but Chicago provided an assistant at the rank of "docent" along with a budget of $1,500 a year. However, Hale's research goals had already grown beyond his telescope's capacity, and in 1892 he persuaded Charles T. Yerkes to underwrite a new observatory. Completed in 1897 on Lake Geneva near Williams Bay, Wisconsin, the Yerkes Observatory contained a forty-inch refracting telescope, the world's largest at the time, complemented by an array of darkrooms and laboratories equipped for advanced experiments in chemistry and physics. The observatory complex led an advance in astronomy from a reliance on untested interpretations of spectrograms from natural phenomena to their validation by comparison with spectrograms from controlled environments in which physicists and chemists replicated "various conditions of temperature and pressure encountered in the stars . . . and . . . the behavior of metals and gases." Hale's Yerkes Observatory design was "revolutionary" because it proved his seminal insight about the necessity of integrating instrument making, observation, and experiment-based verification.

Despite this success, however, by 1903 Hale had begun exploring construction of an even larger instrument in the cool, clear air of Mount Wilson near Pasadena, California. After receiving a grant from the Carnegie Foundation, Hale resigned from Chicago to direct what became the Mount Wilson Solar Observatory. During this period he started a second scientific journal, formed a professional society for American astronomers, and was elected to the National Academy of Sciences, which had been established under federal charter in 1863. His pivotal work on spectrographic studies of solar flares and sunspots and his 1908 discovery of solar magnetic fields would, alone, have established his reputation as one of the twentieth century's leading scientists. Yet equally important were Hale's entrepreneurial and leadership skills as he pioneered the coordination of colleagues, private philanthropy, public policy, institution building, and the popularization of research into what today is called "big science."[1]

Breasted and Hale probably met shortly after the former's arrival on campus in 1895, perhaps through their mutual friendship with George S. Goodspeed and his wife. By 1897 Hale was a contributor to Breasted's Chicago Society of Egyptian Research, and the Breasteds attended the formal inauguration of the Yerkes Observatory. In 1905, after Hale departed for California, he invited the Breasted family to summer in the house he retained in Williams Bay near Yerkes Observatory. After that they fell out of regular contact until probably sometime just prior to a Hale family trip to Egypt in January 1911 for which Hale sought Breasted's advice. Around that time, while passing through Chicago, Hale took him to lunch and provided much-welcomed encouragement at a time when Breasted was feeling disheartened about his career. By 1914 Hale was assisting Breasted's search for research funds, in part by helping him make contacts among philanthropists and opinion leaders, and partly by validating Breasted's work in prominent forums like the National Academy of Sciences.[2]

Looking ahead to the academy's fiftieth anniversary in 1913, Hale thought it a good opportunity to expand its functions beyond meeting annually to do little more than elect new members. Starting in 1912 he launched a reform effort with a series of three addresses based on a study of the major European academies that were subsequently published in *Science*. The first and second addresses, "The Work of European Academies" and "The First Half Century of the National Academy of Sciences," emphasized the accomplishments and influence of academies abroad to show that the American academy was by contrast an underachiever. The third address, "The Future of the National Academy of Sciences," offered suggestions to increase the institution's usefulness and influence.

Hale's recommendations included publishing members' research; educating the public by disseminating news of scientific progress through the Associated Press; supporting science education in the schools, perhaps with a lecture series on evolution "beginning with . . . the constitution of matter" and concluding with "an account of early Oriental peoples, the rise of the Egyptian dynasties, and their influence on modern progress"; and building a permanent headquarters in Washington, DC, complete with meeting rooms, laboratories, and publicly accessible "historical exhibits" on science. Further, Hale decried the impediments flowing from increasing specialization in the sciences, and he explored ways to expand the disciplines represented by the academy's membership. He wondered if the academy should expand its membership beyond "the physical and natural sciences, and in what measure may it recognize successful research in such fields as philosophy, archeology, political economy, and history." Hale believed that "a means of defining our choice of investigators in the humanities may easily be found," and he cited as examples "the classical archeologist or the student of Egyptology or Assyriology." "Would it not be advisable," Hale asked, "when the Academy chooses its next member from outside the domain of the physical and natural sciences, to elect an archeologist from one of these fields?"[3]

The academy's governing council distributed Hale's paper for members' comment prior to meeting again in April 1914. Hale sent a copy to Breasted, inviting the latter's observations as well. His imagination fired by the possibilities, Breasted replied with two letters written the same day. In the first he proposed enlarging the academy's membership categories by adding a "Historico-Philosophical Section" to "represent the Humanities," which would combine the social sciences and humanities in a grouping that included anthropology, psychology, education, political economy, and sociology alongside philosophy, history, and philology. The academy already had a section for archaeology and psychology, with archaeology represented by three anthropologists investigating pre-Columbian and postcontact Native American subjects. In America by then "archaeology, ethnology, physical anthropology, and linguistics [were] regarded as different branches of anthropology." Breasted also recommended a more specific membership breakdown within the fields of history, archaeology, and philology that would add nine new representatives. Under archaeology there would be three: one for Egypt, Assyria, Babylonia, and Asia Minor; one for the Mediterranean; and one for India, China, and Japan.

In his second letter, Breasted anticipated misgivings natural scientists might harbor about the rigorousness of humanities scholarship by arguing that "the methods which aroused such distrust are now long since antiquated. . . . An important illustration . . . is archaeological research. . . . Paleolithic archaeology is furnishing the geologist with a sequence of forms in human industry which enable the geologist to date natural formations by means of artefacts contained in them." "As the period of time under investigation goes on," Breasted conceded, "the two sciences of course part company"; nonetheless, "as man's advance continues, social processes emerge, but their study is carried on exactly as in natural science, with this unavoidable difference, . . . we are not able to repeat the experiment." However, he pointed out, "this limitation" applies to research in the natural sciences, such as astronomy or geology. The real problem was that "research in the humanities is sadly in need of organized assistance in the United States. It possesses no national centre." While the humanities were creating "plural organized worlds" primarily among university departments and scholarly associations, they lacked a mechanism—like the National Academy of Sciences—for communicating with one another or advocating their priorities to national policy makers.[4]

When Hale reported academy members' responses to his proposals, he found that out of seventy-five respondents, fifty-two approved enlarging its membership, with only eight opposed and the balance having no opinion. When it came to adding humanities scholars, eight approved, three opposed, and the vast majority had no opinion. One who approved adding the humanities referred to the academy's founding aims, writing that "we should now aim to reestablish . . . the 'philosophy' which originally was meant to embrace all that is knowable, and which should form the scope of the . . . Academy." Hale also quoted most of Breasted's suggestions referring to him as "one outside of the Academy, in whom I have great confidence." Hale concluded by recommending the election of humanities scholars, suggesting they "should have a real part in the work, and the Academy should do something for them." "We might pick men who have the most scientific viewpoint of their work," Hale suggested. "I know there are those who work . . . exactly as any member might work . . . , and who treat it precisely as a natural scientist treats his work."

Hale positioned Breasted for election to the academy in the next year or two, a step that would bring aboard an ally for Hale's plans while also adding a "scientific" endorsement his friend could show to prospective donors and opinion leaders. But the outbreak of the First World War that summer overshadowed the initiative. Hale foresaw a role for the academy in a national mobilization should the United States be drawn into the war, and he turned to coordinating scientific and industrial planning in preparation for the worst. The National Research Council, established in 1916 under the academy's auspices and continuing to this day, was a result. Hale chaired it until 1919.[5]

He also assisted Breasted's grant-seeking by prodding him to articulate his objectives more clearly. Hale thus posed hypothetical donors' questions: They "may ask how many inscriptions not previously known or deciphered would be copied. Also how much the work would contribute to new knowledge instead of recording what is already known." Breasted replied that "the number of unstudied inscriptions is very large, though the number absolutely unknown is . . . very limited." But, Breasted continued, "You can form no idea of how incomplete, inaccurate and slovenly the old copies . . . are. The difference between an old and modern photograph of a nebula may suggest to you the vast difference between a copy of an inscription made today and a copy made twenty-five years ago. Although in both the case of the nebula and that of the inscription, the <u>original</u> has long been known, only the <u>modern</u> reproduction of it furnishes any adequate basis for study. . . . A copy of an Aswan inscription, made over twenty years ago, tells us . . . a certain official there made ten journeys to a land, the name of which was read by the copyist as [nearby] Punt." However, Breasted continued, "a modern copy . . . shows that the name . . . is Byblos." Because Byblos was located much farther away, on the eastern rim of the Mediterranean, the corrected transcription "throws an almost epoch-making light on navigation . . . and the foreign connections of Egypt" about 2600–2200 BCE. Breasted argued there was an inestimable amount of new information to be discovered by multiplying such findings by the nearly countless lines of inscriptions to be transcribed.[6]

Hale offered to present Breasted's goals to Norman Wait Harris, a Chicago financier and philanthropist friend of Hale's father. Having been a member of Breasted's Chicago Society of Egyptian Research in the 1890s and one of three donors who subsidized the publication of *Ancient Records of Egypt*, Harris already knew him and his work. By May 1914 Breasted completed a "comprehensive plan of research on the Nile" to be forwarded to Harris with a cover letter from Hale. It was nearly identical to the one he submitted to Gates in 1907, including an updated design for a "floating archaeological laboratory" (figure 6.1). The proposal did include two new items. At Hale's behest, Breasted for the first time included excavations in the scheme, but for the purpose of uncovering inscriptions as opposed to the "acquisition of antiquities." Noting that in "recent years . . . the demands of science have tended to be subordinated to the demands of the

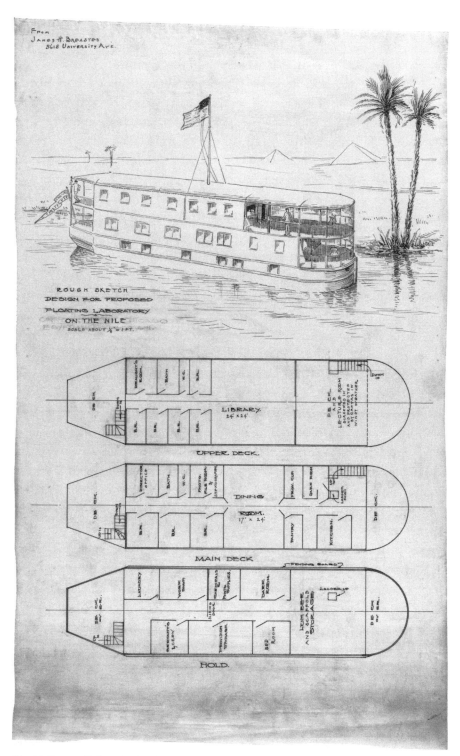

Fig. 6.1 Breasted's "Rough Sketch: Design for Proposed Floating Laboratory on the Nile," prepared ca. April 1907 and revised ca. April 1914. Courtesy of the Oriental Institute, University of Chicago.

museum," Breasted explained he was more interested in undiscovered inscriptions than museum-quality treasures. He also incorporated a development plan: "Once the Nile laboratory is afloat and at work . . . people of means would visit . . . and in watching the 'wheels go round' would soon be interested. One of my hopes is to have a deck auditorium on the boat, where we could seat guests to hear stereopticon lectures." Since the boat would "become a recognized institution" in Thebes, and given the "interest such lectures could be made to arouse, . . . there would be frequent opportunities to present . . . future plans . . . to those interested and able to support them."[7]

Breasted recast the rationale for his project, shifting from ancient Egypt's inherent significance to arguing its importance in filling a knowledge gap between the Stone Age and the rise of ancient Greece and Rome. Drawing on ideas he advanced in *Outlines of European History*, Breasted pointed to Egypt's influence on classical antiquity and the "foundations upon which European culture was built," which in turn led to a fresh observation. He noted that ancient Greece was "connected with the Orient by two links: the Mediterranean and Asia Minor." Breasted commented that the latter area was "filled with ancient city-mounds untouched and unexplored" and comprises a region in which "the problems of the transmission of civilization are to be largely solved." Given the proximity of the floating laboratory to this region, "its files and library could be made the centre for the study of the Eastern Mediterranean." Findings from Egypt and Asia Minor "would converge to be filed in its library," which "would form the best possible clearing-house for bringing together and correlating it all. Visiting scholars would be welcomed and if possible a guest-room or two on the boat should be at their disposal." The laboratory would be aligned with "American organizations like the National Academy," and its publications program would form "a valuable . . . part of the Proceedings" Hale was then establishing. "In conclusion," Breasted wrote, "the floating laboratory could be made a great archaeological institute,—the leading institution engaged in such research,—a centre to which the scientific men of the whole world would habitually turn for authoritative . . . research in the early history of civilization."[8]

Hale's cover letter to Harris, written on academy stationery, began with a report on an evolution lecture series at the academy sponsored by his family. It was inaugurated that spring with a course of papers on the beginning and constitution of matter and would proceed through several stages culminating with "the appearance of man and his first steps on the road toward civilization." "After careful consideration of the best available lecturers," Hale wrote, Breasted was selected "as the one best qualified" to address the last topic. Hale acknowledged Harris's support for *Ancient Records* and reminded him of Breasted's other accomplishments by linking ancient Egypt with the story of evolution and comparing epigraphic methods with science, commenting that his "advances . . . correspond with those . . . in astronomy through the application of new photographic methods." To continue this work, Harris's support would "establish the Harris Egyptian Institute of the National Academy of Sciences . . . which would at once take a unique place in the field of international science." Hale closed by arguing that were Harris to back this work, he "would be doing a truly national service, which would be appreciated by leaders of the state no less than by men of science" and that he would "powerfully aid" expansion of the academy's work into the humanities. In an afterthought Hale wrote, "if by any chance the Egyptian project" did not appeal to Harris, he might consider the "possibility of giving an Academy building."[9]

Harris replied that though he was interested in both projects, he was not financially able to underwrite them. Hale forwarded to Breasted news of Harris's rejection, commenting, "I have had many such experiences . . . and they have always resulted in making me all the more determined." Hale recommended another fund-raising strategy: "My present idea would be to get a number of men to contribute so much a year each, and in this way start a campaign which might be developed later so as to include the whole of your original project." But Hale wondered if the emphasis on epigraphy over excavation remained a stumbling block. "Probably we should have to devote ourselves to excavation . . . at first, as it is so much easier to interest people in this."[10]

Hale and Breasted continued discussing issues dividing what, nearly a half century later, would be characterized as the "two cultures" of the sciences and humanities. At one point Hale invited Breasted to comment on the introduction to a book he was writing about the previous ten years' accomplishments of the Mount Wilson Observatory. Hale proposed that scientists and artists were more alike than different because they shared a creative exaltation in their work. Breasted felt the analogy was flawed and offered "some further analysis." He diagrammed the relations between the subjects and objects of Hale's comparison, noting that Hale was comparing "1" and "4":

	Subject		Object
1.	Astronomer	investigates	Celestial Bodies
2.	Art Historian	investigates	Surviving Works of Art
3.	Nature or a creator	creates	Celestial Bodies
4.	The Artist	creates	Cathedrals, temples, statues, paintings, etc.

Breasted then offered three propositions: "1. There is a supreme beauty in the heretofore hidden visions disclosed by science. 2. The scientist may feel the highest joy in that beauty. 3. This feeling seems . . . akin to that of artistic creation, as in the first glow of discovery [when] the full beauty of the new vista bursts upon the discoverer." Citing paintings by the nineteenth-century British painter J. M. W. Turner, Breasted described the artistic process as being an intermingling of "tradition and the visible world" surrounding the artist, a process of discovery that is "thrust upon <u>him</u> as upon the <u>scientist</u>." Breasted then asked, "Are there not . . . (<u>after</u> observation) two processes here? First, the discovery or disengagement of the bare facts in the new area; second, the creative joy which may ensue after contemplation and presentation of the new area discerned?" Again he diagrammed these relationships:

1.	Turner's <u>discernment</u> of aerial perspective.	$\Big\} = \Big\{$ Astronomer's <u>reconstruction</u> of stellar universe.
2.	Turner's <u>painting</u> of aerial perspective.	$\Big\} = \Big\{$ Astronomer Hale's thrilling <u>picture</u> of the stellar universe. . . .

With regard to the astronomer's "reconstruction" of the universe, Breasted added that he did not mean "the collection of the <u>data</u> . . . , but the <u>discernment</u> of the system based on them." He broke this notion down into three "processes": "1. Observation; 2. Analytical discernment; 3. Constructive presentation."

Breasted's analysis missed his friend's point. Hale was trying to articulate the emotional trials and thrills of discovery rather than the nature of scientific practice. The scientist's "path," he wrote, "is steep and beset with difficulties, but it leads to heights which continually unfold new prospects of ever increasing charm." Hale and Breasted were moving in opposite directions with this colloquy, the scientist striving for poetic expressiveness, the humanist seeking analytical precision. In the end, Hale dropped the comparison.[11]

The following year Hale, who had "a new plan on foot" that made Breasted's presence in Pasadena "very desirable," invited him to give two or three illustrated lectures for an art association Hale had helped establish. He wanted Breasted to meet Henry E. Huntington, a railway baron, financier, and collector of rare books and art, who had a large estate in nearby San Marino. Hale was urging Huntington to create an institution through which his collections would be made publicly available, but he also saw in Huntington and his circle prospects for Breasted's project. Breasted accepted the invitation and proposed three "popular talks," wondering: "Can your people stand so large a dose in such quick succession?" Hale thought they could, and Breasted selected some lantern slides and headed to southern California for the first time.

Though the lectures were well received, the enthusiasm of one person who was interested in Breasted's project was blunted by his discussion of epigraphy. Breasted lamented afterward, "I shall never again make the mistake of smothering . . . interest . . . by too persistent pushing of research without reference to excavation. Evidently we must always carry on some kind of excavation, although I should always regard it as merely a means to an end—a kind of sop, if you will—a concession to popular interest." Hale and Breasted also exchanged ideas about Huntington's readiness to establish a far-reaching institution. Hale was planning a proposal for a "Pasadena Institute for Arts, Letters, and Science"—"Pasadena" a place holder for "Huntington" should he agree to fund it. Hale envisioned a research institution consisting of various discipline-specific divisions including one to be headed by Breasted. He countered with a variation on Hale's plan, calling it an "Academy of Arts, Letters and Science" that would in turn be subdivided into separate institutes, such as: "The Chemical Institute, The Geographical Institute, The Oriental Institute." But nothing immediate came of Hale's proposal.[12]

Breasted did not explain why he would name his division an *Oriental* institute rather than an *Egyptian* institute. The first indication that the scope of Breasted's project might be enlarged beyond ancient Egypt to include the "Orient"—meaning the entire ancient Near East—was in his proposal to Norman Wait Harris in 1914. Over the next two years Breasted clarified this broader if still inchoate vision. Responding to a query from Hale about "pending Oriental research," Breasted distilled his aims into four problems: "1st. Rise of Civilization," exploring the "fundamental processes in the evolution of mankind" from the Stone Age to the advent of classical antiquity; "2nd. The Decipherment of Hittite," capitalizing on the 1915 breakthrough in reading Hittite to "study . . . documents" relevant to ancient Near Eastern history as a whole; "3rd. An Assyrian and Babylonian Dictionary," the compilation of which was necessary to improve reading Assyrian and Babylonian cuneiform; "4th. Egyptian Documents and the Mediterranean Situation," the completion of Breasted's epigraphic survey to preserve surviving inscriptions and reveal the Mediterranean influences of ancient Egypt.

His preference for "Oriental Institute" thus signaled a personal adjustment from Egyptology alone to a broader historical view that coincided with Breasted's textbook writing and changes he and John M. P. Smith brought to their department at Chicago. He also connected this change with current events, claiming that the lessons of ancient history would help explain and correct the "processes still going on" in these lands "as daily illustrated by the . . . operations of the warring nations of Europe and the Near East"—a reference to nearly two years of world war. All these factors, Breasted later explained, resulted in a larger perspective that made an Oriental, rather than an Egyptian, institute necessary and viable.[13]

Breasted adapted the institute concept from a German model wherein it could exist within a university structure *and* function as an independent organization. For Breasted and others working in American research universities, the "institute had a particular appeal . . . because of growing concerns that the essential values of the university were being eroded," especially the value of "disinterested research." The vision of research-university founders like Harper was being compromised as higher education professionalized, bureaucracies grew, and swelling student populations diluted institutional resources. At several of America's leading universities, efforts to "revive the research ideal and preserve the integrity of 'real' university work" found expression in proposals like Breasted's. The research institute "promised a refuge from teaching obligations and the prospect of undisturbed time and funding for investigation" while also protecting specialized projects from competing demands. While Breasted's plan was not unique in American higher education, it was unusual in the realm of ancient Near Eastern studies, and he was ahead of his time in attempting to organize an institution that would serve the field as a whole.[14]

In September 1916, while America's entry into the war was still being debated, Frederick Gates's effusive regard for *Ancient Times* and Hale's encouragement emboldened Breasted to once again pursue Rockefeller support. In acknowledging Gates's plaudits, Breasted wrote at length about recent progress in ancient Near Eastern studies and the "great achievements and undreamed-of revelations [that] still await" systematic research. Looking ahead to the allies' hoped-for victory, Breasted suggested that the inability of "financially crippled European governments" to sponsor such work as they had done in the past imposed on Americans greater-than-ever "responsibilities as well as . . . opportunities." Breasted wondered if Gates might be interested in discussing "the situation and the new possibilities." Gates welcomed the visit, and in early April 1917 Breasted met with him and other officials associated with the Rockefeller philanthropies.

Breasted's meetings with the others were necessary because in the years following the University of Chicago's founding, Gates persuaded the Rockefellers to organize their donations based on "the principle of scientific giving." As a result, they created several foundations governed by separate boards of trustees more or less expert in their various charitable interests. The objective was to "establish efficiency in giving" in order to "attack and improve underlying conditions" rather than respond piecemeal to the myriad symptoms of social ills brought to their attention. As Gates put it, the change meant "laying aside retail giving almost wholly, and entering safely and pleasurably into the field of wholesale philanthropy." Thus, rather than supporting numerous hospitals to care for the sick, the Rockefellers turned to funding medical research and education aimed at wiping out or controlling the spread of fatal diseases. The Rockefeller Institute for Medical Research was established in 1901, a year later the General Education Board and Rockefeller Sanitation Commission appeared, the Rockefeller Foundation—which continues to this day—was chartered in 1913, the Laura Spelman Rockefeller Memorial was formed in 1918, and in 1923 the International Education Board was created. The boards were overseen from the Rockefellers' corporate offices headquartered in New York by an expanding number of individuals, many of whom, like Gates, advised the Rockefellers on both philanthropic and business affairs. Rockefeller senior described his offices as "a sort of a family affair. We talk over all kinds of matters of our common interest. We have not drawn sharp lines between business and philanthropic interests. We have developed both among us as a part of our common daily work."[15]

When Breasted met with Gates, he learned that while Gates could provide entrée to this extended "family," Breasted would have to persuade other key advisors if he were to have any success. Gates's enthusiasm for *Ancient Times* was a symptom of his long-standing interest in ancient history generally. Starting in 1902, he "began to read intensively about the origins and development of human civilization to find out the best means to use the foundations to promote human progress." Although Gates was generally predisposed to welcome Breasted's ideas, convincing others in the Rockefeller offices was a different matter. Breasted visited with General Education Board and Rockefeller Foundation officials and learned that several had been reading *Ancient Times* and were interested in his plans. Teddy Roosevelt's review, which had appeared two months prior, may have helped warm Breasted's reception, and perhaps Gates also greased some wheels. The only person with whom Breasted did not speak was John D. Rockefeller Jr., who by this point had fashioned himself into a "consciously modern" foundations manager, becoming the first "to make his career as a 'professional philanthropist.'" Rockefeller now guided the boards' priorities and would have to be won over by Breasted, a process that would be eased by Abby Rockefeller's note praising *Ancient Times* just a month later. But America had declared war on Germany just a few days before Breasted's visit. Of his time with the Rockefeller officials he wrote, "I shall have to wait until after the war before they can undertake my plans,—but I have their attention, their interest & their confidence."[16]

Upon returning home, Breasted followed up on the information he gleaned in New York with a new "Oriental Institute" proposal. He circulated it to Chicago president Judson (who was also a Rockefeller Foundation trustee), Gates, and Hale so the latter could forward it to yet another trustee with whom Hale was acquainted. The proposal recycled aspects of the one made to Norman Wait Harris, but now related to the growing importance of international affairs in American public policy. Breasted spoke to the prospect of a transformed Middle East after war's end and America's new responsibilities in the region's affairs: "Delivered from Turkish misrule, the lands around the eastern end of the Mediterranean are about to be opened up for the first time to unrestricted exploration and excavation. . . . It is but obvious scientific statesmanship to take advantage of this great opportunity and to do what European governments will feel too financially hampered to do after the war is over. . . . The great opportunity

can be seized and the work efficiently done by the establishment of an ORIEN-
TAL INSTITUTE."[17]

Such work, Breasted explained, would require "research and study on the
spot, just as do the geology or botany of a given region." The institute would thus
have two branches "with a headquarters at the most favorable strategic point in
ASIA, either Beyrut, Damascus or Aleppo, with another headquarters in AFRICA
at Cairo." Yet this kind of effort was well beyond the reach of a scholar "holding
the customary university post" who was limited to a handful of Middle Eastern trips in an entire career. Remedying the situation required ongoing funding
for support personnel and "adequate physical equipment": "Just as chemistry
or astronomy would be helpless without their laboratories and instruments, so
permanent archaeological research in the Near East would be impossible without
a fully equipped archaeological laboratory."

Breasted would have the institute's work begin in Asia rather than Africa in
order to place greater emphasis on excavations. "The first field work . . . would
be a preliminary survey," he explained, "exploring and mapping the almost untouched buried cities of Syria, making full records of their present condition,
with a view to preserving what is already above ground, and to eventual systematic excavation of the most promising places." Breasted then connected his plan
with interests back in the United States: "The monuments discovered by the
Institute could be turned over to the universities and museums of America. In
the course of time oriental collections of world-wide importance . . . would grow
up in America."

Breasted's references to international responsibilities and domestic opportunities resonated with changes being contemplated by foundation officials at
the time. American foundations were considering "new cooperative structures"
involving private-public partnerships to address large needs. The First World
War accelerated these changes as foundations performed services the "government did not do as practice or could not do by law or was restrained from doing
by popular belief." In calling upon Rockefeller officials to consider America's opportunities and obligations in the Middle East and linking his project to the collective weal at home, Breasted was aligning his objectives with the foundations'
growing ambitions.[18]

A National Academy of Humanistic Science

Breasted's initiative was shelved as all turned to the conflict in Europe and a
national mobilization at home. As the widening destruction edged ever closer
to America, he saw one proposal after another "evaporate with . . . news of
the appalling war." "Yet," Breasted wrote, "how insignificant all such projects

[are] in the light of the European conflagration! Heigh-ho! What is it all for?" Breasted's distress over the war's futility deepened as he followed Americans' arguments about the country's stake in the conflict, witnessed a rising tide of anti-Germanism, and learned of European colleagues' sons fighting on opposing sides. At first he was able to keep up correspondence with friends on both sides of the war and thus received sad news of their sons' deaths. Gaston Maspero lost one, Eduard Meyer lost two, Adolf Erman lost one—and there were others. Communication became more difficult over time, and Breasted's impartiality and that of his German colleagues began to waiver, particularly after America was drawn into war. When his son Charles enlisted, Breasted's circumspection was displaced by anxiety, and he succumbed to the torrent of wartime patriotism and anti-German sentiment sweeping the nation. While Charles was in basic training, Breasted sent a small German dictionary used during his Berlin student days with "Dictionary of the Enemy's Language" inscribed on the flyleaf. Fortunately, Charles never needed it. He became ill before shipping out, requiring surgery and hospitalization, and subsequently received an honorable discharge.[19]

Despite Breasted's formidable powers of concentration, he was deeply unsettled by the war and produced little in the way of new scholarship, instead attending to follow-up tasks and new opportunities arising from his textbooks' success. He debated with Henry Hilton the latter's proposal for a more compact edition of *Outlines*, ultimately rejecting it in favor of a "general Oriental History" that would be more extensive than *Ancient Times*, a project that was never realized. Alternatively, Breasted relayed suggestions from Gates and other "important men in the East" that *Ancient Times* be brought out in a trade edition aimed at a broader public audience, a notion that did not appeal to Ginn. He was encouraged by several, including a leading secondary-school expert, to recast *Outlines* for less "mature" audiences, signaling the book's still-growing potential. Nonetheless, he felt all but useless during the war, writing to one colleague, "I only wish I could enlist too, but they wont take me. . . . I am making war speeches wherever the opportunity arises, especially to university and high school students." He published an article on the West's strategic and geopolitical interests in the Middle East, which Breasted circulated to suggest his personal "use in oriental connections," volunteering for service in the British administration in Egypt and Egypt's Antiquities Service. But he was turned down by both.[20]

Breasted's fame as a popular educator prompted an invitation from the National Security League in early fall 1917 to develop a national educational program for high schools. The league was established in 1914 as a militant, prowar advocacy group whose objective was cloaked in its avowed purpose of helping America prepare itself should it be involuntarily drawn into the war. When the nation's hand was forced in 1917, the league took up other causes, including some disreputable efforts such as weeding out political dissenters on college campuses and promoting a wealth-based meritocracy. Breasted was a member of the league by 1916, perhaps at the encouragement of his fellow faculty member Ernest DeWitt Burton. Burton thought Breasted could help with a "speaking campaign among the teachers of the country," the objectives of which were unclear. Breasted may also have been encouraged by Theodore Roosevelt, who, along with *Outlook*'s publisher, endorsed the league's prowar stance.

Despite his friends' urging, Breasted hesitated over the league's objectives. He shared with fellow educators a wariness about allowing a private organization like the league to establish a foothold in American public schools for many reasons, not least of which was its potential for setting a precedent for others such as the Catholic Church. Nonetheless, seeing in the league's invitation an opportunity for a personal contribution to the war effort, Breasted offered a plan "toward replacing the prevalent provincialism of the American outlook with breadth of world-vision." Well ahead of his time, he proposed a sweeping reorganization of the American education system based on a long-term federal mandate that would regard "education as sufficiently important to require a fully equipped Department with a Cabinet Officer at its head." Fearing the loss of qualified teachers during the war, Breasted prepared plans for "organizing 1,250,000 high school pupils [into] a nationwide Patriotic Legion. In accordance with this plan all members of the Legion who would endeavor to remain in high school and go on to higher education . . . would be known as the Gold Star Corps. They would . . . gain all the education and training possible" to teach in place of Americans who died in combat. The league's education director urged Breasted to accept an appointment in the league's New York headquarters from September 1918 until the plan was implemented. His misgivings were reinforced by Judson and others, however, and Breasted declined the offer.[21]

He coped with war news the best way he could, by taking a long view of history to absorb news of the war's unfathomable horrors. Breasted applied himself to general interest writings and lectures on themes associated with his textbooks, usually in educators' journals and conferences. Though his articles reiterated topics treated in the books, they were linked to the present with references to wartime conditions in Europe and the Middle East. In one, he juxtaposes evidence of modern civilization, gun-shell fragments, with that of prehistoric life, stone tools, both of which could be found along the Somme valley in France where one of the war's deadliest battles was fought: "These steel fragments buried here represent man's latest and most terrible effort in the art of self-destruction," while the "flint fist hatchets [are] the earliest surviving weapons of man." In another, while discussing ancient Egypt's military campaigns on the "Asiatic side of the Suez," Breasted notes, "England's operations in this region during the World War have been but a repetition of a military drama enacted over and over again since the sixteenth century B.C. I might read the records still preserved on the walls of the Karnak temple at . . . Thebes, and if I were only to substitute the name of General Allenby for that of Thutmose III, you would almost imagine I was reading the dispatches of the British commander to London during his campaign in Palestine."[22]

In April 1918 Breasted was elected president of the American Oriental Society, one of the nation's oldest scholarly associations. He had been a member since his Yale days and gave his first paper at one of the society's meetings while still a student. The society's president was expected to address its annual meeting at the conclusion of the year-long term, the subject to be "some phase of the progress and significance of Oriental studies." When Breasted's turn came, he drew together ideas he had been pursuing with Hale and the Rockefeller boards. Titled "The Place of the Near Orient in the Career of Man and the Task of the American Orientalist," the address is a summation of changes in his thinking about the discipline, a declaration of independence from what he regarded as outmoded ideas and practices, and an articulation of the direction he believed the field should take.

The timing of his address in April 1919, just months after the First World War's end, provided added impetus for a fresh look at the Middle East as a land of scholarly "responsibility" and "opportunity." By "responsibility," he meant his and his colleagues' obligations to current and previous generations of European scholars, to whose teachings Americans were indebted. In taking up the reins of ancient Near Eastern research, Americans could assist European peers impoverished by war just as American troops aided weary Allies on Europe's battlefields. As "opportunity," Breasted envisioned a synthesis of ongoing and new ancient Near Eastern research that would lead to a more complete understanding of "mankind viewed *as a whole*."[23]

Breasted began by recalling that, in "endeavoring to make . . . the Near East intelligible to American high school boys and girls," he was inspired by the work of anthropologists studying the pre-Columbian period of Native American history. It is unclear how he first learned about their research because a publication he cited as exemplary, Clark Wissler's *The American Indian: An Introduction to the Anthropology of the New World*, was not published until 1917, after *Outlines* and *Ancient Times* were completed. Nonetheless, the anthropologists' concept of "culture traits"—the cultivation of maize, the "cotton complex," pottery, rudimentary metallurgical skills, and the transition "from the pictographic to the phonetic stage" in ancient writing—helped him conceptualize the ancient Near East's development. He was further intrigued by the "Americanists'" method of tracing culture traits' "lines of diffusion" back to their points of origin and how that information revealed the antiquity and crucial role of the "great intercontinental bridge" linking the Americas. These findings sensitized him to prehistoric evidence of the ancient Near East, especially along "the great [Pleistocene] rift in north-eastern Africa, which we call Egypt."

Breasted compared recent research on prehistoric settlements in the Middle East to pre-Columbian findings, likening the origins and seminal role of ancient Near Eastern peoples to those of the ancient peoples of Central America. It led him to conceive of an "Egypto-Babylonian culture-nucleus" spanning an "intercontinental bridge connecting Africa and Eurasia" much as the ancient cultures of pre-Columbian Central America settled the land bridge connecting the North and South American continents and from there nurtured the development of native peoples in both directions. Thus the "Egypto-Babylonian group" is "like the keystone of the arch, with prehistoric man on one side and civilized Europe on the other." Yet, Breasted lamented, research on this "synthesis" was still "hardly begun."[24]

The reason for this, Breasted argued, was the disciplinary narrowness of scholars in classical and ancient Near Eastern studies. "Americanists," he said, "have enjoyed enviable freedom from the traditional prejudices like those of old-school classicists, who felt it [a] sacrilege to acknowledge the . . . Orient . . . , or those of the Egyptologists and Assyriologists, who are often more interested in proving the shores of the Nile or of the Euphrates to have been the oldest home of civilization." The source of the problem, Breasted argued, was the philological origin of research in classical and ancient Near Eastern studies: "The heavy burden of recovering and mastering the lost oriental languages has made of us orientalists chiefly philologists . . . , equipped to utilize *written* documents, and a little perplexed and bewildered in the presence of other kinds of evidence." Speaking "as a fellow-sufferer from this too exclusively philological discipline," Breasted added, "I am not inviting my colleagues to this confessional without being painfully aware that I must kneel there myself!"

In contrast, the "lack of writing throughout most of the . . . New World has saved the Americanists from the regrettable narrowness, limitations, and often pedantry, of the old time philologist." Americanists encompassed "the linguist, the archaeologist, the ethnologist, and the physical anthropologist," and their disciplinary specializations were not "kept in water-tight compartments, but . . . brought to bear on the career of man in the New World." Then, reversing his long-standing aversion to archaeology in favor of epigraphy, Breasted admitted that as "a matter of history the archaeologist has not received a very hospitable reception in the ranks of orientalists." Systematic excavations *would* help answer important questions about the diffusion of culture traits within the ancient Near East and into Asia and Europe. To answer such questions "it is evident that we need the assistance of men thoroughly trained in archaeology, physical anthropology, botany, paleontology, geology, meteorology, and anthro-geography," and zoology and hydrography as well.[25]

The problem remained, however, of how best to integrate the evidence collected by these many disciplines into the "vast cultural synthesis" Breasted envisioned. His solution was establishment of an oriental institute, under American auspices, with two permanent branches, "one in Asia and the other in the Nile valley." Likening it to an astronomer's observatory, Breasted characterized the institute as a "veritable laboratory" containing "*evidence of every kind and character*," whether in originals, reproductions, surveys, maps, notebooks, or publications. "Liberal provision" should be made for postdoctoral research fellows, support staff, darkrooms, drafting rooms, and all the other accouterments necessary so that "not only the methods but especially the equipment of natural science should be applied to our study." The institute "should maintain *close relations with the scientific departments* of the university" of which it is a part, and the "small group of universities capable of" pursuing similar research "should cooperate . . . to . . . avoid unnecessary duplication." Believing "the project can . . . command the respect . . . of our great financial foundations," Breasted concluded that in "seeking support for oriental research, . . . the worth and dignity of our great task should move us to claim all that is conceded to the natural sciences. Are we not engaged upon later phases of the same vast process of development which they are investigating?"[26]

The "vast process" to which Breasted referred was the great arc of evolution from the beginning of cosmological time to the first stirrings of recorded human history. The notion was on his mind because Hale had invited Breasted earlier in 1919 to speak in a National Academy of Sciences series Hale had established in his father's honor, "The William Ellery Hale Lectures on Evolution." They fulfilled one of Hale's 1913 proposals for revitalizing the academy, fostering science education in the schools with a course of lectures on evolution "beginning with . . . the constitution of matter" and concluding with "an account of early Oriental peoples, the rise of the Egyptian dynasties, and their influence on modern progress." Breasted was the last of seven lecturers, the others all prominent scientists of the day, including Ernest Rutherford, a 1908 Nobel Prize laureate who led off the series with a paper on the nature of matter and "the evolution of the elements." The further evolution of the cosmos was traced in subsequent lectures up to the penultimate address, "The Beginnings of Human History from the Geologic Record," presented by John C. Merriam, a leading paleontologist. Breasted picked up the story with two lectures on "The Origins of Civilization": "From the Old Stone Age to the Dawn of Civilization" and "The Earliest Civilization and its Transmission to Europe." He delivered them in late April 1919 at the National Academy of Sciences annual meeting, just days after his outgoing American Oriental Society presidential address.[27]

He began by justifying his presence among the natural scientists, proposing a more permeable boundary between the natural sciences and the humanities.

Breasted cited the transition from the prehistoric era to earliest ancient history as an example:

> There is an enormously long stage in the career of man when the study of him is obviously the task of the natural scientist. . . . At a certain stage . . . , however, we begin to call the study of him and his works archaeology, history, philology, art and literature—lines of study which we sharply differentiate from natural science. . . . The protoplasm is indeed a long way from the idea of liberty and the chimpanzee may antedate by millions of years the conception of social justice, but the transition from the stage of biological to that of social processes is a gradual one.

Breasted fleshed out his argument by devoting nearly two-thirds of his first lecture to an exploration of prehistoric evidence in northeast Africa, dating to about 20,000 BCE when hunter gatherers began converging on the rift zone through which the Nile now flows. He traced the development of flint implements and their makers' locations as they drifted toward the river's increasingly fertile flood plain and acquired skills in animal husbandry, cultivation, and pottery making. Breasted connected these developments to larger climatic processes, such as the advance and retreat of glaciers in Europe, to explain his belief that hostile conditions there retarded human progress, while temperate conditions in North Africa fostered relatively rapid development. It was for this reason, Breasted argued, that ancient Egypt achieved "an industrial superiority over Europe and Asia beginning in the middle of the fifth millennium B.C." that lasted "some four thousand years . . . until the advance of Greek industry and commerce in the sixth century B.C." Breasted's focus on Egypt's prehistory marked a new direction for him in both chronological depth and methodological breadth. As his survey advanced in time, however, he emphasized the early history of the ancient Near East as a whole to link the humanities with the natural sciences while also demonstrating the region's crucial role in shaping European civilization. He illustrated these relationships between prehistory and the origins of ancient civilizations, the sciences and the humanities, and the ancient Near East and Europe with new diagrams (figure 6.2).

The scientists in Breasted's audience were not convinced, and some were offended that a humanist was invited to speak before the academy. One observer was struck by "how disgusted an able young zoologist of Johns Hopkins was when he returned from Washington . . . : an unknown archaeologist and 'language-man' had been asked to give the principal address—what was the field of science coming to when such a thing was possible!"[28]

The juxtaposition of the American Oriental Society and National Academy of Sciences meetings in late April occasioned another Hale-Breasted initiative.

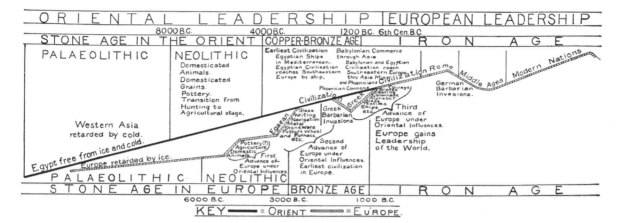

Fig. 6.2 "Diagram Visualizing the Rise of Civilization in the Orient and Its Transition Thence to Europe," figure 134 from Breasted's "Origins of Civilization," *Scientific Monthly* 10, no. 3 (March 1920): 267. Public domain, reproduction by author.

At the society's meeting Breasted led his peers in pursuing an opportunity that arose following the armistice the preceding fall: an international peace conference whose organizers were inviting constituencies of all kinds, including scholars, to participate. However, America had "no nationally representative body of humanistic scholars" to advocate their interests at the conference. The American Oriental Society felt the problem more acutely than other associations because, as Breasted wrote, it had a disciplinary interest in the "territory of the now defunct Ottoman Empire" to be administered by the European Allies. The absence of a nationally representative humanities organization underscored other problems, especially "securing . . . funds for proper support" of humanities research. The society's leadership responded by appointing a committee of three members, chaired by Breasted, "to consider . . . the formation of a National Academy of Humanistic Science." On the eve of Breasted's first lecture at the National Academy of Sciences, Hale arranged for him to present the American Oriental Society's initiative to the academy's governing council. Breasted proposed that the academy "consider the feasibility of taking a list of fifty or sixty names . . . to be furnished by the committee of the Oriental Society and select ten men, asking them to . . . form a National Academy of Humanistic Research under the charter of the National Academy of Sciences."

The academy council's president appointed a committee of three members to "consider some practical scheme for . . . a national organization for humanistic research" and report its findings to the council. Breasted was asked to put his proposal in writing, and the following afternoon he supplied a memorandum on the "Scope, Purpose and Functions of a National Academy of Humanistic Science." It would include archaeology, art, philology, literature, history, sociology, economics, and philosophy; but Breasted limited the "scope" to "the prosecution of <u>research</u> in the career and activities of man historically considered." To assure the scientists of the proposed academy's rigor, eligible members had to be "engaged in applying modern scientific methods of investigation and not solely the creative imagination, as in the case of artists, architects and writers who would not be included." The academy's "purpose" was to be "the correlation of all research in the career of man, resulting . . . in the articulation of the course of historic civilization with the evolutionary stages already traceable in the pre-human stages; the recovery . . . of man's career . . . ; and the construction of a basis of observed fact for philosophical consideration of the whole vast synthesis." Among its "functions" would be the "mutually helpful association" of members, representation of members' interests in matters of national concern such as "the future control of scientific research in the former Ottoman Empire," and "the guidance, encouragement, and support of the researches" outlined above. Breasted's proposal was discussed by the council, but no action was taken; instead, on Hale's recommendation, the committee was to explore the matter further and issue a feasibility study.[29]

The discussions in Washington made it clear, however, that there was little appetite for creating either a separate congressionally mandated humanities academy or for a humanities division within the academy. In reporting his conversations to the American Oriental Society's leadership, Breasted outlined various possibilities, including "action by a convention of . . . all the various humanistic societies and organizations." He was referring to discussions already under way among a number of American associations about creating an umbrella organization. They were motivated by the announcement of a scholarly meeting in Paris to consider forming an international organization of scholarly academies and associations, one that "presupposed the existence in each country . . . of a single body or group authoritatively representative of humanistic studies."

Breasted was unenthusiastic about participating in a conference of all interested parties because he believed the "number of societies carrying on really sound and scientific modern research . . . is very limited." He preferred that "an arbitrary and possibly somewhat autocratic process of selecting the leading soundly scientific organizations should be instituted." By September 1919 another plan overtook Breasted's, however. A group of ten associations, invited by leaders of the American Academy of Arts and Sciences and the American Historical Association, sent representatives to Boston to organize the "American Council of Learned Societies Devoted to Humanistic Studies" (the last four words of the council's title were subsequently dropped). That body, which included American Oriental Society officers, elected delegates to the first meeting of the international group, the newly established Union Académique Internationale.[30]

Breasted's initiative for an academy of humanistic science did not immediately die, however. Its cause was taken up by other members of the American Oriental Society during fall 1919. Although Hale attempted to keep things going, changes in leadership at the society and the National Academy of Sciences bogged down the conversation, and resistance among some academy members persisted. In fall 1920, John C. Merriam, who spoke in the Hale lecture series, concluded that the "Academy does not . . . favor extending its work away from investigations of the strictly scientific type, and the members do not . . . desire to risk expanding the work of the Academy into the field of emotional rather than scientific activity." Nonetheless, he believed that certain "eminent investigators whose approach is strictly scientific should be included . . . regardless of the particular field of knowledge in which the work happens to lie." Merriam urged the academy to periodically accept "the several leaders in the field of humanistic research . . . whose work is clearly scientific. . . . Unquestionably one of the best . . . would be Professor James H. Breasted." Meanwhile there was growing opposition to an academy affiliation from American Oriental Society members who preferred their alliance with the American Council of Learned Societies. Breasted would have been very much in the middle of this debate but for a happy turn of events that found him sailing back to the Middle East.[31]

Founding an Institute, Surveying the Field

A few months after the armistice, in January 1919, Breasted renewed his courtship of the Rockefeller boards. He recast an earlier proposal as a "Plan for the Organization of an Oriental Institute at the University of Chicago" and circulated it to the head of the General Education Board and Judson. Breasted reiterated the opportunities afforded by the Ottoman Empire's collapse, now claiming the "study of these lands is the birthright and the sacred legacy of all civilized peoples." But, Breasted predicted, this opening would lead to "exploitation in mining, railroad building, manufactures and agriculture," which threatened the frail ruins and buried antiquities of the ancient Near East, making the systematic recovery of ancient evidence all the more urgent. In this plan, however, he placed the institute's headquarters in the Haskell Oriental Museum rather than the Middle East.

A "historical laboratory," it would still function as a central repository for records produced by investigators in the field. Breasted continued to emphasize photography's role in rescuing "forever large numbers of written documents and monumental ruins still unsurveyed." Although he felt the institute "might accomplish much" with archaeological explorations, the plan did not contemplate "costly excavation campaigns." Instead it relied on "purchasing original ancient documents and monuments at relatively low prices" to fill out the Haskell collections and support his primary goal: producing "a great history of the Origin and Development of Civilization." The institute would nevertheless support the research projects of other American institutions and scholars by making its library and museum collections available to them.

Breasted, aided by a "small staff of helpers," would be "granted the time and the funds to become a kind of permanent archaeological ambassador-at-large to the Near Orient." In envisioning himself as a representative "on the ground" in the Middle East, he thought he could be of "substantial value," primarily as an advisor to others seeking to acquire antiquities or find fresh sites to excavate. Reports produced by "the Oriental Institute on present-day conditions in the Near East might also be of value to our government, to our educational and relief organizations, and even to our business men." To support all these activities, Breasted requested a $250,000 endowment that would be established at the University of Chicago and yield about $10,000 per year according to his calculations. Breasted hoped he might eventually establish a permanent field office in the Middle East, but he believed that with this inaugural funding he could demonstrate the institute's "efficiency and its possibilities" and thus be in a better position to raise additional support.[32]

Breasted submitted his proposal without prior university endorsement, which—as he later acknowledged—was "putting the cart before the horse." The General Education Board's president replied that establishing something like an institute "belongs to a university administration rather than an organization like ours." Bureaucratic gridlock ensued when university officials would not commit to the plan without an affirmative signal from the foundation, and foundation officials would not accept responsibility for creating a new institution. Frustrated by the logjam, Breasted tried contacting other Rockefeller officials as well as John D. Rockefeller Jr. himself. Using Abby Rockefeller's note of appreciation for *Ancient Times* as an entrée, Breasted wrote that "the career of early man, of which that book offers only a slight sketch, can now be written out in a much fuller form." But, he argued, this would not be possible without support, and he enclosed a copy of the Oriental Institute proposal for Rockefeller's consideration. "You are today one of the great forces in making social, economic, and industrial history," Breasted continued. "The very principles of justice and fair treatment which you are so admirably applying in your present day work, first grew up in the minds and hearts of men in that ancient world of the Near Orient." Appealing directly to Rockefeller's Christian faith, Breasted concluded, the "noblest task in the study of man, is to recover the story of the human career, which culminated in the emergence of a religion of divine fatherhood and human brotherhood."

Rockefeller passed the proposal to one of his personal advisors, Starr J. Murphy, asking him to investigate it more closely. Murphy wrote to Judson wondering if, instead of an endowment, the project might not be financed "for the first few years by annual grants, until the proposition could be tested out," after which time the endowment question could be taken up anew. Judson agreed, suggested a larger annual budget, and recommended the proposal to the General Education Board, writing that the plan was "very sound . . . and no one in the country is better qualified to carry it out than is Mr. Breasted." Sharing Breasted's sense of urgency, Judson added, "Now is the time . . . to move in the matter." Murphy concluded that although the project was "of very great importance," it should not be backed by the General Education Board because of its policy of declining proposals from individuals. Instead, Murphy recommended that Rockefeller either "contribute the whole" or contribute a portion of the grant on condition that "the balance is raised from other private subscribers." Judson was apprised of this suggestion and counseled that should Rockefeller make a personal grant, it ought to be to the university rather than directly to Breasted.[33]

As Breasted perused the daily mail in early May 1919, he came across a personally addressed envelope with an engraving of a fashionable, expensive Virginia resort. Thinking at first it was a solicitation, he was about to fling it "across the dining room into a great Sudanese basket reserved" for the era's equivalent of junk mail when curiosity got the better of him. It contained a letter from John D. Rockefeller Jr. that began with an apology for not replying sooner to Breasted's appeal. Noting that he was "greatly interested" in the project and that he agreed with Breasted's assessment of the situation in the Middle East and believed "no one is better fitted to lead in this enterprise" than Breasted, Rockefeller declared himself "happy to finance" the project for five years at the rate of $10,000 per year, the money to be handled through the University of Chicago. Rockefeller enclosed a copy of a letter to Judson confirming the gift with a few additional contractual details, including a caveat that the "pledge should not be construed to imply any committal . . . beyond the five year period."

Unbeknownst to Breasted, Rockefeller sent a second letter to Judson indicating his agreement that Breasted's budget was too low. Rockefeller pledged an additional $50,000—for a total of $100,000, or $20,000 a year for the five years. "With this confidential understanding," Rockefeller continued, "it would be possible for [Judson] to say to . . . Breasted in discussing the work and budget with him" that should additional support be needed, Judson could claim that Rockefeller's "interest in the enterprise" was such that Judson would "feel free" to ask for the additional money even though it was already on hand. Rockefeller's personal attention to Breasted's proposal was due almost entirely to *Ancient Times*. Breasted "said many times . . . that had he not written the book, there would have been no Institute."[34]

Breasted began organizing his Oriental Institute, arranging its first project—an expedition to survey research opportunities in the Middle East—and seeking additional funds. He structured the institute with himself as director, the Haskell Oriental Museum's administrative secretary as the institute's secretary (augmenting the latter's salary), and four colleagues from the Department of Oriental Languages and Literatures as a "Research Staff" (without additional compensation). Breasted also negotiated an agreement with the university's library for a shared cataloger to help accession objects as well as books.

He viewed the grant as a first step toward creating "a great American Institute in the Near East," despite Rockefeller's caveat that it did not imply support after five years. Breasted's optimism was shared by Hale, who thought the grant would "prepare the way for carrying out a large and comprehensive plan by the Carnegie Institution or the Rockefeller Foundation. The best way to secure [their] support . . . will be to prepare a detailed report, pointing out the possibilities developed by your first survey of the Near East." Breasted did ask Carnegie Institution officials for funding, initially to provide salaries for two geologists to assist his survey expedition, but without success. With regard to his patron, Breasted agreed with Hale, "I have every reason to believe that Mr. Rockefeller's giving along this line has only begun." To a fellow Egyptologist Breasted wrote, "This is merely a beginning of the kind of work which I have always wanted to set going,—pure research without reference to results for public consumption." Breasted also published a brief article in the *American Journal of Semitic Languages and Literatures* to formally announce the institute, justify its creation, and explain its objectives. Breasted concluded by welcoming contacts with individuals and organizations interested in cooperative efforts.

Organizing the institute's survey expedition was his highest priority, however. Breasted had originally planned for a September departure, but the threat of dock strikes in England and the ensuing transatlantic travel congestion they would cause forced him to move up his trip to late August, shortening his preparation time by nearly a month. He asked twenty-one-year-old Charles to remain home and help his mother with the two younger children—James Jr. and Astrid, now eleven and five respectively—while Breasted was on what he anticipated could be a nine- to ten-month sojourn abroad.[35]

Surveying ancient sites in what remained an unstable war zone required the assistance of local governing authorities. Although Egypt continued to be a British protectorate and was comparatively secure, the remainder of the Middle East was experiencing varying degrees of strife. Following the end of the First World War and collapse of the Ottoman Empire, the Covenant of the League of Nations, signed in June 1919, acknowledged the conditional independence of former Arab provinces in the Middle East. However, the extent of their autonomy depended on the leniency of the colonial powers assigned mandates over them that, in theory, were to involve the advice of local communities. However, things did not go so smoothly. For example, a general Syrian congress held in July 1919 implicitly rejected the colonial plan by electing a king of a united Syria, which was to have encompassed Palestine. At the Conference of San Remo, in April 1920, the Allies ignored this and other Arab initiatives and divvied up the Ottoman Empire. As a result, when Breasted was traveling through the region, Britain administered Palestine (now divided between Israel and the Palestinian Authority), Transjordan (now Jordan), and what is now the southeastern half of Iraq from an area northwest of Baghdad to Basra and the Persian Gulf. France administered what are now Lebanon, Syria, and the northwest half of Iraq.

Turmoil in the region arose from nationalist ambitions playing out against a background of tribal rivalries, particularly in the area of modern-day Syria and Iraq. Britain and France, both interested in allowing some measure of local autonomy, were undecided about how to grant it and to whom, all the while keeping a close eye on each other. Given these uncertainties, Breasted had to rely on the connections of British and French colleagues willing to help him obtain letters and guarantees of safe passage, without which his trip would be impossible. Accordingly, he made the rounds of diplomatic and military officials in London and Paris before continuing to Egypt. Breasted's arrival in London coincided with a joint meeting of the Royal Asiatic Society, French Société Asiatique, and American Oriental Society, where he also identified contacts for travel permissions and assistance. He stockpiled expedition equipment and supplies in London as well.[36]

Acquisitions for the Haskell Oriental Museum were also on Breasted's agenda, and he spent a fair amount of time pursuing them in London and Italy on his way to Egypt. Breasted anticipated that large numbers of antiquities would surface among dealers in Europe and the Middle East at war's end, and he was right. Trade and travel restrictions during the war compounded by buyers' depleted assets, especially in Europe, resulted in the availability of large numbers of highly desirable objects. Breasted obtained acquisition funds from the university and Chicago-area donors, and he was also delegated to purchase works for the Art Institute of Chicago and the Saint Louis Art Museum, in the end spending nearly $100,000 on behalf of various interests. Although the search for worthy things was time-consuming and wearying, Breasted enjoyed discovering significant works among traders' dusty backroom holdings, especially those whose value and authenticity could only be discerned through subtle historical clues.

He bemoaned the time needed to make contacts, especially with British and French diplomats and military officials. Yet Breasted savored his access to the powerful and influential, especially those possessing great wealth or diplomatic importance. While his official reporting describes such encounters in a strictly businesslike tone, Breasted's letters home convey a sense of fascination, even flattery, in rubbing elbows with the high born and politically connected. His time in England was filled with meetings and social events populated by a host of notables, including George Herbert, 5th Earl of Carnarvon, a collector of Egyptian antiquities and patron of explorations in Thebes and the Valley of the Kings.

Another was General Edmund H. H. Allenby—whom Breasted had earlier compared to Thutmose III—the commander of Britain's Egyptian Expeditionary Force during a series of victories in 1917 and 1918, culminating in the defeat of the Turkish army and its German advisors in Palestine on the plains below the ancient site of Megiddo, the biblical Armageddon. Allenby had just been named a field marshal in the British army, made a viscount, and appointed high commissioner of Egypt.[37]

Breasted arrived in Egypt in November 1919 and busily pursued acquisitions, made further expedition arrangements, studied works in the Egyptian Museum, and caught up on the latest discoveries. He also persuaded Allenby, who had just taken up residence in Egypt, to authorize an "experimental" aerial photography survey of the sixty-mile string of pyramids stretching south from the Abū Ruwāsh and Giza groups. Allenby had the Royal Air Force put a plane at Breasted's disposal, and the flight was arranged for what turned out to be an "extremely 'bumpy' day." The pilot had to fly higher than Breasted preferred, averaging about 5,000 feet, which meant the physical features he wanted to photograph would appear too distant to be of much scholarly use (figure 6.3). The plane was a two-seat, open-cockpit craft with the passenger sitting behind the pilot but without a windscreen. Outfitted like "Peary in the Arctic," Breasted struggled to photograph the sites, a task imperiled by wind rushing past the fuselage with such force that it crushed the camera's bellows into the picture field. After two hours of intermittent photography interrupted by steep banking, sudden drops, and an undignified bout of "sea-sickness," Breasted gamely declared "the University of Chicago was the first institution to begin archaeological work from the air in Egypt." His experiment helped pioneer the use of aerial photography in archaeology.[38]

To assist him on the expedition, Breasted recruited two of his doctoral students in Egyptology, Ludlow S. Bull and William F. Edgerton, and a junior faculty member in Assyriology, Daniel D. Luckenbill. A former student, William Shelton, joined later in the planning. They met up with Breasted as needed, with Bull and Edgerton arriving first to assist with research in Egypt, and Luckenbill and Shelton meeting the group in early February on the eve of its departure. Breasted originally planned to travel overland from Egypt via Transjordan to the desert in northern Syria, a trip of about 850 miles, where the group would turn southeastward and follow the Euphrates, visiting ancient sites along the way toward the vicinity of Baghdad and Basra, whereupon the expedition would return home (maps 1 and 4). There was still fighting in Transjordan, however, and the British authorities urged Breasted to avoid it. The only alternative was to reverse plans by heading for Basra first. The change required taking a ship from Port Said through the Suez Canal to the Red Sea and Gulf of Aden, eastward across the Arabian Sea to Bombay (now Mumbai), and from there returning across the Ara

Fig. 6.3 Breasted's aerial photograph of the pyramids of Abu Sir, 13 January 1920. The diagonal lines are guy wires securing the plane's overhead wing to its fuselage. Courtesy of the Oriental Institute, University of Chicago.

bian Sea in a northwesterly direction to the Gulf of Oman and then the Persian Gulf—reaching Basra after a nearly 5,000-mile detour. The expedition sailed from Port Said on 18 February 1920, arrived in Bombay eleven days later, and after a forty-eight-hour layover in a rough travelers' shelter, sailed on to Basra, disembarking on 10 March. A few years later Breasted learned that Allenby and other British officials had approved his expedition plans with considerable disquiet because of the rough terrain and politically unsettled conditions ahead. Although Breasted remained fit for a fifty-four-year-old, his white hair made him look older, causing officials to wonder if he would survive the journey.[39]

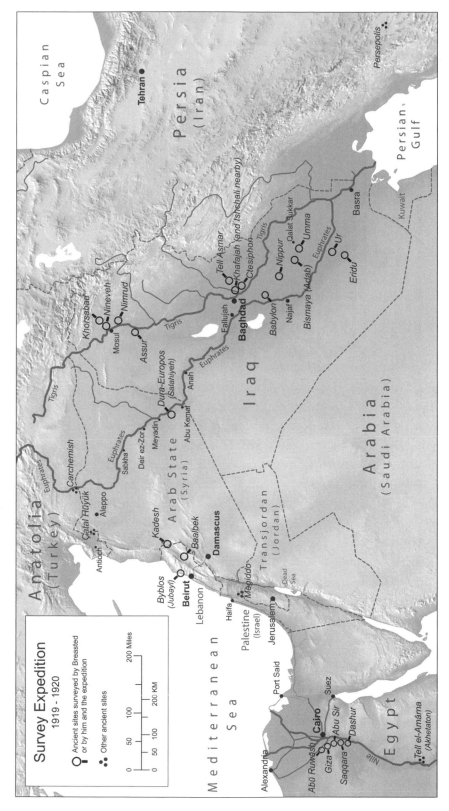

Map 4

Fig. 6.4 Oriental Institute expedition automobile caravan with unidentified Arab drivers near Eridu, ca. 17 March 1920. Courtesy of the Oriental Institute, University of Chicago.

The British were still consolidating their administration in southern Iraq while contending with warring tribes to the northwest. Basra was a major stepping-off point for this effort, and the abundant food, supplies, and equipment in the British commissary stores were offered to Breasted by the regional commander, thus assuring cheap and plentiful provisions. Breasted also hired two Arab helpers for the expedition: "Ali the cook and Abbas the camp boy." On 16 March, after further preparations, the expedition headed north by train toward Baghdad on a specially outfitted rail car to be used as a base for tours overland by automobile or on the Euphrates by boat—all provided by the British. The first stops were the Babylonian city of Ur and what was once the ancient port of Eridu, which, around 2000 BCE, was on the Persian Gulf. Now, because of the accumulation of silt, it is nearly 150 miles from the water's edge (figure 6.4).

The expedition visited the Sumerian sites of Lagash and Umma, the latter requiring a trip on horseback accompanied by a young British colonel, a guard of five armed Arab troops, and the sheikhs of several neighboring tribes who wanted to join the trek (figure 6.5). The sheikhs were hoping to mediate a conflict between the British and another sheikh whom the colonial administration was seeking for an unspecified transgression. Upon riding up the hill of Umma (Tell Yokha), the expedition was met by a larger, armed group, which included the accused sheikh. Being outnumbered and insufficiently armed, Breasted's party felt more than a little threatened despite the Arabs' efforts to show their hospitality and obeisance to British rule. Unpersuaded by this outpouring of sociability, the "imperturbable young Englishman, sitting here unarmed in the midst of a wild

Fig. 6.5 Oriental Institute expedition and Arab escort in the vicinity of Qaḷat Sukkar, 23 March 1920. Courtesy of the Oriental Institute, University of Chicago.

Arab tribe who outnumbered us fifty to one and could have slaughtered us all in a few minutes," refused to pardon the sheikh. The two groups parted without incident.[40]

The expedition continued north and west between the Euphrates and the Tigris, stopping at nearby sites such as Nippur and Babylon. It arrived in Baghdad on 6 April and spent several days there, Breasted visiting antiquities dealers from whom he made significant acquisitions. The group took a day trip to Ctesiphon, once winter capital of the ancient Parthian empire, where nearly all that remains is a giant vaulted space erected in the third century CE (figure 6.6). "I am a fairly hardened observer of great buildings," Breasted wrote, "but I found this magnificent hall simply overwhelming. . . . No other architectural relic of the past, except the great pyramids of Egypt, has filled me with quite the same consciousness of human achievement." On 12 April, the expedition left Baghdad by train, heading north along the Tigris to Ash Sharqāṭ—the end of the rail line—and nearby Assur, the earliest capital of Assyria, dating to at least as early as 3000 BCE. After studying Assur's ruins, the group continued by car caravan further north to Mosul, which it used as a base for trips to the nearby Assyrian sites of Nimrud, Nineveh, and Khorsabad.

These excursions were hazardous because, Breasted learned, "the Arabs here are not yet as well under control as in Babylonia. A big Rolls-Royce armored car fitted with a machine gun will head our column." Initially the expedition concentrated on Nineveh "until an ebullition of the Kurds had settled down," and it was permitted to examine Khorsabad, the palace of Sargon II, king of Assyria during the early seventh century BCE, and Nimrud, which, during the eighth-century BCE reign of Ashurnasirpal II, replaced Nineveh as capital of Assyria (figure 6.7). Breasted was impressed by the potential for rich scholarly and artistic

Fig. 6.6 Remains of third-century CE Sassanian palace, begun by Shāpūr I, Ctesiphon, ca. 10 April 1920. Courtesy of the Oriental Institute, University of Chicago.

Fig. 6.7 Tops of two Assyrian winged bulls flanking palace and temple entrance, Nimrud, ca. 18 April 1920. Courtesy of the Oriental Institute, University of Chicago.

finds among the ancient mounds, writing of Khorsabad, "In following the line of the extensive walls we found that the gates . . . had been structures of monumental architecture. Though now grass-grown hills, each . . . could be excavated with great profit, for the natives uncovered in our presence a large alabaster threshold . . . bearing impressive cuneiform records of the campaigns of Sargon." But dangers remained. "A few days before our arrival," Breasted remarked, "a British officer was murdered by the ruins of Assur. Of the fifteen political officers of the British administration, seven were murdered by natives, five before our arrival and two afterward."[41]

The expedition returned to Baghdad on 23 April, whereupon Breasted learned that an officer stationed at Salahiyeh, along the Euphrates and about 250 miles northwest of Baghdad, had discovered some ancient wall paintings while his troops were digging trenches. The British asked Breasted to record the paintings, and he was willing to do so provided the British allow his expedition to explore some Persian sites first. The officials balked because the troops in Salahiyeh, which was on the western frontier of Britain's zone of command, would soon be withdrawn eastward by nearly a hundred miles. Meanwhile Breasted realized that if he could obtain transportation to Salahiyeh, the expedition would be halfway to Aleppo, whence it could return overland to Egypt along the Mediterranean, thus avoiding a "long, wearisome journey back . . . via Bombay, . . . a saving of almost 5000 miles!" Breasted also knew, however, that the barren region between Baghdad and Aleppo could be dangerous because it was hotly contested among regional clans and it lay between the areas where British and French troops could guarantee safe transit. He consulted a British officer familiar with tribal sheikhs along the route, who replied it was "probable" the expedition could pass through safely.

With that faint assurance, the expedition, consisting of seven cars and military escort provided by the British, left Baghdad on 28 April. By the second day the caravan had lost the trail and then found its way by following the Euphrates' southern bank (figure 6.8). The group planned to stop each night at a British military post, but repeated mishaps and rough terrain slowed its progress, and it had to spend two nights in the open desert. Each evening the cars formed a circle, and the group's members took turns keeping watch. As day turned to night, "across the level river flats we saw Bedouin campfires. We avoided them, but invisible eyes were doubtless watching us." Breasted did his record keeping while the others slept, writing "by the light of a carefully masked globe candle" and stopping every fifteen minutes to "make the round of the camp with my gun in one hand, a shillalah in the other." Two of the cars were lost to accidents and mechanical failures by the time the caravan reached a British outpost at Anah. There the expedition joined a British supply caravan of thirty-four "vans" making its way to Abu Kemal, one of the few remaining British strongholds on the

Fig. 6.8 Oriental Institute expedition along the Euphrates near Fallujah, 28 April 1920. Courtesy of the Oriental Institute, University of Chicago.

Fig. 6.9 British military biplane provided for aerial survey of the desert and Euphrates valley in the vicinity of Salahiyeh, ca. 3 May 1920. Courtesy of the Oriental Institute, University of Chicago.

way to Salahiyeh. The colonel in charge warned the group to stay close because a police escort "had been fired on the day before. . . . The Arabs of this region happen to be excellent marksmen." The convoy arrived in Abu Kemal, about twenty-seven miles short of Salahiyeh, on 2 May. During the brief layover, the commander offered Breasted and Luckenbill an "air reconnaissance in one of his bombing planes, an experience which gave [them] exceedingly valuable impressions of the desert and Euphrates valley" (figure 6.9).[42]

Upon arriving, Breasted learned the British were withdrawing their forces on

5 May, which left just one day to record the ancient paintings. The next morning the expedition headed out to Salahiyeh and spent the day clearing, surveying, and photographing the paintings with the aid of Indian troops, under British command, who had been using the ancient ramparts there as a military outpost. Salahiyeh is the site of Dura-Europos, which began as a Babylonian town that was fortified into a military colony by the Seleucids about 300 BCE. After changing hands among various warring powers in the following centuries, it was conquered by the Romans in 165 CE and remained a thriving caravan city until it was destroyed during yet another conflict about a century later.

The remarkably well-preserved paintings, likened to those discovered at Pompeii, reveal the intermingling of artistic and religious traditions during the first few centuries of the Common Era in a frontier region shared by Asian and European empires (figure 6.10). The paintings constituted the expedition's most significant discovery, and Luckenbill's twenty-four photographs and Breasted's notes led to the production of the inaugural volume in the Oriental Institute Publications series two years later. Despite the paintings' importance and hints of further surviving works remaining to be excavated, the expedition regretfully stopped work as night fell and prepared for an early departure the next morning. At Breasted's urging, the Indian troops re-covered the paintings with sand to protect them for future study.[43]

The following morning, as the British withdrew eastward, Breasted and the others headed west into what had been described to him as a lawless no-man's land between the British and French spheres of interest. The British took the automobiles with them, however, and the expedition transferred its belongings to five locally hired horse-drawn wagons guided by their owners (figure 6.11). An officer arranged for the group to be accompanied by five Arab riflemen as far as the frontier of the British administration at Meyadin, about twenty miles further on. Breasted was advised to fly an American flag to signify the expedition's political neutrality, a step made necessary by the Arabs' hostility toward the French as well as the British. Governance of the area beyond Meyadin was increasingly contested between the French and followers of Faysal Husayn, who had helped lead an Arab army that joined the Allied war effort against the Ottomans and Germans. In March 1920 the Syrian congress elected Faysal king of the united Syria that included Palestine, but the next month the Allies affirmed the mandate system that placed the area of modern Syria and Lebanon under French control and Palestine under British control. The Oriental Institute expedition was passing between the zones of British and French administration just as the new jurisdictions were being imposed on Arab leaders throughout the region.

At Meyadin the expedition experienced these changes firsthand as the Arab riflemen recommended by the British fell away and were replaced by others recommended by the governor of the next town about thirty miles up the Euphrates, Deir ez-Zor, theoretically under French rule but rife with calls for independence. Word of the British withdrawal and the Americans' arrival preceded the expedition, and by the time it pulled into Deir ez-Zor, Breasted found a host of

> Arab sheikhs, Army officers, Government officials . . . all waiting to discuss with me the political future of the Arabs. . . .
>
> I plied them with questions in Arabic, French, and English, and soon found myself favored with a hundred conflicting confidences concerning the domestic and international ambitions of the Arabs, and immersed in the infinite complexities of Near Eastern politics. . . . The one invariable *leit-motif* throughout [was] their hope of assistance from America, and their complete confidence in our ability to help them.
>
> I tried as best I could to explain . . . America's own difficulties, but failed. . . . We were so tremendously powerful, we had such unlimited wealth, ours was the land of liberty and human rights, where all men were treated justly and fairly; surely we could secure . . . the same things for the Arabs who had so long endured despotism.

In retrospect, Breasted was "much amused" at his safety concerns about the journey through Arab-controlled territory: "An Englishman would be in the gravest danger . . . , a Frenchman more so. But Americans may now travel where they like in Arabia, for the Arabs know we are not looking for some advantage out of them." The only danger that lingered in the Americans' minds was "robbery by highwaymen," but Breasted could "recall such occurrences even in America!"[44]

The expedition slowly made its way over the rugged terrain, averaging about four and a half miles per hour from one caravansary to the next, or a maximum of forty-five miles in one leg, by rising at 3:00 a.m. for a 5:00 a.m. departure. By 8 May the group was about 400 miles from Baghdad and 130 from Aleppo, about three to four days away (figure 6.12). The caravansaries, or *khans* in Arabic, seem to become less well kept as the group worked its way west. Ordinarily Breasted obtained second-floor accommodations to be above the noise, dirt, and seemingly incessant commotion below. But at the last *khan* before Aleppo, only the first floor was available. Of it, Breasted wrote:

> We are down among the horses and their attendant mess. The rustic flavor would be bearable but for the swirling wind which picks up all the dried horse droppings in the *khan* and with fiendish accuracy deposits them on ourselves and our belongings. . . . A delicious touch was added to this bouquet of flavors and aromas when the drivers thoughtfully set a leaky petroleum tin on top of my bed-roll.

Fig. 6.10 "The Wall of Bithnanaia in Hall II: The Three Ministrants," Dura-Europos, 4 May 1920. Courtesy of the Oriental Institute, University of Chicago.

Especially effective and penetrating is the smudge from the burning dung, the only available fuel. . . . Our dinner is being cooked *over* it and thanks to the wind, quantities are being cooked *in* it as well. . . .

We are simply alive with fleas, and existence is one long scratch. You incessantly feel them crawling all over you, and resign yourself to misery as best you can.

Fig. 6.11 Oriental Institute expedition wagon drivers at Salahiyeh, 5 May 1920. Courtesy of the Oriental Institute, University of Chicago.

Fig. 6.12 Oriental Institute expedition outside the caravansary at Sabkha, ca. 8 May 1920. Courtesy of the Oriental Institute, University of Chicago.

Of course the locals had to endure these plagues, too, and Breasted was appalled at their apparent tolerance of the unsanitary conditions. Such critiques were invariably tempered by Breasted's capacity for wonder. As the group was about to depart in predawn darkness,

The stars twinkled with marvelous brightness. A half-moon hanging just above the western horizon threw a ghostly light over the huge court, and our wagons made long, broken shadows across the litter and filth of this desolate caravanserai. All at once the place was beautiful, and the spirit of the never-changing East seemed to brood over . . . this station through which the life of the orient had so long ebbed and flowed.

A ruddy light came through a door . . . , and as I stood in the silence of the
night listening to the munching of the horses, the low sound of voices reached
me faintly. Our drivers were sitting inside, earnestly talking with the *khanji* (the
keeper of the *khan*). The scene was like some old Dutch painting of the kitchen
of a wayside inn. . . . The candlelight behind them brought out in illumined sil-
houette the weather-beaten, glistening features of their rugged faces enveloped
in the smoke of cigarettes.

The expedition pulled into Aleppo on 12 May, and Breasted, feeling a sense
of "deliverance" upon entering a hotel and bathing, rejoiced: "From head to foot
I am one mass of red blotches—but I believe that . . . I am now no longer entertaining a single flea." He succumbed to a "raging fever," however, and while local
medical care enabled him to continue, the ailment—which was later determined
to be a rare malady—periodically afflicted him for the rest of his life.[45]

Breasted wanted to visit ancient sites in the vicinity of Aleppo such as
Carchemish and Antioch, but conflicts among local sheikhs and between them
and the French made the trips too risky. Instead, he hired a rail freight car and
armed Arab escort to travel almost due south to study Kadesh, the location of
the battle between Egyptians and Hittites about which Breasted had written
nearly two decades before, and Baalbek, a strategic site successively conquered
and developed by ancient Egyptians, Greeks, and Romans. From Baalbek, the
expedition shifted to a "little cogwheel railway" that took it over the Lebanon
Mountains to Beirut, where it arrived on 18 May. There it was met by Harold H.
Nelson, the former student and American University of Beirut professor whom
Breasted had recruited in 1907 for his ill-fated third epigraphic expedition. Nelson guided the present expedition to ancient Phoenician sites along the Mediterranean coast including Byblos (now Jubayl), as well as to local dealers and a
collector of Phoenician sarcophagi among other ancient works.

Here, too, "turbulent conditions" forced the group to curtail its survey, and
on 28 May it boarded a train to Damascus to visit dealers and ancient sites.
American diplomats there arranged for Breasted to meet French and Arab government officials. These meetings included dinner with Faysal Husayn during
his brief reign as king and a visit to Syria's short-lived Chamber of Deputies.
Breasted witnessed a nascent democracy in action during a parliamentary session that was "quiet, orderly and interesting: the old turbaned sheikhs favored
enforcement of completely centralized government with no local independence;
while the younger men in European clothes and red *tarbushes* (fezes) pled for
local autonomy and wide local liberty."

On 1 June the expedition departed Damascus by train for Haifa. Upon reaching the coastal city, Breasted learned that his hoped-for investigations in Palestine would be "quite impossible" because of local unrest. Accordingly Nelson

returned to Beirut accompanied by Luckenbill, and the others began their return to Cairo via Jerusalem. Breasted wanted to visit Megiddo, but bad directions waylaid the expedition, and the "great mound" was only visible from the
distance. He had to settle for "studying the earliest great battlefield between
Egypt and Asia,—the scene of so many dramatic struggles . . . that it has become proverbial as Armageddon." Breasted also planned to visit important ruins
outside Jerusalem, but even there conditions were too unstable for the British
authorities to assure his safety. He made the rounds of major sites within the
city, an experience that aroused "the religious emotions of one's childhood," and
Breasted also met British officials and scholars to lay the groundwork for future
research in Palestine.

The conversations were disturbing, however, because of rising tensions
among Moslems, Christians, and Jews resulting from the Balfour Declaration
of November 1917. The statement, which affirmed British support for establishing *in* Palestine a national home for the Jewish people, angered Moslems and
Christians, who were confronted with the prospect of a minority Jewish population, estimated then to comprise about 10 percent, achieving disproportionate
power in the land. Meanwhile, Jews were upset that the British did not authorize
the reconstitution of Palestine as *the* national Jewish homeland. By the time of
Breasted's visit, the "money of wealthy Jews everywhere" was "inundating this
country, and is augmented by the money of western Christians . . . caught by the
idea of restoring the Jews to their Promised Land." For their part, Moslems and
Christians were mounting "strong anti-Jewish demonstrations [and] many Jews
have been killed and many more wounded." Breasted feared the situation would
deteriorate into "a conflagration of the most serious proportions."[46]

On 9 June Breasted and the remaining expedition members departed Jerusalem on a newly completed rail line for the then comparatively quick fifteen-hour
trip to Cairo. The expedition staff dispersed, and Breasted remained to oversee
shipment of his acquisitions before returning to Chicago. While there he was
asked by Allenby to report his observations of political conditions in the territories through which he had passed to a meeting of regional British military
officials. Afterward the officials suggested that Breasted stop in London on the
way home to present a similar report to England's prime minister, David Lloyd
George, and foreign minister, George Curzon. Allenby added that he had "repeatedly warned the people at home that their present policy is steering straight for
trouble. But they won't listen to me. Perhaps they will take it from you!" Breasted
accepted the assignment and, at the request of a US military attaché in Egypt,
prepared a similar report for the US War Department. But he anticipated the
London visit with a "depressing sense of complete inadequacy—a pedagogue
meddling minutely in the vast game of the imperial powers. . . . The spectacle of
England and France plotting against each other in the Near East has cured me

of any vestige of such idealistic visions of international amity as I may still have been cherishing when I left America."

Breasted arrived in London on 26 June and shortly thereafter met with Foreign Minister Curzon, to whom he presented three issues:

> First. The dangerous hostility of the Arabs and the threatened general outbreak against the British. I was thus able to forewarn him of the imminent Arab outbreaks which have filled the press . . . the last few weeks. . . .
>
> Second. The dangerous situation in Palestine resulting from the disproportionate amount of power granted the Jews. . . .
>
> Third. The persistent anti-British propaganda carried on by French officials, and the reprisals in kind by the British, introducing into Western Asia a European rivalry which has already had deplorable consequences in Syria and Palestine, as well as in Mesopotamia.

Curzon was deeply interested and "cordial in his thanks," and he arranged Breasted's reimbursement for his London detour. Breasted was both disturbed and beguiled by his encounter with international diplomacy. Having worked with Egyptian Antiquities Service officials, he was certainly no stranger to the interrelations of government and scholarship in the Middle East. But his expedition, especially the contacts it afforded with government leaders, subtly strengthened his confidence in his own powers of observation and persuasion, despite his occasional claims to the contrary. It also revealed the extraordinary access archaeologists would have to Middle Eastern officials, as well as the scholars' home-country diplomats and opinion leaders—a level of entrée that would continue for over a decade, until the clouds of another world war began gathering.[47]

After dashing to Paris for some additional acquisitions, Breasted made his transatlantic return. He arrived in Chicago in mid-July with Ali, the Arab cook—who had become "as devoted as a faithful dog"—still by his side, now to become the Breasted family's housekeeper. Ali, a "small and boyish" twenty-one-year-old, had no remaining ties to his homeland, his family members having died of "privation" during the war. Ali's arrival was described by Breasted's son Charles as potentially a "solution of the servant problem," a subtle reference to difficulties in the Breasteds' home. Once the family could afford housekeepers, these hapless folk bore the brunt of Frances Breasted's frequent, alternating bouts of depression and peevishness, which had resulted in a constant turnover of domestic help. Breasted knew how heavily his nearly year-long sojourn abroad weighed on his wife, and he wanted to ease her burdens by bringing home fresh and, he hoped, more dedicated help.

Charles characterized his father's time away as a "serious trial" for his mother, who painfully endured "weeks of waiting between . . . letters, the dread of every cablegram, the lengthening months of anxiety, and above all the deep, unabating pain of separation from one who embodied her world and was her reason for living." Sadly, as the date of Breasted's return approached, "the possessive nature of her affection . . . had become more and more intensified, and her profound involuntary jealousy of all he had seen and experienced . . . consumed her and made her . . . physically ill." When Breasted arrived, "she lay anguished in a darkened room." Breasted shook off his alarm, "the never-say-die Victorian vanquishing the realist." Charles sensed his father "for the fraction of a moment . . . was wondering . . . whether coming home did not perhaps demand greater courage than the rigors of the field."

In truth, Breasted found refuge in his vocation, writing about a year later, "Of the three great things which constitute a man's life—his home, his friends and his work—the last must for me henceforth largely take the place of the first two. I am always thankful for work, which does not destroy feeling nor render it callous, but is like a faithful friend who gently leads one into a lovely garden of consolation and noble interest where aches and anxieties are soothed into sweet forgetfulness." As for Ali, he was undone by "homesickness and the alien climate," and Breasted arranged his return to the Middle East in late 1921.[48]

7

An Institute, a Calling

A Beginning and a Program

Breasted resumed regular university work in fall 1920, continuing as chair of the Department of Oriental Languages and Literatures, and now directing the Oriental Institute. His establishment of the institute, expedition accomplishments, and invitation to advise British leaders were recognized by the university with a raise to $7,000 a year. That, along with textbook royalty income averaging about $10,000 per annum and lecture fees, increased his annual income to $18,000. Breasted's publications, expeditions, and popular lectures were bringing him a measure of nationwide fame as well. By the 1920s his correspondence files show a steady, almost overwhelming growth in queries, requests, and admiring notes from all walks of American life, including ministers, amateur archaeologists, collectors, and students from other schools. During a conversation with a colleague, Breasted mentioned a letter from a high school student and "his detailed answer." Frances Breasted, who was nearby, remarked, "He spends so much precious time on those letters," to which he replied, "One never knows what young soul may be inspired to something great; I may not be able to answer all letters . . . , [but] I must answer letters from these eager young students."[1]

Not long after his return from the Middle East, Breasted was invited to deliver the university's fall convocation address. The invitation arrived while he was preparing a brief report on the expedition. The report along with the much longer and rhetorically richer convocation address translate the expedition's lessons into a preview of Breasted's ambitions for the institute. The "Report of the First Expedition of the Oriental Institute," a journal-style summary of the expedition and his "Political Mission to England," concludes with "Opportunities & Recommendations." The text also contains an overview of Breasted's antiquities purchases, which numbered about twenty-six hundred objects, as well as other tangible results in the form of photographs and field notes supplemented with "an extensive series of maps, plans, and diagrams exhibiting the geography, topography and ethnology of Western Asia." Breasted concluded the report with a "comprehensive plan of attack" for the ancient Near East "as a whole."[2]

Breasted's emphasis on the region "as a whole" signaled his objective of fielding projects that spanned the ancient Near East. He defined them by civilizations: Egyptian, Phoenician, Assyrian, Babylonian, Hittite, and the "common ground" of Palestine where they mingled. He stuck by his vision of two "headquarters" for the institute's Middle Eastern operations: Cairo during the winter months, when temperatures would allow Egyptian fieldwork, and "on the high cool slopes" overlooking Beirut during the summer months. All the institute's efforts, whether based in Chicago, Cairo, or Beirut, were directed toward a single ultimate purpose: production of "*a work on 'The Origins and Early History of Civilization,' which shall give the first adequate account of human beginnings & the early career of man.*" Breasted did not expect this to happen quickly, however, probably not even in his lifetime: "Before the whole recoverable story drawn out of every available mound is in our hands, it may indeed be a century or two; but . . . I am confident that with sufficient funds and adequate personnel *it will be possible in the next twenty-five or thirty years, or let us say within a generation, to . . . recover and preserve for future study the vast body of human records which they contain.*"[3]

The convocation address, titled "The New Past," called students to a life of scholarship in the ancient Near East. By "New Past," Breasted meant recent discoveries in such fields as paleontology and geology, as well as archaeology and ancient languages, from "the ages of man's prehistoric development and linking these up . . . with the history of the Orient," findings that show ancient history in a new light. Breasted's formulation of a "New Past" was not a methodological manifesto along the lines of James Harvey Robinson's "New History." Rather, it reflected an emerging sensibility among public intellectuals. Similarly, George Ellery Hale published an essay about the same time titled "The New Heavens," in which a "new" universe was being revealed by the ever larger telescopes he was building. Breasted, Hale, and their contemporaries shared a conviction that, thanks to accelerating developments in science and industry, civilization had arrived at the threshold of a new era. Others, however, were not so sure about "the new." Confidence in old verities and settled beliefs was being upset by relentless advances, including the use of new technologies to wreak unfathomable destruction in war. While some, like Breasted and Hale, enthusiastically crossed that threshold, others, particularly religious conservatives, lingered at the door. One contemporary fretted: "This is an age of new things. So many new discoveries—so many new inventions—so many combinations that the people are all at sea. In this age we have new thought, new voices, new books, new theology, new psychology, new philosophy, new religion, and everything that hell can suggest and the devil concoct."[4]

The "New Past" depended on a synthesis of the "two great forces which led men out of the Middle Ages into modern life . . . a vision which looked both *forward* and *backward*, and which not only caught the limitless possibilities of the *future* . . . but also . . . the profoundest inspiration from the . . . *past*." "In these days when emotional religion has so often given way to sober and even prosaic resolution," Breasted continued, "I see in the picture of man's past achievements and progress a powerful stimulus to continue the great adventure on the highest plane. I am convinced that this New Past . . . may be made a great moral power among the youth of our land."

Exploring the "New Past" required "a new type of historian—a cosmopolitan student of man, who is alike anthropologist, archaeologist, ethnologist, comparative religionist, versed in art and literature and acquainted both with the classical and the leading oriental languages of antiquity." To educate this kind of scholar, however, higher learning had to be revolutionized by replacing the old organization of subjects with one that bridged the "chasm . . . between natural and so-called humanistic science" with a new curriculum that presented the "history of the universe, from the fundamental constitution of matter through the . . . appearance of man." "In this way," Breasted explained, "the New Past would enable us to link up the career of man with that of the physical universe out of which he . . . emerged."

The Oriental Institute would do its part by illuminating the critical transition from "Stone Age barbarism" to the first stirrings of civilization, but this called for the "aid of a new generation of young Americans who are willing to spend the years necessary to gain the training and equipment without which the work cannot be done." Breasted acknowledged that his field entailed "a life of some sacrifices," which he rendered in terms evocative of a religious vocation:

> Those who elect to undertake it must set their faces to the East, feeling a deep reverence for the life of man on the earth, and highly resolving to devote their all to this new crusade. . . . [To] them the recovery of the unfolding life of man will not be a toilsome task, but rather a joyful quest, the modern quest for the

Grail, from which arduous journeys and weary exile in distant lands will not deter us. For in this crusade of modern scientific endeavor in the Near Orient . . . we are returning to ancestral shores. And in the splendor of that buoyant life of the human soul which has somehow come up out of the impenetrable deeps of past ages and risen so high, they shall find a glorious prophecy of its supreme future.

Among those in the convocation audience was Breasted's son Charles, who had just graduated from Chicago. He heard in the address a personal appeal to enter his father's field, a step he was unwilling to take. Although Breasted understood his son's decision, he did not give up easily, regarding the institute's work as not merely a job but a calling.[5]

Translation of Breasted's vision into reality required a reconsideration of what constituted the most essential evidence for ancient Near Eastern research and how best to interpret it. He returned to a line of thinking first pursued in a 1912 address, "Oriental History as a Field of Investigation." Mindful of his earlier aversion to excavations and how it illuminated for him the issues dividing archaeologists, epigraphers, and lexicographers, Breasted sought a shared arena in which knowledge produced in each discipline could contribute to a greater whole. The key to crossing these methodological boundaries, Breasted argued, was to reposition the objects of ancient Near Eastern research as *historical* evidence by asking broader, more probing questions concerning "the distribution of land, sources of royal income, the control of vice-kings by over-lords; . . . relations between classes, relation of classes to fiscal system, effect of foreign immigration, etc." By framing the ancient Near East as a historical unknown, Breasted wanted the institute to practice archaeology not as barely legitimized treasure hunting but as a data-collection method on a par with epigraphy and lexicography. The production of the comprehensive ancient Near Eastern history he envisioned was the end point of a process that began with the collection and interpretation of raw evidence of all kinds, objects and texts alike. The various subsidiary programs Breasted began mapping out would funnel that evidence into a single center where it could be sorted, examined, and interpreted. The institute was to become a "historical laboratory," a place where the "expert historian does his work."[6]

Over the course of 1921 Breasted designed the institute's inaugural projects, including several that would distinguish it internationally. One was the institute's publications program, which fulfilled his commitment to disseminating scholarly research and would flower into five separate series and dozens of volumes during Breasted's lifetime. He announced it and other plans in the institute's inaugural publication, *The Oriental Institute of the University of Chicago: A Beginning and a Program*, the first number of the Oriental Institute Communications, published in 1922. Another series, Oriental Institute Publications, would commence two years later with publication of the Dura-Europos discoveries. Whereas the latter series was designed to provide in-depth, definitive results from institute research projects at home and field operations abroad, Oriental Institute Communications was established to circulate relatively brief, initial reports on new projects or recent findings.

A Beginning and a Program is reminiscent of and was likely inspired by William Rainey Harper's *Official Bulletins*, published in the year leading up to the University of Chicago's opening, in which Harper methodically set out detailed plans for the university. Partly working papers, intellectual blueprints, and publicity announcements, the *Official Bulletins* "audaciously [committed] to paper" Harper's vision of what the university would become. Breasted's first communication, in addition to announcing the publications program, reported other new initiatives, recent achievements including the survey expedition and related acquisitions, the establishment of "archives," and the inception of several smaller projects involving Chicago faculty members in cooperative efforts with other institutions.[7]

Discussion of the expedition's acquisitions led Breasted to comment on the Haskell Oriental Museum, where they would be displayed (figure 7.1). Although he considered them "primarily . . . research materials," he declared the institute would "use them also for visualizing the origins and successive stages . . . of early culture." He envisioned a "presentation of ancient culture as a progressive process" through a "chronological arrangement of the original monuments, both within each show case and from case to case." These would be supplemented with "modern restorations combined with the originals," an example being a diorama-like reconstruction of an ancient Egyptian burial. Gaps in the collections would be filled with reproductions and drawings, and all the materials would be correlated with diagrams, such as one illustrating the upward march of civilization that Breasted had used earlier (see figure 6.2). These display techniques were part of his "system" for "making collections educationally available" for the general public.

The archives, on the other hand, were exclusively for research. A combination library and elaborate, card-based reference catalog, the archives involved "nothing less than disengaging, listing, compiling and classifying the available facts and data from the original monuments, published and unpublished, whether in museums or still standing on the original sites in the Near East, or, finally as scattered through the enormous body of treatises and monographs published in many different places by modern scholars." By mid-1922 there were already over twenty thousand cards. Breasted later expanded the plan to include an "Archaeological Corpus" that documented with photography finds made throughout the Near East.

Fig. 7.1 "Collections of the First Expedition of the Oriental Institute . . . Temporary Installation," view from southeast corner of Egyptian Hall, Haskell Oriental Museum, ca. 1921–22. Courtesy of the Oriental Institute, University of Chicago.

The ambition of Breasted's archives is reminiscent of other early-twentieth-century information-gathering projects, especially the "Mundaneum" being developed about the same time in Belgium by the pioneering information theorist Paul Otlet. However, he was aiming for a far more comprehensive source, one that would furnish answers to queries from throughout the world, free of charge, that—supplemented with certain technological advances he envisioned—augured the World Wide Web. Otlet believed his repository would contribute to international understanding and world peace, a vision undone by the Second World War's ravages and ensuing neglect. Breasted's aims were less utopian, but nonetheless grand. He viewed his project as *"one of the most important in the whole range of humanistic research . . . an urgently needed tool"* for which the institute was the "obvious agency." Yet, he admitted, given the "vast range of the ancient civilizations of the Near East, it is hardly conceivable that any organization would be able completely to realize this ideal." Indeed, within a decade Breasted had all but abandoned the archive, conceding the institute could no longer afford it.[8]

Of the projects Breasted outlined in *A Beginning and a Program*, two would become far more enduring parts of the institute's future: the "Assyrian-Babylonian Dictionary" and "Coffin Texts" projects. Breasted announced what would become more familiarly known as the "Chicago Assyrian Dictionary" in spring 1921, and

File Under *nadânu*	Writing { Ideogr. / " w ph. Comp.	Syl, List, Gram, School · Rel (Hymn, Prayer, Psalm, Lit, Rit, Omen, Incan, Hemerol) · Lit (Epic, Prov, Fable) · Hist, Chron, Business, Legal · Law, Medical, Math, Astrol. Assyr. Code	KAV. I, COL. III.

```
                    (24 Cont'd)              2123        (But if the master of the house)
63) us-bu-tu-u-ni i-[di]                           63) knew(that a man's wife) was dwelling (in his
64) 3 a-te i-id-da-an                                   house with his wife),
65) ù šum-ma it-te-ki-e-ir                         64) he shall pay threefold.
66) la-a i-di-e-ma i-ka-ab-bi                      65) But if he denies (it),
67) a-na i-id il-lu-u-ku                            66) says: "I did not know,"
68) ù šum-ma. amêlu ša aššat(at) amêli             67) they shall go to the river.
69) i-na bîti-šu us-bu-tu-u-ni                      68) And if the man in whose house
70) i-na i-id it-tu-u-ra                            69) a man's wife was dwelling,
71) 3 a-te i-id-da-an                              70) returns from the river,
72) šum-ma amêlu ša aššat-su i-na pa-ni-šu         71) threefold he shall pay.
                                                   72) If the man whose wife(of her own accord
                                                        withdrew herself)from his presence
```

Grammar chart:

NOUN, ADJ, PART, INF.				PERSONAL PRONOUN			PRONOMINAL SUFFIX			PRONOUN			VERB (strong,) (md. gem) (pr. hun) (pr. gut) (md. gut) (ter. inf.) (pr. w&i) (quadr.)					I, 2, 3	II, 1, 2, 3	III, 1, 2, 3	IV, 1, 2, 3
	sg.	pl.	du.	nominative gen-acc	sg.	pl.	noun verb	sg.	pl.		sg.	pl.		sg.	pl.	du.					
nom				1st			1st			Demonstr.		mas	1st				Present	a			
gen				2nd			2nd			Rel.		fem	2nd				Preterite				
acc				3rd			3rd			Inter.		neut	3rd	✓			Imperative				
mas	fem	com		mas	fem		mas	fem		Indef.			mas		fem		Infinitive				
PROPER NOUN (incl. gentilic)				NUMERALS									emphatic				Participle				
male	god	star	city	mount.	cardinal		adverbial						dep. clause				Permansive				
female	goddess	temple	land	stream	ordinal		adjectival						ADVERB { encl / pref				PREPOSITION		CONJUNCTION	
underworld				fraction		distributive															

Fig. 7.2 "Assyrian-Babylonian Dictionary" card after editing, figure 57 from Breasted's *The Oriental Institute . . . : A Beginning and a Program* (1922). Courtesy of the Oriental Institute, University of Chicago.

his colleague Assyriologist Daniel D. Luckenbill assumed formal responsibility for it that fall. The dictionary's methods were closely modeled on the Egyptian dictionary's including preprinted cards for recording uses of Assyrian words in context (figure 7.2; compare with figure 2.11). Although Breasted credited Luckenbill with designing the card, its function in the dictionary's editorial procedures was obviously guided by Breasted, as is evident in his description of the project's inception. Work commenced 3 October 1921, a date Breasted hoped would be "memorable . . . in the history of oriental science." At the outset Luckenbill was assisted by another Chicago faculty member along with a team of collaborators working at other institutions, all but one being alumni of Chicago's Department of Oriental Languages and Literatures.

The reach of the project, to survey "all the cuneiform documents now available," demanded an efficient operation that relied on specialized typewriters, filing systems, and other aids to speed the work. Within six months, the team was completing and filing 2,000 cards a week, with the total reaching about 75,000. Breasted wanted to increase the staff by 25 percent to boost its output to over

Fig. 7.3 Photograph of panel interior from the coffin of an ancient Egyptian nobleman, Nefri, "The Steward of the Estate," ca. 2000 BCE, Egyptian Museum, Cairo, no. 28087. The photograph was taken in 1923 by John Hartman for the Coffin Texts project, and the hieroglyphic text is primarily in the lower right quadrant. Courtesy of the Oriental Institute, University of Chicago.

200,000 cards per year. Even with a larger staff, he estimated it could take eight to ten years to bring the dictionary "near completion." Yet the intellectual rigor he sought in his own work and taught to his students retarded the dictionary's progress. As knowledge of Assyrian grew and the standards of scholarly accuracy became ever more exacting, the project evolved into an ongoing language seminar, and the dictionary's compilation slowed to an almost imperceptible pace. More than four decades would pass before the first of an originally projected six volumes was issued, and the project would grow to about 2 million cards and an estimated twenty-one volumes, the dictionary only nearing completion almost ninety years after its launch.[9]

Depicting Picture Writing

The Coffin Texts project began with an observation Breasted made in *Development of Religion and Thought in Ancient Egypt* in 1912. It came in his discussion of Egyptian mortuary practices during the Middle Kingdom (about 1975–1640 BCE), when texts began to be inscribed on coffin interiors to guide the deceased into the afterworld. Egyptologists customarily referred to mortuary texts inscribed in pyramids as "Pyramid Texts." During the Middle Kingdom, Breasted noticed, the Pyramid Texts were "largely appropriated by the middle and the official class. At the same time there emerge similar utterances, identical in function but . . . more suited to the needs of common mortals. . . . Later the Book of the Dead was made up of selections from this humbler and more popular mortuary literature. Copious extracts from both the Pyramid Texts and these forerunners of the Book of the Dead . . . were now written on the inner surfaces of the heavy cedar coffins" (figure 7.3).

The coffin inscriptions are important because they constitute the "earliest literary expression" of Egyptian "ethical consciousness [and] moral responsibility in the life hereafter," and "as a class are sometimes designated as the Book of the Dead." However, Breasted noted, this appellation is misleading because "about half of them are taken from the Pyramid Texts, and the Pyramid Texts are sharply distinguished from the Book of the Dead." Thus "it would seem not only incorrect, but also the obliteration of a useful distinction to term these Middle Kingdom texts the Book of the Dead." Therefore, Breasted continued, "I have for convenience termed them Coffin Texts, a designation drawn from the place in which they are found, and thus parallel with the Pyramid Texts." Breasted later created a table to clarify the distinctions:

Form and Date	Social Class	Contents
I. THE PYRAMID TEXTS		
Engraved in five pyramids, about 2625–2475 B.C.	Exclusively for the pharaohs; sharply distinguished from II and III	Older materials, from about the 35th to the 25th century B.C.
II. THE COFFIN TEXTS		
Written with ink on the insides of wooden coffins (very rarely on papyrus), 23d to 18th century B.C.	For the nobles and the well-to-do; not sharply distinguished from III	A large proportion of Pyramid Texts, with much additional material that later passed into the Book of the Dead
III. THE BOOK OF THE DEAD		
Written on a papyrus roll and placed in the tomb, 16th century B.C. until the Christian era	For all classes of society; not sharply distinguished from II	A large body of Coffin Texts, also other, probably older, material

Because the Coffin Texts contain "the earliest surviving fragments of the Book of the Dead" and had yet to be systematically studied, there was a significant gap in knowledge of the religious beliefs and practices of a growing population outside the pharaonic courts. However, "such documents can never be fully understood," Breasted argued, "until *all* these Coffin Texts have been collected and published as a whole."[10]

When Breasted returned to the Coffin Texts, now a decade later, he sought the advice of British Egyptologist Alan H. Gardiner. The two first met in the Egyptian galleries of the British Museum in early July 1901, just as Gardiner, fourteen years Breasted's junior, was completing his studies at Oxford. They dined together that evening, and Breasted was impressed by the younger man's gifts, expecting him to "do great things in a few years." Shortly thereafter Gardiner moved to Germany, where he studied with Breasted's mentor Adolf Erman and assisted with the Egyptian dictionary project. Coming from a wealthy family, Gardiner could devote his all to research, becoming one of Egyptology's most rigorous and productive scholars. He and Breasted remained in touch over the years, their wives and children became acquainted with one another, and their research interests periodically converged. It was Gardiner's work on the sage Ipuwer that inspired Breasted's ideas regarding "social prophecy," particularly as articulated in *Development of Religion and Thought in Ancient Egypt*.

When, in 1921, Breasted first mentioned to Gardiner the idea of collecting and editing the Coffin Texts, he merely wondered if Gardiner had any observations about it. Gardiner replied that he had already "thought a good deal about [a] scheme" involving a team of perhaps two or three additional collaborators and asked, "Is it impossible that some cooperation should be devised?" The two had previously discussed the benefits of "consulting and incorporating [the] work of other men on a given text." While Breasted agreed with this approach, he did so cautiously because when he examined the work of others, he found that "I was only getting dust in my eyes." He associated this attitude with the nature of his doctoral training and an attendant "isolation of the Berlin school in grammatical research." Breasted was referring to the prevailing methodology of the time, which dictated going back to the original sources whenever possible rather than relying on other scholars' potentially unreliable transcriptions or translations. He recalled that "in the early 90-ties Erman used to say to me: 'When I consult others' research on the difficult points, I find they don't understand them either.'"[11]

In this instance, however, Breasted enthusiastically welcomed Gardiner's collaboration and leaped ahead to a work plan. He suggested that they jointly oversee the project, serve as coeditors, and hire assistants such as Ludlow S. Bull and William F. Edgerton—the doctoral students who accompanied Breasted on the survey expedition—and another one Gardiner knew, Adriaan de Buck, a young Dutchman who was just completing his studies in Germany, where he worked with Kurt Sethe and Adolf Erman. Already thinking about publication, Breasted offered the distinctions he drew among the Pyramid Texts, Coffin Texts, and Book of the Dead, indicating his preference for "Coffin Texts" as the project's title.[12]

Breasted barely touched on methodology beyond suggesting they catalog all known coffins in Egypt and abroad bearing relevant texts and establish "the principle . . . that the enterprise is dependent on securing photographs of everything." At the time, there were 138 coffins documented in museum collections, of which 95 were in the Egyptian Museum, the balance scattered among museums in Europe and America. Gardiner accepted Breasted's suggestions, including the use of photographs "as an essential feature of the work." He also agreed to Breasted's separation of the texts into three divisions based on points of origin, the "Coffin Texts" project title, and the cataloging idea.

Gardiner's most significant contributions to the project's design turned on questions of methodology and rigor. In particular, he argued for a process of cross-checking involving all three participants in reviewing each other's transcriptions before publication, a far more rigorous and time-consuming approach that, up to this point, had not been employed in Egyptology. While each person would be responsible for transcribing a single coffin, once the transcription was complete, it "was to be controlled most carefully by the other two" participants. After the transcription was agreed upon, it was "to be read, and so far as possible translated in a common sitting, so that any mistakes could . . . be eliminated straight away." This approach was necessary, Gardiner observed, because to do the work properly, each coffin, no matter how fragile, had to be disassembled, photographed and studied, and then reassembled—an invasive procedure that could not be repeated: "The first collation must also be the last."[13]

Over the following year the two further refined their methodology, concentrating on recording transcriptions, duplicating them for editorial work, photography, and schedule. They planned to publish the transcriptions in a vertical format corresponding to most of the original inscriptions—a significant decision because some of their contemporaries published vertically oriented inscriptions in horizontal formats to save on publication costs. To speed the editing process, Breasted proposed using standardized prepunched forms that could be collected in loose-leaf ring binders. Most commonly used in business and legal settings at the time, this "technology for updating" would be ideal for assembling and comparing similar texts from many different coffins. Breasted experimented with several techniques for producing worksheet copies and settled on photostats—high-contrast photographic prints especially suited to copying texts. Gardiner was skeptical about the usefulness of photographs in the transcription process, but Breasted prevailed. Priority was given to photographic documentation first, and the transcription process would begin from photographs, with the transcription sheets subsequently "collated," or corrected, against the original inscriptions.

Among their more difficult challenges were painted scenes, patterns, and decorative bands containing hieroglyphic texts. Those texts were usually the names and titles of the deceased who once occupied the coffins, as well as fragments of mortuary prayers, so they had to be included in the transcriptions. However, they are frequently horizontal and separated from the main inscriptions (see the third through fifth bands from the top on the right side of figure 7.3). Breasted

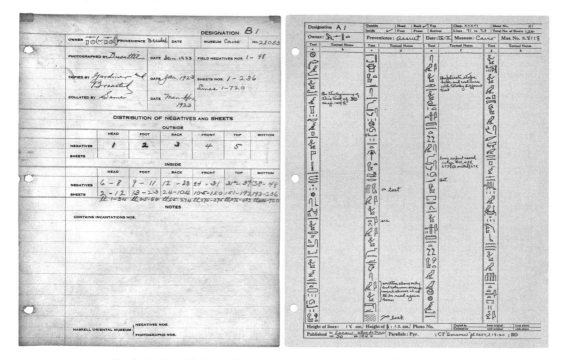

Fig. 7.4 Left, Coffin Texts photographs and transcriptions record form; right, Coffin Texts transcription form. Both forms designed by Breasted, spring 1922; left-hand form filled out by Breasted, January 1923; author and date of right-hand transcription unknown. Courtesy of the Oriental Institute, University of Chicago.

realized the form he was designing would not readily accommodate horizontal texts, but rather than force them into a misleading orientation, he recommended that they be written horizontally on the first page of a coffin's transcription. Significantly, the subjects of paintings that depicted "gifts or offerings, doors, house fronts, sacred eyes, etc.," were "not to be considered." Efficiency no doubt led Breasted to pass over visual evidence that, in other spheres of his work, had become ever more important. Gardiner agreed, though with reservations: "As a general principle I think we ought in collecting to be always on the safe side, including more . . . rather than less. We can always restrict the scope later, but we cannot then widen it."

Breasted followed up with a memorandum of agreement that outlined the participants' responsibilities, succession of publication rights, and "Rules of Work and Arrangement of Manuscript," and he completed designs for two forms: one to log the photographs, the other to record the transcriptions (figure 7.4). The transcription form served several additional purposes: recording linguistic annotations and indicating the texts' positions within coffins, the coffin's present location, its provenance, the height of lines and standard hieroglyphs in the original, and previous citations. Breasted believed the transcriptions and

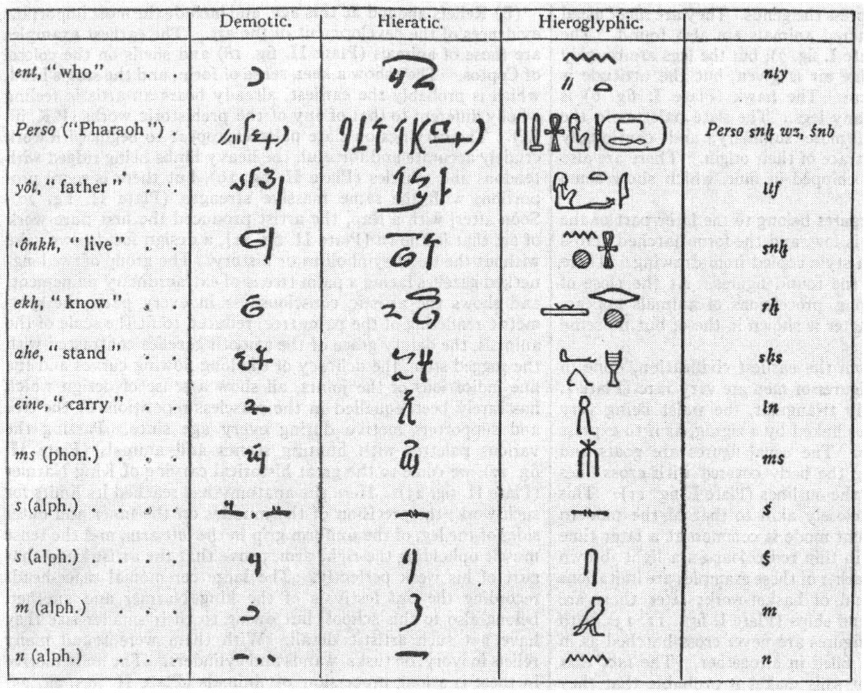

Fig. 7.5 Table of ancient Egyptian writing forms. From *Encyclopaedia Britannica*, 11th ed., 9:65. Public domain, reproduction by author.

related annotations should be kept parallel because the original texts were in a "cursive form of hieroglyphic which not infrequently approaches hieratic. The hand-copying on the . . . form is therefore a transliteration into hieroglyphic and many textual notes will be concerned with matters of transliteration." The problem turned on a crucial difference between the hieratic scripts of the Coffin Text writers, which—like an individual's cursive handwriting—can be highly idiosyncratic, and hieroglyphs, which are more like block lettering (compare the "Hieratic" and "Hieroglyphic" columns in figure 7.5). The task required interpreting sometimes confusing hieratic marks into hieroglyphs, interventions not unlike translating difficult handwriting into typescript—judgments that had to be noted and explained each time they were made. The wider "Textual Notes" columns on Breasted's form were essential for this purpose.

Breasted and Gardiner guessed the Egyptian Museum's coffins contained about 10,000 lines of text, which Breasted estimated would require about 2,500 copies of the forms for their transcription. By May 1922 the forms and related materials were ready, and Breasted shipped a supply to Gardiner. After a few months of delays they agreed to rendezvous in Cairo and start with the Egyptian Museum coffins during the winter 1922–23 season.[14]

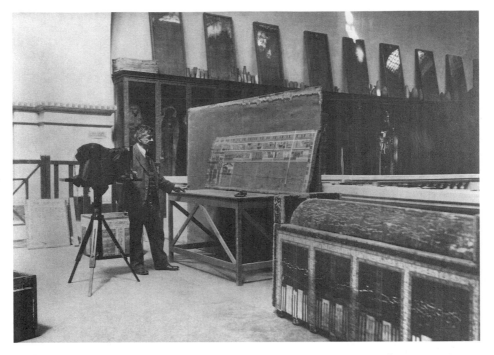

Fig. 7.6 John Hartman photographing a panel for the Coffin Texts project in the Egyptian Museum, Cairo, ca. 1923. Courtesy of the Oriental Institute, University of Chicago.

As planned, they employed assistants in Cairo, including John Hartman, an Austrian living there at the time who was hired to photograph the dismantled coffins (figure 7.6), and one of Breasted's students, Ludlow S. Bull. Pierre Lacau, then head of the Antiquities Service, approved the team's use of an Egyptian Museum side gallery for a work site (figure 7.7). "Breasted took an energetic part in our first season's work," Gardiner wrote, "and I marveled how accurately this many-sided scholar accomplished his copying." Breasted commented, "The work of this first winter really disclosed to us for the first time the formidable difficulty and unforeseen extent of our task." He was grappling with another problem, too, administration of Oriental Institute programs and staff, which repeatedly pulled him away from the project.

The 1923–24 season commenced without Bull, and to replace him and also help fill in for himself, Breasted obtained a five-year grant to hire Adriaan de Buck who, along with a couple of shorter-term assistants, ended up doing most of the transcriptions. Recognizing Gardiner's expanding leadership of the project as Breasted reduced his, Breasted arranged for Gardiner's formal appointment as "Research Professor in Egyptology" at the University of Chicago, accompanied by an annual stipend for travel expenses. Gardiner was "flattered and pleased by the honour," but also guarded. He wanted to avoid "any definite obligation. The

Fig. 7.7 The Coffin Texts project staff at work in a side gallery of the Egyptian Museum, Cairo, 1922–23. In the middle distance, from left to right: Alan H. Gardiner, Breasted, and Ludlow S. Bull. On the far left and far right are Anna MacPherson Davies and Norman de Garis Davies, a couple expert at rendering facsimiles of ancient Egyptian paintings. Mr. Davies was a member of Breasted's 1906–7 Nubian expedition team. Courtesy of the Oriental Institute, University of Chicago.

one thing which I have always considered the greatest blessing of my position in life, has been the independence which it has given me."

Breasted withdrew from active participation early in 1925 and took the occasion to iron out remaining methodological details with Gardiner as they began looking ahead to publishing their findings. The "Revised Memorandum on the Coffin Texts" contains a shift in nomenclature as the individual texts began to be called "spells," a tightening of cataloging specifications for similar texts, and plans to publish in parallel columns alternate versions of spells to ease their comparison (figure 7.8).

As the project was refined, its progress slowed, straining Breasted's relationship with Gardiner. Breasted was eager to push ahead as quickly as possible; Gardiner preferred exactitude over efficiency. They clashed in particular over the role of T. George Allen, a former doctoral student of Breasted's who was born in Rockford, Illinois, Breasted's birthplace. Allen received his degree in 1915, and two years later Breasted appointed him secretary of the Haskell Oriental Museum, a title that changed to secretary of the Oriental Institute when it was established. Breasted wanted Allen to work in an editorial capacity on the Coffin

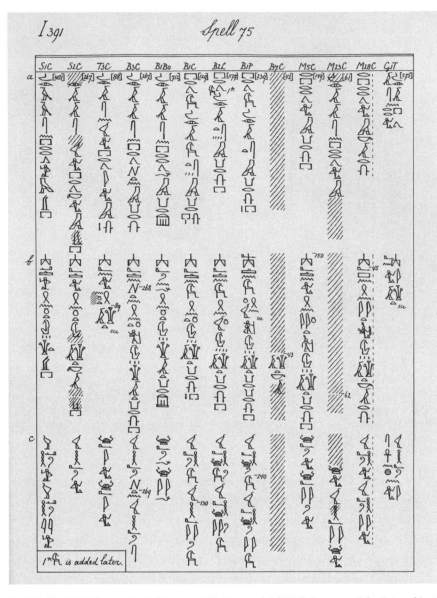

Fig. 7.8 "Spell 75," from de Buck, *Egyptian Coffin Texts*, vol. 1 (1935). Courtesy of the Oriental Institute, University of Chicago.

Texts, correlating them with the Pyramid Texts for the publication. Allen would have to work closely with Gardiner, something Allen was eager to do because he had "a very high opinion" of Gardiner's scholarly acumen. Gardiner, however, thought Allen was out of his depth. Breasted urged his friend to consider the institute's purposes, which included giving students and young scholars "opportunities for gaining indispensable experience" so they could "worthily . . . take our places and carry on after we are gone."

Meanwhile, with Adriaan de Buck assuming ever-greater responsibilities for the project, Gardiner was concerned de Buck would not receive sufficient credit for its success. In the end, Gardiner accepted Allen, and Breasted reassured his partner about de Buck's credit by drafting sample title pages for the publication showing who was responsible for which aspects of the project. By the late 1920s, Gardiner's participation also diminished, and de Buck's correspondingly grew. He completed transcribing the Cairo coffins and those in European collections by 1929–30 and those in America the following winter. De Buck saw the texts through publication, a task that required seven volumes and lasted from 1935 to 1961.

The transcription process took so long because of the complexity of translating the highly personal and abbreviated nature of hieratic script into more easily read hieroglyphs. To carry the analogy of transcribing a person's hard-to-read handwriting into block letters one step further, one has to imagine a page of script in which a certain squiggle that is repeated many times could be either an *n* or an *r*. Solving the problem requires a careful examination of the squiggle in context. If a certain word, such as *are* occurs many times, the precise rendering of the *r* in it may help one interpret other words containing *r* or *n*, such as *over* and *oven*. The challenge of transcribing hieratic writing increased as Egyptologists' appreciation of their nuances of meaning grew, demanding—as de Buck put it—that they "make the veil of transcription as thin as possible." Even the transcription of hieroglyphs was a form of translation, one that depended on comparing many inscriptions to ascertain the shades of meaning represented by subtle differences among *seemingly* similar signs. Breasted's goal of copying the surviving records of Egypt as a means of preserving and disseminating them was becoming ever more complex as Egyptology itself matured.[15]

It's not easy to read a hieroglyphic inscription, especially one located on a remote, crumbling temple. Comparing an inscription to another one located hundreds of miles away is even harder. Yet, to do this kind of comparative study, the nuts and bolts of Egyptology, one needs a method of making accurate copies of the inscriptions. When the inscription is damaged, that pursuit of accuracy means balancing fidelity to what remains of a partially effaced sign against an informed guess of what that sign *was*. To merely record the damaged sign is an act of representation. To guess at what it likely was when whole is a type of translation. It is a conjecture that ideally is informed by a prior knowledge of hieroglyphs, but one that is only as good as the extent of that knowledge at the time the supposition is made. Attempts at rendering, much less understanding, hieroglyphs in the seventeenth century, well before Jean-François Champollion deciphered them, were often comically bad. However, even in the late nineteenth century and well after Champollion's breakthrough, the depiction and interpretation of hieroglyphs left ample room for improvement. It was Breasted's generation of scholars that slowly and meticulously compiled the dictionaries, grammars, and concordances necessary to narrow the remaining gaps in understanding this famously difficult language.

Although copies of inscriptions gradually improved in the nineteenth century, they still contained glaring errors, depending not only on the copyists' fidelity to what they observed but on the level of their training in hieroglyphs and the state of Egyptological knowledge when they were trained. When the reliability of hieroglyphic copying improved, it was largely arm-in-arm with advances in hieroglyphic scholarship. The centuries-long history of attempts to understand hieroglyphs is to an extent a chronicle of repeated failures to recognize the importance of their accurate depiction. Yet the prevailing beliefs of each era in which hieroglyphs were encountered also confused their interpretation. Taken as a whole, successive generations' efforts to represent and translate these intriguing signs reveal more about the "myth of Egypt and its hieroglyphs" in the Western imagination than a growing understanding of them. This also explains why it took so long, even after Champollion forged the keys to reading hieroglyphs, to begin sorting out the problems of depiction and interpretation that preoccupied Breasted's generation.[16]

Hieroglyphs first appeared in ancient Egypt about 3200 BCE, functioning initially as signs both for sounds of speech, or phonograms, and as pictures of objects represented, or ideograms. The phonograms came to express single, double, or triple consonants, the most frequently used being single, or "unilateral," consonants, though they never constituted an alphabet. The phonograms, as consonants, comprise a skeletal language in the sense that they require, like Semitic languages such as Arabic and Hebrew, a prior knowledge of the requisite vowels necessary to vocalize words. Without that knowledge, a group of consonants can be pronounced in different ways, leading to different meanings. For example, our consonants *tdy* could be read, depending on which vowels we supply, as *today*, *tidy*, or *toady*. Around 1985 BCE, some hieroglyphs began to function as determinatives; that is, a given sign when placed after a group of others lost its phonetic or ideogrammatic value and instead determined the meaning of the ones just preceding it. All in all, the many possible meanings of certain hieroglyphs, depending on their placement and adjacent signs, their uses as phonograms, ideograms, or determinatives, as well as potential vowel placements, confounded generations of would-be translators accustomed to strictly alphabetical writing systems. That hieroglyphic texts can be organized in vertical or horizontal lines and, when in vertical columns, from left to right or vice versa did not make things any easier.

The foundation of hieroglyphic writing was in place by about 2500 to 2200 BCE, and it entered its "classic" period around 2000 to 1800 BCE, at which point as many as seven hundred signs were in fairly steady use. Starting as early as the

1550s to 1200s BCE, the language entered a period of very gradual corruption and decline, a process that begins to be especially noticeable after the Persian conquest in 525 BCE and accelerates further after the advent of Ptolemaic rule in 305 BCE. Over time Egyptian writing evolved from stately hieroglyphs to the cursive hieratic and then into the yet more abbreviated demotic (figure 7.5). Yet the underlying structures, functions, and meanings of hieroglyphs remained essentially stable throughout this long history, with changes coming primarily in added shades of meaning, the formation of compound ideograms, and the addition of new ideograms.

For reasons that remain unclear to this day, however, the use and knowledge of hieroglyphs and other Egyptian writing forms gradually began to fade during the late Ptolemaic and Roman periods. Elements survived only in the form of six Coptic letters—the remaining twenty-five letters of the Coptic alphabet descending from ancient Greek. Curiously, though contacts between ancient Greece and Egypt began sometime between 653 and 525 BCE, the Greeks either did not acquire or did not sustain the ability to read hieroglyphs. Herodotus represented the views of many Greeks when he erroneously characterized hieroglyphic inscriptions on monuments as possessing only sacred content and hieratic texts on papyrus as exclusively epistolary writings or the mundane transactions of everyday life. In fact, hieroglyphic texts on monuments also recount historical events and daily routines, while hieratic writings on papyrus are frequently sacred tracts. But the Greeks' certainty about the inherent religious meaning of hieroglyphs lingers in our nomenclature today: the Greeks called the mysterious inscriptions "sacred carvings," whence the word *hieroglyph* derives.

Assuming that hieroglyphs had an intrinsically religious purpose, Greek-influenced scholars such as Plotinus, the founding father of Neoplatonism, believed that they were deliberately cryptic so as to confine knowledge of their meaning to only the most learned, endowing them with a mystical aura as well. With the Renaissance retrieval of classical learning and the translation into Latin of Plotinus's work, published in 1492, his hermetic estimation of hieroglyphs helped inspire Renaissance scholars' searches for hidden meanings in all kinds of curious and ancient things. This sensibility was so wide reaching that, by the early seventeenth century, a fairly accurate depiction of the ritual furnishings and cult objects on an ancient Roman frieze could be labeled as "hieroglyphic effigies" (figure 7.9).[17]

It was not until well into the seventeenth century that scholars began to explore the *linguistic* functions of Egyptian hieroglyphs, principally as a way of ferreting out the origins of European languages. A leader of this effort was the German-born Jesuit Athanasius Kircher, a polymath whose investigations of hieroglyphs began with the study of Coptic. His findings, published in 1636 as *Prodromus Coptus sive Aegyptiacus* (Harbinger of Coptic or Egyptian), show a

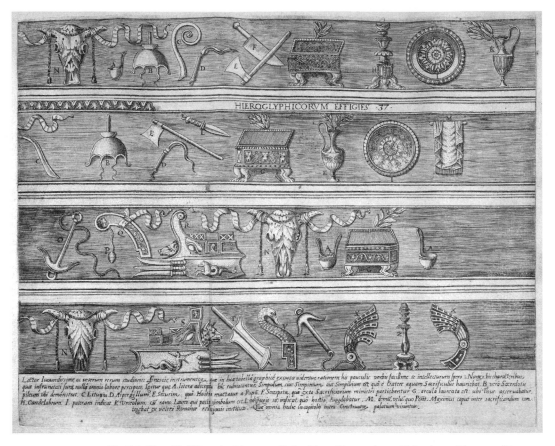

Fig. 7.9 Plate 37, "Hieroglyphicorum effigies," from Hörwarth von Hohenburg, *Thesaurus hieroglyphicorum* (1610). Public domain, reproduction of shelfmark Vet. D2.b.1, plate "Hieroglyphicorum effigies 37," courtesy of the Bodleian Library, University of Oxford.

correct understanding of Coptic as being related to ancient Egyptian, and this insight led him to focus on hieroglyphs. The result, published in three volumes between 1652 and 1654 as *Oedipus aegyptiacus*, is a sprawling compendium of inscriptions, false translations, and commentary in which Kircher got a handful of things right, such as the phonetic value of *mu*, the hieroglyph for water (figure 7.10), but nearly all the rest he got very wrong. Kircher was blinded by the theological assumptions of his milieu, and despite his very real discoveries, he nonetheless pressed on to weave his knowledge of Egypt into a cosmology "governed by the doctrines of Christianity." Not until the late eighteenth century did a fresh interest in antiquities and exploration plant the seeds for what, by the mid-nineteenth century, grew into the beginnings of archaeology and Egyptology, *Egyptologist* first appearing in print in 1859.[18]

When Napoleon invaded Egypt in 1798, his army was accompanied by about 160 scholars, who, along with dozens of artists, fanned out to document the land

Fig. 7.10 Detail from Kircher, *Turris Babel* (1679). The left-hand column shows the hieroglyph, the center column a brief analysis of its meaning, and the right-hand column its phonetic value. Public domain, reproduction courtesy of Asian and Middle Eastern Division, New York Public Library, Astor, Lenox, and Tilden Foundations.

from ancient monuments to contemporary life. It took thirteen years for their records to be published, beginning in 1809, filling twenty-three volumes that include nearly nine hundred plates. Titled *Description de l'Égypte*, it contains engravings of numerous monuments, showing their architecture, bas-reliefs, and some inscriptions rendered with comparative accuracy given that no one understood hieroglyphs at the time. The *Description*'s editors also compiled tables of individual hieroglyphs (figure 7.11, left) and cartouches of royal names (figure 7.11, right), which appeared to offer a basis for systematic studies of ancient Egyptian. Ultimately, however, it was the French army's discovery in 1799 of the Rosetta Stone—with its parallel texts in hieroglyphs, demotic Egyptian, and ancient Greek—that provided the means for translating hieroglyphs (figure 7.12).

Scholars began by associating the stone's demotic inscriptions with ancient Greek passages they could readily translate. By 1818, Thomas Young, a British physician, scientist, and Egyptological pioneer, began relating those demotic marks to hieroglyphs on the stone, and in 1822 Champollion, realizing the differences between hieroglyphs and demotic were largely graphic rather than linguistic, forged the tools for their effective translation. The race to record and translate inscriptions was on. The first epigraphic survey expedition to Egypt was led by Champollion and the father of Egyptology in Italy, Ippolito Rosellini, in 1828–29, and from 1842 to 1845 the German scholar Karl Richard Lepsius, Adolf Erman's teacher, headed an expedition whose transcriptions are considered by many to have anticipated significantly higher standards for epigraphic accuracy and comprehensiveness.[19]

Given the vast numbers of inscriptions to record, however, efficiency was as important as accuracy. In England John Williams, an astronomer and antiquarian, experimented during the 1830s with laying sheets of paper over inscriptions and rubbing inked transfer sheets against them. The technique, though efficient, produced crude results and was soon abandoned (figure 7.13). Others, like Lepsius, made "squeezes," paper or papier-mâché impressions done on site in Egypt

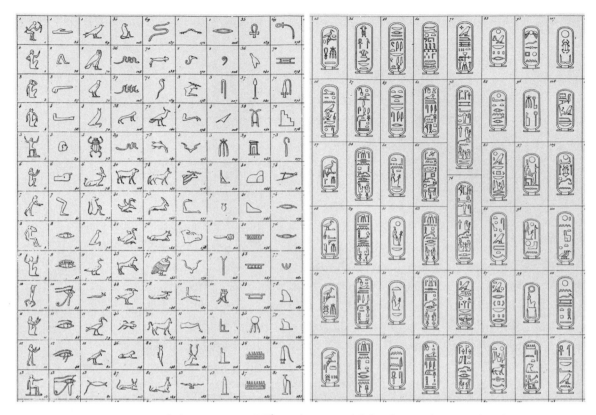

Fig. 7.11 Details from *Description de l'Égypte* (1809–1828): left, volume 5, plate 50; right, volume 5, plate 51. Public domain, reproductions by author.

and shipped back to Europe. But they were fragile and difficult to reproduce in publications (figure 7.14). Hand-rendered copies posed their own problems. Egyptologists lacking sufficient drawing skills were unable to capture valuable paleographic nuances, typically rendering hieroglyphs in overly spare, almost abstracted forms. An example by British Egyptologist Percy Newberry, who had some knowledge of hieroglyphs, is crude and childlike in comparison to one by his countryman Howard Carter (figure 7.15). Newberry and Carter worked side by side in the same set of tombs, and though Carter could not read hieroglyphs at the time, he was a trained artist, and his skill shows in the fidelity and delicacy of his copies. Yet, even as Egyptologists' knowledge advanced during the early twentieth century, they accepted simplified transcriptions, particularly for compilations of texts from various sources in which uniformity of presentation took precedence over accuracy. Good examples are the edition of Pyramid Texts published between 1908 and 1922 by Breasted's fellow student Kurt Sethe (figure 7.16), which helped inspire Breasted's *Development of Religion and Thought in Ancient Egypt*, and the Coffin Texts transcriptions (figure 7.8).[20]

Fig. 7.12 Rosetta Stone (196 BCE), named for the site in Egypt, Rashīd, where it was found in 1799. Photograph © Trustees of the British Museum.

Fig. 7.13 Rubbing, by John Williams, of the stela of Tunennekhebkhŏns, ca. 1830s. Reproduced with permission of Griffith Institute, University of Oxford. The stela is now in the British Museum, registration no. 1905, 1115.2.

Fig. 7.14 (*facing page, top*) Papier-mâché squeeze, "Doc. 44. Chapelle-crypte du temple de Mout., Estampage de l'inscription A. Paroi S.," plate 69, from Jean Leclant, *Montouemhat, quatrième prophète d'Amon, prince de la ville* (Cairo: Imprimerie de l'Institut Français d'Archéologie Orientale, 1961). © Institut Français d'Archéologie Orientale.

Fig. 7.15 (*facing page, bottom*) Details of plates from Newberry and Griffith, *El Bersheh* [1893–94?]. Left, "Tomb No. 5," rendering by Percy Newberry, vol. 2, plate 17; right, "Tomb No. 2," rendering by Howard Carter, vol. 1, plate 16. Public domain, reproductions by author.

RIGHT HAND WALL.

FRONT WALL, RIGHT SIDE.

INNER CHAMBER.

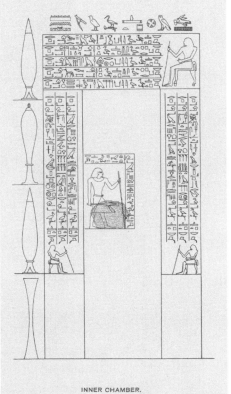

INNER CHAMBER.
GATEWAY TO THE TEMPLE.

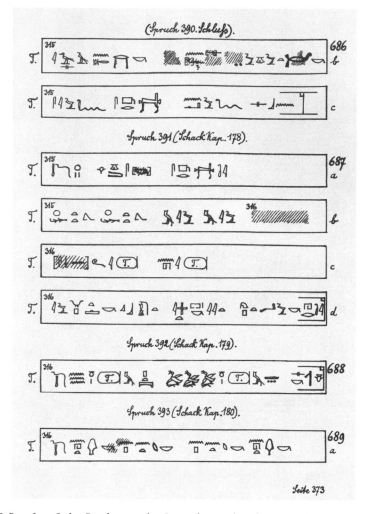

Fig. 7.16 Page from Sethe, *Die altägyptischen Pyramidentexte* (1908), 1:323. Public domain, reproduction by author.

At first photography seemed to simultaneously solve the problems of accurate and efficient documentation. Indeed, just days after the announcement of Louis Daguerre's invention in 1839, François Jean Arago declared to France's Chamber of Deputies:

> Upon inspecting some of the pictures . . . , everyone will think of the immense advantage which could have been derived during the expedition to Egypt[;] . . . if photography had been known in 1798, we would have today faithful images of a good number of the typical scenes of which the greed of the Arabs and the vandalism of certain travelers, have forever deprived the learned world.

> To copy the millions and millions of hieroglyphs which cover . . . the great
> monuments of Thebes, of Memphis, of Karnak, etc., would require scores of
> years and legions of draftsmen. With the Daguerreotype, a single man could
> carry out this immense work.[21]

By referring to the Egyptian expedition and copying millions of hieroglyphs to
extol the advantages of photography, Arago was reminding his audience of the
slow, labor-intensive preparation of the *Description de l'Égypte*—a work that
would have been familiar to most educated Frenchmen. It is striking to find,
almost at the moment of photography's birth, the first of many optimistic pre-
dictions of its speed and accuracy in recording endangered monuments.

The photography of ancient Near Eastern sites began soon after the technology's invention. But the vast majority of the images taken during the nineteenth century—like concurrent explorations by dilettantes, adventurers, and
those digging for buried treasures—aimed to satisfy the West's fascination with
what was imagined to be the Middle East's exoticisms and mysteries. The era's
photographs are mostly views of picturesque landscapes, architecture, or people
in strange costumes. While one might point to photographs featuring ancient
monuments as a starting point for what would become archaeological photography, very few of the images satisfied even the most rudimentary standards of
scholars of the day attempting to document sites. This was particularly true for
epigraphers, whose work demanded images of particular fidelity and clarity.[22]

There were attempts to photographically record inscriptions well before
Breasted came on the scene. Lepsius hoped to use the new medium during his
1842–45 expedition, but his camera was damaged before any photographs were
taken. An American expatriate living in France, John Beasley Greene, made two
trips to Egypt between 1853 and 1855 that yielded several photograph albums
and one volume of hand-drawn transcriptions. The latter, published in 1855,
are from an interior pylon at Medinet Habu that Greene prepared alongside his
photographs. The transcriptions prompted some late-twentieth-century scholars to conclude erroneously that Greene, well ahead of his time, invented a then
secret, special technique whereby he outlined in ink the hieroglyphs recorded in
his photographs and chemically removed the photographic emulsions, leaving
only the drawn outlines. Such was not the case, however. Rather, after scraping
away earth covering an inscription along the bottom of a pylon, Greene realized
he had created a trench that was too dark and narrow to photograph the now-
revealed hieroglyphs. He solved the problem by taking papier-mâché squeezes
of the inscriptions and photographing the squeezes in better light. Greene
treated his idea as a great advance, which he kept secret until after the book was
published.

The first person to photograph inscriptions with a high degree of precision and then use the images for direct transcriptions was Frenchman Félix Guilmant in his 1907 publication of a Valley of the Kings tomb transcription. One scholar thought Guilmant created his transcriptions by using the drawing and chemical-bleaching process attributed to Greene. However, a careful comparison of his photographs with the related transcriptions reveals that he used either tracing or transfer paper to outline the hieroglyphs for publication.[23]

By the early 1920s, Breasted's exploitation of photography had spanned nearly the full range of possibilities: teaching and popular-lecture illustrations, tourist-oriented images for *Egypt through the Stereoscope*, visual notes for the Egyptian dictionary project, annotated documents of the 1905–7 upper-Nile expeditions, aerial survey aids, and intermediary records for the Coffin Texts project. He found, however, that while photography was a speedy and cost-effective technique for recording inscriptions, the resulting prints were often not clear enough to serve the purposes of Egyptology, especially if the ancient reliefs were worn or damaged. The annotation method Breasted developed during the 1905–6 expedition was a step in the right direction. But his hand-marked photographs were hardly publishable or sufficiently precise to satisfy the increasingly rigorous demands of modern Egyptology. Breasted continued to ponder how photography might help in the production of accurate, rapid, and *publishable* records of inscriptions.

A Man, Not a Recognized Branch of Science

Breasted's administrative responsibilities took a toll on his research during the 1920s. Aside from textbook revisions, an encyclopedia entry, and a handful of reviews and occasional pieces, he found little time for original scholarship. He did complete a publication of the Dura-Europos findings and commenced work on an ancient medical papyrus that would occupy him for nearly a decade. But launching and sustaining the Oriental Institute's projects, alongside chairing his department at Chicago, were Breasted's primary concerns. Looking for personal assistance, he continued trying to entice Charles into a career in ancient Near Eastern studies, hoping his son might pursue graduate training in the field. But Charles preferred literature, ideally as a creative writer and playwright. Eventually Breasted wore down his son's resolve, and in fall 1922 Charles agreed to assist with Egypt travel plans involving the entire family—that is, all except Harriet Breasted, who had died in 1921 at the age of eighty-five. Within a few years, Charles went from periodically serving as his father's aide-de-camp and general factotum to long-term assistant for special projects and finally to a full-time paid position, ultimately becoming an Oriental Institute staffer as executive secretary and later assistant director. He never lost his interest in writing and gradually applied his skills to public relations, working with journalists to both publicize and manage coverage of his father's and the institute's activities.[24]

The Egypt trip was occasioned in part by a potential donor's invitation to a Nile tour, Breasted's family tagging along as guests while he served as tour guide. Breasted departed ahead of the others to address a Parisian conference marking the centenary of Champollion's translation of hieroglyphs. The conference invitation was one of many indications of Breasted's rising international reputation. That same fall he was awarded an honorary doctorate by Oxford University, and a number of comparable honors would be conferred in subsequent years by learned institutions throughout Europe. At home he was elected to the National Academy of Sciences in spring 1923, his nomination made by John C. Merriam, with Hale lobbying behind the scenes. The covert campaigning was necessary because there were plenty of scientists who either opposed electing humanists or resented Hale's advocacy of Breasted and their joint effort to formally accommodate "humanistic science" within the academy. After Hale succeeded in raising money for the academy's new home on the National Mall in Washington, he invited Breasted to address the building's dedication ceremonies in April 1924. Of the scientists and dignitaries gathered under the building's dome, only Hale knew Breasted had drafted the legend encircling its mosaic interior: "Science, Pilot of Industry, Conqueror of Disease, Multiplier of the Harvest, Explorer of the Universe, Revealer of Nature's Laws, Eternal Guide to Truth."

On his way to and from Egypt in 1922, Breasted met with scholars in England, France, and Italy, and he also spent several weeks in Germany seeking the advice of colleagues and consulting the Egyptian dictionary project files for his medical papyrus study. He renewed friendships with all his old friends and mentors save Eduard Meyer, who—still bitter over the war—relayed word to Breasted that he "could have no intercourse with an American." Being fairly prosperous at a time when Germany was economically drained by postwar reparations, Breasted tried to repay the many kindnesses received during his student days. Gardiner, during a subsequent visit to Berlin, learned of "how exceedingly good and helpful" Breasted had been and reported that Breasted's generosity "cheered and heartened" their German colleagues. "Perhaps," Gardiner mused, "we may live to see a real, wholehearted cooperation once again."[25]

Soon after returning to Chicago in spring 1923, Breasted began a proposal for renewing his Rockefeller grant, which was to end the following year. However, Breasted wanted more than just a continuation of the funding. He wanted a grant sufficiently large to endow the institute and create a new building better suited to the particular needs of ancient Near Eastern research and large enough to house its growing collections. Breasted crafted a new proposal, "Future and Development of the Oriental Institute," which addressed the institute's staff and operations in Chicago, prospective efforts in the Middle East, and the new building. He introduced it with a discussion of Louis Agassiz, the natural scientist whose work Breasted cited toward the conclusion of *Development of Religion and Thought in Ancient Egypt*. Breasted recalled Agassiz's establishment, in 1859, of the Museum of Comparative Zoology at Harvard University as a means of advancing natural sciences research in America. He further observed that paleontology, anthropology, and ethnology had been similarly developed in the United States through an infrastructure of museums and university departments.

Yet, Breasted argued, this proliferation of disciplines and institutions left an important gap. With the aid of a diagram, he pointed out that what Agassiz had done for the "first two stages of life on earth now remains to be done for the third," by which Breasted meant "the one that lifted man from savagery and made him what he is":

	Successive Stages of Life on Earth	Name of Science	Organizations for Research
I	Evolution of Lower Animal life up through Mammals and Rise of Physical Man	Palaeontology	Numerous Museums & University Departments
II	Primitive Man and Races of Men	Anthropology & Ethnology	
III	Origins of Civilization and Early History of Civilized Societies (down through Hebrew History)	No Name	Only the Oriental Institute of the University of Chicago
IV	Later Civilized Society	History and Sociology	University Departments & Historical Societies & Museums

He positioned the Oriental Institute as the *only* institution qualified to investigate that next stage, the "Origins of Civilization and Early History of Civilized Societies." "Shall we not do for <u>man</u>," Breasted asked, "what is now being done everywhere for the <u>lower animals</u>?"[26]

Breasted sought money for modest salary increases for a full-time staff of two and part-time staff of sixteen—the latter also salaried by the university. He wanted to increase the full-time staff by four to assist with museum work, publications, and the library, as well as more money for acquisitions and to print publications. The total request came to $50,000 a year, a five-fold increase over the institute's founding annual budget. However, Breasted was asking for far more because he sought that support "in perpetuity"; that is, he wanted an endowment large enough to yield $50,000 a year. He also floated the idea of resurrecting his beloved epigraphic survey and starting excavations at several of the sites he mentioned in his 1920 expedition report, all of which would come to another $15,000 per annum. The new building—designed to accommodate the institute's multiple functions as museum, library, research center, teaching facility, and publication office with work-support areas for photography, drafting, and collections and records storage—would cost $775,000 and require a $150,000 endowment for its operating support.[27]

While Breasted was preparing his proposal, in July 1923, Harry Pratt Judson retired from the university's presidency, and he was succeeded by Breasted's old friend and colleague Ernest DeWitt Burton. He backed the plan, and the two traveled to New York that November to present it personally to Rockefeller Jr. His reaction stunned them. Rockefeller said that he had told Judson two years earlier that he would not support the institute after the five-year gift was spent. He viewed his role as having been "called in at the birth" and supporting the "child" only long enough for the university to find other funding for the institute. However, "understanding the embarrassment of the position" in which Breasted and Burton found themselves, Rockefeller offered to consider the proposal "as an entirely new proposition." In following up, Burton apparently suggested to Breasted that they engage Rockefeller's Christian sympathies by specifically emphasizing the institute's potential contributions to biblical studies. Breasted declined, however, remarking, "I know his interest in the lands which brought forth the Bible and the life of Jesus will reenforce this appeal. But the work must stand on its own merits; its vital importance must be its own appeal."[28]

Burton agreed and wrote to Rockefeller endorsing the proposal by prioritizing it in the context of the university's other programs: "While research at the University in the Physical Sciences is well established and has yielded large results, it seems to me very important that the work in this field should be balanced by not less successful research in reference to the whole history of man and of human society." Rockefeller responded by extending his original gift for one year, upping it to $50,000, so that Breasted could continue his work without sudden disruption and Rockefeller could more thoroughly evaluate the new proposal. However, in announcing the extension, Rockefeller noted it was made "without any committal, expressed or implied, beyond it." Rockefeller then turned to Frederick T. Gates for counsel, confiding that he was inclined to support the request because it was for an "enterprise which is less appealing to the average man, hence the more difficult to raise money for."

During this period, Rockefeller and the boards were receiving applications from other institutions seeking money for Middle Eastern research, no doubt inspired by word of the institute's past support. Rockefeller's advisors, including

Gates, sought Breasted's recommendations, and he replied that they were all worthy, but—seizing the opportunity to advance his own cause—Breasted also argued the findings of such programs could not be properly utilized without an organization like the Oriental Institute to serve as a "clearing house" because the institute's staff was uniquely "able to deal with all ancient documents in Egyptian, Coptic, Babylonian, Assyrian, Hittite, Hebrew, Aramaic, Arabic, etc."[29]

Gates endorsed Breasted's prioritization of compiling and interpreting known records over more excavations, adding: "Discovery has gone infinitely beyond utilization. . . . The Museums of America and also of the old world are stuffed with material undeciphered and . . . unpacked." Regarding Breasted's leadership, Gates commented, "Even his weaknesses, if he has them, are his excellencies carried to excess. . . . His staff is so well chosen, his enthusiasm is so contagious, his organizing and executive capacity is so great that it would seem to be wasteful and a false economy to cut him off entirely from research and confine him to routine departmental instruction." However, Gates cautioned, the institute's success relied *so* heavily on Breasted that the endowment request should be declined. "Breasted is himself [its] very life and soul. . . . He is the Atlas that carries it on his back. His like has not arisen and he will leave no successor. At fifty-eight he has, let us hope, a dozen years at least of health. After that the University will have to readjust itself to a new situation. It should not have its hands tied by endowment confined to specific ends." Gates recommended Rockefeller decline the building proposal as well, leaving that to "local wealth."

Just as Gates was completing his report, Breasted passed through New York on his way to Egypt. The Rockefellers invited him to stay overnight with them so they could discuss arrangements, made at Breasted's suggestion the previous summer, for a wintertime two-month-long Nile tour that he would guide. The plan fell through, however, when Abby Rockefeller concluded that their younger children should not miss that much school. Gates's report reached Rockefeller during Breasted's visit, and on the eve of his departure Rockefeller accompanied him to his guest bedroom to say he would continue his support for an additional four years—a total extension of five years—at a rate of $50,000 per year. Rockefeller said he was not supporting an endowment or paying for a new building because "he was supporting a <u>man</u>, not a recognized branch of science."

While this emphasis on the individual rather than the institution adhered to a philanthropic principle Rockefeller and the boards were following with greater frequency, it suited the personal regard Rockefeller and his wife had for Breasted. Rockefeller's letter to Burton formalizing the grant also stated that it was based on Breasted's personal gifts rather than the intrinsic value of the institute or ancient Near Eastern studies. Nonetheless, Breasted confided to Hale: "In five years more we shall get on so far that they will not be willing to see us shut up shop."[30]

The Chicago House Method

Within a few weeks of his arrival in Egypt, the institute's future now secure for five more years and with far more generous funding at his disposal, Breasted began implementing new plans. The first was his "old project for saving the inscriptions of Egypt," an epigraphic survey to record hieroglyphic texts on surviving monuments. The seventeen years since Breasted had to terminate his earlier expedition tempered his ambitions, however. He narrowed his focus to the temples of ancient Thebes—those in the vicinity of modern Luxor, especially the complexes of Luxor and Karnak along the east side of the Nile, and the Ramasseum and Medinet Habu on the western side beyond the flood plain.

To launch the project, Breasted turned to his former student Harold H. Nelson, who was still a professor at the American University of Beirut. In January 1924, Breasted formally invited Nelson to head the survey as the "directing epigrapher" and supervise a seasonal staff of three—a draftsman, photographer, and local foreman—along with other local workers as needed. Breasted would have a "comfortable house" erected on site to accommodate Nelson, his wife and daughter, and the draftsman and photographer and to provide staff workrooms. Because of Egypt's intense summers, the survey's work would go from the late fall to early spring, leaving Nelson free to keep his faculty position at the American University, though in a reduced capacity.

Breasted was flexible on the details and eager to work out an arrangement that best suited Nelson. He offered Nelson $3,500 a year plus travel expenses for him and his family, as well as living expenses while they were in Egypt. Nelson accepted, arranged a reduced teaching load at the American University, and agreed to launch the program the following fall. Breasted proposed Medinet Habu (figure 7.17) as the survey's first subject because it was "still as a whole practically unpublished," an observation he first made in 1903. He acquired land nearby to erect a building for the staff and its work spaces, and by early April he had prepared a design and hired a retired architect-engineer from Britain now living in Egypt to oversee the building's construction.[31]

By May Breasted was back in Chicago, where he planned the survey's methodology. He decided to rely on a combination of Egyptological expertise, photography, and drawing to record the inscriptions. Breasted had concluded that the "current impression" that photographs alone provide a sufficiently complete record is "fundamentally incorrect" because

> any straight line carved on the face of a stone wall, . . . largely and indeed often
> *wholly* disappears in a photograph if the straight line . . . is parallel with the
> rays of light illuminating the wall. . . . The [only] sculptured lines which are ade-
> quately recorded in the negative [are those] which . . . lie transversely across the

Fig. 7.17 Aerial view of Medinet Habu showing the mortuary temple of Ramses III (center), and Amon temple (lower right), 1933. Photograph by James Henry Breasted Jr. Courtesy of the Oriental Institute, University of Chicago.

path of the rays of light falling on the wall. In that case the illumination throws a high light on one side of the transverse line and a shadow on the other, producing contrasts which thus emphasize the line and give it a plastic character and sharp definition. . . . In order to secure all that the camera might record, it would be necessary to take at least eight negatives of every inscription, each with a different illumination—that is, with the light . . . coming from top, bottom, right, left, and diagonally from each of the four corners. Even a group of eight such negatives would not record all that the wall discloses to the . . . epigrapher . . . ; for a badly weathered inscription . . . contains much which is visible to the trained and experienced eye, but which nevertheless is too faint and confused to be recorded photographically.

At best a photograph is only "an invaluable partial record," which must somehow be "supplemented and completed by the discerning eye" of an experienced Egyptologist. However, it's impractical to expect an Egyptologist to be "a sufficiently good draftsman to make a satisfactory facsimile of all that he might add to the photograph." The Egyptologist must be assisted by "the best available artist." Accordingly, the "ideal recording system . . . must unite in one record three things: the speed and accuracy of the camera, the reading ability of the experienced orientalist, and the drawing skill of the accurate draftsman." The challenge lay in assuring the resulting images were both highly accurate and sufficiently legible so they could be reproduced with modern, cost-effective printing methods and distributed in sufficient quantities to serve other scholars throughout the world.[32]

Breasted's prescription may have been inspired by techniques used to prepare his textbook illustrations. As printers began adapting photography for mass-produced illustrations in the late nineteenth and early twentieth centuries, they discovered that the reproduction of photography's continuous tones demanded specialized plates and papers that drove up their printing costs. As an alternative, engravers invented a technique for quickly translating the shapes and continuous tones in photographs into crisp "cuts" or black-and-white engravings more suitable for commercial printing. It involved drawing over photographic prints with pens using waterproof india ink and then immersing the prints in chemical baths to bleach away the photographic emulsions. The resulting black-line drawings could then be photomechanically reproduced on metal plates, or photoengraved, for printing on the same papers and presses as were used for conventional metal type.

Breasted did not know the particulars of the technique, however, and in May 1924 he wrote to the Eastman Kodak Company for its paper recommendations by explaining that the starting point, large photographs of inscription-covered walls, had to possess two characteristics. First, they had to be printed on "paper of such hard finish that the draughtsman can ink in the contours and outlines . . . with waterproof India ink. . . . The inked-in lines will be highly elaborate, covering practically the entire surface of the enlargement." Second, the "paper must chemically be of such a formula that after the draughtsman's work is completed the entire enlargement can be put into a bath and the photographic record completely faded out. This fading out must be sufficient to permit the photo-engraver to make his zinc plate by rephotographing from the inked-in enlargement." An Eastman Kodak representative sent a handful of sample photographs on various types of papers, adding that many "concerns over the country do work of this nature" and offering a bleaching formula that "has been used successfully by many photographic workers." Breasted experimented with the papers by drawing on them with india ink (figure 7.18) and calling in a photographer associated with the institute to assist with the bleaching. A paper was selected, the chemical process fine tuned for conditions in Egypt, and the information forwarded to Nelson. Breasted also selected the photographic equipment and darkroom supplies so they could be on hand when Nelson arrived in Luxor.[33]

Over the spring and summer, Breasted and Nelson corresponded about the

ARTURA CARBON BLACK
GRADE D

Fig. 7.18 Eastman Kodak Company photographic paper sample, india ink outlining by Breasted, May 1924. Courtesy of the Oriental Institute, University of Chicago.

construction and furnishing of the "epigraphic survey expedition house." By early June Breasted shortened its unwieldy moniker to "the Luxor house," and by the end of the month Nelson began calling it "Chicago House." By the fall "Chicago House" stuck and became a shorthand for both the site and title of the project, which was at first the "Epigraphic Expedition" and later the "Epigraphic Survey." Nelson made a brief trip to Luxor to check on construction progress and begin ordering furnishings, but he and his family did not move there until September. In addition to housing the epigraphic staff and Nelson's family, Chicago House was designed for occasional visitors such as Breasted, other institute "home" staff, and scholars who might contribute to the work. Concerned about the budget, however, Breasted wanted to find the right balance between collegiality and hosting freeloaders. He proposed that Nelson establish a modest per diem fee that visitors, including Breasted, would pay as a way of discouraging hangers-on.

A more delicate problem was how welcoming the staff should be to the wealthy or well-connected who were stopping off in Luxor as its tourism reputation grew. Acquaintances of Breasted's, friends of the university, and others would no doubt want to drop by Chicago House—as visitors did at other expedition sites in Egypt—and want to see the Epigraphic Survey's work firsthand. Despite his concerns about the costs and distractions of being too hospitable, Breasted explained to Nelson that "we are in a position where the interest of American friend[s] may be of great value . . . , and we must be careful . . . that those who ought to do so shall see our work and know about it. . . . On the whole it will be better to be imposed on once in a while than to offend anyone who may be of value to science," especially potential donors.[34]

Well before the photography and drawing began, Nelson began wondering about the physical dimensions of the volumes to be published. Though it seemed as though he was putting the cart before the horse, the graphic emphasis of the publications had a direct bearing on the size of the drawings to be reproduced. Larger volumes would allow bigger and more detailed drawings; smaller volumes would force the reduction of drawings to the point that crucial details would be lost. Given the enormous dimensions of the temple inscriptions, if the drawings were printed on smaller pages, but without reducing them, they would have to be broken into many small plates, necessitating a scheme for showing how one section fit with the next.

Another of Nelson's concerns was collation of the new drawings with earlier publications, particularly if the previous copies or photographs showed passages that were now illegible or missing. That kind of checking was virtually impossible in Luxor because the Egyptological libraries there were thin and assembled for expeditions for other sites, and the collections in Cairo were inconveniently distant.

There were other questions too: Did Breasted want the volumes to include translations or a bibliography of relevant publications? Was he contemplating the inclusion of specialized studies on philological or historical problems raised by troublesome inscriptions? Finally, where among Medinet Habu's vast inscriptions did Breasted want to begin? "Personally," Nelson wrote, "I should like to begin with as well-preserved a wall as possible so that we may get into the swing of the work before we reach too many difficulties."[35]

Breasted decided the Medinet Habu volumes would not include translations. These, if ever done, would be part of the institute's new "Ancient Records Series" that he was launching. If there were to be any special studies, they could be published in the Oriental Institute Communications series. As for collations with previous publications, Breasted originally intended to send relevant books and articles to Chicago House on an as-needed basis, but he changed his mind, proposing instead that the work be done in European or American libraries. Perhaps, Breasted thought, "as time goes on the available library in the field will contain the more necessary things."

The publication was to be nearly thirteen inches tall by about ten and a half inches wide. He based his decision on the already-settled plan of using up to

Fig. 7.19 Chicago House at its point of greatest expansion, viewed from the rear and looking east, with the Colossi of "Memnon" (Amenhotep III) in the middle distance and the Nile and Luxor beyond, ca. late 1920s. Medinet Habu is about one-third of a mile to the right (out of view). Courtesy of the Oriental Institute, University of Chicago

eight- by ten-inch photographic negatives for most images, which, when necessary, could then be published at full size to capture the most detail. Breasted's decision also took into account an analysis of hieroglyphic lines on one of the tallest walls at Medinet Habu. He and Nelson based their analysis on the average height of a certain sign, which—after transcription, reduction to about a quarter of an inch, and multiplication by the number of lines on the wall—ostensibly showed the minimum page size needed for legible reproduction. As for a starting place, Breasted recommended the temple exterior on the north side (figure 3.5).[36]

After innumerable difficulties shipping furnishings and equipment, completing Chicago House construction (figure 7.19), and organizing staff, Nelson reported that work commenced on 17 November 1924—about thirty years to the day after Breasted first set foot in Egypt. The professional staff included John Hartman, the photographer employed on the Coffin Texts project, and Alfred Bollacher, who had extensive experience copying hieroglyphs. Of the three, Nelson had the least field experience, and although he was trained in Egyptology, he was reluctant to settle questions of epigraphic standards and policies that

Fig. 7.20 Epigraphic Survey staff at work on the first pylon at Medinet Habu, 1925. From left to right, John Hartman, Harold H. Nelson, and Alfred Bollacher with unidentified Egyptian assistants. Courtesy of the Oriental Institute, University of Chicago.

came up in the field. His letters to Breasted that fall and winter were filled with questions about such details as whether or not masonry joints between stones should be indicated in drawings, how to handle photographic distortions that cause vertical and horizontal lines to converge toward the edges of large images, and to what extent the staff should fill in missing parts of signs when their likely form can be guessed—and if such fragmentary passages *are* completed, should they be rendered with solid or broken lines, the latter to indicate they are "restorations." Nelson also wondered whether or not Breasted or another more seasoned Egyptologist should check the work.

There were a host of other technical problems: inscriptions behind columns that could not be photographed without a special right-angle lens, the absence of an accurate ground plan to plot the locations of photographs and transcriptions, and a disparity between the speed of the photography and the far slower work of drawing and checking as Hartman far outpaced Bollacher and Nelson (figure 7.20). The initial plan, Nelson wrote, was:

Hartman and I go over the wall together and map out the work. . . . I do this
with him, for he can tell me how much he can take on a single plate. Then he
takes the photographs, develops them and makes his enlargements. . . . Then I
work over the enlargement, placing a piece of tracing paper over the photo and
drawing in on the tracing paper such signs as are difficult to make out or which
are broken. . . . Then Bollacher draws on the enlargement with a pencil, using
my data and notes. Then I check up on his work. After that he draws in with
pen and Hartman [bleaches] the photo, leaving Bollacher's drawings. So far, we
have not gone beyond the pencil drawings, as I want an opportunity to collate
with earlier publications. . . . I believe it would be wise for me to make a visit . . .
to Cairo . . . collating in the Museum library. I am afraid that if I do not do that,
we shall omit some material. . . . I shall not make the final pen drawings till I
hear from you.

Breasted decided masonry joints should be drawn, and he had a ground plan
prepared in Chicago which he sent along with scholarly publications relevant to
Medinet Habu.[37]

With regard to recording damaged or difficult-to-read inscriptions, Breasted
replied, "The whole question of what is really on the wall and what you know . . .
must have been there, must be solved by adopting a very rigid principle, as follows: Insert in the ordinary black lines only what is visible on the stone. . . .
Completion of many imperfect scenes and broken passages . . . should, without
exception, be indicated by dotted lines." He then added further guidelines:

Another class of insertions of matter no longer visible on the stone will of
course come in from the old publications. [They] would probably better be included in brackets.

These matters raise the whole question of collation, both of the original
wall and of the old publications. . . . [The] only safe rule is the one . . . adopted
for the Coffin Texts,—that is, that no one man's readings shall be accepted as
final, no matter who he is. . . .

Our procedure . . . should therefore be as follows: After you have done
all you can in the collation of the original wall, there should be two more . . . :
(1) A collation with the old publications, which will always result in a list of
queries which can only be settled by a re-examination of the original wall.
(2) A collation by Gardiner and myself . . . [to settle] the queries . . . , and for
general examination of every fragmentary and badly weathered passage.

Gardiner was interested in the Epigraphic Survey, but Breasted had not discussed
with him the possibility of his regular involvement at Medinet Habu.[38]

Before Breasted returned to Luxor in February 1925, Nelson had acquired a car to transport people and goods from the Nile to Chicago House, about two and a half miles distant. It also came in handy for picking up notables Breasted steered Nelson's way with growing frequency, despite the former's concerns about distractions. By this point Nelson had already entertained the son of Chicago mercantilist and philanthropist Julius Rosenwald, Otis Elevator Company president Edmund A. Russell, and a pair of Chicago-area steel-company executives. Breasted personally guided Cyrus Hall McCormick, formerly head of International Harvester Company and son of the inventor, through Luxor and on a private Nile voyage to Abu Simbel and back. Meanwhile it became clear that Chicago House was too small, and it needed a research library to speed the collation process. These unforeseen needs had Breasted seeking new funding sources, a task to which Nelson applied himself as well. For the remainder of the 1924–25 season and much of the 1925–26 season, their correspondence—and correspondence between Nelson and support staff in Chicago—was filled with endless details ranging from the installation of electrical generators and insect abatement to darkroom equipment and interior decorating.[39]

Over the course of the first season, Nelson gained confidence and began taking a firmer hand in monitoring work quality. As the Epigraphic Survey continued, however, its progress was slowed by a number of unanticipated discoveries that heightened Nelson's awareness of the paleographic issues at stake. As he scrutinized the hieroglyphs, he realized the survey's transcriptions had to capture for posterity not only the minute paleographic details of the hieroglyphs' exact forms but any clues that revealed the methods by which they were carved as well. Nelson reported to a colleague, "I have been working for about a week on one small section which has been doubly inscribed. . . . The wall is not in good condition, and the reliefs were at one time filled with plaster. Moreover, most of this portion of the inscription is very badly carved." In passages where the ancient Egyptians made errors, plastered them over, and then recarved the hieroglyphs, should the epigraphers show only the final versions? What if the plaster has fallen out, leaving only the errors? Is not the corrective procedure important historical evidence that should be recorded?

While Breasted and Nelson struggled with these issues, Gardiner was questioning the rigor of collations with earlier publications. Breasted replied that the survey's pencil tracings could be used for this purpose and proposed sending some to Gardiner so he could collate them with publications in London's Egyptology libraries. A "preliminary trial," Breasted continued, could be done by putting "readings in ink of a special colour," using the initials of authors' last names as keys to the sources. In view of the two types of collations needed as the drawings were refined—those that checked the tracings against the actual inscriptions and others that checked the tracings against previous publications—the tracings became valuable as working studies. If the tracings were mailed to

Gardiner, however, they could not be used for on-site collations against the inscriptions or vice versa. Toward the end of the first season, Nelson discussed the problem with Hartman, and they concluded, as Nelson wrote, "that we could make blue or brown prints of my tracings which could be easily multiplied to any number desired. I am putting into my requests for next year, paper for making blue print paper. Hartman, who knows how to make blue print paper, says it is much better to buy the plain paper and then prepare it at Luxor so that it will be fresh when needed." Nelson introduced blueprint copies the following season, thereby enabling several Egyptologists to simultaneously participate in the collation process.[40]

Toward the end of the first season, Nelson noted that in dividing his time between Chicago House and the American University he could "do justice to neither enterprise." He wanted to give his all to the Epigraphic Survey and felt he would be far more productive if he could spend the survey's off-seasons on library research. About the same time, Breasted began considering a staff expansion so that the collation process could keep up with the photography. He estimated the survey needed two additional Egyptologists and another draftsman. The staff shortage was exacerbated by Nelson's absences from Medinet Habu to collate drawings against publications in Cairo's research libraries. These needs were on Breasted's mind during a June 1925 visit to the Rockefeller offices, where he was becoming a more frequent advisor on other institutions' archaeological proposals. Commenting on one such request he noted the shortage of qualified personnel in the field, and a General Education Board officer pursued the question, inviting Breasted to outline a solution.

His formal response, titled "A New Area of Humanistic Research and a Plan for Beginning its Investigation," summarized recent statements he had made about the state of ancient Near Eastern research. He emphasized now-familiar observations about the gap between the humanities and sciences, the institute's unique position in closing that gap, and how this "already existent machine" could provide training opportunities in "humanistic research" if it had some additional funds. The money would be used to hire and train two additional epigraphers and two additional draftsmen for the Epigraphic Survey, two additional catalogers for the archives in Chicago, an executive secretary and three support staff for the museum, and for an entirely new project—a "geological-paleontological survey of . . . the Nile valley for the recovery of evidences of human occupation in geological ages"—a "surface geologist" and paleontologist. Breasted's budget request came to about $38,000 a year for five years, or a little over $190,000.[41]

Rockefeller learned of this correspondence and offered to Breasted up to $50,000 per year above the grant renewal he made in late 1923. Should the General Education Board fund Breasted's request, Rockefeller wrote, he would supply the difference, $12,000 per year, as a "contingent fund" for Breasted to hire a personal assistant and additional project staff, to procure equipment, or to use "in any other way which in your judgment will add most to the productiveness of your work." Rockefeller prefaced his pledge by observing, "The most important factor in the advancement of . . . Mankind is men and women, well-trained, with high purpose and fine spirit. No finer service can be rendered than to hold up the hands of exceptional people of this type. You are such [a] one—unique in your field. . . . The possibilities for useful service during these ripening years of your life, who can estimate?"

Breasted was sixty years old by this point and was beginning to show his age with minor but increasingly frequent health problems. He tried to keep to an "abstemious diet and regular habits," which included exercise. But he worked long hours and, though "high strung," kept "his nerves under remarkable control"— factors that no doubt led to periodic bouts of what students described as "nervous indigestion." Rockefeller gently suggested that, in offering the additional backing, he hoped Breasted would "make the careful preservation of your own health of paramount importance." Rockefeller's letter, Breasted replied, "touched me so deeply that anything I am able to put on paper as a reply is a very feeble expression of what I feel." Breasted put the additional money toward publications and support staff for institute projects, though he assured Rockefeller his admonition regarding personal assistance would be "carefully heeded." The General Education Board approved Breasted's request, allocating $200,000 over five years, and Rockefeller topped it with an additional $50,000. The grant inaugurated the board's foray into humanities funding and sparked other Rockefeller philanthropies to do the same. Their combined support for humanities projects grew substantially in subsequent years and spread to other universities, a policy change that was due almost entirely to Breasted's persistent advocacy.[42]

Progress during the 1925–26 season was halting. The additional funds Breasted obtained required expanding Chicago House to accommodate more staff. By early January 1926 Nelson found himself once again overwhelmed as the jobs of architect, general contractor, and interior decorator were piled on top of his other responsibilities. He was further distracted by a steady flow of visitors—many sent by Breasted, who was courting potential donors, opinion leaders whose endorsements might prove useful, or repaying debts for past assistance. Nelson loyally entertained all comers, though he wondered if the enlarged budget might allow for a "social secretary," and he acquired a "Who's Who" to prepare himself for unfamiliar members of the social elite. Such entertaining did pay off, however. After visits to Medinet Habu by Julius Rosenwald, who shortly thereafter became a General Education Board officer, Rosenwald donated funds to add a research library and work spaces, and the General Education Board allocated book-acquisition funds.[43]

When Nelson *was* able to concentrate on the Epigraphic Survey, he found problems aligning the survey's approach with the publication format Breasted originally envisioned. The plan did not take into account the extent to which hieroglyphic texts sometimes occurred in the midst of dramatic pictorial reliefs. Nelson realized that if the survey's transcriptions isolated the inscriptions from the reliefs, the results would drain both of meaning. To present both as they appeared while also scaling the hieroglyphs large enough so they were readable, however, meant publishing such passages in a larger format.

While Nelson wrestled with this problem, Gardiner began to question Nelson's ability to maintain sufficient Egyptological standards during the on-site collation process. Breasted tried to reassure him but suggested that Gardiner work closely with Nelson and the new staff members he was recruiting in an apprentice-like relationship. Nelson subsequently met with Gardiner, who said he didn't have the time to provide such guidance. Even so, Gardiner was "keen on recording the exact form" of hieroglyphs and complained to Nelson that Bollacher's renderings were too schematic and "not conforming to the proper canons of paleographic accuracy." Breasted was beginning to tire of Gardiner's criticisms and confided to Nelson that he found in them a touch of condescension typical of other critiques of American research as being naive and shoddy. Nelson replied, "Personally, I am anxious . . . to turn out a distinctly American piece of work of the highest excellence."[44]

Near the beginning of the 1926–27 season, the Epigraphic Survey's third, Breasted offered Nelson a permanent, full-time appointment in the institute as head of the survey and research professor at the University of Chicago. The promotion solved work-flow problems they had discussed over the previous two years, while also recognizing Nelson's growing responsibilities and leadership. The Chicago House expansion was mostly done by this time, and the research library was a major addition to the survey's "equipment." Nelson learned that it "excited the envy of our fellow archaeologists. We shall have a good many using our library. . . . But that is what it is here for." The staff was enlarged with three epigraphers, William F. Edgerton—who accompanied Breasted on the 1919–20 survey expedition—and two of Breasted's other doctoral students, Caroline Ransom and John A. Wilson. An Italian cartographer formerly with Egypt's survey department, Virgilio Canziani, joined the group as a draftsman. With an enlarged staff, research library, and modern facilities, work on Medinet Habu should have accelerated. Instead it intensified. Although the additional epigraphers meant in theory that collations of the draftsmen's renderings against the walls and earlier publications could proceed more quickly, in practice the scholars' discussions and cross-checking revealed fresh insights and questions of interpretation that slowed the drawings' completion.

Breasted came to Chicago House in January 1927 to assist Nelson in guiding the work, settle questions of standards and practices, and figure out ways to quicken the process. One of the first problems they discussed was how to transcribe hieroglyphic texts that appeared among pictorial reliefs. Breasted agreed with Nelson's recommendation that they adopt a larger publication format, which "necessitated redrawing some of the more complicated reliefs." As the work progressed and the beauty and dynamism of the reliefs were clarified through the copying process, Breasted came to admire each "stunning composition as a work of art."[45]

Conversations about such matters as the transcription of damaged hieroglyphs, the restoration of missing hieroglyphs based on comparable texts at other sites, collation standards, and now the reliefs' artistic qualities drew the staff into a searching reevaluation of the survey's methodology. After many discussions, Nelson observed "several limitations . . . became apparent":

> In the first place, the drawing of less common signs was seen to be paleographically inadequate. The pictographic character of the Egyptian system of writing adds to many words a fulness which was lost unless the details of each individual hieroglyph could be clearly given. The determinatives of many words graphically supplement the bare root meaning by additional shades of thought unavoidably lost in the smaller scale of reproduction which was at first used. In the second place, the reliefs . . . proved to be full of new, picturesque, interesting and important details necessarily omitted in the sketchy drawings at first contemplated. . . . In the third place, it soon became clear that the value of the reliefs as works of art was of a higher order than has generally been accredited to them. The limited scale of reproduction at first proposed failed largely to bring out effectively the *artistic* value of these great temple reliefs.

The problem was due to the project's initial emphasis on hieroglyphs only, leading to completed drawings that were scaled just large enough to assure the bare legibility of hieroglyphs as simplified signs. Despite the use of photography as a starting point, rendering the hieroglyphs on such a small scale inadvertently systematized them—almost like type—and the paleographic nuances that conveyed the "additional shades of thought" were lost. That smaller scale of drawing in turn diminished depictions of the reliefs.[46]

In the end, the epigraphers were "confronted by a clearly defined question: Were we ready to adopt the principle of making our facsimiles a complete and final record of the original wall, including both reliefs and inscriptions?" The answer was yes, which meant they had to "scrap the work of the first two seasons and redraw the plates on a larger and more adequate scale which would make them paleographically, archaeologically, and artistically as final and complete a record of the entire original wall as human fallibility could reasonably expect to attain." In addition, the transcription method was fine tuned to assure a higher degree of fidelity to the inscriptions and reliefs, principally by means of the collation process. Each surface was now

1. Photographed on an 8 × 10–inch film, from which was then made an enlargement, generally for one-fourth to one-third larger than the final printed plate of the publication [figure 7.21]. The enlargement was made of sufficient size to insure the clear definition of as great a number of details as possible [and] to allow convenient handling by the artist, no sheet being more than [about 20 by 24 inches].

2. The enlargement was then taken by one of the staff artists to the temple wall, where in the presence of the original, at such close range as to be able to touch [it] with his hand . . . , he carefully entered every line in pencil on the photograph itself. Subsequently in the drafting-room . . . , the lines . . . were entered . . . in waterproof India ink, and the results were later verified by the artist before the original.

3. The enlargement . . . was then submitted to a chemical treatment that bleached out the photograph completely. . . . There was thus produced a black-and-white drawing. . . .

4. From this drawing, by contact printing in sunlight, was then made a sepia paper negative from which could be produced a blueprint positive. By this method the subsequent steps in the extensive process of correction could . . . utilize blueprints instead of the original drawing, which would have been seriously injured by much handling.

5. The inexpensive blueprint was next cut up in small sections 3 or 4 inches square, each of which was pasted on a sheet of foolscap paper, leaving . . . a wide margin on which any corrections or additions could be entered by the epigraphers. These . . . "collation sheets," were then taken out to the temple and in the presence of the wall were submitted to a searching comparison, line by line, with the original. Each drawing was thus collated by at least two members of the epigraphic staff until no more un-entered traces of the design could be recovered and all errors by the artist had been corrected. At the same time archaeological or philological observations . . . of value . . . were entered on the collation sheets for future reference [figure 7.22].

6. The very numerous corrections and additions . . . were then entered on the drawings by the artist, but again only after he had compared them with the original; and these changes were afterward checked by the epigraphic staff. This process was repeated until nothing more that the staff could observe on the wall remained to be entered on the plates.

7. Any . . . restorations of entire signs or of missing parts of signs or figures were entered in dotted lines. Restorations . . . merely resting on deductions . . . have been bracketed. In a few cases copies were made long ago. . . . Such old

copies have always been fully collated, and any additional signs, words, or figures thus available have been inserted. . . . Such restorations from early copies . . . have been entered without brackets. The reasons for such restorations and the authority from which they were drawn will be stated in the volume of textual notes.

    8. These textual notes . . . appear in a separate volume, thus freeing the present volume from such critical material and making the notes more convenient for comparison with the plates.

The resulting ink-line drawings (figure 7.23) could thus be reproduced as they were in large-format folios that faithfully showed everything from enormous reliefs to small hieroglyphs in brilliant detail.

The most significant changes from the method first worked out by Breasted and Nelson were the elimination of intermediate pencil tracings—the initial drawing was now done directly on the photographs—and the production of handy blueprint-based collation sheets for cross-checking. Now, while the collation process was under way, the artists could move on to the next photographs, speeding up the drawing process, and when the artists incorporated the epigraphers' additions and corrections, they were made directly on the already-inked drawings, accelerating the correction process. Over time, the collation sheets became "valuable for the future editing and understanding of the inscriptions and reliefs," significant resources in their own right as records of the epigraphers' thinking. Most important of all, as a result of following the photographs so closely as foundations for the drawings, the transcriptions were indeed much closer to facsimiles.[47]

This new procedure, which came to be known as the "Chicago House method" and which the Epigraphic Survey has largely followed to this day, furnished some though not all the results Breasted sought. The publications emanating from the Epigraphic Survey *have* become invaluable records of monuments that continue to decay. Yet the Chicago House method did not yield the speed Breasted sought. To the contrary, it led to a gradual slowing as checking, cross-checking, and scholarly consultations among epigraphers increased. In part this was due to the rigor and commitment of the epigraphers, the first generation of whom were either current students or recent doctoral graduates. As they immersed themselves in the intricacies of the hieroglyphs and reliefs, the survey became more like an ongoing research seminar than a sleek copying machine, especially when old lions of Egyptology like Breasted and Gardiner were around (figure 7.24). "<u>Chicago House . . . is really a graduate outpost of the University of Chicago</u>," Breasted exulted. The epigraphers' widening knowledge only magnified their caution, however. Sixty years later, one of Nelson's Chicago House successors observed that the "degree of accuracy required for . . . a true facsimile

Fig. 7.21 Preparatory photograph, ca. October 1927, for plate 43, "Ramses III Presenting Captives of the Libyans and the Sea Peoples to the Theban Triad," from *Medinet Habu*, vol. 1, *Earlier Historical Records of Ramses III* (1930). The superimposed outline shows the area represented in the plate (see figure 7.23). Courtesy of the Oriental Institute, University of Chicago.

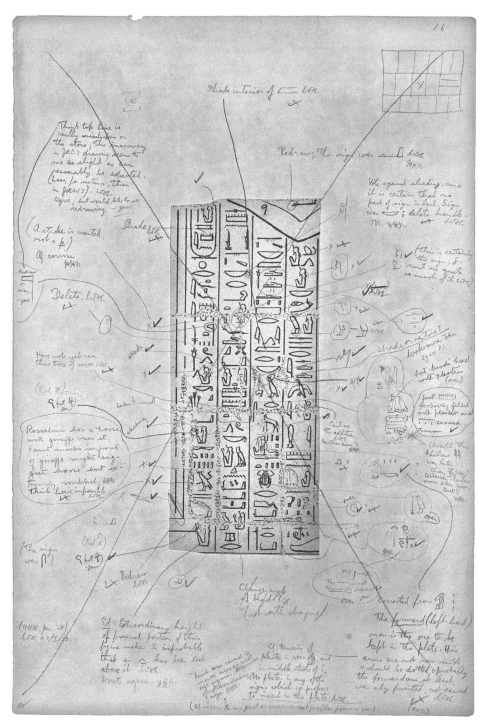

Fig. 7.22 Collation sheet, ca. January 1928, for plate 43, "Ramses III Presenting Captives of the Libyans and the Sea Peoples to the Theban Triad," from *Medinet Habu*, vol. 1, *Earlier Historical Records of Ramses III* (1930). The blueprint pasteup is the section below the pharaoh's raised arm in the center of figure 7.21. Collated by Harold H. Nelson, John A. Wilson, and William F. Edgerton. Courtesy of the Oriental Institute, University of Chicago.

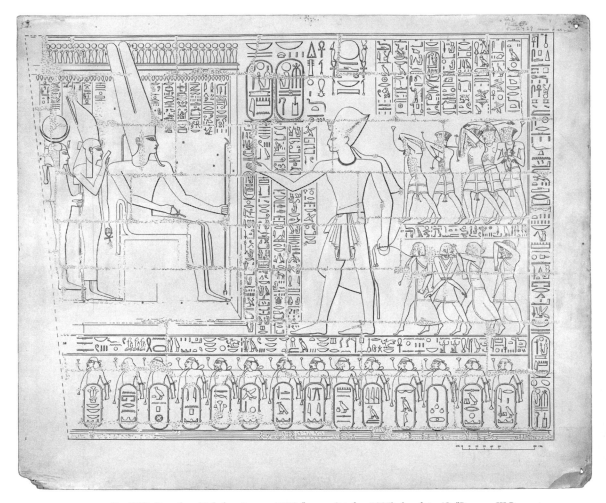

Fig. 7.23 Completed ink drawing, ca. 1928 (begun October 1927), for plate 43, "Ramses III Presenting Captives of the Libyans and the Sea Peoples to the Theban Triad," from *Medinet Habu*, vol. 1, *Earlier Historical Records of Ramses III* (1930). Drawing by J. Anthony Chubb. Courtesy of the Oriental Institute, University of Chicago.

remains a subject of some concern: how accurate is 'accurate' and how complete is 'complete'?" The difference between historical evidence worth recording and inessential detail remains a live issue.

As the Medinet Habu volumes were published in subsequent years, they received glowing reviews that cited the Chicago House method as "close to perfection" and one that "could not be bettered." A telling review of the fifth volume, published in 1957, concentrated on just the kind of evidentiary minutiae the survey regularly netted. In studying the book's drawings, the reviewer noted a "series of small deep holes" along doorways leading into the temple's forecourts, holes that cut through inscriptions and were thus added later. Placement of the

Fig. 7.24 Breasted and Gardiner in the second court of Medinet Habu, the latter holding a fly whisk by his face, ca. 1927–28. Courtesy of the Oriental Institute, University of Chicago.

holes led some scholars to theorize they are traces of panels installed over the original inscriptions by adherents of a form of ancient Egyptian popular worship tangentially related to what remained of the old priestly cults. The reviewer used this evidence to explore the hypothesis at Medinet Habu and other sites. He closed by commenting "in testimony" to the survey's "well known" accuracy that its drawings furnished most of the "examples mentioned in the preceding discussion. The detail in question might easily have been omitted even by the most observant and conscientious copyists."[48]

In 1929 Nelson calculated "it will take us about twenty-one years more to finish Medinet Habu at the present rate," an estimate that turned out to be too conservative. The sheer quantity of inscriptions to be recorded, details to be considered, and continual revisiting of questions once thought settled resulted in a grueling process, the duration of which no one had anticipated. The physical demands alone of collating drawings at walls where one had to "stand on a ladder for four hours at a stretch" peering at lines and lines of hieroglyphs in the bright Egyptian sun could be daunting. Breasted thought they might accelerate the work by adding yet more staff members, but Nelson was not so sure: "Too large a personnel decreases the initiative of the individuals and tends to a shifting of responsibility. One becomes a cog in a machine, grinding out plates for publication, rather than an enthusiastic investigator devoted to independent research. This I feel is a very real difficulty." Enthusiasm, in Nelson's view, was "the very

Fig. 7.25 Epigraphic Survey staff for the 1926–27 season, family members, and visitors at Chicago House, ca. early February 1927. Left to right, front row: Irene Louise Nelson (daughter of Harold H. and Libbie Nelson), Phoebe Byles (Chicago House librarian, British), John A. Wilson (survey epigrapher), Mary Rouse Wilson (Wilson's wife); second row: Mrs. Ransom (Caroline Ransom's mother), Libbie Nelson, Harold H. Nelson (survey director), Breasted, Frances Hart Breasted, Jean Edgerton (wife of William F. Edgerton), William F. Edgerton (survey epigrapher); third row: [unidentified], Caroline Ransom (survey epigrapher), Clarence S. Fisher (Megiddo expedition director), Alfred Bollacher (survey artist, German), Mrs. Bollacher (Bollacher's wife, German), Alan H. Gardiner, Uvo Hölscher (Medinet Habu architectural survey director, German), Edward L. DeLoach (Megiddo expedition surveyor); back row: [Roger Barr (Breasted's secretary)?], Mrs. Canziani (wife of Virgilio Canziani, Italian), Virgilio Canziani (survey artist, Italian), Adriaan de Buck (Coffin Texts project editor, Dutch). Courtesy of the Oriental Institute, University of Chicago.

life of the whole undertaking that we must not kill. I do not believe we can have scientific mass production."

Breasted tried to head off morale problems by building and furnishing Chicago House to accommodate the staff's personal needs, even providing space for family members. As a result, by 1928 not only was "the household" of professional staff members cosmopolitan—with members from America, England, Germany, Italy, and Austria—there were also "several wives, a child, and various attendants" (figure 7.25). Before long, not "counting a few regular visitors, twenty-two persons from five different countries sat down for three meals a day.

At the end of an intensive six-month season they would be heartily tired of one another." Although Chicago House was part of a small community of expeditions in Thebes that included a group from the Metropolitan Museum of Art, a German contingent, and others, they "were too busy for much social activity." These problems were on Breasted's mind and, during a "lantern slide stunt," he mentioned "the long evenings without diversion of any sort" at Chicago House. To his delight, two university alumni responded by donating a combination Victrola and radio cabinet accompanied by a "good library of Victrola records." Nelson, appreciating his younger colleagues' hunger for more "creative work," suggested alleviating the tedium by offering opportunities for personal research studies based on Medinet Habu findings. Breasted readily found money for the initiative.[49]

The Epigraphic Survey showed that Breasted's ultimate goal of compiling material for a comprehensive history of the ancient Near East was evolving into ever more complex questions of evidence and methodology—issues that flowed naturally from the rigorous standards and ideals he inspired among his earnest young associates. Where Breasted hoped to map a forest, his subordinates were finding more and more varieties of interesting and important trees. However, he was uncomfortable with forcing junior colleagues to compromise their work to meet his larger aims when their discoveries proved to be so intriguing and valuable. Furthermore, the enthusiasm that, in Nelson's words, was Breasted's "greatest asset, aside from unusual mental power," was not readily sustained by staff during long seasons of fieldwork in distant places. The sense of adventure that captured the American imagination at home foundered on the day-to-day "grind" of fieldwork in upper Egypt.

The energy required to motivate his staff added yet another unforeseen burden to the responsibilities Breasted shouldered in founding the institute. Still he enjoyed rallying his associates far more than attending to administrative details, and he feared becoming a "roll-top-desk functionary" and ceasing to be a productive scholar. He admitted these contradictory feelings to Hale, who counseled Breasted to temper his ambitions, acknowledging the advice to be "rather incongruous, especially in view of the fact that I have spent so much of my life in building up research institutions." Nonetheless, Hale argued, "Many men can be found who are competent as administrators and organizers, but very few appear in the course of a century who have your great powers of research." That being said, Hale appreciated Breasted's dilemma, noting that the "true investigator in science . . . must try to shape his life's work so as to secure the greatest possible accomplishment, even if it means a sacrifice of his . . . personal research."[50] Hale's letter arrived at a time when Breasted was contemplating yet another daring scheme.

8

Permanence

King Tut

While on his family's Nile trip in December 1922, Breasted received a note from the Earl of Carnarvon hinting of a magnificent discovery. Carnarvon collected Egyptian antiquities, and the two probably first met around the turn of the century when Breasted was periodically in England recording inscriptions for the Egyptian dictionary project. In 1919 he visited Carnarvon's castle with Gardiner, and their paths no doubt crossed in Egypt as well. Carnarvon began wintering in Egypt in 1903, and three years later he began obtaining permits from the Egyptian Antiquities Service to search for the buried tombs of pharaohs and nobles with the assistance of explorers for hire. The permitted sites were in the Theban necropolis, an area west of the Nile near Luxor that included not only large mortuary temples like Medinet Habu but hundreds of small tombs cut deep into the rising slopes and hills beyond. Carnarvon's archaeological interest was neither scholarly nor philanthropic.

In those days Antiquities Service permits allowed a division of finds between archaeologists, or their sponsors, and the Egyptian Museum—provided the site was no longer intact. Undamaged tombs were almost never found, however. Thebes had a millennia-long history of tomb plundering, especially during times of military collapse and political turmoil when tombs were left unguarded, as was the case toward the end of Ramses IX's reign, around 1108 BCE, when the Egyptian empire began disintegrating. Egyptian beliefs dictated that tombs be furnished with the day-to-day accouterments of life to serve the deceased in the afterlife. Some tombs, like those of the pharaohs, contained richly ornamented furnishings and sarcophagi. However, no wholly intact pharaonic tombs had yet been found. The certainty among Egyptologists that great treasures once resided in the tombs was based on the recurring evidence each time another tomb was uncovered of its being previously looted and on the discovery of small precious things robbers had overlooked.[1]

In 1909 Carnarvon asked Howard Carter to head up his explorations. Carter was the British artist who copied inscriptions alongside Egyptologist Percy Newberry in the 1890s. Carter expanded his skills by training with others including Flinders Petrie, from whom he acquired some knowledge of modern excavation techniques. In 1899 he became an inspector for the Antiquities Service and continued in that capacity until October 1905 when he resigned after a fracas provoked by French tourists was ignored by the service's director, who was also French. Carter remained in Egypt and turned to freelance archaeology and copying, and he and Breasted likely met shortly after this incident, just as the latter was launching his 1905–6 expedition.

Although Carter had a mercurial temperament, he was among the more skillful and well-connected persons available when Carnarvon hired him. Carter had some modest success in the necropolis, locating several tombs of scholarly interest, though not the kinds of treasures Carnarvon hoped to find. In 1917, after work was curtailed during the First World War, Carnarvon obtained a permit to explore in a special area within the Theban necropolis: the Valley of the Kings. Actually a small cleft in the hills just beyond a tall bluff overlooking western Thebes, the valley was the secluded and exclusive burial site for pharaohs and royal notables during the New Kingdom period, roughly 1539–1075 BCE. Distributed within its confines are over sixty tombs chiseled out of solid limestone, many very elaborate. Its proximity to the Nile, readily defensible boundaries, and location near a pyramid-shaped mountain made the valley an especially prized location.

By the time Carter began work there, the area had been thoroughly explored by others, and many assumed there was nothing else to find. Carter believed otherwise and drew up a grid of the valley, and by following the grid section by section, he planned to dig through the surface to bedrock until he had thoroughly checked the valley from one end to the other. After five seasons, however, Carter had little to show for his efforts, and Carnarvon was pulling out. Prior to the beginning of the 1922–23 season, Carter offered to excavate the one remaining

Fig. 8.1 Valley of the Kings, vicinity of Luxor, Egypt, today. The arrow indicates the location of the tomb of Tutankhamun in the valley floor and the entrance to the tomb of Ramses VI just above it. Photograph by author.

unexplored plot at his own expense if Carnarvon allowed him to do so under his permit. Carnarvon agreed but insisted on paying for this last round of work.[2]

In early November 1922, Carter started clearing the unexplored plot, an area on the valley floor covered with limestone chips and the foundation stones of ancient "huts." They were below the entrance to the tomb of Ramses VI, who died about 1137 BCE, and workmen lived in the huts while they carved out the pharaoh's tomb (figure 8.1). The limestone chips were debris from the tomb's creation. Just days after the clearing began, Carter discovered rock-cut stairs descending into the solid limestone valley floor. By the next afternoon, the stairway had been cleared down to an entryway neatly filled with stone blocks that were plastered over and stamped with New Kingdom necropolis seals indicating it was the portal to an ancient chamber—one that appeared to have survived intact. Carter had his workmen refill the stairwell to conceal its existence, placed a guard nearby, and hastened to Luxor, where he cabled Carnarvon of the news. The earl promptly booked passage to Egypt, arriving in Luxor in late November.

With his patron now on hand, Carter had the stairway cleared again and found that the blocked entry opened into a steep, downward-sloping corridor, also filled with debris. After two additional days of clearing, Carter found a second blocked opening, this one also stamped with ancient seals. As Carnarvon, his daughter, and an assistant stood by, Carter chiseled a small hole in the upper left-hand corner of the blockage, determined there was another large space beyond, and enlarged the opening so he could lift a candle through it and peer inside. As his eyes adjusted to the dark interior, Carter recalled, "Details of the room within emerged slowly . . . strange animals, statues and gold—everywhere the glint of gold. For . . . an eternity it must have seemed to the others standing by—I was struck dumb with amazement, and when Lord Carnarvon, unable to stand the suspense any longer, inquired anxiously, 'Can you see anything?' it was all I could do to get out the words, 'Yes, wonderful things.'"[3]

It was the tomb of Tutankhamun. The pharaoh died young, in about 1322 BCE, just fourteen or so years after the death of his illustrious predecessor Amenhotep IV the "heretic." His was one of the few pharaonic tombs of the New Kingdom not to have been previously found. Carter among others suspected, because of scattered evidence bearing the king's name found in nearby locations, that it had to have existed in the Valley of the Kings. At first, however, Carter was not certain what he had found. This is because the location—in the valley floor rather than along the sides—was inauspicious, and the entrance seals appeared to Carter to have been of a much later date. After removing the remaining entryway blockage, he invited a few others, including Antiquities Service director Pierre Lacau and a London *Times* reporter, to attend an official viewing on 29 November. Afterward, Carter once again closed up the chamber and filled the stairway with limestone debris. The *Times* reporter published an article the next day that was immediately picked up by newspapers around the world, electrifying readers with hints of even more magnificent finds: "What adds interest to this discovery is there is still yet a third sealed chamber, which, significantly, . . . two figures of the king . . . are guarding." This possibility drew to the valley more journalists, whose competition for "inside" stories and scoops devolved into a media frenzy replete with half-truths and wild speculations.

Carter and Carnarvon prepared for the most immediate problems: responsible documentation, care, and removal of the objects; security of the objects in the valley and during shipment to the Egyptian Museum amid a crush of uninvited visitors and tourists; and management of publicity as individual works were revealed. Carter left to assemble supplies, equipment, and a qualified staff to help him with the tasks that lay ahead. Carnarvon returned to England to personally recount the discovery to King George V and Queen Mary, bask in its glory, and prepare for a longer-than-usual stay in Luxor as the tomb's contents were removed. While in London, he agreed to license to the *Times* exclusive worldwide rights to report the story as it unfolded, setting up hostile relations with other papers, especially the Egyptian press.[4]

In mid-December Carter returned with supplies and prefabricated gates to secure the chamber. By 18 December, the stairway and corridor leading into it had been cleared again and the gates installed, and Carter was prepared to reenter the tomb. He invited a few scholars to join him that day, including Breasted and Herbert Winlock, who was directing the Metropolitan Museum of Art's ex-

Fig. 8.2 Antechamber, tomb of Tutankhamun, view toward left from tomb entryway. Photograph by Harry Burton, ca. December 1922. Copyright: Griffith Institute, University of Oxford.

cavations in Thebes. Carter prepared for their arrival by covering the gate with a sheet, and after they arrived, he dramatically pulled it away to reveal a chamber filled with treasures (figure 8.2). "Literally stunned with surprise," Breasted wrote, "Winlock and I could only utter one ejaculation of amazement after another, and then turn to shake Carter's hand. I was almost in tears. . . . [For] all about us lay a completely new revelation of ancient life, far surpassing anything of which we had ever known before." Breasted tried to maintain his "critical faculties," but "emotion struggled with the habit of years to observe and understand." He "felt the cultural values of the ancient world shifting so rapidly that it made one fairly dizzy. I wandered up and down . . . , aimlessly fingering notebook and pencil. Of what use were notes made in such a state of mind, with a whirling myriad of thoughts and details crowding for record all at once?" Breasted did notice, however, that the chamber was a mess. "The first impression that the royal tomb equipment was undisturbed, was incorrect. Evidences of disturbance and robbery were unmistakable," he wrote. "Sumptuous openwork designs in heavy sheet gold which had filled the spaces between the legs of finer chairs had been wrenched out and carried away" by ancient looters. "Besides being a Sherlock Holmes task of unusual interest, it was . . . a matter of importance to . . . gain some rough approximation of when they forced their entrance."[5]

Carter assumed the chamber was a vault and not a tomb and that it was created during antiquity to hide a cache of royal funerary objects removed from several nearby pharaonic tombs. Because of its location in the valley floor and his reading of the seals, Carter theorized the vault was made during disturbances around the time of Ramses IX, when no tomb was safe from looting. Even though Carter was not fluent in hieroglyphs, he based his theory on the seals, which he thought were from Ramses IX's reign. But as Breasted pointed out, Carter's suppositions did not take into account other facts. As Carter was clearing the blocked entrances, he discovered small holes that had previously been knocked through them, refilled, plastered over, and stamped with seals. Further, the chamber entrance was found underneath workmen's huts and debris associated with the creation of the tomb of Ramses VI, a pharaoh who predated Ramses IX. Taken together, this evidence showed that the disturbance to Carter's find occurred *before* the turmoil of Ramses IX's reign. Finally, Breasted doubted Carter's readings of the seals. Carter preserved fragments of the stamped plaster from the entryways (figure 8.3), and he invited Breasted to examine them. Breasted discovered that the seals used over the originally plastered entryways and the patched holes were the same and that they were from Tutankhamun's reign. This meant the looting took place shortly after the pharaoh's death and burial. There was one important question to be answered, however: Was this a tomb or royal cache?[6]

At one end of the chamber was evidence of yet another blocked entryway, which was also plastered over and stamped with seals. Because it was flanked by two nearly life-sized pharaonic sentinel statues (figure 8.4), the blockage strongly suggested that something of great importance was on the other side. Carter invited Breasted to examine those seals as well, and later, with his eight-year-old daughter, Astrid—who was with the Breasted family tour—in tow, he returned to examine them. Breasted's preliminary study indicated that they, too, contained Tutankhamun's name, but the crowded conditions and poor lighting meant a more complete investigation would have to wait until the space was cleared, a slow, laborious process that began in late December. The anteroom was mostly emptied by early February 1923, and just prior to breaking through the blocked entryway, Carter asked Breasted to reexamine the seals. He spent the better part of two days studying them and confirmed that they were from Tutankhamun's reign.

On 16 February, before a small but distinguished audience gathered in the chamber, which included Breasted and Gardiner, the Carnarvons, the Allenbys, Antiquities Service officials, and others, Carter removed the blockage. To the great satisfaction of the small assembly, the entry opened into another chamber that contained the outermost of a series of nested, elaborately decorated and perfectly preserved burial shrines, at the center of which rested the mummy of

Fig. 8.3 Plaster fragment from the blocking over the first doorway, tomb of Tutankhamun. The oblong markings, or cartouches, are seal impressions made by ancient Egyptian funerary officials. Photograph by Harry Burton, ca. January–February 1923. Copyright: Griffith Institute, University of Oxford.

Tutankhamun. Following a quiet celebration, Breasted remained two days more to continue working on the seal impressions, later compiling a report for Carter (which remains unpublished).[7]

Possessing a showman's flair for theatricality, Carter took advantage of nearly every significant step that followed in the tomb's clearing to create special invitation-only events like those of the first few months of discovery. Things soon spun out of control, however, and Carter found himself being pressed for special viewings by visiting royalty, wealthy elites, friends of Carnarvon, and many others. Egyptian government and Antiquities Service officials noticed the hubbub and especially its ramifications for both Egyptian society and international tourism. All this occurred in the context of an upsurge in Egyptian nationalism and a corresponding relaxation of British control, developments that affected the public context of Carter's discovery.[8] But first some background.

From the beginning of the sixteenth century until Napoleon's invasion in 1798, Egypt was under Ottoman rule. With Napoleon's invasion of Egypt and ensuing French studies, capped off by publication of *Description de l'Égypte* and

Fig. 8.4 Antechamber, tomb of Tutankhamun, view toward right from tomb entryway showing sentinel figures. The wall stains between the figures reveal some of the plaster covering the opening into the burial chamber; the seal impressions studied by Breasted were in that plaster. Photograph by Harry Burton, ca. December 1922. Copyright: Griffith Institute, University of Oxford.

Champollion's decipherment of hieroglyphs, France established a foothold as the first among equals with a stake in Egypt's antiquities. After the French had been pushed out of Egypt by the British and Ottomans in 1801 and the British then withdrew, the Ottomans failed to reestablish complete control. Over the following decades a succession of strong-willed local rulers became increasingly independent of Istanbul. However, they permitted or sometimes were forced to grant special French and British access for various projects such as the Suez Canal, begun in 1856.

French influence in antiquities-related matters continued; in 1858 a Frenchman, Auguste Mariette, was appointed conservator of Egyptian monuments (later director-general of the Antiquities Service) by Sa'īd Pasha, Egypt's leader at the time, and the French established the Institut Français d'Archéologie Orientale in Cairo in 1880. To quell a rising tide of protests against European and Turkish hegemony in Egypt, the British reinvaded the country in 1882, and in 1904 Britain and France signed the Entente Cordiale, which formalized French oversight of the Antiquities Service while preserving Britain's oversight of Egyptian governance and defense. By then the director-general's purview had expanded to encompass supervision of the Egyptian Museum and approval of archaeological excavations. During that period the quantity of finds foreigners could ship home was determined by the director-general on an ad hoc basis, but an antiquities law approved in 1912 limited foreign excavators to no more than half their finds, with the majority going to the Egyptian Museum. When Carter was exploring in the Valley of the Kings, permits tended to be limited to a year at a time, and they were often written to address the particular conditions of individual sites.[9]

These laws remained unchanged when the British declared Egypt a protectorate at the beginning of the First World War, erasing the remaining vestiges of Ottoman rule on the eve of the Ottoman Empire's final collapse. Things did change, however, after the war's end as both pro-Western and nationalist Egyptians began agitating for independence. The British conceded a measure of autonomy and preempted the more militant Egyptians, led by Saad Zaghlul and his *Wafd* party, by declaring Egypt "independent" in early 1922. But the British retained control in four spheres: security of British communications, defense of Egypt against foreign aggression, protection of foreign interests and minorities in Egypt, and control of the Sudan. After the protectorate was abolished, the Antiquities Service director-general, by then Pierre Lacau, started tightening excavation-permit terms, including divisions of finds, along lines that were more in step with the nationalist sensibilities of Egyptian politicians and opinion leaders.

Lord Carnarvon died suddenly in April 1923, toward the end of Carter's first season in Tutankhamun's tomb, and Lacau signaled that while he would happily approve future permits for Carter, the terms would be less generous. When, in October 1923, Carter sought a new permit—now under the sponsorship of Lady Carnarvon—both he and the Antiquities Service sought more advantageous terms in light of the discovery. Carter wanted to assure a fair division of the finds and total control over all aspects of the tomb's clearance and publicity. For its part, the Antiquities Service wanted to retain all the finds, alter the London *Times* agreement so that news releases could be issued simultaneously by the *Times* and the local Egyptian press, and require Egyptian inspectors on site to monitor Carter's work. The two sides struggled over the details, even seeking mediation by British officials, who begged off because of the political sensitivities involved. After about a month a new permit was granted that accommodated both sides' demands, but it was hedged with reservations and deep mistrust. Not content to leave well enough alone, and angered by subsequent Antiquities Service requests, Carter fired off an angry letter to Lacau that was shared with others, including the press. Relations between Carter and Lacau, and between their allies, continued to fray, with most Western Egyptologists lining up on Carter's side.

Some of Carter's supporters, including Gardiner and Breasted, were not especially interested in the specifics because they were not heading any excavations. However, they *were* alarmed by the prospect of the Antiquities Service impeding their access in order to satisfy Egyptian nationalists who, the Westerners believed, did not really care about Egypt's antiquities. Almost to a person, European and American Egyptologists underestimated the importance of Egypt's pharaonic past in the formation of modern Egyptian identity, a relationship that was well established prior to Carter's discovery. Further, in overlooking Egypt's interest in its heritage, most members of the Egyptology community perceived the government as not caring about antiquities except when important discoveries were made. Most Egyptologists thus regarded the government's inability to preserve and protect antiquities as evidence of official neglect and disinterest rather than poverty and more pressing priorities.

When the Egyptians sought more control over the Tutankhamun finds, Breasted and his colleagues regarded the initiative as either nationalist political posturing or crass opportunism in anticipation of future tourist revenues. The Egyptologists believed that only they could fully understand and adequately care for the antiquities, while the Egyptians believed the Westerners were interested only in carrying off Egypt's national patrimony. Carter, for his part, just wanted to continue his work without Antiquities Service interference. His allies sought more: long-term assurance the Antiquities Service's powers would be limited so as to allow European and American Egyptologists the autonomy they had enjoyed in the past. The "chance conjuncture of partial Egyptian independence and the discovery of Tutankhamun's tomb" marked the moment when "Egyptology and nationalism became more tightly intertwined than ever before." When viewed in this context, the clash between Lacau and his Egyptian superiors on one side and Carter and his allies on the other is "a striking illustration of nationalist sensitivity to western cultural imperialism."[10]

Tensions between Carter and Lacau intensified as minor aggravations accumulated. In January 1924, dispatches about Carter's finds and difficulties with the Antiquities Service began appearing in the *Christian Science Monitor* and *Chicago Daily News*, scooping the Egyptian press in violation of his agreement with Lacau. They were filed by a mysterious journalist, "George Waller Mecham," who appeared to have inside access to the unfolding story. The reporter was Charles Breasted, recently arrived in Egypt to assist his father, writing under a pseudonym. The younger Breasted made the newspaper arrangements on his own but with his father's blessing and Carter's acquiescence. Then a misunderstanding arose over a private viewing Carter arranged, without Lacau's approval, of the opening of two of the nested shrines housing Tutankhamun's sarcophagus. Things had barely settled down from that dustup when Carter contacted Lacau about planning a special audience for the sarcophagus opening on 12 February. In an aside, Carter mentioned he wanted to schedule another viewing the following day for wives of his colleagues. One of Lacau's superiors, the Egyptian head of the country's Department of Public Works, vetoed the plan.

It was the last straw for Carter, who promptly issued a public statement—typed by Charles Breasted—accusing the Department of Public Works and the Antiquities Service of "impossible restrictions and discourtesies" impeding the tomb's clearance. In protest, Carter announced he was stopping work in the tomb and locking it down until the problems were resolved. Carter then filed a lawsuit against the two agencies, tactlessly hiring a British lawyer in Egypt who, during the protectorate, had prosecuted the Public Works official for treason, resulting in a short prison sentence. The Egyptians replied with a lawsuit of their own, the minister of Public Works cancelled Carter's excavation permit, and Lacau's staff seized control of the tomb, breaking off Carter's locks and replacing them with their own to bar his access.

In rejecting the Egyptians' largely symbolic oversight of the tomb's clearance, Carter's timing couldn't have been worse. Egypt's first general election since declaring independence had been held the previous month and it swept the nationalist *Wafd* party—led by Saad Zaghlul, now an Egyptian hero—into power. Speaking on behalf of his Egyptian superiors, Lacau recognized Carter's "scientific" skill, but, he continued, "it so happens that the work is carried out in a land in which we are the guests . . . and which believes it necessary to remind excavators of its rights."[11]

Outraged by the Egyptians' countermoves, Carter raced down to Cairo to press his case. All involved were eager to avoid a protracted legal battle, however, and representatives of the Egyptian government, Lady Carnarvon, and Carter asked Breasted to mediate an out-of-court settlement. None of the parties indicated why they turned to him. Breasted made no secret of his support for Carter's position, allying himself with other Western Egyptologists lobbying for Carter in public declarations and behind-the-scenes maneuvers involving the American and British diplomatic corps. One reason could have been Breasted's nationality. As an American, he was from a country that had no history of colonial rule in Egypt, and unlike France, America had not been involved in Egypt's antiquities administration. Yet none of the other Americans working in Egypt were asked to mediate the dispute.

There were, however, two additional considerations that distinguished Breasted from his fellow Americans. First, unlike his countrymen, he was not doing any excavations; his work was concentrated exclusively on recording inscriptions, and when Breasted *had* sought permission to move earth, it was only to get a better look at them. Second, after his 1919–20 expedition reports to British military and diplomatic officials, Breasted was perceived to understand the political interests of Middle Eastern peoples and relations between them and the European powers. More than likely, the contending parties regarded Breasted as possessing the requisite disinterest and diplomatic skill to negotiate an agreement that respected each side's concerns.[12]

Breasted, who was at Chicago House, traveled to Cairo and began negotiating a settlement. He recommended postponing a court hearing scheduled for each side to set out its case, a notion Carter rejected, believing that his views would prevail if given a proper airing. After the hearings began, the Antiquities Service unexpectedly agreed to the preliminary terms Breasted had submitted to both sides, with one exception. Breasted left the division of the Tutankhamun finds for another day, but the Antiquities Service insisted instead that Carter and Lady Carnarvon renounce any claims to them and drop their lawsuit. While the court case continued, Breasted worked feverishly to find a common ground on which all could agree. Finally, by early March 1924 they had come to terms and were about to sign an agreement when Carter's lawyer, during one of the hearings, characterized the Egyptian government's seizure of the tomb as akin to breaking in "like a bandit." The Egyptians were insulted and broke off negotiations, and the minister of Public Works suggested Breasted take over the tomb's clearance from Carter, a step Breasted regarded as "utterly unthinkable." He sought an eleventh-hour resolution, but to no avail.

Breasted withdrew from the negotiations after having "spent five weeks on this thankless task, and after having been kicked effectively by both sides." Carter left for England and then continued to the United States for a lecture tour, and the tomb remained closed for nearly a year. He retained another lawyer skilled at navigating Egyptian politics, and while Carter was abroad, the lawyer worked quietly behind the scenes. Then, in November 1924, the British commander in chief of the Egyptian army and governor of Sudan was assassinated, an act for which the British held Saad Zaghlul, now prime minister, responsible. He resigned and was succeeded by a moderate politician who, while friendlier to Britain's interests, had far less parliamentary support than Zaghlul. The nationalists didn't trust the moderates, and both sides were even more wary of British motives. Despite these changes, by the time Carter returned to Egypt that December both he and his Egyptian counterparts were prepared to compromise, but in the end, he gave up far more than they. He was allowed to resume work in the tomb in January 1925 and continued his slow, meticulous documentation and clearing until it was completed in early 1932, *all* the finds to be permanently housed and displayed in the Egyptian Museum. Lacking a scholar's temperament, Carter never published a full account of the tomb's contents and did not pursue other explorations, instead entering a period of gradual decline, dying in England in 1939.[13]

Breasted felt his role in the controversy was entirely a waste of time, and he believed his work on the seal impressions and negotiations between Carter and the Egyptian government was unappreciated. But in fact his participation in the negotiations increased his stature, and it broadened his access to the arenas of Egyptian politics and diplomacy.

From the very beginning of his investigation on the tomb's identification, Breasted related his experiences to Rockefeller. The first report came in a detailed letter that he concluded by suggesting the Rockefeller family take a Nile tour Breasted would help organize—the plan that would subsequently be put off. Rockefeller read the letter to his father and other members of the family who had already been following news reports of the discovery, possibly including one citing the "authority of the world famous Professor Breasted." The Rockefellers appreciated his insider's account of the story and his contextualization of it, with his "intimate knowledge" of Egyptian history, which "added enormously to its vividness, interest and charm." In the summer following the discovery, Breasted obtained Carter's permission for the Rockefellers to attend the burial chamber's opening should they be on the planned Nile trip when the opening occurred. Breasted's Tutankhamun letters to Rockefeller were hardly out of the ordinary. He reported frequently to Rockefeller on the Oriental Institute's projects, either in long letters or with cover notes accompanied by journal articles or institute publications.

His relationship with Carter, however, brought an added dimension. It furnished Breasted with privileged information and access to the tomb at a time when it seemed the entire world was captivated by the story but very few enjoyed such entrée. The flurry of publicity swirling around Carter's find provided Breasted with a rare opportunity not only to firm up his patron's commitment but to recruit others to his cause as well. Breasted's realization was accompanied by a bit of discomfort, however. Since the beginning of his lecture-circuit days, he had struggled to find a happy medium between benefitting from the public's "Egyptomania" and maintaining his intellectual integrity. Now, with Carter's discovery and the public infatuation that had transformed an obscure pharaoh, known as Nebkheperure Tutankhamun among Egyptologists, into "King Tut," Breasted was in an ideal position to divert some of that passion into support for the Oriental Institute.[14]

After assisting with the tomb seals, Breasted was asked by Carter to provide ongoing consultations while the tomb's contents were documented and to contribute to the "historical side" of the discovery's final publication. In return Breasted wanted lantern slides of key finds to illustrate future lectures. He wasn't interested in stealing the spotlight from Carter, however. On the contrary, Breasted advised him on the possibilities and pitfalls of the American lecture tour Carter subsequently made. Breasted knew that despite the Carnarvons' patronage, Carter was not a wealthy man and his only potential gain from the discovery would come from publications and lecture tours, enterprises with which Carter had relatively little experience.

In much the same way that Breasted counseled Carter on how best to profit from King Tut, George Ellery Hale advised Breasted on how to turn the public craze to *his* advantage. Their conversation about the uses of popular interest had begun a couple of years earlier. Starting in January 1920, after Rockefeller's gift establishing the Oriental Institute and in the midst of Breasted's survey expedition, he began thinking about creating a "Cairo Oriental Institute" that might be underwritten by "the Rockefeller millions." The new institute would complement his Chicago program by serving as a base in Egypt and as a stepping-off point for work throughout the Middle East. In 1921 Breasted calculated he would need as much as $5 million for the project and began exploring a variety of sources, including the Carnegie Institution and the National Research Council. Hale advised him that the sum of money was too great, given the postwar financial travails in America and urged Breasted instead to stick with Chicago and "build up . . . from small beginnings." Hale felt "Mr. Rockefeller's interest [could] probably be developed still further" as the Oriental Institute's work advanced. In the meantime, Hale urged Breasted to "present your scheme to a wide public" through articles in scholarly and popular journals, offer plans for "gradual development," and indicate "phases of the work" that could be achieved with smaller gifts.[15]

When Hale and his wife arrived in Egypt for a long-planned visit, by coincidence shortly after Carter's discovery, Hale urged Breasted to promote his own projects by tapping into the King Tut phenomenon. Breasted agreed that "now is the time to strike the public for funds," and Hale offered to help by writing a couple of popular-journal articles toward that end. Referring to his epigraphy project, which he had not yet set under way, Breasted replied, "I have not entirely abandoned the plan for the photographing campaign. . . . I should be very grateful . . . if you would call attention . . . to the great necessity for such a plan." Hale followed through, writing two essays for the public-affairs monthly *Scribner's Magazine*, which had a subscriber base of about eighty-three thousand around this time.

The first piece, "Recent Discoveries in Egypt," included several quotations from Breasted's publications, referring to him as "the leading historian of Egypt." The second one, "The Work of an American Orientalist," summarized Breasted's scholarship, the logic of his plan for what would become the Epigraphic Survey, and the Oriental Institute's projects to date, including the Assyrian dictionary and Coffin Texts. Hale concluded with a direct appeal: "When we are so fortunate as to possess a scholar competent to write the most important chapter in the history of the evolution of man, we should hasten to give him as complete an equipment and as large a staff of associates as our leading investigators in the physical, biological, and medical sciences already enjoy." Hale's *Scribner's* articles were published in the months leading up to the renewal of Breasted's institute grant, and he subsequently wrote to Hale that they were "immensely valuable to the cause I am trying to put through" and "accomplished a great deal of good."[16]

By this point Hale had written frequently for *Scribner's*, often arguing for "science's link to the pragmatic activities of everyday life," a position consistent with the editorial policies of public-affairs magazines of the era. The percentage of science articles they featured "increased in the 1920s as did the presence of scientists as authors. Moreover, these scientists represented a particular influential group within the research community: those involved in the budding national politics of science." Hale was not only a leader of that group, he was also the second-most-prolific author or subject in American popular magazines—after Thomas A. Edison—between 1910 and 1955. Hale's prominence and that of similarly active scientist-writers "came not from their position[s] or scientific accomplishments but because of their articulateness. . . . They could describe even arcane topics in terms that laypersons could understand." Breasted learned from Hale's example and tried his hand at writing for a broader public, as exemplified in a short, illustrated article he contributed to an issue of *Popular Mechanics*, "Feats of Old Egyptians Rival Modern Works of Engineers," on the quarrying, transport, and erection of large stone obelisks. Hale's guidance was so useful to Breasted because they faced comparable challenges. Just as "when scientists wrote articles . . . , they were not just relating scientific facts; they were also attempting to advance the cause of science and to mold the public's images of science," so too Breasted wanted the public to understand that Egyptology consisted of far more than treasure hunting and that ancient Egypt contributed more to civilization than superstitions.[17]

An Unbuilt Museum

While mediating the Carter dispute in March 1924, Breasted was visited by George E. Vincent, then president of the Rockefeller Foundation. Breasted showed Vincent around Cairo's sites, including the Egyptian Museum. The building, which opened in 1902 and remains in use to this day, is a sprawling, two-story stucco-over-masonry structure. The museum was designed by a French architect in a polychrome, beaux-arts neoclassical style—complete with tributes to European Egyptologists—and it is as much a monument to the French colonial presence as to Egypt's ancient past. By the 1920s the building was already overcrowded and had fallen into disrepair. Its "roof leaked in the winter rains, . . . plaster of ceilings and walls had crashed down upon and damaged irreplaceable historical items; [and] basement storage magazines . . . were regularly flooded at high Nile." Vincent was disturbed by the museum's condition and thought Rockefeller might be interested in underwriting its repair. The idea was not far-fetched. After a trip to France in 1923, during which Rockefeller saw the poor conditions of Versailles, Fontainebleau, and the Reims cathedral, he offered $1 million to the French government for their restoration. That gift was being negotiated while Vincent was in Egypt, and France accepted it two months later.[18]

Upon returning to New York, Vincent shared his observations with Raymond A. Fosdick, one of Rockefeller's philanthropic gatekeepers, "principal colleague and chief interpreter of the outside world, . . . lawyer, adviser, friend, and, eventually, biographer." In October 1924 Fosdick wrote to Breasted seeking advice on the matter, not for the Rockefeller Foundation, of which he was a trustee, but on behalf of "other sources." While Fosdick thought there might be some interest in addressing the museum's needs, he wanted to be certain the Egyptian government could not afford the necessary repairs. If not, he also wondered how a major donation would be handled given the "present political situation in Egypt," a reference to disputes between moderate and more militant Egyptian nationalists and between them and British authorities. Breasted replied that the museum's neglect was due to insufficient funds. However, he added, the museum's disrepair was a symptom of two interlocking problems: the incompetence of the Antiquities Service's French managers—who were responsible for the museum—and Egyptian malfeasance.

Breasted sidestepped the question of Egyptian political stability, declaring instead, "Such a contribution from the New World to the Old,—from the youngest of the great nations to the oldest, . . . would by its very presence in the greatest city of Islam, form a moral lesson of tremendous power. It would go far toward healing the present unhappy breach between the Near East and the West; it would proclaim to the men of the Orient the sacredness of their past, which brought forth the great religions of the modern world; and it would demonstrate to them the unselfish zeal of the men of the West to preserve forever the priceless spiritual values which they find in our great common heritage from the Ancient Orient."

Fosdick was unpersuaded and brought up the "upset conditions in Egypt" again. Breasted claimed to be "in possession of . . . conclusive facts bearing on this situation" based on his "intimate confidential contact" with top British and Egyptian officials since the 1919–20 expedition report and continuing through the Tutankhamun negotiations. He declared the British were there to stay, the Egyptians knew this, and the periodic eruptions of political unrest in Egypt amounted to nothing more than the "noise they make in opposition . . . simply for home consumption." However, he excused the "troublesome native inefficiency" of the Egyptians "in carrying on their own government." After all, he pointed out, there had not "been any more trouble in getting the Egyptian Government machinery into motion, and certainly . . . less time spent, than was the case with the beginnings of government under our fathers in these United States."[19]

Placated, Fosdick met with Breasted in November to outline a proposal for Rockefeller's consideration. Breasted followed up the meeting with a plan that expanded the project beyond repair of the museum building to address what he considered the root causes of its neglect. Breasted argued the need for "preservation of the priceless collections" as well as their "permanent future accessibility," that is, for Western scholars. His mechanism for bringing this about was the establishment of an "Egyptian Antiquities Board" made up of four Americans, two Egyptian-government representatives—the minister of Public Works and the director-general of the Antiquities Service—and perhaps a British official. The board would be legally constituted and have the power to hold and disburse funds to repair or replace the current Egyptian Museum, maintain it in perpetuity "for the benefit of foreign scientists," and provide "permanent representation of the scientific interests of the foreign world in Egypt." Breasted proposed the board have its own facility, a building adjacent to the museum with offices for staff and visiting scholars, as well as a research library. And he mapped out an elaborate scheme to present the plan to the Egyptian government, with separate sections on "relations" with the British and Egyptians.

In January 1925 Breasted traveled to New York, where he and Fosdick presented their observations to Rockefeller, who was interested in their ideas but wanted more details and a menu of practical solutions. Breasted continued to Egypt, where he ran the plans by Allenby, who was still high commissioner there. Allenby sent the plans to his superiors in London, who authorized him to support the effort. The following June, Breasted, Fosdick, and Rockefeller met again and settled on plans for a new museum building, a separate "archeological research building," and a substantial operating endowment at a total cost of $10 million. Rockefeller intended to personally donate the entire package to the Egyptian people, and he asked Breasted and Fosdick to supervise its implementation.[20]

The project advanced with the "customary thoroughness" characteristic of Rockefeller's larger endeavors. In late August, Rockefeller paid for a tour of major American museums by Breasted, Welles Bosworth (the architect designate), Fosdick, V. Everit Macy—another of Rockefeller's advisors—and a civil engineer. The group visited the art museums of Boston, Cleveland, Minneapolis, and Chicago and studied blueprints of the Detroit Institute of Arts building, just being erected at the time. Although their observations helped shape the Egyptian museum building program, Breasted specified many details, communicating directly with Bosworth. In October 1925, Breasted, Fosdick, and Macy met in Rockefeller's office to sign an indenture that stipulated the project's terms and conditions, including Rockefeller's designation of the three others as project trustees with Breasted as their chair.

Breasted was also delegated to present the proposed gift to King Fuʿād I, Egypt's titular leader since its independence declaration in 1922. Breasted was to bring with him the indenture for the Egyptian government's approval and a lavishly printed and illustrated booklet ostensibly intended to explain the nature and purpose of the project. Titled *The New Egyptian Museum and Research Institute at Cairo*, the booklet's text was written by Breasted, and he supervised its design and production with two more subtle purposes in mind: first, to impress Fu'ād and other Egyptian leaders with the project's grandeur and importance for Egypt and, second, to provide Fu'ād and the Egyptian government a means of publicizing the project as a great Egyptian accomplishment.

The plans were discussed extensively with British officials in London and Egypt, in part because the scheme initially required that the British relinquish the site of a military barracks along the Nile adjacent to the current Egyptian Museum. However, at no point was any *Egyptian* official consulted. For diplomatic and security reasons, the British specifically advised Breasted against consulting with either the Egyptians or French. Breasted had no qualms about the British advice because he was confident that Egyptian leaders, overwhelmed and flattered by Rockefeller's generosity, would gratefully accept the offer and—with the booklet—proudly announce it to the Egyptian people and the world.[21]

The financial and legal frameworks underlying the plan are mapped out in the indenture, which stipulates (1) a $5.4 million fund to construct the new museum building and a separate "Institute of Archeological Research" building; (2) a $4.6 million endowment to be administered by a newly established independent and international "Egyptian Archeology Foundation"; (3) establishment of an international "Egyptian Museum Commission" to oversee the museum once construction was completed; and (4) a procedure for transferring control of the museum and its administration back to the Egyptian government thirty-three years after the building's completion. The research institute would remain the Egyptian Archeology Foundation's property for no less than fifty years and potentially in perpetuity.

The Egyptian Museum Commission was to be composed of the Egyptian minister of Public Works, the director-general of the Egyptian Antiquities Service, and the directors of the Egyptian Archeology Foundation. Because of their numerical superiority, however, members of the Egyptian Archeology Foundation—the majority of whom were Westerners—would dominate the commission: "The . . . Foundation shall be composed of two representatives each of the United States, Great Britain and France, and, if the Foundation . . . so decides . . . one or two representatives of another, or . . . two other nations, preferably nations conducting archeological work in Egypt." Because the American members were to be appointed, one each, by the National Academy of Sciences and the Metropolitan Museum of Art, Breasted, as a member of the National Academy of Sciences and its only Egyptologist, was assured a directorship of the Egyptian Archeology Foundation and thereby membership on the commission.

Income yielded by the foundation's endowment was for "scientific and educational purposes, and in general to foster and maintain archaeological research and study in any part of the world and to preserve and make available for scientists and scholars monuments of ancient culture wherever located; . . . [and] to provide and maintain museums, libraries, laboratories, schools, and other facilities appropriate to the general objects of the Foundation." However, for the thirty-three-year duration of the agreement, the foundation was also to pay the museum's operating costs, including staff salaries. It is unclear how the museum was to be funded after that period if the foundation chose to use the money for other purposes. The Institute of Archeological Research was to "carry on researches dealing with monuments in the Museum or elsewhere, and publish the results of its researches, to maintain a library of Oriental Archeology, and to furnish research facilities for other institutions or individuals." Its "Research Director" was to be "the person who is now the Director of the Oriental Institute."[22]

The indenture also specified that the new museum and its collections would be controlled by the Egyptian Museum Commission. The Egyptian Archeology Foundation would own the Institute of Archeological Research and its endowment in perpetuity. Taken together, these stipulations placed the museum, its collections, and its budget under the commission's control, and the Egyptian Archeology Foundation, through its power of the purse, had final say over the commission. If they accepted the terms, the Egyptians would be ceding governance of these institutions and resources for the thirty-three-year duration of the agreement. Breasted felt the time was necessary "because . . . America required a period of about thirty years to develop a generation of Egyptologists," implying Egypt would train a corps of Egyptian scholars during this time to take over the museum and research institute when the agreement ended. But other than hoping the project would "contribute . . . to the success of Egypt in training and developing her own scientists," neither the indenture nor the accompanying brochure offered assistance toward this goal.[23]

The museum building was to be "the finest modern monument in Egypt" and "a temple of the unfolding life of man . . . erected in forms of nobility and impressiveness" (figure 8.5). Noting that the "first such institution," the Museum of Alexandria, was erected in Egypt, Breasted wrote, "It is indeed appropriate that the capital of a new and independent Egypt should now be embellished with . . . the most magnificent museum of modern times." According to architect Bosworth, it was designed to relate "harmoniously with what it is to contain, or as Viollet-le-Duc phrases it in his definition of style, 'an expression in every respect to its use.'" Thus, "In harmony with the ancient buildings of the land . . . the exterior . . . shall be of solid ashlar stone masonry," with an entrance portico supported by twelve columns of "granite from the same Assuan quarries whence

Fig. 8.5 Proposed Egyptian museum building complex viewed from across the Nile; the museum is
on the right, the research institute on the left. Rendering by William Walcot after designs by Welles
Bosworth, from *The New Egyptian Museum and Research Institute at Cairo* [1925]. Courtesy of the
Oriental Institute, University of Chicago.

the ancient Egyptian architects hewed their granite, from the days of the first
pyramids to the vast obelisks of Luxor and Karnak."

The museum was to face the Nile with a facade engraved with the words
"Erected in the Reign of His Majesty King Fuad I" in Arabic, English, and French.
The entry vestibule would be lined with the busts "of the great Egyptologists of
the past, now standing in the old museum . . . ranged on either side as in a kind
of Hall of Fame." Beyond the vestibule the visitor would have a vista "down the
axis of the building [through] a deep perspective of courts and colonnades" all
lined with "tall flower columns . . . suggested by the great colonnade of the Karnak hypostyle." In the rearmost court, "what may be termed the 'holy-of-holies'
of this temple of ancient life," would be a "deep apse-like hall" containing statues
of "the most splendid of Egyptian emperors, Amenhotep III, enthroned by his
lovely queen Tiy," representing "the culmination of ancient Egyptian power and
genius" (figure 8.6).

The enormous halls would use high sidelighting to illuminate spaces subdivided by lower partition walls tall enough to enclose large statuary without
blocking the windows. Bosworth's appropriation of ancient Egyptian architec-

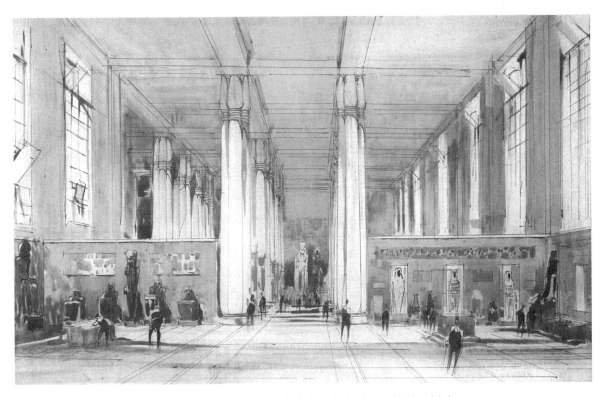

Fig. 8.6 Proposed Egyptian museum exhibition hall illustrating displays and high sidelighting. Rendering by William Walcot after designs by Welles Bosworth, from *The New Egyptian Museum and Research Institute at Cairo* [1925]. Courtesy of the Oriental Institute, University of Chicago.

tural forms for the proposed museum's facade and interiors represents a distinctly Western perception of the most appropriate style for a modern Egyptian building of great symbolic importance. The Islamic revival style, then fashionable among Cairo's Egyptian and foreign architects, would have been a viable alternative consistent with the historicist tastes of the era.[24]

The plan allowed installation of "the collections all on one plane with unsurpassed clearness of chronological and genetic sequence." They were to be experienced as a reification of ancient Egyptian history similar to the narration of art history in major European and American "survey" museums. Breasted's rendition of that history favored a particular thematic thrust, the story of "human development as it will be possible to follow it . . . from primitive savagery to a highly refined culture expressing itself in marvelous monuments and works of art, through a magnificent culmination to a decline which eventually resulted in European supremacy, and after the Sixth Century B.C. in European leadership of civilization." His focus on ancient Egypt as the birthplace of European civilization was intended to explain why the West was so keen on preserving modern Egypt's heritage. Never mind that the notion of Egypt's history ending in "European supremacy" might be regarded differently by Egyptian leaders struggling for independence and asserting a new national identity. The plan was thought to support them by catering to the interests of a contemporary Egyptian public. Yet Breasted focused far more on Western tourists, anticipating "steamship cruises, which carry increasing thousands . . . every succeeding year, [and which] will always include [the museum] in their itineraries as they pass through the Suez Canal."[25]

Only the "finest objects" were to be displayed on the main floor, however, while "monuments of somewhat inferior worth" were to be stored on the museum's ground floor. In reality a basement, the ground floor was nonetheless designed to be above the Nile's highest annual inundation (figure 8.7). However, this was no ordinary storage vault. The minimum height of the ground floor was to be nearly eighteen feet so that it could "furnish a type of storage such that monuments placed there can be . . . made available to scholars, scientists and institutions all over the world." To this end, Breasted included special facilities "which should form a part . . . of every complete museum": for the collections, a conservation laboratory; for "museums and educational institutions throughout the world," casting rooms and a photography lab for the "production of facsimiles," lantern slides, and photographs that could be acquired though printed catalogs; and for visiting scholars, "a series of cool, light and conveniently equipped work rooms" furnished with "small . . . dark-rooms" so "each visiting scientist [could make] his own photographic records."[26]

Next door to the museum would be the Institute of Archeological Research with its own staff and equipment because the "administrative duties devolving upon the staff of a great museum leave them little or no time for scientific work." Its stately three-story building was to be constructed in a similar architectural style (figure 8.5), and it was linked to the museum by a tunnel between the museum's ground-level storage halls and the institute's ground level. The tunnel would be used to move museum objects to the institute, especially new finds, so researchers could study them and furnish labels for their installation in the museum. The institute's ground level was also to include a photographic laboratory specialized to help prepare materials for publication. The third floor would contain workrooms for visiting scholars, drafting rooms, and "quarters for native servants." Also behind the scenes, "to facilitate uninterrupted access to their papers and records, the Research Director and the Research Secretary, when in Cairo, will doubtless reside in the building; and apartments for them might well occupy a part of the second floor."[27]

Dominating the main floor was the institute's library (figure 8.8). The remaining space was to contain a suite of offices, seminar rooms, and a meeting room for the Egyptian Archeology Foundation board. The "Research Staff [to be] recruited from among the best obtainable scholars and scientists" would have

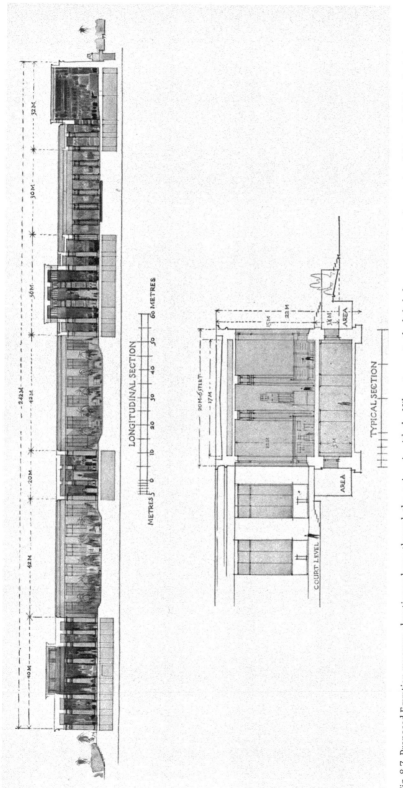

Fig. 8.7 Proposed Egyptian museum elevations: above, through the main axis with the Nile entrance to the left; below, across axis of a sample exhibition hall. The shaded portions below elevations are ground-floor storage areas. Rendering by William Walcot after designs by Welles Bosworth, from *The New Egyptian Museum and Research Institute at Cairo* [1925]. Courtesy of the Oriental Institute, University of Chicago.

Fig. 8.8 Proposed research institute library interior. On the far wall is a map of the Nile, its north-south axis oriented horizontally with the delta to the right. Rendering by William Walcot after designs by Welles Bosworth, from *The New Egyptian Museum and Research Institute at Cairo* [1925]. Courtesy of the Oriental Institute, University of Chicago.

consisted of a research director, research secretary, their personal secretaries, library staff, a general office pool, and visiting scholars. The institute's special features—library, drafting rooms, and photography facilities to produce publication illustrations—conformed with Breasted's priorities of interpretation and publication. Of the specific tasks Breasted outlined for the research institute, only one, a study of prehistoric remains theoretically below the alluvial floor of the Nile valley, would have required new excavations. Breasted's other objectives were an architectural survey of ancient Egyptian buildings, a general handbook of Egyptian archaeology "such as we possess for Greece and Rome," a history of the development of Egyptian hieroglyphs, an investigation of Egypt's surface geology "by natural scientists working hand in hand with prehistoric archaeologists and paleontologists," and an examination of "the relations between prehistoric Egypt and neighboring Asia."

As an independently and very well-funded creature of the Egyptian Archeology Foundation and a privileged partner of the Egyptian Museum, the research institute would have dominated Egyptology in Egypt. This role is hinted by the map—showing the reach of ancient Egypt—looming over the institute's library, its scale and placement calling to mind a futuristic command-center screen. The large globe in the middle of the floor is a reminder that the institute's "researches would not be" hampered by "geographical or cultural restrictions . . . [permitting] the extension of its investigations to follow the lines of diffusing culture in all directions and if necessary into other continents."[28]

What began as a restoration of the old museum was inflated by Breasted into a research program. "Never in the history of humanistic science and certainly never in the history of oriental science has research been equipped and endowed on so grand a scale," Breasted crowed. "The . . . Museum will be transformed into a great archeological . . . research enterprise with $10,000,000 behind it." In effect, the museum had been turned into a resource for a research center designed for Western scholars and their constituencies. Consistent with the expanding breadth of Breasted's Oriental Institute program, the project's apparent focus on Egyptology was also enlarged so it could serve "scientific research in the ancient lands of the *Near East as a whole*." The project's evolution from a museum restoration project into a research institution that injected Western scholarship into the Middle East was consistent with Rockefeller's and other American philanthropists' initiatives overseas. It exemplified an emerging trend among the nation's benefactors of "promoting stability and orderly change" in emerging nations while also "extending the 'benefits' of Western science, technology, and value systems abroad."[29]

In mid-January 1926 Breasted, accompanied by an American diplomat, visited King Fuʿād, who had received the proposal and booklet about a week earlier. The king's response was cool because he was concerned about the project's "international control over funds and administration." The king referred the plan to the prime minister, Ahmad Ziwar, who in turn passed it to the Egyptian legal ministry for analysis. The Egyptians countered with alternative proposals that led to several weeks of testy negotiations between the Americans and Egyptians and extensive side consultations with the British. All but one of the revisions were accepted by Rockefeller, and a revised indenture was returned to Prime Minister Ziwar for his final approval.

To the consternation of Breasted and his associates, Ziwar turned down the plan. In rejecting it he is quoted as having said, "The conditions are absolutely unacceptable, they infringe upon the sovereignty of Egypt! My colleagues in the council of ministers decline to consider the matter until the conditions of the contract have been fundamentally revised!" The two sides entered into further negotiations that lasted nearly two more months, Rockefeller and Breasted agreed to several changes proposed by the Egyptians, and the Americans drafted a revised proposal for the Egyptian government's approval in March. Ziwar found the new proposal lacking on one point and sought an amendment. Discussions continued, but Rockefeller and his advisors had already told Breasted that they regarded "the bargaining period as definitely ended." The Americans eventually lost patience and in late April gave Ziwar and his ministers a week to reconsider, but they received no reply, and the proposal was formally withdrawn.[30]

Accounts in the West suggest it was a lost opportunity the blame for which was placed on Egyptian "bickering and petty politics." This was hardly the case. The project required the Egyptians to cede control over part of their national patrimony to a handful of American and European scholars for more than three decades. At the time of the negotiations, the Egyptian government was in the midst of a political crisis, the most volatile issue of which was colonial rule. An immediate conflict under way at the time of the Breasted-Rockefeller proposal pitted the king and Ziwar's ministry, who sought some measure of accommodation with the British, against the popular and far more anticolonial *Wafd* party that dominated the Egyptian parliament. With a parliamentary election approaching about one month after Breasted's final offer, Ziwar no doubt believed the plan's acceptance would further excite a mounting level of nationalist opposition to his already weak government. "Will recent governmental changes in these parts affect your plans in any way?" Nelson asked Breasted. "What one party accepts may be utterly repudiated by the next when it gets into power." Finally, the king and his allies were annoyed by the presumptuousness of presenting them a completed contract and announcement without first consulting them. Even a British consulate official understood their vexation at the way the gift was "thrown at the heads" of the Egyptian government. If Breasted's diplomatic skills were as great as his confidence in them, he should have been more sensitive to Ziwar's predicament and worked more strenuously to alleviate it.[31]

Another of Breasted's miscalculations was his expectation of unanimous backing from Western Egyptologists. Despite their occasional rivalries, he thought they would close ranks in supporting the project, if for no other reason than professional self-interest, and that their assent would translate into additional diplomatic pressure on Egypt. Following his mediation of Carter's problems in early 1924, Breasted joined colleagues in lobbying Western diplomats to obtain a relaxation of the Antiquities Service restrictions Lacau had set in place a few years earlier. In May 1925, after starting to discuss the museum project with Rockefeller and his aides, Breasted wrote to several prominent American museum officials urging them to contact the secretary of state about the restrictions. To the Metropolitan Museum of Art's director Breasted also confided:

> The importance of this protest just at this juncture is . . . : I am expecting to [have a] conference in London with Sir Frederick Kenyon [British Museum director] and the British Foreign Minister [regarding]: (1) The proper

maintenance and scientific use of the collections in the National Museum at Cairo, (2) Fair, enlightened and scientific control of foreign expeditions . . . in Egypt. . . . I shall be taking with me influences of such weight that there is little doubt we shall be able to insure the continuance of <u>Western</u> control of the Cairo Museum. Such a project may, of course, influence the second of the above interests."

Breasted was parlaying Western indignation over tightening Antiquities Service restrictions into support for the Egyptian museum project, arguing his plan would help assure Western "scientific control" of the Antiquities Service as well. It was a strategic blunder. By linking the museum project to the Antiquities Service dispute and placing so much emphasis on Western oversight of the new building, he overreached, plunging the entire scheme into the center of Egyptian politics at a time of considerable volatility. Had he remained true to his own scholarly interests, which—after all—did not depend on excavations and divisions of finds, Breasted might well have seen the new museum building, the research institute, and an enormous research endowment created on terms that would have served his purposes while also satisfying Egyptian ambitions for greater sovereignty.[32]

Breasted's missteps were due in part to his overestimation of Britain's readiness to intervene in Egypt's antiquities policies. Breasted's take on Britain's power and range of interests in Egypt's internal affairs was influenced by several British friends, especially Gardiner. Starting in late 1917, in anticipation of the First World War's end and collapse of the Ottoman Empire, Gardiner joined other British Egyptologists in an effort to establish a greater presence in Egypt. Knowing that Britain's Foreign Office was developing plans for a British protectorate in Egypt, Gardiner and his colleagues lobbied the Foreign Office to give British scholars a voice in the Antiquities Service, reorganize the museum's management, and establish a "British Imperial Institute of Archaeology" in Cairo. Nothing came of their proposals. However, when the British statesman Alfred Lord Milner was appointed to head a commission on Egypt's postwar administration, British Egyptologists again mobilized to press their case. They enlisted Breasted in their cause, and while he was passing through Egypt on his 1919–20 expedition, Breasted was consulted by the Milner commission regarding Egyptian Museum and Antiquities Service matters, and he is quoted in its report.

As before, the document did not change British policy because diplomats were unwilling to irritate either the Egyptians or the French over Antiquities Service policies. When Breasted went to London as the emissary of Rockefeller's gift, he naively assumed the warmth of his reception in the highest circles of the British government represented firm British backing. Although the British were more than happy to offer Breasted advice, they did not regard the matter a "foreign interest" worthy of their intervention. Further, he ignored a valuable insight delivered confidentially by the Foreign Office's Egyptian expert, who told Breasted that the Egyptians didn't think Americans were necessarily any more trustworthy than the British when it came to their internal affairs.[33]

The project's flawed handling was also born of the differences between how Breasted thought about ancient Egyptians and the people of modern Egypt. Breasted's attitudes toward contemporary Egyptians were complicated, inconsistent, and often affected by immediate circumstances. He found the squalor of impoverished Egyptians' living conditions shocking and incomprehensible. And he was outraged by what he perceived as vandalism when the more enterprising among Egypt's poor lugged away ancient stonework for building materials or stripped monuments of reliefs for visiting tourists and the international antiquities market. On the other hand, Breasted was humane, too, interrupting his survey expeditions along the Nile to attend to sick and malnourished Egyptians. Breasted did not write about the plight of impoverished Egyptians except when he crossed paths with those living in the shelter of ancient monuments or hustling for tourist dollars. Even then, his observations tended toward the descriptive, almost ethnological, unless he was annoyed by a problem, in which case he was fully capable of condemning a hapless peasant in painfully harsh terms.

Breasted was severely critical of most Egyptian officials, whom he regarded as generally lazy and corrupt. To a certain extent he recognized that the government inefficiencies and dereliction he encountered in Egypt were learned from colonial bureaucrats who brought bad attitudes from Europe, where he witnessed abuses as well. Nonetheless, being incapable of anything less than a tireless work ethic, Breasted regarded Egyptian officials' work habits and their neglect of fellow Egyptians' needs as unconscionable. It simply did not occur to Breasted that this behavior arose in a context in which generations of colonial rule engendered passivity among Egyptian officials as a form of political resistance. Furthermore, the function of baksheesh as a bureaucratic lubricant and foundation of the tourist economy, cast a pall over most Egyptian transactions that led many Westerners, including Breasted, to assume that official corruption reached the highest levels of the government. Taken together, these experiences and false impressions clouded Breasted's judgment. At an early planning stage of the museum project, Breasted described to George Ellery Hale his "plan of protecting the administration of the antiquities out here from ignorant native control. What these modern Egyptian Nationalists want, is not liberty or independence, but merely easy posts and fat salaries." A few months later, Breasted said about his booklet that with "this ammunition I hope to intoxicate the King and give him such a pipedream of the Arabian Nights possibilities . . . that we shall be able to stampede him and his whole group into it. . . . When he says the word [it will be sent] to all the leading people and institutions of the world! If that doesn't get a vain and self-conscious Oriental, nothing else will."[34]

Rockefeller and his advisors expressed "perfect confidence in [Breasted's] diplomacy and good judgment" and thus did not appreciate the political difficulties their project would create for Egypt's leadership. In first proposing the booklet, Breasted did note that "the King's chief apprehension will be that his people will regard the . . . Project as an unwarranted concession to foreign influence." But rather than accept the validity of nationalist concerns, Breasted and the others worked to bypass them, even if that meant taking advantage of political instability to put the plan through: "[Ziwar] can hardly expect to last beyond the . . . next Parliament, which is . . . pretty certain to be strongly nationalist in complexion. . . . Our advisors all agreed that the time to submit the project was immediately, while Ziwar was in power, and that we should bend every effort to have it a 'fait accompli' before his fall." For their part, the Egyptians made a good-faith effort to reach a mutually satisfactory agreement. During negotiations, when pressured by Rockefeller and his aides to maintain a hard line, Breasted reported the Egyptians had "gone as far . . . as any Egyptian Government can be expected to go and survive." One of Rockefeller's lawyers, who was present in Cairo for some of the negotiations, commented on the "many points on which [the Egyptians] yielded," and that they "were moved by a sincere desire to aid in the consummation of the project."[35]

Recounting the project's collapse, Charles Breasted—who was in Egypt and assisting his father at the time—wrote that the Americans "approved the Egyptian government's revised version of the contract without a single change." In failing to accept the Americans' final offer, he implied, the Egyptians spurned "a contract drawn by the Egyptian government itself." However, the text approved by Rockefeller and returned for the Egyptians' final approval, *did* contain certain pivotal revisions. The changes tightened Western control of the Egyptian Museum Commission and museum personnel hiring and compensation. The Americans' less-than-honorable intentions are evident in the recommendation of Rockefeller's lawyer that it wasn't necessary to call the changes to the Egyptians' attention. Regardless of "just how far good faith" required Breasted to go in disclosure, the lawyer added, "Mr. Rockefeller must . . . be completely protected . . . against any charge or suggestion that he is trying to put something over on the Egyptian Government." It is tempting to regard the project as a case study in the annals of Western cultural imperialism. Yet the dominance sought by Breasted and his associates was plainly understood by the Egyptians, weighed within a domestic political context, and rejected when the Americans refused to accommodate Egyptian wishes.[36]

The seed of the project's failure was contained within its very conception. The great *Egyptian* museum Breasted proposed could not be realized without the Egyptians ceding control over their antiquities. What Breasted envisioned as "[forming] a prospect of which every citizen of Egypt will be proud . . . in the midst of the greatest Moslem city of the world, housed in the most splendid modern buildings of Egypt's capital," Fu'ād and Ziwar viewed as a monument to their political weakness. A project the Americans offered as an enticing emblem of international benevolence the Egyptians received as a sign of Western hegemony. That the museum would have been the best modern building in Cairo, a Moslem city and the capital of Egypt, only intensified its faults. To the Egyptian leadership, the project raised the specter of a highly visible capitulation of Egyptian sovereignty, a political liability they could ill afford in a time of nationalist turmoil.

The collapse of the project also dramatized the functions of museums as public symbols. By using the Egyptian museum to leverage Western control of Egypt's antiquities, Breasted hoped to sweeten the politically bitter medicine of his terms with a new national monument for Egypt. The museum was thus understood by all to be a powerful symbol. In the end, however, it was the potential meaning of the symbol to the constituencies it represented that divided the parties' understanding of it. As one of the project's critics asked Breasted, "Would your proposal have the slightest chance at success shorn of the attractive bait of a fine museum[?] This is I think the acid test."[37]

Shortly before the museum project's demise, Breasted made a trip to Jerusalem, where he found there, too, "existed a great need for a museum building" to replace the current one. It was a dark and dilapidated old house that was so overcrowded fragile works had to be stored out of doors. Later that spring, after the debacle in Cairo, Breasted outlined to Fosdick the value of a modern museum building in Jerusalem for Palestinian archaeology. Fosdick liked the idea and thought it would appeal to Rockefeller. Breasted wrote to Rockefeller, whose initial response, in light of the Egyptian experience, was cool, but Rockefeller did provide $20,000 to study the situation and purchase an option on some property. In mid-January 1927 Breasted reported to Rockefeller "Suggestions for the Development of the Jerusalem Museum Plans." Drawing on his experience with the Egyptian project, Breasted recommended a configuration that combined key features of the museum and research institute plans under one roof, albeit on a much smaller scale. Rockefeller approved the general thrust of Breasted's plans, and the project quickly advanced, in part because of what—from the Westerners' point of view—was the more favorable political climate in Palestine.[38]

When Palestine became a British mandate in 1920, the first in a succession of high commissioners was appointed to oversee the civilian administration. The terms of the mandate charged Britain with responsibility for "the development of self-governing institutions." Arab opposition to the Balfour Declaration, however, resulted in political stalemate. As a result, the power and autonomy of the high commissioner's office only grew, and, in contrast to the situation in Egypt, the British exercised almost total control over Palestinian domestic affairs. The British School of Archaeology in Jerusalem was assigned to establish a Palestine Department of Antiquities to administer permits for archaeological excavations, division of finds, and a museum. In 1926 the administrative ties between the British School and the Department of Antiquities were severed, setting the stage for the Palestine museum initiative.[39]

In early April 1927, while passing through New York on his way to the Middle East, Breasted met with Rockefeller and Fosdick to review the plans. Rockefeller "was interested but noncommittal, and took the ground that [Breasted] was planning a whole series of museums in the Orient and expecting [Rockefeller] to contribute money." Nonetheless, about two weeks later he pledged $2 million for the project, half for the building and half for endowment. Breasted went to Jerusalem and met with several mandate officials, including High Commissioner Lord Herbert Plumer and Public Works Department architect Austen St. Barbe Harrison, who would design the museum. The British proposed a site on a rise, overlooking the northeast corner of Jerusalem's Old City, which had been reserved for the high commissioner's new official residence. Breasted agreed with the recommendation and guided the building plan, sharing with Harrison information on modern museum design and furnishings he had collected for the Egyptian museum project.[40]

To receive Rockefeller's gift, the British had to provide the land and accept responsibility for erecting the building and administering it as part of its Department of Antiquities "in such . . . relations with an International Advisory Committee as the Palestine Government may deem feasible." The building plans developed swiftly, so fast in fact that a sticking point arose over the disparity between the gift stipulations for the Egyptian and Palestinian projects. The Egyptians had been asked to cede control to Western authorities, but no comparable terms were attached to the Palestinian project.

The difference can be attributed to the dissimilar political contexts of Egypt and Palestine. The Egyptians were moving toward establishing sovereignty over their nation and its institutions, while in Palestine Britain's mandate authority was still very much in place and conditions looked to remain that way for a long time to come. Breasted, Rockefeller, and Fosdick were all aware of the disparity, the latter noting: "We are treating the Palestine Government far more liberally than we offered to treat the Egyptian Government. The reasons for it are obvious: we can deal with the English in Palestine where it is impossible to deal with the Egyptians in Egypt." They realized that if the "Egyptian proposition should ever be reopened, the terms upon which Mr. Rockefeller had offered to contribute his money to Palestine, if publicly known, might seriously embarrass the situation." Accordingly, they suggested that the terms of the gift already negoti-

Fig. 8.9 View of the Palestine Archaeological Museum from the Mount of Olives, Jerusalem, ca. 1935–39. The wall of the Old City is visible on the left. G. Eric and Edith Matson Photograph Collection, Library of Congress, Prints and Photographs Division, LC-DIG-matpc-03381.

ated be set out in a request from the British to Rockefeller and he could make his donation in response. Plumer agreed and replied with a request structured so that Rockefeller was able to accept the terms with "a letter of gift containing not a reference to or . . . statement of conditions. Plumer [could] then publish [the] letter of gift without offending sensitive Egyptians by the easy conditions so much in contrast with those exacted of Egypt."[41]

Construction of the Palestine Archaeological Museum, as it was officially named, was not completed until 1935, and it opened to the public in January 1938. The building was designed in a style one observer called "Mediterranean modernism." The overall masses of the building, which include an octagonal tower and two wings with interior courtyards, and its simple lines, arched windows, and stepped facade hugging the site's gentle slope (figure 8.9) allude to the traditional building motifs of Jerusalem's Old City. The confluence of typical eastern Mediterranean architectural features, integrating southern Italian influences with those of traditional Arab design and stonework, is evident in the uses of repeated arches, colonnades, and thick walls. The exterior is clad in the distinctive "Jerusalem limestone" that comes from a quarry along the road to Jericho. One wing was designed to house the Department of Antiquities. It also includes a lecture hall with an unusual feature: a backlit screen for projecting images from behind, designed so projectors could not be seen or heard by the audience. The other wing contained the museum's offices and support facilities.[42]

The galleries, arranged around a central open-air court with a reflecting pool, provided a chronologically arranged survey of ancient Near Eastern history beginning with prehistoric objects and concluding with works dating no later than about 1700 CE. Preparing display labels was a particular challenge, however, because they had to be written in the three official languages—Arabic, English, and Hebrew—reflecting "the peculiar conditions prevailing in Palestine." The task of translating English descriptions into Arabic and Hebrew required "considerable labour, involving the creation of many new terms in both languages, in consultation with linguistic and archaeological authorities in those languages."[43]

The museum's administrative structure was unclear, suggesting that, as in Egypt, the director of the Department of Antiquities was likely to be the museum's de facto head. The director was assisted by an Archaeological Advisory Board "created in response to a wish of Mr. Rockefeller that there should be some channel through which international opinion could be brought to bear on the control of antiquities in Palestine." However, its role was confined to settling disputes that might arise between the Department of Antiquities and "any archaeologist or other member of the public." The board consisted of "the heads of the principal archaeological schools in Palestine, with representatives of the religious communities."

At that time, the British School of Archaeology in Palestine and the American Schools of Oriental Research were two of the major players in Palestinian archaeology, and Breasted was a trustee of the American Schools from 1926 until his death. The other archaeological programs included a Jerusalem branch of the Pontifical Biblical Institute as well as French and German institutions. Prior to the mandate's termination in 1948, the British entrusted the museum to the Archaeological Advisory Board. In 1967, after the Six-Day War, during which Israel captured the part of Jerusalem containing the museum, Israel assigned its antiquities responsibilities and collections to the Israel Department of Antiquities, which in turn asked the Israel Museum (located in west Jerusalem) to manage the displays and collections. To avoid any hint of recognizing Palestine, the Israeli authorities have referred to the institution as "The Rockefeller Museum" ever since.[44]

The Egyptian museum project remained on Breasted's mind, and in May 1926, just months after its collapse, he confided to Nelson that he did not regard it as "dead." Breasted returned to it because of the research institute and endowment ideas, which if realized would have provided the Middle Eastern base and funding for which he yearned. In March 1927 Breasted responded to word of King Fu'ād's desire to reopen negotiations with a revised proposal that contained two noteworthy changes: one was a plan for cultivating a new generation of archaeologists by providing positions for young Western scholars and archaeological training and employment for promising Egyptian students; the other changed the name of the "Egyptian Archeology Foundation"—which was to manage the endowment—to simply the "Archeology Foundation." The name change signaled that while the new entity could still pursue the ideas in the original plan, with a handsome building fund and endowment still at its disposal, it would be far less closely wedded to work in Egypt. However, neither news of the king's interest nor Breasted's response aroused any enthusiasm among Rockefeller's advisors. In a subsequent "Report on the Cairo Museum Project," Breasted all but conceded the initiative was indeed dead: "While our experience . . . involved very regrettable expenditures of time and strength it taught both sides a great deal. . . . I hope these results are worth all they have cost."[45]

Endless Details and Larger Plans

The Egyptian museum project's demise did not diminish Rockefeller's regard for Breasted. To the contrary, the difficulties encountered in Egypt seem only to have strengthened the bonds of friendship they had formed in previous years. As a result, Rockefeller began to underwrite Breasted's initiatives with less and less scrutiny. When the Egyptian dictionary project began to founder during the German economic crisis following the First World War, Breasted sought assistance from Rockefeller, who, on Breasted's word alone, provided the funds necessary to complete the project. Rockefeller's confidence in Breasted was matched by that of the philanthropist's associates.[46]

While the Palestine museum plans were firmed up, Breasted sought and received a five-year $250,000 grant from the General Education Board that included $175,000 for field expeditions in Asia Minor focusing on Hittite sites and $75,000 to set up an Oriental Institute "contingent fund." Shortly thereafter the General Education Board allocated another $250,000 to the University of Chicago to endow the Epigraphic Survey and $50,000 for Oriental Institute publications. Meanwhile Rockefeller pledged another $75,000 to be distributed over five years for the salary and travel expenses of an assistant for Breasted—his son Charles—and to hire a business manager for the institute. This tide of cash prompted Breasted to speculate about the $8 million left from the money Rockefeller had set aside for the Egyptian Museum project, and he wondered if it might be redirected toward other initiatives. He also noticed that "the Rockefeller foundations, while steadily augmenting their support of the . . . Institute, were becoming more and more interested in the whole field of Near Eastern and Mediterranean archaeology."

Around that time, Rockefeller officials encouraged Breasted to "draw up large-scale plans," asking for a systemic, long-term program rather than continually returning to them with piecemeal proposals to problems and opportunities of ancient Near Eastern research. Breasted was more comfortable with asking for smaller grants because past experience taught him that big visions usually failed.

After he sent a particularly circumspect "Memorandum on Scientific Research in the Ancient Orient," a Rockefeller official concluded that Breasted had become too timid: "Professor Breasted has for so many years been accustomed to getting on with little that he is a poor adept at the gentle art of asking. He was indeed, as he explained, so fearful that he would get nothing that he asked only for the barest necessities." Breasted's backers were now ready for a larger vision; they pressed him for more, and he happily complied.[47]

In August 1927 he submitted to Rockefeller an audacious $32.5 million plan that was breathtaking in its sweep and ambition. His "Beginning and Development of the Archeology Foundation" took as its point of departure elements of the proposal Breasted had developed during the Egyptian museum project's last gasp. To be called either the "Archeology Foundation" or the "Rockefeller Archeology Foundation," the body Breasted now had in mind would serve as another Rockefeller philanthropic arm like the General Education Board or the Rockefeller Foundation. Its resources would be designated for (1) training future generations of "young archeological scientists" by endowing professorships at several universities, (2) sponsoring "field expeditions in a wide-spread and systematic effort to salvage the vast body of perishing archeological evidence throughout the ancient world," (3) publishing findings from fieldwork, and (4) "allocation to museums and educational institutions of such monuments as are awarded to America" from expeditions' divisions of finds.[48]

Breasted organized the teaching program around the creation of a permanent "commanding" or "leading center," which in turn would be supplied students by a group of "selective feeders" designated to "select and prepare students for more specialized work at the leading center." The "leading center," of course, was to have been the Oriental Institute. To develop its teaching capacity, Breasted proposed endowing nine professorships, ten annual fellowships, four assistant professorships, and travel expenses for all. The "selective feeders" consisted of a number of American and European universities, including Harvard, Yale, Princeton, Oxford, Liverpool, London, and Paris, and each was to have received one to three endowed professorships. Because the excavation program was to be launched right away, however, extensive consultations should begin immediately with the "leading archeologists in America, England, France, Germany, and Austria" to identify available and qualified personnel.

Breasted strongly emphasized the "establishment of archeological <u>research</u> on a permanent basis." Accordingly, "the Oriental Institute should be permanently endowed like any such laboratory in natural science. As a scientific clearing house for the correlation of results the Institute will be even more necessary after the proposed field work of the Archeology Foundation has begun." The plan included a new building for the Oriental Institute as well. Next, Breasted sought the "establishment of permanent research centers in the Near East," which included the enhancement or construction of facilities for, and endowment of, existing American Schools of Oriental Research operations in Jerusalem and Baghdad. Finally, he wanted to provide for "conservation of the ancient evidence" through the construction and endowment of museums in Baghdad and Beirut, as well as the one in Palestine, the gift for which was being finalized about this time.[49]

According to Charles Breasted, "Neither the boards nor Mr. Rockefeller appeared to be taken aback" by the $32.5 million proposal. Yet they did not endorse it either. Rather, discussions continued over the course of the following fall, during which Breasted and Rockefeller officials looked for ways to align their objectives. These "successive conferences" led to Breasted's "thoughts [being] greatly clarified. . . . Seeming failure at times always resulted in clearer definition of needs and purposes." He began to see a way to accomplish his goals. Research and teaching at the Oriental Institute would be supported by the General Education Board, and field operations abroad would be personally supported by Rockefeller.

Overall, however, Breasted's most crucial insight concerned the question of permanence. Rockefeller's willingness to support the Palestine museum project, even after the Egyptian museum project's failure, and his continued backing of Breasted throughout, revealed that Rockefeller could be persuaded to underwrite projects Breasted deemed worthwhile. But when it came to permanently institutionalizing ancient Near Eastern studies with an endowment, Rockefeller retreated. If Breasted were to make the Oriental Institute permanent, it would be through the Rockefeller boards. And that meant a change in strategy, away from his personal strengths—which were particularly important for Rockefeller—to the significance of ancient Near Eastern studies as a "humanistic science," which was especially important to the boards. To paraphrase Rockefeller's observation in 1923, Breasted the "man" was not the issue; rather, it was the Oriental Institute as a mainstay of an "established branch of science."[50]

Breasted's new approach was presented in a "Brief on Scientific Education in the Study of Early Man, Popularly Called Archeology." Although reminiscent of his last "Archeology Foundation" proposal, it focused almost exclusively on the "commanding center" idea. In justifying it he offered a fresh analogy: "Imagine a medical student obliged to visit one university for the elements of physiology, another institution for the elements of anatomy, a third place for the study of therapeutic, and that there were no institutions . . . where he could pursue at the same time the . . . training of a good physician. That has always been the situation of scientific education in archeology." Breasted used the medical analogy because it corresponded to the Rockefellers' long-term, international commitments to medical research and education. The new proposal still called for endowed faculty positions and fellowships, construction of a new building, and a publication endowment. Noting the institute was in its eighth year and had a long list of accomplishments, Breasted believed it had proven its "efficiency and usefulness." The cost of his new scheme, excluding the expeditions that he hoped would be covered by Rockefeller, was $11 million.[51]

Casting his ideas as a "brief" rather than a proposal, Breasted failed to elicit an immediate reaction. In part it was overshadowed by an offhand suggestion in his earlier "Archeology Foundation" plan, consultations with "the leading archeologists in America, England, France, Germany, and Austria." Rockefeller and his associates liked the idea and assumed that he would conduct the study. But he begged off, and it was assigned to a General Education Board official. Breasted assisted by compiling a "List of Men to Be Visited in Connection with the Archeology Foundation" that included the names, contact information, and strikingly candid comments on eighty-two scholars, including recommendations of two to avoid.[52]

The study turned out to be more thorough than Breasted imagined. It included visits to the Oriental Institute and Chicago House while Breasted was away, and, not content with site visits and meetings with archaeologists, the General Education Board had another staffer survey a variety of published sources ranging from scholarly journals to institutional annual reports. The result was a detailed study on "Archaeological Excavations" complete with a table showing the locations, sponsors, directors, and—when known—costs of thirty-six expeditions then underway around the world, including Central America and China. That report concluded: "Whether it be in Maya lands, Bible lands or the land of the Pharaohs the cry of the archaeologist is for trained workers and for money and more money. If our knowledge is to be added to, three things seem necessary: 1. Endowment of schools to train workers; 2. Subsidy of operations; 3. Endowment to provide for living wage for the advanced archaeologist. . . . On the whole this science has had comparatively little attention and support."[53]

Although Breasted's endowment drive was eliciting positive signals, the slow pace of the evaluation process worried him. His current grants would run out in the following year, and he had heard that the notion of a "gradual endowment" rather than a single large outlay was being considered, meaning that it could be several years before the full income stream would be in place. In May 1928 he explored a five-year "emergency subvention" totaling $200,000 to tide the institute over until a longer-term plan was in place. A Rockefeller official rejected the request, writing to a colleague that "no attention should be given . . . to further small contributions. The work has been supported in that way long enough. These details are without end." Yet, he observed, "It seems to me that the establishment of an Oriental Institute at Chicago on a sound basis is perhaps the most important single opportunity in the field of humanities . . . at the present time."[54]

Breasted was also concerned about leadership changes in Rockefeller's offices and at Chicago. The Rockefeller philanthropies had had an influx of new trustees and staff members whom Breasted needed to court. About the same time, the president of the University of Chicago suddenly resigned and was replaced by an acting president, Frederic Woodward, who was not familiar with the institute or Breasted's current fund-raising effort. Breasted introduced himself to the new arrivals, liberally sprinkling institute publications as he went. He bolstered his campaign with two heavily illustrated articles for the popular media. One, "A Laboratory for the Investigation of Early Man," was written in July and published in November 1928 in *Scribner's Magazine*. It summarized Breasted's now-familiar observations about the vital importance of ancient Near Eastern research and the institute's accomplishments, arguing that there was now an "unparalleled need and opportunity [that] can only be met by a <u>permanent</u> research organization." Copies of the manuscript and then preprints of the article were a frequent enclosure in his correspondence with Rockefeller and Chicago officials in the following months.[55]

Breasted's change in strategy had the desired effect, and officials in Chicago and New York edged toward a consensus. Rockefeller staffers summarized his goals as $1.5 million for a new building, $2.2 million endowment for faculty and student fellowships, $5.75 million endowment for research including excavations, and $1 million endowment for publications—$10.45 million total. But they had to work around an internal policy: "A large part of the program is in the East to which the General Education Board cannot give." They decided the International Education Board could underwrite a major share of the plan, with the remaining parts picked up by the Rockefeller Foundation, Rockefeller himself, or—for only those aspects based in America—by the General Education Board. Questions remained, however, about granting large endowments versus a more incremental approach.

Breasted replied with a memorandum and detailed cost projections that explored the alternatives. But he was leery of leaving the impression that short-term funding would be sufficient and continued to press for endowment. While an individual investigation might be completed in a few years, he acknowledged, "the larger investigation of which it is a part is permanent. In the same way, for example, a temporary study of [a certain] microbe may be part of the larger <u>permanent</u> field of bacteriological investigation." Similarly, most of the institute's current projects "cannot be completed, any more than Hale's study of the sun can be regarded as completing research in astronomy . . . , or the investigations of [a doctor] at the Rockefeller Institute of Medicine can be looked upon as completing research in medicine. . . . [The] field program of the Oriental Institute, therefore, . . . will be going on for centuries, and . . . is as permanent as the researches in astronomy, physics, chemistry or any natural science."[56]

After consultations among Breasted, his Chicago superiors, and Rockefeller officials, they concluded, in light of Chicago's other pressing needs, that his proposal could be trimmed and still address the highest priorities. A revised plan found a middle ground between large endowments and a long-term commitment to annual grants, and in November 1928 the General Education and International Education Boards formally considered it. The General Education Board appropriated $2 million, most of which went into the Oriental Institute's teaching endowment. The International Education Board appropriated $1.5 million for a new building and endowment to maintain it, $1.5 million for teaching endowment, another $1 million matching grant for teaching endowment that required Chicago to raise another $1 million for a research endowment, and a bit over $2.2 million for ten years of annual grants to support research, field expeditions, and publications. All told, Breasted obtained about $8.2 million, of which about $6 million was for endowment, achieving his dream of making the Oriental Institute a permanent fixture in the landscape of ancient Near Eastern studies. By coincidence, earlier that year the International Education Board had allocated $6 million to Hale to fulfill his dream of creating a 200-inch reflecting telescope and establishing the Mount Palomar Observatory. Breasted and Hale celebrated this congruity, enjoyed the fact that their grants were the two largest ever made by the International Education Board, and then turned to the enlarged tasks they had created for themselves. For Breasted, however, there was a more immediate obligation.[57]

The Rockefeller family's much-discussed and delayed Middle East trip was rescheduled to embark in early January 1929, about a month after Breasted's grants were announced. He planned and led the three-month tour for an eleven-person party that included John and Abby Rockefeller; the youngest of their six children, David, who was thirteen at the time; a tutor for him; the family doctor; Breasted; and his son Charles (figure 8.10). The itinerary included brief stops in Gibraltar, Algiers, Naples (including a side trip to Pompeii), and Syracuse before tourists and leader arrived in Alexandria for the Egyptian leg of the trip. They spent two weeks in Cairo taking day excursions to sites in the area before embarking on a steam-powered *dahabiyya* for a leisurely trip up the Nile, during which they visited major sites along the way and spent four days in Luxor exploring the many temple complexes there, as well as Chicago House, and observing the Epigraphic Survey's work. After reaching Abu Simbel, they continued to Palestine, lingering in Jerusalem before visiting Nazareth, Tiberias, Haifa, Megiddo, and Damascus. They returned via Beirut, Haifa, and other sites along the Mediterranean coast, spending about two weeks altogether in Palestine, Syria, and Lebanon.[58]

Prior to their departure, Rockefeller relayed to Breasted through Fosdick a "friendly but frank request to raise no financial questions during the voyage."

Fig. 8.10 The Rockefellers, Breasted, and Megiddo expedition staff at Megiddo, ca. late February 1929. From left to right: P. L. O. Guy (expedition director), A. Murray Dyer (David Rockefeller's tutor), David Rockefeller, Geoffrey Morgan Shipton (expedition acting recorder), Mary Todhunter Clark (later married Nelson A. Rockefeller), Edward L. DeLoach (expedition surveyor), Robert Scott Lamon (expedition draftsman and surveyor), Abby Aldrich Rockefeller, John D. Rockefeller Jr., Breasted, Ralph Bernard Parker (expedition assistant), unidentified Arab assistant. Courtesy of the Oriental Institute, University of Chicago.

Breasted had no intention of doing so. Their mutual regard and affection had reached the point that months before, when lunching with Rockefeller, Breasted avoided bringing up a money matter because he didn't want to place his patron "in the embarrassing position of making any such decision face to face with a friend." Yet the circumstances of the trip, and Breasted's zeal to make it educational as well as enjoyable, rendered the topics of his research and goals unavoidable. He prepared for the trip by having a "slide trunk specially built" and bringing along a lantern-slide "outfit" to illustrate nightly lectures on the next day's sites. Rockefeller, writing to his other children at home, commented, "Doctor Breasted has made all of these things live for us with his intelligent lantern slide talks night after night. Friends whom we have met and invited to these lectures . . . have uniformly been thrilled at what they saw and heard."

Charles recalled that the "month's voyage by private steamer up the Nile became a vitalized synopsis of [Breasted's] *History of Egypt*, and a motor journey through Palestine and Syria, a vivification of his *Ancient Times*." Rockefeller followed Breasted's explanations closely, at one point asking him "many questions . . . regarding the chronological outline of periods and dynasties. He . . .

carefully wrote down all the main dates . . . so that he could study them." Rockefeller also "bought hundreds of photographs," and to Breasted's "amazement and
delight he was absorbed in these a great deal of the time," Breasted sitting "with
him by the hour while he scribbled . . . notes on the back of each photograph."[59]

As a result, Rockefeller acquired a much better understanding of Breasted's
work. While viewing reliefs at Abydos he told Breasted, "I can quite understand
your anxiety to see these things saved." After observing an Egyptologist reas-
sembling broken statues for museum display, Rockefeller remarked that "he
regards such work, of securing museum pieces, as very limited indeed, when
compared with the kind of [epigraphic] work [the institute] was doing." Later
Rockefeller commented that "he regarded [the institute's] work as of more importance than the [Egyptian] museum project." While Rockefeller's attitude
about endowing ancient Near Eastern studies did not change, his personal commitment to Breasted's work redoubled. One of his advisers observed, "He has
now got something which he wants to support because he is deeply interested
in it and not because it is his duty to do so, as is the case with most of the things
he does." Toward the end of the trip, Breasted wrote, the two "by [Rockefeller's]
desire, often rode together, and he talked frequently of Inst. affairs. . . . On the
long drive from Damascus to Beirut, [Rockefeller] discussed the whole budget of
the Inst. item by item. . . . We talked for hours."[60]

On the return voyage to America, Rockefeller handed Breasted "a long pencil
memo, and asked if it was correct. It contained the leading items of the present Inst. Budget, but added those of the needs still unprovided for." The total
amounted to nearly $2.2 million. "Also," Breasted wrote, Rockefeller "examined
me thoroughly on my own personal work," compiling another list that included
updated editions of *Ancient Records of Egypt*, *A History of Egypt*, trade and school
adaptations of *Ancient Times*, a critical edition of the medical papyrus, and work
on "Egyptian Religion." Within a few weeks of their return, Breasted was invited
to New York for meetings on the projects Rockefeller had itemized. During a day
of fund-raising conversations Breasted characterized as "reckless," he confirmed
Rockefeller's notes, and in May 1929 the International Education Board allocated
an additional $1.94 million to the Oriental Institute, almost precisely as specified
by Rockefeller.[61]

He continued to mull over Breasted's personal projects and the demands
of overseeing a growing institution. Now nearly sixty-four years old, Breasted
fatigued more easily and was beginning to experience more acute health problems. Yet he seemed generally fit by all outward appearances. Breasted still cut a
"well-knit figure" and possessed a posture that suggested a "strong and active"
body, and his "firm jaw and erect carriage bespoke the man of resolution and
action," an impression also owing to his lifelong habit of being a "brisk, lively
walker" who plowed ahead with head "slightly bowed." He was conscious of his

health and continued to exercise and monitor his diet. Breasted also realized the Oriental Institute's future rested to a large extent on perceptions of his physical capacity to lead it. Prior to his most recent New York trip, Breasted's left arm "suddenly became enormously swollen and turned purple." Because he felt no pain, he continued with the meetings, struggling to keep his left hand out of view "lest the rumor get about that I was unwell just at this critical juncture when everything was going so splendidly." The problem turned out to be a thrombosis, which dissipated after about three weeks of treatment. Nonetheless, those who knew him well—including Rockefeller—were worried about Breasted's stamina under the stresses of leading the institute.

Wanting to help further Breasted's personal projects without adding to his administrative load, but knowing him well enough to appreciate that his work was more meaningful to him than anything else, in July 1929 Rockefeller wrote: "Because you have given so generously, not only of time and strength but of your means as well, to the advancement in its various phases of the project to which your life has been devoted, because of my admiration for what you have done and are doing, my genuine affection for you, and also because I am anxious to do anything that I wisely can to insure your good health and your freedom from unnecessary care and anxiety and your being most fit for the furtherance of your work, it is my pleasure to set aside $100,000 for your personal use, as distinguished from the various enterprises to which you are committed." Concerned the management of such a large sum of money might, in itself, become burdensome for Breasted, Rockefeller further offered to hold it on account and have his office distribute regular interest payments at the rate of 6 percent per year—leaving to Breasted's preference the most congenial arrangement.

Breasted was stunned. After a day of reflection he replied, "It is a marvel to me that in the midst of all your great affairs you have been able to give any thought to my difficulties. . . . These words of friendship, of sympathy and confidence, are in themselves a new draught of courage and inspiration." By this point in his life, Breasted had received numerous scholarly awards and honorary degrees and considerable public acclaim. Even so, Breasted was often surprised and embarrassed by such recognition: "All these things fill me with sudden apprehension, or seem like some grotesquely impossible dream—a case of absurdly mistaken identity." While listening to the conferral of his honorary degree from Oxford University in "polished Latin," Breasted pictured himself as "a dusty, bare-footed youngster standing at the door of a cluttered smithy in a little village in northern Illinois, watching the big blacksmith shoeing his father's only horse. And here was a learned Oxonian . . . saying all these ridiculous things to this lad! Of course somebody would find out . . . I looked about me in anxiety, thinking it might occur at any moment."[62]

9

A Historical Laboratory

An Institute, Not a Museum

On 28 April 1930 Breasted wrote in his diary, "At ten o'clock this morning, the members of the Oriental Institute, the Dep't. of Oriental Languages, the History and Art Departments, in a procession headed by Pres. Hutchins, Dean Laing, and the Director of the Institute marched from Haskell Museum to the site at 58th St. and University Ave., where [I] was given the ceremonial spade and formally 'broke ground' for the new Oriental Inst. building. In the background stood the steam shovel, and as I write I can hear it already at work."

Breasted's laconic account belied the ceremony's importance for him. It marked the culmination of seven years of efforts to create a home especially designed for the institute's particular needs. When he first asked for a new building in 1923, it was to alleviate crowded conditions in the Haskell Oriental Museum resulting from its being shared by the Department of Oriental Languages and Literatures, the Oriental Institute, and Chicago's Divinity School—the latter occupying about half the building's space. At the time, university officials did not expect to find another home for the Divinity School any time soon and shared Breasted's hope that Rockefeller, in renewing his 1919 gift for another five years, might throw in a new building as well. When Rockefeller didn't, Breasted looked elsewhere, even approaching the American-born London department-store magnate Harry Gordon Selfridge, whom Breasted had probably met in the early 1900s when Selfridge was still a junior partner of Chicago merchant Marshall Field.[1]

Not long after Ernest DeWitt Burton became Chicago's president, he launched a fund-raising campaign for buildings and endowment that quickly yielded gifts for a "Theology Group," including a Divinity School building. After the Divinity School moved out of Haskell in 1926, the Oriental Institute took over the top three floors, and Oriental Languages and Literatures remained on the lower level. Breasted allocated the first and third floors for galleries; and he obtained funds for new exhibition cases, placing a high priority on professionally installing materials for "Public Exhibition" in which collections were to be "educationally available."

The chronologically organized display he planned earlier in the decade was only partially implemented, and only for the Egyptian collections. The third-floor display included sections on Palestine, Mesopotamia, and western Asia, but it was mostly left "incomplete and temporary" because Breasted expected to augment the holdings with acquisitions from excavations and purchases. The first-floor installation of the Egyptian collections, in contrast, was far more thoroughly articulated, reflecting the much larger quantity of objects on hand thanks to Breasted's aggressive acquisition efforts. Half the floor was designated for "chronological exhibits" and the other half for "topical exhibits." Visitors were advised to go through the chronologically arranged side first, following the lettered sequence of alcoves in alphabetical order and within each alcove to follow the numerical sequence of display cases. The chronological side ran from the prehistoric, "before 3000 B.C.," to the Ptolemaic and Roman periods, "about 400 A.D." The topically arranged section was similarly organized as a sequence of alcoves and cases. It illustrated a range of subjects from "Plant Remains" and "Color" to "Games" and "Toilet Articles."[2]

Shortly after taking over most of Haskell, however, Breasted began lobbying for more space to accommodate facilities then unavailable there, including a large classroom or lecture hall and especially "room for research work." Installing the Haskell exhibits heightened Breasted's awareness of the differences between public education and scholarly research and how these differences affected the disposition of space within a "museum." In addition to the first- and third-floor public galleries, for example, there was a room for "museum study collections" on the second floor, which was closed off to the public because it was reserved for administration and research. Located just outside Breasted's office, the study-collection room—which was equivalent in size to about two-thirds of a gallery on the other floors—was reserved for teaching and research rather than public display, and apparently Breasted needed yet more space for "research work."

At the same time, Breasted was contemplating the potential of public exhibitions for donor cultivation as well as community education. Commenting on the new installation, Breasted added, "We must have an opening . . . at which our Chicago friends . . . may have an opportunity to look over the Museum. Our work is attracting great interest and I hope that such an exhibition may contribute to the development of this interest and bring us additional support." He also decided to issue "an illustrated brochure . . . with pictures . . . and other highly interesting and attractive features of our work. . . . We have done very little . . . printed propaganda, and I want to see that literature of this kind shall be available at this opening so that our friends will carry away a very brief outline, graphically indicating what we are trying to do." The resulting booklet, *The Oriental Institute*, was the first in what became a series of "handbooks." Published in time for the Haskell exhibits' public opening on 9 December 1926, it was an introduction to the institute's research programs at home and abroad, however, not a gallery guide.[3]

The exhibits garnered praise from the press and individuals alike, as well as Chicago's board of trustees. A display on Medinet Habu that contained a photograph of a relief, a drawing derived from it, and related materials was arranged to illustrate the work of the Epigraphic Survey. Breasted was amazed by the public's enthusiastic response and wrote to Nelson, "You would be surprised to hear the admiring comments offered by all visitors as they contemplate [the drawing] as a work of art." When planning the Medinet Habu publications the following year, Breasted remarked, "Since putting in the exhibit . . . my ambitions . . . have grown considerably." He now wanted to include more photographs along with the drawings, all "on as large a scale as possible" so as to permit "the temple and its records to make the impression of a great work of art as well as a body of historical records." This interplay of education and cultivation, display and discovery, research and publication strengthened Breasted's conviction that, as he said at the public opening, "This is not a museum, it's a workshop."[4]

When the Haskell Oriental Museum opened in 1896, it was the first discipline-specific, university-based, and purpose-built structure for the collection and study of ancient Near Eastern objects. It was intended to house not just exhibition galleries but museum storage, offices for faculty (some of whom, like Breasted, doubled as curators), museum staff, a research library, and classrooms. Although the university compromised the museum's original functions, Breasted hoped to restore them when he reclaimed Haskell for the institute. He found, however, that the institute's collections were beginning to outgrow Haskell's capacity and that the building's design was not well suited for the other functions of a "workshop." As Breasted began to imagine a building to replace Haskell, the facility he had in mind incorporated all the types of specialized spaces that existed in Haskell—and by then many other museums, but with a crucial difference. The priority of space for public exhibitions versus that for research was inverted. Whereas public museums allocated most space to galleries, the building Breasted contemplated shrank exhibition space to less than a quarter of the physical plant. While exhibitions remained an important feature of the institute's public service and development, like the place of textbooks in Breasted's personal scholarship, exhibitions were nonetheless secondary to research and graduate training.[5]

Laboratory, workshop, institute—these terms typically served a rhetorical function in Breasted's drive to create an ideal, permanent research center. While this nomenclature often corresponded to the predispositions of his audiences, especially the language of "scientism"—as in "historical laboratory," Breasted was groping for the right characterization of an institutional structure that did not yet exist. Designing the research institute that was to have been part of the Egyptian museum project clarified Breasted's ideas about the kind of building he wanted. When it became clear that nationalist movements throughout the Middle East meant a permanent, Western-owned research institute there was untenable, Breasted merged the most essential features of the Egyptian plan—museum, research institute, endowment—with the educational mission of a university. The result was a center in Chicago equipped with its own building and endowed funds adequate to support research and teaching at home and in the Middle East.

After receiving the grant for the institute's new home, Breasted was offered the possibility of naming the new building "The Oriental Institute, Haskell Oriental Museum" to satisfy the terms of the Haskell gift once the institute moved to the new building and was replaced in Haskell by other university departments. He turned down the idea. The new building was to be a research and teaching center, and having "museum" in its name would imply the institute was placing a higher priority on public service than was actually the case. A few years later Breasted reiterated that "the Institute disavows being a museum and its exhibits of monuments are purely incidental."[6]

The architectural plans for the new building were developed over the course of 1929 under Breasted's close supervision. The principal architect was Oscar Harold Murray, a junior associate of the better-known Bertram Grosvenor Goodhue, who had all but finished designing Chicago's University Chapel before his death in 1924. Murray joined with two others to create a successor firm to Goodhue's and completed plans for the chapel, which opened in 1928. The land allocated for the institute is diagonally across the block that houses the chapel and, as Breasted noted, "Because of the nearness of the Chapel, the new Institute building was planned to harmonize with it externally." The result is a building in a somewhat modernized Gothic style in which exterior features—such as win-

Fig. 9.1 Oriental Institute building from the northwest, designed by Oscar Harold Murray and completed in 1931, ca. 1931. Courtesy of the Oriental Institute, University of Chicago.

dow enclosures and faux buttresses—are flattened, and the overall design is less heavily ornamented than earlier neo-Gothic buildings (figure 9.1).

By the time the building plans were completed, in late February 1930, the stock-market crash of the previous fall had depressed construction costs, allowing the university to erect "a more extensive building" in size and finish than initially planned. Exterior decorations such as stone medallions, plaques, and a tympanum above the main entrance, as well as relatively rich interior decorations in the building's more public spaces, reflect the substantial funds available. Breasted specified sources for ornamental designs, selected symbols, and corrected errors in depictions of ancient Near Eastern images. Nowhere is his involvement more evident than in the tympanum over the building's main entrance.[7]

Breasted wanted a "scene which will suggest the flow of time and the gradual unfolding of the human career." Breasted recommended a central feature be "the disk of the sun, with some indication of radiating brilliance, diffused over the whole scene." He thought the background might contain symbols from the ancient past, such as the pyramids at Giza, and the foreground might show recent motifs such as "human figures and buildings of an unmistakably" modern type to illustrate "later human development." Breasted was far more precise about

Fig. 9.2 Clay maquette for tympanum over Oriental Institute building entrance, conceived by Breasted and sculpted by Ulric Ellerhusen, ca. 1931. Courtesy of the Oriental Institute, University of Chicago.

what he didn't want: "The plow and the anvil have been rather overworked in such connections; ships and steam locomotives likewise. Probably modern architecture would serve the purpose better." The resulting design, titled by Breasted "East Teaching the West," represents a now-favorite theme: the ancient Near East as the wellspring of Western civilization with pride of place going to Egypt and America (figure 9.2):

> The East is represented by an Egyptian figure. . . . On his shoulder hangs an Egyptian writing outfit consisting of a little vase for water and a tube for . . . reed pens . . . , and a palette. . . . The West is symbolized by a youth who reverently holds in his hands a fragment bearing the hieroglyphic words ". . . We behold thy beauty."
>
> The figure of the East is flanked by a lion of Amenhotep III, . . . the figure of the West, with a bison.
>
> Above and between the figures is a Sun Disk with the Symbol of Life and diverging rays terminating in human hands. Ancient ruins are indicated by broken blocks . . . , a broken capital from the Temple of Sahure, and the Step-Pyramid at Saqqara. Above the animals, outstanding figures of Eastern and Western civilizations are shown.

The most remote figure in Eastern history . . . , placed in upper row nearest central group, is King Zoser; followed by Hammurapi and Thutmose III. In middle row Assurnasipal and Darius, and in the . . . left hand corner the Sassanian king Chosroes.

Back of the figure of the West . . . , in the upper row nearest center is Herodotus. . . . Behind Herodotus is Alexander the Great; then Emperor Augustus of Rome. In the middle row a Crusader and a Field Archaeologist. In the lower right . . . a Museum Archaeologist examining a vase. On the left the columns of Persepolis, the Sphinx, and three pyramids . . . indicate the Art and Architecture of the East; while on the right the Parthenon, the Cathedral of Notre Dame and the Nebraska State Capitol represent . . . the West.[8]

The iconographic symmetry seems strikingly off balance in places. Why, for example, are the ancient rulers on the left complemented by archaeologists on the right? Perhaps Breasted conceived of them as students eager to learn from their forebears as did, one might argue, Herodotus and Alexander. The crusader makes less sense in this reading, although he might represent a very different sentiment on Breasted's part. Rather than signifying the medieval warriors dispatched by Christendom to seize the Holy Land from Muslim control, Breasted may have been drawing on a more personal analogy. Starting with the 1920 convocation address attended by his son, Breasted began using "crusade" to express the zeal with which he hoped a new generation of students would pursue ancient Near Eastern studies. He reworked and expanded the address eight years later for delivery to an American Historical Association conference at the conclusion of his term as its president. It was titled "The New Crusade."[9]

Another tympanum image, the thirty-four-story tower of the Nebraska state capitol—visible for miles on the plains surrounding Lincoln—is an homage to Bertram Grosvenor Goodhue, who designed it. However, there is an even more subtle image in the tympanum, one that would be lost on most save those Egyptologists who took the time to study it closely. In the background behind the figures representing "East" and "West" are rays of light emanating from the sun disk. The rays end with hands that appear to be touching the heads and arms of the two figures before cascading further down the scene. This distinctive configuration of sun disk, rays, and hands is taken from depictions of Ikhnaton after the advent of the pharaoh's religious revolution (compare with figures 1.12 and 3.7).

The inspiration for its use in this context may have come from George Ellery Hale. After retiring from his directorship of the Mount Wilson Observatory in 1922, Hale built a solar observatory for his personal work in Pasadena on the edge of Henry Huntington's estate, now home of the Huntington Library. Completed in 1925, the tiny observatory permitted Hale to resume the solar studies

Fig. 9.3 Tympanum over Hale Solar Observatory entrance, conceived by George Ellery Hale and completed by Lee Lawrie, ca. 1924–25. Detail of photograph of Walter Adams (out of view) by the observatory entrance. This item is reproduced by permission of The Huntington Library, San Marino, California.

that launched his career, and he made important discoveries there. In it "Hale became in truth . . . the 'Priest of the Sun.'" Thanks to his lifelong friendship with Breasted, Hale was familiar with Ikhnaton and the centrality of the sun as symbol and life source in the pharaoh's new religion. Hale incorporated two references to Ikhnaton in the observatory, one a copy of an ancient portrait relief in the observatory's interior, the other a sun disk and rays on the tympanum over its entrance (figure 9.3). Breasted, who visited the observatory about a month before the groundbreaking for the Oriental Institute's new building, wrote that

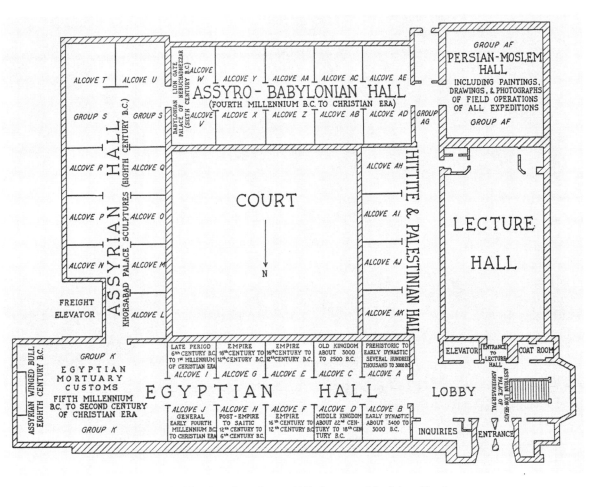

Fig. 9.4 Oriental Institute building first-floor plan, ca. 1931. Courtesy of the Oriental Institute, University of Chicago.

its Ikhnaton references "touched my imagination." Of the many traces of Breasted's hand in the institute's conception and design, Ikhnaton's sun symbol is his most personal.[10]

The building is three stories tall with a lower level that extends just high enough above grade to include windows. It was designed so future growth could be accommodated with additions to the building's south face "without disturbing the unity and symmetry of the whole." The institute's public areas are confined to the first floor, which contains a lecture hall and suite of galleries framing an interior open-air courtyard (figure 9.4). The lecture hall seats about 270 people and was "equipped with every modern device" to illustrate "scientific lectures, including automatic curtains for daytime darkening and . . . a projection chamber . . . with openings for . . . two cinemas . . . and two still-life projectors. Here the Institute will hold talking 'movie' lectures showing its field operations." Upon

Fig. 9.5 Egyptian Hall, Oriental Institute, ca. 1931, with human-headed winged bull, limestone, Khorsabad, Palace of Sargon II, ca. 721–705 BCE visible in the distance. Courtesy of the Oriental Institute, University of Chicago.

entering the building, visitors were directed to the Egyptian Hall, where an al-phabetical arrangement of gallery alcoves was employed to help visitors follow the exhibit's chronological organization (figure 9.5). But after the Egyptian Hall it was not "practicable to continue the chronological arrangement," so visitors were advised to follow the "circuit of the halls" and reenter the building lobby via the "Hittite-Palestinian Hall." One gallery, designated "Persian-Moslem Hall," was off the "circuit" and used for displays on the institute's expeditions then in the field. To further aid visitors, "each important exhibit is accompanied by a map of the Near East . . . on which a red arrow indicates the site at which the monument or monuments was discovered." The map also showed institute ex-pedition locations throughout the Middle East (figure 9.6).

The machinery of research, instruction, and museum work was behind the

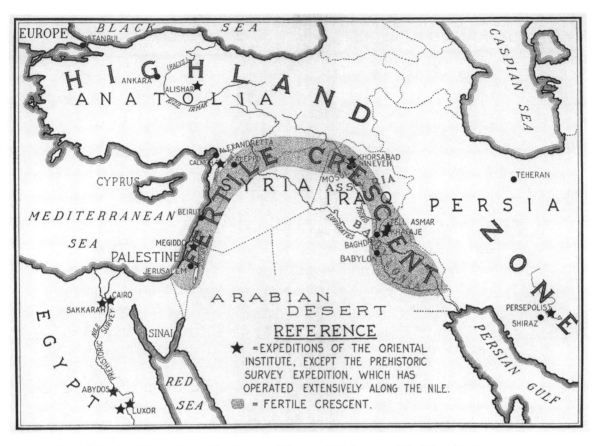

Fig. 9.6 Map highlighting Oriental Institute expeditions, ca. 1931. Courtesy of the Oriental Institute, University of Chicago.

scenes. The lower level was designated for collections storage, workshops, and equipment for conservation and exhibit preparations—including presses for label printing and four photography labs for publications, research, and record keeping. A ground-level loading dock opens onto a freight elevator with a six-ton capacity for lowering large statuary down to the basement, where a "trolley rail" running along the ceiling through the workshops allows "a single workman to shift stones weighing several tons." The second floor contains offices for the institute's administration, research and teaching faculty, publications, and a spacious library reading room. Each faculty office is sufficiently large to accommodate small seminars. Because Breasted did not expect the institute to host many large classes, only two classrooms were incorporated in the design. The third floor contains library stacks, space for projects like the Assyrian dictionary, and offices for research fellows and doctoral students.[11]

The new building opened 5 December 1931 with a program attended by about three hundred members of Chicago's elite and visiting dignitaries including the

Egyptian minister to the United States. Dedication addresses were given by John H. Finley, Raymond Fosdick, and Breasted. Finley was an associate editor of the *New York Times*, whose professional life included stints in higher education as well as journalism, and a public intellectual whose writings were often "sprinkled with quotations from the ancients," and Fosdick represented Rockefeller and his foundations. Robert Maynard Hutchins, who had been appointed University of Chicago president a few months before the institute's groundbreaking, was the master of ceremonies.

Finley's speech, "The West Orienting Itself," discussed the institute's accomplishments in illuminating the West's indebtedness to and interests in the ancient Near East. In a play on a Greek word from Homer's *Odyssey*, Finley saluted Breasted "as *Ptolisoter*, the 'saver of ancient cities.'" Fosdick's speech, "Archeology the Interpreter," likened archaeology to astronomy but as a more "sobering science" because unlike astronomy, which impresses us with our insignificance in the immensity of the universe, archaeology reminds us of the "impermanence of human institutions." Thus, although "bricks and mortar are not substitutes for creative scholarship, . . . sometimes creative scholarship can be given a reasonable degree of permanence if it is suitably clothed." Fosdick compared Breasted to Louis Pasteur and Niels Bohr, for whom, Fosdick said, "we erect monuments while they yet live—institutes and laboratories by which . . . their contributions to human knowledge can be made more effective."

Breasted's address, "The Rise of Man," recapitulated some favorite themes before turning to a topic that was becoming increasingly important for him: "man's earliest triumph over material forces." The Egyptians, in discovering "inner values," evolved "from savagery to civilization," signaling the "dawn of conscience . . . the emergence of social idealism." In his boldest terms yet, Breasted declared that this step occurred "entirely independent of religion." It was not "projected from the outside into a world of unworthy men by some mystic process which our old school theologians called inspiration or revelation"; rather, it arose "out of man's own life illumining the darkness of social disillusionment and inner conflict." Indeed, Breasted marveled, "It is the greatest discovery in the whole course of evolution . . . , a new realm at whose gates we are still standing hesitant," when "evolution of man passed to a higher level than that of merely biological processes." Breasted dedicated the building to more fully understanding this "highest process in the Universe . . . *the unfolding life of man.*"[12]

The institute's opening attracted widespread press coverage, including a cover story in *Time* magazine and months of follow-up pieces, many of which featured Breasted's life and work (figures E.2 and 9.7). A groundswell of popular interest ensued, "very greatly to the surprise of all members of the Institute." Twenty-three thousand people visited in the first three months, attendance totaled over 50,000 just past the six-month mark, and by May 1935 it had reached 250,000.

Fig. 9.7 "Orientalist," one of a series of 1930s drawings called "Topnotchers" by a cartoonist who signed his work as "Ket." The image was copyrighted and distributed in fall 1932 by the Western Newspaper Union, no longer in business, which provided news and feature services to a consortium of papers. This particular copy appeared in the Bristol, Pennsylvania, *Courier*, 14 September 1932. Public domain, reproduction by author.

"The situation . . . proved to be embarrassing," Breasted wrote, "for a great many of these visitors came in companies representing clubs, educational institutions of all sorts, . . . social organizations, etc.," wanting guided tours. Of ninety-five such groups in the first three months, eighty-one requested tours, overwhelming the museum's administrative secretary, who called on other institute staffers for assistance. Breasted realized that each group, in organizing its visit, became "itself a center of advertising" that further swelled its ranks. He cited the

Geographic Society of Chicago, whose "party consisted of approximately 200 members." Breasted hoped a third, enlarged version of the institute's handbook might alleviate this distraction by facilitating self-guided tours. However, that edition, like the first two, only introduced the institute's research programs and field operations. There was also a flyer containing the gallery floor plan and brief self-guided tour instructions; but Breasted admitted that "all these provisions, however well intended, were totally inadequate." He thought one solution might be a "talking movie." If the institute had a "movie lecture" that could be screened several times daily in the institute's lecture hall, visitors would "be able to . . . inspect the exhibits much more intelligently" on their own.[13]

Outposts

Not long after establishing the institute, Breasted began receiving leaves from teaching. Early in the 1920s they were for research projects like the Coffin Texts and Epigraphic Survey, but by the mid-1920s the leaves compensated for his growing administrative responsibilities. He continued to chair the Department of Oriental Languages and Literatures and to oversee a gradual merging of its curriculum and research programs with the institute's. By fall 1925, after Breasted had reached his sixtieth year, his relief from regular teaching became permanent, though he continued to supervise doctoral students and teaching fellows. He missed teaching, however, remarking, "My head is now all woozy because I can not sharpen it on the minds of those bright young men." Breasted's salary grew as the institute expanded, from $7,000 to $8,000 a year in 1923 and to $10,000 in 1927, when he was appointed distinguished service professor. Two years later he was given the first of two named professorships, the second established by Rockefeller in 1930 in honor of Breasted's old friend Ernest DeWitt Burton.

Breasted reached the nominal retirement age of sixty-five that year, but his workload and salary continued as before. It wasn't until 1933 that Breasted retired from his department's chairmanship, but he carried on as the institute's director. He had become a skillful administrator, and the institute's increasingly large staff at home and abroad depended on his leadership. With the renewal and enlargement of Rockefeller's personal support in 1923, augmented with ever-larger grants from his foundations, the institute expanded from a handful of staff to thirty-eight in 1926, fifty-one in 1928, and seventy-three in 1931—numbers that did not include Department of Oriental Languages and Literatures faculty, teaching fellows, and institute collaborators like Gardiner. Breasted's dream of a publishing program also became a reality, and he assumed another large task as its editor in chief. Between the institute's founding and 1926, it issued four publications, in the next three years twelve more, and in the following three years another twenty-three, with many more planned or under way. There were times when Breasted wondered if he had bitten off too much. To Hale he lamented, "You call it Americanitis and I think that about right."[14]

Most of the institute's growth came from field projects throughout the Middle East (the starred locations in figure 9.6; see also map 1). The first was at Megiddo in Palestine. Although others had probed it before, Breasted believed the site held great scholarly potential if subjected to a systematic excavation that cleared the entire very large mound down to bedrock. In 1921, Rockefeller pledged support for the project if Breasted could raise matching funds. None were found, and in 1925 Breasted turned again to Rockefeller, who funded the entire plan with a $215,000 grant for five years' work. Next was an architectural survey at Medinet Habu that involved excavating the twenty-acre site surrounding the main temple. Begun in 1927, it was one of the few field projects to be completed during Breasted's lifetime. In addition to important discoveries of pharaonic building foundations, it also yielded two statues of Tutankhamun, one of which is now in the Oriental Institute (figure 9.8). Also in Egypt were two copying projects: tomb paintings and reliefs in the necropolis at Saqqara, begun in 1930, and similar works in the temple of Seti I at Abydos, begun in 1929 in collaboration with the Egypt Exploration Society.

Beyond Egypt and Palestine there were expeditions focusing on the Hittites. They resulted from institute surveys between 1926 and 1929 that singled out two sites, one in Anatolia, or modern-day Turkey, at a mound east of Ankara near the village of Alishar, the work there beginning in 1927, and the other in western Syria, west of Aleppo, at a site called Çatal Hüyük that Breasted conjectured was the biblical town of Calneh, where work began in 1931–32. Along the eastern side of the Fertile Crescent, Breasted launched three excavations between 1928 and 1930, all at sites he had visited during the 1919–20 survey: the Assyrian city and palace of Sargon II at Khorsabad, fifteen miles northeast of Mosul in present-day Iraq, where the institute obtained a great human-headed, winged bull (rear of figure 9.5), and Mesopotamian sites in the Diyala region twenty-five miles northeast of Baghdad—Tell Asmar, Khafajah, Ishchali, and Tell Agrab.

The most distant expedition started excavating sites principally of the Achaemenian period (about 560–330 BCE) in 1931 in and around Persepolis, northeast of Shiraz in southern Persia, or modern-day Iran. All the projects were funded by Rockefeller or the Rockefeller foundation boards with the exception of Persepolis, which was underwritten with a $100,000 gift from Ada Small Moore, widow of a somewhat less-than-reputable financier and promoter. Overall, in "selecting projects for research and sites for excavation," one scholar later observed, Breasted pursued "fundamental undertakings [over] easy and sensational ones. All credit must be given him . . . for having made his choices with such discrimination."[15]

The challenges of successfully pursuing a large number of field projects, most

Fig. 9.8 Colossal statue of Tutankhamun, quartzite and pigment, temple of Aye and Horemheb (Medinet Habu), New Kingdom, 18th dynasty, ca. 1332–1322 BCE, photograph ca. 1931. The onlooker is Watson Boyes, Oriental Institute museum secretary. Courtesy of the Oriental Institute, University of Chicago.

in remote locations scattered along a 2,000-mile "front" nearly half a world away, were considerable. There were unanticipated problems, such as a malaria outbreak at Megiddo spawned by a nearby wetland. There were the occasional appointments of personnel who didn't work out and had to be fired. And there were the difficulties that arose when individuals from different countries and cultures were thrown together in close quarters for months at a time in isolated outposts.

"Internationalism in the abstract," Breasted wryly observed, "is a very different thing from internationalism in daily practice on an expedition!" There were also the intrigues and frictions of negotiating permits and security agreements with six different governments and their antiquities officials, as well as settling mutually agreeable terms for allocating finds. Breasted justly maintained that the institute's fieldwork was "not conditioned on a division of antiquities," but he was determined to assure that his expeditions received their fair share of finds in comparison to other institutions in the field. All in all, Breasted concluded, "from the beginning of the Institute's development . . . , one of its most important activities has unavoidably been the creation and maintenance of a diplomatic sphere of action, which has demanded a great deal of thought and investigation, a large body of correspondence, and much of [my] time and energy."[16]

Few knew better than Breasted how arduous life could be for those dispatched to digs in often remote and inhospitable conditions. He firmly believed "the rigorous conditions of field work demand a reasonable measure" of staff comfort that required erecting "suitable" buildings comparable to Chicago House to house staff and facilitate fieldwork. As the expeditions multiplied, the nature of the buildings varied in accordance with "each expedition's probable period of occupation," its annual working season, and its staff size. Breasted expected the institute to work for a long time in the vicinity of Luxor and, with additional Rockefeller support, acquired land along the east bank of the Nile about halfway between the Luxor and Karnak temple complexes to build a second Chicago House that was larger, more durable, and readily secured during off-seasons (figure 9.9). Breasted anticipated a similarly long-term commitment to excavations in ancient Babylonia and built near Tell Asmar an expansive expedition headquarters (figure 9.10). At Persepolis, the expedition cleared and reconstructed what remained of an ancient palace, built a "modern roof" over it, and housed the expedition's staff and workrooms at the back. A colonnaded hall at the front was restored into "a museum where the sculptures and smaller monuments discovered . . . [were] set up as the nucleus of a national museum of Persian art, the gift of the Oriental Institute to the people of Persia." By contrast, believing the institute's work in Alishar would be less long-lived, Breasted authorized less extensive accommodations: a few plain buildings, sheds, and tents (figure 9.11).

The better of the institute's outposts were criticized for being needlessly grand. The Tell Asmar headquarters was denounced as a "palace" and a "scandal among expedition houses." Such condemnations were not uncommon among archaeologists. The Metropolitan Museum of Art's Egyptian expedition created a new base in the 1920s that one scholar called "a Ritz among dig-houses." On the other hand, as another scholar said of the Tell Asmar complaint, it was undeniable "that members of the institute's expeditions were generally healthier than those at other excavations." The trend toward establishing better working

Fig. 9.9 Second, and current, Chicago House, Luxor, Egypt, completed in 1931. Library, work rooms, and offices on the left; residence and dining facilities on the right; support facilities in the rear. The Nile access and most of the land between the buildings and the Nile have since been taken by the Egyptian government for a corniche and related walks and parkways. Photograph 1933 by James Henry Breasted Jr. Courtesy of the Oriental Institute, University of Chicago.

Fig. 9.10 Iraq expedition headquarters, Tell Asmar, Iraq, completed in 1930. Courtesy of the Oriental Institute, University of Chicago.

Fig. 9.11 Anatolian-Hittite expedition camp, Alishar, Anatolia (Turkey), 1929. Courtesy of the Oriental Institute, University of Chicago.

conditions was spearheaded by several American institutions, but the Oriental Institute led the way, as noted by the British archaeologist and historian Seton Lloyd, who worked at Tell Asmar between 1930 and 1937:

> Most European institutions . . . appeared to grudge every penny beyond the absolute minimum necessary to keep their expeditions in the field. . . . The result was a tradition . . . of personal austerity and discomfort. . . . In the early 1930s this circumstance was sharply emphasized by the arrival . . . of better-equipped and more heavily subsidized expeditions sponsored by the richer American universities. Notable among these was Chicago's Oriental Institute. . . . Breasted's conception for the institute . . . accorded with and even anticipated improvements in communications and security which were then beginning to appear. . . . These excavating establishments need no longer be envisaged as groups of intrepid explorers braving the perils and hardships of a savage country in the cause of science. They were to be research centres . . . established in these countries with the collaboration and protection of the local government. . . .
>
> It may well be imagined that such . . . developments in the field caused some raising of eyebrows in circles where vocational austerity was still the order of the day.

The stock-market crash and deflation that made the institute's new Chicago quarters less expensive lowered expedition costs too. Within a couple of years, however, the economy slipped into the Great Depression, and Rockefeller officials scrambled to honor past pledges and more closely scrutinized grant recipients as the several boards' assets shrank. An officer monitoring the Oriental Institute reported an "impression of lavishness" in its operations, and as the Depression deepened, uncertainty grew about whether "in comparison with other archaeological work, . . . the work of the Institute was being expensively conducted." The concern was "not so much that money is being wasted but that a degree of completeness and accuracy is being obtained which [is not] always justified." Rockefeller stood by Breasted, regarding such judgments as "a matter of opinion" and countering that "there was no use to do the work at all unless it were perfectly done."[17]

Social Responsibilities

When Rockefeller asked about Breasted's personal work during their Middle Eastern tour, the latter's reply broadened into what he viewed as "the social responsibilities of the modern scientist, to make his technical results more widely of use to society." Breasted had been writing various types of essays for popular consumption, but he was thinking specifically about his textbooks, which he continued to update. In their various iterations and translations, *Outlines of European History* and *Ancient Times* were finding ever-larger audiences around the world, by 1920 reaching an annual circulation of nearly 100,000 and by 1923 over 125,000. Breasted's royalties came to about $750 a month, and he was grateful for the added income, but he was also aware that the books' growing circulation had "enormously increased" the influence of his ideas. He began contemplating a trade edition of *Ancient Times* aimed at an adult readership. Because "A. T. did more than anything I have ever written to advance our interests," Breasted wrote to his wife, "I am convinced I could not do a better piece of work for oriental science than to get the book out in form for wide circulation among our people."

Ginn and Company did not have this kind of reach, so Breasted and his partner for *Outlines of European History*, James Harvey Robinson, agreed to issue popular versions of their books with the trade publisher Harper and Brothers. Initially, Breasted was going to retitle his book "Victorious Man." After discussing it with Robinson and a Harper editor, however, he settled on "The Conquest of Civilization," with Robinson's book to be titled "The Ordeal of Civilization." Harper planned to issue the books as a boxed set, as well as individually, and the box title—at Breasted's suggestion—was "The Human Adventure." *Conquest*, issued in 1926, was closely based on *Ancient Times*. The most obvious changes were the removal of teaching aids and additions on recent discoveries such as the paintings at Dura-Europos and the tomb of Tutankhamun.

The critical response to *Conquest* was tepid. Reviewers knew of Breasted's ability to make "the ancient past live again" and of *Ancient Times* as "one of the most fascinating books that was ever written," so they looked forward to what they thought was an entirely new book. They were disappointed to find that *Conquest* was essentially a repackaged *Ancient Times* and, in rather backhanded compliments, reviewers expressed their dismay by underscoring his achievement with *Ancient Times*. Because the textbook was "printed beautifully, profusely illustrated, and impressive in format," it transcended mere pedagogy to attract and inspire a much broader audience, setting a high standard that the only slightly revised but more costly *Conquest* did not surpass.[18]

Among Breasted's revisions in *Conquest* was a brief discussion and accompanying illustration of a seventeenth-century BCE papyrus containing remarkable insights about human anatomy, diagnoses of medical ailments, and treatments including surgical procedures. It was the Edwin Smith Papyrus, named after an American adventurer, amateur student of hieroglyphs, and dealer who found his way to Luxor, where he lived between 1858 and 1876. While there, Smith acquired the over-fifteen-foot-long and remarkably well-preserved scroll and brought it to America, and his daughter donated it to the New York Historical Society in 1906. One of Breasted's former doctoral students, Caroline Ransom Williams, then curator of Egyptian antiquities for the society, brought the relatively unknown papyrus to his attention in 1920, and he immediately realized its significance. Breasted decided it merited publication in a critical edition, not only because of its subject, but because the text included a great many previously unknown or exceedingly rare usages, suggesting it had been copied in antiquity from a much earlier source. Breasted published two preliminary studies on the papyrus, one for a general readership and another for Egyptologists, in 1922. He hoped to finish the critical edition in 1923, but the task took most of the 1920s, as Breasted's attention was diverted to institute affairs and other projects.[19]

Preparation of the critical edition returned Breasted to the type of research that marked the beginning of his career, requiring the deep knowledge and rigor that informed his first major publication, *Ancient Records of Egypt*. Breasted's analysis of the papyrus included comparisons with relevant texts, research in the Egyptian dictionary files in Berlin, and consultations on "difficult passages" with old colleagues like Kurt Sethe, who had now succeeded Erman as head of Berlin's Egyptology program. The result, published in 1930 as *The Edwin Smith Surgical Papyrus*, reflects not only the breadth of his knowledge in ancient Egyptian language and history but his awareness of the study's potential meaning for a world of scholarship outside Egyptology as well. Breasted's task was complicated by the papyrus's compilation: one side contains the medical treatise; the other contains incantations and recipes associated with ancient magical rituals. He treated both sides with equal care. But Breasted underscored differences between the two to highlight the medical text's significance while downplaying the magical text as a "grotesquely incoherent hodge-podge" to head off its adoption by those interested only in promoting mistaken beliefs about Egyptian occultism.

Breasted mustered generous resources and a lifetime of publishing experience to produce a text both scholarly and handsome. The work was produced in two volumes, the first a larger-than-standard six-hundred-page-long translation with an extensive scholarly apparatus, and the second an even larger folio containing a full-size foldout facsimile of the papyrus divided into twenty-two plates with hieroglyphic transcriptions of the original hieratic text, hand-lettered by two of Breasted's colleagues, on facing pages. The typesetting, photoengraving, and printing were done by the same pairing of forces that produced the Egyptian museum-project booklet.[20]

While *Smith* was intended for Egyptologists, Breasted added several features to make it accessible for others. These include "General Explanatory Notes, for Physicians and Other Non-Egyptological Readers" and a separate "Consecutive Translation" of both sides of the papyrus so readers could peruse the texts without being distracted by the scholarly apparatus. He hoped these steps would render the book more approachable "to medical men and historians of science." In the introduction Breasted highlighted what he considered the papyrus's most notable aspects: a remarkably accurate understanding of human physiology—including the earliest words for *brain* and *pulse*, a strikingly modern diagnostic method, and numerous glosses, which Breasted saw as its "most valuable . . . materials"—and the designation of corrections with a marginal cross mark that Breasted called the "earliest known asterisk." The corrections, along with paleographic comparisons with other papyri, suggested to him that the papyrus was a copy of a yet more ancient text.

The many glosses, in turn, caused Breasted to wonder if they were necessary because the copyist's source was, itself, an edited version of a yet earlier papyrus. Based on a minute analysis of the hieratic signs, Breasted conjectured that such "scientific and pedagogic" explanations would not have been necessary unless, at some point between when the original text was written and the source papyrus for the present copy was made, the meanings of certain concepts and terms had already been forgotten. Breasted dated the original text to the beginning of the Old Kingdom, around 2600 BCE, and the glossed version—from which the Smith Papyrus was copied—to the end of the Old Kingdom, or about five hundred years later. The Smith Papyrus, which he placed at around the seventeenth century BCE, thus contained text from almost a thousand years earlier, or about forty-five hundred years before Breasted's study.

Most striking of all, however, was the papyrus's division into forty-eight "cases," each subdivided into an "examination," "diagnosis," and "treatment." Among these Breasted found evidence of three diagnostic methods: "ocular," "olfactory," and "tactile," the last very similar to palpation. The translation and commentary follow, and the rest of the first volume is filled with pages of transcriptions set in hieroglyphic type and interwoven with translations, comments, and notes, often with hieroglyphic annotations laced into the commentary as well (figure 9.12).[21]

Reviews of *Smith* focused approvingly on the papyrus's medical interest, and when it was thought to have gone out of print in the late 1970s, a press specializing in reprints of medical "classics" issued a limited-edition facsimile of the first volume. George Sarton, representing the young discipline of the history of science, wrote an essay-length review because he believed *Smith* to be of such great significance. Midway through the review he was so taken with the papyrus's content that he interrupted himself to ask: "When did science begin?" Sarton recognized that the origin of science in antiquity was a subject that, as Breasted showed, could be illuminated by humanists, and Sarton saw it as a place to build bridges of understanding between the sciences and humanities. Breasted had begun corresponding with Sarton years before, in 1916, they remained in touch over the years, and in 1926 Breasted was elected the second president of the History of Science Society, which Sarton helped found. Breasted followed Sarton's writings, particularly when the latter began articulating what he called the "new humanism," a theory that paralleled Breasted's notions concerning "humanistic science."

Despite their mutual regard and shared interests, however, Sarton's review was thoroughly objective. Though impressed with the scholarship in *Smith*, Sarton encountered instances in which Breasted overstated the insights of the papyrus's author and the successor who glossed it. Regarding Breasted's declaration that they discovered the human pulse and its association with the circulatory system, Sarton commented, "It is unwise to exaggerate the achievements of those early Egyptian physicians. . . . It is better to understand their limitations. The greatest of these, with regard to this case, was their failure to distinguish between blood vessels, tendons, and nerves." Although Sarton was devoted to the humanities, he was a scientist by training and uncomfortable with Breasted's literary ebullience.[22]

When Breasted explained to Rockefeller the importance of making "technical results more widely of use to society" and modern scientists' "social responsibilities," Breasted was also contemplating how he might apply his knowledge to society's moral and spiritual renewal. Breasted believed his struggles with the religion of his parents, and the calming inspiration he drew from his research, might be relevant to the young people of his time. He shared with his contemporaries a sense that the "cumulative impact of a half-century of social, economic,

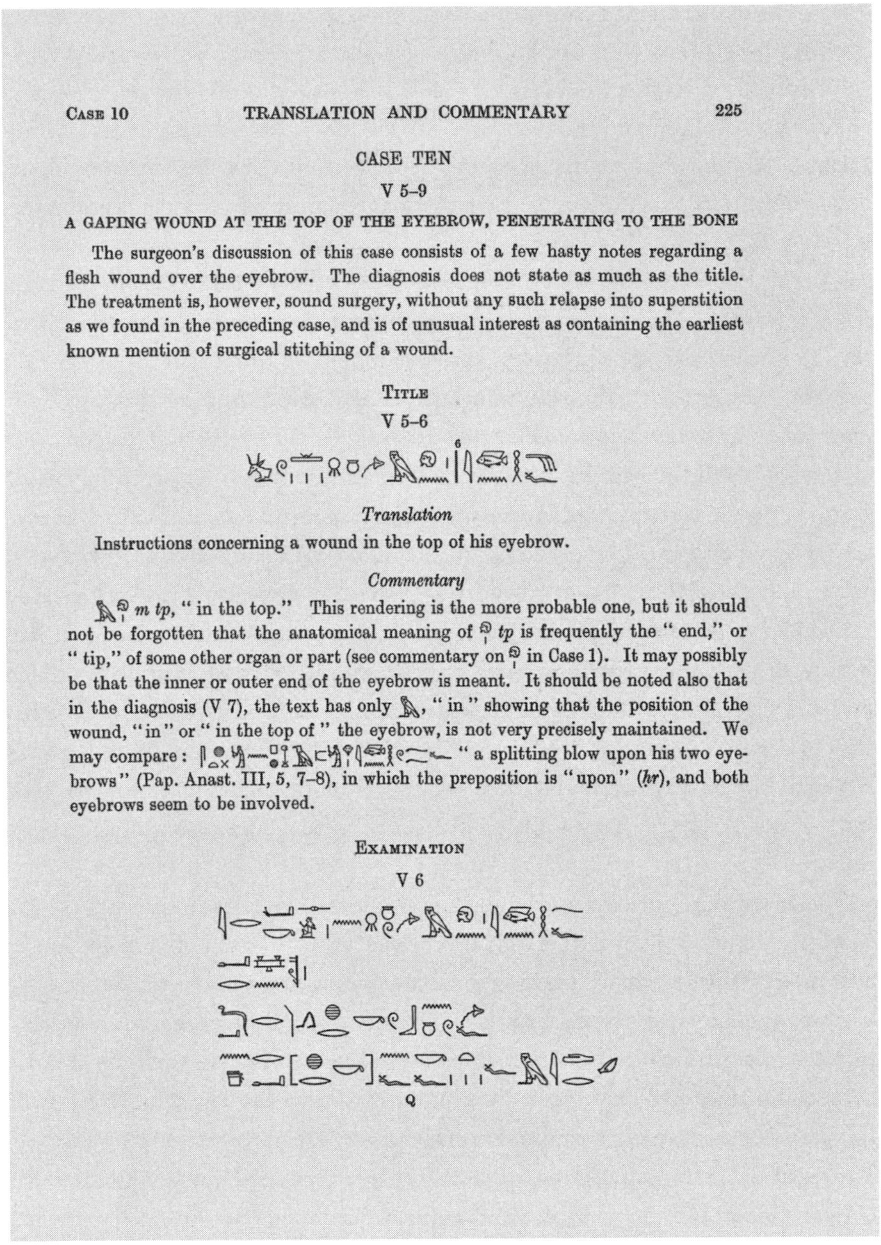

Case 10   TRANSLATION AND COMMENTARY   225

CASE TEN

V 5–9

A GAPING WOUND AT THE TOP OF THE EYEBROW, PENETRATING TO THE BONE

The surgeon's discussion of this case consists of a few hasty notes regarding a flesh wound over the eyebrow. The diagnosis does not state as much as the title. The treatment is, however, sound surgery, without any such relapse into superstition as we found in the preceding case, and is of unusual interest as containing the earliest known mention of surgical stitching of a wound.

TITLE

V 5–6

Translation

Instructions concerning a wound in the top of his eyebrow.

Commentary

m tp, "in the top." This rendering is the more probable one, but it should not be forgotten that the anatomical meaning of tp is frequently the "end," or "tip," of some other organ or part (see commentary on in Case 1). It may possibly be that the inner or outer end of the eyebrow is meant. It should be noted also that in the diagnosis (V 7), the text has only , "in" showing that the position of the wound, "in" or "in the top of" the eyebrow, is not very precisely maintained. We may compare: "a splitting blow upon his two eyebrows" (Pap. Anast. III, 5, 7–8), in which the preposition is "upon" ($ḥr$), and both eyebrows seem to be involved.

EXAMINATION

V 6

Fig. 9.12 Page from Breasted's *Edwin Smith Surgical Papyrus*, vol. 1 (1930). Courtesy of the Oriental Institute, University of Chicago.

and intellectual changes, as well as the host of new forces unleashed by the [First World] war, . . . created a new America. . . . [They] contributed significantly to changes in morals, manners, and mobility. . . . As old ways changed, so did old certainties. . . . Gone was that 'ineffable certainty which made God and his plan as real as the lamp-post.'"

Being an activist by nature, Breasted had long wanted to confront these changes. In 1916 he observed to Frederick Gates:

> The current false impression of the origin, nature and career of man, gained by the average person largely from religious teaching, have formed a serious obstacle to human progress. My own early training in an orthodox religious home . . . has made clear to me . . . how much we need a tactful but uncompromising presentation of the main facts of man's career. . . . Such a presentation intelligible to the youth of the country would contribute essentially toward the creation of a reverence for man and his spiritual possibilities, which would help to fill the void left by the inevitable displacement of the old emotional type of religious faith.[23]

Yet Breasted recognized that the research of his generation helped displace the "old emotional type of religious faith," and as a result the "human career has thus . . . gained a secular aspect, as we suddenly see it placed against a background of geological ages and . . . evolution." That "secular aspect" not only undermined religious faith, it dehumanized society, rendering "the Universe . . . for us and our youth only the action of a vast machine." Accordingly, Breasted believed, "there is now a grave responsibility to avoid such stark materialism, and to aid in disclosing the full story of man and his introduction of spiritual values into an otherwise mechanistic universe." He considered the institute's work a means toward this end but also recognized its limitations. In 1924, writing about organized worship to Frances Breasted, he remarked:

> The service is a good thing. It brings about an attitude of mind which is reassuring and consoling; but its forms have buried deep and far out of ordinary reach the greatest truths we know. To create a new literature of religion, a new service and a new ritual built up out of our experience . . . , but enriched also from our new knowledge of nature and of the human career,—that is the great task of coming generations. I like to think that our Oriental Institute will contribute a body of new fact which will one day take its place in future efforts along this line; although it would be a great mistake to make this a motive for our work. We are organized merely to discover and recover the truth. It is for the future to do with it what it will.

His views on this point never changed, but Breasted believed the "secular aspect" had grown into a more urgent problem, and by early 1931 he had decided to address it in a book. He chose the title before the book was written: "The Dawn of Conscience."[24]

Breasted expected it to be "especially timely in our present situation when the younger generation has very largely cast off the old moorings and doesn't like the word 'conscience.'" The book would be a "reply to the current disillusionment regarding the future of mankind, but based of course entirely on his past." While Breasted hoped it would be a "work of real importance, which will substantially influence human life and character," he feared it might instead turn into "an academic performance" of little interest. In the end he decided to organize the text around one goal: "the first <u>historical</u> demonstration that the evolutionary process, which seems to have operated so largely in the rise and development of <u>material</u> forms, has culminated in ideals of human conduct and has thus given rise to an age of character, which we have little more than begun. For the first time our world, if not the universe, is <u>historically</u> demonstrated to possess a value and a meaning." He completed the manuscript in June 1933 and published *The Dawn of Conscience* the same year.[25]

It is based on his *Development of Religion and Thought in Ancient Egypt* with additions from two unpublished lecture series, one presented at Cornell University in a program "devoted to 'Evolution,'" the other delivered at Bryn Mawr College. Other additions consist of new findings; reinterpretations of known sources, including results from the Coffin Texts project; and fuller treatments such as those addressing Ikhnaton's theological innovations. The result consists of a core—*Development* revised and enlarged—with new front and back material including a fresh foreword, additional first chapter and last chapters, and an epilogue. The main points of Breasted's argument are contained in these new materials. In the foreword he notes: "Some of these ancient sources are delightfully picturesque oriental tales, and such the reader will traverse with ease and even pleasure. Others," Breasted admits, "are not so easily assimilated and if the young reader . . . finds himself mired in rather heavy going and inclined to give up, I suggest he read at least the epilogue."[26]

"The most pressing need of America at the present critical juncture," Breasted declared, "is not more mechanisation but more character." He singled out for particular scorn "technocrats": social scientists and theorists of the time who believed the Great Depression resulted from governmental and economic inefficiencies. The technocrats believed neither "business nor representative government were capable of bringing about the required adjustments" and that certain "dominant institutions and values" blocked the "path of the massive social engineering project the crisis demanded." Their "clarion call for technicians to plan and engineer the new order" came in 1932 and 1933, just as Breasted was completing *Dawn*, and he was responding to the technocrats just as the national debate they provoked was rising to a crescendo. A lifelong advocate of technology and the efficiencies it offered his own field, he was not opposing the spirit of technological innovation. Rather he feared the fascination with "technocracy" would replace schools' humanities curriculums with "a vague miscellany called 'civics' or 'social studies.'"

Breasted believed the way out of the Great Depression was not through more grim "mechanisation" but rather through the inspiration of "the dawn of conscience, the rise of the earliest ideals of conduct, and the resulting Age of Character—a development not only wonderfully fascinating to follow step by step, but also a new vision of hope in times like these." Explaining that the book was "especially for the new generation," Breasted burnished his credentials with youth doubting traditional religious verities by recalling "disquieting experiences" from his younger years. He told the story of discovering an imperfection in the Ten Commandments and hoped "the present generation of young people, who may be troubled with such fundamental questions," would be inspired by the development of morality in ancient Egypt.[27]

An aspect of Breasted's Ten Commandment story, that the Egyptians articulated a moral code superior to the Decalogue long before the latter was "revealed," was characteristic of an argument running through *Dawn*: "Our moral heritage . . . derives from a wider *human* past enormously older than the Hebrews, and it has come to us rather *through* the Hebrews than *from* them." While scholars had been exploring Egyptian influences on Old Testament writings for a while, Breasted knew the notion was still new and even radical to the general public, and he was particularly concerned about its implications for the Jewish community. He underscored his "admiration of Hebrew literature," noting that he had taught Hebrew for years, that his students included "many future rabbis," and that "among modern Jews he has many valued friends." Breasted went to such lengths because of Nazism's rise. In "a world in which anti-Semitic prejudice is still regrettably evident it seems appropriate to state that the book was not written with the slightest anti-Semitic bias." Nonetheless, he refused to compromise. The truths he found were "a result of the social experience of *man himself*" and were not "projected from the outside into a world of unworthy men by some mystic process. . . . It is the greatest discovery in the whole sweep of the evolutionary process."[28]

Breasted's reference to evolution signaled an additional step in his thinking that had begun years before. Though he was not a strict Darwinist in the sense that he never discussed natural selection, Breasted believed the model of evolution was applicable to the development of conscience. He foreshadowed this idea in addresses and grant proposals written for, or inspired by, his collaborations with Hale in the 1910s, and it was refined in subsequent years. In *Dawn* Breasted pointed to the continuity of Egypt's long history as an "isolated social laboratory"—an evolutionary crucible—where "during some three thousand years, beginning about 4000 b.c. . . . human society . . . moved from stage to stage of the longest ethical evolution which we can follow in the career of any human society." The incremental "emergence of conscience as a social force" was an essential feature of this "great transformation." Thus, Breasted argued, the "career of man, like other processes of nature, is a slow development, and the great transformation may be as slow in completion as the process of man's physical evolution." By declaring that morality was not revealed, but the product of an evolutionary process, Breasted was not only clarifying an idea that had been solidifying over the course of the past two decades, he was also affirming his side in one of the great disputes of his day.[29]

The conflict, which pitted fundamentalist Christians against adherents of evolutionary theory, began brewing in the late 1910s and boiled over with the "Scopes Monkey Trial" in July 1925. As the author of textbooks that incorporated evolution in their treatment of early history, Breasted was invited to testify as an "authority" during the Scopes trial. The invitation came from Clarence Darrow, the attorney defending the public-school teacher—John T. Scopes—who had violated a Tennessee state law prohibiting the teaching of evolution. Darrow lived in Chicago, and he contacted "distinguished colleagues" of Breasted's at the University of Chicago, who recommended him. The unspecified colleagues could have been either scientists or Divinity School faculty. The Divinity School might seem an odd place for Darrow to contact, but several of its faculty members noisily opposed the fundamentalists. In the school's "relatively open [theological] atmosphere Biblical criticism and liberal theological tendencies appeared early among Baptists in the Northern United States and soon flourished as in no other evangelical denomination, except perhaps the Congregationalist"—the denomination in which Breasted was raised. Under Harper's leadership, the mostly Baptist Divinity School became "the leading American center for aggressive theological liberalism."

Breasted was traveling abroad when Darrow's invitation arrived and did not testify, although there is some evidence that Darrow drew on *Ancient Times* during the trial. A few months later, while reworking it into *Conquest of Civilization*, Breasted commented to Hale that the changes "made it distinctly a presentation of certain chapters in evolution, and I expect to have an awful row with the fundamentalists. I have some apprehensions that it may affect unfavorably the use of <u>Ancient Times</u> in the schools."[30]

In bringing *Dawn* to a close, Breasted reiterated the "sources of our moral heritage" with particular emphasis on Egyptian influences on Hebrew scripture: that the name *Moses* is Egyptian, that Moses "enjoined his countrymen to adopt an enormously ancient Egyptian custom, the rite of circumcision," and that the Old Testament psalms echo Ikhnaton's writings. "It would be interesting to know also," Breasted speculated, "what place the hymn of Ikhnaton may have had among the influences which gradually led the Hebrews to monotheism." All in all, this evidence reveals that the process of moral development is ongoing and the "incompleteness of the great transformation" provides an incalculable opportunity. If people recognized "the nature of moral progress . . . to have been a product and an outgrowth of social experience, modern man [would be] for the first time in a position to put forth his hand and . . . influence and expedite the process of moral advancement."[31]

The beginning and conclusion of *Dawn* come closer to a public expression of personal faith than anything else Breasted published. If judged by his uses of biblical literature to contextualize ancient Near Eastern research, he might appear to be a devoted adherent of some Christian denomination. But that was not the case. Although he attended church services throughout his life, he was hardly a pious or attentive participant. During dull moments in church, Breasted would jot notes for projects he had under way. After hearing a minister speak, Breasted once remarked, "There is such a lot of dry sticks in this world that I often wonder why there is not a tremendous conflagration, . . . if someone should touch a match to it, what a lot of cut & dried theology would go up in smoke." To a friend who was also a minister, Breasted wrote, "You would probably be scandalized if I were to tell you that I think there is more of the reality and sincerity of religion in the native beliefs of our Southwest Indians than I can find anywhere in the Christian Church."

Although Breasted's beliefs shifted early in his life from a faith in the authority of biblical scripture to a far more complex understanding of human spirituality and morality, he continued to believe in God. Breasted articulated his beliefs in response to a survey of a thousand "persons of different professional and occupational classes of America" conducted in 1921 by a group of Chinese students at Chicago. They posed three questions: "(1) What is your idea of God?; (2) Do you believe in God?; (3) Why?" In replying, Breasted changed the order, taking up the second and third questions first:

> (2) I do believe in God, although this belief has undergone great changes in the course of my life.
>
> (3) I cannot conceive of an intelligible universe like that in which we live, without a guiding intelligence controlling it. Furthermore that universe is not static but is evidently passing through successive stages, which [is] very tangibly illustrated in the course of the human career, which we are now able to follow for probably several hundred thousand years . . . to a lofty and humane civilization which brought forth teachers like Jesus, Confucius, Buddha, Zoroaster, and the Hebrew prophets. This progress has gradually lifted us to a level where we not only possess teachers like these . . . , but where great multitudes

of men . . . are devoted to such visions and ideals, and are striving to follow
them, in spite of such vast and tragic mistakes as the world war just concluded.
To me these facts constitute a logical and convincing basis for belief in God.

(1) A Being who controls the universe for purposes glorious beyond my full
comprehension, but of whose glorious work, if not of himself, I catch some
gleams in the splendor of the universe and the inspiring career of man. That
career inspires me with the belief that he is interested in my efforts not only
toward a worthy life and character for myself, but also toward the uplifting of
all my fellow men, of whatever race, to attain similar ideals. In this way I am
thrilled with the belief that I am aiding and sharing in his purposes.

As one scholar wrote of the time, "God became the world, man, and his dreams;
religion became human experience."[32]

Dawn of Conscience attracted more reviews than any of Breasted's previous
books, in all manner of print media including scholarly journals in several disciplines, popular magazines, and newspapers. Breasted clearly had raised a topical
issue. With the exception of one scathing critique from a *Theosophical Quarterly*
reviewer, who couldn't abide Breasted's decidedly nonmystical treatment of
Egypt, the reviews are mostly laudatory with some reservations. Two reviewers
focused on what they perceived as inconsistencies in Breasted's argument, such
as that between the power of Egypt's top-down theological system and the force
of its bottom-up ethical insights or between Egypt's function as an isolated "social laboratory" and the fact that its most novel changes came during times of
conflict and contacts with neighboring cultures.

Another reviewer complained Breasted used his sources "as a springboard
for diving into the treacherous waters of philosophical speculation and moral"
disquisitions and as "an excuse for preaching a sermon" inappropriate in "a sober
scientific study." The same author, writing for a Jewish scholarly journal, noted
that Breasted was "anxious to put over the point that too much credit is commonly given the Hebrews for our moral legacy. . . . His enthusiasm . . . , however,
almost leads him to make the infinitely more serious error, understandable but
not forgivable, of reversing the situation." A scholar writing for a second Jewish journal expressed the concerns of others who challenged Breasted's claims
of originality for the Egyptians by asking, "May it not be that each people was
adding to its own culture while digesting creations of other peoples, far and
near?"[33]

Cultural anthropologist Ruth Benedict, who pioneered the application of psychological theory to the comparative study of culture groups, wrote that *Dawn*
was in effect "a treatise in the history of ethics, and students of comparative
ethics . . . will wish that [Breasted] had not interpreted the birth of conscience as
such a primal miracle. . . . Psychology and ethics and history are at one in accept-

ing conscience as the individual's reaction to the mores of his country and his age." Because "conscience is inevitable in human culture" and all "peoples . . . in terms of their customs distinguish good from bad," Benedict argued, "when such a distinction is found it does not by any means connote, as Professor Breasted assumes, that high ethical standards are associated with it."[34]

Another probing assessment came from William Foxwell Albright, an American Orientalist who helped improve archaeological standards in Palestine. Like Breasted he was interested in ancient Near Eastern religious beliefs, but from a foundation in biblical archaeology, a particular subset within the larger field that is guided by the interanimations of archaeological investigation and biblical studies. Unlike Breasted, Albright remained a faithful Christian throughout his life, and he believed the teachings of Christianity to be both unassailable and the best navigational aids for interpreting ancient Near Eastern finds. Whereas he regarded Breasted as America's leading proponent of "atheistic humanism," others knew Albright as the chief advocate of what he called "Christian humanism." As Albright saw it, Breasted "stressed the view that man is the creator of his own achievements, possessing boundless capacity for self-improvement." In responding to Breasted's oft-repeated assertion that man's destiny is to "rise," Albright countered that the "theist" would "contend that man has been raised in spite of his nature, by infinitely skillful manipulation on the part of a superhuman agency." Albright labeled Breasted's approach "individualistic meliorism" and attributed it to Breasted's falling under the sway of "theological liberals of the Divinity School, who reacted more and more vigorously against the place attributed to the Bible and historical Protestantism and saw religion primarily as a social and ethical phenomenon." In this environment, Albright contended, "it was impossible to escape the conviction that man's destiny is to improve steadily and irresistably. In such remorseless progress a teleological goal is inevitable."

Perhaps the biggest challenge Breasted posed to Albright and other biblical archaeologists was his then radically different rationale for Western interest in the ancient Near East. John A. Wilson, one of Breasted's former students, who later developed an interest in historiography, put it best. Both sides believed that "archaeology would recover a story which was *our story*," but the "we" trying to "recover our story" functioned within almost diametrically opposed belief systems. Thus Breasted's "logic was different from the argument" of biblical archaeologists: "it was no longer our story because Near Eastern archaeology would prove the accuracy of the biblical account; it was our story because our secular beginnings were in that ancient world."[35] Yet of all the thinkers who seriously engaged with Breasted's ideas, the most original was an amateur antiquities student and collector, Sigmund Freud.

Having been educated in the canons of Western literature and history, Freud was well prepared to read widely outside the professional works of his field. He possessed a particular affinity for the myths of ancient civilizations, and they became touchstones for a number of his most penetrating insights in human psychology. Freud's writings abound with references to mythological and literary figures—Thanatos, Eros, Narcissus, Sphinx, Antigone, and most famously, Oedipus. His interests included antiquities as well, and he began collecting them in 1899. By the 1930s visitors to his consulting room and study could not help but notice the small sculptures and vessels filling glass-front cabinets or arrayed across virtually every flat surface, including his desk. Freud particularly sought representations of figures from ancient history and mythology, especially those of Greece, Rome, and Egypt. His book collecting embraced archaeological studies too.

Freud's fascination with antiquity coincided with his attempts to explain psychoanalytic theory, and in the process archaeology became a "mighty metaphor" for the practice of psychoanalysis. Freud characterized a person's lifetime of memories as being like an archaeological mound and analysis like the archaeologist's meticulous digging down through the accumulated layers. The top levels, or most recent recollections, are encountered first, and as the archaeologist/analyst probes more deeply, ever-earlier stages of the past come into view. The archaeology metaphor served another purpose as well: to explain psychoanalytic theory's differentiation between surface appearances or the symptoms of neuroses and the "buried" causes that underlay them.

Among the works Freud collected and read were three by Breasted: the 1906 British edition of *History of Egypt*; the 1934 British edition of *Dawn of Conscience*; and, unbeknownst to many because Breasted's name doesn't appear on the volume's title page, his contribution to the second volume of *The Cambridge Ancient History*. Breasted wrote six chapters, over 150 pages, covering the period from the eighteenth dynasty (about 1539 BCE) to the end of the twentieth dynasty (about 1075 BCE). Breasted's *History of Egypt* was among a handful of books that "delighted" Freud, and if we may judge by the frequency of Freud's underlinings and marginal notations, he studied all the books closely—especially *Dawn*. All three became sources for Freud's last and perhaps most controversial work, a small, troubling collection of three essays titled *Moses and Monotheism*. Despite his best intentions in writing *Dawn*, Breasted may inadvertently have helped set Freud's project in motion.[36]

Freud began contemplating the cultural ramifications of the Moses story before the turn of the century. The first public manifestation of this interest was an essay on Michelangelo's statue of Moses that Freud published anonymously in 1914. Around 1933 Freud turned to the figure of Moses per se, and in the summer of 1934, not long after the British edition of *Dawn* was issued, he began writing the first two essays for what ultimately became *Moses and Monotheism*. They were completed and published in a journal in 1937, the final essay was completed in 1938, and the three were issued together in simultaneous German and English editions the next year.

Within the first few pages of the first essay, Freud has an extensive quotation from *Dawn*, Breasted's proof that the name *Moses* is Egyptian. Freud was struck by the fact that several scholars had made similar observations but none, including Breasted—even after his thorough study—arrived at what Freud considered to be an obvious deduction: Moses had an Egyptian name because he *was* Egyptian. In the remainder of the first two essays, based in part on numerous citations of Breasted's work, as well as the work of other scholars including Breasted's friends Adolf Erman and Eduard Meyer, Freud spins out an astonishing scenario.[37]

Moses, Freud asserts, was not only Egyptian but probably the governor of an eastern Egyptian province at the time of Amenhotep IV's theological revolution. Inspired by the monotheism of Amenhotep-cum-Ikhnaton, and distraught by the pharaoh's death and the religion's demise, Moses gathered a following of tribes and led them eastward beyond Egypt's control. Freud theorizes that Moses's followers met up with other tribes in the Sinai with whom they shared a common proto-Jewish heritage though the latter had no experience of Egyptian rule and religion. Indeed, the tribes to the east had evolved their own magical-ritual cult based on a "volcano god," "Jahve" (Yahveh or Yahweh). Freud derived the notion from Breasted's observation in *Dawn* that the "peculiar manifestation of Yahveh as 'a pillar of fire' or 'a pillar of cloud' and his appearance on Mount Sinai *by day* with 'thunders and lightnings and a thick cloud' are obviously volcanic phenomena."

According to Freud, as Moses's followers intermingled with the eastern tribes, he imposed an even more severe version of Ikhnaton's monotheism. But things did not go well. The volcano-god worshipers chafed against the elimination of their cult, which resulted in the golden-calf incident and other defiant acts. Freud, inspired by the speculations of German theologian and biblical archaeologist Ernst Sellin, concluded their fury was so great that they murdered Moses. Out of guilt, however, the volcano-god worshipers made peace with his followers. The Judaism we know today is thus an amalgam in which elements of Egyptian monotheism and the magical-ritual cult uneasily coexist, but the cause of that forced coexistence—guilt over the murder of Moses—seemed to have faded with the passage of time.

Drawing on the "documentary paradigm" of biblical criticism, Freud points out the separate literary traditions from which the five books of Moses were composed. He concentrates on two literary sources that are identified by the different names each gives to God, specifically the "J" source for Yahweh and the "E" source for Elohim. The latter name is literally the Hebrew plural for *El*, or God; thus *Elohim* means "gods," though in the Jewish tradition the name is understood to mean "the one God." Freud, however, chose to read *Elohim* literally, seeing in it evidence of many gods in the same presumably monotheistic text, and he regarded that internal dissonance as proof of the ancient merger of two disparate traditions after a long-forgotten crisis, a "traumatic experience," at the very moment of Judaism's creation. It was that notion of cultural trauma that led Freud to his third essay.[38]

Having "established historically" the forgotten origins of Judaism, Freud explains how they had been buried in collective memory by expanding his concept of individual "psychopathology, in the genesis of human neurosis," to the scale of "mass psychology." By this means Freud could apply to an entire people the "formula" he established for explaining the development of individual neuroses: "early trauma—defense—latency—outbreak of the neurosis—partial return of the repressed material." The "early trauma" was the murder of Moses, the "defense" was the guilty merger of monotheistic and polytheistic religions, and "latency" was the period in which the conflicting tribal beliefs were integrated in sacred texts and historical traditions. For the last two steps in his formula, Freud moves beyond the ambit of Judaism to Christianity.

In a yet more remarkable turn, Freud describes "a growing feeling of guiltiness" that "seized the Jewish people." It went on, Freud writes, until

> Paul, a Roman Jew . . . , seized upon this feeling of guilt and correctly traced it back to its primeval source. This he called original sin; it was a crime against God that could be expiated only through death. . . . In reality this crime . . . had been the murder of the Father [Moses] who later was deified. The murderous deed itself, however, was not remembered; in its place stood the phantasy of expiation. . . . A Son of God, innocent himself, had sacrificed himself, and had therefore taken over the guilt of the world. It had to be a Son, for the sin had been murder of the Father.
>
> The Mosaic religion had been a Father religion; Christianity became a Son religion. The old God, the Father, took second place; Christ, the Son, stood in his stead.

Judaism is reduced to a neurosis and, with an Oedipal twist, Christianity is born in a "return of the repressed."[39]

Freud's reliance on Breasted in particular is evident throughout the first two essays. In addition to Breasted's observations on the Egyptian origin of Moses's name and circumcision, Breasted's writings on Amenhotep IV are essential for Freud's purposes. He acknowledges his account "follows closely" *History of Egypt*, *Dawn*, and the Cambridge chapters, and he even adopts Breasted's spelling of "Ikhnaton" over the by-then equally common "Akhenaton." However, where

Breasted responded to rising anti-Semitism in the 1930s by issuing a disclaimer, Freud moved in the opposite direction. Although well aware of the incendiary nature of *Moses* for Jews, Freud wrote, "To deny a people the man whom it praises as the greatest of its sons is not a deed to be undertaken lightheartedly—especially by one belonging to that people. No consideration, however, will move me to set aside truth in favour of supposed national interests."

Despite this declaration, Freud initially suppressed the particularly inflammatory third essay. His reason is abundantly clear. Between 1934 and 1938, when Freud wrote *Moses*, anti-Semitism in Germany and Austria had escalated from hateful speech and government-approved discrimination into the murderous violence and destruction of *Kristallnacht*. After the forced *Anschluss* (union) that bound Austria to Germany in early 1938, what few illusions of security Austrian Jews like Freud could entertain quickly dissipated. His family and friends hustled the elderly and ailing Freud out of Vienna to London, where he died a year later. Freud was in Vienna in March 1938 when he filed the third essay away; he changed his mind three months later, only after arriving in the relative safety of London.

At a time of worldwide economic and social distress, Breasted and Freud drew very different lessons from ancient Egyptian and biblical texts. *Dawn* is infused with Breasted's belief in humanity's destiny to "rise," while *Moses* is permeated with Freud's belief that the dark "mental residue of those primeval times has become a heritage which, with each new generation, needs only to be awakened."[40] The Egyptologist probed the past to inspire a better future, while the physician probed the past to explain a troubled present.

New Prospects, Old Constraints

While in the midst of completing *Dawn*, Breasted was asked to report on the Oriental Institute for the University of Chicago Survey, a series of book-length studies sponsored by the General Education Board. Designed to foster a searching self-examination of the university's accomplishments, problems, and prospects, it was aimed at "students of education literature" and focused primarily on academic-administration issues such as institutional growth, enrollment, physical plant, and instructional problems. Breasted's contribution, *The Oriental Institute*, was the twelfth and final volume in the series and the only one on a research program. He completed most of the nearly 450-page text "in rough state, . . . in 60 days" by drawing heavily on previously published papers, reports, and institute handbooks. Many passages are new, however, particularly those summarizing the latest results from projects at home and abroad. Taken as a whole, the book is the most comprehensive single account of the institute's origins, development, and accomplishments through the mid-1930s. Although Breasted had long argued for a systematic and broad approach to ancient Near Eastern studies, the book contains his first and only statement of how the institute's programs corresponded with that large view:[41]

Stages of Human Development	Oriental Institute Projects
A. Prehistory	
Earliest human evidences down to fourth millennium B.C.	Prehistoric Survey, Persian Expedition, Megiddo Expedition, Anatolian Expedition
B. History of civilization: the rise and development of *nations*	
1. Earliest advance in control of material world	
a) Earliest pictorial representations of human activity . . .	Sakkarah (Memphis) Expedition
b) Development of material life and government in Western Asia	Iraq Expedition (Babylonian . . .), Anatolian Expedition, Persian Expedition
2. Earliest advance in . . . human conduct and mind	
a) Dawn of conscience . . .	Coffin Texts
b) Initial steps toward inductive science	Edwin Smith Surgical Papyrus
c) Earliest art in the historic age	Sakkarah Expedition, Iraq Expedition (Babylonian . . .)
3. Earliest advance in business and economic life	
a) Creation of earliest commercial and economic world	Assyrian Dictionary, Iraq Expedition
b) Origin of business practices and their documentary forms	
C. History of civilization: the rise and development of *empires*	
1. Egypt . . .	
a) Political history	
(1) Historical records of . . . Theban temples . . .	Epigraphic Expedition
(2) Historical records of . . . Abydos Temple of Seti I	Abydos Expedition (jointly with Egypt Exploration Society)
b) Art and architecture	
(1) Paintings of . . . Theban cemetery	Davies-Gardiner Paintings
(2) Paintings of . . . Abydos Temple of Seti I	Abydos Expedition (jointly with Egypt Exploration Society)
(3) . . . Medinet Habu	Architectural Survey

Stages of Human Development	Oriental Institute Projects
2. Western Asia . . .	
a) Hittite Empire . . .	Anatolian Expedition
b) Assyrian Empire . . .	Iraq Expedition (Assyrian . . .)
c) Babylonian Empire . . . ⎫	
d) Chaldean Empire . . . ⎭	Iraq Expedition (Babylonian . . .)
e) Persian Empire . . .	Persian Expedition
f) Palestine and the Hebrews . . .	Megiddo Expedition
g) Roman Empire	
(1) Forerunners of Byzantine	Preliminary Reconnaissance Expedition
art . . .	[1919–20]
(2) Syriac Christianity	Peshitta
3. Civilization of Islam	
a) Moslem wisdom . . .	Kalīlah wa-Dimnah

Although *The Oriental Institute* was ostensibly for higher-education scholars and administrators, reviews suggest it was read most closely by scholars in ancient Near Eastern studies. None could resist commenting on the institute's financial resources, it being "the first to be able to carry out a programme on a proper scale unhampered by lack of funds." Awareness of the institute's comparative wealth was heightened by the Depression because the "generosity of the Institute's supporters has enabled it to employ the best men available . . . , and to skim the cream from most of the dormant or defunct expeditions which have suffered from lack of funds."

By the time *The Oriental Institute* was published, however, pressure was increasing for Breasted to economize. His annual budget passed the $677,000 mark during the 1929–30 academic year, well before the new Chicago building was completed. As the financial crisis deepened, Chicago began cutting its budget, and in the fall of 1931 Breasted was asked to reduce his university appropriation of about $5,300 by 10 percent. He complied and was subsequently told that his salary was to be cut by about a third as well, the assumption being that the sum—$3,000—could be made up out of institute funds. Breasted was offended, partly because he had worked hard to raise that money for other purposes, and partly because the institute was paying over $71,000 to the university for faculty salary subventions and student fellowships. He was also upset by the timing. The cut was demanded on the very day the institute dedicated its new building. Breasted sent an angry response that concluded with his resignation. The cuts and his resignation were mutually withdrawn.[42]

While Breasted could face down his superiors at Chicago, Rockefeller officials were much tougher. The Depression all but erased the International Education Board's assets, and the General Education Board and Rockefeller Foundation stepped in to honor its pledges, including those to the institute. A representative announced the plan to Hutchins and Breasted in April 1932, assuring that the foundation would continue to support the institute but demanding that "substantial reductions . . . be made." Breasted reduced his spending across the board, suspending the Hittite expedition and "virtually wiping out" the antiquities-purchasing fund. He pushed back as well, however, arguing that further cuts would mean "scattering of personnel built up by years of labor, loss of idle equipment, decay of unoccupied field headquarters, forfeiture of concessions and sacrifice of political influence indispensable to operations under oriental governments." The Rockefeller officials were unmoved, and moreover a few were uncomfortable with the institute's spending priorities, one commenting on the lavishness of its building and more. "Permanent looking and extremely comfortable headquarters have been built or are being built at each excavation," he wrote. "The motion picture record of all the work has recently been completed. . . . [Yet] B[reasted] is talking about necessity for more space." Charles Breasted, as the institute's executive secretary, was singled out in particular for his "extravagance."[43]

The references to a motion picture and Charles Breasted were connected. In 1932 Hutchins contracted with an educational film company to produce a series of "sound films under the direction of the university faculty." Charles Breasted seized the opportunity to create a two-part film initially titled "The New Past." The plan was to present the "scientific ideas and ideals" that led to the institute's creation, to show its new "headquarters" building, and by using a "carefully selected group of . . . significant objects" from the institute's collections and "editing in especially taken 'shots,' . . . show the work of its field expeditions in active operation." He began by having over eight reels of film shot of his father. The scene was his father's institute office, where, with "artifacts and other vividly illustrative materials, [he] . . . described in a clear, dignified, human, and almost epic manner, the advent of the creature man and his amazing . . . upward struggle." The footage closed with "a scene of [Breasted] descending the stairs in the main lobby [of the institute] to lead his invisible audience through the exhibition halls." This aspect of the project was comparatively inexpensive, however. To film expeditions distributed across the Middle East required a plane to swiftly traverse the long distances between sites. Charles Breasted estimated an additional cost of about $12,000 to $15,000.

He could not proceed, however, without university permission to reallocate funds within the institute's budget. The reallocation would be accomplished with "presumably temporary" assessments of field-expedition budgets. Charles justified the levies by asserting they supported production of a "highly desirable scientific record." Because his father was traveling abroad at the time and Charles wanted to start shooting in the Middle East right away, he proposed the plan to a university official by arguing essentially two benefits. First, he believed the "possibilities are definite for earning a substantial return on this investment and at the same time fulfilling the educational purposes for which it was made." He offered a few income-producing schemes such as multiple daily showings in the institute's lecture hall at fifty cents a head or at other locations, such as the city's Orchestra Hall, for one dollar a head, "especially if introduced . . . by the Director in person." Charles also believed the film could be a cost-saving measure by relieving institute staff from introducing the collections to visitors and touring groups, an expense he calculated as equaling "at least two salaried guides." The second benefit would be its "value as propaganda of the most desirable and dignified sort for the University."

His father concurred with the reallocation, if uneasily. Breasted knew the university was "taking the lead in the preparation of such films" and that it expected to "profit both educationally and financially." He noted as well that "one of the most serious and intelligent of the Hollywood directors stated . . . that there is a wide spread public demand for short . . . films, especially showing instructive travel and history, and carrying people away from home and its present shadows of depression and discouragement." He also envisioned a day when such films "will form permanent sections in school, college and university courses" and felt "some responsibility in this matter; just as I did to put out such a book as Ancient Times." The university approved Charles's request, but his father remained cautious: "I am a somewhat venturesome, even at times reckless, individual; but the amounts of money we are venturing give me concern. 'Et haec olim meminisse juvabit' [time heals all things], perhaps."[44]

Filming in the Middle East began in December 1932, and after it was about half done, in mid-February 1933, Breasted, his wife, and their younger son, James Jr., joined Charles and the cinematographer to complete the remainder. At the airfield in Heliopolis, Egypt, they boarded a trimotor airplane—designed for six passengers and two crew members—chartered from Imperial Airways, a British company. For almost four weeks, through mid-March, they hopscotched to expedition sites throughout the Middle East. It was strenuous flying, however, with a number of very bumpy passages that took a toll on the entire group but especially the older Breasteds—Frances had turned sixty a few months prior, and Breasted was sixty-seven. They collected many hours of footage, and Charles needed more than a year to winnow it down to about seventy minutes. It premiered at the University of Chicago with two screenings in early June 1934, the first introduced by Breasted, the second by Charles.[45]

The film, called *The Human Adventure*, opens with production credits superimposed over the institute building's tympanum (figure 9.2), credits for James Henry Breasted's "scientific supervision" and Charles Breasted's authorship and narration superimposed over the institute's Khorsabad bull (figure 9.8), and a depiction of a cuneiform panel that morphs into an inscription dedicating the film to the institute's "devoted personnel both at home and abroad." The credits are accompanied by the tempestuous opening of Felix Mendelssohn's *Die Hebriden* (The Hebrides), the only music in the film with the exception of a repeated measure at the very end. The movie proper begins with its title seen against deep space through which the viewer flies toward a distant sphere that, as it looms closer, turns out to be Earth. The film then cuts to scenes of volcanic and tectonic activity, whereupon Charles begins speaking. Delivered in a grandiloquent style, not unlike old-fashioned theatrical declamation, his narration starts with the beginnings of life, the dinosaur period, the transition from hominids to *Homo sapiens*, and the advent of tool making and speech, with parts of the narrative illustrated with motor-animated dinosaurs and cavemen. The animated figures were filmed at a Sinclair Oil Company exhibit titled "The World a Million Years Ago" at the Century of Progress Exposition along Chicago's lakefront in 1933–34. The Sinclair company, mindful of oil's origins in the dinosaur age, adopted a brontosaurus (now known as apatosaurus) image as its trademark and included one in its exhibit along with other scenes from prehistory.[46]

Charles concludes the introductory section with a sequence of quotes from his father's writings, ending: "[The] promise of man's future lies in the story of his past. Where shall we learn of man's conquest of civilization?" The Oriental Institute, of course, and views of the Chicago building accompanied by a description of its work follows. Charles then introduces his father, shown standing in his institute office behind a desk arrayed with artifacts ranging from flints to cuneiform tablets, with a map of the Middle East on an easel to one side (figure 9.13). The elder Breasted welcomes the audience with a brief overview of ancient history, from hunting and gathering to commerce and the "dawn of conscience." His discussion leads from the historical background to the sites where that history took place as a way of setting up the expeditions tour that will follow. His delivery is enlivened by his picking up and explaining objects and walking over to the map, where, with a pointer, he shows the centers and reach of ancient civilizations.

One is struck by the stiffness of Breasted's delivery, however. Although there are brief moments of soaring oratory, for the most part his speech seems mechanical and awkward as he looks downward to collect his thoughts or off camera as though seeking a response from a crew member or perhaps his son. It's hard to believe this is the man who was regarded by colleagues, students, and the public as such a captivating and inspiring speaker. But he was disarmed by the circumstances. Prior to being filmed Breasted wrote, "My chief worry is to learn a speech <u>verbatim</u>. . . . There are 16 paragraphs in my speech. Fifteen seconds additional in each paragraph would mean 4 minutes excess and add 360 feet of film. My speech must not exceed 10 minutes at the utmost. There are . . . 900

Fig. 9.13 Movie still, James Henry Breasted, from Charles Breasted's *The Human Adventure*, 1934. Courtesy of the Oriental Institute, University of Chicago.

feet of film in ten minutes. A reel is a maximum of 1000 ft. long. If I add 360 ft. my speech will exceed the reel! And I forget the actual terse wording of my speech as fast as I learn it! Humiliating experience!" Breasted realized that "the very ease with which I can find the words for extemporaneous delivery is my undoing."[47]

The expeditions tour begins in Egypt with aerial views of Cairo and the pyramids of Giza before heading south to the institute's fieldwork at Saqqara and Thebes, the latter with shots of the Epigraphic Survey working at Medinet Habu and in the large temple complex of Karnak. Among the lovely overhead and ground-level scenes of the temples and Chicago House are images of Breasted walking with institute workers or inspecting inscriptions. The next stop is much farther south, near Aswan and the quarries from which obelisks were cut and transported to Thebes. The scenes include a brief view of Breasted and his wife walking on an unfinished obelisk abandoned in the quarry. From there the tour turns north, crossing Jerusalem and Haifa to Megiddo, where aerial and ground views include the staff's uses of a balloon for overhead photography. The sections from Megiddo and a later stop, Tell Asmar, contain disquieting footage of child laborers and Charles's often condescending remarks about the adults.

A few years earlier the Union Internationale de Secours aux Enfants (Save the Children International Union) had complained to the university about a clearance project at Medinet Habu. The union's report focused mainly on a Metropolitan Museum of Art expedition nearby, but the Epigraphic Survey was also accused of employing children and harsh working conditions, including the use of whips by Egyptian foremen. Nelson disputed some aspects of the report while also explaining certain practices, arguing in essence that this was the way things were done, noting, for example, that foremen routinely carried whips as signs of authority. Further, Nelson added, the institute fully compensated its workers and concluded each season with a festival for employees that consisted of entertainment, feasts, sports, and games.

The union's secretary-general was mostly understanding but did not accept the local-standards argument, countering, "Western institutions employing native labour . . . have a noble opportunity of showing a good example." Nelson agreed. Up to that point large work crews had not been employed by the Epigraphic Survey. Things changed in 1927 when Breasted authorized the architectural survey of Medinet Habu that required clearance of the surrounding site, a project that employed hundreds of laborers over five seasons. To oversee the project, Breasted appointed a German Egyptologist, Uvo Hölscher, who insisted that he report directly to Breasted rather than through Nelson. Prior to the union complaint, Nelson had told Hölscher that Americans found his practices objectionable. The latter replied that the Egyptians were an "undisciplined people" and "rough" treatment was justified, and he ignored Nelson. In the end, Nelson felt the union's criticism was "just," and he asked to be excused from defending Hölscher's conduct any further.

By growing the institute so quickly and relying on an ever-larger corps of subordinates to whom he delegated considerable autonomy, Breasted exposed the institute to this kind of problem. Shortly after receiving the grants that enabled the institute's expansion into fieldwork, Breasted commented, "The hobgoblin that haunts me now is the question where I am to find the young men to man these projects." As John A. Wilson later observed, "The rapid growth of the institute was not wholly to its good. Many of the new persons appointed were inexperienced, and some of them were temperamental." Often loyal to a fault, Breasted's instinct was to defend his lieutenants first and ask questions later. In most cases, the people he recruited to head the institute's field operations proved to be effective leaders and productive scholars in their own right—examples being Henri Frankfort, who headed expeditions in Iraq, and Ernst Herzfeld, who headed the work at Persepolis. When things went wrong and Breasted was slow to react, however, the results reflected poorly on the institute in ways that contradicted the high professional standards he espoused.[48]

The last stop of *The Human Adventure* is Persepolis. The aerial and ground views of the palace complex and adjacent sites make up one of the longer segments in the film as it recapitulates themes established earlier including the contrast of ancient ruins and the technologies of modern archaeology, important discoveries, the behavior and incomprehension of local workers, and the "timeless" grandeur and "immortality" of the site. Charles's narration concludes there, observing that "the trooping sunset clouds above Persepolis give warning that our own day too is done." It's an abrupt and inconclusive end by today's cinematic standards, but that did not disturb contemporary audiences, who were enthusiastic about the film. A Chicago critic reported that the audience there regarded it as "vivid and exciting," and a New York critic remarked that "although the picture falls within the unhappy category known as 'educational films,' it is nevertheless entertainment in a full sense."

The New York showing took place in fall 1935 at Carnegie Hall, which was rented by the institute for four screenings. An endorsement from the United Parents Associations of New York was lined up in advance, and the showings were locally advertised. To the surprise of Carnegie Hall's management, its theater was filled "almost [to] capacity" for all the showings. The hall's president commented that, from "long experience, we fully appreciate the difficulty of successfully producing entertainment of high informative value. . . . [It] is no small feat to crowd an Auditorium seating approximately 3000 persons with an attraction of this nature." School showings were equally popular. The head of the New Jersey State Normal School (now Kean University) was "moved to write" that *The Human Adventure* attracted so much interest that it had to "run six matinees and four evening performances" to accommodate the nearly six thousand people wanting to see it. Charles publicized the film's Carnegie Hall showings to Rockefeller officials and followed up with attendance reports. He also reported the Carnegie Hall box-office income, which, despite the large attendance, barely covered the screening costs, much less its production. In his eagerness to transmit this information, Charles hardened impressions of his "extravagance" by sending the report to the Rockefeller offices via air mail special delivery—an unnecessary indulgence in a time of fiscal distress.[49]

Throughout 1934 and into 1935 the Depression continued to take a toll, and the elder Breasted struggled to maintain the institute's funding with budget maneuvers and appeals to Rockefeller or his associates, but without much success. Around June 1935, Rockefeller officials began debating a plan for Breasted to gradually wind down expeditions for which his annual grants would end in 1939 and to operate on endowment income alone. Though they did not say as much, a consensus was forming that the institute's ten-year expedition grant would not be renewed and Breasted and his colleagues ought to prepare for this change. Rockefeller was apprised of the discussions and told Fosdick it seemed "unthinkable" that Breasted "should not be fully and amply supported so long as he lives." On the other hand, Rockefeller acknowledged, "I fancy the officers are opposed to the work. . . . How this feeling . . . can be reversed tactfully and wisely is the question." His associates were particularly wary of doing anything to encourage future requests from Breasted. One officer, noting Breasted's pattern of leveraging new opportunities into fresh appeals, worried, "Now he might discover something else. I should like the limitation of approved budgets." Another replied, "The more it is nailed down, the better."[50]

Breasted contemplated the ten-year grant's conclusion with rising alarm. Despite his previous cuts, the institute's budget had grown to a projected $660,000 for the 1935–36 fiscal year. When that grant ended, the institute's budget would shrink to about $150,000 per year. In October 1935, Breasted turned to Rockefeller yet again. He recalled the beginnings of their association, expressed gratitude for Rockefeller's backing, and confided, "That I can now seek your advice as a friend is to me a precious privilege." Breasted sought his patron's counsel on "whether the work of the Oriental Institute is to be made permanent or become a memory." He estimated that, on the basis of the current year's budget, it would require an additional endowment of about $15 million to permanently sustain its present level of activities. "I am really standing with my back to the wall," Breasted wrote, "fighting for the survival of the noble scientific organization which you have made possible. I will be most grateful if you will tell me as a friend whether you think it wise in times like this for me to . . . struggle" to maintain the institute's many projects.

Although Breasted and Rockefeller had a warm and durable relationship, it remained courtly, and Breasted treaded lightly around funding questions, seeking Rockefeller's "advice" rather than asking directly for money. Breasted hoped his friend would once again either move things behind the scenes or personally tender the needed cash. Rockefeller understood this. But the Depression, his philanthropies' struggles to meet prior commitments, and the growing independence of their trustees and staff—which Rockefeller sought and carefully nurtured—had altered his sense of the Oriental Institute's needs.

Rockefeller replied to Breasted's appeal by observing that the institute's situation was "both unsound and precarious" and that it called for a "complete review . . . having in mind its future." With regard to Breasted's implied hope for Rockefeller's personal assistance, the latter responded, "In making the contributions . . . in the earlier years of its development, . . . I did not for a moment assume I was putting myself in the position of becoming the patron of the vast enterprise that has since developed." His personal commitment, Rockefeller continued, did not extend "beyond what each gift was specifically intended to cover." More to the point, he wrote:

> I have been as enthusiastic as you . . . about the great central purpose of your work. . . . However, I cannot but feel, much as I regret to say so, that in your enthusiasm you have been led to expand the scope of your operations far beyond

what was prudent or permanently possible to maintain. I have no thought of making further contributions . . . , and much of the pleasure which I have had in contributing to the various specific projects . . . would have been taken away had I felt for a moment that gifts that I made . . . for specific matters could be construed by you as evidences of a larger and more enduring interest in the whole enterprise on my part. . . .

. . . Were I in your place, I would feel very uneasy and insecure until I had very greatly deflated the whole enterprise at any early date.

Breasted's entreaty was sent from Egypt, and he was still traveling in the Middle East when Rockefeller's reply, written about a month later, was mailed. Breasted never saw it.[51]

Keen as a Boy

The filming trip through the Middle East took a particular toll on Frances Breasted's health, and by the fall of 1933, just months after their return to America and a vacation in the Southwest, it began to decline. By May 1934 she had "been confined to bed for months," suffering from bacterial endocarditis, and she died in mid-July at the age of sixty-one. Her funeral service, held in Bond Chapel on Chicago's campus, "was marked by its simplicity—a short tribute, the reading of several poems, prayer, and at the beginning and end almost joyous music" performed by a string quartet. Breasted was a devoted husband, and he wrote to her almost daily when he was away. The letters may also have been his way of helping her alleviate what seems to have been a lifelong struggle with depression. Charles felt "the fact that everyday life was for my mother such a constant struggle caused my father the profoundest distress of mind. Yet by his own admission he 'had not the courage to face the reality'; and as always, with a fine Victorian chivalry, he attributed to their relationship whatever it may have lacked." At one point Frances wrote in her diary, "Among my husband's trials and problems the greatest has been my peculiar temperament. . . . Not even my intense love for him has helped me to conquer it."[52]

Breasted mourned her death and sought solace on a trip to Alaska and the Canadian Rockies, places he had not yet visited, with his daughter, Astrid, who was then about twenty. As ever, he derived his greatest comfort from work. He published a long review of the first of the eleven volumes of *The Story of Civilization*, titled *Our Oriental Heritage*, by the popularizing historian and philosopher Will Durant, and he completed an article-length manuscript on a bronze base for a small Ramses VI sculpture discovered at Megiddo. Before long he also rediscovered romance. Sometime in the months following Frances's death, Breasted began seeing her younger sister, Imogen. She was previously married to a New York stock broker she had met in France during the war while he was an intelligence officer and she was doing "Y. M. C. A. social work." They had two children, but the marriage fell apart "on grounds of incompatibility," and Imogen raised them alone. After a courtship of well less than a year, Breasted and Imogen married in early June 1935, he approaching the age of seventy, she at fifty. That fall he took her to Italy and the Middle East. They toured Palestine, especially Jerusalem and the recently completed Palestine Archaeological Museum, and of course Egypt.

The trip combined business with pleasure, and the itinerary included visits to several of the institute's expedition sites. Just as the institute's funding successes depended on Breasted's personal leadership, his presence was vital to raising morale among its workers in the field, a point Nelson periodically made in appealing for the "inspiration" of Breasted's visits. The journey buoyed his spirits and energy immeasurably. "I have never seen him more youthful or exhilarated than he was this season," Harold Nelson wrote. "I only hope that he did not overdo for he was game for any enterprise that was suggested." Breasted continued to keep in shape by doing a "daily dozen" fitness routine, and he enjoyed competing "with the young men of the staff in athletic exercises."[53]

Although he caught a debilitating cold on the voyage home, Breasted was "keen as a boy" to return to Chicago and revise his *History of Egypt*. "Think of it!" he wrote. "Not a syllable of all the results which all my expeditions have been bringing in for sixteen years nor any of my own researches for over thirty years, have gone into the book." A year prior, hinting at thoughts of retirement, he wished he "were not obliged to live such a busy life" and fretted about not having "time to think," being so occupied "merely . . . assembling evidence." Ideally, Breasted wrote, he would like to "contemplate the evidence with some tranquility of soul and some feeling of leisure." Yet he was torn about retiring from the institute's directorship, fearing he would miss its many activities and conceding that he would just as soon "die in the harness."

The shipboard cold turned into strep throat complicated by "a latent malarial condition" that may have dated back to his 1919–20 expedition. When Breasted's ship arrived in New York, he was rushed to the hospital, where for five days doctors tried to cure him. They were able to quell the malaria, but the strep infection proved fatal, and Breasted died 2 December 1935. In a twist he would have enjoyed, his five attending physicians issued "a signed statement" on the precise cause of his death. As solemnly reported by the *New York Times* and picked up by the *Chicago Daily Tribune*, "The emphasis placed . . . on a post mortem substantiation of the diagnosis was . . . to eliminate any possibility that Dr. Breasted's death might be attributed to the oft-discredited story of 'King Tut's curse.' According to this fable, a fatal curse was fastened on the scientists, of whom Dr. Breasted was one, who in 1922 entered the tomb of King Tutankhamun."

Within a day, word of Breasted's death spread across America, Europe, and the Middle East, touching not only friends, but many others who expressed their sadness in letters to Breasted's family. Several came from fellow Egyptologists. Percy Newberry, who first met Breasted during his honeymoon trip in 1894–95, consoled the family with words of Breasted's "great success . . . achieved in the later years of his life for he had a very hard struggle in the earlier part," declaring that "every one interested in the study of ancient history owes him an immense debt of gratitude for it was he more than anyone, who raised the standard of Egyptological scholarship in the world." Others came from American pre-Columbian archaeologists such as Alfred Kidder, who recalled that "it was, in fact, the reading of his 'History of Egypt' . . . just after I'd left college which turned the scales, for me, between archaeology and business."

Condolences arrived from prominent figures like the Allenbys and the Egyptian ambassador to the United States, and from "the humble folks of Luxor and Kurna. [They] felt the touch of [Breasted's] personality." A note to Charles arrived from Hamed Abdalla, "Dragoman, Luxor," who wrote, "With deepest sorrow, hearing the sudden death of your kind father, it is a great loss to his Luxor friends." Breasted's students were especially stricken. Caroline Ransom Williams wrote, "I never had a truer, kinder, more helpful friend." Harold Nelson wrote to John A. Wilson, "I am having difficulty in adjusting my thoughts to a situation in which he no longer figures. I constantly think of many . . . things that turn up in the course of the day's work which I know would interest him." Even students of former students were saddened. One recalled "having read from one of his books while I was in the eighth grade" and later finding "'The Dawn of Conscience' . . . was an inspiration to read . . . while in seminary. . . . I feel the loss of this man; he has been so much a part of me, although I have never known him personally."[54]

In accordance with Breasted's wishes, there was no funeral. His body was cremated, and the urn containing his ashes was buried in the Breasted family plot, located in Greenwood Cemetery, Rockford, Illinois, during a private family gathering. While settling his estate, the family also helped plan a public memorial service that took place in early April 1936 in Chicago's University Chapel. The program was led by Hutchins and included his remarks "For the University," quotes from Breasted's writings read by Hutchins, and selections from works by Schubert, Wagner, and Beethoven performed by the Chicago Symphony Orchestra. The closing half hour of the memorial was broadcast live "over the nation-wide network of the Columbia Broadcast System."[55]

There had been some conversations among Hutchins, Rockefeller officials, and Breasted about his eventual successor as the Oriental Institute's director, but they had been leisurely at best. Charles had decided a couple of years prior to his father's death that he wanted to leave, ideally by June 1936. But even if he had aspirations to rise from his current position as assistant director, he lacked the scholarly background to qualify. It was decided to groom a current staff member to take over, perhaps in another year or two when the elder Breasted was finally ready to retire. By consensus that person was John A. Wilson, who was by then an associate professor of Egyptology, secretary of the Department of Oriental Languages and Literatures, and on the Epigraphic Survey staff. Hutchins regarded Wilson as a "careful and economical administrator," and Breasted felt he had the requisite scholarly skills. A plan to begin easing Wilson into the institute's administration was barely under way, however, when Breasted died. The university was forced to issue a statement calming its trustees, who could not imagine the institute without Breasted, assuring them that he had "left an organization . . . entirely capable of carrying on the work." Wilson was appointed acting director in January 1936, Charles agreed to remain on until October, and Wilson became director that summer. His first task was to begin scaling down the institute's activities at home and abroad, an assignment that occupied almost all his time for the next two years.[56]

During the period of the institute's most rapid growth, there were at least a few university administrators and trustees who believed the Rockefeller boards' "large grants to the . . . Institute were out of line with the other needs of the University." But they, like the foundation officials, understood Breasted's special relationship with Rockefeller and kept out of the way. All that changed after Breasted's death, throwing into even sharper relief his personal influence as one of the university's most powerful "academic entrepreneurs." Rockefeller stepped back, and his associates along with university officials asked Wilson to plan for immediate reductions. By early March 1936 he, with Charles Breasted's assistance, presented a 50 percent reduction in the coming year's budget. Officers of the Rockefeller Foundation took the lead in monitoring the planning, and though they were "favorably impressed" by Wilson and felt he showed "a refreshing modesty in his outlook," they believed the cutbacks should go "much further." They were also willing to provide some additional support, provided the university commit itself to the institute's long-term future. Shortly thereafter the trustees recorded their "conviction that the Institute should be continued as a major enterprise of the University in teaching and research."[57]

Over the next few months, the Rockefeller Foundation and the university agreed to slash the institute's annual budget from total expenditures of nearly $711,000 during the 1935–36 fiscal year to $205,000 by 1938–39. Most of the cutbacks were accomplished by either shutting down or drastically shrinking expeditions, and Wilson and Rockefeller officials helped the staff of canceled expeditions find other work. The plan preserved the Epigraphic Survey on a much smaller scale, although consideration was given to selling or leasing out the new Chicago House and retreating to the old one. On one point, however, Wilson stood his ground. "The goal of all our work is publication," he declared, and only if the need to publish new results slackened would money be redirected to expeditions. Meanwhile, research and teaching at the institute's Chicago headquarters would continue as before to the extent possible. Rockefeller kept an eye on the institute's financial situation, communicating confidentially with Wilson, and he was active behind the scenes in maintaining "vital features of the work." The Rockefeller Foundation and General Education Board honored their commitments, added $1 million more to fill in for a matching grant the university was to have raised from other sources, and worked to ease the institute into a financially sustainable future. All told, the institute's endowments raised by Breasted came to about $5 million. However, taking advantage of the terms of one of the grants that allowed the university to reassign funds in a financial emergency, Hutchins transferred $2 million to other purposes in the mid-1940s. A trustee later regretted the move, commenting that he had "no doubt . . . this transfer was completely legal, but . . . thinks the ethics involved, to say nothing of the wisdom, is questionable." Of the more than $11.85 million Breasted raised from Rockefeller and his philanthropic boards, a sufficient amount remained as endowment to assure the institute's permanence.[58]

A Lengthened Shadow

During his remarks at the Oriental Institute's building dedication, Raymond Fosdick quoted Ralph Waldo Emerson's observation that "an institution is the lengthened shadow of one man." "If there had been no Breasted," Fosdick continued, "there would have been no Oriental Institute." For scholars and others who followed the latest archaeological news from the Middle East, the institute and Breasted were synonymous, and there were few articles that mentioned one without referring to the other. Wilson and his colleagues wanted to memorialize that association by renaming the institute's building "James Henry Breasted Hall." The university's trustees agreed, but the action didn't quite stick. The building is known on campus as the Oriental Institute, and Breasted's name is attached only to the building's first-floor auditorium. But despite the institute's Depression-era cutbacks, it not only survived but has remained one of if not *the* world's leading center of ancient Near Eastern studies, whether gauged by faculty, research at home, expeditions abroad, or publications. To a striking degree, the institute today is very much the one Breasted envisioned in its continuation of programs such as the Epigraphic Survey, its wide geographic distribution of archaeological explorations, its philological studies and compilation of lexicons, its training of new generations of scholars, and its firm commitment to publishing results, and it reflects his appetite for adapting new technologies to attack old problems. Although Breasted's name has long since faded from collective memory, the institute's steady stream of news-making accomplishments have assured the university's association with Middle Eastern archaeology in the public mind. Where else would Indiana Jones have studied archaeology?[59]

In the years following Breasted's death, there were moments of recollection. One was sparked by publication of Charles Breasted's *Pioneer to the Past: The Story of James Henry Breasted, Archaeologist*, in 1943. That flurry of attention may have prompted the naming of a Second World War "Liberty Ship" the *James Henry Breasted* the following year. Years later, in 1985, a "longtime member" of the American Historical Association endowed the James Henry Breasted Prize for the "best book in English in any field of history" prior to 1000 CE. Neither these nor the Oriental Institute comprise the whole of Breasted's "lengthened shadow," however, and when Fosdick quoted Emerson, he was using "institution" a bit differently than the poet and essayist intended. The full quote begins: "Every true man is a cause, a country, and an age; requires infinite spaces and numbers and time fully to accomplish his design;—and posterity seems to follow his steps as a train of clients." After listing great figures from history and their lasting influence on civilization, Emerson continues, "An institution is the lengthened shadow of one man; . . . and all history resolves itself very easily into the biography of a few stout and earnest persons."

The "institution" Breasted left behind is more subtle and deeply imbedded in American culture than the Oriental Institute. It comprises many insights and ideas, ranging from the expression *Fertile Crescent* to a persistent conviction among American scholars and teachers that ancient history, especially of the Near East, is not only fascinating but still relevant to modern life. "Sharing with other Americans of his time the sense of living in an amorphous and traditionless present," one writer observed, Breasted "was impelled toward an all-embracing past, as if the past alone, being secure, could give meaning to the present."[60]

The scholars who wrote obituaries, research-journal memorials, and later works encapsulating Breasted's life approached it as though to illustrate Emerson's dictum on history's resolving itself into biography. Breasted's peers shared Charles's view of his father as a pioneer, though not necessarily to the past, but rather as a harbinger of his discipline's future, especially in America. Breasted was "the real founder of Egyptology in the New World"; he "more than any other . . . persuaded the American academic community that archaeology is a . . . necessary part of the study of man"; he was "the first American Orientalist to be regarded by competent European judges as fully equal to their best" and "the first American humanist scholar to be so highly respected in Europe"; he was mainly responsible for the "incomparably improved climate for humanities research in America"; for generations "the sense educated Americans had of the pre-classical era came from him"; and "he did for Egypt and the Fertile Crescent, what Pearl Buck did, in a different way, for China."

These themes recurred decades later in an opinion piece published in 1998 by the Archaeological Institute of America's president at the time, Stephen L. Dyson. Titled "An American Pioneer," it was written for the fiftieth anniversary issue of the association's magazine *Archaeology*. The group had just held its annual conference in Chicago, and the experience "roused memories and associations" for Dyson because it was Breasted's example "more than any other" that inspired him to pursue archaeology. A few years prior he had traveled to Rockford, Illinois, to give a lecture for the Archaeological Institute's local chapter, "which mustered its usual overflow audience," prompting Dyson to remark, "Breasted's spirit must be pleased to see such vigorous amateur interest in his hometown." Recalling that Breasted's ashes were in a Rockford cemetery, Dyson visited it to see "the grave in his native Midwestern soil." Having just completed a book on the history of classical archaeology in America, Dyson was particularly attuned to the field's historiography, and it heightened his regard for Breasted's career as "very much an American academic success story" and his life "the model of the American archaeologist."[61]

There are many terms that have been used to characterize Breasted's career: *Egyptologist, Orientalist, philologist, epigrapher, archaeologist, historian, teacher, mentor, humanist, academic entrepreneur, public intellectual, popularizer*, and more. *American* is the most commonly used one of all, but it is an awkward addition because birthplace is hardly a vocation. Yet his contemporaries and successors seemed compelled to add it to whichever one of the other terms they used. Perhaps from the perspective of other American scholars it is to lay claim to Breasted as one of their own. Perhaps from the perspective of scholars abroad it recognizes the distance of his origin, whether viewed from Europe or from the Middle East. Yet Breasted's work bridged not only widely separated lands but civilizations and eras as well. The juxtaposition of "American" with the other roles he played may, in the end, speak best to the trajectory of his life from the American Midwest to ancient Egypt and how that experience fired his passion to understand and shorten the distances between the worlds he traversed.

Epitaph

As Breasted reached his later years, "his talk . . . turned more frequently to the old days in Europe and Egypt, to the experiences of
his boyhood. He found and hung on the walls of his room old photographs" of his parents, the places he lived in Downers Grove and
Rockford, "where, as he had done more and more often . . . , he revisited the family plot in the old cemetery and lingered for an hour
of quiet self-communion." The plot is near a narrow drive that leads
up from the Greenwood Cemetery's main entrance to a small chapel
and Rockford Cemetery Association office next door. When Breasted
visited his parents' graves, he would drop by the office "for a little
chat" with the association's managing secretary. His family now all
passed, the family grave was Breasted's one tangible, remaining connection with Rockford, for which he retained a "warm sentiment and
a deep loyalty."

American burial customs are as diverse as the many peoples who
originally populated the continent or later migrated to it. Some Native Americans created permanent graves, others didn't. Immigrants
brought the practices of a variety of religious traditions. Religiously
like-minded settlers during the early colonial period, when most immigrants were Christian, cohered into religious communities and
placed their graveyards by churches they built in the midst of their

neighborhoods. Starting in the 1830s, with the advent of the "rural" cemetery movement, these practices began to change. Inspired by trends in France and England, and compelled by increasingly congested neighborhoods, Americans established graveyards on "elevated viewsites" at cities' outskirts. Greenwood Cemetery exemplifies that change. It was established in 1845, on 114 acres of land toward what was then the western edge of Rockford, along a rise above the Rock River. Like other American cemeteries established during the era, it represents changing fashions in landscape and monument design that occurred over the years. Some areas are neatly manicured with small grave markers set flush with the ground so they afford "unbroken lawn scenery" and a sense of "common" open space. Others have tall sheltering trees and scattered bushes among which are situated large monuments bearing statues or elaborate reliefs and even a few architecturally flamboyant mausoleums.

Although Breasted preferred cremation after his death, he left no guidance about where his ashes should be buried. Breasted's preference of cremation followed a trend that began after the Civil War. Reformers at the time, concerned about land conservation and public sanitation, pressed for "the practice of incineration and urn burial" as the best way to preserve and safely use dwindling open space as towns grew more crowded. The cremation movement expanded around the turn from the nineteenth into the twentieth century and no doubt influenced Breasted's thinking. But that's as far as his expressed preferences went, and the family had to decide where his ashes should be placed. Charles and the rest of the family were confident Breasted would want his ashes interred in Greenwood Cemetery, ample room remained in the family plot, and the urn's burial was readily arranged. One important detail remained, however: whether and how the grave might be marked.

Charles took the lead and decided the family should place over Breasted's grave a "simple stone from . . . Egypt." "To my mind," Charles wrote, "it is singularly fitting . . . that his ashes should be protected under" a stone "from a land to the study of whose wonderful history his life was so largely devoted." Charles hoped to "secure a block of the most weather-resisting stone from one of the several . . . historic sites in Egypt of which we know he was especially fond." Depending on the source, it could be sandstone, limestone, or granite. Charles thought it might be left "rough-hewn" and the family could add "a small bronze medallion or tablet bearing a minimum of appropriate wording and identification." The Cemetery Association secretary recommended granite because Rockford's weather was too hard on the softer stones. With the assistance of Harold Nelson, Charles sought a granite block from a still-working Aswan quarry in an area from which the stone for ancient Egypt's obelisks and statuary was extracted. Nelson traveled upriver to Aswan from Luxor and, working with a government school training workers to quarry the granite, he picked out an ap-

Fig. E.3 Aswan granite block for Breasted's grave marker, as delivered to Rockford, Illinois, 1937. Courtesy of the Oriental Institute, University of Chicago.

propriate shade and grain of stone. Charles "was deeply gratified" that Nelson handled the matter because the elder Breasted's affection for Nelson "was that of a father."[1]

Charles remained undecided about whether to have a bronze plaque mounted on the stone or to have the stone itself engraved. He was persuaded of the latter approach by Nelson, who could more clearly envision how the granite might be dressed and inscribed, perhaps because of his studies of ancient Egyptian inscriptions. As shipped, the stone was not quite square, measuring a bit over thirty-two inches on its longest sides, and it weighed over a ton. Although modern conveyances made its transport easier than it would have been in ancient Egypt, the block's weight required direct shipment from its port of entry to Rockford before Charles could see it. He was concerned about its being "covered with ugly and irregular chisel marks" because he wanted it to appear "as if it had been simply broken away from the quarry" and he wondered if its quality was good enough "that an inscription could be successfully cut." The Rockford memorial maker who received the stone sent photos showing there were chisel marks (figure E.3), and he recommended sandblasting the stone to remove them. He was confident he could engrave it and that it would bear up well. He also proposed creating a slightly recessed and smoothed "panel" into which he would carve a "deep sunk sandblast letter of a square Gothic or Roman Architectural type," a treatment reminiscent of ancient Rome's Latin inscriptions.[2]

The text had not been settled, however, and Charles turned to his siblings and stepmother for advice. To get the discussion going, he proposed six variations on the same basic wording, each of which contained certain elements: an opening line explaining the stone was from Aswan, Breasted's name, his birth and death dates with or without locations, and a closing line that summarized his profession with or without a quote from his writings. In a cover note to his sister, Charles wrote, "It is . . . a curious exercise of the mind, to attempt in a brief epitaph to summarize the life and career of any man of achievement." "This is especially true," he continued, for one "with whose work I was so intimately associated. If the resulting suggestions seem a little impersonal, it is because . . . I have tried to be especially objective. Good taste and common sense dictate that an inscription of this sort should be strictly devoid of sentimentality."

Among the six variations, the greatest differences were near the end, where Breasted's professions were listed: "Orientalist and archeologist, historian of the early world," "Archeologist and historian of the early world," and the last, by Charles's wife, simply "Historian and Archeologist." All concluded with slightly different iterations of one of Breasted's favorite themes: "The course of human progress is a rising line" or "trail." But the family concurred, as Imogen Breasted put it, that "brevity makes for dignity," and the agreed-upon inscription eliminated any quotation. If not for the reference to Aswan, Breasted's lifelong association with Egypt would not be evident. Perhaps they assumed the connection would be obvious, but its subtlety and the decision to identify Breasted as a historian and archaeologist rather than an Orientalist or Egyptologist were not discussed.[3]

For unknown reasons Charles asked the Cemetery Association secretary to keep the family's grave-marker plan "in strictest confidence" until it was decided. Once done, however, he felt "it would be appropriate to issue a brief statement to the Rockford press," which Charles volunteered to prepare. After a few months the stone was ready to be set in place, Charles apparently notified a *Rockford Morning Star* editor, and on a snowy day in January 1938 a photographer was dispatched to Greenwood Cemetery to capture the event. The result, a low-angle view that makes the quite heavy stone appear all that more massive (figure E.4), is reminiscent of how illustrators imagined ancient Egyptians dragged pyramid blocks into place.

Along with the photograph, the *Morning Star* ran an editorial titled "An Enduring Stone." The editors noted there "was no ritual" when the gravestone was set in place. "None was required. The simple placing of a stone kindred with the tombs and temples of Egypt above the ashes of James Henry Breasted, greatest of our Egyptologists, had its own meaning. He took his nurture from our valley, in death he returned to it, but near him in his sleep is a symbol of that far valley of the Nile to whose study" he devoted his life. The editors expressed the community's gratitude to the family for thus "enduringly linking through the memory of a great man our little midwestern river and the Nile," and they pledged

Granite Block Marks Grave Of Noted Archeologist

Fig. E.4 News photo of Breasted's grave marker being set in place, from *Rockford Morning Star*, 20 January 1938. Copyright *Rockford Register Star*. Used with permission.

that Breasted's "monument and memory and . . . spirit . . . will be revered as long as our river runs to the sea."[4]

A paradox of Egyptology is that most of what has been learned about ancient Egyptian life has been gleaned from works created to honor Egyptians in death and serve them in the hereafter. Like other Egyptologists, Breasted spent much of his life with the surviving evidence of virtually every aspect of ancient Egyptian death customs—mortuary temples, funerary chapels, grave stelae, coffin texts. The pharaohs and nobles who commissioned these material legacies poured fortunes and time into preparing for their sojourn in the afterlife. The hints of their daily lives that occasionally glimmer through these works are incidental to other, more somber purposes.

One might think that Breasted, as a scholar who spent so much time dwell-

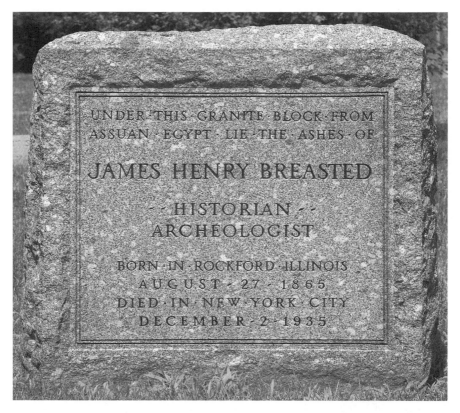

Fig. E.5 Breasted's grave marker inscription, completed ca. January 1938, Greenwood Cemetery, Rockford, Illinois. Photograph by author, June 2009.

ing in that particular valley of death, would have had more to say about how he wanted his to be handled. But as he reached the time of life when people might begin contemplating such things, he was far more interested in using his knowledge to mediate the travails of modern life and help the young prepare for an uncertain future. Unguided by his wishes, his heirs chose to mark his remains with a foreign stone inscribed with words that joined the most salient aspects of his life and accomplishments. In juxtaposing his American roots with his life's work in distant places, the curiously out-of-place stone in a conventional American cemetery also embodies the confrontations of tradition and change that he both lived and led.

Acknowledgments

This book began as a study of museums and pedagogy about two decades ago while I was working at the University of Chicago's Smart Museum of Art. The seed for the idea was planted a few years prior, however, during my conversations with the late Robert Rosenthal, who then headed what is now Chicago's Special Collections Research Center and was my supervisor as I ran its exhibitions program. He along with his good friend Neil Harris, Preston and Sterling Morton Professor Emeritus of History, University of Chicago, introduced me to the cultures of collecting and exhibitions through many discussions, some especially memorable for their settings: amid the aisles of Chicago's extraordinary rare book and manuscript collections.

I was fortunate to be working in Special Collections at a moment when the lives of several wonderful individuals intersected there. Our work routines were leavened by interesting discoveries among the books and archives that led to ideas for exhibitions or the simple pleasures of insights shared. Coffee breaks were a daily ritual, and chats about work were, for me, opportunities to learn about colleagues' areas of expertise and their ways of approaching larger questions. Among my fellow coffee breakers, there are three to whom I am especially indebted: Michael T. Ryan, now Director of the Rare Book and Manuscript Library of Columbia University; Daniel Meyer, now Associate Director of the Special Collections Research Center and University Archivist of the University of Chicago; and the late Jean F. Block, a volunteer who contributed her knowledge to many projects, the most memorable of which was transforming her work processing Chicago's first four decades of architectural records into the exhibition and catalog *The Uses of Gothic: Planning and Building the Campus of the University of Chicago, 1892–1932*. My wife once said that although I had earned undergraduate and graduate degrees well before starting work in Special Collections, my real education was acquired there. She's right.

My museums and pedagogy research started with the University of Chicago's museums and was supposed to branch out from there. The Oriental Institute proved so fascinating, however, that I never got beyond it. Figuring out how to proceed stymied me. I stopped work on that project to write another book, and I might not have completed this one without the encouragement of Jason Thompson. Scholars know him through his fundamental research on the history of Egyptology and others readers through his recent history of Egypt. I know him as an unusually kind and thoughtful friend who not only nudged me in just the right directions at just the right times but who also read and commented on the manuscript for this book. His advice on travel and study in Egypt, along with his personally guided tour of medieval Cairo, made my research in that remarkable country both productive and all the more meaningful.

The interrelations of ancient Near Eastern studies, the history of Egypt and other ancient civilizations, and the contexts of modern intellectual history in which scholars of Breasted's generation trained and worked are dizzyingly complex. Several scholars provided me with indispensable navigational aids, asked challenging questions, offered valuable advice, and shared their own research. Along with Jason Thompson, they include Donald M. Reid, Professor Emeritus of History, Georgia State University and Bruce Kuklick, Roy F. and Jeanette P. Nichols Professor of American History, University of Pennsylvania. William Kelly Simpson, Professor Emeritus of Egyptology, Yale University, and William Sumner, former Oriental Institute director and Professor Emeritus of Chicago's Department of Near Eastern Languages and Civilizations, were also very helpful.

J. Alex Schwartz, formerly Senior Editor of the University of Chicago Press, signed my project on and made several important suggestions that helped sharpen its focus and accelerate my writing. After Alex left, Susan M. Bielstein, Executive Editor of the Press, enthusiastically embraced the book and assisted me in further improving it; and Anthony Burton, Illustrations Editor, thoughtfully and skillfully guided it through the production process. I am also indebted to copy editor George Roupe for his many insightful suggestions, as well as his scrupulous care.

Some of my research was previously published in journals. Marcia Pointon, formerly editor of *Art History* and Professor Emeritus of Art History, University of Manchester, provided very clarifying advice on my article for her journal, and I am grateful to her as well as John L. Foster, formerly editor of the *Journal of the American Research Center in Egypt*, and the late Helene E. Roberts, formerly editor of *Visual Resources* and head of Visual Collections of the Fine Arts Library, Harvard University, for their support in seeing my research into print.

At the Oriental Institute, Karen Wilson, Research Associate and formerly Museum Curator, generously shared her knowledge with me over the years. Geoffrey Emberling, formerly Chief Curator of the Museum and Research Associate, mightily improved the manuscript for this book with his many searching and detailed comments. At Chicago House, I am obliged to W. Raymond Johnson, Director of the Epigraphic Survey, who graciously welcomed me for my research there, invited me to observe the survey's work at Medinet Habu and Luxor temple, and offered indispensable advice for my visits to other ancient sites in the area.

Much of my research was done in archival collections. The effectiveness of that kind of investigation depends entirely on the assistance of archivists overseeing them. It was my good luck to be assisted by friendly and generous professionals at each repository I consulted. Far and away the largest amount of this work was done in the Oriental Institute archives, and I was especially fortunate to have John Larson, Archivist, as my guide. Not only is John deeply familiar with Breasted's papers, he is an expert on Breasted's biography, the Oriental Institute's history, and the lore of Egyptology and ancient Near Eastern archaeology, and he generously shared that knowledge on many occasions. John is responsible for a very large repository of archaeological materials that are actively used by Oriental Institute research staff and students, as well as scholars from all over the world. Despite the unforeseen problems that often arise in such actively used collections, he always provided a warm welcome and was invariably patient and helpful. This book would simply not have been possible without his assistance.

The other archivists and curators to whom I am also beholden are my friend Daniel Meyer, University Archivist, University of Chicago; Kenneth W. Rose, Associate Director of Research and Education, and Thomas E. Rosenbaum, Archivist, Rockefeller Archive Center; Judith R. Goodstein, University Archivist Emeritus, California Institute of Technology; Janice F. Goldblum, Archivist, and Daniel Barbiero, Assistant Archivist, National Academy of Sciences; Jaromir Malek, Keeper of the Archive, Griffith Institute, Oxford University; and John Strom, Carnegie Institution of Washington. Several others helped me through correspondence: Janet Wallace, Museum Archivist, and Christopher Date, Assistant Museum Archivist, British Museum; Kimberly J. Butler, Archivist and Associate Director of Archives, North Central College; Cherie Miller, Registrar, and Joan Blocker, former Librarian and Archivist, Chicago Theological Seminary; and the late Ornit Ilan, former Curator, Rockefeller Museum, Israel. I am also grateful to Wayne State University Library's interlibrary loan staff for its assistance over the years.

My many archival research trips were underwritten by travel grants from the National Endowment for the Humanities, the Rockefeller Archives Center, and Wayne State University's Division of Research. Time to write was made possible with a summer-stipend grant from the National Endowment for the Humanities and research grants from Wayne State's Division of Research, Humanities Center, and College of Fine, Performing, and Communication Arts. I wish to acknowledge my college's former dean, Sharon Vasquez (now Provost of the University of Hartford) and Gloria Heppner, my university's Associate Vice President for Research, for their timely support with funds for illustrations and permissions. Thanks are also due to my colleagues in the James Pearson Duffy Department of Art and Art History, the college, and the university for approving two sabbaticals during which I worked on this book. And I am indebted to Marie Persha, the office supervisor of my department, for her tireless help in conducting the innumerable fiscal transactions associated with my grants and research trips.

There are many others to whom I am obliged for their assistance in large and small ways, and in neglecting to list their names I am no less grateful. In thanking the many colleagues who assisted me, I wish only to recognize how much I have learned from them. Because I'm a less than ideal student, however, errors of fact or interpretation no doubt found their way into this book, and I accept full responsibility for them.

I'm lucky to have friends and family members who are brilliant, probing intellects and who honor me with their interest in my work. Tom Meites and Lynn Frackman plied me with rigorous questions that pushed me to think harder and dig deeper as the book proceeded, their queries always accompanied by excellent food and wine in the comfort of their lovely home where I often stayed during my Chicago visits. My brother-in-law, John Paquette, tested my assumptions during our annual Clear Lake, Iowa, rendezvous in the warm and welcoming home of my mother-in-law, Joyce Paquette. Mary Paquette-Abt, my best friend and wife for a long time now, encouraged me when my spirits flagged and offered painful but necessary critiques when I strayed off the mark. Although we work in very different fields, her passions and interests broaden my own and make my endeavors all that much richer.

Notes

Abbreviations

AHA   American Historical Association

AHG   Alan H. Gardiner

AHoE   James Henry Breasted. *A History of Egypt: From the Earliest Times to the Persian Conquest*. New York: Charles Scribner's Sons, 1905.

AHotAE   James Henry Breasted. *A History of the Ancient Egyptians*. New York: Charles Scribner's Sons, 1908.

AR   [University of Chicago]. *Annual Register*. Chicago: University of Chicago, 1893–1930.

ARoE   James Henry Breasted, ed. and trans. *Ancient Records of Egypt: Historical Documents from the Earliest Times to the Persian Conquest*. 5 vols. Chicago: University of Chicago Press, 1906–7.

AT   James Henry Breasted. *Ancient Times: A History of the Early World, an Introduction to the Study of Ancient History and the Career of Early Man*. Boston: Ginn, 1916.

BTM   Board of Trustees Minutes, University of Chicago

CB   Charles Breasted (JHB's son)

CIW   Carnegie Institution of Washington Archives

CPI   Consumer Price Index, figures calculated at Samuel H. Williamson, "Seven Ways to Compute the Relative Value of a U.S. Dollar Amount—1774 to Present," MeasuringWorth.com, http://measuringworth.com/calculators/uscompare (accessed January 2011).

DOC   Director's Office Correspondence, Oriental Institute Archives, University of Chicago

DoRaT   James Henry Breasted. *Development of Religion and Thought in Ancient Egypt*. New York: Charles Scribner's Sons, 1912.

EttS	James Henry Breasted. *Egypt through the Stereoscope: A Journey through the Land of the Pharaohs*. New York: Underwood & Underwood, 1905.
FB	Frances (Hart) Breasted
FO	Foreign Office
FTG	Frederick T. Gates
GEB	General Education Board (a Rockefeller family foundation)
GEH	George Ellery Hale
GEHP	George Ellery Hale Papers, California Institute of Technology Archives
GI	Griffith Institute, Oxford University
HHN	Harold H. Nelson
IEB	International Education Board (a Rockefeller family foundation)
JDR Jr.	John D. Rockefeller Jr.
JHB	James Henry Breasted
JHBP	James Henry Breasted Papers, Oriental Institute Archives, University of Chicago
JHR	James Harvey Robinson
LtFHB	Letters to Frances Hart Breasted
LtP	Letters to Parents
NAS	National Academy of Sciences
NA	National Archives, United Kingdom
OI	Oriental Institute, University of Chicago
OIA	Oriental Institute Archives, University of Chicago
OoEH	James Henry Breasted and James Harvey Robinson, *Outlines of European History, Part I*. Boston: Ginn, 1914.
OMR	Office of the Messrs. Rockefeller
PP	Office of the President, General Files
PttP	Charles Breasted. *Pioneer to the Past: The Story of James H. Breasted, Archaeologist*. New York: Charles Scribner's Sons, 1943.
PttP:AA	Geoff Emberling, ed. *Pioneers to the Past: American Archaeologists in the Middle East, 1919–1920*, Oriental Institute Museum Publications, no. 30 (Chicago: Oriental Institute, University of Chicago, 2010).
RAC	Rockefeller Archive Center
RBF	Raymond B. Fosdick
RF	Rockefeller Foundation
RFA	Rockefeller Family Archives
RFH	Robert Francis Harper
RG	Record Group
TDoC	James Henry Breasted. *The Dawn of Conscience*. New York: Charles Scribner's Sons, 1933.
TOI	James Henry Breasted. *The Oriental Institute*. University of Chicago Survey, vol. 12. Chicago: University of Chicago Press, 1933.
UCA	University of Chicago Archives
WRH	William Rainey Harper
WWWE	Warren R. Dawson, Eric P. Uphill, and M. L. Bierbrier. *Who Was Who in Egyptology*. 3rd edition. London: Egypt Exploration Society, 1995.

Epigraph

1. "East Gone West," *Time* 18, no. 24 (14 December 1931): 23–24. By the 1930s JHB was heard on radio broadcasts across the nation, and his addresses were published in major newspapers: "To Broadcast," *Los Angeles Times*, 27 May 1932; "WSBT-WFAM Radio Highlights," *South Bend* [IN] *Tribune*, 26 May 1932; "The New Deal 4,000 Years Old, Study of Egyptian Life Shows," *New York Herald Tribune*, 30 December 1934.

2. Rockford's citizens followed JHB's career throughout his lifetime; see, for example,

"Rockford Man New Line Chief, Prof. James H. Breasted to Direct New University Department at Chicago," *Rockford Register-Gazette*, 5 August 1915; "Breasted's Work," *Rockford Illinois Republic*, 9 April 1929. For a more recent treatment: Jon W. Lund, *Rockford: An Illustrated History* (Chatsworth, CA: Windsor Publications, 1989), 81. On Freud, see chapter 9 of the present volume. While the influence of JHB's ideas in the worlds of scholarship and teaching has been explored to some extent, such cannot be said of his impact on literature. An exception is work on the poet and novelist H.D. (Hilda Doolittle): Marsha Bryant and Mary Ann Eaverly, "Egypto-Modernism: James Henry Breasted, H.D., and the New Past," *Modernism/ Modernity* 14, no. 3 (September 2007): 435–53. The poet and author Edgar Lee Masters was moved to write a poem titled "Ikhnaton" after reading JHB's *TDoC*, adding in a cover note to JHB, "It is a good thing for this world, for our country in particular, to have this historical a department so lucidly presented and with such satisfying authority." Edgar Lee Masters to JHB, 1 March 1934, JHB section in Pamphlet Files, OI Library. Unfortunately the poem appears to be lost. *Concise Dictionary of American Literary Biography: Realism, Naturalism, and Local Color, 1865–1917*, s.v. "Edgar Lee Masters." *Raiders of the Lost Ark*, 35 mm, 115 min., Lucasfilm, Ltd., San Rafael, CA, 1981. Lawrence Kasdan (screenplay) and George Lucas (story), *Raiders of the Lost Ark*, revised third draft (University City, CA: Medway Productions, August 1979). Anne Merrifield (Secretary to George Lucas) to Jeffrey Abt, 26 August 2003. The most concise but comprehensive overview of Lucas's work is in *Authors and Artists for Young Adults*, vol. 23, s.v. "George Lucas."

Chapter 1

1. William P. Schenk, "James Henry Breasted," *The Red and White of the Lake View High School of Chicago* (December 1932): 13, 26. *PttP*, 7–11, 34, 91. The Breasted's first child, a daughter, was born ten years before JHB and died before she reached her first birthday. Ida Breasted is buried in the family plot in Greenwood Cemetery, Rockford, Illinois: John Larson to Jeffrey Abt, 11 September 2009. On Charles Breasted's hardware business and travels for the Michigan Stove Company, see his business cards and correspondence in JHBP. His territory was later reduced to upper Illinois: Charles Breasted to JHB, 16 January 1887, LtP, JHBP. Charles Breasted addressed JHB as "Jimmy" through his teenage years and later as "Jim." See, for example, Charles Breasted to JHB, 23 February 1880, LtP, JHBP. [CB and JHB], publicity release, "Biographical Sketch of James Henry Breasted," 1 December 1935, Archival Biographical Files, UCA, 1–2. The release was written by CB in 1927–28 and edited by JHB between 1932 and 1934: "Biographical Sketch of James Henry Breasted," [n.d.], JHBP. JHB, "Sketchbook, Animals and Objects," 1877, JHBP.

2. *PttP*, 1, 11–13, 83–84, 91, 113. Schenk, "Breasted": 13, 26. The cannon story is from two slightly varying versions as told by JHB's sons: CB, manuscript, "Insert for Page 31" [for *PttP*], [ca. 1939–40]; and James Henry Breasted Jr. to CB, 21 July 1938, JHBP. The Breasted family's copy of the Layard book was the Harper and Brothers 1859 edition. It is inscribed "To Charles Breasted with a Merry Christmas from Hatty, 1869": Carla Hosein to John Larson, 20 September 2001 (e-mail note copied to Jeffrey Abt by John Larson). "Hatty" (or Hattie) was Charles Breasted's nickname for Harriet Breasted: *PttP*, 92. JHB occasionally mentioned the book: JHB, "The New Past," *University* [of Chicago] *Record*, new ser., 6, no. 4 (October 1920): 239; and *TDoC*, 3. JHB inherited it after his parents' deaths: "Schedule A of agreement executed August 18, 1937 between [James H.] Breasted [Jr.] and the University of Chicago," JHBP. Gordon Waterfield, *Layard of Nineveh* (New York: Frederick A. Praeger, 1968), passim (the Breasteds' edition is indexed under "*Nineveh and Babylon*"). See also Frederick N. Bohrer, "The Printed Orient: The Production of A. H. Layard's Earliest Works," *Culture and History* 11 (1992): 85–105.

3. *PttP*, 10, 13–14. The science exhibit quote and classmate's recollection are from Dean Kirn, "Old Friends—Pay Tribute," *The College Chronicle* [of North Central College], 10 December 1935, 2. North-Western, now called North Central College, was founded in 1861 as Plain-

field College in Plainfield, Illinois, by the Evangelical Association's "Conferences" of Illinois and several adjacent states. Its name was changed to North-Western in 1864, and it moved to Naperville in 1870, its name changing to North Central in 1926. By the time of JHB's enrollment it probably numbered about three hundred students. Clarence N. Roberts, *A Clear and Steady Light: A Brief History of North Central College* (Naperville, IL: North Central College, 1981). On JHB's course of study: Kimberly J. Butler (archivist/associate director of archives) and Karen Masden (student record keeper), both of North Central College, to Jeffrey Abt, 6 and 11 November 2002, respectively. On JHB's illness and his specialization in literature: JHB, "Vita," in "De hymnis in solem sub Rege Amenophide IV conceptis" (Ph.D. diss., Friedrich Wilhelm University [University of Berlin], 1894), n.p. The Latin original reads: "ut me totum litteris traderem, sed vere ineunte anni LXXXI domum redire gravi morbo vexatus coactus sum. Qua de causa mense Septembri anni LXXXIII demum studia litterarum intermissa in academia." For an example of his college work: JHB, manuscript, "Our Commonwealth, Oration for Cicero," [1883], JHBP. On the back of it JHB later observed, "Much merriment it has afforded me,—freshman eloquence par excellence."

On the trip east: JHB, "From Chicago to the Seashore via Washington" (sent to Charles and Harriet Breasted), 4 June 1884, and JHB to Charles and Harriet Breasted, 8 June 1884, LtP, JHBP. JHB's remarkable writing skills are evident even earlier: JHB, manuscript, "A Trip in a Schooner from Chicago to Green Bay," n.d. [ca. 1870s?], JHBP.

4. On JHB's pharmacy training: *The Alumni Record of the University of Illinois, Chicago Departments: Colleges of Medicine and Dentistry, School of Pharmacy*, ed. Carl Stephens (University of Illinois, 1921), [unpaged] "Class of 1886" listing. On resuming his pharmacy studies in fall 1885: "Boys and Girls Abroad," *North-Western College Chronicle* 7, no. 2 (November 1885): 10. The graduation appears to have been in February: "Local Brevities," *North-Western College Chronicle* 7, no. 5 (February 1886): 10. The degree was called a "Ph.G." Once an independent institution, the Chicago College of Pharmacy is now the College of Pharmacy, University of Illinois: College of Pharmacy, University of Illinois at Chicago, *History of the College of Pharmacy*, http://www.uic.edu/pharmacy/about_the_college/history.php (accessed July 2011). On JHB's illness: "Boys and Girls Abroad," *North-Western College Chronicle* 8, no. 7 (April 1887): 10.

5. For examples of Backus's religious ardor: Theodocia Backus to JHB, 26 February 1884, JHBP; and *PttP*, 21–22. Gaius Glenn Atkins and Frederick L. Fagley, *History of American Congregationalism* (Boston: Pilgrim, 1942), 342. *PttP*, 16–17. The Fiske quote is from Schenk, "Breasted": 13, 26. Daniel Taggart Fiske was a Congregationalist minister who graduated from Andover Theological Seminary (now Andover Newton Theological Seminary). He became a trustee in 1861 and was board of trustees president from 1885 to 1899. He is probably best known for his response to a theological controversy: D[aniel] T[aggart] Fiske, *The Creed of the Andover Theological Seminary* (Boston: Cupples, Upham, 1887). JHB to May Breasted, 26 October 1887, JHBP. On the dates of JHB's seminary attendance, see also "Local Brevities" and "Broadcast," *North-Western College Chronicle* 9, no. 2, and 10, no. 1 (November 1887 and October 1888): 12 and 8, respectively.

The seminary numbered 115 students when JHB entered but rose to 143 the following year. It moved to Hyde Park and affiliated with the University of Chicago in 1914. On its history: Arthur Cushman McGiffert Jr., *No Ivory Tower: The Story of the Chicago Theological Seminary* (Chicago: Chicago Theological Seminary, 1965); for the period from its founding through JHB's attendance: G. S. F. Savage, "A Chapter of the Early History of the Chicago Theological Seminary," *Illinois Society of Church History* 1 (1895): 11–23. On its association with Congregationalism: [Committee, Board of Directors, Chicago Theological Seminary], *Chicago Theological Seminary: Quarter Centennial Historical Sketch* (Chicago: Jameson & Morse, 1879), 7, 53ff.

For JHB's actual graduation date: North-Western College Register, College Department, entry for J. H. Breasted, 12 June 1890, Office of the Registrar, North Central College. JHB's diploma is dated 12 June 1888, but the last four digits of the Roman numerals were altered, suggesting that the original date was different, plausibly 1890. Diploma, Bachelor of Liberal Arts, North Western College, 12 June [1890?], Certificates, Diplomas, Medals folder, JHBP. JHB probably changed the date himself because he finished two years earlier: "revocare potui atque maturitatis examine perfunctus admissus sum anno LXXXVIII ad gradum 'Baccalaurie Artium'" (having completed my final examinations I was admitted in the year '88 to the degree of Bachelor of Arts): JHB, "Vita," in "De hymnis," n.p.

6. For a concise and still useful discussion of the Higher Criticism in biblical studies: *Encyclopaedia Britannica*, 11th ed., s.v. "Bible, (A) Old Testament, 3. Textual Criticism, 4. Higher Criticism," and "Bible, (B) New Testament, 3. Textual Criticism, 4. Higher Criticism." Curtiss literally imported the tools of the Higher Criticism to Chicago in the form of "the first critical, scholarly Old Testament library to be set up in America": *Dictionary of American Biography*, Base Set 1928–36, s.v. "Samuel Ives Curtiss, 1844–1904." Samuel Ives Curtiss, "Twenty-Five Years as a Seminary Professor, 1878–1903," *Chicago Seminary Quarterly* 3 (July 1903): 6–8. Siegfried Wagner, *Franz Delitzsch: Leben und Werk* (Munich: Kaiser, 1978). On Curtiss's affinity with Delitzsch: Samuel Ives Curtiss, *Franz Delitzsch: A Memorial Tribute* (Edinburgh: T. & T. Clark, 1891). On Americans and the Old Testament: James P. Wind, *The Bible and the University: The Messianic Vision of William Rainey Harper* (Atlanta: Scholars Press, 1987), 34n21. On Hebrew in America: Shalom Goldman, *God's Sacred Tongue: Hebrew and the American Imagination* (Chapel Hill: University of North Carolina Press, 2004).

7. *PttP*, 17–20, 22. JHB taught himself Greek as well during 1887–88: [CB and JHB], "Biographical Sketch," 2–3; "Quarum elementa nullo adiutore assecutus eram" (I acquired the rudiments in this field with no outside help), JHB, "Vita," in "De hymnis," n.p. JHB later used homemade flip cards to learn Aramaic, Syriac, Assyrian, Babylonian, Egyptian hieroglyphs (including hieratic and demotic), and Coptic, as well as modern Arabic, French, German, and some Italian. On JHB's Hebrew prize, "Broadcast," *North-Western College Chronicle* 10, no. 3 (December 1888): 9. For the context of Curtiss's Hebrew program: McGiffert, *No Ivory*, 76–77. The Ward quote is from Schenk, "Breasted," 26. The journal edited by Ward, the *New York Independent*, was a Congregationalist weekly that was distinguished by its strong antislavery position. *Dictionary of American Biography*, Base Set 1928–36, s.v. "William Hayes Ward." CB's story in *PttP* (pp. 22–23) about JHB's "wavering" and the conversation with his mother is told a bit differently by CB's younger brother: James Henry Breasted Jr. to CB, 14 September 1938, JHBP.

8. For a prehistory of the Higher Criticism in the United States: Jerry Wayne Brown, *The Rise of Biblical Criticism in America, 1800–1870: The New England Scholars* (Middletown, CT: Wesleyan University Press, 1969); and Ira V. Brown, "The Higher Criticism Comes to America, 1880–1900," *Journal of the Presbyterian Historical Society* 38, no. 4 (December 1960): 193–212, which also addresses the immediate theological and historical contexts of WRH's work, as well as his own contributions. Curtiss, "Twenty-Five": 9–10. The "documentary paradigm" observation is from John W. Boyer, "'Broad and Christian in the Fullest Sense': William Rainey Harper and the University of Chicago," *University of Chicago Record* 40, no. 2 (5 January 2006): 5. For WRH on Delitzsch: Wind, *Bible*, 56, 59. JHB's comment on WRH is in JHB, "John Merlin Powis Smith," *University* [of Chicago] *Record*, new ser., 19, no. 1 (January 1933): 72. For an uncritical but fairly comprehensive biography of WRH: Thomas Wakefield Goodspeed, *William Rainey Harper, First President of the University of Chicago* (Chicago: University of Chicago Press, 1928).

9. On the similarities in JHB's and WRH's backgrounds: Daniel Lee Meyer, "The Chicago Faculty and the University Ideal, 1891–1929" (Ph.D. diss., University of Chicago, 1994), 33. WRH's intellectual beginnings are treated in Wind, *Bible*, 27–37 (his dissertation title is from p. 30); and Boyer, "Broad," 3–4. *Dictionary of American Biography*, Base Set 1928–36, s.v. "William Dwight Whitney." See also Bruce Kuklick, *Puritans in Babylon: The Ancient Near East and American Intellectual Life, 1880–1930* (Princeton, NJ: Princeton University Press, 1996), 19–20.

10. Wind, *Bible*, 37–40 (the American Institute of Hebrew, which later became the Amer-

ican Institute of Sacred Literature, faded from the scene in the 1940s, p. 148); Boyer, "Broad," 4–6. The various permutations of the two journals are *The Hebrew Student* (1882–83), *The Old Testament Student* (1883–89), *The Old and New Testament Student* (1889–92), *The Biblical World* (1893–1920), and *The Journal of Religion* (1921–present); *Hebraica* (1884–95), *American Journal of Semitic Languages and Literatures* (1895–1941), and *Journal of Near Eastern Studies* (1942–present). *Biblical World* reached a circulation of about five thousand by the turn of the century. Boyer, "Broad": 23n33. On the journal's place in WRH's work: Wind, *Bible*, 49–50, 81–86. For the context of WRH's initiatives: Robert Lee Carter, "The 'Message of the Higher Criticism': The Bible Renaissance and Popular Education in America, 1880–1925" (Ph.D. diss., University of North Carolina at Chapel Hill, 1995). For the quote on *The Hebrew Student* and the Higher Criticism: Brown, "Higher Criticism," 200. See also William R. Hutchinson, *The Modernist Impulse in American Protestantism* (Cambridge, MA: Harvard University Press, 1976), 194.

11. Theodore Morrison, *Chautauqua: A Center for Education, Religion, and the Arts in America* (Chicago: University of Chicago Press, 1974), 73ff. On WRH's teaching: Brown, "Higher Criticism," 201. Wind, *Bible*, 40–46, on his work ethic, p. 5; on WRH's biblical theology and "messianic vision": Boyer, "Broad," 5–6. See also Joseph E. Gould, *The Chautauqua Movement: An Episode in the Continuing American Revolution* (Freedonia, NY: State University of New York, 1961).

12. *PttP*, 20–21, 24. On JHB's church services in Naperville and at his alma mater: "Broadcast" and "Chapel Diary," *North-Western College Chronicle* 10, 8 (May 1889): 10–11. $10 = $241 CPI 2009.

13. *PttP*, 9, 23–24. Charles Breasted Jr.'s birth and death dates, 10 May 1878 and 15 August 1889, are from his tombstone in the Breasted family plot in Greenwood Cemetery, Rockford, Illinois. JHB's only public acknowledgment of his grief over his brother's death is in Schenk, "Breasted," 26. JHB is listed as a partial registrant at the Chicago Theological Seminary during 1890. Joan Blocker (librarian and archivist) and Sheri Miller (registrar), Chicago Theological Seminary, telephone interviews by author, 11 November 2003.

14. Morrison, *Chautauqua*, 76. JHB supplemented his preparations for Yale by attending other summer sessions taught by WRH: [CB and JHB], "Biographical Sketch," 3. JHB to Charles Breasted, 20 July 1890, LtP, JHBP. Herbert Ershkowitz, *John Wanamaker: Philadelphia Merchant* (Conshohoc[k]en, PA: Combined Publishing, 1999), 43ff, 130ff. Wanamaker's tenure as postmaster general was colored by his religious beliefs as well as his entrepreneurial experience. He ended Sunday mail deliveries shortly after assuming the post (p. 91). For the national and international "Sunday School" movements in which Wanamaker was so active: E. Morris Fergusson, *Historic Chapters in Christian Education in America* (New York: Fleming H. Revell, 1935). JHB to Harriet Breasted, 29 June 1890, LtP, JHBP. On "problems of vocation": Robert M. Crunden, *Ministers of Reform: The Progressives' Achievement in American Civilization, 1889–1920* (New York: Basic Books, 1982), 278. For JHB's depiction of the sign: JHB to Breasted family, 27 July 1890, LtP, JHBP.

15. JHB to WRH, 1 September 1890, PP 1889–1925, 9:14, UCA. Thomas Wakefield Goodspeed, *A History of the University of Chicago: The First Quarter-Century*, 3rd ed. (Chicago: University of Chicago Press, 1972); Richard J. Storr, *Harper's University: The Beginnings* (Chicago: University of Chicago Press, 1966). On WRH's offer from Yale: Boyer, "Broad," 10; and Meyer, "Chicago Faculty," 53. JHB to Harriet Breasted, 25 September 1890, LtP, JHBP (emphasis JHB's).

16. *PttP*, 26. JHB to Charles Breasted, 2 November 1890, LtP, JHBP (emphasis JHB's). The course list follows the plan outlined in his Yale enrollment form, which was completed the same day he wrote home about his meeting with Harper. The form was for Yale's doctor of philosophy program, and Breasted indicated, in response to a question about his future course of study, "Probably Semitic Studies as <u>major</u> & philosophy as <u>minor</u>": JHB, "Enrollment Form," 25 September 1890, James Henry Breasted Student Folder, Manuscripts and Archives, Yale University Library (emphases JHB's). On RFH's "new scheme": JHB to Harriet

Breasted, 16 November 1890, LtP, JHBP. On RFH: J. Dyneley Prince, "Robert Francis Harper, 1864–1914," *American Journal of Semitic Languages and Literatures* 31, no. 2 (January 1915): 89–92; and *Dictionary of American Biography*, Base Set 1928–36, s.v. "Robert Francis Harper." For Friedrich Delitzsch, see closing paragraph of *Encyclopaedia Britannica*, 11th ed., s.v. "Franz Delitzsch." See also Kuklick, *Puritans*, 7, 18, 125–26, 177–78.

17. JHB to Charles Breasted, 24 November 1890, LtP, JHBP. On the Baptist community's role in the university's founding: Goodspeed, *History*, 1–97; and Storr, *Harper's*, 3–52. On WRH's reservations: Goodspeed, *History*, 107–29 (the quote is from p. 124). See also Boyer, "Broad," 9.

18. Charles Breasted to JHB, 9 November and 24 December 1890 (emphasis Charles Breasted's), JHB to Harriet Breasted, 15 February, (emphasis JHB's), JHB to Charles and Harriet Breasted, 8 March, JHB to Harriet Breasted, 13 March 1891, LtP, JHBP (emphases JHB's).

19. Charles Breasted to JHB, 18 April, JHB to Harriet and Charles Breasted, 22 April and 1 May 1891, LtP, JHBP. *PttP*, 30.

20. Laurence R. Veysey, *The Emergence of the American University* (Chicago: University of Chicago Press, 1965), 125–36. Carl Diehl, *Americans and German Scholarship, 1770–1870* (New Haven, CT: Yale University Press, 1978); Jurgen Herbst, *The German Historical School in American Scholarship: A Study in the Transfer of Culture* (Ithaca, NY: Cornell University Press, 1965); Wanda Durrett Bigham, "The Germanic Impact on the American Professor in the Late Nineteenth Century" (Ph.D. diss., University of Kentucky, 1978). For an entertaining and succinct study of Ranke relevant to this discussion: Anthony Grafton, *The Footnote: A Curious History* (Cambridge, MA: Harvard University Press, 1997), 34–93. *WWWE*, s.v. "(Karl) Richard Lepsius" and "Heinrich Ferdinand Karl Brugsch."

21. JHB to Charles Breasted, 18 April 1891, LtP, JHBP. The chart in figure 1.7 accompanies this letter; another version, apparently prepared for JHB's teaching ca. 1904–5, is located in JHB section, Pamphlet Files, OI Library. The revised chart was probably for a more general history course on ancient Near Eastern history JHB began offering about that time. He was added to Chicago's Department of History faculty roster, and "Oriental History" was added to his title in the 1904–5 academic year. On Playfair, the "father of modern graphical display": Howard Wainer, *Graphic Discovery: A Trout in the Milk and Other Visual Adventures* (Princeton, NJ: Princeton University Press, 2005). For a broader historical treatment of information graphics, including Minard's: Edward R. Tufte, *The Visual Display of Quantitative Information* (Cheshire, CT: Graphics Press, 1983). See also James Elkins, "Schemata," in *The Domain of Images* (Ithaca, NY: Cornell University Press, 1999), 213–35.

22. JHB to Charles Breasted, 6 May 1891, LtP, JHBP. The research was published as JHB, "The Order of the Sentence in the Hebrew Portions of Daniel," *Hebraica* 7, no. 4 (July 1891): 245–52. On the connection between JHB's *Hebraica* article and master's thesis: JHB, "Vita," in "De hymnis," n.p. As late as early July JHB had a different master's topic in mind—prayer as understood and practiced in the Old Testament: JHB to WRH, 3 July 1891, PP 1889–1925, 9:14, UCA.

23. *PttP*, 33. The date on JHB's Yale diploma originally read, in Roman numerals, "1892," but the last "I" was scraped off so that it now reads "1891." Diploma, Master of Arts, Yale University, [1891], Certificates, Diplomas, Medals folder, JHBP. As he had apparently done after completing his degree requirements at North-Western College earlier than his diploma indicated, JHB must have corrected his Yale diploma himself after completing that degree a year earlier than the diploma showed. Confusion over the doctoral residence requirement explains the degree's delay: [CB and JHB], "Biographical Sketch," 3; JHB, "Vita," in "De hymnis," n.p.

24. *PttP*, 34–39.

25. JHB to Harriet Breasted, 19 August and 11 September 1891, LtP, JHBP. *PttP*, 36–37. During JHB's studies at the Chicago Theological Seminary, it had a program to teach prospective ministers German so they could "work among the Germans in their own language": Cur-

tiss, "Twenty-Five Years,": 11. *Dictionary of American Biography*, Base Set 1928–36, s.v. "Hermann Eduard von Holst, 1841–1904." On von Holst's recruitment: Meyer, "Chicago Faculty," 95–96. On JHB's role in the "Berlin Collection" acquisition: Robert Rosenthal, "The Berlin Collection: A History," in *The Berlin Collection: Being a History and Exhibition* . . . (Chicago: University of Chicago Library, 1979), 3–20. On JHB's activities with the Harper family: JHB to WRH, 26 December 1891, PP 1889–1925, 9:14, UCA.

26. Bradner continued at Berlin through the 1892–93 academic year, whereupon he returned to the United States for a career in the Episcopal ministry and later the Episcopal Church's national education organization: Janet Elaine Gertz, "Biographical Sketch," in *Guide to the Lester Bradner Papers*, Manuscripts and Archives, Yale University Library (1982). *Dictionary of American Biography*, Base Set 1928–36, s.v. "Charles Foster Kent." On Humboldt's work outside of government: *Encyclopaedia Britannica*, 11th ed., s.v. "Karl Wilhelm von Humboldt." On the breadth of Berlin's curriculum and faculty specialties: "Table 6: Disciplines at the Philosophical Faculty of Berlin University, 1890–1930," in Peter Lundgreen, "Differentiation in German Higher Education," in *The Transformation of the Higher Learning, 1860–1930*, ed. Konrad H. Jarausch (Chicago: University of Chicago Press, 1983), 149–79. *PttP*, 41 (emphasis JHB's).

27. *WWWE*, s.v. "Jean Pierre Adolphe (Adolf) Erman." *PttP*, 39–40 (emphasis JHB's). JHB's University of Berlin transcript is in JHBP. JHB's translation of the Arabic text reads:

Berlin. Nov. The 22nd day.
I write to you on the day when we give praise unto God for his merciful provision unto us. Hence I heard a sermon in the church to-day upon this subject.—The speaker said: "Praise be unto God the one, the sole, the only, the unchangeable, the eternal, who was before created things when time was not, nor place. And he said 'Let it be' and there was light far-reaching which he shed forth from his secret place. Then he created from light, fire flaming, and the sea from the raging waters full of billows. Then he created from the waters and the fire the vault of heaven with its pinnacles and the stars and the clear-burning lights. And as for the heavens he formed them and the earth and the mountains he spread them out.—Therefore praise ye his name."

Arabic text and translation: JHB to Charles Breasted, 22 November 1891, LtP, JHBP. On JHB's practicing and mastering Arabic: *Dictionary of American Biography*, supplements 1–2: To 1940, s.v. "James Henry Breasted" (entry written by his former student Edith W. Ware); and W. F. Albright, "James Henry Breasted, Humanist," *American Scholar* 5, no. 3 (Summer 1936): 288.

28. JHB to WRH, 26 December 1891, PP 1889–1925, 9:14, UCA (emphases JHB's). JHB to Charles Breasted, [January? 1892], and to Breasted family, 1 May 1892, LtP, JHBP. For the full list of JHB's probable courses under Erman: Erika Endesfelder, *Die Ägyptologie an der Berliner Universität—Zur Geschichte eines Fachgebietes* (Berlin: Humboldt-Universität zu Berlin, 1988), 89–90 (for 1891–1894). Erman's teaching program is addressed on pp. 18–32.

29. Sethe later became one of the leading Egyptologists of the era and eventually succeeded Erman at Berlin, *WWWE*, s.v. "Kurt Heinrich Sethe." *PttP*, 43–48. The only other person mentioned by JHB was a "Smend," identified by his son as an Old Testament scholar and thus almost certainly Rudolf Smend, who would then have been teaching at the University of Göttingen. *Biographisch-bibliographisches Kirchenlexicon*, s.v. "Rudolf Smend," http://www.bautz.de/bbkl/s/smend_r.shtml (accessed May 2006). $0.88 = $21 CPI 2009.

30. *PttP*, 40, 48 (emphases JHB's). JHB to Harriet Breasted, 23 October and JHB to Charles Breasted, 13 November 1892, LtP, JHBP. BTM, 21 June 1892, 1:64, UCA. JHB also mentions a stipend from the University of Chicago in JHB, "Vita," in "De hymnis," n.p. JHB to Charles and Harriet Breasted, 19 December 1892, LtP, JHBP.

31. JHB to Charles and Harriet Breasted, 14 April 1893, LtP, JHBP. *WWWE*, s.v. "Urbain Bouriant." The Egyptian Museum building under Bouriant was, from 1863 to 1889, the pre-

decessor of today's museum: Donald Malcolm Reid, *Whose Pharaohs? Archaeology, Museums, and Egyptian National Identity from Napoleon to World War I* (Berkeley: University of California Press, 2002), 104–7. On JHB's museum-based studies: JHB to WRH, 26 December 1891, 25 April and 22 May 1892, PP 1889–1925, 9:14, UCA; JHB to Charles and Harriet Breasted, 20 November 1892, LtP, JHBP. The New Museum is one of five Berlin museums located on the Museuminsel (Museum Island) in the Spree River, which runs through the center of Berlin. For a brief sketch of the museum's and the collection's history prior to German unification: Virginia Jackson et al., eds., *Art Museums of the World*, (Westport, CT: Greenwood, 1987), s.v. "German Democratic Republic, Berlin, East."

32. JHB, "The Development of the Priesthood in Israel and Egypt—a Comparison," *Biblical World* 2, no. 1 (July 1893): 19–28. Adolf Erman, *Egyptian Grammar, with Table of Signs, Bibliography, Exercises for Reading, and Glossary*, translated with preface by James Henry Breasted (London: Williams and Norgate, 1894). On the grammar's importance: Warren R. Dawson, "James Henry Breasted," *Journal of the Royal Asiatic Society* (1936): 180. Charles Breasted to JHB, 12 July, JHB to Charles and Harriet Breasted, 17 October, JHB to Charles and Harriet Breasted, 12 November 1893, LtP, JHBP. On travel and acquisition funds: JHB to WRH, 17 March 1894, PP 1889–1925, 9:14, UCA. JHB to Charles and Harriet Breasted, 12 February 1894, LtP, JHBP. *PttP*, 49.

33. JHB to Charles and Harriet Breasted, 12 February 1894, LtP, JHBP. $10 = $257 CPI 2009. JHB to Charles and Harriet Breasted, 22 April 1894, LtP, JHBP. On the Hartford Theological Seminary: http://www.hartsem.edu/pages/about-us/history.aspx (accessed July 2010). BTM, 3 April 1894, 1:192, UCA. $800 = $21,100 CPI 2009. JHB stopped by the seminary on his return to Germany after visiting home in late summer 1893, apparently to explore job prospects there, and his father later approved of JHB's decision to accept the Chicago offer because it was closer to the family: Charles Breasted to JHB, 15 October 1893 and 6 May 1894, LtP, JHBP. Storr, *Harper's*, 60–61, 196; Wind, *Bible*, 81–86.

34. JHB to Charles and Harriet Breasted, 25 March 1894, 22 April 1894, LtP, JHBP (emphases JHB's).

35. On the setting and contents of JHB's examination: *PttP*, 52–57 (emphasis JHB's). *Encyclopaedia Britannica*, 11th ed., s.v. "Eberhard Schrader," "Eduard Zeller," and "Theodor Mommsen." Zeller published a number of books. It's likely that Breasted prepared with Zeller's *Die Philosophie der Griechen in ihrer geschichtlichen Entwicklung*, 3 vols. (Leipzig: O. R. Reisland, 1879–92) or an earlier edition of the same.

36. On the printing process for JHB's dissertation: JHB to Charles and Harriet Breasted, 25 March 1894, LtP, JHBP; and Luis Nadeau, "Office Copying & Printing Processes," in *Guide to the Identification of Prints and Photographs: Featuring a Chronological History of Reproduction Techniques* (Fredricton, NB: Luis Nadeau, 2002), 5 ("Autographic Process"). JHB, "De hymnis." The German text survives in what appears to be a working manuscript used to abridge and translate it into Latin. All the rectos contain the German text and hieroglyphic transcriptions, while the facing pages (versos) have the Latin translation with blanks left for the hieroglyphs, an approach that conforms with JHB's description of the autograph process. There is also space to the right of the Latin text with annotations in a hand other than JHB's. The German dissertation is about a third longer than the Latin version, with the additional material following in a separate section that JHB may originally have intended to publish in a second volume (see *DoRaT*, 329n1). Curiously titled "Einleitung," it contains about forty pages of additional hieroglyphic transcriptions with notes and German translations, the material consisting of forty texts divided into six sections. JHB, "De hymnis in solem sub Rege Amenophide IV conceptis. Comparantur cum hymnis polytheismum professis" (Ph.D. diss. [German text], Friedrich Wilhelm University [University of Berlin], [ca. May 1894]), JHBP. The subtitle, "Comparantur cum hymnis polytheismum professis" (Compared with hymns of the polytheistic confession), is not included in the Latin version.

37. *PttP*, 57. *WWWE*, s.v. "Ludwig Borchardt," "Carl Schmidt." JHB to Charles Breasted, 27 May 1894, LtP, JHBP (emphases JHB's). [Editorial staff], "George Stephen Goodspeed,"

Biblical World 25, no. 3 (March 1905): 169–72; *PttP*, 134. JHB and Goodspeed were close colleagues at Chicago until their friendship was cut short by the latter's untimely death in 1905.

38. JHB to WRH, 21 July and 11 September 1894, PP 1889–1925, 9:14, UCA. On Harper's plans for university museums: Goodspeed, *History*, 135, 366; and Jean F. Block, *The Uses of Gothic: Planning and Building the Campus of the University of Chicago, 1892–1932* (Chicago: University of Chicago Library, 1983), 34–41. JHB to Charles Breasted, 10 October 1894, LtP, JHBP. On the leave and acquisitions money: BTM, 25 September 1894, 1:258–59, UCA. $500 = $12,900 CPI 2009.

39. *PttP*, 26–28, 49–51 (emphasis JHB's). On JHB's serial courtships and the Rockford engagement: James Henry Breasted Jr. to CB, 14 September 1938, JHBP. Frances Hart's mother, Helen Watkins Hart (1845–1919), was the widow of George Hart (1834–88), originally of Lynchburg, Virginia, who evidently left her a "fortune": David Johnson, "Mountain View Cemetery," http://files.usgwarchives.org/ca/alameda/cemeteries/mtvview-h1.txt (accessed May 2006). *James Henry Breasted*, White's Biography Brochures ["From the National Cyclopedia of American Biography"] (New York: James T. White, 1927), n.p. JHB, "The Ladies," toast delivered at "Ambassador's Dinner in Berlin, Thanksgiving Day," 30 November 1893, JHBP. The Bible classes were initially taught at the American Church in Berlin, the pastor of which was instrumental in Harper's "Berlin Collection" acquisition: Rosenthal, "Berlin Collection," 4.

40. *PttP*, 50–51. JHB's father congratulated them on their engagement in Charles Breasted to JHB, 18 November 1893; his comment on Hart is in Charles Breasted to JHB, 15 April 1894, LtP, JHBP. JHB to Charles and Harriet Breasted, 22 April and 26 August 1894, LtP, JHBP.

41. *PttP*, 58–60. JHB was laying plans with Schmidt as early as April 1894: Charles Breasted to JHB, 13 May 1894, LtP, JHBP. On the "pocket camera": "Saver of Cities Sailing Today for Near East," *New York Tribune*, 4 February 1933; on the Kodak: JHB, "The New Crusade," *American Historical Review* 34, no. 2 (January 1929): 221; and on the "tupenny" camera: "Prof. Breasted Famous U. of C. Historian, Dies," *Chicago Daily Tribune*, 3 December 1935. On JHB's parents' approval and Erman: JHB to Charles and Harriet Breasted, 26 August 1894, LtP, JHBP. Hart's indecisiveness caused more than a little confusion for JHB's parents: Charles Breasted to JHB, 23 September, JHB to Harriet Breasted, 1 October, and JHB to Charles Breasted, 5 October 1894, LtP, JHBP. On the Reisners' attendance at the wedding, which came about because Reisner and JHB first met at an Archaeological Institute of America conference in 1890 while the former was a postgraduate student at Harvard and the latter was at Yale, and they met again in Berlin when JHB introduced Reisner to Erman: George A. Reisner, "James Henry Breasted: An Appreciation," *Egyptian Gazette* (14 December 1935). *WWWE*, s.v. "George Andrew Reisner." On Reisner's studies in Berlin: Endesfelder, *Die Ägyptologie*, 27. On picking up the pieces: James Henry Breasted Jr. to CB, 14 September 1938, JHBP.

42. *PttP*, 51–52. On Egypt's political background in relation to the development of Egyptology during this period: Reid, *Whose Pharaohs?*, 21–136.

43. *PttP*, 62–64, 66–67. JHB to Harriet and Charles Breasted, 4 November 1894, LtP, JHBP. On modes and costs of transportation in Egypt at the time: Reid, *Whose Pharaohs?*, 84–86. $10 = $264 CPI 2009.

44. JHB to WRH, 26 January 1895, PP 1889–1925, 9:14, UCA. *PttP*, 64–65. *WWWE*, s.v. "Jacques Jean Marie de Morgan" and "Émile Charles Adalbert Brugsch." On the Antiquities Service and Egyptian Museum: Reid, *Whose Pharaohs?*, 7–8, 56, 63, 93, 100, 104–6, 167.

45. *PttP*, 69, 71–72, 79.

46. *PttP*, 72–75. On the tomb's discovery: John A. Wilson, *Signs and Wonders upon Pharaoh: A History of American Egyptology* (Chicago: University of Chicago Press, 1964), 81–85.

47. *PttP*, 75–77. *WWWE*, s.v. "(Sir) William Matthew Flinders Petrie." JHB to Harriet and Charles Breasted, 2 February 1895, LtP, JHBP (emphases JHB's). On progressive history:

Ernst A. Breisach, *American Progressive History: An Experiment in Modernization* (Chicago: University of Chicago Press, 1993); see also chapter 5 of the present volume.

48. On the vandalism incident at el-Amârna and its influence on JHB's thoughts about transcription as preservation: Ludlow Bull, Ephraim A. Speiser, and Albert T. E. Olmstead, "James Henry Breasted, 1865–1935," *Journal of the American Oriental Society* 56 (1936): 119 and JHB to WRH, 26 January 1895, PP 1889–1925, 9:14, UCA. *PttP*, 78–80. On tourism in Egypt: Reid, *Whose Pharaohs?*, 64–92.

49. *PttP*, 80–83. *WWWE*, s.v. "(Charles) Paul Pierret" and "Gaston Camille Charles Maspero." JHB, "The Nations of the Ancient East," review of *The Struggle of the Nations: Egypt, Syria, and Assyria*, by G. Maspero, *The Dial* 22, no. 261 (1 May 1897): 282–84.

50. *PttP*, 80, 83–86. *WWWE*, s.v. "Earnest Alfred Thompson Wallis Budge."

Chapter 2

1. Jean F. Block, *Hyde Park Houses: An Informal History, 1856–1910* (Chicago: University of Chicago Press, 1978), 1–67; Block, *The Uses of Gothic: Planning and Building the Campus of the University of Chicago, 1892–1932* (Chicago: University of Chicago Library, 1983), 2–19, Walker Museum treated on pp. 34–36. *TOI*, 27. [CB and JHB], publicity release, "Biographical Sketch of James Henry Breasted," 1 December 1935, Archival Biographical Files, UCA, 4.

2. Meyer, "Chicago Faculty," 31, 69, 78; Boyer, "Broad," 16; Wind, *Bible*, 105, 129.

3. Goodspeed, *History*, 134–35; Storr, *Harper's*, 60–63. All the quotations are from Meyer, "Chicago Faculty," 58, 69, 74–75, 77–78, 137, except the one on Harper's work ethic: Boyer, "Broad," 12.

4. On the Baptist Union Theological Seminary's absorption into Chicago as its Divinity School and its relationship with Semitic Languages and Literatures: Wind, *Bible*, 72–80; and Boyer, "Broad," 10, quote on professional theology from p. 17. On the early years of biblical studies at Chicago and their connections with "ancillary disciplines": Robert W. Funk, "The Watershed of the American Biblical Tradition: The Chicago School, First Phase, 1892–1920," *Journal of Biblical Literature* 95, no. 1 (March 1976): 4–22. The bulwark observation is from John A. Wilson, "James Henry Breasted—The Idea of an Oriental Institute," in *Near Eastern Archaeology in the Twentieth Century: Essays in Honor of Nelson Glueck*, ed. James A. Sanders (New York: Doubleday, 1970), 42. On faculty recruitment: Storr, *Harper's*, 65–85; and Meyer, "Chicago Faculty," 81–130, especially pp. 121–27 for the first faculty's composition; quote from p. 122. BTM, 1 October 1894, 1:192, UCA. As an "Assistant," JHB held a nonstandard rank that was about in the middle of what would become the university's academic pecking order. From lowest to highest, the ranks were scholar, fellow, lecturer, reader, docent, tutor, assistant, instructor, assistant professor, associate professor, nonresident professor, professor, and head professor—the last being reserved for heads of departments: Meyer, "Chicago Faculty," 73. On JHB's promotion and additional appointments: BTM, 10 March and 28 April 1896, 1:408, 421, UCA.

5. $800 = $21,100 CPI 2009. When he was promoted to "Instructor" in 1896, JHB's salary was increased to $1,200 = $31,600 CPI 2009. Chicago's faculty salaries in its early years were competitive with leading American universities: Meyer, "Chicago Faculty," 81–84. JHB's parents moved to Englewood in anticipation of his university job but also for its good rail connections, probably for Charles Breasted's business travels: Charles Breasted to JHB, 11 January and 16 April 1891, LtP, JHBP. *PttP*, 89, 91–92; F.A.M.E. quote from p. 96. JHB, Notebook ["Pastor's Pocket Record"], 2 April 1895–17 March 1899, JHBP. JHB's talks were frequently publicized in local papers, see for example: "'Folklore of Ancient Egypt,' Subject Discussed by Dr. Breasted . . . ," *Chicago Daily Tribune*, 16 January 1896. Donald M. Scott, "The Popular Lecture and the Creation of a Public in Mid-Nineteenth-Century America," *Journal of American History* 66, no. 4 (March 1980): 791–809 (for another reference to "F.A.M.E.," see p. 793).

6. For a general history of Egyptomania that emphasizes its visual culture: James Stevens Curl, *The Egyptian Revival: Ancient Egypt as the Inspiration for Design Motifs in the West* (London: Routledge, 2005). See also the series of anthologies "Encounters with Ancient Egypt," published by the University College London Press, each of which contains essays on the reception of ancient Egypt in the West, such as Sally MacDonald and Michael Rice, eds., *Consuming Ancient Egypt* (London: Institute of Archaeology, UCL Press, 2003). On representations of Egypt at world's fairs and expositions: Reid, *Whose Pharaohs?*, 125–30, 304, 306, and see pp. 228–29, 253, for the World's Columbian Exposition. See also the beginning of Bruce G. Trigger, "Egyptology, Ancient Egypt, and the American Imagination," in *The American Discovery of Ancient Egypt*, ed. Nancy Thomas (Los Angeles: Los Angeles County Museum of Art and American Research Center in Egypt, 1995), 21–28. On Little Egypt and Orientalism in American burlesque and popular dance-theater culture: Donna Carlton, *Looking for Little Egypt* (Bloomington, IN: IDD Books, 1994). *PttP*, 96.

7. JHB, "Looking Eastward," summer 1896, Notes for address to Chicago Women's Club, JHBP. Peter Washington, *Madame Blavatsky's Baboon: A History of the Mystics, Mediums, and Misfits Who Brought Spiritualism to America* (New York: Schocken Books, 1995), 51ff. "The term 'theosophy' has in recent years [1910–11] obtained a somewhat wide currency in a restricted signification as denominating the beliefs and teachings of the Theosophical Society": *Encyclopaedia Britannica*, 11th ed., s.v. "Theosophy" (from subsection titled "Oriental Theosophy"). One scholar sets the Theosophical Society's rise in the context of other religious innovations, all formed in response to the "social disarray and pluralism of ways of life" in late-nineteenth-century America: Wind, *Bible*, 22.

8. On the department name change: Harry Pratt Judson to JHB, 6 October 1911, PP 1889–1925, 9:18, UCA. Edward W. Said, *Orientalism* (New York: Random House, 1978). There are a number of excellent responses to Said's argument: Albert Hourani, "Wednesday Afternoons Remembered," and "Islamic History, Middle Eastern History, Modern History" in *Islam in European Thought* (Cambridge: Cambridge University Press, 1991), 61–73, 90–115 (interestingly both essays quote JHB); and Kuklick, *Puritans*, 199–201, quote from p. 201.

9. On JHB's Pilgrim Congregational Church lectures: "Egypt and the Nile," *The Eye* (February 1896). *Prospectus of the Kenwood Centre of University Extension* (n.p.: n.p., 1896), which notes: "Many of the Lantern Views are from negatives made by Mr. Breasted in Egypt." JHB, *The History and Civilization of Egypt*, University Extension, Lecture-Study Department Syllabus no. 75 (Chicago: University of Chicago Press, 1898), 6, 9, 12.

10. JHB, *Egyptian Art: Syllabus of a Course of Six Lecture-Studies*, University Extension, Lecture-Study Department Syllabus no. 120 (Chicago: University of Chicago Press, 1898), 18.

11. *PttP*, 101.

12. On Haskell's design: Block, *Uses*, 36–41. Of the scant published information on Cobb, the best is "Henry I. Cobb Dies; a Noted Architect," *New York Times*, 28 March 1931. On the Haskell donation: Goodspeed, *History*, 277, 297–300. For the dedicatory speeches: [University of Chicago], *The President's Report*, Decennial Publications, 1st ser., vol. 1 (Chicago: University of Chicago Press, 1903), 543–44.

13. Goodspeed, *History*, 135–36, 366. Block, *Uses*, 34–36. [University of Chicago], *The President's Report*, cxxv–cxxvii, 440. [Board of Libraries, Laboratories, and Museums], Minutes, 30 January 1904, Board of Libraries, Laboratories, and Museums, UCA.

14. [Committee on Museums], Report, 5 April 1904, Board of Libraries, Laboratories, and Museums, UCA (emphases Committee's). On the existing museums under consideration, "The Department Museums recognized in the University Budget are Walker, Haskell, Zoology, Botany, History, Commerce": [Board of Museums], Minutes, 21 January 1905, Board of Libraries, Laboratories, and Museums, UCA.

15. [WRH], *Official Bulletin* [University of Chicago] 2 (April 1891), 23. On the university's library-system debates: Meyer, "Chicago Faculty," 249–310, quotes from pp. 249, 310. Frank R. Lillie to WRH, 19 January 1905, Board of Libraries, Laboratories, and Museums, UCA. On the university's increasingly constrained finances: Storr, *Harper's*, 341–58.

The leader among faculty members pressing Harper for more museum space was Thomas Chrowder Chamberlin, a prominent geologist recruited from the University of Wisconsin's presidency to be a member of Chicago's first faculty, head the geology department, and direct the Walker Museum. Chamberlin joined the faculty early enough to take part in the Walker Museum's planning; Harper appointed him director of museums within the Board of Libraries, Laboratories, and Museums, and his was a prominent voice in the museums study. Susan F. Schultz, "Thomas C. Chamberlin: An Intellectual Biography of a Geologist and Educator" (Ph.D. diss., University of Wisconsin–Madison, 1976), 13; Goodspeed, *History*, 368; Block, *Uses*, 34–36. Chamberlin likely studied in the museums of Beloit College and the University of Michigan. On their museums: http://www.beloit.edu/logan/history.php (accessed July 2010); Lewis B. Kellum, "The Museum of Paleontology," in *The University of Michigan: An Encyclopedic Survey*, ed. W. A. Donnelley, W. B. Shaw, and R. W. Gjelsness (Ann Arbor: University of Michigan Press, 1956), 487–502.

On the history of college museums in America in particular and their larger social context: Sally Gregory Kohlstedt, "Curiosities and Cabinets: Natural History Museums and Education on the Antebellum Campus," *Isis* 79, no. 3 (September 1988): 405–26; Kohlstedt, "Museums on Campus: A Tradition of Inquiry and Teaching," in *The American Development of Biology*, ed. Ronald Rainger, Keith R. Benson, and Jane Maienschein (Philadelphia: University of Pennsylvania Press, 1988), 15–47; Joel J. Orosz, *Curators and Culture: The Museum Movement in America, 1740–1870* (Tuscaloosa: University of Alabama Press, 1990).

16. For a brief sketch of museum history that sets the context for America's contributions: *Dictionary of Art*, s.v. "Museum, I. History." Daniel M. Fox, *Engines of Culture: Philanthropy and Art Museums* (New Brunswick, NJ: Transaction Publishers, 1995). Winifred E. Howe, *A History of the Metropolitan Museum of Art*, 2 vols. (New York: Metropolitan Museum of Art, 1913–46); Walter Muir Whitehill, *Museum of Fine Arts, Boston: A Centennial History*, 2 vols. (Cambridge, MA: Belknap Press, Harvard University, 1970); Vera L. Zolberg, "The Art Institute of Chicago: The Sociology of a Cultural Organization" (Ph.D. diss., University of Chicago, 1974); Jeffrey Abt, *A Museum on the Verge: A Socioeconomic History of the Detroit Institute of Arts, 1882–2000* (Detroit: Wayne State University Press, 2001).

The Art Institute of Chicago originated with the Chicago Academy of Design, founded in 1869, which was reorganized as the Chicago Academy of Fine Arts in 1879. It assumed its current name in 1882, the year Hutchinson became its president. The Columbian Museum of Chicago was renamed the Field Columbian Museum in 1894 to recognize Chicago merchant Marshall Field's $1 million donation to help make it permanent, and it was given its present name in 1905: [Field Museum of Natural History], *Handbook: Information Concerning the Museum—Its History, Building, Exhibits, Expeditions, Endowments and Activities*, 9th ed. (Chicago: Field Museum of Natural History, June 1940), 8–10. See also Paul D. Brinkman, "Frederic Ward Putnam, Chicago's Cultural Philanthropists, and the Founding of the Field Museum," *Museum History Journal* 2, no. 1 (January 2009): 73–100. There was talk of collaboration between the Columbian Museum and the university: see the correspondence between WRH and F. W. Skiff in Board of Libraries, Laboratories, and Museums file, UCA; Kohlstedt, "Museums," 28.

On cultural patronage in Chicago during this period: Helen Lefkowitz Horowitz, *Culture and the City: Cultural Philanthropy in Chicago from the 1880s to 1917* (Lexington: University Press of Kentucky, 1976). Appendix A, "Participation of the Cultural Philanthropists," 229–34, lists several Chicago leaders (including Ryerson and Hutchinson) along with their institutional affiliations throughout the city. *Dictionary of American Biography*, Base Set 1928–36, s.v. "Martin Antoine Ryerson" and "Charles Lawrence Hutchinson." On the Trustees' Committee on Buildings and Grounds: Block, *Uses*, 8–13.

17. The Museums Association of Great Britain was established in 1889 and the American Association of Museums was founded in 1906: Geoffrey Lewis, *For Instruction and Recreation: A Centenary History of the Museums Association* (London: Quiller, 1989); and Philip D. Spiess II, Terry Zeller, and Wilcomb E. Washburn, "75th Anniversary Issue," *Museum News*

75, no. 2 (March–April 1996): 38–63. Shortly after assuming his duties at Haskell, JHB sought the advice of others in the museum field, including Cyrus Adler, then a senior administrator of the Smithsonian Institution, for advice about planning Haskell's displays and collection development. WRH probably recommended Adler to JHB because they moved in the same circles, the former having trained in Semitic languages and literature at Johns Hopkins University, where he also taught in the Semitics department. Adler organized the United States contribution to the World's Columbian Exposition as well. Cyrus Adler to JHB, 14 June 1895, DOC. *Dictionary of American Biography*, supplements 1–2: To 1940, s.v. "Cyrus Adler."

Ayer collected books (which he donated to the Newberry Library in Chicago) and Native American artifacts (which he donated to the Field Museum), and he was instrumental in persuading Marshall Field to make his $1 million naming donation (see n. 16 above). *Dictionary of American Biography*, Base Set 1928–36, s.v. "Edward Everett Ayer." On his Field Museum acquisitions: Frank J. Yurco, "The Egyptian Collection and the Legacy of Edward E. Ayer," *Bulletin of the Field Museum of Natural History* 59, no. 10 (November 1988): 20–21. JHB to WRH, 26 January 1895, PP 1889–1925, 9:14, UCA. JHB to Edward E. Ayer, 2 and 7 January 1902, DOC; Edward E. Ayer to JHB, 6 and 8 January 1902, DOC.

18. WRH to JHB, 27 April and 2 September 1896, DOC; JHB to WRH, 6 September 1896, PP 1889–1925, 9:14, UCA. On JHB's collection-development activities, see also Goodspeed, *History*, 492; and *TOI*, 104. Some details on the sources of funding and objects received are in JHB, "Abstract of Report (and Views Used) before the 1st Annual Meeting of the C. S. E. R. (Chicago Society of Eg. Research)," lecture notes, 3 December 1897, JHBP. The society's member list includes Charles Hutchinson, Martin A. Ryerson, and another Chicago philanthropist JHB would later approach for assistance, Norman W. Harris: see JHB, List of Members, Chicago Society for Egyptian Research, 1898, DOC. $5 = $133 CPI 2009. The money for Petrie's work was initially directed through his Egyptian Research Account, which later became the British School of Archaeology in Egypt, and then through the Egyptian Exploration Fund, which later changed its name to the Egyptian Exploration Society. Some of the funding went to two Egyptologists trained by Petrie, James E. Quibell and Bernard P. Grenfell, and to Édouard Naville: *WWWE*, s.v. "James Edward Quibell," "Bernard Pyne Grenfell," and "(Henri) Édouard Naville." On the Egyptian Exploration Society, see T. G. H. James, ed., *Excavating in Egypt: The Egypt Exploration Society, 1882–1982* (Chicago: University of Chicago Press, 1982). *AR*, 1905–6, 122. On visualization: JHB to WRH, 8 March 1898, PP 1889–1925, 9:14, UCA.

Regarding the inventory: JHB to WRH, 23 June 1905, PP 1889–1925, 9:17, UCA; on the museum reorganization: JHB to WRH, 5 August 1902, PP 1889–1925, 9:15, UCA. JHB's plan included placing the "Assyrian Museum" and "Comparative Religion" on the first floor's south and north ends, respectively, and the "Palestinian Museum" on the south end of the third floor.

19. JHB, "Report of J. H. Breasted as a Member of the Committee Appointed on the Proposed Reorganization of Haskell Oriental Museum," memorandum to WRH, 7 July, JHB to WRH, 11 July 1905, PP 1889–1925, 9:17, UCA. *PttP*, 121–22, 132. On RFH's reputation elsewhere, which may have colored JHB's perceptions: Kuklick, *Puritans*, 31–33. For an instance where JHB wrongly complained about RFH: WRH to JHB, 22 May 1901, PP 1889–1925, 9:15, UCA. For the quote about RFH: *Dictionary of American Biography*, Base Set 1928–36, s.v. "Robert Francis Harper." The entry was written by George A. Barton, a fellow expert in Semitic languages: *Dictionary of American Biography*, supplement 3: 1941–45, s.v. "George Aaron Barton."

20. JHB, "A Sketch of Egyptian History with Special Reference to Palestine Down to about 950 B.C.," *Biblical World* 7, no. 6 (June 1896): 438–58. JHB, "The Nations of the Ancient East," review of *The Struggle of the Nations: Egypt, Syria, and Assyria*, by G. Maspero, *The Dial* 22, no. 261 (1 May 1897): 282–84 (the three-volume series was originally published as *Histoire ancienne des peuples de l'Orient classique* and this volume as *Premières mêlées des peuples*). JHB, review of *A History of Egypt*, vol. 2, *The XVIIth and XVIIIth Dynasties*, by W. M. Flinders Petrie, *American Historical Review* 2, no. 2 (January 1897): 324–27.

21. JHB, "Ramses II and the Princes in the Karnak Reliefs of Seti I," *Zeitschrift für ägyptische Sprache und Alterthumskunde* 37 (1899): 130–39. After on-site studies, JHB's Chicago successors found his conjectures were not entirely correct: The Epigraphic Survey, *Reliefs and Inscriptions at Karnak*, vol. 4: *The Battle Reliefs of King Sety I*, Oriental Institute Publications, no. 107 (Chicago: Oriental Institute, University of Chicago, 1986), 91–94; and William J. Murnane, appendix 5, "The Mysterious Mehy," in *The Road to Kadesh: A Historical Interpretation of the Battle Reliefs of King Sety I at Karnak*, Studies in Ancient Oriental Civilization, no. 42 (Chicago: Oriental Institute, University of Chicago, 1985), 163–75.

22. *PttP*, 102–3; JHB dates the origins of the documentary sources project to 1895 in *TOI*, 196. JHB's proposal is in JHB to WRH, 2 September 1898, PP 1889–1925, 9:14, UCA. The repositories JHB visited included the museums of "Berlin, London (British Museum, University College, Petrie Collections), Paris (Louvre, Bibliothèque Nationale, Musée Guimet), Vienna (Hofmuseum), Leyden, Munich, Rome (Vatican, and Capitoline), Florence (Museo Archeologico), Bologna, Naples, Turin, Pisa, Geneva, Lyons, Liverpool, and some others." *ARoE*, 1:xvi.

23. Some hints regarding the types of lenses JHB used during this period are in Gayton A. Douglass to JHB, 14 July 1899, DOC. JHB to Harriet Breasted, 17 September (on glass plates and itinerary) and 19 November 1899, LtP, JHBP (emphasis JHB's). On JHB's photography in Florence: JHB to Harriet Breasted, 21 October 1899, LtP, JHBP; on his photography in the Louvre: JHB to Harriet Breasted, 27 January 1901, LtP, JHBP. The photography did not go well at first, and within a few days of arriving in Vienna he reported difficulties processing his negatives, which at first he attributed to problems with the film, the camera, or underexposure. After a long night of experimenting in his hotel room, he discovered he was not fully mixing a prepared chemical cartridge. JHB to FB, 23 and 24 September 1899, LtFHB, JHBP. The stela in figure 2.10 was translated by JHB in *AHoE* (p. 170) as "I was one having goodly gardens and tall sycamores; I built a wide house in my city, and I excavated a tomb in my cemetery-cliff. I made a canal for my city and I ferried [people] over it in my boat. I was one ready [for service], leading my peasants until the coming of the day when it was well with me [day of death], when I gave it [his wealth] to my son by will." On photographing the stela: *AHoE*, 170n1. The article based on joined photographs (with illustration) is JHB, "King Harmhab and His Sakkara Tomb," *Zeitschrift für ägyptische Sprache und Alterthumskunde* 38 (1900): 47–50.

24. One of JHB's major discoveries that almost certainly would have caught Erman's attention was an important early religious text on a stela in the British Museum. It had been previously overlooked because it was difficult to read—the stela had been recycled as a millstone in antiquity. Breasted published a hand-drawn copy, edited transcription, and interpretation of it in several publications: JHB, "The Philosophy of a Memphite Priest," *Zeitschrift für ägyptische Sprache und Alterthumskunde* 39 (1901): 39–54; JHB, "The First Philosopher," *The Monist* 12, no. 3 (April 1902): 321–36; JHB, "The Philosophy of a Memphite Priest," *Open Court* 17 (1903): 458–79. The text was subsequently important to his observations about the religious revolution of Amenhotep IV (see chapters 3 and 5 of the present volume). JHB describes working on the stela in *DoRaT*, 43–47, and, more colorfully, in *TDoC*, 30–31. See also JHB to Harriet Breasted, 4 August 1901, LtP, JHBP.

On the beginning of JHB's work on the Egyptian dictionary: JHB to Harriet Breasted, 4 March 1900, LtP, JHBP; JHB to WRH, 27 March 1900, PP 1889–1925, 9:15, UCA; BTM, 26 June 1900, 2:414, UCA. *PttP*, 102–3.

25. JHB compared the English and Egyptian dictionary projects in the context of the Oriental Institute's Assyrian dictionary project, which began in October 1921: JHB, *The Oriental Institute of the University of Chicago: A Beginning and a Program* [preprint of article in *American Journal of Semitic Languages and Literatures* 38 (July 1922): 233–328] (Chicago: University of Chicago Press, 1922), 60–64; see also *TOI*, 383–87. JHB's earliest account of the project is in JHB, "Egyptian Dictionary, Germany's Great Contribution to Egyptology," *Current Encyclopedia: A Monthly Record of Human Progress* 1, no. 5 (November 1901): 598–600.

For the *New English Dictionary*'s origins and compilation, see "Historical Introduction," in *A New English Dictionary on Historical Principles*, ed. James A. H. Murray et al. (Oxford: Clarendon, 1888–1933), 1:v–xxiv. Jacob Grimm and Wilhelm Grimm, *Deutsches Wörterbuch*, 8 vols. (Leipzig: S. Hirzel, 1965). The *Deutsches Wörterbuch* was cited by one of the *New English Dictionary*'s earliest editors as a lexicographical model and, with regard to speedy completion, a rival. The *Deutsches Wörterbuch* wasn't completed until 1960: Lynda Mugglestone, "'Pioneers in the Untrodden Forest': The New English Dictionary," in *Lexicography and the OED: Pioneers in the Untrodden Forest*, ed. Lynda Mugglestone (Oxford: Oxford University Press, 2000), 4–5. *Encyclopaedia Britannica*, 11th ed., s.v. "Dictionary [under "Methods"]." *PttP*, 51.

26. The dictionary was published as *Wörterbuch der aegyptischen Sprache*, ed. Adolf Erman and Hermann Grapow, 13 vols. (Leipzig: J. C. Hinrichs, 1926–63). JHB's contributions are cited in 1:iii–vi. For some historical background on the dictionary: http://aaew .bbaw.de/dateien/informationen/geschichte.html (accessed July 2010). The *zettel* have been digitized and can be searched through another link on the same website: http://aaew.bbaw .de/dateien/dza/einfuehrung.html (accessed July 2010). The *zettel* copies retained by JHB are pasted into bound volumes: JHB, "Wörterbuch der aegyptischen Sprache: Zettel," 4 vols. (n.d.), JHBP.

27. *PttP*, 103–8. Heinrich Schaefer, *The Songs of an Egyptian Peasant*, translated by Frances Hart Breasted (Leipzig: J. C. Hinrichs, 1904). The Breasteds must have become acquainted with Schaefer (Schäfer in German) because he also was a student of Erman's. Schäfer later became director of the New Museum and a professor at the University of Berlin. *WWWE*, s.v. "Heinrich Schäfer." The 134 songs were collected primarily during 1900–1 from a guard working for the Egyptian Antiquities Service at Saqqara while Schäfer was excavating in the area. The text contains transliterations from the Arabic and FB's translations from Schäfer's German renderings, although she referred to the original Arabic with the assistance of Schäfer and her husband: "Author's Preface," vii–xiv, and "Translator's Preface," xv–xvi. JHB's flute lessons were with Emil Prill of the Berlin Royal Opera from 1892 to ca. 1927, who, CB says, was also *Kapellmeister* for Kaiser Friedrich Wilhelm II. CB continued to refer to the Ermans as his German uncle and aunt into his adulthood. See his correspondence with Käthe Erman in the 1936–39 file in CB's *PttP* correspondence records, OIA (Adolf Erman died in 1937). FB's quote is from Ps. 69:1–2. On CB's toy: JHB to "Englewoodenheads," 21 January 1900, LtP, JHBP. On JHB's time management: *Dictionary of American Biography*, supplements 1–2: To 1940, s.v. "James Henry Breasted" (entry written by his former student Edith W. Ware) and JHB to FB, 13 January 1924, LtFHB, JHBP. Charles Scribner's Sons Publishers, "The Egyptians," publication contract with JHB, 12 July 1898, Contracts with Publishers, JHBP. The series edited by Kurt Sethe was Untersuchungen zur Geschichte und Altertumskunde Aegyptens and included over twenty titles including JHB's. JHB to Charles and Harriet Breasted, 15 July 1900, LtP, JHBP (emphasis JHB's).

Chapter 3

1. JHB to Charles and Harriet Breasted, 15 July 1900, LtP, JHBP (emphasis JHB's). Underwood & Underwood to JHB, 31 July 1901, DOC.

2. William C. Darrah, *The World of Stereographs* (Gettysburg, PA: W. C. Darrah, 1977), 18–19, 46–48. On the beginnings of photography in the Middle East: Nissan N. Perez, *Focus East: Early Photography in the Near East, 1839–1885* (New York: Harry N. Abrams, 1988). On the beginnings of photography in Egypt: Deborah Bull and Donald Lorimer, *Up the Nile: A Photographic Excursion, Egypt 1839–1898* (New York: Clarkson N. Potter, 1979); and Kathleen Stewart Howe, *Excursions along the Nile: The Photographic Discovery of Ancient Egypt* (Santa Barbara, CA: Santa Barbara Museum of Art, 1993). For JHB's endorsement: *A Trip around the World* (New York: Underwood & Underwood, 1899). Underwood & Underwood to JHB, 31 July and 25 October 1901, DOC.

The photographer's name was Charles H. Baker, and JHB discusses the instructions in *EttS*, 14–15. JHB to Underwood & Underwood, 27 August 1903, DOC. JHB to Horace C. Fiske, 18 July 1905, DOC. A. E. Osborne to JHB, 10 February and 17 March 1905, DOC. Complete sets of the stereographs are hard to come by, but they have been published in a cleverly assembled CD-ROM version complete with cardstock 3-D viewing glasses: *Egypt through the Stereoscope: One Hundred Underwood & Underwood Stereographs, 1908*, CD-ROM, (n.p.: Golden Age Publishing, 2001). For printed reproductions of the images accompanied by an abridged version of JHB's narrative: JHB, *Egypt: A Journey through the Land of the Pharaohs*, abridged republication of *EttS* (New York: Camera/Graphics Press, 1979). An online transcription of the book interlaced with page scans, the images, maps, and—on the contents pages—hyperlinks to related online resources, is at http://scholarship.rice.edu/handle/1911/9166 (accessed July 2010). See also http://oi.uchicago.edu/pdf/stereoscope.pdf (accessed July 2010). Some of the original negatives are in Underwood & Underwood Glass Stereograph Collection, Archives Center, National Museum of American History, Smithsonian Institution, Washington, DC.

For a study of *EttS* that sets it in the context of Underwood & Underwood's other publications: Elaine A. Evans, "In the Sandals of Pharaoh: James Henry Breasted and the Stereoscope," McClung Museum, University of Tennessee, 12 July 2003, http://mcclungmuseum.utk.edu/newresearch/stereoscope/stereoscope.htm (accessed August 2006). However, the article contains some errors concerning JHB's biography and the history of Egyptology. On *EttS* as an example of "virtual travel": Lisa Spiro, "Egypt through the Stereoscope: Stereography and Virtual Travel," Connexions, Travelers in the Middle East Archives, http://cnx.org/content/m13785/latest/ (accessed December 2006).

3. *EttS*, 11–52, 352. For the source of JHB's *EttS* endorsement: [Underwood & Underwood], *The Underwood Travel System: What Is It?* (New York: Underwood & Underwood, n.d.), 9, reproduced in T. K. Treadwell, ed., *Underwood & Underwood's 1890 Stereoview Catalog and Other Documents* (n.p.: Institute for Photographic Research, 1995).

4. *EttS*, 122–25. The Baedeker map most likely used as JHB's source is from *Egypt: Handbook for Travelers*, 5th ed., [ed. Georg Steindorff] (Leipzig: Karl Baedeker, 1902), between pp. 112–13. On Steindorff's role in revising that edition, including maps and plans, see p. vi. *WWWE*, s.v. "Georg Steindorff." Belzoni was an early-nineteenth-century Italian explorer and excavator: *WWWE*, s.v. "Giovanni Battista Belzoni."

5. On one of the earliest uses of figures to establish scale in Egyptian photographs: Julia Ballerini, "The In Visibility of Hadji-Ishmael: Maxime Du Camp's 1850 Photographs of Egypt," in *The Body Imaged: The Human Form and Visual Culture since the Renaissance*, ed. Kathleen Adler and Marcia Pointon (Cambridge: Cambridge University Press, 1993), 147–60.

6. *EttS*, 294–95. The Medinet Habu scene is first listed in: *The Land of the Pharaohs through the Perfecscope, Describing a Series of One Hundred Original Stereoscopic Photographs* (New York: Underwood & Underwood, 1897). JHB discusses contemporary Egyptian life in positions 5, 7–9, and 67, and Westerners show up in positions 34, 43–44, and 87. On this type of Orientalist photography: Sarah Graham-Brown, *Images of Women: The Portrayal of Women in Photography of the Middle East, 1860–1950* (New York: Columbia University Press, 1988), 1–64, which includes, on p. 11, an Underwood & Underwood stereograph that almost certainly was taken on the same day and close to the very same location as figure 3.3: "Fig. 4—'Luncheon in the Temple of Medinet Habu, Thebes, Egypt,' Underwood & Underwood, 1897." This is a good example of the sort of Orientalist imagery, replete with erotic overtones, that JHB avoided. The last quote is from Howe, *Excursions along the Nile*, 27.

7. Darrah, *World*, 48. The price is from a 1908 "Underwood Travel System" price list reproduced in Treadwell, *Underwood & Underwood's*. $19 = $478 CPI 2009.

8. JHB to WRH, 28 July 1901, and WRH to JHB, 6 August 1901, PP 1889–1925, 9:15, UCA. BTM, 1 May 1902, 4:28, UCA. $2,083 = $53,600 CPI 2009.

9. *PttP*, 102; *TOI*, 196. JHB, *A New Chapter in the Life of Thutmose III*, Untersuchungen zur Geschichte und Altertumskunde Aegyptens, vol. 2, no. 2, ed. Kurt Sethe (Leipzig: J. C.

Hinrichs, 1900). JHB, "The Battle of Kadesh," in *Investigations Representing the Departments: Semitic Languages and Literatures, Biblical and Patristic Greek*, Decennial Publications, 1st ser., vol. 5 (Chicago: University of Chicago Press, 1904), 81–127; quote from p. 82. For a more recent treatment, including battlefield diagrams: John Baines and Jaromir Malek, "The Army," in *Cultural Atlas of Ancient Egypt*, rev. ed. (Abingdon, UK: Checkmark Books, 2000), 202–3.

10. *ARoE*, 1:xvii, 5:vi. The contract for *ARoE* was signed in 1901: University of Chicago [Press], publication contract with JHB for "Ancient Records of Egypt," 21 October 1901, Contracts with Publishers, JHBP. JHB dedicated *ARoE* to his father in the manuscript, but prior to publication—and without notifying JHB—WRH altered the dedication to acknowledge three donors who supported its publication: Martin A. Ryerson, Norman W. Harris, and Mary H. Wilmarth. BTM, 13 February 1905, 5:162–65, UCA. On Ryerson: chapter 2, n. 16 of the present volume; on Harris: chapter 6, n. 7. The change deeply angered JHB: *PttP*, 168.

Olof Alfred Toffteen was the student who compiled the indexes. He earned a baccalaureate degree in Sweden before immigrating to the United States, where he studied at Johns Hopkins prior to attending Chicago. He completed his doctorate in 1905 and remained in the area teaching Semitic languages and literatures for a short while at the Western Theological Seminary, then in Chicago. Toffteen did similar kinds of editorial work for others and published a handful of books and articles. *Who Was Who in America*, s.v. "Olof Alfred Toffteen." There are eleven indexes: "Divine Names," "Temples," "Kings of Egypt," "Persons," "Titles, Offices, and Ranks," "Geographical," "Miscellaneous [terms]," "Egyptian [words]," "Hebrew [words]," "Arabic [words]," and a concordance to Lepsius's *Denkmäler aus Aegypten und Aethiopien* (1849–59).

11. *ARoE*, 1:vi–vii. JHB, "Translator's Preface," in Erman, *Egyptian Grammar*, vi.

12. *ARoE*, 1:viii–xii.

13. *ARoE*, 1:vii, 3. JHB's discussion of the Seti I reliefs is in 3:59–68 (the illustration is on p. 61); his description of the Medinet Habu relief scenes and inscription translations are from 4:40–41.

14. *ARoE*, 1:xiii–xiv, xlii. All the typographical features of *ARoE* were in common use by this time, including numbered paragraphs for cross-references and citations. See, for example, Kurt Sethe, *Die Thronwirren unter den Nachfolgern Königs Thutmosis' I., Ihr Verlauf und ihre Bedeutung*, Untersuchungen zur Geschichte und Altertumskunde Aegyptens, vol. 1, ed. Kurt Sethe (Leipzig: J. C. Hinrichs, 1896), which JHB would have known because his book on Thutmose III was published in the same series.

15. *ARoE*, 1:3–4, 16–17.

16. *ARoE*, 1:17–20. John Ruskin, *Mornings in Florence, Being Simple Studies of Christian Art for English Travellers*, 3rd ed. (n.p.: George Allen, 1889). JHB's copy was a gift from FB while he was in Florence photographing inscriptions: JHB to FB, 20 October 1899, LtFHB, JHBP.

17. *ARoE*, 1:20–21.

18. *ARoE*, 1:25–48. On the current state of thinking about Egyptian chronology: Rolf Krauss, *Sothis- und Monddaten: Studien zur astronomischen und technischen Chronologie Altägyptens* (Hildesheim: Gerstenberg, 1985).

19. *ARoE* was initially sold for $12 per set and soon increased to $15 ($369 CPI 2009). The price information is from a University of Chicago Press advertisement in *Outlook* 83, no. 6 (9 June 1906): 2. F[rancis] Ll[ewellyn] Griffith, review of *ARoE*, vol. 1, *English Historical Review* 21, no. 83 (July 1906): 545–47; Griffith, review of *ARoE*, vols. 2–5, *English Historical Review* 23, no. 89 (January 1908): 109–10. *WWWE*, s.v. "Francis Llewellyn Griffith."

20. Christopher Johnston, review of *ARoE*, 5 vols., *American Historical Review* 12, no. 4 (July 1907): 858–61. Paul Haupt, "Christopher Johnston," *Journal of the American Oriental Society* 36 (1916): 339–41.

21. The 1923 and 1962 reprints were by the University of Chicago Press, the 1988 reprint in London under the Histories & Mysteries of Man imprint, and the 2001 reprint by the University of Illinois Press. The Arabic version is *Kitab tarikh Misr min aqdam al-'usur ilá al-fath al-Farisi*, ed. and trans. JHB, Hasan Kamal, and Muhammad Hasanayn Ghamrawi (Cairo: al-

Matba 'ah al-Amiriyah, 1929). *ARoE* is available online as pdf scans, and links to each volume are at http://onlinebooks.library.upenn.edu/webbin/book/lookupid?key=olbp12727 (accessed August 2010). Peter A. Piccione, "Introduction to the Illinois Paperback," in *Ancient Records of Egypt: Historical Documents from the Earliest Times to the Persian Conquest*, edited and translated by JHB, 5 vols. (Chicago: University of Chicago Press, 1906–7; reprint, Urbana: University of Illinois Press, 2001), 1:xxx, xxxvii, xli–xlii. On the extent to which Egyptological scholarship has advanced since *ARoE*'s publication, see the "Supplementary Bibliographies" Piccione compiled for the Illinois reprint edition: 5:vii–xix.

22. JHB's parents wrote often to him of Kent's visits, including the latter's take on university news and his unhappiness at Chicago, foreshadowing his departure for Brown: Charles Breasted to JHB, 5 November 1893, LtP, JHBP. Charles Scribner's Sons Publishers, "The Egyptians," publication contract with JHB, 12 July 1898, Contracts with Publishers, JHBP. JHB to Harriet Breasted, 28 January 1900, LtP, JHBP.

23. JHB to Charles and Harriet Breasted, 15 July 1900, LtP, JHBP. Charles Scribner's Sons to JHB, 21 September, 11 November, and 7 December 1903, Contracts with Publishers, JHBP. JHB to Charles Scribner's Sons, 4 October 1903, Contracts with Publishers, JHBP. *PttP*, 122.

24. Charles Scribner's Sons to JHB, 22 November 1904, 31 March 1905, Contracts with Publishers, JHBP. *PttP*, 138; *ARoE*, 5:vi; *AHoE*, xv. The preface is dated 1 September 1905. JHB's family also assisted his proofreading for *Ancient Records*: *ARoE*, 1:xvii.

25. On the Egyptian design motifs used on the cover, see the glossary in Curl, *Egyptian Revival*. The sale price is from "A History of Egypt," promotional flyer (New York: Charles Scribner's Sons, 1905). $5 = $126 CPI 2009.

26. *AHoE*, vii–xii (emphases JHB's). *Dictionary of Art Historians*, s.v. "Johannes Overbeck," http://www.dictionaryofarthistorians.org/overbeckj.htm (accessed August 2006).

27. *AHoE*, xii–xiv.

28. Bull, Speiser, and Olmstead, "Breasted," 115.

29. *AHoE*, 235–36, 240–41, 243–44.

30. *AHoE*, 356–58 (emphasis JHB's).

31. *AHoE*, 359–60, 363–64.

32. *AHoE*, 364–66, 371, 376; the parallel quotes are from pp. 373–74. The Aton hymn is not translated in *ARoE* because JHB considered it a religious text. An English translation based on the transcription in JHB, "De hymnis" was made by Francis Llewellyn Griffith for W. M. Flinders Petrie's *A History of Egypt: During the XVIIth and XVIIIth Dynasties* (London: Methuen, 1896), 214–18. JHB's translation in *AHoE* is similar though not identical, but he divides it into subsections similar to Griffith's. JHB was aware of the translation: *ARoE*, 2:403nb (which also indicates he planned to render another English translation in a subsequent [*ARoE*?] series "devoted to religion" that he never compiled).

33. *AHoE*, 376–78, 392. For a historiography of Amenhotep IV/Ikhnaton scholarship from the beginnings of Egyptology through the present that largely accepts JHB's findings: Erik Hornung, *Akhenaten and the Religion of Light*, trans. David Lorton (Ithaca, NY: Cornell University Press, 1999).

34. *AHoE*, 403, 474, 595.

35. Griffith, review of *ARoE*, vol. 1, 545. W. Max Müller, review of *AHoE*, *American Historical Review* 11, no. 4 (July 1906): 866–68. *WWWE*, s.v. "Wilhelm Max Müller."

36. Franklin H. Giddings, review of *AHoE*, *Political Science Quarterly* 21, no. 3 (September 1906): 529–31. *Dictionary of American Biography*, supplements 1–2: To 1940, s.v. "Franklin Henry Giddings"; *Encyclopedia of World Biography*, 2nd ed., s.v. "Franklin Henry Giddings." There are nearly twenty other unsigned reviews in the clippings file for *AHoE* in JHB section in Pamphlet Files, OI Library. They are virtually unanimous in echoing Giddings's praise. For a sampling, see "A New History of Egypt," *Book Buyer* (November 1905), and "The New History of Egypt," *Times Literary Supplement*, 30 March 1906, weekly edition.

37. The 1909 edition of *AHoE* was JHB's only revision. The dates of Scribner's reprints do

not follow a discernible rhythm and instead tend to suggest connections with spikes in public interest in Egypt: 1912, 1919 (end of World War I?), 1923, 1924 (discovery of Tutankhamun's tomb in 1922?), 1928, 1937, 1945, 1946 (publication of *PttP* in 1943?), 1948, 1950, 1951 (turmoil in the Middle East?), 1959, 1964. Other US editions were published by Bantam Books (1964, 1967), Simon Publications (2001), and Kessinger Publishers (2003). All the British editions were published by Hodder & Stoughton. The German edition is JHB, *Geschichte Aegyptens*, trans. Hermann Ranke (Berlin: K. Curtuis, 1910), reprinted by Phaidon in 1936 and 1954; the Russian edition is JHB, *Istoriia Egipta: s drevnieishikh vremen do persidskago zavoevaniia*, trans. V. Vikent'ev (Moscow: Kn-vo M. i S. Sabashnikovykh, 1915); the French edition is JHB, *Histoire de l'Egypte depuis les temps les plus reculés jusqu'à la conquête persane*, trans. Mahmoud Saba (Brussels: Vromant, 1926); the Hebrew edition is JHB, *Divre yeme mitsrayim: min ha-zeman ha-ḳadum be-yoter ve-'ad le-kibush ha-Parsi* (Tel Aviv: Sh. Fridman, 1956). The first Braille edition was published in 1910 and reissued in 1979. Piccione, "Introduction to the Illinois," xxxiv. The quote cited by Piccione is in *WWWE*, s.v. "James Henry Breasted."

38. *PttP*, 321, 130 (emphases JHB's).

Chapter 4

1. JHB to Harriet Breasted, 5 April 1900, LtP, JHBP (emphasis JHB's). On fund-raising to establish the University of Chicago: Goodspeed, *History*, 69–97, 273–96; Storr, *Harper's*, 35–52, 244–80. Rexmond C. Cochrane, *The National Academy of Sciences: The First Hundred Years, 1863–1963* (Washington, DC: National Academy of Sciences, 1978). Robert H. Bremner, *American Philanthropy*, 2nd ed. (Chicago: University of Chicago Press, 1988), 85–115. On "tackling" Yerkes: JHB to Harriet Breasted, 26 May 1901, LtP, JHBP. *Dictionary of American Biography*, Base Set 1928–36, s.v. "Charles Tyson Yerkes." On his observatory donation: Goodspeed, *History*, 307–18.

2. On the Carnegie Institution's founding: Nathan Reingold, "National Science Policy in a Private Foundation: The Carnegie Institution of Washington," in *The Organization of Knowledge in Modern America, 1860–1920*, ed. Alexandra Oleson and John Voss (Baltimore: Johns Hopkins University Press, 1979), 313–41. See also Howard S. Miller, *Dollars for Research: Science and Its Patrons in Nineteenth-Century America* (Seattle: University of Washington Press, 1970), 166–81.

3. On the Carnegie proposal: JHB to Daniel C. Gilman, 17 February 1902, JHB file, CIW. [Jean-François] Champollion, "Note remise au vice-roi pour la conservation des monuments de l'Égypte (Alexandrie, Novembre 1829)," in *Lettres écrites d'Égypte et de Nubie en 1828 et 1829* (Paris: Didot Frères, 1833), 454–61. George R. Gliddon, *An Appeal to the Antiquaries of Europe on the Destruction of the Monuments of Egypt* (London: James Madden, 1841). *WWWE*, s.v. "George Robins Gliddon." The incidental erosion and deliberate destruction of Egypt's antiquities continue to the present day: Edward Brovarski, "Epigraphic and Archaeological Documentation of Old Kingdom Tombs and Monuments at Giza and Saqqara," in *The American Discovery of Ancient Egypt: Essays*, ed. Nancy Thomas (Los Angeles: Los Angeles County Museum of Art, 1996), 25–26; and Chris Hedges, "Muslims' Ire Falls on Mummies, Too," *New York Times*, 23 July 1993.

4. JHB to Daniel C. Gilman, 17 February 1902. $10,000 = $257,000 CPI 2009.

5. JHB to Daniel C. Gilman, 17 February 1902. *Dictionary of American Biography*, Base Set 1928–36, s.v. "Daniel Coit Gilman." On Gilman's start at the Carnegie Institution: David Madsen, "Daniel Coit Gilman at the Carnegie Institution of Washington," *History of Education Quarterly* 9, no. 2 (Summer 1969): 154–86. See also *Carnegie Institution of Washington Year Book* [for 1902] (Washington, DC, January 1903), 174–81; and James Trefil and Margaret Hindle Hazen, *Good Seeing: A Century of Science at the Carnegie Institution of Washington, 1902–2002* (Washington, DC: Joseph Henry, 2002), 21–35, 44–47.

6. RBF, *John D. Rockefeller, Jr.: A Portrait* (New York: Harper and Brothers, 1956), 104, 107. FTG, *Chapters in My Life* (New York: Free Press, 1977), 91–124, 189–98. See also Good-

speed, *History*, passim; Storr, *Harper's*, passim. *Dictionary of American Biography*, Base Set 1928–36, s.v. "Frederick Taylor Gates." Besides JHB, the other Semitic department signatories to the application were Emil G. Hirsch (rabbinical literature and philosophy), Ira M. Price (Semitic languages and literatures), George S. Goodspeed (comparative religion and ancient history), RFH, James Richard Jewett (Arabic language and literature), W. Muss-Arnolt (biblical philology), and John M. P. Smith (Semitic languages and literatures). On JHB's role in the proposal's preparation: JHB to Harriet Breasted, 24 August 1907, LtP, JHBP.

7. JHB et al. to JDR Jr., 20 May 1903, RFA/RG 2, OMR/Educational Interests series, box 108, University of Chicago, folder Pledge—Bible Land Exploration, RAC. RBF, *Rockefeller, Jr.*, 125–33; Albert F. Schenkel, *The Rich Man and the Kingdom: John D. Rockefeller, Jr., and the Protestant Establishment*, Harvard Theological Studies 39 (Minneapolis: Fortress, 1995), 23–29.

8. WRH to FTG with attachment, "Estimate of Expense . . . for Exploration and Excavation in Bible Lands," 8 June 1903, RFA/RG 2, OMR/Educational Interests series, box 108, University of Chicago, folder Pledge—Bible Land Exploration, RAC (emphasis JHB's). $17,000 = $428,000 CPI 2009.

9. JDR Jr. to John D. Rockefeller, 18 June 1903, and John D. Rockefeller to JDR Jr., 25 June 1903, RFA/RG 2, OMR/Educational Interests series, University of Chicago, box 104, RAC. JDR Jr. to Martin A. Ryerson, 3 July 1903, RFA/RG 2, OMR/JDR Jr., Personal Papers, 48; Fosdick notes, vol. 18, RAC.

10. BTM, 23 June 1903, 4:282, UCA. *AR* (1904–5), 146. JHB to WRH, 18 September 1903, PP 1889–1925, 9:16, UCA; and WRH to JHB, 5 November 1903, PP 1889–1925, 9:16, UCA. *Dictionary of American Biography*, Base Set 1928–36, s.v. "Charles Lawrence Hutchinson." Trefil and Hazen, *Good Seeing*, 24. JHB to Charles L. Hutchinson, 27 August 1903, JHB file, CIW (emphases JHB's). JHB may also have written Hutchinson because he had been to Egypt in 1894 and, according to his friend Charles Kent, came back "very enthusiastic over the wonders of that ancient country": Charles Breasted to JHB, 24 June 1894, LtP, JHBP. It appears that neither JHB nor any of the others attempted to match the Rockefeller grant after this point.

11. WRH was very familiar with RFH's work at Nippur and the Babylonian Exploration Fund: see their correspondence, PP 1889–1925, 51:5–6, UCA. On RFH's association with the Babylonian Exploration Fund: Kuklick, *Puritans*, 31–34, 47, 55–56 (Kuklick also discusses the Babylonian Exploration Fund's founding, history, and intellectual context, pp. 26ff). Homer E. Moyer, ed., *Who's Who and What to See in Florida* (St. Petersburg: Current Historical Company of Florida, 1935), s.v. "Edgar James Banks"; and Edgar James Banks, *Bismya; or, the Lost City of Adab* (New York: G. P. Putnam's Sons, 1912), 2–4 (the story of the Ur committee is on pp. 4–17). On Banks's life into the 1940s, but not without factual mistakes and errors of interpretation: Ewa Wasilewska, "The Forgotten Indiana Jones," *The World & I* 15, no. 8 (August 2000): 160. Edgar James Banks, "Eight Oracular Responses to Esarhaddon," *Hebraica* 14, no. 4 (July 1898): 267–77. Edgar James Banks to WRH, 4 and 9 April 1900, PP 1889–1925, 51:7, UCA. Edgar James Banks, *A Plan for the Excavation of Mugheir, or Ur of the Chaldees, a Buried Babylonian City, the Birth-Place of the Biblical Abraham and Sarah* (Cambridgeport, MA: Louis F. Weston, [ca. 1889–1900]).

On the Rockefeller proposal and WRH's assistance: Edgar James Banks to WRH, 3 October and 12 November 1900, PP 1889–1925, 51:7, UCA; WRH to Edgar James Banks, 15 October 1900, PP 1889–1925, 51:7, UCA. WRH's *Biblical World* offer is in WRH to Edgar James Banks, 23 September 1901, PP 1889–1925, 51:7, UCA. Word of Banks's business dealings came from the Methodist Episcopal Church bishop in Washington, DC: John F. Hurst to WRH, 6 May 1902, PP 1889–1925, 51:7, UCA. On the terms of Banks's appointment and Bismaya expedition: BTM, 20 October 1903, 4:354–58, UCA. The beginning of the Bismaya expedition is recounted in Banks, *Bismya*, 24–33; see also Kuklick, *Puritans*, 109–10. WRH observed to the son of one of the "Ur Committee" members, "We feel that we are the heirs of the work of the first committee, and that we have inherited very much that is of value."

WRH to Henry Samuel Morton, 26 October 1903, PP 1889–1925, 51:7, UCA. On the excavations in the context of Assyriology more generally: C. Wade Meade, *Road to Babylon: Development of U.S. Assyriology* (Leiden: E. J. Brill, 1974), 64–70.

12. JHB was due back in Chicago to teach in the 1904 spring and summer quarters, but his leave was extended to balance his department's staffing: WRH to JHB, 25 January 1904, PP 1889–1925, 9:16, UCA. *WWWE*, s.v. "Eduard Meyer." *PttP*, 128–30.

13. Rumors concerning Bismaya legal problems and RFH's efforts to smooth them over are suggested in Hermann V. Hilprecht to WRH, 6 January 1905, PP 1889–1925, 51:7, UCA; WRH to Hermann V. Hilprecht, 9 January 1905, PP 1889–1925, 51:7, UCA; RFH to Hermann V. Hilprecht, 25 March 1905, PP 1889–1925, 51:7, UCA. On Banks's severance: Edgar James Banks to RFH, 27 April 1905, PP 1889–1925, 51:7, UCA; and Edgar James Banks, RFH, and WRH, Memorandum of Agreement, 27 April 1905, PP 1889–1925, 51:7, UCA. See also Banks, *Bismya*, passim (note the guarded prefatory note by Chicago's president). The entire text was reviewed by Chicago officials prior to publication "so as to avoid any difficulty": Edgar James Banks to Harry Pratt Judson, 9 October 1911, PP 1889–1925, 51:7, UCA; and [unsigned, secretary to the president, University of Chicago] to J. S. Dickerson, 20 May 1914, PP 1889–1925, 51:7, UCA. Also on the Bismaya expedition's demise: Kuklick, *Puritans*, 109–11; and Meyer, "Chicago Faculty," 346. On the expedition's archaeological yield: Karen Wilson, *Bismaya: Recovering the Lost City of Adab*, Oriental Institute Publications no. 137 (Chicago: Oriental Institute, University of Chicago, 2010). *PttP*, 132.

14. *PttP*, 140, 146, 155–56. On JHB's supplementary funding request and its rejection: BTM, 13 February 1905, 5:290, UCA. The resulting budgetary implications are addressed in JHB, field notes, "U of C Expedition—1905–06—Book I," 19 November 1905 [unpaged], JHBP. For a concise overview of Nubian history that sets the context for JHB's expedition, see John A. Larson, introduction to *Lost Nubia: A Centennial Exhibit of Photographs from the 1905–1907 Egyptian Expedition of the University of Chicago*, Oriental Institute Museum Publications, no. 24 (Chicago: Oriental Institute, University of Chicago, 2006), vii–x.

15. *PttP*, 156. JHB's equipment does not survive, but it is possible to get a sense of its specifications from his correspondence: Dr. Pulfrich (of Carl Zeiss company) to JHB, 23 October 1905, and [signature illegible] (of Curt Bentzin company) to Carl Zeiss (company), 24 October 1905, DOC; JHB, field notes, "U of C Expedition—1905–06—Book I," 19 November 1905 [unpaged], JHBP. JHB, "First Preliminary Report of the Egyptian Expedition," *American Journal of Semitic Languages and Literatures* 23, no. 1 (October 1906): 4–6. Nowhere does JHB identify the type of glass-plate negatives used. In the report just cited he indicates that orthochromatic plates were definitely not employed because they "do not keep in a warm climate like that of Nubia" (p. 48). The surviving prints suggest a fine-grain, high-contrast emulsion was used, which would also explain the long exposure times discussed below. In addition to the single large-format camera, he also purchased "a number of smaller instruments," including "a small camera" to photograph the recording process in action, as well as "remarkable architectural details": *PttP*, 181.

16. JHB, "First . . . Report," 6. On the Nadar lamp's design and operation: Chris Howes, *To Photograph Darkness: The History of Underground and Flash Photography* (Gloucester: Alan Sutton, 1989), 145. JHB's first photograph under artificial light may have been during the "honeymoon" trip when he took one in the interior of a pyramid "by calcium light": H. A. S., "James Henry Breasted, Ph.D.," [North-Western] *College Chronicle* 16, no. 8 (April 1895): 8. A calcium light was a lamp constructed by projecting a flame into a lime cylinder with a lens at the opposite end to concentrate the light. It was once used for stage lighting, hence the expression *limelight*.

17. *PttP*, 156–57. JHB, "First . . . Report," 12. JHB had heard that Persons was prone to illness and made provisional arrangements to hire Norman de Garis Davies (see below), who was then working in the Valley of the Kings, should Persons not be able to complete the trip: JHB, field notes, "U of C Expedition—1905–06—Book I," 26 December 1905 [unpaged], JHBP. On Koch and Persons, see Larson, *Lost Nubia*, xi. On the beginnings of American

Egyptology: Gerry D. Scott III, "Go Down into Egypt: The Dawn of American Egyptology," in *The American Discovery of Ancient Egypt*, ed. Nancy Thomas (Los Angeles: Los Angeles County Museum of Art, 1995), 37–47. See also Wilson, *Signs and Wonders*. On the beginnings of American epigraphic studies in Egypt and American studies in Nubia: James P. Allen, "The American Discovery of Middle Kingdom Texts," and Timothy Kendall, "The American Discovery of Meroitic Nubia and the Sudan," both in *The American Discovery of Ancient Egypt: Essays*, ed. Nancy Thomas (Los Angeles: Los Angeles County Museum of Art and American Research Center in Egypt, 1996), 44–47, 150–54.

18. JHB to Harriet Breasted, 30 December 1905, LtP, JHBP (emphasis JHB's). The boat's crew cost twenty-three Egyptian pounds per month: JHB, field notes, "U of C Expedition—1905–06—Book I," 26 December 1905 [unpaged], JHBP.

19. JHB, Field notes, "U of C Expedition—1905–06—Book I," 11 January 1906 [unpaged], JHBP. For the relationship between blueprints and cyanotypes: Luis Nadeau, "Office Copying & Printing Processes," in *Guide to the Identification of Prints and Photographs: Featuring a Chronological History of Reproduction Techniques* (Fredericton, NB: Luis Nadeau, 2002), 4. See also *Encyclopaedia Britannica*, 11th ed., s.v. "Sun Copying." Several cyanotypes taken and printed on site at Wadi Halfa survive. Most are labeled in red ink on the back in JHB's hand and collated, also in red ink, on an accompanying ground plan. See "Photo 2322, Neg. 1384/Halfa, Large Temple/Jan. 1906/Door IV (36 Temple No.)" and "Page of Notebook 1, Wadi Halfa, Thutmose III," in "Egypt: Wadi Halfa" photo file, OIA. That the cyanotypes proved ineffective in their first week of use is evident from another photograph bearing a typed label along the bottom edge that reads: "Black and white photo is much clearer than this blue print." See "Photo 2303, Neg. 1365/Halfa, Large Temple/Jan. 1906/(17 Temple No.)," in "Egypt: Wadi Halfa" photo file, OIA. The scale rod at the bottom of figure 4.2 was fashioned by Koch: JHB to Harriet Breasted, 14 January 1906, LtP, JHBP.

20. JHB, "First . . . Report," 10–12 (emphases JHB's). *Encyclopaedia Britannica*, 11th ed., s.v. "Philae."

21. The Wadi Halfa photography statistics are from JHB, field notes, "U of C Expedition—1905–06—Book I," 12 January 1906 [unpaged], JHBP. JHB, "First . . . Report," 6–10.

22. JHB, "First . . . Report," 27, 30; *PttP*, 166–67. The masthead was on a *dahabiyya* belonging to artist Henry Roderick Newman: JHB, field notes, "U of C Expedition—1905–06—Book I," 15 February 1906 [unpaged], JHBP; and *Dictionary of American Biography*, Base Set 1928–36, s.v. "Henry Roderick Newman."

23. *PttP*, 165–66.

24. *PttP*, 167, see also p. 125. WRH died of cancer: Goodspeed, *History*, 409–10. JHB to WRH, 26 March 1904, PP 1889–1925, 9:16, UCA. William Clark, *Academic Charisma and the Origins of the Research University* (Chicago: University of Chicago Press, 2006).

25. JHB, "First . . . Report," 38, 60–62.

26. JHB, "First . . . Report," 62–64; *PttP*, 169–72 (emphasis JHB's).

27. Goodspeed, *History*, 411–13; Meyer, "Chicago Faculty," 221–22. JHB, "First . . . Report," 1–64. The "snow" discovery was at Abu Simbel in a text where "Ramses [II] is praying that the winter journey of his Hittite visitors, as they pass through the northern countries . . . to Egypt, may be free from 'rain and *s-r-ḳ*.' In two different places the two words occur together, showing that their association is something natural and common. . . . It was curious indeed to come to snowless Nubia to find such a word for the first time" (pp. 26–27). *PttP*, 173.

28. On Schliephack and Davies: Larson, *Lost Nubia*, xi; and *WWWE*, s.v. "Norman de Garis Davies." *PttP*, 173–74, 181; JHB, "Second Preliminary Report of the Egyptian Expedition," *American Journal of Semitic Languages and Literatures* 25, no. 1 (October 1908): 3–4.

29. *PttP*, 174; JHB, "Second . . . Report," 3–4.

30. *PttP*, 176–77 (emphasis JHB's); JHB, "Second . . . Report," 4–5, 10–12.

31. *PttP*, 172, 178, 180–81.

32. *PttP*, 183–87; JHB, "Second . . . Report," 19–23. Decades later a marker was found

upriver from where JHB began looking, about halfway between the fourth and fifth cataracts: Vivian Davies, "Kurgus 2000: The Egyptian Inscriptions," *Sudan & Nubia* 5 (2001): 46–58. My thanks to Geoff Emberling for bringing this to my attention.

33. *PttP*, 189–91; JHB, "Second . . . Report," 25.

34. *PttP*, 193–200; JHB, "Second . . . Report," 39, 41–51.

35. *PttP*, 200; JHB, "Second . . . Report," 51–82. Quotes regarding the Gem-Aton temple are on pp. 77–78. See also JHB, field notes, "Notebook no. 8—Napata to Soleb, 1906–1907," 21–22 January 1907, pp. 56–63, JHBP. Heinrich Schaefer (Schäfer) was the scholar who compiled the Egyptian folk songs FB translated into English; see chapter 2 of the present volume.

36. JHB, "Second . . . Report," 83–96. Quotes regarding the Soleb temple are on pp. 87–88.

37. JHB, "Second . . . Report," 96–109; *PttP*, 205–6 (emphasis JHB's).

38. FTG to JHB, 16 October 1906, RFA/RG 1, JDR, Letterbooks, 1877–1918, vol. 358, ltr. 120, RAC. JHB had sent the book much earlier, probably in June when he sent a copy to JDR Jr.: JDR Jr. to JHB, 28 June 1906, RFA/RG 1, JDR, Letterbooks, 1877–1918, vol. 272, ltr. 233, RAC. JHB to FTG, 20 November 1906, RFA/RG 2, OMR/Educational Interests series, box 108, University of Chicago, folder Pledge—Bible Land Exploration, RAC (emphasis JHB's). FTG to JHB, 26 December 1906, RFA/RG 2, OMR/Educational Interests series, box 108, University of Chicago, folder Pledge—Bible Land Exploration, RAC.

39. JHB to FTG [draft letter/proposal], 13 April 1907, DOC. The final version appears to have been lost.

40. JHB to FTG, 13 April 1907. One estimate for construction of a boat is Hamburg and Anglo-American Nile Co. Nile Engine Works, "Specification and Estimate," 16 April 1907, DOC. $14,000 = $330,000 CPI 2009. The idea of a floating base station was pursued by others, some earlier and some later. For an earlier example, see Scott, "Go Down," 44–45 (figure 19); Allen, "American Discovery," 46; and Wilson, *Signs and Wonders*, 101–2. For a later example, see the illustration of "The Nile steamer *Fostat*, used as a floating field camp by several archaeological expeditions and later berthed in Cairo as the ARCE [American Research Center in Egypt] field office (1968–92)," in Nancy Thomas, "American Institutional Fieldwork in Egypt, 1899–1960," in *The American Discovery of Ancient Egypt*, ed. Nancy Thomas (Los Angeles: Los Angeles County Museum of Art, 1995), 71 (figure 41).

41. JHB to FTG, 13 April 1907. $354,450 and $434,450 = $8.35 and $10.20 million CPI 2009. "Goose" quote is from *PttP*, 209–10 (although CB is incorrect about the mailing date).

42. FTG to RFH, 16 May 1907, and RFH to FTG, 21 May 1907, RFA/RG 2, OMR/Educational Interests series, box 108, University of Chicago, folder Pledge—Bible Land Exploration, RAC. JHB learned of RFH's appointment to take over WRH's duties as head of Semitic Languages and Literatures, and thus the Oriental Exploration Fund, while still abroad the previous spring: RFH to JHB, 14 March 1906, DOC. For more details on the transition: Clara Z. Havill to CB, 26 April 1940, JHBP. FTG to JHB, 28 May 1907, RFA/RG 1, JDR, Letterbooks, 1877–1918, vol. 275, ltr. 477, RAC. JHB to FTG, 12 June and 26 June 1907, RFA/RG 2, OMR/Educational Interests series, box 108, University of Chicago, folder Pledge—Bible Land Exploration, RAC. JHB's "wandering life" confession is in JHB to RFH, 24 June 1907, DOC.

43. RFH to FTG [w/enc. draft letter RFH to JHB], 24 July 1907, RFA/RG 2, OMR/Educational Interests series, box 108, University of Chicago, folder Pledge—Bible Lands Exploration, RAC. On Judson's ascent to the presidency: Goodspeed, *History*, 413–14. RFH to FTG, 30 July, 31 July, and 1 August 1907, RFA/RG 2, OMR/Educational Interests series, box 108, University of Chicago, folder Pledge—Bible Lands Exploration, RAC. *WWWE*, s.v. "Harold Hayden Nelson." Cable quotations are from JHB to Harriet Breasted, 24 August 1907, LtP, JHBP.

44. JHB had been suspicious of RFH for several years by this point, see chapter 2. Examples of RFH's backing JHB are in RFH to JHB, 26 October 1906 and 10 April 1907, DOC; the $500 supplement is discussed in RFH to JHB, 17 January 1907, DOC. On his encourage-

ment concerning the FTG initiative: RFH to JHB, 22 April and 1 May 1907, DOC. His efforts to secure alternate sources after the FTG proposal failed are in RFH to JHB, 31 May and 17 June 1907, DOC. On JHB's mixed signals: JHB to RFH, 21 May, 28 June, and 31 July 1907, DOC. RFH's peace offerings are in RFH to JHB, 6 November and 17 December 1907 and 18 March 1908, DOC.

45. The letter to Burton is quoted from JHB to Harriet Breasted, 24 August 1907, LtP, JHBP. Ernest D. Burton to JHB, 11 September 1907, JHBP (emphasis Burton's). Thomas Wakefield Goodspeed, *Ernest De Witt Burton: A Biographical Sketch* (Chicago: University of Chicago Press, 1926); see also *Dictionary of American Biography*, Base Set 1928–36, s.v. "Ernest De Witt Burton." On the university's finances during this period: Storr, *Harper's*, 341–58. *PttP*, 212–13.

46. JHB to Harriet Breasted, 24 August 1907, LtP, JHBP. Sale of the equipment to the Berlin academy is mentioned in JHB to GEH, 1 May 1914, GEHP; see also JHB to J. M. Powis Smith, 1 February 1909, DOC, and *TOI*, 408–9. The sale was probably stimulated by a request from Henry George Lyons, then director in chief of Egypt's Survey Department, who had called on JHB "for the purpose of securing a resume of [JHB's recording] methods, which the government desires to apply to the work of copying and publishing the records in the temple of Philae and other temples immediately above the Assuan dam, as the government is about to raise the dam, and is making an effort to secure records of the monuments endangered by the . . . rise of the waters." See JHB to FTG [draft letter/proposal], 13 April 1907, DOC. *WWWE*, s.v. "Henry George Lyons." RFH planned to use the equipment after the Germans; it was shipped to Beirut but not used and eventually returned to Chicago: RFH to JHB, 4 April 1909, DOC. RFH tried to obtain a permit to dig at "Mugheir" (Muqaiyir, site of the Babylonian city of Ur, about a hundred miles northwest of Basra, Iraq) in 1908 and apparently gave up the following year: Harry Pratt Judson to FTG, 14 May 1908, RFA/RG 2, OMR/Educational Interests series, box 103, Univ. of Chicago, 1899–1909, misc., RAC; and RFH to Harry Pratt Judson, 28 September 1908, PP 1889–1925, 51:7, UCA. The photographic equipment used by the expedition is not preserved at the OI, a loss partially explained by JHB's loan of "a complete set of Zeiss lenses of large size" to Koch prior to the First World War for unspecified "scientific work. Late in the war he carried them off to the Balkans for use in making war pictures and lost them there": JHB to AHG, 23 December 1921, DOC. See also HHN to T. George Allen, 24 July 1925, DOC. Fortunately Koch survived the war.

On JHB's subsequent attitude toward RFH: *PttP*, 214, 216; JHB's colleagues had their own reservations about RFH. See, for example, John M. P. Smith to RFH, 2 December 1908, and John M. P. Smith to JHB, 8 September 1909, DOC. On the gradual dissipation of the Oriental Exploration Fund: Harry Pratt Judson to FTG, 14 May 1908, RFA/RG 2, OMR/Educational Interests series, box 103, Univ. of Chicago, 1899–1909, misc., RAC; Harry Pratt Judson to FTG, 12 January 1910, RFA/RG 2, OMR/Educational Interests series, box 108, University of Chicago, folder General: 1903–1930, RAC. Five thousand dollars remained from the initial gift in 1910, and Judson wondered if the donor still wanted to pursue FTG's idea of seeking a permit for renewed excavations in Mesopotamia: Harry Pratt Judson to JDR Jr., 31 October 1910, RFA/RG 2, OMR/Educational Interests series, box 108, University of Chicago, folder Pledge—Bible Lands Exploration, RAC. In response to Judson's letter, JDR Jr. sought the advice of FTG, who counseled they should "retire from the field of private exploration" and leave it to England, France, Germany, and other governments: FTG to JDR Jr., 5 November 1910, RFA/RG 2, OMR/Educational Interests series, box 108, University of Chicago, folder Pledge—Bible Lands Exploration, RAC. One hundred dollars remained on account by 1919: JHB to Harry Pratt Judson, 17 May 1919, PP 1889–1925, 9:19, UCA. On the Harvard proposition: JHB to Harriet Breasted, 20 October 1907, LtP, JHBP.

The quantity of photographs taken is an estimate based in part on their OIA accession card (accession no. 201, 18 August 1919), the contents of which were conveyed to me by John A. Larson, museum archivist, OIA: Larson to Abt, 14 May 1997. George Reisner mentions JHB's sharing the photographs with fellow scholars in Reisner, "James Henry Breasted."

JHB hoped the materials would be published as late as 1933, by which point he had turned over the project to one of his OI colleagues: *TOI*, 29–30, 408. See also John A. Wilson, *Thousands of Years: An Archaeologist's Search for Ancient Egypt* (New York: Charles Scribner's Sons, 1972), 65. Reproductions of nearly eleven hundred of the two expeditions' epigraphic studies, landscape views, and contemporary scenes are available in microfiche: *The 1905–1907 Breasted Expeditions to Egypt and the Sudan: A Photographic Study* (Chicago: University of Chicago Press, 1975) and on the worldwide web, http://oi.uchicago.edu/museum/collections/pa/breasted/intro.html (accessed December 2010). A selection of views with excerpts from JHB's field notebooks is included in Larson, *Lost Nubia*. On JHB's failure to return to Nubia: *PttP*, 208.

Chapter 5

1. *PttP*, 210–15. RFH to JHB, 17 December 1907 and 18 March 1908, DOC. JHB, "Second . . . Report."

2. *AHotAE* is dedicated to JHB's father. For the inception of *AHotAE*, see chapter 3 of the present volume. *Dictionary of American Biography*, Base Set 1928–36, s.v. "Frank Knight Sanders." On the Historical Series for Bible Students: *AHotAE*, ii; an identical statement was published in the other volumes, for example, George Stephen Goodspeed, *A History of the Babylonians and Assyrians* (New York: Charles Scribner's Sons, 1902). On positivist, "scientific" historical writing in America and its links with the German training and scholarly traditions to which Kent and JHB were heirs: John Higham, *History: Professional Scholarship in America*, updated ed. (Baltimore: Johns Hopkins University Press, 1989), 92–103.

3. *AHotAE*, viii–ix (emphasis JHB's). "Book Notes," *Political Science Quarterly* 24, no. 1 (March 1909): 176–77. There are nearly thirty reviews in the clippings file for *AHotAE* in the JHB section in Pamphlet Files, OI Library. They are virtually unanimous in echoing this reviewer's praise. The publication pattern for reprints is similar to *AHoE*'s: see chapter 3, n. 37, in the present volume.

4. The Divinity School appointment was originally in its Department of Old Testament Literature and Interpretation, but in the 1897–98 academic year was moved to the newly formed "Divinity Conference," made up of faculty members "whose work is closely related" to the Divinity School: *AR*, 1897–98. JHB's appointment in the Department of General Literature ("formerly Department of Literature [in English, which] has for its theoretic basis the unity of all literatures") ran from 1904 to 1909 only: *AR* for those years inclusively. On the Department of Archaeology's founding: [University of Chicago], *The President's Report*, Decennial Publications, 1st ser., vol. 1 (Chicago: University of Chicago Press, 1903), 6; see p. 188 for a summary of the frequency of and enrollment in JHB's course offerings from 1895 to 1902. The Department of the History of Art's inaugural year is inferred from *AR*. He offered his first course as a professor of "Oriental History" in June 1908: JHB, diary entry, 12 October 1908, JHBP.

5. Harry Pratt Judson to JHB, 6 October 1911, PP 1889–1925, 9:18, UCA. *AR*, 1914–15, 188. Regarding the departmental name change and JHB's appointment: BTM, April 1915, 9:55–57, UCA. JHB appears to have become the department's interim chair after RFH's death in August 1914: JHB to John M. P. Smith, 10 August 1914, DOC.

6. For changes under JHB's leadership: *AR*, 1914–15, 188–97; and JHB to John M. P. Smith, 10 August 1914, DOC. On the shift toward historical interpretation: JHB, "John Merlin Powis Smith," *University* [of Chicago] *Record*, new ser., 19, no. 1 (January 1933): 72–73 (emphasis JHB's). On the ancient history meeting: Albert T. E. Olmstead, "Breasted the Historian," *Open Court* 50, no. 936 (January 1936): 1–2. Olmstead, who was writing about himself and other newly minted professors, ended up at the OI from 1929 until his death in 1945. *Dictionary of American Biography*, supplement 3: 1941–45, s.v. "Albert Ten Eyck Olmstead."

7. *AR*, 1914–15, 195, 197–98.

8. Wilson, *Thousands of Years*, 42–43; HHN, "Biography of Prof. Breasted: One of Our Greatest Scholars," *Chicago Daily Tribune*, 11 April 1943.

9. JHB, notes, "Children of the Sun, A Romance of the Early World," 26 October–21 November 1909, JHBP (emphasis JHB's). See also JHB, notes for play, [n.d.], JHBP. Years later JHB mentioned starting a "tremendous novel" in which he had "every kind of hope"; however, it is unclear if he was referring to this or another effort: William P. Schenk, "James Henry Breasted," *The Red and White of the Lake View High School of Chicago* (December 1932): 13.

10. The recollection is from *TDoC*, xi–xii. JHB to May Breasted, 24 March 1891, LtP, JHBP; JHB to WRH, 3 July 1891, PP 1889–1925, 9:14, UCA (emphases JHB's). The master's thesis idea was not pursued; see chapter 1, n. 22 in the present volume. JHB to Breasted family, 21 January 1900, LtP, JHBP (emphases JHB's). In 1903, then in Berlin as a married scholar, JHB wrote to his mother: "We went up to the Museum this morning and took a last look at our beloved Durer's and Botticelli's and Rafael's . . . and the rest of the heavenly things. . . . It was better than going to church!" JHB to Harriet Breasted, 8 March 1903, LtP, JHBP.

11. JHB, manuscript, "A Neglected Source of Moral and Religious Enthusiasm," 10 February 1909, JHBP. For the complete text of "De Profundis": Alfred, Lord Tennyson, *Ballads, and Other Poems* (Boston: James S. Osgood, 1880), 95–98. JHB misquoted Tennyson, writing "out of the deeps" (plural) as opposed to Tennyson's "out of the deep," a mistake JHB repeated in later works.

12. JHB, manuscript, "The Study of History and the Idea of Inspiration," 20 April 1910, JHBP (emphases JHB's). George W. Stocking Jr., "On the Limits of 'Presentism' and 'Historicism' in the Historiography of the Behavioral Sciences," *Journal of the History of the Behavioral Sciences* 1, no. 3 (July 1965): 211–18.

13. JHB, "The Earliest Social Prophet," *American Journal of Theology* 14 (1910): 114–16 (emphasis JHB's). The reviewed text is: AHG, *The Admonitions of an Egyptian Sage: From a Hieratic Papyrus in Leiden (Pap. Leiden 344 recto)* (Leipzig: J. C. Hinrichs, 1909). For more on AHG, see chapter 7 of the present volume. See also JHB's review of a text on Egypt's influence on the Bible: Daniel Völter, *Aegypten und die Bibel* (Leiden: E. J. Brill, 1909); the review is JHB, "Egypt and the Bible," *American Journal of Semitic Languages and Literatures* 27, no. 1 (October 1910): 95–96.

14. JHB, manuscript, "The Old Historical Method," 21 January 1911, JHBP (emphasis JHB's). *Encyclopedia of World Biography*, 2nd ed., s.v. "Guglielmo Ferrero." The Ferrero work to which JHB was in all likelihood referring is Guglielmo Ferrero, *The Greatness and Decline of Rome*, 5 vols. (New York: G. P. Putnam's Sons, 1907–9). *Encyclopaedia Britannica*, 11th ed., s.v. "Leopold von Ranke."

15. JHB, manuscript, "Revelation a Historical Process," 6 June 1912, JHBP (emphasis JHB's).

16. JHB, "Old Historical Method" (emphasis JHB's).

17. Francis Brown to JHB, 11 January, and JHB to Francis Brown, 17 January 1911, DOC. Flyer, *The Morse Lectures, 1912: Religion and Thought in Ancient Egypt* (New York: Union Theological Seminary, [ca. February 1912]). JHB to Francis Brown, 16 November, and Francis Brown to JHB, 20 November 1911, DOC. *DoRaT*.

18. JHB to Charles and Harriet Breasted, 22 April 1894, LtP, JHBP (emphases JHB's). *DoRaT*, xi.

19. John A. Wilson, "James Henry Breasted, 1865–1935," *National Academy of Sciences, Biographical Memoirs* 28, no. 5 (1937): 102. *DoRaT*, vii, xi–xii. The Pyramid Texts edition to which JHB referred is Kurt Sethe, *Die Altägyptischen Pyramidentexte: Nach den Papierabdrücken und Photographien des Berliner Museums*, 4 vols. (Leipzig: J. C. Hinrichs, 1908–22). On JHB's work on the Pyramid Texts: JHB, diary entry, 12 May 1912, JHBP; Bull, Speiser, and Olmstead, "Breasted," 116.

20. *DoRaT*, 49, 90.

21. *DoRaT*, 165–66, 180–81.

22. *DoRaT*, 188ff, 198–99, 215.

23. *DoRaT*, 314–15, 319, 322. JHB's *AHoE* discussion of Ikhnaton's religious revolution is summarized in chapter 3 of the present volume.

24. *DoRaT*, 323–24, 331–32, 334–35, 343.

25. *DoRaT*, 348–49, 354, 364–65, 369–70. *American Eras*, vol. 7, *Civil War and Reconstruction, 1850–1877*, s.v. "Robert Green Ingersoll." The quote is a chiasmus based on Alexander Pope's "An honest man's the noblest work of God," a line from the poem "Epistle IV, Of the Nature and State of Man with Respect to Happiness," in his *An Essay on Man*, 4 vols. (London: J. Wilford, 1733–34). There is no evidence JHB knew this, however. *Dictionary of American Biography*, Base Set 1928–36, and *Encyclopedia of World Biography*, 2nd ed., both s.v. "Jean Louis Rodolphe Agassiz."

26. Nathaniel Schmidt, review of *DoRaT*, *American Historical Review* 19, no. 1 (October 1913): 133–35. *Dictionary of American Biography*, supplements 1–2: To 1940, s.v. "Nathaniel Schmidt." Review of *DoRaT*, *The Nation* 95, no. 2471 (7 November 1912): 434. W. M. Flinders Petrie, review of *DoRaT*, *Ancient Egypt* 1, no. 4 (1914): 42–43. *DoRaT* was reissued in 1959 with an introduction by one of JHB's most accomplished students, John A. Wilson, who observed, "All subsequent studies of ancient Egyptian religion and thought have been indebted to this book": John A. Wilson, "Introduction to the Torchbook Edition," in James Henry Breasted, *Development of Religion and Thought in Ancient Egypt*, Harper Torchbooks (New York: Harper and Row, 1959), xi. That edition was reissued by the University of Pennsylvania Press in 1972, 1986, and 1999 and remains in print today. An Arabic translation was published in 1961: JHB, *Tatawwur al-fikr wa-al-din fi Misr al-qadimah*, trans. Zaki Sus ([Cairo]: Dar al-Karnak lil-Nashr wa-al-Tab' wa-al-Tawzi', 1961).

27. On JHB's salary history: BTM, 1 May 1902 and 6 July 1903, 4:28, 302, UCA. His compensation apparently remained unchanged until around 1911: BTM, 18 Apr 1911 and 25 March 1913, 7:197, 8:10, UCA. $2,500 = $62,900, and $4,500 = $101,000 CPI 2009. Oddly, CB does not mention his siblings in *PttP*. JHB Jr. received his baccalaureate degree from Princeton University and continued with studies in Egyptology and Near Eastern archaeology at the University of Heidelberg and Queens College, Oxford, before earning a master's degree in art history at the University of Chicago. He pursued a career in teaching and museum work and authored a book on ancient Egyptian servant statues; he died in 1983. *The Dictionary of Art Historians*, http://www.dictionaryofarthistorians.org/, s.v. "James Henry Breasted Jr." (accessed July 2010); and *Contemporary Authors Online* (Detroit: Gale, 1998), in *Literature Resource Center*, http://go.galegroup.com.proxy.lib.wayne.edu/ps/i.do?&id=GALE%7CH1000011706&v=2.1&u=&it=r&p=LitRC&sw=w, s.v. "James Henry Breasted, Jr." (accessed July 2010). There is virtually no published information about Astrid Breasted's life save that she died in 1985. *Social Security Death Index*, http://ssdi.rootsweb.ancestry.com, s.v. "Astrid Hormann" (actually Hörmann, her married name, accessed July 2010).

JHB, diary entry, 12 August 1912, JHBP; and *PttP*, 221. On JHB's expanding use of stereographs from *EttS*: JHB to A. E. Osborne, 3 June 1909, and A. E. Osborne to JHB, 5 August 1909, DOC. JHB, "A Reading Journey through Egypt," *Chautauquan* 56, no. 1, and 58, no. 3 (September 1909, May 1910). Charles Scribner's Sons, publication contract [with JHB], "A work on the entire Nile Country from Khartoum to the Sea . . . title . . . not yet decided," 15 February 1910; and Scribner's, publication contract [with JHB], "Two Thousand Miles up the Nile," 21 October 1910, Contracts with Publishers, JHBP. The book's basis in the *Chautauquan* series is evident from the surviving manuscript, which consists largely of published pages from the series, cut and pasted on larger backing sheets for ease of editing and expansion: JHB, manuscript, "Two thousand miles up the Nile," n.d., JHBP. JHB began work on the manuscript, which he expected to be about six hundred pages long, in June 1910 and stopped after October 1910: JHB, diary entries, 20 June and 1 October 1910, JHBP. He expected to complete it not long after finishing *DoRaT* in 1912: 323n2 in the latter; and JHB, diary entry, 12 May 1912, JHBP. He was still thinking of reviving it as late as 1931: JHB to Charles Scribner Jr., 12 May 1931, DOC.

28. On JHB's ancient history course: Bull, Speiser, and Olmstead, "Breasted," 117; and

Wilson, "James Henry Breasted," 101. Henry Hoyt Hilton, *Observations and Memories with Ginn and Company from Eighteen Ninety to Nineteen Forty-Six* (Boston: Ginn, 1947), 61. See also: O[range] J[udd] Laylander, *The Ginn Sketchbook* (Boston: Athenaeum, 1933), 13–18. *PttP*, 221–22. On Ginn in general and JHB's association with the company in particular: Thomas B. Lawler, *Seventy Years of Textbook Publishing: A History of Ginn and Company, 1867–1937* (Boston: Ginn, 1938), 170–71. JHB, diary entries, 19 August 1912 and 23 September 1915, JHBP. $5,000 = $114,000, and $1,200 = $27,400 CPI 2009.

29. JHB to Harriet Breasted, 17 January 1904, LtP, JHBP. JHB to AHG, 7 January 1913, Gardiner MSS, 42.37.21, GI. An indication of JHB's recruitment into the historians' ranks is an invitation from Chicago's Department of History to present a lecture at an American Historical Association annual conference on its behalf because "no one can more brilliantly represent the faculty of history here than yourself": James Westfall Thompson to JHB, 26 January 1914, DOC. JHB to FB, 3 April 1911, LtFHB, JHBP (emphasis JHB's). *Encyclopedia of World Biography*, 2nd ed., s.v. "Thomas Henry Huxley."

30. JHR, *An Introduction to the History of Western Europe*, 2 vols. (Boston: Ginn, 1902–3). *Dictionary of American Biography*, supplements 1–2: To 1940, s.v. "James Harvey Robinson." See also Luther V. Hendricks, *James Harvey Robinson, Teacher of History* (Morningside Heights, NY: King's Crown, 1946). JHB joined the American Historical Association in May 1910: Waldo G. Leland to JHB, 13 May 1910, DOC. "Meeting of the American Historical Association in Indianapolis," *American Historical Review* 16, no. 3 (April 1911): 457 (JHR's paper is reported on pp. 470–72). Quotes regarding his paper are from Benjamin Keen, "Editor's Foreword," in JHR, *The New History: Essays Illustrating the Modern Historical Outlook* (1912; reprint, Springfield, MA: Walden, 1958), unpaged; and Breisach, *American Progressive History*, 73. JHB to FB, 1 and 3 April 1911, LtFHB, JHBP.

31. JHR to JHB, 3 August and 17 December 1911, and JHB to JHR, 12 August 1911, DOC. "Anticlerical" quote is from *Dictionary of American Biography*, s.v. "Robinson." JHB to JHR, 11 November 1912, DOC. JHB, review of *The New History: Essays Illustrating the Modern Historical Outlook*, by JHR, *Journal of Philosophy, Psychology, and Scientific Methods* 9, no. 21 (10 October 1912): 585–87. Keen, "Editor's Foreword," unpaged.

32. Breisach, *American Progressive History*, 43–45, 52–53, 62, 66, 68, 72. On the broader context of historical research in America during this period: John Higham, *History*, especially the chapters "Scientific History: The American Orthodoxy" and "Postscript: Objectivity Reexamined."

33. JHB, diary entries, 1 June, 12 August, and 1 September 1913, and 1 January and 4 August 1914, JHBP. $500 = $11,200 CPI 2009. JHR to JHB, 10 February, 24 May, 25 October, and 24 November 1913; JHB to JHR, 29 May and 11 October 1913, DOC.

34. JHB to Underwood & Underwood, 18 March 1913, DOC. JHB to JHR, 14 February 1913, DOC. JHB to Henry H. Hilton, 30 September 1913, DOC (emphasis JHB's). JHB to Edward K. Robinson, 22 June 1914, DOC (emphases JHB's). JHB to AHG, 7 January 1913, Gardiner MSS, 42.37.21, GI.

35. JHB to Edward K. Robinson, 10 June and 16 October 1913, and Edward K. Robinson to JHB, 3 October and 13 November 1913, DOC. JHB to Henry H. Hilton, 30 September 1913, DOC (emphases JHB's). JHR to JHB, 24 November and 12 December 1913, and JHB to JHR, 26 November 1913, DOC.

36. JHB, diary entries, 4 August 1914 and 25 September 1915, JHBP (emphases JHB's). JHB to Dana W. Hall, 29 October 1914, DOC. C. H. Thurber to JHB, 6 October 1914, DOC. *OoEH*, part I, iv–v, 697–98 (emphasis JHB's). For JHB's understanding with Underwood & Underwood, see JHB to Underwood & Underwood, 18 March 1913, JHB to A. E. Osborne, 10 and 18 April 1913, and A. E. Osborne to JHB, 15 April 1913, DOC.

37. JHB to Henry H. Hilton, 16 November 1914, DOC (emphases JHB's).

38. JHB, "The Ancient History of the Near East (with Remarks on Western Asia, by Daniel David Luckenbill)," *American Journal of Semitic Languages and Literatures* 30, no. 2 (January 1914): 125–37. JHB, review of *The Ancient History of the Near East from the Earliest Times to*

the Battle of Salamis, by H. R. Hall, *American Historical Review* 19, no. 3 (April 1914): 582–86. JHB to Henry H. Hilton, 16 November 1914, DOC. For a good example of the lantern-slide lectures JHB was giving about this time: JHB, "The Eastern Mediterranean and Early Civilization in Europe," *Annual Report of the American Historical Association for the Year 1914*, 2 vols. (Washington, DC: American Historical Association, 1916), 1: 103–12 ("This address was delivered with illustrations . . . ," p. 105, n. 1).

39. *OoEH*, iii (emphases JHB's and JHR's), 86.

40. *OoEH*, 186–93.

41. *OoEH*, 56–57 (the map, titled "The Ancient Orient," is inserted between these two pages). On the map's last-minute revision: JHB to W. H. Greeley, 15 and 16 June 1914, DOC. George Stephen Goodspeed, *A History of the Ancient World* (New York: Charles Scribner's Sons, 1904), 5–6. Bruce Kuklick was the first to notice this connection: Kuklick, *Puritans*, 241. Albert T. Clay, "The So-Called Fertile Crescent and Desert Bay," *Journal of the American Oriental Society* 44 (1924): 186–201.

42. JHB, diary entry, 25 September 1915, JHBP. $655 = $14,400 CPI 2009. *OoEH* initially sold for $1.50 ($33 CPI 2009): Edward K. Robinson to JHB, 30 November 1914, DOC. JHB, *A Short Ancient History* (Boston: Ginn, 1915). Subsequent editions of *Outlines* include JHB and JHR, *A History of Europe, Ancient and Medieval* (Boston: Ginn, 1920), and rev. ed. (1929); JHB, JHR, and Emma Peters Smith, *A General History of Europe, from the Origins of Civilization to the Present Time* (Boston: Ginn, 1921), revised and published as *Our World Today and Yesterday* (1924); JHB, JHR, and Emma Peters Smith, with the assistance of Edith Williams Ware, *A History of Civilization, Earlier Ages* (Boston: Ginn, 1937). Some editions continued publication through the 1950s. The sales estimate is from Hendricks, *James Harvey Robinson*, 108. Henry Noble Sherwood, review of *OoEH*, part I, *School Review* 23, no. 8 (October 1915): 571–72. See also Wayland J. Chase, review of *OoEH*, *History Teacher's Magazine* 6, no. 8 (October 1915): 266. Henry H. Hilton to JHB, 6 April 1915, DOC. *OoEH*, 279.

43. JHB to Henry H. Hilton, 8 October 1914, DOC (emphases JHB's). Hutton Webster, *Ancient History* (Boston: D. C. Heath, 1913). Webster (1875–1955) was a professor at the University of Nebraska. Henry H. Hilton to JHB, 5 January and 5 February 1914, DOC. JHB to Henry H. Hilton, 13 September 1913, DOC.

44. JHB to A. E. Osborne, 30 July 1914, DOC. As an example of JHB's close involvement in the illustrations' preparation, see the more than ten letters he exchanged with E. K. Robinson between 14 January and 21 July 1915, DOC, concerning a single illustration: "Transportation of Queen Hatshepsut's 350-Ton Obelisks down the Nile," in *AT*, 83 (figure 61). On head- and tailpieces: JHB to Edward K. Robinson, 20 August 1914, and Edward K. Robinson to JHB, 25 August 1914, DOC.

45. On the new book's design: W. H. Greeley to JHB, 4 and 8 August 1914, and JHB to W. H. Greeley, 6 August 1914, DOC. On cross-reference methods: JHB to W. H. Greeley, 21 October and 9 November 1914, W. H. Greeley to JHB, 30 October 1914, C. H. Thurber to JHB, 12 November 1914, and JHB to C. H. Thurber, 17 November 1914, DOC.

46. JHB to Edward K. Robinson, 7 May 1915, DOC. *AT*, 199, 217, 240–41. G. A. T. [?] to C. H. Thurber, 9 August 1916, C. H. Thurber to JHB, 10 August 1916, and JHB to C. H. Thurber, 14 August 1916, DOC.

47. C. H. Thurber to JHB, 8 May, JHB to C. H. Thurber, 11 May and 1 June, W. H. Greeley to JHB, 8 June, and JHB to W. H. Greeley, 12 June 1916, DOC.

48. Henry H. Hilton to JHB, 1 March, and JHB to Henry H. Hilton, 4 March 1915, DOC. *AT*, vii. [Unidentified Ginn and Company reader], report, "Ancient Times, James Henry Breasted, Ginn and Company," 1916, DOC. [JHR], handwritten note on galley proof for *Ancient Times*, [ca. March] 1916, JHB section of Pamphlet Files, OI Library.

49. JHB, diary entries, 1 February and 14 August 1916, JHBP. Philip Van Ness Myers, *Ancient History*, rev. ed. (Boston: Ginn, 1906). The book was originally published as *Outlines of Ancient History, from the Earliest Times to the Fall of the Western Roman Empire, A.D. 476 . . .* (New York: Harper Brothers, 1882). Ginn acquired its publication rights and began issuing it

as *Ancient History* in 1888. The revised edition to which JHB referred was issued in 1916 by Ginn under the same title. Myers, who was one of the most prolific history textbook authors of the era, was an unlikely competitor. His highest degree was in law, and he appears to have spent a substantial portion of his career as an academic administrator before becoming a professor of history and political economy at the University of Cincinnati: "Professor P. V. Myers, Retired Educator," *New York Times*, 21 September 1937, 25. On student populations and their textbooks: Arthur Leslie Woodward, "Teaching Americans about Their Past: History in Schools, 1880–1930," Ph.D. diss., (University of Illinois at Urbana-Champaign, 1982), 8; for an in-depth analysis of the publishing histories of textbooks by Myers and Robinson (including *Outlines*), see pp. 149–72; see also 35–40, 45 (tables 4 and 8), 107–16, 238–40, quote from pp. 9–10. Robert Dale Cremer, "An Analysis of the Development of High School World History Textbooks and Enrollments from 1900 to 1959" (Ph.D. diss., State University of South Dakota, 1963), 248, 251. Another researcher finds a trend between about 1900 and 1920 toward an increasing use of maps, illustrations, and teaching aids like questions at the ends of chapters: Albert E. Rinsch, "An Analysis of World History Textbooks for High Schools to Determine Modern Trends," (MS thesis, Indiana State Teachers College, 1936).

50. JHB, diary entry, 14 August 1916, JHBP. *AT*, iii–vii. *AT*'s initial cost was $1.60 ($32.30 CPI 2009); the price information comes from reviews (see n. 51).

51. *AT*, vii. The wall maps are, JHB and Carl F. Huth Jr., eds., *Breasted Ancient History Series* (Chicago: Denoyer-Geppert, 1916–20). JHB began work with the map publisher while *AT* was in the final production stages: JHB to L. P. Denoyer, 20 May 1916, and L. P. Denoyer to JHB, 25 September 1916, DOC. The maps were as popular as *AT* and over a thousand sets were sold at the National Education Association's 1917 annual meeting: L. P. Denoyer to JHB, 6 March 1917, DOC. For a contemporaneous overview of wall maps: W. L. G. Joerg, "Recent American Wall Maps: A Review," *Geographical Review* 14, no. 3 (July 1924): 456–64. JHB and Carl F. Huth Jr., *A Teacher's Manual Accompanying the Breasted-Huth Ancient History Maps* (Chicago: Denoyer-Geppert, 1918). The desktop atlas is JHB, Carl F. Huth Jr., and Samuel Bannister Harding, eds., *Ancient and European History Atlas, Reductions from Large Wall Maps* (Chicago: Denoyer-Geppert, [1920]). *Dictionary of American Biography*, Base Set 1928–36, s.v. "Lewis Henry Morgan." The "Barbarism-Civilization" sequence is identical to Morgan's theory of the three-step evolution of ancient societies: the first, "savagery," being the hunting and gathering stage; next, "barbarism," marking the transition to agriculture-based settlements; and last, "civilization," characterized by the formation of urban societies. Lewis H[enry] Morgan, *Ancient Society; or, Researches in the Lines of Human Progress, from Savagery through Barbarism to Civilization* (New York: Henry Holt, 1877). It is unclear whether or not JHB was familiar with Morgan's work or if the former assimilated the latter's theory through other sources, a distinct possibility given Morgan's widespread influence.

52. Many of the *AT* reviews are in JHB section of Pamphlet Files, OI Library. Jacob Hoschander, "Survey of Recent Biblical Literature, V. Archaeology," *Jewish Quarterly Review*, new ser., 7, no. 2 (October 1926): 199–200. Review of *AT*, *Ancient Egypt* 4 (1917): 86–87; Ralph Van Deman Magoffin, review of *AT*, *Classical Weekly* 10, no. 25 (30 April 1917): 199–200. The quote regarding JHB's influence on ancient historians and European leaders is from David Fromkin, *A Peace to End All Peace: Creating the Modern Middle East, 1914–1922* (New York: Henry Holt, 1989), 24. "Book Table," *Journal of Education* 85, no. 3 (18 January 1917): 77; review of *AT*, *American Education* 20 (June 1917): 629–30.

53. For a concise sketch of Roosevelt's career: *Dictionary of American Biography*, Base Set 1928–36, s.v. "Theodore Roosevelt." For the period in question: Patricia O'Toole, *When Trumpets Call: Theodore Roosevelt after the White House* (New York: Simon and Schuster, 2004). "Meeting of the American Historical Association at Indianapolis," *American Historical Review* 16, no. 3 (April 1911): 473–74; "Meeting of the American Historical Association at Buffalo and Ithaca," *American Historical Review* 17, no. 3 (April 1912): 474. It's possible, though unlikely, that JHB first met Roosevelt during one of two campus visits the president made in April 1899 and April 1903: Boyer, "Broad," 19. Theodore Roosevelt, "History as Literature,"

American Historical Review 18, no. 3 (April 1913): 476, 481–87. Weigall was another Egyptologist: *WWWE*, s.v. "Arthur Edward Pearse Brome Weigall." JHB had thought a lot about the strategic nature of the region in ancient history. It was the topic of JHB, "Battle of Kadesh," and he treated it several times in *AHoE*, passim. Theodore Roosevelt to JHB, 4 October 1916, R. H. Post [telegram on behalf of Roosevelt] to JHB, 22 October 1916, and Theodore Roosevelt to JHB, 9 January 1917, DOC. The inception of the relationship between Roosevelt and JHB, as well as their Chicago meeting, are discussed by CB in *PttP*, 229, 232–34. His dates are wrong, however. Theodore Roosevelt to JHB, 5 December 1916, Gilbert T. Grosvenor to Theodore Roosevelt, 18 December 1916, and JHB to Theodore Roosevelt, 11 December 1916, DOC.

54. O'Toole, *When Trumpets Call*, 21–22, 93; Ira V. Brown, *Lyman Abbott, Christian Evolutionist: A Study in Religious Liberalism* (Cambridge, MA: Harvard University Press, 1953), 66–67, 77–78, 168, 189–92, 240. Abbott was the editor of *Outlook* during this period; the magazine was absorbed by another in 1927, and the new version ceased publication in 1935: Brown, *Lyman Abbott*, 233. Theodore Roosevelt, "The Dawn and Sunrise of History," *Outlook* 115, no. 7 (14 February 1917): 272–75.

55. The circulation figure includes a subsequent abridged version: JHB to GEH, 21 December 1920, GEHP. *AT* went through a number of reprints well into the 1960s. JHB revised it for a trade edition, however, in 1926 (see chapter 9 of the present volume). It was published in Arabic translation in 1926: see Orit Bashkin, "The Arab Revival, Archaeology, and Ancient Middle Eastern History," in *Pioneers to the Past: American Archaeologists in the Middle East, 1919–1920*, ed. Geoff Emberling, Oriental Institute Museum Publications, no. 30 (Chicago: Oriental Institute, University of Chicago, 2010), 91–94. Myers's *Ancient History* began to decline in use in the late 1910s and 1920s with the advent of newer competition, including Webster's *Ancient History*, *Outlines of European History, Part I*, and *Ancient Times*, but then only gradually: Woodward, "Teaching Americans," 110–14, especially tables 26, 27, 28; quote from p. 116. FTG to JHB, [ca. September 1916], DOC; see also *PttP*, 230. Abby A[ldrich] Rockefeller to JHB, 18 May 1917, DOC. *Dictionary of American Biography*, supplement 4: 1946–50, s.v. "Abby Greene Aldrich Rockefeller."

Chapter 6

1. CB to F[rederick] H. Seares, 3 April 1939, JHBP. Helen Wright, *Explorer of the Universe: A Biography of George Ellery Hale* (New York: E. P. Dutton, 1966), 108–10, 185–86. See also Walter S. Adams, "George Ellery Hale, 1868–1938," *Biographical Memoirs* (National Academy of Sciences) 21, no. 5 (1940): 181–241; and Frederick H. Seares, "George Ellery Hale: The Scientist Afield," *Isis* 30, no. 2 (May 1939): 241–67. Goodspeed, *History*, 307–13, 317–18. $1,500 = $36,500 CPI 2009. Rexmond C. Cochrane, *The National Academy of Sciences: The First Hundred Years, 1863–1963* (Washington, DC: National Academy of Sciences, 1978), 185–87. "Big science" is believed to have been coined in Alvin M. Weinberg, "Impact of Large-Scale Science in the United States," *Science* 134, no. 3473 (21 July 1961): 161–64. Although most, including Weinberg, attribute the big science phenomenon to the mobilization of scientific research for the Second World War—especially the Manhattan Project—it's clear that the seeds for those efforts were planted by Hale during the First World War and the following years. The notion of disciplinary bigness spilled over into archaeology as well: Allen E. Rogge, "Little Archaeology, Big Archaeology: The Changing Context of Archaeological Research" (Ph.D. diss., University of Arizona, 1983).

2. Wright, *Explorer*, 92, 133, 266–67, and the figure opposite p. 113. JHB to GEH, 5 January 1897, GEHP. *PttP*, 137–39, 224–27. On the ca. 1911 meeting in Chicago: JHB to GEH, 25 April 1931, GEHP.

3. GEH to Charles D. Walcott, 25 January 1908 and 17 May 1912, and Charles D. Walcott to GEH, 25 May 1912, GEHP. Wright, *Explorer*, 307–9; Cochrane, *National Academy*, 194–99. GEH's NAS articles were combined and reprinted as GEH, *National Academies and the Progress*

of Research (Lancaster, PA: New Era, 1915), quotes from pp. 123–24, 135, 158–60. GEH first articulated a plan using evolution to structure an educational program some years earlier: GEH, "A Plea for the Imaginative Element in Technical Education," *Technology Review* 9, no. 4 (October 1907): 467–81.

4. GEH to JHB, 6 April 1914, JHBP. On the NAS's archaeology representatives at the time: GEH, *National Academies*, 155. On Americanist anthropology: Bruce G. Trigger, *A History of Archaeological Thought* (Cambridge: Cambridge University Press, 1989), 110–11. On archaeological research in the Americas: Gordon R. Willey and Jeremy A. Sabloff, *A History of American Archaeology*, 3rd ed. (San Francisco: W. H. Freeman, 1993). JHB to GEH, 7 April 1914, GEHP; JHB to GEH, 7 April 1914, JHBP.) Laurence R. Veysey, "The Plural Organized Worlds of the Humanities," in Alexandra Oleson and John Voss, eds., *The Organization of Knowledge in Modern America, 1860–1920* (Baltimore: Johns Hopkins University Press, 1979), 51–106.

5. GEH, report, "Summary of Opinions of Members Re Suggestions in Mr. Hale's Paper: 'The Future of the National Academy of Sciences,'" 27 November 1914, GEHP. "Report of Mr. George E. Hale," Minutes of the Academy, 21 April 1914, NAS Archives, insert between pp. 25–26. See also GEH's annotated copy in GEHP. On the founding and first few years of the National Research Council: Cochrane, *National Academy*, 200–256; *A History of the National Research Council*, Reprint and Circular Series of the National Research Council (Washington, DC: National Research Council, 1933); and Wright, *Explorer*, 285ff.

6. GEH to JHB, 15 April, and JHB to GEH, 18 April 1914, GEHP (emphases JHB's).

7. "N. W. Harris, Banker . . . ," *New York Times*, 17 July 1916. JHB to GEH, 1 May 1914, GEHP. The budget was $30,000 for the boat and equipment and $25,000 per year for fifteen years. $25,000 = $504,000 CPI 2009.

8. JHB to GEH, 1 May 1914, GEHP.

9. GEH to [Norman Wait] Harris, 8 May 1914, JHBP (emphasis GEH's).

10. N[orman] W[ait] Harris to GEH, 29 June 1914, GEHP. GEH to JHB, 14 July 191[4], JHBP. *PttP*, 226–27.

11. The expression "two cultures" appears to have first been used by C. P. Snow in 1959, see C. P. Snow, *The Two Cultures: And a Second Look* (Cambridge: Cambridge University Press, 1964). See also Stefan Collini, "Introduction," in C. P. Snow, *The Two Cultures* (Cambridge: Cambridge University Press, 1998), vii–lxxiii. For a more recent essay that explores the two-cultures debate: John Guillory, "The Sokal Affair and the History of Criticism," *Critical Inquiry* 28, no. 2 (Winter 2002): 470–508. See also Fritz Machlup, *Knowledge: Its Creation, Distribution, and Economic Significance* (Princeton, NJ: Princeton University Press, 1980), 59–90. JHB to GEH, 18 November 1914, GEHP (emphases JHB's). Hale's book was published as GEH, *Ten Years' Work of a Mountain Observatory* (Washington, DC: Carnegie Institution, 1915). For excerpts from the introductory matter GEH probably sent to JHB, from which the final quote comes, and GEH's decision to drop it: Wright, *Explorer*, 283–84. *International Dictionary of Art and Artists*, s.v. "J(oseph) M(allord) W(illiam) Turner." JHB viewed Turner's paintings in the National Gallery in London on his way home from the 1919–20 expedition and commented specifically on the paintings' "aerial deeps": JHB to CB, 27 June 1920, JHBP.

12. GEH to JHB, 25 May 1915, JHBP. *Dictionary of American Biography*, Base Set 1928–36, s.v. "Henry Edwards Huntington." JHB to GEH, 27 May and 24 June 1915 and 18 January 1916, JHBP. Almost a decade later GEH devised a plan that was realized as the Huntington Library and Art Gallery. GEH apprised JHB of the new plan: GEH to JHB, 29 August 1925, GEHP; and GEH, manuscript, "The Future Development of the Huntington Library and Art Gallery" [ca. October 1925, sent to JHB with cover letter dated 25 October 1925], JHBP. The new institution bore no relation to the one GEH and JHB envisioned earlier: Wright, *Explorer*, 371–86; John E. Pomfret, *The Henry E. Huntington Library and Art Gallery: From Its Beginnings to 1969* (San Marino, CA: Huntington Library, 1969), 40–59.

13. JHB to GEH, 9 June 1916, GEHP. On Smith and the OI: JHB, "John Merlin Powis Smith," 73.

14. Meyer, "Chicago Faculty," 334–35, 398–401. On the German model: Charles E. Mc-

Clelland, *State, Society, and University in Germany, 1700–1914* (Cambridge: Cambridge University Press, 1980), 275. See also Robert E. Kohler, *Partners in Science: Foundations and Natural Scientists, 1900–1945* (Chicago: University of Chicago Press, 1991), 217–19.

The OI plan's focus on the ancient Near East differed from subsequent similarly named research institutions like the School of Oriental and African Studies, University of London (founded in 1917, which Edward Said discusses in *Orientalism* [New York: Random House, 1978], 214–15) and the Oriental Institute of Oxford University (established in 1957). Those are geographically broader or chronologically more inclusive—going from antiquity to the present to embrace the modern (Islamic) period: C. H. Phillips, *The School of Oriental and African Studies, University of London, 1917–1967: An Introduction* (London: School of Oriental & African Studies, University of London, 1967); and G. R. Driver, "Oriental Studies and the Oriental Institute," *Oxford* 17, no. 2 (May 1961): 56–67. See also Jerrold S. Cooper, "From Mosul to Manila: Early Approaches to Funding Ancient Near Eastern Studies Research in the United States," *Culture and History* 11 (1992): 133–37; and, on a curious effort to establish a national "Oriental Seminary" for Philippine studies in Washington, DC, pp. 155–57.

15. JHB to FTG, 22 September 1916 and 21 March 1917, and FTG to JHB, 24 March 1917, DOC. Barbara Howe, "The Emergence of Scientific Philanthropy, 1900–1920: Origins, Issues, and Outcomes," in Robert F. Arnove, ed., *Philanthropy and Cultural Imperialism: The Foundations at Home and Abroad* (Boston: G. K. Hall, 1980), 27–28; Barry D. Karl and Stanley N. Katz, "Donors, Trustees, Staffs: An Historical View, 1890–1930," in *The Art of Giving: Four Views on American Philanthropy* (North Tarrytown, NY: Rockefeller Archive Center, 1979), 3, "family affair" quote from p. 10. For a historical overview, see Robert H. Bremner, *American Philanthropy*, 2nd ed. (Chicago: University of Chicago Press, 1988). On the boards: Daryl L. Revoldt, "Raymond B. Fosdick: Reform, Internationalism, and the Rockefeller Foundation" (Ph.D. diss., University of Akron, 1982), 376–77; RBF, *Adventures in Giving: The Story of the General Education Board* (New York: Harper and Row, 1962); RBF, *The Story of the Rockefeller Foundation*, reprint of 1952 edition with an introduction by Steven C. Wheatley (New Brunswick, NJ: Transaction Publishers, 1989); George W. Gray, *Education on an International Scale: A History of the International Education Board* (New York: Harcourt, Brace, 1941).

16. Howe, "Emergence of Scientific Philanthropy," 28. Karl and Katz, "Donors, Trustees, Staffs," 9. JHB to FB, 10 April 1917, LtFHB, JHBP.

17. JHB to Harry Pratt Judson and FTG, 11 May 1917, DOC; JHB to GEH, 19 May 1917, GEHP. JHB, "Plan for an Institute of Oriental Archaeology in the Eastern Mediterranean World," 19 May 1917, GEHP (emphasis JHB's).

18. JHB, "Plan for an Institute" (emphases JHB's). Karl and Katz, "Donors, Trustees, Staffs," 6, 10.

19. JHB, diary entry, 4 August 1914, JHBP. *PttP*, 227–29, 234–36, 325, 386–87.

20. JHB to Henry H. Hilton, 20 and 23 April and 28 November 1917, and Henry H. Hilton to JHB, 21 April 1917, DOC. One of JHB's best-known correspondents regarding *OoEH* was Bessie L. Pierce: "Dr. Bessie Louise Pierce Dies . . . ," *New York Times*, 5 October 1974. She briefly addressed *OoEH* in Bessie Louise Pierce, *Public Opinion and the Teaching of History in the United States* (New York: Alfred A. Knopf, 1926), passim. JHB, "The Bridgehead of Asia Minor," *The Nation* 106, no. 2762 (8 June 1918): 676–78. On JHB's offers to work in Egypt: JHB to J. E. Quibell, 25 July, J. E. Quibell to JHB, 6 August, JHB to F. R[eginald] Wingate, 29 July, and [F.] Reginald Wingate to JHB, 12 October 1918, DOC.

21. Robert D. Ward, "The Origin and Activities of the National Security League, 1914–1919," *Mississippi Valley Historical Review* 47, no. 1 (June 1960): 51–65. See also John Carver Edwards, *Patriots in Pinstripe: Men of the National Security League* (Washington, DC: University Press of America, 1982), especially chapter 5, "The Committee on Patriotism through Education," 91–110. On JHB's National Security League involvement: Harry H. Merrick to Members, National Security League, 23 March 1916, DOC; JHB to FB, 8 September 1917, LtFHB, JHBP; JHB to R[obert] M[cNutt] McElroy, 19 June, 7 July, and 23 September 1918, DOC; [JHB?], file memorandum, [after ca. 7 September] 1918, DOC; and Robert McNutt

McElroy, *Annual Report upon the Educational Work of the National Security League*, Patriotism through Education Series, vol. 39 (New York: National Security League, 1918). McElroy was education director of the National Security League. JHB to Harry Pratt Judson, 25 January 1919, PP 1889–1925, 9:19, UCA. The idea for a cabinet-level department of education and welfare was first proposed by President Warren Harding in 1923, but it was not until the Eisenhower administration, in 1953, that the Department of Health, Education, and Welfare was established. The Department of Education was carved out as a separate cabinet-level agency during the Carter administration in 1979–80.

22. JHB to FB, 20 March 1918, LtFHB, JHBP. JHB, "Ancient Egypt and the Modern World," *History Teacher's Magazine* 8, no. 7 (September 1917): 214; JHB, "The Earliest Internationalism," in *The Semicentenary Celebration of the Founding of the University of California, with an Account of Conference on International Relations* (Berkeley: [University of California Press], 1919), 203.

23. "Proceedings of the American Oriental Society," *Journal of the American Oriental Society* 38 (April 1918): 334. JHB to Charles and Harriet Breasted and family, 26 October 1890 and 6 May 1891, LtP, 1877–1908, JHBP. Nathaniel Schmidt, "Early Oriental Studies in Europe and the Work of the American Oriental Society, 1842–1922," *Journal of the American Oriental Society* 43 (1923): 1–14, quote regarding presidential addresses from p. 1. JHB, "The Place of the Near Orient in the Career of Man and the Task of the American Orientalist," *Journal of the American Oriental Society* 39 (1919): 159–84, quotes from pp. 159–60 (emphasis JHB's).

24. JHB, "Place of the Near Orient," 160–61, 165, 168. Clark Wissler, *The American Indian: An Introduction to the Anthropology of the New World* (New York: Douglas C. McMurtrie, 1917). On JHB's regard for Wissler's work: JHB to Clark Wissler, 15 November 1920, DOC; and *TOI*, 4–5. Some of Wissler's notions, specifically those related to cultural diffusion, have not stood the test of time: George W. Stocking, in *Dictionary of American Biography*, supplement 4: 1946–50, s.v. "Clark Wissler." On the origins and early development of "diffusionism" as an archaeological concept: Trigger, *History*, 150ff, 244ff.

25. JHB, "Place of the Near Orient," 161, 163, 169–71, 180 (emphasis JHB's).

26. JHB, "Place of the Near Orient," 180–84 (emphases JHB's).

27. GEH, *National Academies*, 119, 123–25. GEH, "The William Ellery Hale Lectures on Evolution" [ca. 26 July 1919], GEHP. *Notable Scientists: From 1900 to the Present*, s.v. "Ernest Rutherford." JHB, list of two lecture titles, 14 March 1919, GEHP. *Dictionary of American Biography*, supplement 3: 1941–45, s.v. "John Campbell Merriam." The lectures were published in six parts: JHB, "The Origins of Civilization," *Scientific Monthly* 9, nos. 4–6, and 10, nos. 1–3 (October–December 1919 and January–March 1920).

28. JHB, "Origins," *Scientific Monthly* 9, no. 4:289, 312 (see also 9, no. 6:577 and 10, no. 2:183). The zoologist's reaction to JHB is from Albright, "James Henry Breasted," 292.

29. "Important Actions Taken by the Board of Directors at the Philadelphia Meeting, April 23–25, 1919," *Journal of the American Oriental Society* 39 (April 1919): 153. Cochrane, *National Academy*, 244–45. Minutes, National Academy of Sciences Council, 27 and 28 April 1919, NAS Archives. JHB, "Scope, Purpose, and Functions of a National Academy of Humanistic Science," [27–28 April 1919], GEHP (emphasis JHB's).

30. JHB, manuscript, "Report . . . on Negotiations with the National Academy of Science Regarding the Creation of a National Academy of Humanistic Science," [ca. late April/early May 1919], DOC. *Proceedings of the Conference of American Learned Societies Devoted to Humanistic Studies* (Boston: American Council of Learned Societies Devoted to Humanistic Studies, 1919), n.p. JHB to Frederick J. Teggart, 21 May 1919, DOC. Teggart was a prominent historian who, at the time, was associated with the newly formed Institute of International Education, which was closely associated with efforts to represent American interests at the Paris convention. *Dictionary of American Biography*, supplement 4: 1946–50, s.v. "Frederick John Teggart." See also Stephen Mark Halpern, "The Institute of International Education: A History" (Ph.D. diss., Columbia University, 1969). "The American Council of Learned Societies," *Journal of the American Oriental Society* 40 (1920): 77–80. Ariel De, "International Un-

derstanding and World Peace: The American Council of Learned Societies, 1919–1957" (Ph.D. diss., City University of New York, 2004).

31. Charles J. Ogden to JHB, 3 October 1919, and JHB to Charles J. Ogden, 9 November 1919, DOC; Morris Jastrow Jr. to GEH, 21 October and 12 November 1919, and GEH to Morris Jastrow Jr., 4 and 20 November 1919, GEHP; John C. Merriam to GEH, 5 November 1919, GEHP. Another attempt to revive JHB's initiative is reflected in Minutes, National Academy of Sciences Council, 27 April 1920, and Charles D. Walcott to GEH, 12 May 1920, GEHP. The Merriam quote is from what, in effect, was a report terminating the initiative: Minutes, National Academy of Sciences Council, 15 November 1920, GEHP. An abbreviated version is in "Annual Meeting Minutes," *Report of the National Academy of Sciences for the Year 1921* (Washington, DC: Government Printing Office, 1922), 10–12. An example of dissension among the Orientalists is Charles R. Lanman to [John C.] Merriam and GEH, 23 January 1920, GEHP. After the GEH/JHB initiative, the academy hardened its disciplinary boundaries for good: A. Hunter Dupree, "The National Academy of Sciences and the American Definition of Science," in *The Organization of Knowledge in Modern America, 1860–1920*, ed. Alexandra Oleson and John Voss (Baltimore: Johns Hopkins University Press, 1979), 342–63. See also James R. Angell, memorandum, "Announcement of the National Research Council," 12 December 1919, NAS-NRC: Organization, Policy, 1919–1923, NAS Archives.

32. JHB to Wallace Buttrick, 13 January 1919, and JHB to Harry Pratt Judson, 25 January 1919, PP 1889–1925, 9:19, UCA. JHB, "Plan for the Organization of an Oriental Institute at the University of Chicago," 16 January 1919, GEB/2324.2, Oriental Inst./series I, subseries 4, box 659, folder 6851, RAC. $250,000 and $10,000 = $3.10 million and $124,000 CPI 2009. For a published transcription of the plan: *PttP:AA*, appendix A, 115–19.

33. Wallace Buttrick to JHB, 28 January and 1 March 1919, and JHB to Wallace Buttrick, 16 February 1919, GEB/2324.2, Oriental Inst./series I, subseries 4, box 659, folder 6851, RAC. On JHB's campaign to rally support among other Rockefeller officials: JHB to Abraham Flexner, 18 February 1919, and to Wallace Buttrick, 24 February 1919, GEB/2324.2 Oriental Inst./series I, subseries 4, box 659, folder 6851, RAC (the latter on JHB's cultivation of Julius Rosenwald); JHB to FTG, 28 February 1919, DOC. JHB to JDR Jr. with enclosure, "Plan for the Organization of an Oriental Institute at the University of Chicago," 16 February 1919, RFA/RG 2, OMR/JDR Jr. series, Educational Interests subseries, box 112, folder Univ. of Chicago, Oriental Inst., 3 yr. pledge–5 yr. pledge, RAC. Murphy was brought to JDR Jr.'s attention by FTG and became one of JDR Jr.'s closest advisors until Murphy's untimely death in 1921. "Starr J. Murphy Dies in Florida," *New York Times*, 5 April 1921. See also RBF, *Rockefeller, Jr.*, 412. Starr J. Murphy to Harry Pratt Judson, 5 March 1919, and Harry Pratt Judson to Starr J. Murphy, 7 March and 10 April 1919, RFA/RG 2, OMR/JDR Jr. series, Educational Interests subseries, box 112, Univ. of Chicago, Oriental Inst., 3 yr. pledge–5 yr. pledge, RAC. Starr J. Murphy to JDR Jr., 14 and 19 April 1919, RFA/RG 2, OMR/JDR Jr. series, Educational Interests subseries, box 112, folder Univ. of Chicago, Oriental Inst., 3 yr. pledge–5 yr. pledge, RAC.

34. *PttP*, 240. JDR Jr. to JHB, 2 May 1919, and JDR Jr. to Harry Pratt Judson [with enclosure, JDR Jr. to JHB, 2 May 1919], 2 May 1919, RFA/RG 2, OMR/JDR Jr. series, Educational Interests subseries, box 112, Univ. of Chicago, Oriental Inst., 3 yr. pledge–5 yr. pledge, RAC. For a reproduction of JDR's letter to JHB: Geoff Emberling and Emily Teeter, "The First Expedition of the Oriental Institute, 1919–1920," in *PttP:AA*, 33. The quote regarding *AT* is from Hilton, *Observations*, 61.

35. JHB to JDR Jr., 7 May 1919, RFA/RG 2, OMR/JDR Jr. series, Educational Interests subseries, box 112, Univ. of Chicago, Oriental Inst., 3 yr. pledge–5 yr. pledge, RAC. On organizing the OI and its library: JHB to Harry Pratt Judson, 17 May 1919, PP 1889–1925, 9:19, UCA; JHB to Ernest D. Burton, 10 July 1919, JHBP. JHB, diary entry, 7 May 1919, JHBP; GEH to JHB, 17 May 1919, JHBP; JHB to GEH, 26 July 1919, GEHP; JHB to Alan H. Gardiner, 9 May 1919, Gardiner MSS, 42.37.17, GI. When JHB affiliated the Department of Oriental Languages and Literatures faculty with the OI, he inaugurated a process through

which the department became ever more closely associated with the OI. The former is now called the Department of Near Eastern Languages and Civilizations, and it is housed in the OI building. Most faculty members have joint appointments with the department and the OI, and some are also associated with the Center for Middle Eastern Studies, founded in 1965, and housed in another building on Chicago's campus. On the Carnegie request: JHB to Robert S. Woodward, 28 August 1919, and Robert S. Woodward to JHB, 16 September 1919, JHB file, CIW. *PttP*, 242.

36. *PttP*, 242–43; JHB, "Report of the First Expedition of the Oriental Institute of the University of Chicago," [after ca. 3 September] 1920, PP 1925–45, 62:1, UCA, 2–3. JHB to Harry Pratt Judson, 7 December 1919, PP 1889–1925, 9:19, UCA. On conditions in the Middle East on the eve of the expedition: Geoff Emberling, "Archaeology in the Middle East before 1920: Political Contexts, Historical Results," in *PttP:AA*, 15–21; and James L. Gelvin, "The Middle East Breasted Encountered, 1919–1920," in *PttP:AA*, 21–29. On the expedition per se, from inception to conclusion: Emberling and Teeter, "The First Expedition," 31–84. JHB's correspondence home during the expedition is available online at the Oriental Institute Digital Archives, http://oi.uchicago.edu/research/pubs/catalog/oida/oida1.html (accessed July 2010).

37. On JHB's anticipation of acquisition opportunities, subsequent negotiations, and actual purchases: JHB to JDR Jr., 16 August 1919, DOC; *PttP*, 241, 250–58, 275; JHB, "Report of the First Expedition," 6–8, 18–19, 21. $100,000 = $1.24 million CPI 2009. See also Emberling and Teeter, "The First Expedition," 41–49. On hobnobbing with dignitaries: JHB, "Report of the First Expedition," 2–3, 8–9; and *PttP*, 243–46. *WWWE*, s.v. "George . . . Herbert, 5th Earl of Carnarvon." *Historic World Leaders*, s.v. "Edmund H. H. Allenby."

38. JHB, "Report of the First Expedition," 5; *PttP*, 258–61. Aerial photographs were first taken in the mid-nineteenth century, not long after the invention of photography, initially from hot-air balloons. The first systematic investigations of aerial photography for archaeological purposes were by Englishman O. G. S. Crawford in 1922: O. G. S. Crawford, "History and Bibliography of Archaeology from the Air," in *Wessex from the Air*, ed. O. G. S. Crawford and Alexander Keiller (Oxford: Clarendon, 1928), 3–7; and Crawford, "A Century of Air-Photography," *Antiquity: A Quarterly Review of Archaeology* 28, no. 112 (December 1954): 206–10. For a survey of the subject, see Leo Deuel, *Flights into Yesterday: The Story of Aerial Archaeology* (New York: St. Martin's, 1969), 24ff on Crawford's experiments. Some years later JHB's OI colleagues would methodically use aerial photography: P. L. O. Guy, "Balloon Photography and Archaeological Excavation," *Antiquity: A Quarterly Review of Archaeology* 6, no. 22 (June 1932): 148–55; Erich F. Schmidt, *Flights over Ancient Cities of Iran*, Special Publications of the Oriental Institute of the University of Chicago (Chicago: Oriental Institute, University of Chicago, 1940).

39. JHB, "Report of the First Expedition," 4, 6, 9. Leroy Waterman, "Daniel David Luckenbill, 1881–1927," *American Journal of Semitic Languages and Literatures* 44, 1 (October 1927): 1–5; *WWWE*, s.v. "Ludlow Sequine Bull" and "William Franklin Edgerton." For additional biographical information, including Shelton's: *PttP:AA*, appendix C, 148–51. *PttP*, 242–43, 253, 261–62, 265–66.

40. JHB, "Report of the First Expedition," 10; *PttP*, 253, 268–73, quote from p. 273. On the names of the two Arab helpers: JHB to CB, 21 March 1920, JHBP.

41. *PttP*, 273–81, Ctesiphon and Rolls-Royce quotes from pp. 275 and 278 respectively. JHB, "Report of the First Expedition," 10–12.

42. JHB, "Report of the First Expedition," 12–14; *PttP*, 281–85.

43. JHB, "Report of the First Expedition," 14; *PttP*, 285–88. JHB, *Oriental Forerunners of Byzantine Painting: First-Century Wall Paintings from the Fortress of Dura on the Middle Euphrates*, Oriental Institute Publications, no. 1 (Chicago: University of Chicago Press, 1924), 52–61. On the site's subsequent excavations and interpretation: Clark Hopkins, *The Discovery of Dura-Europos*, ed. Bernard Goldman (New Haven, CT: Yale University Press, 1979). The murals studied by JHB are in a space now called the Temple of Palmyrene Gods, ca. 115 CE.

44. JHB, "Report of the First Expedition," 14–15; *PttP*, 288–96, quotes from pp. 292 and 296. On the flag, which JHB almost certainly found in the Middle East because it was either very old or fabricated on the basis of an old photograph: Emberling and Teeter, "The First Expedition," 72 (the OI still has the flag—see figure 4.60 on the same page).

45. JHB, "Report of the First Expedition," 15; *PttP*, 294–300 (emphases JHB's).

46. JHB, "Report of the First Expedition," 15–18; *PttP*, 300–309.

47. JHB, "Report of the First Expedition," 18–21; JHB to Curzon quote from p. 21. *PttP*, 309–14. On archaeologists and international relations in the Middle East: James F. Goode, *Negotiating for the Past: Archaeology, Nationalism, and Diplomacy in the Middle East, 1919–1941* (Austin: University of Texas Press, 2007). Changes in access are addressed on p. 226.

48. *PttP*, 218–19, 313, 315–16, 321. On the description of Ali: JHB to FB, 23 May 1920, LtFHB, JHBP.

Chapter 7

1. JHB's base salary went from $4,500 to $5,500 between 1919 and 1920, while his annual supplement for directing the OI remained at $1,500: BTM, 8 April 1919 and 1 and 13 July 1920, 11:65, 432, 440, UCA. On royalty and other income: JHB, diary entry, 1 July 1922, JHBP. $18,000 = $216,000 CPI 2009. Thanks to GEH, JHB's accomplishments were also honored by his appointment to the National Research Council in July 1920: Charles D. Walcott to JHB, 15 May 1920, and JHB to Clark Wissler, 15 November 1920, DOC. JHB was appointed to the Division of Anthropology and Psychology, then chaired by Clark Wissler, the anthropologist whose work stimulated JHB's ideas about cultural diffusion; see chapter 6 of the present volume. On the student's letter: Olmstead, "Breasted the Historian," 3.

2. JHB, "Report of the First Expedition of the Oriental Institute of the University of Chicago," [after ca. 3 September] 1920, PP 1925–45, 62:1, UCA: 19, 23 (emphasis JHB's). A retyped office-copied version is in the JHB section in the Pamphlet Files, OI Library: "Report of the Director of the Oriental Institute of the University of Chicago on the Expedition to Egypt, Mesopotamia, Arabia, and Palestine in the Interest of the Institute, 1920." It was prepared at Judson's request for distribution to Chicago's trustees and JDR Jr.'s advisers: JHB to CB, 17 October 1920, JHBP. JHB also used the report for fund-raising purposes: JHB to John C. Merriam, 24 December 1920, DOC (Merriam was then president of the Carnegie Institution). For a published transcript of the report: *PttP:AA*, appendix B, 121–46. For a condensed version illustrated with expedition photographs and views of key acquisitions: JHB, *Oriental Institute . . . Beginning and Program*, 2–45. On the number of acquisitions: JHB, "Budget Recommendation for the Year 1921–22, Department of Oriental Institute and Haskell Oriental Museum," [ca. January–February?] 1921, PP 1889–1925, 51:8, UCA.

3. JHB, "Report of the First Expedition," 23–27 (emphases JHB's).

4. JHB, "The New Past," *University* [of Chicago] *Record*, new ser., 6, no. 4 (October 1920): 237–56, quote from p. 244. JHR, *The New History*. GEH, "The New Heavens," *Scribner's Magazine* 68, no. 4 (October 1920): 387–402, subsequently republished as *The New Heavens* (New York: Charles Scribner's Sons, 1922). For "age of new things" quote: Baxter F. McLendon, *The Story of My Life and Other Sermons* (Lynchburg, VA: Brown-Morrison, 1923), 38, cited in Willard B. Gatewood Jr., *Controversy in the Twenties: Fundamentalism, Modernism, and Evolution* (Nashville: Vanderbilt University Press, 1969), 5. See also Breisach, *American Progressive History*, 61.

5. JHB, "New Past," 238, 241, 246–47, 250, 256 (emphases JHB's). The essay formed the basis for at least two subsequent addresses and two publications: JHB, "The New Past," in *The New Past and Other Essays on the Development of Civilization*, ed. Edward H. Carter (Oxford: Basil Blackwell, 1925), 1–16; JHB, "The New Orient," address [in Jerusalem], 27 March 1928, JHBP; and JHB, "The New Crusade," address [as president of the American Historical Association], 2 November 1928, JHBP. The latter was revised and published under the same

title in *American Historical Review* 34, no. 2 (January 1929): 215–36. Regarding CB's recollection of the address, see *PttP*, 316–18.

6. JHB, manuscript, "Oriental History as a Field of Investigation," [December 1912], JHBP. The text is dated December 1913 and labeled as being read at the "American Historical Society." For the correct date and location—the American Historical Association annual conference: "Meeting of the American Historical Association . . . , *American Historical Review* 18, no. 3 (April 1913): 452–53. JHB was invited to give the paper in an ancient history session on "the most profitable fields now open for investigation": Charles H. Haskins to JHB, 9 October 1912, DOC. [JHB], *A Historical Laboratory: How the Expert Historian Does His Work* (Boston: Ginn, 1922).

7. JHB, *Oriental Institute . . . Beginning and Program*, 2. A listing of the OI's publications, complete through 1991 and organized by series (which grew to twelve), is in Thomas A. Holland, ed., *Publications of the Oriental Institute, 1906–1991*, Oriental Institute Communications, no. 26 (Chicago: Oriental Institute, University of Chicago, 1991). Holland's history of the OI's publications program is on pp. xi–xiv. Oriental Institute Communications and Oriental Institute Publications were later counted, respectively, as the second and third OI publication series. The first, Ancient Records: English Translations of Historical Documents of the Ancient Near East, Especially Egypt, Babylonia, and Assyria, was relatively short lived. JHB began it anachronistically, with his *ARoE*, and the only other publication was that by his former student Daniel D. Luckenbill, *Ancient Records of Assyria and Babylonia*, 2 vols. (Chicago: University of Chicago Press, 1926–27). On Harper's *Official Bulletins*, see Meyer, "Chicago Faculty," 68–69.

8. JHB, *Oriental Institute . . . Beginning and Program*, 54, 87–88. On the display "system": JHB, "Budget Recommendation . . . 1921–22." Françoise Levie, *L'Homme qui voulait classer le monde: Paul Otlet et le Mundaneum* (Brussels: Impressions Nouvelles, 2006). On the further development and end of JHB's "Archives and Archaeological Corpus": *TOI*, 401–7 (emphasis JHB's).

9. JHB, *Oriental Institute . . . Beginning and Program*, 65–73. The starting date is from JHB to AHG, 12 October 1921, DOC. See also *TOI*, 378–400; Erica Reiner, *An Adventure of Great Dimension: The Launching of the Chicago Assyrian Dictionary*, Transactions of the American Philosophical Society, vol. 92, pt. 3 (Philadelphia: American Philosophical Society, 2002); Matthew W. Stolper, "The Chicago Assyrian Dictionary at Seventy," *Oriental News and Notes*, 129 (May–June 1991): 1–2, 10; and Martha T. Roth, "How We Wrote the Chicago Assyrian Dictionary," *Journal of Near Eastern Studies* 69, no. 1 (April 2010): 1–21. For an up-to-date list of published volumes: http://oi.uchicago.edu/research/pubs/catalog/cad (accessed August 2010).

10. *DoRaT*, 272–73n1; JHB, *Oriental Institute . . . Beginning and Program*, 74–77. *TOI*, 152–55 (emphasis JHB's), table from pp. 152–54.

11. JHB credits Danish Egyptologist Hans Lange with suggesting the Coffin Texts project as a fitting first initiative for the OI: JHB to AHG, 31 July 1921, DOC. *WWWE*, s.v. "Hans Ostenfeldt Lange." *WWWE*, s.v. "Alan Henderson Gardiner"; AHG, *My Working Years* (London: Coronet, 1962). The latter contains a somewhat flawed account of the Coffin Texts project's inception (pp. 34–35), which the present discussion corrects. On his relationship with JHB, AHG regarded it warmly and as "a much valued friendship, [that] is shabbily disguised or rather ignored in [*PttP*]," pp. 34, 52. JHB's and AHG's first meeting is recounted on p. 52, although AHG's recollection of the date is off by a year. JHB to Harriet Breasted, 7 July 1901, LtP, JHBP. On JHB's and AHG's correspondence and mutual interests, see, for example, JHB to AHG, 13 August 1905, Gardiner MSS, 42.37.25, and 3 September 1912, Gardiner MSS, 42.37.22, GI. On the importance of AHG's Ipuwer book for JHB's work, see chapter 5 of the present volume. JHB to AHG, 18 May, and AHG to JHB, 27 June 1921, DOC. On consulting the work of others: JHB to AHG, 7 January 1913, Gardiner MSS, 42.37.21, GI. JHB's quote of Erman was in German: "Wenn Ich die schwierigen [S]tellen bei anderen nachschlage, so finde

Ich das die anderen auch nichts verstanden haben." My thanks to Donald Haase, professor of German, Wayne State University, for his advice on the translation.

12. JHB to AHG, 31 July 1921, DOC. *WWWE*, s.v. "Adriaan de Buck." Partial accounts of the Coffin Texts project are in *TOI*, 149–68; and Adriaan de Buck, introduction to *The Egyptian Coffin Texts*, 7 vols., Oriental Institute Publications, nos. 34, 49, 64, 67, 73, 81, 87 (Chicago: University of Chicago Press, 1935–1961), 1:ix–xv. On the larger Egyptological context of the Coffin Texts project: James P. Allen, "The American Discovery of Middle Kingdom Texts," in *The American Discovery of Ancient Egypt: Essays*, ed. Nancy Thomas (Los Angeles: Los Angeles County Museum of Art, 1996), 44–55.

13. JHB to AHG, 31 July 1921, and AHG to JHB, 12 September 1921, DOC. On the coffins census: *TOI*, 164. AHG to JHB, 21 September 1921, Gardiner MSS, 42.38.2, GI.

14. On vertical versus horizontal formatting of transcriptions: AHG to JHB, 21 September 1921, Gardiner MSS, 42.38.2, GI; JHB to AHG, 12 October, and AHG to JHB, 13 October 1921, DOC. *TOI*, 158–59. Howard T. Senzel, "Looseleafing the Flow: An Anecdotal History of One Technology for Updating," *American Journal of Legal History* 44, no. 2 (April 2000): 115–97. JHB to AHG, 25 October, and JHB, manuscript, "Memorandum of Agreement," 26 October 1921, DOC. AHG to JHB, 4 December, and JHB to AHG, 23 December 1921, DOC. AHG to JHB, 27 January, JHB to AHG, 15 May, JHB, manuscript, "Rules of Work and Arrangement of Manuscript," [ca. 15] May, JHB to AHG, 23 May, and AHG to JHB, 18 September 1922, DOC. JHB, *Oriental Institute . . . Beginning and Program*, 79. On Coffin Texts photography: JHB to AHG, 19 November 1922, DOC.

15. On AHG's comment on JHB: AHG, *My Working Years*, 36. *TOI*, 159–61. BTM, 12 June 1924, 14:199, UCA. JHB to AHG, 12 June, and AHG to JHB, 19 June 1924, DOC. JHB, "Revised Memorandum on the Coffin Texts," 30 July 1925, Gardiner MSS, 42.38.3, GI (another copy is in DOC). *WWWE*, s.v. "Pierre Lucien Lacau" and "(Thomas) George Allen." JHB to AHG, 19 October, and JHB, "Memorandum of a Conversation between Alan H. Gardiner and James H. Breasted, London," 20 October 1925, DOC. See also AHG to JHB, 16 January, and JHB to AHG, 6 February 1930, DOC. De Buck, introduction, *Egyptian Coffin Texts*, 1:xiii. Clearly, de Buck was influenced by the views of AHG, whose work he cites in particular: AHG, "The Transcription of New Kingdom Hieratic," *Journal of Egyptian Archaeology* 15 (1929): 48–55. For a clear and concise discussion of hieroglyphic paleography: Henry G. Fischer, "Archaeological Aspects of Epigraphy and Palaeography," in *Ancient Egyptian Epigraphy and Palaeography* (New York: Metropolitan Museum of Art, 1976), 27–50.

16. Much of the following discussion is based on Erik Iversen, *The Myth of Egypt and Its Hieroglyphs in European Tradition*, 2nd ed. (Princeton, NJ: Princeton University Press, 1993).

17. Iverson, *Myth of Egypt*, 45–46, 60–73, 86–87. *Encyclopaedia Britannica*, 11th ed., s.v. "Plotinus." Plotinus, *Enneads* [*Prohemium Marsilii Ficini Florentini in Plotinum . . .*] (Florence: Antonio Miscomini, 1492). Hans Georg Hörwarth von Hohenburg, *Thesaurus hieroglyphicorum è museo . . .* ([Munich?: Hörwarth von Hohenburg?], 1610).

18. Iverson, *Myth of Egypt*, 92–98; quote from p. 97. Athanasius Kircher, *Turris Babel, sive Archontologia qua prime priscorum . . .* (Amsterdam: Janssonius van Waesberge, 1679); and Kircher, *Oedipus aegyptiacus, hoc est vniuersalis hieroglyphicae . . .* (Rome: V. Mascardi, 1652–54). On Kircher's transcriptions of hieroglyphs: Helen Whitehouse, "Towards a Kind of Egyptology: The Graphic Documentation of Ancient Egypt, 1587–1666," in *Documentary Culture: Florence and Rome from Grand-Duke Ferdinand I to Pope Alexander VII*, ed. Elizabeth Cropper, Giovanna Perini, and Francesco Solinas (Bologna: Nuova Elfa Editoriale, 1992), 63–79. *The Compact Edition of the Oxford English Dictionary* (1971), s.v. "Egyptology."

19. *Description de l'Égypte*, 19 vols. (Paris: Imprimerie Impériale, 1809–28). *WWWE*, s.v. "Thomas Young" and "(Niccolo Francesco) Ippolito Baldessare Rosellini." My overview is not a probing examination of Egyptology's history, a topic wanting systematic scholarly treatment. This gap will be filled by Jason Thompson's forthcoming book tentatively titled *Wonderful Things: A History of Egyptology* (Cairo: American University in Cairo Press, forth-

coming). Wilson, *Signs and Wonders* contains a broad, if brief survey despite the limited scope implied by its subtitle: pp. 1–123. Although the text is not accompanied by footnotes, it does include a chapter-by-chapter bibliography. A concise, up-to-date summary, followed by a fine bibliography, that concludes with art history considerations is *The Dictionary of Art*, s.v., "Egypt, Ancient, XVIII, Rediscovery." See also Baines and Malek, "The Study of Ancient Egypt," in *Cultural Atlas of Ancient Egypt*, 22–29.

20. For an excellent overview of epigraphic techniques, see Ricardo A. Caminos, "The Recording of Inscriptions and Scenes in Tombs and Temples," in *Ancient Egyptian Epigraphy and Palaeography*, 2nd. ed. (New York: Metropolitan Museum of Art, 1979), 3–25. See also Peter F. Dorman, "Epigraphy and Recording," in *Egyptology Today*, ed. Richard H. Wilkinson (Cambridge: Cambridge University Press, 2008), 77–97. JHB did a fine job of setting Egyptian epigraphy in the context of Egyptology's beginnings, and he did it often. See, for example: *TOI*, 187–98. A more thorough study, by one of JHB's students, emphasizes America's contributions in its later chapters: Wilson, *Signs and Wonders*. More recent essays on American contributions to Egyptology, including its epigraphic work, are collected in Nancy Thomas with essays by Gerry D. Scott III and Bruce G. Trigger, *The American Discovery of Ancient Egypt* (Los Angeles: Los Angeles County Museum of Art and American Research Center in Egypt, 1995); and Thomas, ed., *The American Discovery of Ancient Egypt: Essays*, (Los Angeles: Los Angeles County Museum of Art and American Research Center in Egypt, 1996). The evolution of epigraphic techniques continues: Peter Der Manuelian, "Digital Epigraphy: An Approach to Streamlining Egyptological Epigraphic Method," *JARCE* (*Journal of the American Research Center in Egypt*) 35 (1998): 97–113. Careful readers will note that many of these works incorrectly characterize the history of JHB's epigraphic efforts leading up to the development of the "Chicago House method" (discussed below). See chapters 2 and 4 of the present volume for accurate information. Finally, there are significant differences between epigraphy and drawings made to document archaeological excavations. One can discern these differences by comparing, for example, the Caminos essay cited above with Stuart Piggott, "Archaeological Draughtsmanship: Principles and Practice. Part I: Principles and Retrospect," *Antiquity* 39, no. 155 (September 1965): 165–76.

WWWE, s.v. "John Williams" and "Percy Newberry." For a discussion of John Williams's rubbings, see Rosalind Moss, "Some Rubbings of Egyptian Monuments Made a Hundred Years Ago," *Journal of Egyptian Archaeology* 27 (1941): 7–11. Percy E. Newberry and F. L. Griffith, *El Bersheh*, 2 vols., Archaeological Survey of Egypt, nos. 3–4 (London: Egypt Exploration Fund, [1893–94?]). T. G. H. James, *Howard Carter: The Path to Tutankhamun*, rev. pbk. ed. (London: Tauris Parke, 2001); on Carter's copying, see pp. 56–57. Kurt Sethe, *Die altägyptischen Pyramidentexte: Nach den Papierabdrücken und Photographien des Berliner Museums*, 4 vols. (Leipzig: J. C. Hinrichs, 1908–22). *DoRaT*, vii–ix. Some Egyptologists, especially the French, reduced their copies of hieroglyphic inscriptions to typesetting, lending to their transcriptions a typographic severity quite foreign to the original sources. See, for example, Émile Chassinat, *Le Temple de Dendara*, vol. 5, part 1 (Cairo: Institut Français d'Archéologie Orientale, 1952).

21. M. [Dominique François Jean] Arago, *Rapport de M. Arago sur le daguerréotype* (Paris: Bachelier, 1839), 25–26. *WWWE*, s.v. "(Dominique) François Jean Arago." The translation is mine. The full original text reads:

A l'inspection de plusieurs des tableaux qui ont passé sous vos yeux, chacun songera à l'immense parti qu'on aurait tiré, pendant l'expédition d'Égypte, d'un moyen de reproduction si exact et si prompt; chacun sera frappé de cetté réflexion, que si la photographie avait été connue en 1798, nous aurions aujourd'hui des images fidèles d'un bon nombre de tableaux emblématiques, dont la cupidité des Arabes et le vandalisme de certains voyageurs, ont privé à jamais le monde savant.

Pour copier les millions et millions d'hiéroglyphes qui couvrent, même a l'extérieur, les grands monuments de Thèbes, de Memphis, de Karnak, etc., il faudrait des vingtaines d'années et des légions de dessinateurs. Avec le Daguerréotype, un seul homme pourrait mener à bonne fin cet immense travail.

22. On the history of photography in the Middle East in general and Egypt in particular, see chapter 3 of the present volume and nn. 2, 5, and 6 in that chapter. Scholarship on tourist and travel photography has grown markedly in recent years, particularly in the contexts of colonialism and cultural imperialism. See, for example, Eleanor M. Hight and Gary D. Sampson, eds., *Colonialist Photography: Imag(in)ing Race and Place*, (London: Routledge, 2002); and James R. Ryan, *Picturing Empire: Photography and the Visualization of the British Empire* (Chicago: University of Chicago Press, 1997). The usefulness of this work for understanding the origins and development of archaeological photography is quite limited, however, because of a tendency to confuse photography of ancient sites made for the tourist trade, or popular consumption at home, with photographs made for archaeological study. A history concentrating on photography's role in archaeology would be most helpful but remains to be written. There are only a few brief sketches, such as Peter G. Dorrell, "The Early Days of Archaeological Photography," in *Photography in Archaeology and Conservation* (Cambridge: Cambridge University Press, 1989), 1–7. Work along these lines is more advanced among anthropology historians, and some of their insights are applicable to the development of archaeological photography. See, for example, Elizabeth Edwards, ed., *Anthropology and Photography, 1860–1920* (New Haven, CT: Yale University Press, 1992); and the exhibition catalog Melissa Banta and Curtis M. Hinsley, *From Site to Sight: Anthropology, Photography, and the Power of Imagery* (Cambridge, MA: Peabody Museum Press, 1986).

23. Perez, *Focus East*, 191. J. B. Greene, *Fouilles exécutées à Thèbes dans l'année 1855, textes hiéroglyphiques et documents inédits* (Paris: Librarie de Firmin Didot Frères, 1855). Greene was so proud of his squeeze-based work-around that he sent a secret announcement to France's Academy of Sciences, causing a stir and then disappointment when his innovation was found to be so cumbersome and modest. One of the copies I examined, in the Chicago House research library, Luxor, Egypt, is accompanied by a second oblong volume (titled *Fouilles exécutées à Thèbes*, 1855), an album of photographs including close-up views of inscriptions, sections of statues, sections of walls, etc., that appear to be study images or visual notes. A careful examination of all the transcriptions and source photographs—in the Chicago House and University of Glasgow copies—clearly shows that his drawings were done freehand. See also Bruno Jammes, "John B. Greene, an American Calotypist," *History of Photography* 5, no. 4 (October 1981): 305–24; and Andre Jammes and Eugenia Parry Janis, *The Art of the French Calotype* (Princeton, NJ: Princeton University Press, 1983), 121n186. An example of the misunderstanding regarding Greene's work is Lanny Bell, "New Kingdom Epigraphy," in *The American Discovery of Ancient Egypt: Essays*, ed. Nancy Thomas (Los Angeles: Los Angeles County Museum of Art, 1996), 105. Félix Guilmant, *Le tombeau de Ramsès IX* (Cairo: Imprimerie de l'Institut Français d'Archéologie Orientale, 1907). On the assertion concerning Guilmant's use of a chemical-bleaching process: Caminos, "Recording of Inscriptions," 10. Caminos offers only the book itself as evidence, but the book does not contain any text other than title pages and plate labels. The only evidence of Guilmant's use of photography in the book is the inclusion of three excellent but unaltered "détails photographiés" following the ninety-three drawings that constitute the book's contents.

Early in the history of photography, it was used to publish hieroglyphs by photographing a hand-drawn transcription and making a limited number of photographic prints from the negative: Ricardo A. Caminos, "The Talbotype Applied to Hieroglyphics," *Journal of Egyptian Archaeology* 52 (1966): 65–70. JHB's colleague and fellow American George Reisner, who helped pioneer truly systematic and fully documented excavation techniques, began experimenting with photography to record finds in situ starting in 1899 and by the early 1900s was employing it regularly. Peter Der Manuelian, "George Andrew Reisner on Archeological Photography," *JARCE* (*Journal of the American Research Center in Egypt*) 29 (1992): 1–34; and Joan Knudsen and Patricia Podzorski, "Focus on Egypt's Past," *KMT: A Modern Journal of Ancient*

Egypt 5 (Spring 1994): 62–69, 87. The differences between JHB's and Reisner's research programs—epigraphy versus excavation—surfaced in their respective photographic problems and solutions, a topic that also warrants further historical study.

24. JHB, *Oriental Forerunners*. For JHB's initial assessments of the medical papyrus: JHB, "The Edwin Smith Papyrus: An Egyptian Medical Treatise of the Seventeenth Century before Christ," *New York Historical Society Quarterly Bulletin* 6 (1922): 3–31; and JHB, "The Edwin Smith Papyrus: Some Preliminary Observations," in *Recueil d'études égyptologiques dédiées à la mémoire de Jean-François Champollion . . .* (Paris: E. Champion, 1922), 385–429. JHB to CB, 6 January and 17 October 1920, JHBP. *PttP*, 316–18, 324–25. CB began drawing a salary related to JHB's work when he started assisting his father as a "secretary" with the ill-fated Egyptian Museum project in August 1925 (see chapter 8 of the present volume), and he joined the OI's payroll 1 July 1927 as assistant to the director: JHB, diary entries, 27 July 1925 and 24 December 1927, JHBP; and *PttP*, 398–99.

Regarding Harriet Breasted, JHB's sister, May, married a Robert S. Padan, and they were in Chicago by 1902, when Harriet Breasted moved in with them. Padan ceased to be in the picture by 1909, however, and May and Harriet remained apartment mates until May's death in 1914. *Chicago Blue Book*, 1890–1915, http://libsysdigi.library.illinois.edu/oca/Books2007 -10/chicagobluebooko/ (accessed August 2010); and "Obituary," *Chicago Daily Tribune*, 2 March 1914.

25. *PttP*, 324. For a nearly complete list of JHB's honors and awards: Wilson, "James Henry Breasted," 112–14. See also: J[ean] M. R[oberts] to CB, 20 November 1934, JHBP. *Report of the National Academy of Sciences for the Year 1923* (Washington, DC: Government Printing Office, 1924), 18. GEH to John C. Merriam, 31 July 1919, GEHP; and Minutes, National Academy of Sciences Council, 15 November 1920 and 13 November 1922, GEHP. On members' opposition to JHB's election: Edwin B. Wilson to William M. Davis, 17 November, and William M. Davis to Edwin B. Wilson, 23 November 1922, Members: Breasted, J. H., 1923, NAS Archives; Edwin B. Wilson to William M. Davis, 25 November 1922, and Edwin B. Wilson to Edward B. Van Vleck, 30 April 1923, E. B. Wilson Papers, General, 1922–23, NAS Archives. On JHB's hand in drafting the NAS building legend: JHB, diary entry, 16 March 1925, JHBP; see also Wright, *Explorer*, 316. The dedication address is JHB, address, "Historical Tradition and Oriental Research," 29 April 1924, JHBP; the published version is JHB, "Historical Tradition and Oriental Research," *Proceedings of the National Academy of Sciences* 10, no. 7 (15 July 1924): 289–94. Three years after JHB's visit to Germany, Meyer's emotional wounds from the war were less raw; he too warmly greeted JHB. JHB, diary entries, 1 July, 4 November (source of Meyer quote), and 2 December 1922 and 16 March 1925, JHBP; and AHG to JHB, 21 September 1921, Gardiner MSS, 42.38.2, GI.

26. JHB, proposal, "Future and Development of the Oriental Institute," 23 November 1923, PP 1898–1925, 51:9, UCA (emphases JHB's). The Museum of Comparative Zoology was administratively joined with two other Harvard University natural science museums in 1998 to form the Harvard Museum of Natural History. For a brief historical sketch and link to a bibliography on the zoology museum: http://www.mcz.harvard.edu/about/history.html (accessed October 2008).

27. JHB, "Future and Development" (emphases and parenthetical comments JHB's). $50,000 = $628,000, and $775,000 = $9.74 million CPI 2009.

28. On Burton's ascent to the presidency and the immediate university context of JHB's proposal: Meyer, "Chicago Faculty," 411–28. JHB to JDR Jr., 24 November 1923, RFA/RG 2, OMR/JDR Jr. series, Educational Interests subseries, box 111, Univ. of Chicago, Oriental Inst., env. 1, RAC. JDR Jr. to Ernest D. Burton [copy to JHB], 26 November 1923, RFA/RG 2, OMR/JDR Jr. series, Educational Interests subseries, box 112, Univ. of Chicago, Oriental Inst., 3 yr. pledge–5 yr. pledge, RAC. JHB to Ernest D. Burton, 30 November 1923, PP 1898– 1925, 9:20, UCA.

29. Ernest D. Burton to JDR Jr., 1 December 1923, RFA/RG 2, OMR/JDR Jr. series, Educational Interests subseries, box 112, Univ. of Chicago, Oriental Inst., 3 yr. pledge–5 yr.

pledge, RAC. JDR Jr. to Ernest D. Burton, 4 December 1923, PP 1898–1925, 51:8, UCA. JDR Jr. to FTG, 4 December 1923, RFA/RG 2, OMR/JDR Jr. series, Educational Interests sub-series, box 112, Univ. of Chicago, Oriental Inst., Dec. 29, 1923 Pledge, RAC. JHB to FTG, 17 December 1923, DOC.

30. FTG to JDR Jr., 26 December 1923, RFA/RG 2, OMR/JDR Jr. series, Educational Interests subseries, box 111, Univ. of Chicago, Oriental Inst., env. 1, RAC. The Rockefellers' trip to Egypt was prompted by an invitation JHB had arranged, from Howard Carter, for them to be present at the opening of Tutankhamun's sarcophagus later that winter: JHB, diary entry, 16 March 1925, JHBP. JHB to GEH, 31 December 1923, GEHP (emphasis JHB's). JDR Jr. to Ernest D. Burton, 29 December 1923, PP 1889–1925, 51:8, UCA. On the developing relationship between JHB and the Rockefellers: JHB to FB, 1–6 January 1924, LtFHB, JHBP.

31. JHB to FB, 25 March 1924, Material relating to the Tomb of Tut-ankh-amun, JHBP. JHB to HHN, 31 January 1924, DOC. $3,500 = $43,900 CPI 2009. See also TOI, 69–70; and JHB, diary entry, 16 March 1925, JHBP. JHB to Charles L. Hutchinson, 27 August 1903, JHB File, CIW. HHN to JHB, 14 February 1924, DOC. JHB to A. R. Callender, 2 April 1924, DOC. Callender was the construction supervisor. WWWE, s.v. "Arthur Robert Callender."

32. TOI, 203–4 (emphasis JHB's). The same observations are presented in slightly different form in JHB, foreword to Medinet Habu, vol. 1, Earlier Historical Records of Ramses III, Oriental Institute Publications no. 8 (Chicago: University of Chicago Press, 1930), x–xi.

33. JHB to Eastman Kodak Company, 15 May 1924, and N. L. Ferris to JHB, 21 May 1924, DOC. JHB to HHN, 6 June 1924, DOC. The paper chosen was "Eastman P.M.C. Bromide #9." T. George Allen to JHB, 23 May and 10 June 1924, DOC.

34. The project titles "Epigraphic Expedition" and "Epigraphic Survey" were used interchangeably until the early 1930s, when its publications began to be issued under the latter. JHB seems to have preferred the former; see TOI, 187ff. JHB to HHN, 6 June, HHN to JHB, 30 June and 28 July, and JHB to HHN, 16 September 1924, DOC.

35. HHN to JHB, 10 August and 4 September 1924, DOC.

36. JHB to HHN, 1 October 1924, DOC.

37. HHN to JHB, 18, 22, and 27 November and 3 December 1924, DOC.

38. JHB to HHN, 19 December 1924, DOC (emphases JHB's).

39. JHB to HHN, 10 January 1925, and JHB, diary entry, 16 March 1925, JHBP. Dictionary of American Biography, Base Set 1928–36, s.v. "Julius Rosenwald." Dictionary of American Biography, supplements 1–2: To 1940, s.v. "Cyrus Hall McCormick" (1859–1936). For examples of the many details surrounding the Epigraphic Survey's beginnings: T. George Allen to HHN, 18 February, HHN to JHB, 27 September, and HHN to JHB, 9 December 1925, DOC.

40. HHN to T. George Allen, 26 January 1925, DOC. JHB to AHG, 28 March, HHN to JHB, 22 April 1925, DOC. The initial plan was for 16″ × 20″ blueprints; see HHN to JHB, 10 May 1925, DOC.

41. Regarding HHN's future: HHN to JHB, 25 May and 7 December 1925, DOC. The staff shortage was apparent to JHB during the survey's first season: JHB to AHG, 28 March 1925, DOC. He brought it up with HHN early in the second season: JHB to HHN, 13 October, and HHN to JHB, 24 November 1925, DOC. JHB, diary entry, 7 June 1925, JHBP; JHB to Abraham Flexner, 5 June 1925, GEB/2324.2, Oriental Inst./series I, subseries 4, box 659, folder 6851, RAC. JHB, proposal, "A New Area of Humanistic Research and a Plan for Beginning Its Investigation," [ca. late September 1925], PP 1920–80, 12:9, UCA. In 1919 and 1924 JHB unsuccessfully proposed to the Carnegie Institution studies similar to the "geological-paleontological survey"; see, respectively, chapter 6 of the present volume and JHB to John C. Merriam, 6 June 1924, JHB File, CIW. After being funded by the GEB the project was renamed the "Prehistoric Survey." On its inception and first few publications: TOI, 73–74, 129–44.

42. JDR Jr. to RBF, 7 October, JDR Jr. to JHB, 8 October, and JHB to JDR Jr., 12 October 1925, RFA/RG 2, OMR/JDR Jr. series, Educational Interests subseries, box 112, Univ. of Chicago, Oriental Inst., Egyptian Research, RAC. On JHB's diet and health: Bull, Speiser,

and Olmstead, "Breasted," 118. The university rounded the request up to $200,000: Trevor Arnett to Wickliffe Rose, 1 December, and W. W. Brierley to Max Mason, 5 December 1925, GEB/2324.2, Oriental Institute/series 1, subseries 4, box 659, folder 6851, RAC. $200,000 = $2.45 million, and $50,000 = $612,000 CPI 2009.

On the boards' support for the humanities: RBF, *Story of the Rockefeller Foundation*, 237–51; and Abraham Flexner, *Funds and Foundations: Their Policies Past and Present* (New York: Harper and Brothers, 1952), 125–35. The influence of JHB's thinking on GEB policy can be seen in Abraham Flexner, "Memorandum on Humanities," 24 March, and Abraham Flexner to W. W. Brierley with enclosure, memorandum, "Humanities," 15 April 1926, GEB/2324.2, Oriental Institute/series 1, subseries 4, box 659, folder 6851, RAC. JHB continued to advocate the humanities to the GEB even in situations that had no bearing on the OI: JHB to Trevor Arnett with enclosure, "Memorandum on the Development of Humanistic Studies," 28 May 1928, GEB/2324.2, Oriental Inst./series 1, subseries 4, box 659, folder 6852, RAC. Whether the humanities were all that neglected by the time the GEB began to invest in them is an open question. For a nearly contemporaneous study of the subject: Frederic Austin Ogg, *Research in the Humanistic and Social Sciences* (New York: Century, 1928). Other scholars in the following decade noted a general shift toward humanities funding and often commented on the OI's outsized share of such grants: Frederick Paul Keppel, "Philanthropy and Learning," in *Philanthropy and Learning, with Other Papers* (New York: Columbia University Press, 1936), 27; and Ernest Victor Hollis, *Philanthropic Foundations and Higher Education* (New York: Columbia University Press, 1938), 259. See also Kathleen D. McCarthy, "The Short and Simple Annals of the Poor: Foundation Funding for the Humanities, 1900–1983," *Proceedings of the American Philosophical Society* 129, no. 1 (March 1985): 3–8.

43. JHB, diary entry, 22 December 1927, DOC; and *TOI*, 72. JHB to HHN, 3 January, HHN to T. George Allen, 7 January, and HHN to JHB, 13 January 1926, DOC. On book orders: T. George Allen to HHN, 16 July, and HHN to T. George Allen, 22 July 1926, DOC.

44. On publishing "reliefs, in which the inscriptions appear as part of the scene": HHN to JHB, 22 October 1926, DOC. JHB to AHG, 8 May and 16 August, HHN to JHB, 1 April and 2, 26, and 29 August 1926, DOC.

45. *TOI*, 198–200. HHN to JHB, 3 December 1926, DOC. *WWWE*, s.v. "Caroline Louise (*née* Ransom) Williams" and "John Albert Wilson." See also the latter's autobiography: Wilson, *Thousands of Years*. JHB to HHN, 2 December 1926, DOC. On the research library: HHN to JHB, 5 October 1926, DOC. HHN to T. George Allen, 27 January 1927, DOC. For one of JHB's several comments on the reliefs' artistic merits: JHB to HHN, 25 October 1927, DOC. Despite the strict procedures of the Chicago House method, the individual styles of the draftsmen and artists who transcribed the reliefs are very evident: [John Carswell], *Artists in Egypt: An Exhibition of Paintings and Drawings by Artists Employed by the Oriental Institute in Egypt, 1920–1935* (Chicago: Oriental Institute, University of Chicago, 1977).

46. HHN, "The Epigraphic Survey," in *Medinet Habu, 1924–1928* (Chicago: University of Chicago Press, 1929), 12–13 (emphasis HHN's). On the circumstances of the survey's methodological changes, see also Wilson, *Thousands of Years*, 52–53. In relation to Wilson's account, see also HHN, "Epigraphic Survey," 30–31 and figures 17–20. JHB hints at the adoption of what would become the new method in: JHB to HHN, 12 February 1927, DOC. On the translation of hieroglyphs into actual typographic fonts: *The Dictionary of Art*, s.v. "Egypt, Ancient, XVIII Rediscovery (3. Epigraphers)"; and Caminos, "Recording of Inscriptions," 11. On the Coffin Texts approach to the transcription of hieroglyphs, see, in addition to the treatment above, de Buck, introduction to *Egyptian Coffin Texts*, 1: xiii–xiv.

47. Although the decision to revamp the process was made jointly by JHB and HHN, the initiative to do so appears to have come from HHN earlier in the 1926–27 season: HHN to JHB, 3 December 1926, DOC. The description of the Chicago House method is from HHN, introduction to *Medinet Habu*, vol. 1, *Earlier Historical Records of Ramses III*, Oriental Institute Publications, no. 8 (Chicago: University of Chicago Press, 1930), 10.

Additional information is drawn from JHB's longer and more detailed description in *TOI*, 204–12. The new method was characterized earlier in JHB, foreword to HHN, *Medinet Habu, 1924–1928*, ix.

48. JHB to Harold H. Swift, 2 August 1927, H. H. Swift Papers, 168:3, UCA (emphasis JHB's). The quote on "accuracy" in the Chicago House method is from Lanny Bell, "The Epigraphic Survey: The Philosophy of Egyptian Epigraphy after Sixty Years' Practical Experience," in *Problems and Priorities in Egyptian Archaeology*, ed. Jan Assmann, Gunter Burkard, and Vivian Davies (London: KPI, 1987), 47. See also Lanny Bell, William Murnane, and Bernard Fishman, "The Epigraphic Survey (Chicago House)," *NARCE* (*Newsletter of the American Research Center in Egypt*) 118 (1982): 3–18.

Questions surrounding the creation of epigraphic images have moved beyond practice to theory. The context of Bell's observation on accuracy cited above is a discussion of the role of conjecture and judgment in completing damaged texts or scenes. The Egyptologist's uses of photographs and direct studies of inscriptions restrain but do not prohibit the application of his or her prior knowledge of Egyptian hieroglyphs and culture in the collation process. Thus, Bell observes, the Epigraphic Survey is "in reality producing *rationalized* facsimile copies." Bell, "The Epigraphic Survey," 47 (emphasis Bell's). Relevant to this inquiry is the function of "aesthetic" considerations in astronomers' preparations of their images for publication. See, for example, Michael Lynch and Samuel Y. Edgerton Jr., "Aesthetics and Digital Image Processing: Representational Craft in Contemporary Astronomy," in *Picturing Power: Visual Depiction and Social Relations*, ed. Gordon Fyfe and John Law (London: Routledge, 1988), 184–220. Lynch and Edgerton discuss astronomers' "cleaning" of their images as a means of "composing visible coherences, discriminating differences, consolidating entities, and establishing evident relations," p. 212. See also Stephanie Moser and Sam Smiles, "Introduction: The Image in Question," in *Envisioning the Past: Archaeology and the Image*, ed. Stephanie Moser and Sam Smiles (Oxford: Blackwell, 2005), 1–12.

The reviews, in order of quotation, are S. R. K. Glanville, review of *Medinet Habu*, vol. 3, *The Calendar, The "Slaughter-House," and Minor Records of Ramses III*, by the Epigraphic Survey, *Journal of Egyptian Archaeology* 25, no. 1 (June 1939): 122; T. Eric Peet, review of *Medinet Habu*, vol. 1: *Earlier Historical Records of Ramses III*, and vol. 2, *Later Historical Records of Ramses III*, by the Epigraphic Survey, *Journal of Egyptian Archaeology* 20, no. 1–2 (June 1934): 123–24; and Henry George Fischer, *Medinet Habu*, vol. 5, *The Temple Proper, Part I*, by the Epigraphic Survey, *American Journal of Archaeology* 63, no. 2 (April 1959): 195–98. Excerpts of more recent reviews of Epigraphic Survey publications are in Lanny Bell, "The Epigraphic Survey and the Rescue of the Monuments of Ancient Egypt," in *The Ancient Eastern Mediterranean*, ed. Eleanor Guralnick (Chicago: Archaeological Institute of America, 1990), 7–15. The Epigraphic Survey has issued a large number of books: Holland, *Publications of the Oriental Institute*, 6–11. For the most current list, which includes free pdf downloads of most of the Epigraphic Survey publications: http://oi.uchicago.edu/research/pubs/catalog/egypt.html (accessed August 2010).

49. HHN to CB, 19 January and 26 May 1929, DOC. The Epigraphic Survey's work at Medinet Habu continues, and new volumes are in preparation as of this writing. On life at Chicago House: Wilson, *Thousands of Years*, 56–59. On the Victrola: JHB to HHN, 18 June 1926, DOC. Two years later CB picked out more records, "at least 64, nicely divided between mellifluous jazz of the less strident kind and some very delightful classical things of the sort which will gratify the cosmopolitan tastes of Chicago House": CB to HHN, 1 September 1928, DOC; see CB to HHN, 5 September 1928, DOC, for a list of the records. The still-working Victrola and record collection remain at Chicago House. On staff research: HHN to JHB, 9 August, and JHB to HHN, 14 September 1927, DOC. JHB honored his commitment to publishing Epigraphic Survey staff members' research, and the earliest vehicle was the Oriental Institute Communications series. See, for example: Uvo Hölscher and John A. Wilson, *Medinet Habu Studies, 1928/29*, Oriental Institute Communications, no. 7 (Chicago: University of Chicago Press, 1930).

50. The functionary quote is from JHB, diary entry, 16 March 1925, JHBP. GEH to JHB, 26 May 1925, JHBP.

Chapter 8

1. JHB, diary entry, 16 March 1925, JHBP; *PttP*, 243, 330. *WWWE*, s.v. "George Edward Stanhope Molyneux Herbert, 5th Earl of Carnarvon." See also JHB to Harry Pratt Judson, 7 December 1919, PP 1889–1925, 9:19, UCA. T. Eric Peet, *The Great Tomb Robberies of the Twentieth Egyptian Dynasty . . .*, 2 vols. (Oxford: Clarendon, 1930).

2. James, *Howard Carter*, 1–247; *WWWE*, s.v. "Howard Carter." *PttP*, 161–62, 327–30. For additional information on the Theban necropolis in general and the Valley of the Kings in particular: http://www.thebanmappingproject.com (accessed November 2008).

3. James, *Howard Carter*, 251–57, quote from p. 257.

4. James, *Howard Carter*, 263–84. "An Egyptian Treasure," *Times* (London), 30 November 1922. Nicholas Reeves, *The Complete Tutankhamun: The King, the Tomb, the Royal Treasure* (London: Thames and Hudson, 1990).

5. James, *Howard Carter*, 272–73. JHB, diary entry, 16 March 1925, JHBP. *WWWE*, s.v. "Herbert Eustis Winlock." Quotes regarding JHB's first visit are from JHB to JDR Jr., 29 December 1922, DOC; and JHB, *Some Experiences in the Tomb of Tutenkhamon*, Alumni Pamphlets, no. 2 (Chicago: University of Chicago, 1924), 1–10, reprinted from article under same title in *Art and Archaeology*, 17 (1924): 3–18. There are some contradictions among published sources about the dates of the Tutankhamun discovery and excavation process. The most reliable chronology is Carter's diary: http://www.griffith.ox.ac.uk/gri/4elres.html (accessed November 2008).

6. JHB to JDR Jr., 29 December 1922, DOC; JHB, *Some Experiences*, 10–13.

7. JHB, *Some Experiences*, 13–14. On JHB's assistance with the seals, see also Howard Carter and A. C. Mace, *The Tomb of Tut-Ankh-Amen: Discovered by the Late Earl of Carnarvon and Howard Carter*, 3 vols. (London: Cassell, 1923), 1:109, 178; 3:100; and Margaret Gardiner, "Tut'ankhamun and My Long-Lived Father," in *A Scatter of Memories* (London: Free Association Books, 1988), 102–3. On Astrid's presence: JHB, "Archaeology," in *Compton's Pictured Encyclopedia* (Chicago: F. E. Compton, 1935), 1:249–50. JHB, [Report on seal impressions], Tutankhamun Archive, i.3.22 (folder ii), GI.

8. James, *Howard Carter*, 288–92. On publicity stresses, see also *PttP*, 345.

9. Jacques Berque, *Egypt: Imperialism and Revolution*, trans. Jean Stewart (London: Faber and Faber, 1972); and Afaf Lutfi al-Sayyid-Marsot, *Egypt's Liberal Experiment: 1922–1936* (Berkeley: University of California Press, 1977). *WWWE*, s.v. "François Auguste Ferdinand Mariette." On the history of Middle Eastern antiquities laws: Morag M. Kersel, "The Changing Legal Landscape for Middle Eastern Archeology in the Colonial Era, 1800–1930," in *PttP:AA*, 85–90.

10. James, *Howard Carter*, 302–3, 314–15, 320–30. *PttP*, 346–47, 355. Elliott Colla, *Conflicted Antiquities: Egyptology, Egyptomania, Egyptian Modernity* (Durham, NC: Duke University Press, 2007), 183–210; John A. DeNovo, *American Interests and Policies in the Middle East, 1900–1939* (Minneapolis: University of Minnesota Press, 1963), 375–76; Goode, *Negotiating*, 67–97. Donald Malcolm Reid, "Nationalizing the Pharaonic Past: Egyptology, Imperialism, and Egyptian Nationalism, 1922–1952," in *Rethinking Nationalism in the Arab Middle East*, ed. James Jankowski and Israel Gershoni (New York: Columbia University Press, 1997), 129–33. See also Reid, *Whose Pharaohs?*, passim. Closing quotes are from, respectively, Reid, "Nationalizing," 129; and DeNovo, *American Interests*, 376.

11. James, *Howard Carter*, 327–28, 329–46, quotes from pp. 337, 340. *PttP*, 354–55, 358–68.

12. Howard Carter to JHB, 26 and 27 February, and JHB to Howard Carter, 26 February 1924, Material relating to the Tomb of Tut-ankh-amun, JHBP.

13. James, *Howard Carter*, 347–84, 437, 439–68. *PttP*, 368–72, "bandit" and subsequent

quotes from pp. 370–71. "Kicked" quote is from JHB, diary entry, 16 March 1925, JHBP. JHB was evenhanded in the negotiations to the extent that he suspected the motives of all involved: JHB to GEH, 22 and 25 March 1924, Material relating to the Tomb of Tut-ankh-amun, JHBP. JHB used a pair of lectures to the Egyptians' Historical Society of Egypt, delivered in Cairo, to steer public opinion about the controversy by allying Western and Egyptian interests in the antiquities. He closed the first lecture, which was attended by Egypt's minister of education, with a summation of ancient Egypt's "unique position when all the rest of the world was in complete savagery" and the West's debt to ancient Egypt, and then—claiming that he was not there to "preach a sermon"—he nonetheless remarked that he hoped his Egyptian audience would "remember that in inheriting that civilization, you have a great responsibility. The great past of your ancestors calls upon you to be worthy of it." "Egypt's Place in History. Prof. Breasted's Lecture," *Egyptian Gazette* 27 March 1923. Carter's niece donated his papers, including his records of the tomb's clearance, to the Griffith Institute, Oxford University: http://www.griffith.ox.ac.uk/gri/4records.html, s.v. "Howard Carter" (accessed August 2010).

14. The Rockefellers may have read the JHB reference in "Times Man Views Splendors of Tomb of Tutankhamun," *New York Times*, 22 December 1922. JHB to JDR Jr., 29 December 1922, JDR Jr. to JHB, 2 February 1923, DOC. On the Rockefeller Nile trip and tomb visit: JHB, diary entry, 16 March 1925, JHBP. James Stevens Curl, *Egyptomania, the Egyptian Revival: A Recurring Theme in the History of Taste* (Manchester: Manchester University Press, 1994); Jean-Marcel Humbert, Michael Pantazzi, and Christiane Ziegler, *Egyptomania: Egypt in Western Art, 1730–1930* (Ottawa: National Gallery of Canada, 1994).

15. JHB to Howard Carter, 9 July, and Howard Carter to JHB, 12 July 1923, Material relating to the Tomb of Tut-ankh-amun, DOC. On the publication assistance, see also James, *Howard Carter*, 293; on the slides, lecturing, and eventual publications, pp. 305–6, 393–94; on Carter's eventual American lecture tour, pp. 356–63, 371–73; and on an appearance at the University of Chicago hosted by JHB, pp. 359–61. JHB began receiving invitations to write and speak about the Tutankhamun discovery right away: Wm. B. Shaw (editor of *American Review of Reviews*) to JHB, 2 February, and Louis J. Alber (manager of "Lecture Celebrities") to JHB, 26 March 1923, DOC. JHB declined in both cases and in the latter noted Carter's upcoming tour: JHB to Louis J. Alber, 22 August 1923, DOC.

The "Cairo Oriental Institute" plan is sketched out in JHB to CB, 6 January 1920, JHBP. Minutes, Division of Anthropology and Psychology National Research Council, 22 April 1921, Anthro. & Psych.: Meetings, annual: 1920–1924, NAS Archives; Clark Wissler to JHB, 26 May, and JHB to GEH, 18 July 1921, JHBP. On the $5 million plan and Hale's advice: GEH to JHB, 14 August, and JHB to GEH, 1 September 1921, JHBP. $5 million = $59.90 million CPI 2009.

16. GEH's vacation was to recover from a "nervous breakdown" in 1921: Walter S. Adams, "George Ellery Hale, 1868–1938," *Biographical Memoirs* (National Academy of Sciences) 21, no. 5 (1940): 213. Wright, *Explorer*, 344–45. JHB to GEH, 5 February 1923, GEHP. GEH, "Recent Discoveries in Egypt," *Scribner's Magazine* 74 (July 1923): 34–49. GEH, "The Work of an American Orientalist," *Scribner's Magazine* 74 (October 1923): 392–404. On JHB's remarks to GEH about the articles: Frederick H. Seares, "George Ellery Hale: The Scientist Afield," *Isis* 30, no. 2 (May 1939): 263–64.

17. Marcel C. LaFollette, *Making Science Our Own: Public Images of Science, 1910–1955* (Chicago: University of Chicago Press, 1990), 32–33, 45, 50–51. JHB, "Feats of Old Egyptians Rival Modern Works of Engineers," *Popular Mechanics* 42, no. 3 (September 1924): 403–8. On the cultivation of public interest more generally: Merle Curti, "Scholarship and Popularization of Learning," in *The Growth of American Thought* (New York: Harper and Row, 1943), 564–87.

18. *PttP*, 374. RBF, *Rockefeller, Jr.*, 351ff. $1 million = $12.50 million CPI 2009. On predecessors of the Egyptian Museum, its creation, and its function within the context of other Cairo-based museums through the first few decades of the twentieth century: Reid, *Whose*

Pharaohs?, 3–8, 22, 25, 103–7, 182–83, 192–95. The architect was Marcel Dourgnon. For overviews of the museum's contents: Virginia Jackson et al., eds., *Art Museums of the World* (Westport, CT: Greenwood, 1987), 231–39; and Veronica Seton-Williams and Peter Stocks, *Blue Guide Egypt*, 3rd ed. (London: A & C Black, 1993), 194–211.

19. RBF, *Story of the Rockefeller Foundation*, viii. RBF was also a prominent New York civic figure; see RBF, *Chronicle of a Generation: An Autobiography* (New York: Harper and Brothers, 1959). On the gatekeeper reference, see: Revoldt, "Fosdick," 315. RBF to JHB, 2 and 28 October, and JHB to RBF, 7 and 30 October 1924, DOC.

20. JHB to RBF, 6 December 1924, DOC. JHB to Edmund H. H. Viscount Allenby with enclosure, "Memorandum on . . . Cairo Museum," 3 February, Edmund H. H. Viscount Allenby to J. Austen Chamberlain, 6 February, JHB to Edmund H. H. Viscount Allenby with Egyptian museum project documents, 10 March, and Edmund H. H. Viscount Allenby to JHB with British Foreign Office documents, 19 March 1925, FO 141/629, NA. Other materials in folder FO 141/629, NA, show that JHB regularly sent to the British government Egyptian museum project details and related legal documents. JHB, diary entry, 16 March 1925, JHBP. $10 million = $122 million CPI 2009.

21. JHB to GEH, 26 September 1925, GEHP. See also JHB, diary entries, 16 March to 9 April 1926, JHBP; and *PttP*, 373–97. Bosworth worked for Shepley, Rutan and Coolidge and for Frederick Law Olmsted, among other distinguished firms, before establishing his own practice. Bosworth's work included homes for the well-to-do, buildings for academic clients such as MIT and Brown University, and corporate headquarters for businesses like AT&T and Western Union. He also designed the gardens for John D. Rockefeller's Pocantico Hills estate and a house for JDR Jr. and oversaw the Rockefeller-funded restoration projects at Versailles, Fontainebleau, and the Reims cathedral. Quentin Snowden Jacobs, "William Welles Bosworth: Major Works" (MA thesis, Columbia University, 1988). Macy was trained as an architect but never practiced, eventually becoming an independent entrepreneur who developed a personal interest in Middle Eastern exploration: *Dictionary of American Biography*, Base Set 1928–36, s.v. "Valentine Everit Macy." See also Goode, *Negotiating*, 32–33, 38–40.

JHB to Welles Bosworth, 9 February 1925, DOC; JHB to JDR Jr., 4 September 1925, RFA/RG 2, OMR/series Cultural Interests, subseries Cairo Museum, box 25, folder 258, RAC; JHB to JDR Jr., 13 September 1925, RFA/RG 2, OMR/series Cultural Interests, subseries Cairo Museum, box 25, folder 261, RAC. *PttP*, 382–83. King Fuʻād I (Ahmed Fuʻād) reigned from 1922 until his death in 1936. He served in a number of government administration posts during the British protectorate until he became sultan of Egypt in 1917. When Britain began unwinding the protectorate in 1922, it supported a government headed by a king and prime minister in a structure similar to Great Britain's in which Fuʻād became king.

"Cairo Museum Agreement" [indenture], 10 March 1926, RFA/RG 2, OMR/series Cultural Interests, subseries Cairo Museum, box 25, folder 260, RAC. [JHB], *The New Egyptian Museum and Research Institute at Cairo* ([New York: privately printed, 1925]). Although five thousand copies of the booklet were produced, it is now very rare. The copies I examined are in the OIA and the RAC (for the latter, see RFA/RG 2, OMR/series Cultural Interests, subseries Cairo Museum, box 25, folder 258A, RAC). It was printed at Oxford University Press with color plates produced by Emery Walker and contains thirty-seven letterpress-printed text pages, sixteen color plates tipped on backing sheets with letterpress-printed captions, and a frontispiece photogravure portrait of King Fuʻād. The OIA copy contains an engraved card, which suggests most of the edition was distributed after the project's collapse.

On the Foreign Office's advice to withhold information about the project from the Egyptians: John Murray to JHB, 13 July, and JHB to John Murray, 15 July 1925, FO 141/629, NA.

22. "Cairo Museum Agreement," 1–2, 4–5, 14–16.

23. [JHB], *The New Egyptian Museum*, 13, 36–37. In *The New Egyptian Museum*, JHB indicates the period of foreign control is thirty years; the indenture, which was completed later, specifies thirty-three years. The reason for the change is unknown. Once word of JHB's plan began to circulate in Egypt, one critic of it wrote to JHB, "Why doesn't America found an

Institute & train [Egyptians] here . . . ?" Cecil M. Firth to JHB, 8 February 1926, JHBP. By the mid-1920s there had been a long history of undervaluing or actively blocking Egyptian participation in Egyptology: Reid, *Whose Pharaohs?*, 186–212. There was ample reason to believe that JHB, along with his British and French colleagues, could have promoted an academic program in Cairo that would have attracted plenty of highly capable Egyptian students: Goode, *Negotiating*, 103, 112, 118–19.

24. [JHB], *The New Egyptian Museum*, 14, 22–26. On "pharaonic" and Egyptian-revival architecture: Donald Malcolm Reid, "French Egyptology and the Architecture of Orientalism: Deciphering the Facade of Cairo's Egyptian Museum," in *Franco-Arab Encounters: Studies in Memory of David C. Gordon*, ed. L. Carl Brown and Matthew S. Gordon (Beirut: American University of Beirut Press, 1996), 35–69. See also Reid, *Whose Pharaohs?*, 3–7, 237–42.

The Egyptian museum's grandiose conception is reminiscent of imaginary museums designed by ancien régime architects Étienne-Louis Boullée (1728–99) and Claude-Nicolas Ledoux (1736–1806): Helen Rosenau, *Boullée and Visionary Architecture* (London: Academy Editions, 1976); Jean Marie Pérouse de Montclos, *Étienne-Louis Boullée* (Paris: Flammarion, 1994); Claude-Nicolas Ledoux, *Claude-Nicolas Ledoux: Unpublished Projects* (Berlin: Ernst & Sohn, 1992); and Anthony Vidler, *Claude-Nicolas Ledoux: Architecture and Social Reform at the End of the Ancien Régime* (Cambridge: MIT Press, 1990).

The new museum site, adjacent to the current Egyptian Museum, was then occupied by British army barracks and parade grounds (where a Hilton Hotel now stands). The British intended but then declined to give up the property after concluding it was needed for strategic purposes. While CB and subsequent observers devoted considerable attention to negotiations over the location, in the end it made little difference: *PttP*, 377, 381, 386; Wilson, *Signs and Wonders*, 182. The subsequently chosen site was equally prominent and conveyed a distinctly Western, Hausmann-like use of the museum to create a dramatic vista of and from it. On museums and planning urban vistas: Daniel J. Sherman, *Worthy Monuments: Art Museums and the Politics of Culture in Nineteenth-Century France* (Cambridge, MA: Harvard University Press, 1989), 154ff; and Ingrid A. Steffensen-Bruce, "Marble Palaces, Temples of Art: Art Museums, Architecture, and American Culture, 1890–1930" (Ph.D. diss., University of Delaware, 1994), 115ff. However, the museum's design and placement could be said to have been profoundly at variance with the traditional "inner structures" of society in an Islamic city like Cairo. Timothy Mitchell argues that efforts to impose an "urban order" of architecture to portray a city's "interior life" were not appropriate to older Middle Eastern cities and not likely to be successful: Timothy Mitchell, *Colonising Egypt* (Cambridge: Cambridge University Press, 1988; reprint, Berkeley: University of California Press, 1991), 56ff. See also Tarek Mohamed Refaat Sakr, *Early Twentieth-Century Islamic Architecture in Cairo* (Cairo: American University in Cairo Press, 1993); and Mark Crinson, *Empire Building: Orientalism and Victorian Architecture* (London: Routledge, 1996).

25. [JHB], *The New Egyptian Museum*, 24, 26, 37. Carol Duncan and Alan Wallach, "The Universal Survey Museum," *Art History* 3, no. 4 (December 1980): 448–69.

26. [JHB], *The New Egyptian Museum*, 29–30.

27. [JHB], *The New Egyptian Museum*, 31–33. As indicated in JHB's earlier proposals, he had long hoped to establish a research "headquarters" in Cairo. A more recent inspiration may have been the French Institute in Cairo, housed then and now in a former palace: JHB to FB, 14 December 1919, LtFHB, JHBP. It is noteworthy, however, that while he previously contemplated establishing an American institute in Cairo, he decided instead that the new one should be international.

28. [JHB], *The New Egyptian Museum*, 32, 34, 36.

29. JHB, diary entry, 2 June 1925, JHBP (emphasis JHB's). [JHB], *The New Egyptian Museum*, 36 (emphasis JHB's). Arnove, introduction to *Philanthropy and Cultural Imperialism*, 5.

30. JHB to Curtisite (law offices of Curtis, Fosdick, and Belknap), 13 January, and JHB to FB, 13 January 1926, LtFHB, JHBP. Ziwar (1864–1945) was prime minister from 1924 to 1926. *PttP*, 396–97. Chauncey Belknap to JHB, 10 March 1926, JHBP. RBF, JHB, and V. Everit

Macy to Prime Minister Ahmad Ziwar Pasha, RFA/RG 2, OMR/series Cultural Interests, sub-series Cairo Museum, box 25, folder 261, 27 April 1926, RAC.

31. Wilson, *Signs and Wonders*, 183. Ziwar's cautiousness was well founded. His party was defeated in the election, and he tenuously remained in office for barely another year.

To this day, some Egyptologists familiar with the project believe that its failure should be attributed to opposition by French and British archaeologists: William Kelly Simpson to author, 1 March 1996. Some opponents were employees of the Antiquities Service: Cecil M. Firth to Edmund H. H. Viscount Allenby, 29 January 1926, FO 141/629, NA. To an extent, this version reflects a spin put on the project's collapse by JHB and others: *PttP*, 390; and Wilson, *Signs and Wonders*, 182. The outcome might have appeared that way if civil servants from the Antiquities Service, such as Lacau, had lobbied Ziwar's nationalist opponents by informing them of the project's hidden agenda. In any event, subsequent accounts of the project's demise obscured the facts by dwelling on scholars' professional rivalries, thus shifting attention away from its hegemonic objectives. Typical is an apologia that confuses individual resentments with national sovereignty: "An admirable idea crashed on the irrational reefs of international and personal politics. Although Egyptian and Arab nationalism in the 1920s was political rather than cultural, the control of archaeology soon became a battleground for national ambition. A good antiquities law might be administered as an instrument against foreign excavators, but the basic motivation was that understandable emotion, self-determination, and such hostile possessiveness frustrated good field work." Wilson, *Thousands of Years*, 121.

US State Department and British Foreign Office officials clearly assisted the initiative: Chauncey Belknap, report, "Egyptian Museum Negotiations, 1925–1926," [ca. 8–28] February 1926, JHBP; and Goode, *Negotiating*, 99–125. The French government's position is not entirely clear but may, as Goode suggests, have been compromised by France's acceptance of JDR Jr.'s $1 million gift to restore French monuments: RBF, *Rockefeller, Jr.*, 351–57.

HHN to JHB, 1 June 1925, DOC. For the British consulate quote: N[eville] H[enderson], Minute, Residency of the High Commissioner, Egypt, 30 January 1926, FO 141/629, NA. See also "Rockefeller Reply to Egypt Withheld," *New York Times*, 3 April 1926. The most comprehensive and accurate account of the Egyptian government's position in the negotiations is "The Rockefeller Offer, Egyptian Government Makes Its Position Clear," *Egyptian Mail*, 30 April 1926.

32. GEH was also involved in the lobbying effort: Seares, "George Ellery Hale," 264; and JHB to GEH, 22 March 1924, JHBP. JHB to Edward Robinson [Metropolitan Museum of Art director at the time], 10 May 1925, DOC (emphasis JHB's). On linking the Antiquities Service restrictions with the Egyptian Museum project: Goode, *Negotiating*, 111. See also cover form and enclosures regarding "Project to establish new museum in Cairo . . . ," J. Austen Chamberlain to Edmund H. H. Viscount Allenby, 1 July 1925, FO 141/629, NA.

The Anglo-American effort to reimpose Western preferences on the Antiquities Service failed. A more favorable division of archaeological finds and granting of excavation permits for foreign Egyptologists would not recur until the mid-1960s. The changes came after the successful international effort to survey and salvage antiquities to be submerged by the Aswan High Dam: Wilson, *Signs and Wonders*, 194–96.

33. "Memorandum on the Antiquities of Egypt Addressed by the Egypt Exploration Fund to the Foreign Office," [ca. December] 1917, Gardiner MSS, 39.25, GI; British Academy, "Memorandum Addressed to the Foreign Office on the Antiquities of Egypt," [ca. December?] 1917, Gardiner MSS, 39.26, GI. *Encyclopedia of World Biography*, 2nd ed., s.v. "Alfred Milner." *PttP*, 313. JHB is quoted in confidential leaflet [printed for the Foreign Office], "Memorandum by the Special Mission to Egypt on the Antiquities Department," 9 December 1920, Gardiner MSS, 39.26, GI. See also "The memorandum of the Milner Mission made the following specific recommendations as regards policy . . . ," [21 July?] 1921, FO 141/629, NA. JHB pursued a similar effort with the US State Department about the same time: Emberling and Teeter, "The First Expedition of the Oriental Institute, 1919–1920," in *PttP:AA*, 32. On JHB's

involvement in a dispute over antiquities laws that similarly involved the British government, this time in Iraq: Magnus T. Bernhardsson, *Reclaiming a Plundered Past: Archaeology and
Nation Building in Modern Iraq* (Austin: University of Texas Press, 2005), 176–77, 184, 187,
190–94, 217.

On Britain's advice: JHB, diary entry, 6 July 1925, JHBP. Several officials encouraged
JHB to keep the plans from the French: JHB, diary entries, 26 June and 15 July 1925, JHBP.
On the Foreign Office expert's advice: JHB, diary entries, 22 and 26 June 1925, JHBP.

34. *PttP*, 68, 164–65. JHB to GEH, 23 February 1925, GEHP. JHB to GEH, 20 July 1925,
JHBP.

35. JDR Jr. to JHB, 30 November 1925, JHBP. JHB briefly entertained a foray into diplomacy in an official capacity: Goode, *Negotiating*, 89, 114, and for the larger context of this
interest, pp. 16–17. JHB to RBF, 30 May 1925, JHBP. Belknap, "Egyptian Museum," 3–4, 16,
19. JHB to RBF, 8 February 1926, JHBP.

36. *PttP*, 392, 397; Fosdick, *Rockefeller, Jr.*, 362. Chauncey Belknap to JHB, 10 March
1926, JHBP. On cultural imperialism in the Middle East: Said, *Orientalism*. However, as several scholars have pointed out, Said's study is reductionist at certain junctures and does not
take into account mediations between the West and its Arabic and Islamic others through
which *both* sides identify, interpret, and manage relations with their opposites; see, for example, James Clifford, "On *Orientalism*," in *The Predicament of Culture: Twentieth-Century
Ethnography, Literature, and Art* (Cambridge, MA: Harvard University Press, 1988), 255–76.
Timothy Mitchell critiques Said's methodological guide, Michel Foucault, in terms directly
applicable here, arguing, "Colonial subjects and their modes of resistance are formed *within*
the organizational terrain of the colonial state, rather than some wholly exterior social
space": Mitchell, *Colonising Egypt*, xi (emphasis Mitchell's).

Our understanding of the interrelations of philanthropy, culture, and their sociopolitical
contexts in the United States is, if not comprehensive, certainly quite substantial. For an introduction: Bremner, *American Philanthropy*. However, this research has only begun to follow
the expansion of American philanthropy abroad, and the use of philanthropy as a lubricant of
American cultural imperialism represents relatively uncharted scholarly territory. A start was
made in Arnove, *Philanthropy and Cultural Imperialism*.

37. [JHB], *The New Egyptian Museum*, 37. Cecil M. Firth to JHB, 8 February 1926, JHBP.

38. *PttP*, 393–93, 397–98, 400; and RBF, *Rockefeller, Jr.*, 362–63. JHB may have been
apprised of the need for a new building a bit earlier: Austen St. B. Harrison to JHB, 25 January 1926, DOC. JHB, diary entry, 24 December 1927. JDR Jr. to JHB, 24 December 1926,
RFA/RG 2, OMR/series Cultural Interests, subseries Jerusalem Museum, box 25, folder 263,
RAC. $20,000 = $242,000 CPI 2009. JHB, "Suggestions for the Development of the Jerusalem Museum Plans," 18 January 1927, DOC.

39. T. Khalidi, "Palestinian Historiography: 1900–1948," *Journal of Palestine Studies* 10,
no. 3 (Spring 1981): 59–76. J. H. Iliffe, "The Palestine Archaeological Museum, Jerusalem,"
Museums Journal 38, no. 1 (April 1938): 1, 18.

40. On the JDR Jr. quote: JHB, diary entry, 24 December 1927, JHBP. *Merriam-Webster's
Biographical Dictionary*, s.v. "Herbert Charles Onslow (1st Viscount) Plumer." Rachel Kudish-
Vashdi and Yuval Baruch, "The Rockefeller Museum: The Architect," Israel Antiquities Authority, http://www.antiquities.org.il/article_Item_eng.asp?sec_id=39&subj_id=156&id
=158&module_id=12 (accessed May 2009); and "West Meets East: The Story of the Rockefeller Museum, Austen St. Barbe Harrison, 1891–1976," Israel Museum, Jerusalem, http://
www.imj.org.il/rockefeller/eng/Harrison.html (accessed May 2009). Austen St. B. Harrison
to JHB, 25 January 1926, JHB, meeting notes, 9–13 April 1927, JHB, "Report on the Palestine Museum Project," 10 May, JHB to RBF, 27 July 1927, DOC. $2 million = $24.70 million
CPI 2009.

41. When the British mandate was about to end, it established an international council
of trustees to oversee the museum: Rachel Kudish-Vashdi and Yuval Baruch, "The Rockefeller
Museum: The International Council," Israel Antiquities Authority, http://www.antiquities

.org.il/article_Item_eng.asp?sec_id=39&subj_id=156&id=170&module_id=12 (accessed May 2009). RBF to JHB, 5 August 1927, DOC. JDR Jr. to H. E. Field Marshall Lord Plumer, 11 October, H. E. Field Marshall Lord Plumer to JDR Jr., 6 November 1927, RFA/RG 2, OMR/series Cultural Interests, subseries Jerusalem Museum, box 25, folder 263, RAC. On the letter-of-gift arrangement: JHB, diary entry, 24 December 1927, JHBP.

42. "Rockefeller's Museum Completed in Jerusalem," *New York Times*, 20 June 1935. Iliffe, "Palestine Archaeological Museum," 1–7, 17–18; and "The Palestine Archaeological Museum, Jerusalem," *Architect and Building News*, 6 September 1935, 214, 263–65.

43. Iliffe, "Palestine Archaeological Museum," 8–11.

44. Iliffe, "Palestine Archaeological Museum," 19. Philip J. King, *American Archaeology in the Mideast: A History of the American Schools of Oriental Research* (Philadelphia: American Schools of Oriental Research, 1983), 52–53, 108. On the other schools: Shimon Gibson, "British Archaeological Institutions in Mandatory Palestine, 1917–1948," *Palestine Exploration Quarterly* 131 (July–December 1999): 115–43. *Encyclopaedia Judaica*, s.v. "Rockefeller Museum."

45. JHB to HHN, 10 May 1926, DOC. JHB, "Memorandum on Reorganization of Cairo Museum Project," 7 March 1927, JHBP. JHB, "Report on the Cairo Museum Project," 12 May 1927, DOC.

46. On the Egyptian dictionary project: JHB to AHG, 18 December 1923, DOC; JHB, diary entry, 16 March 1925, JHBP; and *PttP*, 376–80.

47. JHB to RBF, 13 December 1926, and W. W. Brierley to Max Mason, 1 March 1927, GEB/2324.2, Oriental Institute/series 1, subseries 4, box 659, folder 6851, RAC. BTM, 14 April 1927, 17:152, UCA. See also JHB, diary entries, 22 and 24 December 1927, JHBP. $250,000 = $3.03 million CPI 2009. On the Hittite expeditions: *TOI*, 265–309. BTM, 13 October 1927, 17:335, UCA. On the endowment and staff-support gifts: JHB diary entries just cited and BTM, 14 October 1926, 16:412–13, UCA; on the publications fund: BTM, 9 December 1926, 16:464, UCA. $75,000 = $909,000 CPI 2009. *PttP*, 397–98. JHB, "Memorandum on Scientific Research in the Ancient Orient," 15 February 1926, JHBP. On JHB's fund-raising timidity: Abraham Flexner to W. W. Brierley with enclosure, memorandum, "Humanities," 15 April 1926, GEB/2324.2, Oriental Institute/series 1, subseries 4, box 659, folder 6851, RAC.

48. JHB began developing ideas for the proposal earlier in 1927: JHB to HHN, 28 July 1927, DOC. JHB, memorandum, "Beginning and Development of the Archeology Foundation," 12 August 1927, DOC. $32.5 million = $401 million CPI 2009.

49. JHB, "Beginning and Development." On the Jerusalem and Baghdad programs: King, *American Archaeology*.

50. *PttP*, 397. JHB to Abraham Flexner, 23 November 1927, GEB/2324.3, Humanities/series 1, subseries 4, box 659, folder 6856, RAC. JHB, diary entry, 25 December 1927, JHBP. The man-not-science quote is from JHB to GEH, 31 December 1923, GEHP.

51. JHB, "A Brief on Scientific Education in the Study of Early Man, Popularly Called Archeology," 9 December 1927, GEB/2324.2, Oriental Inst./series 1, subseries 4, box 659, folder 6855, RAC. A copy of the same paper in JHBP, lists the Rockefeller board officials to whom JHB circulated it. On the Rockefellers' support for medical research and education: RBF, *Adventures in Giving*, 150–73. See also RBF, *Story of the Rockefeller Foundation*, passim. $11 million = $136 million CPI 2009.

52. On JHB's begging off the archaeological study: JHB to AHG, 29 November 1927, DOC. JHB, "List of Men to Be Visited in Connection with the Archeology Foundation," 16 February 1928, DOC. See also JHB's introduction to the list: JHB to Thomas B. Appleget, 16 February 1928, DOC.

53. On the OI visit: William C. Graham, memorandum, "Conversation with Mr. Appleget," 20 March 1928, DOC; on the Chicago House visit: JHB to GEH, 1 March 1928, GEHP. Ruth Savord, report, "Archaeological Excavations," 6 October 1928, GEB/2324.2, Oriental Inst./series 1, subseries 4, box 659, folder 6852, RAC.

54. JHB to George E. Vincent with enclosure, "Oriental Institute Emergency Subven-

tion," 10 May 1928, RF/RG 1.1/series 216R, subseries Univ. of Chicago, Oriental Inst., box 17, folder 236, RAC. JHB to RBF, 17 May (on gradual endowment), and Wickliffe Rose to RBF, 25 May 1928 (on details without end), GEB/2324.2, Oriental Inst./series 1, subseries 4, box 659, folder 6852, RAC.

55. On new Rockefeller personnel: JHB to HHN, 3 May 1928, DOC. The previous Chicago president, Max Mason, left to become president of the Rockefeller Foundation: "Woodward Quits Friday as U. of C. Vice President," *New York Times*, 23 August 1939. JHB briefed Woodward: JHB to Frederic Woodward, 28 July 1928, H. H. Swift Papers, 168:5, UCA. A copy of JHB, manuscript, "A Laboratory for the Investigation of Early Man," 20 July 1928, was enclosed with JHB's letter to Woodward (emphasis JHB's). It was published as JHB, "A Laboratory for the Investigation of Man," *Scribner's Magazine* 84, no. 5 (November 1928): 516–29. JHB enclosed a preprint of it with JHB to Trevor Arnett, 23 October 1928, IEB/series 1, subseries 1008.1, Univ. of Chicago, Oriental Inst., box 18, folder 269, RAC; and he had twenty-five additional copies forwarded to trustees of the GEB. The other article was JHB, "Recovering New History," *Scientific American* 138 (May 1928): 397–99.

56. Trevor Arnett, "Doctor James H. Breasted," 20 September 1928, RF/RG 1.1/series 216R, subseries Univ. of Chicago, Oriental Inst., box 17, folder 236, RAC. Frederic Woodward to [University of Chicago] Board of Trustees with enclosures, "Memorandum Regarding Plans of the Oriental Institute" and "Proposed Oriental Institute Financial Programme," 8 October 1928, Rosenwald Papers, 9:2, UCA. BTM, 11 October 1928, 18:214–16, UCA. On the GEB's limitation: [Trevor Arnett], meeting minutes, "Oriental Institute—Chicago," 9 October 1928, GEB/2324.2, Oriental Inst./series 1, subseries 4, box 659, folder 6852, RAC. $10.45 million = $131 million CPI 2009. JHB, "Memorandum on the Cost of Projects, Past, Present and Proposed," 16 October 1928, H. H. Swift Papers, 168:5, UCA (emphasis JHB's).

57. [Trevor Arnett], meeting minutes, 18 October 1928, GEB/2324.2, Oriental Inst./series 1, subseries 4, box 659, folder 6852, RAC. Frederic Woodward to Trevor Arnett, 26 October 1928, IEB/series 1, subseries 1008.1, Univ. of Chicago, Oriental Inst., box 18, folder 269, RAC. IEB, minutes, 23 November 1928, RF/RG 1.1/series 216R, subseries Univ. of Chicago, Oriental Inst., box 17, folder 235, RAC. W. W. Brierley to Frederic Woodward, 6 December 1928, IEB/series 1, subseries 1008.1, Univ. of Chicago, Oriental Inst., box 18, folder 269, RAC. $8.2 million = $103 million CPI 2009. On GEH's IEB grant, see Wright, *Explorer*, 387–99; and Gray, *Education*, 37–44. Gray summarizes JHB's IEB grant and juxtaposes it with GEH's: pp. 78–83.

58. The family physician was a "Dr. Rutledge" and the tutor was A. Murray Dyer. The other members of the party were Robert W. Gumbel, one of JDR Jr.'s business assistants at the time; Mary T. Clark, a personal guest of Abby Rockefeller; JDR Jr.'s "man," William Johnson; and Abby Rockefeller's maid, recorded only as "Marta." JHB, diary entry, 24 March 1929, JHBP. On Gumbel: RBF, *Rockefeller, Jr.*, 412–13. "Outline—Egyptian Trip," [ca. December 1928], LtFHB, JHBP.

59. *PttP*, 400–401. JHB to RBF, 17 May 1928, GEB/2324.2, Oriental Inst./series 1, subseries 4, box 659, folder 6852, RAC. On the slide preparations and JDR Jr.'s interests: JHB to GEH, 2 April 1929, GEHP; and JHB to FB, 3 February 1929, LtFHB, JHBP. The JDR Jr. quote is from RBF, *Rockefeller, Jr.*, 364. Additional excerpts from JDR Jr.'s letters home are published in *John D. Rockefeller, Jr. Centenary Exhibition* (Chicago: Oriental Institute, University of Chicago, 1974), 15–16.

60. The JDR Jr. quotes regarding Egyptological work are all from the letters cited in the previous note save one: JHB to FB, 9 February 1929, LtFHB, JHBP. JDR Jr.'s advisor's quote is from JHB to GEH, 2 April 1929, GEHP. JHB, diary entry, 24 March 1929, JHBP.

61. JHB, diary entry, 24 March 1929, JHBP. On JDR Jr.'s notes: JDR Jr. to Trevor Arnett with enclosure, "Memorandum re Dr. Breasted," 11 April 1929, RFA/RG 2, OMR/JDR Jr. series, Educational Interests subseries, box 111, Univ. of Chicago, Oriental Inst., env. 1, RAC. Trevor Arnett, interview notes with enclosure, "Memorandum on Gaps in Present Oriental Institute Programme as Made Out by J. D. R., Jr.," 22 April 1929, IEB/series 1, subseries

1008.1, Univ. of Chicago, Oriental Inst., box 18, folder 270, RAC. BTM, 9 May 1929, 19:126–28, UCA. W. W. Brierley to Frederic Woodward, 11 June 1929, IEB/series 1, subseries 1008.1, Univ. of Chicago, Oriental Inst., box 18, folder 270, RAC. $1.94 million = $24.3 million CPI 2009. The "reckless" quote is from JHB, diary entry, 6 May 1929.

62. On JHB's walking and posture: JHB to FB, 13 January 1924, LtFHB, JHBP; Bull, Speiser, and Olmstead, "Breasted," 118–19; *Dictionary of American Biography*, supplements 1–2: To 1940, s.v. "James Henry Breasted" (written by JHB's former student Edith W. Ware). *PttP*, 401. JDR Jr. to JHB, 8 July, and JHB to JDR Jr., 16 July 1929, RFA/RG 2, OMR/JDR Jr. series, box 49, Friends and Services, Friends and Relations, James H. Breasted Gift, RAC. $100,000 = $1.25 million CPI 2009; 6 percent interest per annum on $100,000, or $6,000 = $75,100 CPI 2009. JHB expected a $3,000-per-year pension, which he believed would leave his finances "painfully pinched," so the gift brought a "great sense of relief": JHB, diary entry, 4 September 1929, JHBP. *PttP*, 2.

Chapter 9

1. JHB, diary entries, 28 April 1930, JHBP. "Pres. Hutchins" is Robert Maynard Hutchins (see below); "Dean Laing" is Gordon Jennings Laing, who was dean of the Humanities Division at Chicago, of which the OI became a part after the division was formed in 1931 (the OI is today an independent entity within Chicago's academic administration). On the new building initiative: JHB, "Memorandum of Conversation with Martin A. Ryerson," 30 October 1923, PP 1889–1925, 51:8, UCA. *Oxford Dictionary of National Biography*, s.v. "Harry Gordon Selfridge."

2. On creating the Theology Group: Block, *Uses*, 126–43, 226. On JHB's claims on and equipping of Haskell exhibition space: JHB to Martin A. Ryerson, 1 June, and JHB to Harold H. Swift, 2 October 1925, H. H. Swift Papers, 168:3, UCA; JHB, diary entry, 7 June 1925, JHBP; and BTM, 8 October 1925 and 14 October 1926, 15:398, 16:412–13, UCA. The Divinity School possessed a small collection of East Asian objects that were displayed in Haskell before it moved out: *TOI*, 104–5; and Jeffrey Abt and Richard A. Born, "A History of the Collection," in *A Guide to the Collection: The David and Alfred Smart Museum of Art, University of Chicago* (New York: Hudson Hills, 1990), 14. *Haskell Oriental Museum: Contents and Floor Plans* (Chicago: [Oriental Institute], University of Chicago, [1926]).

3. *TOI*, 106. About this time JHB renewed his appeal to JDR Jr. for a building gift. The latter inadvertently provided an opening when he decided to purchase the Wimbourne Collection, an important collection of Assyrian bas-reliefs, and sought JHB's advice on museums to which he might donate them. JHB included the OI among his recommendations, using the topic to discuss the OI's building needs: JHB to JDR Jr., 19 December 1927, RFA/RG 2, OMR/Educational Interests series, box 117, Gift of Assyrian Bas-Reliefs, RAC. On the Wimbourne Collection and JDR Jr.'s donation of it to the Metropolitan Museum of Art: John Malcolm Russell with Judith McKenzie and Stephanie Dalley, *From Nineveh to New York: The Strange Story of the Assyrian Reliefs in the Metropolitan Museum and the Hidden Masterpiece at the Canford School* (New Haven, CT: Yale University Press, 1997), 128–72. On the opening and brochure: JHB to HHN, 26 October 1926, DOC. JHB, *The Oriental Institute* (Chicago: University of Chicago Press, [1926]).

4. The trustees' invitation is in JHB to Harold H. Swift, 2 August 1927, H. H. Swift Papers, 168:3, UCA. JHB to HHN, 25 October 1927, DOC. The Medinet Habu materials on display would have been similar to figures 7.22–7.24. The last quote is from James O'Donnell Bennett, "Making Ancients Live Again Keeps Breasted Young," *Chicago Daily Tribune*, 10 December 1926.

5. There were earlier university-based museums, but none focused on the ancient Near East. One of the first, a general-purpose institution that continues to exist and is now focused primarily on art and archaeology, is Oxford University's Ashmolean Museum, established in 1683: R. F. Ovenell, *The Ashmolean Museum, 1683–1894* (Oxford: Clarendon,

1986). In America, a less well-documented but specialized example is the Allen Memorial Art Museum at Oberlin College, which opened in 1917. Another is what was once called the University Museum at the University of Pennsylvania (now called the University of Pennsylvania Museum of Archaeology and Anthropology). Founded in 1887 and given its own building in 1899, it served the interests of archaeology and anthropology almost from the beginning, and its collections extend beyond the Middle East to include the Americas, Africa, East Asia, and the Pacific islands: Percy C. Madeira Jr., *Men in Search of Man: The First Seventy-Five Years of the University Museum of the University of Pennsylvania* (Philadelphia: University of Pennsylvania Press, 1964). See also "Architectural History of the Museum," University of Pennsylvania Museum of Archaeology and Anthropology, http://www.museum.upenn.edu/new/about/masterplan/history.shtml (accessed June 2009). For two other particularly relevant examples built almost simultaneously in Europe and America for art history: Kathryn Brush, "Marburg, Harvard, and Purpose-Built Architecture for Art History, 1927," in *Art History and Its Institutions: Foundations of a Discipline*, ed. Elizabeth Mansfield (London: Routledge, 2002), 65–84. The Harvard reference is to the university's Fogg Art Museum, which, incidentally, was assisted with funds from JDR Jr. and the GEB: Kathryn Brush, *Vastly More Than Brick and Mortar: Reinventing the Fogg Art Museum in the 1920s* (Cambridge, MA: Harvard University Art Museums, 2003), 62, 187. Several natural-science museums were built in the latter part of the nineteenth century on American college campuses, but these were general-purpose institutions and not relevant to the issues of disciplinary focus addressed here. See my discussion of Chicago's departmental museums in chapter 2 of the present volume and n. 15 to that chapter.

6. On "scientistic" language: "By scientism I mean the belief that the objective methods of the natural sciences should be used in the study of human affairs; and that such methods are the only fruitful ones in the pursuit of knowledge": Dorothy Ross, "The Development of the Social Sciences," in *The Organization of Knowledge in Modern America, 1860–1920*, ed. Alexandra Oleson and John Voss (Baltimore: Johns Hopkins University Press, 1979), 131n7. For an overview of science in American higher education in the late nineteenth and early twentieth century, as both "faith" and practice: Veysey, *Emergence*, 133–79.

[JHB], *A Historical Laboratory: How the Expert Historian Does His Work* (Boston: Ginn, 1922). JHB was not the only humanist with a fondness for the "laboratory" analogy: David Van Zanten, "Formulating Art History at Princeton and the 'Humanistic Laboratory,'" in *The Early Years of Art History in the United States*, ed. Craig Hugh Smyth and Peter M. Lukehart (Princeton, NJ: Department of Art and Archaeology, Princeton University, 1993), 175–82. JHB to GEH, 31 December 1923, GEHP. On the new building's name: L. R. Steere to Committee on Buildings and Grounds [University of Chicago], 29 May 1929, Buildings and Grounds Department Papers, 25:6, UCA. On the disavowal: JHB to Max Mason, 6 June 1932, RF/RG 1.1/series 216R, subseries Univ. of Chicago, Oriental Inst., box 17, folder 237, RAC. On the sense of "museum" as by definition "public": Jeffrey Abt, "Origins of the Public Museum," *Blackwell Companion to Museum Studies*, ed. Sharon J. Macdonald (Oxford: Blackwell, 2006), 115–34.

7. On the OI building design: Block, *Uses*, 152–61. Richard Oliver, *Bertram Grosvenor Goodhue* (New York: Architectural History Foundation, 1983). The successor firm to Goodhue's was Mayers, Murray and Phillip, which disbanded in 1940. "Oscar H. Murray," *New York Times*, 26 April 1957. The name of the University Chapel was changed to Rockefeller Chapel after Rockefeller senior's death in 1937. Additional details on the building's planning are in *TOI*, 108. On JHB's involvement in the architectural design: JHB, diary entries, 2 September and 29 December 1929 and 20 January 1930, JHBP. For one of JHB's corrections, the correct rendering of a hieroglyphic cartouche for a royal name: JHB to Emery B. Jackson, 30 September 1930, Buildings and Grounds Department Papers, 25:6, UCA.

8. [JHB], memorandum, "Subjects for 8 Medallions on the North Front of the New Oriental Institute Building," 6 May 1930, Buildings and Grounds Department Papers, 25:6, UCA. Jean M. Roberts to Emery B. Jackson, 14 July, with attachment, [JHB], "Oriental Institute

Symbolism," 13 July 1932, Buildings and Grounds Department Papers, 25:6, UCA. The design was executed by Ulric Ellerhusen: Block, *Uses*, 178–79. See also Thomas, *Publications of the Oriental Institute*, x. For a study of the ornamentation throughout the OI building, including the tympanum: Emily Teeter and Leslie Schramer, "Some Decorative Motifs of the Oriental Institute Building," *Oriental Institute News and Notes* 199 (Fall 2008): 14–19.

9. JHB, "The New Past," *University* [of Chicago] *Record*, new ser., 6, no. 4 (October 1920): 237–56. See also chapter 7 of the present volume. JHB, manuscript, "The New Crusade," 2 November 1928, JHBP, published as JHB, "The New Crusade," *American Historical Review* 34, no. 2 (January 1929): 215–36, quote from p. 236.

10. Eric Scott McCready, "The Nebraska State Capitol: Its Design, Background, and Influence," *Nebraska History* 55, no. 3 (Fall 1974): 325–461. On GEH's observatory: Wright, *Explorer*, 349–51. The observatory is no longer used for scientific purposes, but it is on the National Register of Historic Places: "Hale Solar Observatory," National Park Service, http://www.nps.gov/history/online_books/butowsky5/astro4a.htm (accessed June 2009). The tympanum for the Hale observatory was designed and carved by Lee Lawrie: Joseph F. Morris, ed., *Lee Lawrie* (Athens: University of Georgia Press, 1955), 61. For JHB's discussions of the sun rays ending in hands: *AHoE*, 370; *DoRaT*, 320; *TDoC*, 278–79; and, most vividly, JHB, *Encyclopaedia Britannica*, 14th ed. (1929), s.v. "Ikhnaton." On the "Symbol of Life" superimposed over the sun disk: *TDoC*, 47. By this point in their friendship, GEH was so familiar with Egyptian history that he could tease JHB with elaborate pharaonic jests: GEH to JHB, 12 November 1929, DOC. On visiting GEH's observatory: JHB to GEH, 2 April 1930, GEHP.

11. *TOI*, 108–26. *Floor Plan of the Exhibition Halls* (Chicago: Oriental Institute, University of Chicago, January 1932). The building was subsequently expanded to the south with a two-story addition, for conservation labs and collections storage, completed in 1997. The project included renovation of the first floor galleries: Karen L. Wilson, "Construction . . . report," https://oi.uchicago.edu/OI/info/legacy/crrpr.html (accessed July 2009). JHB used the analogy of the machine when discussing the OI building or its operations, and that nomenclature was in the air. On museums and the "ideology of the machine age": Andrew McClellan, *The Art Museum from Boullée to Bilbao* (Berkeley: University of California Press, 2008), 71ff.

12. "Dedication of the New Oriental Institute Building," [ca. November] 1931, GEHP. Harry Scott Ashmore, *Unseasonable Truths: The Life of Robert Maynard Hutchins* (Boston: Little, Brown, 1989); and Mary Ann Dzuback, *Robert M. Hutchins: Portrait of an Educator* (Chicago: University of Chicago Press, 1991). Quote on Finley: *Dictionary of American Biography*, supplements 1–2: To 1940, s.v. "John Huston Finley." Other quotations are from "The Oriental Institute: The New Building Dedicated," *University* [of Chicago] *Record*, new ser. 18, no. 1 (January 1932): 1–16 (emphasis JHB's).

13. "East Gone West," *Time* 18, no. 24 (14 December 1931): 23–24. On visitor numbers and related matters: JHB to HHN, 4 April 1932, DOC; JHB to Emery T. Filbey, 14 March 1932, PP 1920–1980, 29:19, UCA; "250,000 Persons Visit Oriental U. of C. Museum," *Chicago Tribune*, 12 May 1935; *TOI*, 125–26. [JHB], *The Oriental Institute of the University of Chicago*, 3rd. ed. (Chicago: University of Chicago Press, 1931). *Floor Plan of the Exhibition Halls* (Chicago: Oriental Institute of the University of Chicago, 1932).

14. On merging Oriental Languages and Literatures and OI: *TOI*, 126–28. Regarding JHB's leaves, salary, and distinguished professorships, BTM, 11 April 1922, 8 May 1923, and 13 August 1925, 12:374, 380, 13:148, 181, 15:344–45, 17:369, UCA. $10,000 = $124,000 CPI 2009. Distinguished service professors were elected by faculty colleagues, and JHB received the second-highest number of votes, after Nobel laureate Albert A. Michelson in the first year the ballot was held: Meyer, "Chicago Faculty," 480. On relief from teaching: *PttP*, 380. The "woozy" remark is quoted in Olmstead, "Breasted the Historian," 4. On the Burton professorship and subsequent appointments: JDR Jr. to Frederic Woodward, 10 February 1930, RFA/RG 2, OMR/JDR Jr. series, Educational Interests subseries, box 111, Univ. of Chicago, Oriental Inst., env. 1, RAC. BTM, 13 July and 10 August 1933, 23:100, 169, UCA. Around this time the formula for JHB's appointment was changed, boosting his annual salary to $15,000,

but it was reduced when he retired from his faculty position, bringing it to $11,350 per year, which began to be paid entirely out of the OI budget. When he retired from his faculty position, his appointment as OI director went to a year-by-year basis, as opposed to the four-year-term appointments before. BTM, 10 May 1934 and 11 July 1935, 24:75, 25:98, UCA. Martin Sprengling, a Semitic languages professor, was chair of the Department of Oriental Languages and Literatures between 1933 and 1936, when he was succeeded by JHB's former student John A. Wilson. Clara Z. Havill to CB, 26 April 1940, JHBP. Nabia Abbott, "Martin Sprengling, 1877–1959," *Journal of Near Eastern Studies* 19, no. 1 (January 1960): 54–55. The staff counts are from [JHB], *The Oriental Institute* ([1926]); [JHB], *The Oriental Institute of the University of Chicago*, general circular no. 2 (Chicago: University of Chicago Press, August 1928); and [JHB], *The Oriental Institute of the University of Chicago*, 3rd ed. of the handbook (Chicago: University of Chicago Press, 5 December 1931). For a chronological list of OI publications through 1933: *TOI*, 435–38. JHB began issuing separate OI publication catalogs in 1929: *Publications, the Oriental Institute of the University of Chicago* (Chicago: University of Chicago Press, [1929]); and *Buried History: Publications of the Oriental Institute* (Chicago: University of Chicago Press, 1934). JHB to GEH, 18 May 1929, GEHP; see also Wright, *Explorer*, 400–401.

15. On Megiddo: JHB to Harry Pratt Judson, 7 March 1921, JHB to RBF, 15 May, and RBF to Harold H. Swift, 6 July 1925, RFA/RG 2, OMR/JDR Jr. series, Educational Interests subseries, box 112, Univ. of Chicago, Excavations at Megiddo, RAC; BTM, 21 June 1921 and 9 July 1925, 12:113, 15:283–84, UCA; and JHB, diary entry, 2–5 June 1925, JHBP (see also entries for 28 September and 3 October 1925 and 23 March 1926). The OIA now has the first five seasons of Megiddo expedition–related correspondence available internally in digital, searchable transcriptions. $215,000 = $2.63 million CPI 2009. For a concise survey of the expeditions and related publications during JHB's lifetime: *TOI*, 91–92, 145–48, 169–86, 224–377. On the Diyala region, see also Karen Terras, "James Henry Breasted and the Iraq Expedition: The People and Politics of the 1935 Division," *Oriental Institute News and Notes* 202 (Summer 2009): 3–6. On obtaining the King Tut sculpture during division of the Medinet Habu finds: JHB, diary entry, 2 April 1933, JHBP. JDR Jr.'s excavation support is briefly discussed in the *TOI* citations listed above in this note. On the Moore gift: JHB to Mrs. William H. Moore, 17 April 1930, DOC; BTM, 8 January 1931, 21:1, UCA. On Moore's late husband: *Dictionary of American Biography*, Base Set 1928–36, s.v. "William Henry Moore." $100,000 = $1.41 million CPI 2009. On the Assyrian and Persian explorations in the context of American and European Assyriology: Meade, *Road to Babylon*, 93–104, 114–18. The summary observation is from Albright, "James Henry Breasted," 293.

16. On malaria at Megiddo: *TOI*, 75–77, 238–40. JHB was far too discrete to even hint at personnel problems in print, but they surface in his private correspondence and diary; for example, JHB, diary entries, 24 December 1927, 4 September and 29 December 1929, and 6 May 1933, JHBP. On internationalism: JHB to HHN, 16 September 1927, DOC. Regarding negotiations and diplomatic conflicts surrounding OI excavations at Tell Asmar and Persepolis: Goode, *Negotiating*, 141–83, 195–96, 204–19, division-of-finds quote on p. 206. The diplomatic sphere quote is from *TOI*, 35.

17. A brief but effective summation of the hardships and their effects is in Kuklick, *Puritans*, 3–4. On Chicago House: *TOI*, 99–102, and the figures between pp. 189 and 202; introductory and Persepolis quotes from pp. 99, 323. Several factors led to JHB's decision to build a second Chicago House in a new location: the need for a larger physical plant to accommodate a growing library collection, workrooms, and living quarters for an expanded staff; plans, once Medinet Habu was completed, to commence work at Karnak along the Nile's east bank; problems maintaining the Chicago House building owing to soil conditions; and troubles with the local water supply: HHN to JHB, 24 April 1928, and JHB to HHN, 10 April 1929, DOC; and JHB to GEH, 2 April 1929, GEHP. HHN was concerned about the new Chicago House being too comfortable and thus engendering an "air of leisureliness" that would make efficient, speedy work difficult to achieve: HHN to CB, 4 July, and HHN to JHB,

24 August 1929, DOC. The old Chicago House building was acquired by a local sheikh in the 1940s and for some time served as a combination artists' retreat and lodging for the culturally minded. More guest rooms were added in the 1970s, and since then it has declined and then been improved as it passed through various hands. Known as the Marsam Hotel ("marsam" being Arabic for an artist's studio or atelier), it continues in operation as of this writing: http://www.luxor-westbank.com/marsam_e_az.htm (accessed August 2010). See also Reham El-Adawi, "At Home with the Nobles," *Al-Ahram Weekly On-Line*, no. 520 (8–14 February 2001), cached version at http://weekly.ahram.org.eg/ (accessed August 2010).

On the Tell Asmar, Persepolis, and Alishar expedition houses and camps: *TOI*, 340–42, 321–23, 277–81. The Tell Asmar critique is quoted in Goode, *Negotiating*, 96; the follow-up observation is in 196n25. The Ritz quote is from James, *Howard Carter*, 168. For a summation of the Metropolitan Museum's work in Egypt: Nancy Thomas, "American Institutional Fieldwork in Egypt, 1899–1960," in *The American Discovery of Ancient Egypt*, ed. Thomas (Los Angeles: Los Angeles County Museum of Art and American Research Center in Egypt, 1995), 60–64. Seton Lloyd, *Foundations in the Dust: The Story of Mesopotamian Exploration*, rev. and enl. ed. (London: Thames and Hudson, 1980), 190–91. *Contemporary Authors Online*, s.v. "Seton (Howard Frederick) Lloyd." For a more extensive and approving discussion of the OI's expedition outposts: Noel F. Wheeler, review of *TOI*, *Antiquity* 9, no. 33 (1935): 110. On JHB's views of the critiques: Wilson, *Signs and Wonders*, 172. Thomas B. Appleget, file memorandum, "Afternoon Spent with Dr. James H. Breasted, Oriental Institute," 21 November 1932, RF/RG 1.1/series 216R, subseries Univ. of Chicago, Oriental Inst., box 17, folder 238, RAC; and Trevor Arnett, file memorandum, "Mr. John D. Rockefeller, Jr.," 4 March 1935, RF/RG 1.1/series 216R, subseries Univ. of Chicago, Oriental Inst., box 18, folder 241, RAC.

18. JHB, diary entry, 24 March 1929, JHBP. Of JHB's contributions to general-interest collections, two were written specifically for school-age audiences: JHB, "History," in *Paths to Success: Sixteen Essays on Secondary School Subjects Written by Eminent Educators of America*, ed. Harold G. Black (Boston: D. C. Heath, 1924), 65–85; and JHB, "Archaeology," in *Compton's Pictured Encyclopedia* (Chicago: F. E. Compton, 1935), 1:249–54. Those for adult audiences include JHB, chapter 3, "The Foundation and Expansion of the Egyptian Empire," chapter 4, "The Reign of Thutmose III," chapter 5, "The Zenith of Egyptian Power and the Reign of Amenhotep III," chapter 6, "Ikhnaton, the Religious Revolutionary," chapter 7, "The Age of Ramses II," and chapter 8, "The Decline and Fall of the Egyptian Empire," in *The Egyptian and Hittite Empires to c. 1000 B.C.*, ed. J. B. Bury, S. A. Cook, and F. E. Adcock, vol. 2 of *The Cambridge Ancient History* (Cambridge: Cambridge University Press, 1924), 40–195; and JHB, "Ikhnaton."

On textbook abridgements: JHB, diary entry, 7 May 1919, JHBP. On sales: JHB to GEH, 21 December 1920, GEHP; JHB to AHG, 25 October 1923, DOC; and *PttP*, 231. On royalties: JHB, diary entry, 1 July 1922, and JHB to FB, 25 October 1925, LtFHB, JHBP. $750 = $9,950 CPI 2009. On *AT*'s influence and trade version: JHB to FB, 25 May 1925, LtFHB, JHBP. "Victorious Man" is mentioned in JHB to GEH, 26 September 1925, GEHP. On the book and box titles: JHB to FB, 2 October, LtFHB, and JHB, diary entry, 3 October 1925, JHBP. JHB, *The Conquest of Civilization* (New York: Harper and Brothers, 1926), viii. The review quotes are from, respectively: William MacDonald, "Civilization Surveyed," *New York Times*, 19 December 1926; and Fanny Butcher, "Breasted-Robinson Book Brings Back Two Old Friends," *Chicago Daily Tribune*, 2 October 1926. Both reviews addressed Robinson's book as well. There were very few scholarly journal reviews of *Conquest*, all were very brief, and all treated it as an another edition of *Ancient Times*. See, for example, Robert W. Rogers, review of *The Conquest of Civilization*, by JHB, *American Historical Review* 32, no. 4 (July 1927): 830–31.

19. JHB, *Conquest*, 88 and plate 5. The papyrus is now in the collections of the New York Academy of Medicine. JHB, "The Edwin Smith Papyrus: An Egyptian Medical Treatise of the Seventeenth Century before Christ," *New York Historical Society Quarterly Bulletin* 6, no. 1 (April 1922): 3–31; and JHB, "The Edwin Smith Papyrus: Some Preliminary Observations," in *Recueil d'études égyptologiques dédiées à la mémoire de Jean-François Champollion . . .* (Paris:

E. Champion, 1922), 385–429. For additional observations and JHB's initial deadline: JHB, *Oriental Institute . . . Beginning and Program*, 90–93. The project was never far from JHB's mind during the 1920s: *PttP*, 325–26, 390–91; and JHB, diary entries, 1 July 1922, 16 March and 3 October 1925, and 24 March and 29 December 1929, JHBP.

20. JHB, *The Edwin Smith Surgical Papyrus*, 2 vols., Oriental Institute Publications, nos. 3–4 (Chicago: University of Chicago Press, 1930); on research and consultations: 1:xix; on the differences between the surgical treatise and magical text: 1:5–6, 469–70.

21. JHB, foreword and general introduction, *Edwin Smith*, 1:xiii–xxiv, 1–29; On paleographic evidence: 1:25–29 (see especially JHB's hand-drawn "Comparative Table of Paleographic Forms"); on glosses: 1:61–71; on the asterisk and palpation: 1:19 and 7 respectively.

22. JHB, *The Edwin Smith Surgical Papyrus*, facsimile reprint of the 1930 ed., vol. 1 [with only a sample page in reduced form from vol. 2] (Birmingham, AL: Classics of Medicine Library, 1984). The first edition was thought to have sold out because when it was first issued in 1930, of the 2,000 copies printed, only 1,100 were bound. Then, in 1963, the OI's publications secretary discovered that the remaining 900 unbound copies remained with Oxford University Press. Five hundred copies were bound and sold, and by 1977 it was believed to be out of print once again—and this was when the Classics of Medicine Library edition was issued. Then, in 1989, during a warehouse cleaning at Oxford, the remaining four hundred unbound sets were discovered. The OI had them bound in a "reissue" edition with an additional page of front matter and corrigenda. That edition is now sold out. See: T[homas] A. Holland, "Brief History of the Discovery, Study, and Publication of *The Edwin Smith Surgical Papyrus*," in JHB, *The Edwin Smith Surgical Papyrus*, 1991 binding of 1930 ed. sheets, 2 vols., Oriental Institute Publications, nos. 3–4 (Chicago: University of Chicago Press, 1991), flyleaf.

"A Most Ancient Harvey," *New York Times*, 5 October 1930; "Harvey" refers to William Harvey. George Sarton, review of *The Edwin Smith Surgical Papyrus*, by JHB, *Isis* 15, no. 2 (April 1931): 355–67, quotes from pp. 355 and 364. *Dictionary of American Biography*, supplement 6: 1956–60, s.v. "George Alfred Leon Sarton." On the relationship between Sarton, the History of Science Society, and JHB: George Sarton, "James Henry Breasted (1865–1935): The Father of American Egyptology," *Isis* 34, no. 4 (Spring 1943): 289–91. George Sarton, *The History of Science and the New Humanism* (New York: Henry Holt, 1931). JHB read and complimented: George Sarton, *Introduction to the History of Science: From Homer to Omar Khayyam*, vol. 1 (Baltimore: Williams and Wilkins for the Carnegie Institution of Washington, 1927).

23. Gatewood, *Controversy*, 4. The "ineffable certainty" quote is from Walter Lippmann, *A Preface to Morals* (New York: Macmillan, 1929), 21. JHB to FTG, 22 September 1916, DOC.

24. JHB to Abraham Flexner, 5 June 1925, GEB/2324.2, Oriental Inst./series I, subseries 4, box 659, folder 6851, RAC. JHB, "Some Notes on the Oriental Institute as a Laboratory for the Investigation of Early Man and the Training of Specialists to Undertake Such Investigations," attached to JHB to Trevor Arnett, 23 October 1928, IEB/series 1, subseries 1008.1, Univ. of Chicago, Oriental Inst., box 18, folder 269, RAC. JHB to FB, 13 January 1924, LtFHB, JHBP. The title of *TDoC* first appears in JHB to Charles Scribner Jr., 20 January 1931, DOC. JHB subsequently thought of calling it "The Dawn of Conscience and the Age of Character" but then dropped the longer version: JHB to Charles Scribner Jr., 25 March 1931, DOC. The title may consciously or subconsciously have been derived from a work by one of JHB's old friends, W. M. Flinders Petrie, *Religion and Conscience in Ancient Egypt: Lectures Delivered at University College, London*, 2nd ed., (London: Methuen, 1920); the first edition was published in 1898. JHB's *DoRaT* roughly resembles *Religion and Conscience* in organization if not content. The context and effect of JHB's "secular aspect" is suggestive of the climate of intellectual efficiency and neutrality that was permeating the modern university, what one scholar calls "methodological secularization": George M. Marsden, *The Soul of the American University: From Protestant Establishment to Established Nonbelief* (Oxford: Oxford University Press, 1994), 156ff.

25. JHB to Charles Scribner Jr., 12 May 1931 and 25 March 1932, DOC. JHB to CB,

23 August 1932, JHBP (emphases JHB's). See also JHB to Charles Scribner Jr., 20 January 1933, DOC. *TDoC*, xvii.

26. *TDoC*, xii–xiii, x–xi; examples of the updates include 30–33, 140–41, 116n1, 235–40, 278–79.

27. William E. Akin, *Technocracy and the American Dream: The Technocrat Movement, 1900–1941* (Berkeley: University of California Press, 1977), x–xi. *TDoC*, ix–xii.

28. *TDoC*, xv–xvi (emphases JHB's).

29. *TDoC*, 7, 23, 394, 398 (emphases JHB's). The adoption of evolutionary theory by social scientists and humanities scholars is addressed in several works. See especially Peter J. Bowler, *Evolution: The History of an Idea* (Berkeley: University of California Press, 1984); and Carl N. Degler, *In Search of Human Nature: The Decline and Revival of Darwinism in American Social Thought* (Oxford: Oxford University Press, 1991).

30. For an excellent overview of the fundamentalist disputes leading up to the Scopes trial, see George M. Marsden, *Fundamentalism and American Culture: The Shaping of Twentieth-Century Evangelicalism, 1870–1925* (Oxford: Oxford University Press, 1980); quote regarding the Chicago Divinity School is on p. 105. See also Gatewood, *Controversy*, 16–17. Clarence Darrow to JHB, 10 July 1925, DOC. For the larger context of the debate before and after the Scopes trial: David N. Livingstone, *Darwin's Forgotten Defenders: The Encounter between Evangelical Theology and Evolutionary Thought* (Grand Rapids, MI: Wm. B. Eerdmans, 1987). For a fairly complete Scopes trial record, including information on all the major participants: Leslie H. Allen, ed., *Bryan and Darrow at Dayton: The Record and Documents of the "Bible-Evolution Trial"* (1925; reprint, New York: Russell and Russell, 1967). *Dictionary of American Biography*, supplements 1–2: To 1940, s.v. "Clarence Seward Darrow." CB suggests *AT* featured more prominently in the trial than the stenographic record indicates: *PttP*, 230. There is some faint evidence that Darrow and a defense witness culled information from *AT* for use during the trial: *The World's Most Famous Court Trial: Tennessee Evolution Case* (Cincinnati: National Book, 1925), 261, 291, 293. JHB to GEH, 26 September 1925, GEHP (emphasis JHB's).

31. *TDoC*, 350, 353, 369, 405–6.

32. Two of the following entries are annotated as being made "At Church": JHB, notes, "Children of the Sun, A Romance of the Early World," 26 October–21 November 1909, JHBP. JHB to Charles and Harriet Breasted, 4 June 1894, LtP, JHBP. JHB to William Horace Day, 12 September 1933, DOC. See also *PttP*, 47–48. K. S. Wang et al. to JHB, [ca. February], and JHB to K. S. Wang, 28 February 1921, DOC. The results of the survey do not appear to have been published. For a nationwide survey, done in the 1910s, addressing similar questions among American scientists, sociologists, historians, and psychologists: James H. Leuba, *The Belief in God and Immortality: A Psychological, Anthropological and Statistical Study* (Chicago: Open Court, 1921), 219–80. Gatewood, *Controversy*, 44.

33. T. D., review of *TDoC*, *Theosophical Quarterly* 32, no. 1 (July 1934): 87–89. On inconsistencies: Stanley Casson, review of *TDoC*, *Antiquity: A Quarterly Review of Archaeology* 8 (1934): 477–78; and George A. Barton, review of *TDoC*, *American Historical Review* 39, no. 2 (April 1934): 498. *Dictionary of American Biography*, supplement 3: 1941–45, s.v. "George Aaron Barton." On sermonizing and Hebrew sources: Ralph A. Habas, "Breasted's Dawn of Conscience," *Jewish Quarterly Review*, new ser., 25, no. 2 (October 1934): 151–54. Shlomo Marenof, review of *TDoC*, *Jewish Education* 6, no. 1 (January–March 1934): 55.

34. Ruth Benedict, "The Sense of Social Justice in Ancient Egypt," Books, *New York Herald Tribune*, 21 January 1934. *Dictionary of American Biography*, supplement 4: 1946–50, s.v. "Ruth Fulton Benedict."

35. *Dictionary of American Biography*, supplement 9: 1971–75, s.v. "William Foxwell Albright." For an up-to-date study on biblical archaeology: Thomas W. Davis, *Shifting Sands: The Rise and Fall of Biblical Archaeology* (Oxford: Oxford University Press, 2004). Davis characterizes the OI as "purely secular, having no religious interest or input" thanks to JHB's leadership (p. 61) and quotes another scholar who observed that the OI "never had a Biblical archaeologist on its staff" (p. 104). Biblical archaeology pursued other agendas as well: Neil

Asher Silberman, *Digging for God and Country: Exploration, Archeology, and the Secret Struggle for the Holy Land* (New York: Alfred A. Knopf, 1982); and Silberman, "Desolation and Restoration: The Impact of a Biblical Concept on Near Eastern Archaeology," *Biblical Archaeologist* 54, no. 2 (June 1991): 76–87.

William Foxwell Albright, "Toward a Theistic Humanism," in *History, Archaeology, and Christian Humanism* (New York: McGraw-Hill, 1963), 6. Albright, "James Henry Breasted," 296–97. Albright republished the latter essay, under the same title but with minor modifications and additions, in the 1963 collection just cited. On Albright's take on JHB's "meliorism" in the context of the former's own work and beliefs: Kuklick, *Puritans*, 188–92. Wilson, "James Henry Breasted—The Idea," 49 (emphasis Wilson's).

TDoC elicited more personal responses as well, including a "chapel talk" prepared by a Lawrence College zoology professor "perhaps [to] be labeled as a 'book review'": R. C. Mullenix to JHB with address, "Symbiosis," 19 May 1934, JHB section in Pamphlet Files, OI Library.

36. On Freud's collecting in the context of his life and work: Peter Gay, *Freud: A Life for Our Time* (New York: W. W. Norton, 1988), 47–48, 170–73. On his collecting per se: Lynn Gamwell and Peter Gay, eds., *Sigmund Freud and Art: His Personal Collection of Antiquities* (New York: State University of New York, 1989), particularly Gamwell's essay, "The Origins of Freud's Antiquities Collection," 21–32, and Donald Kuspit, "A Mighty Metaphor: The Analogy of Archaeology and Psychoanalysis," 133–51. The information on Freud's copies of JHB's books, including his annotations, is from the CD-ROM in J. Keith Davies and Gerhard Fichtner, eds., *Freud's Library: A Comprehensive Catalogue* (London: Freud Museum and Edition Diskord, 2006); the "delighted" quote is from p. 28. *TDoC* and *AHoE* are items number 348 and 349, respectively; the Cambridge volume is number 438 (for the full citation of the latter, see n. 18 in this chapter). Sigmund Freud, *Moses and Monotheism*, trans. Katherine Jones (New York: Alfred A. Knopf, 1939; reprint, New York: Vintage Books, 1967). See also Carl E. Schorske, "Freud's Egyptian Dig," *New York Review of Books* 40, no. 10 (27 May 1993).

37. Gay, *Freud*, 604–8, 632–34, 643–48. There is a large and growing literature on *Moses and Monotheism*. For a text by an Egyptologist that does an excellent job of situating Freud's work in the history of prior writings on Moses and Ikhnaton, especially JHB's: Jan Assmann, *Moses the Egyptian: The Memory of Egypt in Western Monotheism* (Cambridge, MA: Harvard University Press, 1997). Assmann addresses Freud's and Breasted's works throughout the text, but the key chapter is "Sigmund Freud: The Return of the Repressed," pp. 144–67. See also his discussion of "cultural forgetting," which is central to his own argument and the role of Freud's analysis in it, pp. 215–18. See also Yosef Hayim Yerushalmi, *Freud's Moses: Judaism Terminable and Interminable* (New Haven, CT: Yale University Press, 1991). On the name of Moses: Freud, *Moses*, 4–6; *TDoC*, 350.

38. Freud, *Moses*, 3–65. The discussion of the "J" and "E" traditions and the matter of trauma are on pp. 27–28, 47, 50, 65. *TDoC*, 351 (emphasis JHB's). On the documentary paradigm, see also chapter 1 of the present volume. Ernst Sellin, *Mose und seine Bedeutung für die israelitisch-jüdische Religionsgeschichte* (Leipzig: A. Deichert, 1922).

39. Freud, *Moses*, 73, 91, 101, 109–11.

40. On circumcision: Freud, *Moses*, 30; *TDoC*, 353. For the JHB quotes and cites: Freud, *Moses*, 5–6, 21–26, 62. On the decisions to suppress and then publish the third essay with the others: Freud, *Moses*, 66–71; quotes from pp. 4, 170. On Freud's determination to publish *Moses* despite its controversial nature, appeals of others not to do so, and its immediate reception: Gay, *Freud*, 604–5, 608, 643–48.

41. *TOI*, flyleaf, vii, x; the table is on pp. 96–98 (emphases JHB's). JHB, diary entry, 13 February 1933, JHBP.

42. The reviews were all approving; see, for example, E. A. Speiser, review of *The Oriental Institute*, by JHB, *Journal of Higher Education* 56–58, no. 3 (March 1934): 173–74; and O. E. Ravn, "New Contributions to Assyriology," *Acta Orientalia* 14 (1936): 70–74. *Dictionary of American Biography*, supplement 7: 1961–65, s.v. "Ephraim Avigdor Speiser." E. A. Wallis

Budge, review of *The Oriental Institute*, by JHB, *Journal of the Royal Asiatic Society* (1934): 845–46. On OI's generous funding: Wheeler, "The Oriental Institute," 109–10. BTM, 13 June 1929, 19:159–61, UCA. $677,000 = $8.48 million, and $3,000 = $37,600 CPI 2009. JHB, memorandum to Gordon J. Laing, "University Support of the Oriental Institute," 7 December 1931, DOC.

43. Trevor Arnett, interview notes, meeting with Robert M. Hutchins and JHB, 26 April 1932, RF/RG 1.1/series 216R, subseries Univ. of Chicago, Oriental Inst., box 17, folder 237, RAC. Regarding the assumption of the IEB pledges by the GEB and RF: Robert M. Hutchins to Trevor Arnett, 13 May, W. W. Brierley to Robert M. Hutchins, 19 May, and W. W. Brierley to "Mr. Beal," 16 September 1932, GEB/2324.2, Oriental Inst./series 1, subseries 4, box 659, folder 6853, RAC; BTM, 9 June, 14 July, and 11 August 1932, 22:145–47, 158, 229–33, UCA. The RF's more active role also resulted from a reorganization of the boards that had been completed just a couple of years earlier: Revoldt, "Fosdick," 376–412. On JHB's push back and budgets: JHB to Max Mason with enclosure, "The Oriental Institute: Comparative . . . Budgets for 1931–32 and 1932–33," 6 June 1932, RF/RG 1.1/series 216R, subseries Univ. of Chicago, Oriental Inst., box 17, folder 237, RAC; BTM, 13 October 1932, 22:256–58, UCA. $540,000 = $8.48 million CPI 2009. Thomas B. Appleget, notes of meeting with JHB, 16 June 1932, RF/RG 1.1/series 216R, subseries Univ. of Chicago, Oriental Inst., box 17, folder 238, RAC. On lavishness and extravagance: Thomas B. Appleget, file memorandum, "Afternoon Spent with Dr. James H. Breasted . . . ," 21 November 1932, RF/RG 1.1/series 216R, subseries Univ. of Chicago, Oriental Inst., box 17, folder 238, RAC; JDR Jr. to RBF, 20 August 1935, RFA/RG 2, OMR/JDR Jr. series, Educational Interests subseries, box 111, Univ. of Chicago, Oriental Inst., Env. 1, RAC.

44. The film company was ERPI, Electrical Research Products, Inc. On its history and relationship with Chicago: Paul Saettler, *The Evolution of American Educational Technology*, rev. ed. (Englewood, CO: Libraries Unlimited, 1990), 104–5. CB to Gordon J. Laing, 4 February 1932, PP 1920–1980, 29:19, UCA; and JHB to HHN, 7 March 1933, DOC. JHB's reservations are conveyed in JHB to CB, 14 February 1932, JHBP. $12,000 = $188,000 CPI 2009.

45. John Larson to Jeffrey Abt, 7 November 2002. JHB, diary entries, 15 February to 13 March 1933, JHBP. No doubt the Breasteds' daughter would have joined the flight, but she was in college at Vassar. The cinematographer was Reed Haythorne (1904–87), who was associated with a handful of subsequent educational and entertainment films. On Imperial Airways and the plane (an Avro 618 Ten): http://www.imperial-airways.com (accessed July 2009). On the film's completion date: JHB to GEH, 9 May 1934, GEHP. The film's original length is variously listed as seventy-two or seventy minutes: http://imdb.com, s.v. *The Human Adventure* (accessed July 2009); and http://tcm.com/tcmdb/, s.v. *The Human Adventure* (accessed July 2009). Announcement, *The Oriental Institute . . . Announces the Premiere Showing of the Human Adventure*, [ca. early May 1934], GEHP. The premiere and a second showing the next day were at International House, both as benefits for the University of Chicago Settlement.

46. *The Human Adventure*, produced by the Oriental Institute, University of Chicago [1934]. Script, direction, and narration by Charles Breasted; cinematography by Reed N. Haythorne; technical assistance by ERPI Picture Consultants, Inc. Quotations from the narrative are courtesy of the OI, and they are from a DVD copy of what may be the solitary surviving 16 mm print, generously provided to me by John Larson, archivist, OI. Felix Mendelssohn, *Die Hebriden* (The Hebrides, also called "Fingal's Cave"), op. 26, 1830–32. The film credits neither the music nor the orchestra that recorded it. I'm grateful to David Buch, University of Chicago, who identified the music by listening to the film's very scratchy audio track over the phone. On the Sinclair exhibit: http://cityclicker.net/chicfair/dinosaurs.html (accessed February 2010).

47. JHB to FB, [ca. November–December 1933], LtFHB, JHBP (emphasis JHB's).

48. W. A. MacKenzie to The [University of Chicago] President with enclosed report, "Young Boys, Youths and Men Working under Semi Slave Conditions . . . ," 26 September

1929, PP 1945–1950, 29:19, UCA. JHB to HHN, 21 October, and HHN to JHB, 13 November 1929, DOC. HHN, "Report on the Conditions under Which Workmen Are Employed at Medinet Habu," 13 November 1929, DOC. JHB to David H. Stevens, 6 December 1929, PP 1945–1950, 29:19, UCA. David H. Stevens to W. A. MacKenzie, 10 December 1929, DOC. The secretary-general's quote is from W. A. MacKenzie to David H. Stevens, 10 January 1930, PP 1945–1950, 29:19, UCA. J. M. de Morsier to David H. Stevens with enclosure, 31 January 1930, W. A. McKnight to W. A. MacKenzie, 7 February 1930, PP 1945–1950, 29:19, UCA. HHN to JHB, 13 February 1930, DOC. On the architectural survey: *TOI*, 169–86. *WWWE*, s.v. "Uvo Hölscher." The "hobgoblin" quote is from JHB, diary entry, 2–5 June 1925, JHBP. Wilson, *Thousands of Years*, 66.

On the Iraq and Persepolis expeditions during JHB's lifetime: *TOI*, 310–77. Pinhas Delougaz and Thorkild Jacobsen, "Henri Frankfort," *Journal of Near Eastern Studies* 14, no. 1 (January 1955): 1–3; David Wengrow, "The Intellectual Adventure of Henri Frankfort: A Missing Chapter in the History of Archaeological Thought," *American Journal of Archaeology* 103, no. 4 (October 1999): 597–613. Ann C. Gunter and Stefan R. Hauser, eds., *Ernst Herzfeld and the Development of Near Eastern Studies, 1900–1950* (Leiden: Brill, 2005).

49. "Story of Man Is Put in a Talkie by Dr. Breasted," *Chicago Daily Tribune*, 2 June 1934. F. S. N., "At Carnegie Hall. The Human Adventure . . . ," *New York Times*, 30 October 1935. On the Parents Associations endorsement: announcement, "The First New York Presentation of 'The Human Adventure' . . . ," [ca. October] 1935, RF/RG 1.1/series 216R, subseries Univ. of Chicago, Oriental Inst., box 18, folder 243, RAC. On Carnegie attendance: M. Murray Weisman to Wendell G. Shields, 1 November 1935, RF/RG 1.1/series 216R, subseries Univ. of Chicago, Oriental Inst., box 18, folder 243, RAC. On the New Jersey showings: M. Ernest Townsend to CB, 5 November 1935, RF/RG 1.1/series 216R, subseries Univ. of Chicago, Oriental Inst., box 18, folder 243, RAC. On publicity and earnings reports: Wendell G. Shields to Warren Weaver, 22 October, and CB to David H. Stevens, 5 November 1935, RF/RG 1.1/series 216R, subseries Univ. of Chicago, Oriental Inst., box 18, folder 243, RAC. The film continued to remain in circulation well into the late 1940s at least: "'The Human Adventure' Is Next on Forum Association Film Series," *The Argus* (of Illinois Wesleyan University) 45, no. 20 (7 March 1939); and Helen Clifford Gunter, "Audio-Visual Aids and the Classics," *Classical Journal* 44, no. 2 (November 1948): 152.

50. JHB to Max Mason, 1 March 1934, RF/RG 1.1/series 216R, subseries Univ. of Chicago, Oriental Inst., box 17, folder 240, RAC. JHB to JDR Jr., 1 March, JHB to David H. Stevens, 6 March, JDR Jr. to Thomas B. Appleget, 12 March 1935, RF/RG 1.1/series 216R, subseries Univ. of Chicago, Oriental Inst., box 18, folder 241, RAC. On winding down the OI: David H. Stevens, minutes of staff conference, 13 June 1935, RF/RG 1.1/series 216R, subseries Univ. of Chicago, Oriental Inst., box 18, folder 242, RAC. JHB to CB, 13 August 1935, JHBP. JHB to David H. Stevens, 12 August, and JDR Jr. to Max Mason, 16 August 1935, RF/RG 1.1/series 216R, subseries Univ. of Chicago, Oriental Inst., box 18, folder 243, RAC. JDR Jr. to RBF, 20 August 1935, RFA/RG 2, OMR/JDR Jr. series, Educational Interests subseries, box 111, Univ. of Chicago, Oriental Inst., env. 1, RAC. David H. Stevens, minutes of staff conference, 20 September 1935, RF/RG 1.1/series 216R, subseries Univ. of Chicago, Oriental Inst., box 18, folder 243, RAC.

51. For a detailed analysis of the OI's budget history up to that point: meeting minutes, Rockefeller Foundation Executive Committee, 11 December 1935, RF/RG 1.1/series 216R, subseries Univ. of Chicago, Oriental Inst., box 17, folder 235, RAC. $660,000 = $10.3 million CPI 2009. JHB to JDR Jr., 25 October 1935, DOC. JDR Jr. to JHB, 26 November 1935, RFA/RG 2, OMR/JDR Jr. series, Educational Interests subseries, box 111, Univ. of Chicago, Oriental Inst., env. 1, RAC. On JHB's never seeing JDR Jr.'s reply: CB to JDR Jr., 11 December 1935, RFA/RG 2, OMR/JDR Jr. series, Educational Interests subseries, box 111, Univ. of Chicago, Oriental Inst., env. 3, RAC. JDR Jr. to CB, 19 December 1935, RFA/RG 2, OMR/JDR Jr. series, box 49, Friends and Services, Friends and Relations, James H. Breasted, RAC; and JDR Jr. to CB, 19 December 1935, RFA/RG 2, OMR/JDR Jr. series, Educational Interests

subseries, box 111, Univ. of Chicago, Oriental Inst., env. 3, RAC. $15 million = $234 million CPI 2009.

52. JHB to GEH, 9 May 1934, GEHP. "Mrs. Breasted, Wife of Noted Orientalist, Dies," *Chicago Daily Tribune*, 16 July 1934. "Simple Service Conducted for Mrs. Breasted," *Chicago Daily Tribune*, 18 July 1934. *PttP*, 218–19, 411. She was cremated and her ashes buried in her parents' plot in the Mountain View Cemetery, Oakland, California. See David Johnson, "Mountain View Cemetery," http://files.usgwarchives.org/ca/alameda/cemeteries/mtvview -b2.txt (accessed August 2009). Credit goes to John Larson, archivist, OI, for discerning the connections that led from the burial plots of George and Helen Watkins Hart to those of their daughters, including FB.

53. *PttP*, 411–13. JHB, "Interpreting the Orient," *Saturday Review* 12, no. 11 (13 July 1935): 3–4, 14. *Contemporary Authors Online*, s.v. "Will(iam) (James) Durant." JHB saluted Durant's literary style and skills at synthesis but criticized his factual errors. JHB, manuscript, "Bronze Base of a Statue of Ramses VIth Discovered at Megiddo: A Preliminary Report," 23 February 1935, JHB section in Pamphlet Files, OI Library. The manuscript remains unpublished. "Dr. J. H. Breasted Weds Sister of His First Wife," *Chicago Daily Tribune*, 8 June 1935. Imogen died in 1961 and was buried alongside her sister, FB, and their parents in Oakland, California: David Johnson, "Mountain View Cemetery," http://files.usgwarchives.org/ ca/alameda/cemeteries/mtvview-b2.txt (accessed August 2009). On boosting morale: HHN to JHB, 23 October 1932, DOC; on the visit: HHN to CB, 30 November 1935, DOC; on JHB's exercise routine and competitions with OI staff: JHB, diary entry, 30 April 1933, JHBP. The "daily dozen" was a set of exercises developed for the navy during the First World War by sports entrepreneur Walter Camp: *Dictionary of American Biography*, Base Set 1928–36, s.v. "Walter Chauncey Camp."

54. JHB to "Children," 21 November 1935, JHBP. On the busy-life quote: George Sarton, "James Henry Breasted (1865–1935): The Father of American Egyptology," *Isis* 34, no. 4 (Spring 1943): 290. On the harness quote: John A. Wilson to HHN, 30 December 1935, DOC. "Prof. Breasted Famous U. of C. Historian, Dies," *Chicago Daily Tribune*, 3 December 1935; and "Dr. Breasted Dies; Noted Orientalist," *New York Times*, 3 December 1935. *PttP*, 348–49, 412–13. For one of many efforts to debunk the curse story that includes a statement from JHB: James, *Howard Carter*, 426–28. The Associated Press, in trying to downplay the story while reporting JHB's death, nonetheless gave it a fair amount of column space: Associated Press, "Breasted Dies; Pharaoh Tomb 'Curse' Derided," *Washington Post*, 3 December 1935.

Percy E. Newberry to CB, 3 December 1935, JHBP. A. V. Kidder to CB, 16 December [1935], JHBP. *Dictionary of American Biography*, supplement 7: 1961–65, s.v. "Alfred Vincent Kidder." Lord Edmund H. H. Viscount and Lady Allenby to CB, [ca. 3 December], and M. Amine Youssef [Egyptian minister to the US] to CB, 4 December 1935, JHBP. The "humble folk" quote is from HHN to Imogen Breasted, 6 December 1935, JHBP. Hamed Abdalla to CB, 19 December 1935, JHBP. Caroline Ransom Williams to Imogen Breasted, 4 December 1935, JHBP. HHN to John A. Wilson, 10 December 1935, DOC. The quote from a student of a student is in A. Philip Tuttle to O. R. Sellers, 3 December 1935, JHBP. Tuttle apparently studied with Sellers (who forwarded the former's letter to CB) at the Presbyterian (later McCormick) Theological Seminary in Chicago, and Sellers took "Egyptian classes" for three years as an undergraduate with JHB: O. R. Sellers to CB, 5 December 1935, JHBP. Ovid Rogers Sellers (1884–1975), who took his doctorate at Johns Hopkins, went on to become a prominent Old Testament scholar and archaeologist.

55. On JHB's wishes, see CB to HHN, 16 December 1935, DOC; and "Dr. Breasted Dies; Noted Orientalist," *New York Times*, 3 December 1935. JHB's ashes were interred in May 1937: CB to HHN, 1 July 1937, JHBP.

JHB's estate came to a bit over $180,000, including JDR Jr.'s gift but not real estate or other property. CB was the executor. Estate of James H. Breasted, deceased (as of 2 December 1935), [ca. December 1935], JHBP. $180,000 = $2.79 million CPI 2009. JDR Jr. transferred his $100,000 gift, plus $2,000 accumulated interest, to the Breasted estate about two months

after JHB's death: CB to Robert W. Gumbel, 31 January 1936, RFA/RG 2, OMR/JDR Jr. series, box 49, Friends and Services, Friends and Relations, James H. Breasted Gift, RAC. Other
possessions, including a "corner cabinet made by Dr. Breasted" and sixty-three "17th and
18th century oriental rugs" he collected, were sold at auction: "Auction, Extraordinary, The
Personal Collection and Home Furnishings of Professor James H. Breasted," *Chicago Daily
Tribune*, 25 May 1936. JHB's scholarly library went to his son James, who was then preparing
for a career in archaeology before later turning to art history. The other books were sold at
auction: "Put Collection of Dr. Breasted Up for Auction," *Chicago Daily Tribune*, 24 May 1936.
A portion of JHB's professional library, including offprints and ephemera, went to the OI:
[John A. Wilson and James Henry Breasted Jr.], contract, "Agreement . . . between Breasted
and the University of Chicago," 18 August 1937, JHBP. After completion of Chicago's Regen-
stein Library in 1968 and the ensuing consolidation of several departmental libraries, the
OI's holdings were transferred there. File cabinets containing offprints and ephemera, includ-
ing JHB's materials, were returned to the OI and are now distributed throughout: Pamphlet
Files, OI Library.

   CB distributed possessions of JHB to the latter's friends, including a stone scarab CB
gave to Theodore W. Robinson. In an accompanying note CB wrote: "This piece my father
prized more than any antiquity in his possession. [It has] the name of my father's favorite
personage, King Ikhnaton. . . . A hundred thousand times I have seen him fingering" it.
FB had found and purchased it from a Cairo dealer for JHB. CB to Theodore W. Robinson,
19 May 1936, JHBP. Robinson was a wealthy industrialist and collector of ancient glass, and
part of his collection ended up at the Art Institute of Chicago: "T. W. Robinson, Retired Steel
Executive, Dies," *Chicago Daily Tribune*, 31 December 1948; "Art Institute Opens Show of Ancient Glass," *Chicago Daily Tribune*, 3 July 1940.

   On details of the memorial: *Service in Memory of James Henry Breasted*, "Reprint of Program" (Chicago: University of Chicago, 1 April 1936). The copy I saw is in Biographical Files:
J. H. Breasted, UCA.

   56. On CB's departure plans: CB to JDR Jr., 11 December 1935, RFA/RG 2, OMR/JDR Jr.
series, Educational Interests subseries, box 111, Univ. of Chicago, Oriental Inst., Env. 3, RAC.
For Hutchins on Wilson quote: Max Mason, interview notes, 4–7 June 1934, RF/RG 1.1/se-
ries 216R, subseries Univ. of Chicago, Oriental Inst., box 17, folder 240, RAC. On grooming
Wilson: JHB to HHN, 22 November 1934, DOC. Frederic C. Woodward to Board of Trustees,
University of Chicago, 5 December 1935, H. H. Swift Papers, 168:13, UCA. Rockefeller officials also raced to cope with the new circumstances: David H. Stevens, interview notes, 16
and 20 December 1935, RF/RG 1.1/series 216R, subseries Univ. of Chicago, Oriental Inst.,
box 18, folder 243, RAC. On Wilson's and CB's transitions: Robert M. Hutchins to Max Mason, 21 January 1936, RF/RG 1.1/series 216R, subseries Univ. of Chicago, Oriental Inst., box
18, folder 244, RAC. On Wilson's first couple of years as director: Wilson, *Thousands of Years*,
74–80.

   57. On university attitudes regarding the OI's funding: RBF to CB, 27 March, and CB to
RBF, 31 March 1952, JHBP. See also RBF, *Adventures in Giving*, 237. W. B. Devall, "The Academic Entrepreneurs: New Men of Power," *Liberal Education* 54, no. 4 (1968): 566–72. [John
A. Wilson and CB], report, "The Oriental Institute, Financial Report [revised]," 2 March 1936,
H. H. Swift Papers, 168:6, UCA. Trevor Arnett, diary notes, 9 March 1936, RF/RG 1.1/series
216R, subseries Univ. of Chicago, Oriental Inst., box 18, folder 244, RAC. BTM, 12 March
1936, 26:33, UCA.

   58. Minutes, Rockefeller Foundation Board of Trustees, 15 April 1936, RF/RG 1.1/series
216R, subseries Univ. of Chicago, Oriental Inst., box 17, folder 235, RAC. BTM, 14 May 1936,
26:49–51, 53, UCA. [John A. Wilson], report, "Financial History of the Oriental Institute,"
20 May 1936, H. H. Swift Papers, 106:11, UCA. $205,000 = $3.17 million CPI 2009. On OI
publications: John A. Wilson, "Plans for the Immediate Future of the Oriental Institute,"
15 July 1936, RF/RG 1.1/series 216R, subseries Univ. of Chicago, Oriental Inst., box 18,
folder 244, RAC. On Chicago Houses: HHN to CB, 31 March 1937, JHBP. On Wilson's confi-

dential communications with JDR Jr.: John A. Wilson to JDR Jr., 3 February 1937, RF/RG 1.1/series 216R, subseries Univ. of Chicago, Oriental Inst., box 18, folder 245, RAC. On vital features: JDR Jr. to CB, 19 December 1935, RFA/RG 2, OMR/JDR Jr. series, Educational Interests subseries, box 111, Univ. of Chicago, Oriental Inst., env. 3, RAC. On the endowment transfer: Harold H. Swift, "Oriental Institute," 7 December 1953, H. H. Swift Papers, 106:11, UCA. See also John D. Rockefeller to Trustees of the University of Chicago, 30 September 1930, inserted in BTM, 9 October 1930, 20:[n.p.], UCA. Former OI director William Sumner believed the OI's current annual allocation from the university might be greater than would be the yearly investment income if the endowments remained in place: telephone interview, William Sumner and Jeffrey Abt, 16 June 1994. For the most accurate accounting of the combined Rockefeller gifts and grants for OI: Dana S. Creel to JDR Jr., memorandum, "Dr. Breasted's Work and the Oriental Institute," 23 March 1959, RFA/RG 2, OMR/JDR Jr. series, subseries Educational Interests, box 111, Univ. of Chicago, Oriental Inst., env. 3, RAC. On the OI's development through the late 1940s and related changes in mission: Thorkild Jacobsen and John A. Wilson, "The Oriental Institute: Thirty Years and the Present," *Journal of Near Eastern Studies* 8 (January–October 1949): 236–47.

59. On the RBF quote: "The Oriental Institute: The New Building Dedicated," *University [of Chicago] Record*, new ser., 18, no. 1 (January 1932): 6. On renaming the building: BTM, 13 February 1936, 26:17, UCA. On the OI's activities today: http://oi.uchicago.edu/ (accessed July 2010). See in particular the links under "Research": "Research Projects," "Publications," "CAMEL," and "Computer Laboratory." In a move that would have intrigued and delighted JHB, the OIA is making an increasing number of its publications available online and as free, downloadable pdf files via the catalog link: http://oi.uchicago.edu/research/pubs/catalog/ (accessed August 2010; note that the free pdf versions are designated with a special icon).

60. *PttP*. Reviews of the biography were generally favorable, but nearly all commented on certain problems. Herbert Jenkins neatly captured the most common sentiments: "The chief defect is a lack of dates. . . . The style (like the title) is sometimes tiresomely journalistic. . . . There is a certain amount of autobiography scattered through the book, but perhaps this was inevitable; what there is is quite interesting, but rather irrelevant. We could have wished instead for a little more about the work of the Oriental Institute and of Breasted the Archeologist. But we are grateful for the life of Breasted the Man": Jenkins, "In the Morning of Man," *Times Literary Supplement*, 29 November 1947. See also Nelson, "Biography"; John T. Frederick, "A Life of James Breasted, Historian and Orientalist," *Chicago Sun*, 16 May 1943; Orville Prescott, "Books of the Times," *New York Times*, 12 April 1943; Sarton, "James Henry Breasted"; and H. P. Lazarus, "By Way of Egypt," *The Nation* 157, no. 2 (10 July 1943): 50. The *SS James Henry Breasted* was launched in February 1944 and sank after being bombed the following December: http://www.usmm.org/libertyships.html (accessed July 2009). The Breasted Prize was endowed by Joseph O. Losos: see http://historians.org/prizes/index. cgm?PrizeAbbrev=BREASTED (accessed February 2007). For the Emerson quote: Ralph Waldo Emerson, "Self-Reliance," in *The Collected Works of Ralph Waldo Emerson*, ed. Alfred R. Ferguson and Jean Ferguson Carr (Cambridge, MA: Belknap Press of Harvard University Press, 1979), 2:35–36. On JHB's relationship to the past: Lazarus, "By Way of Egypt," 50.

61. The quotes are from, respectively: *WWWE*, s.v. "James Henry Breasted"; G. Ernest Wright, "The Phenomenon of American Archaeology in the Near East," in *Near Eastern Archaeology in the Twentieth Century: Essays in Honor of Nelson Glueck*, ed. James A. Sanders (New York: Doubleday, 1970), 16; Albright, "James Henry Breasted," 298; William Foxwell Albright, "How Well Can We Know the Ancient Near East?" in *History, Archaeology, and Christian Humanism* (New York: McGraw-Hill, 1963), 129; Kuklick, *Puritans*, 112; and Sarton, "James Henry Breasted," 289. Pearl Buck was a novelist and essayist who won a Nobel Prize in literature and a Pulitzer Prize, principally for her writings about Chinese peasant life, and she is widely credited for expanding understanding of China in America and Europe. *Concise Dictionary of American Literary Biography*, supplement: Modern Writers, 1900–98, s.v. "Pearl S. Buck." Stephen L. Dyson, "An American Pioneer," *Archaeology* 51, no. 1 (January–

February 1998): 8. The Archaeological Institute of America was established in 1879: Stephen L. Dyson, *Ancient Marbles to American Shores: Classical Archaeology in the United States* (Philadelphia: University of Pennsylvania Press, 1998). The founding date of the Rockford chapter of the Archaeological Institute is unknown, but it remains active to this day and takes pride in JHB's connection with the city: http://www.rockfordaia.org/ (accessed July 2009).

Epitaph

1. *PttP*, 412. CB to F. Sidney Mariner, 11 July, and F. Sidney Mariner to CB, 17 July 1936, JHBP. For a concise overview and bibliography on American burial traditions: Elisabeth Walton Potter and Beth M. Boland, "Burial Customs and Cemeteries in American History," in *Guidelines for Evaluating and Registering Cemeteries and Burial Places*, National Register Bulletin, no. 41 (Washington, DC: US Department of the Interior, 1992), 3–7. HHN to CB, 31 March and 21 April, and CB to HHN, 1 July 1937, JHBP.

2. CB to HHN, 1 July, HHN to CB, 7 July, and CB to HHN, 9 July 1937, JHBP. On the stone's condition and inscription: CB to W. A. Tobinson, 16 July, and W. A. Tobinson to CB, 27 July 1937, JHBP. The memorial maker was Robert Trigg and Sons.

3. CB to Astrid B[reasted] Hoarmann, 12 August, and CB to James Henry Breasted Jr., 12 August 1937, JHBP. Carbon copies of the six epitaph versions were attached to the previous letters. Imogen Breasted to CB, 15 August, and James Henry Breasted Jr. to CB, 16 August 1937, JHBP.

4. On publicity surrounding the marker: CB to F. Sidney Mariner, 11 July 1936, JHBP. "An Enduring Stone," *Rockford Morning Star*, 20 January 1938. The paper is now the *Rockford Register Star*.

Bibliography

Archives

British Museum Archives
California Institute of Technology Archives
Carnegie Institution of Washington Archives
Chicago Theological Seminary Archives
Griffith Institute, Oxford University
National Academy of Sciences Archives
National Archives, United Kingdom
North Central College Archives
Oriental Institute Archives, University of Chicago
Rockefeller Archive Center
University of Chicago Archives

Cited Publications by Breasted

(For a more complete bibliography: Wilson, "James Henry Breasted, 1865–1935," under General Works.)

Breasted, James Henry. "Ancient Egypt and the Modern World." *History Teacher's Magazine* 8, no. 7 (September 1917): 214–15.

———, ed. and trans. *Ancient Records of Egypt: Historical Documents from the Earliest Times to the Persian Conquest*. 5 vols. Chicago: University of Chicago Press, 1906–7.

———. *Ancient Times: A History of the Early World, an Introduction to the Study of Ancient History and the Career of Early Man*. Boston: Ginn, 1916.

———. "Archaeology." In *Compton's Pictured Encyclopedia*, 1:249–54. Chicago: F. E. Compton, 1935.

———. "The Battle of Kadesh." In *Investigations Representing the Departments: Semitic Languages and Literatures, Biblical and Patristic Greek*. Decennial Publications, 1st ser., vol. 5. Chicago: University of Chicago Press, 1904.

———. "The Bridgehead of Asia Minor." *The Nation* 106, no. 2762 (8 June 1918): 676–78.

———. Chapter 3, "The Foundation and Expansion of the Egyptian Empire"; chapter 4, "The Reign of Thutmose III"; chapter 5, "The Zenith of Egyptian Power and the Reign of Amenhotep III"; chapter 6, "Ikhnaton, the Religious Revolutionary"; chapter 7, "The Age of Ramses II"; chapter 8, "The Decline and Fall of the Egyptian Empire." In *The Egyptian and Hittite Empires to c. 1000 B.C.*, edited by J. B. Bury, S. A. Cook, and F. E. Adcock, vol. 2 of *The Cambridge Ancient History*, 40–195. Cambridge: Cambridge University Press, 1924.

———. *The Conquest of Civilization*. New York: Harper and Brothers, 1926.

———. *The Dawn of Conscience*. New York: Charles Scribner's Sons, 1933.

———. "De hymnis in solem sub Rege Amenophide IV conceptis." Ph.D. diss., Friedrich Wilhelm University [University of Berlin], 1894 [published Latin text].

———. "De hymnis in solem sub Rege Amenophide IV conceptis. Comparantur cum hymnis polytheismum professis." Ph.D. diss., Friedrich Wilhelm University [University of Berlin], [ca. May 1894, unpublished German text].

———. *Development of Religion and Thought in Ancient Egypt*. New York: Charles Scribner's Sons, 1912.

———. "The Earliest Internationalism." In *The Semicentenary Celebration of the Founding of the University of California, with an Account of Conference on International Relations*, 192–214. Berkeley: [University of California Press], 1919.

———. "The Earliest Social Prophet." *American Journal of Theology* 14 (1910): 114–16.

———. "The Edwin Smith Papyrus: An Egyptian Medical Treatise of the Seventeenth Century before Christ." *New York Historical Society Quarterly Bulletin* 6, no. 1 (April 1922): 3–31.

———. "The Edwin Smith Papyrus: Some Preliminary Observations." In *Recueil d'études égyptologiques dédiées à la mémoire de Jean-François Champollion . . .* , 385–429. Paris: E. Champion, 1922.

———. *The Edwin Smith Surgical Papyrus*. 2 vols. Oriental Institute Publications, nos. 3–4. Chicago: University of Chicago Press, 1930.

———. "Egypt and the Bible." *American Journal of Semitic Languages and Literatures* 27, no. 1 (October 1910): 95–96.

———. *Egypt through the Stereoscope: A Journey through the Land of the Pharaohs*. New York: Underwood & Underwood, 1905.

———. *Egyptian Art: Syllabus of a Course of Six Lecture-Studies*. University Extension, Lecture-Study Department Syllabus no. 120. Chicago: University of Chicago Press, 1898.

———. "Egyptian Dictionary, Germany's Great Contribution to Egyptology." *Current Encyclopedia: A Monthly Record of Human Progress* 1, no. 5 (November 1901): 598–600.

———. "Die Eigennamen auf dem Vatikanskarabäus Amenhoteps III." *Zeitschrift für ägyptische Sprache und Alterthumskunde* 39 (1901): 65–66.

———. "Feats of Old Egyptians Rival Modern Works of Engineers." *Popular Mechanics* 42, no. 3 (September 1924): 403–8.

———. "The First Philosopher." *The Monist* 12, no. 3 (April 1902): 321–36.

———. "First Preliminary Report of the Egyptian Expedition." *American Journal of Semitic Languages and Literatures* 23, no. 1 (October 1906): 1–64.

———. "Foreword." In *Medinet Habu, 1924–1928*, vii–xiv. Oriental Institute Communications, no. 5. Chicago: University of Chicago Press, 1929.

———. "Foreword." In *Medinet Habu*, vol. 1, *Earlier Historical Records of Ramses III*, ix–xi. Oriental Institute Publications, no. 8. Chicago: University of Chicago Press, 1930.

[———]. *A Historical Laboratory: How the Expert Historian Does His Work*. Boston: Ginn, 1922.

———. "Historical Tradition and Oriental Research." *Proceedings of the National Academy of Sciences* 10, no. 7 (15 July 1924): 289–94.

———. "History." In *Paths to Success: Sixteen Essays on Secondary School Subjects Written by Eminent Educators of America*, edited by Harold G. Black, 65–85. Boston: D. C. Heath, 1924.

———. *The History and Civilization of Egypt*. University Extension, Lecture-Study Department Syllabus no. 75. Chicago: University of Chicago Press, 1898.

———. *A History of Egypt: From the Earliest Times to the Persian Conquest*. New York: Charles Scribner's Sons, 1905.

———. *A History of the Ancient Egyptians*. New York: Charles Scribner's Sons, 1908.

———. "Ikhnaton." In *Encyclopaedia Britannica*, 14th ed. 1929.

———. "John Merlin Powis Smith." *University* [of Chicago] *Record*, new ser., 19, no. 1 (January 1933): 69–73.

———. "King Harmhab and His Sakkara Tomb." *Zeitschrift für ägyptische Sprache und Alterthumskunde* 38 (1900): 47–50.

———. "A Laboratory for the Investigation of Man." *Scribner's Magazine* 84, no. 5 (November 1928): 516–29.

———. "The Nations of the Ancient East." Review of *The Struggle of the Nations: Egypt, Syria, and Assyria*, by G. Maspero, edited by A. H. Sayce and translated by M. L. McClure. *The Dial* 22, no. 261 (1 May 1897): 282–84.

———. *A New Chapter in the Life of Thutmose III*. Untersuchungen zur Geschichte und Altertumskunde Aegyptens, vol. 2, no. 2. Kurt Sethe, gen. ed. Leipzig: J. C. Hinrichs, 1900.

———. "The New Crusade." *American Historical Review* 34, no. 2 (January 1929): 215–36.

———. *The New Egyptian Museum and Research Institute at Cairo*. [New York: privately printed], 1925.

———. "The New Past." *University* [of Chicago] *Record*, new ser., 6, no. 4 (October 1920): 237–56.

———. "The New Past." In *The New Past and Other Essays on the Development of Civilization*, edited by Edward H. Carter, 1–16. Oxford: Basil Blackwell, 1925.

———. "The Order of the Sentence in the Hebrew Portions of Daniel." *Hebraica* 7, no. 4 (July 1891): 245–52.

———. *Oriental Forerunners of Byzantine Painting: First-Century Wall Paintings from the Fortress of Dura on the Middle Euphrates*. Oriental Institute Publications, no. 1. Chicago: University of Chicago Press, 1924.

———. *The Oriental Institute*. University of Chicago Survey, vol. 12. Chicago: University of Chicago Press, 1933.

———. "The Oriental Institute of the University of Chicago." *American Journal of Semitic Languages and Literatures* 35, no. 4 (July 1919): 196–204.

———. *The Oriental Institute of the University of Chicago: A Beginning and a Program*. Chicago: University of Chicago Press, 1922.

———. "The Origins of Civilization." *Scientific Monthly* 9, nos. 4–6, and 10, nos. 1–3, October 1919–March 1920.

———. "The Philosophy of a Memphite Priest." *Zeitschrift für ägyptische Sprache und Alterthumskunde* 39 (1901): 39–54.

———. "The Philosophy of a Memphite Priest." *Open Court* 17 (1903): 458–79.

———. "The Place of the Near Orient in the Career of Man and the Task of the American Orientalist." *Journal of the American Oriental Society* 39 (1919): 159–84.

———. "Ramses II and the Princes in the Karnak Reliefs of Seti I." *Zeitschrift für ägyptische Sprache und Alterthumskunde* 37 (1899): 130–39.

———. "A Reading Journey through Egypt." *Chautauquan* 56, no. 1, through 58, no. 3 (September 1909–May 1910).

———. "Recovering New History." *Scientific American* 138 (May 1928): 397–99.

———. Review of *A History of Egypt*, by E. A. W. Budge. *American Historical Review* 9, no. 1 (October 1903): 120–26.

————. Review of *A History of Egypt*, vol. 2, *The XVIIth and XVIIIth Dynasties*, by W. M. Flinders Petrie. *American Historical Review* 2, no. 2 (January 1897): 324–27.

————. Review of *The Ancient History of the Near East from the Earliest Times to the Battle of Salamis*, by H. R. Hall. *American Historical Review* 19, no. 3 (April 1914): 582–86.

————. Review of *The New History: Essays Illustrating the Modern Historical Outlook*," by James Harvey Robinson. *Journal of Philosophy, Psychology, and Scientific Methods* 9, no. 21 (10 October 1912): 585–87.

————. "The Rise of Man and Modern Research." In *Smithsonian Institution Annual Report for 1932*, 411–35. Washington, DC: U. S. Government Printing Office, 1933.

————. "Second Preliminary Report of the Egyptian Expedition." *American Journal of Semitic Languages and Literatures* 25, no. 1 (October 1908): 1–110.

————. "A Sketch of Egyptian History from the Fall of the Native Kings to the Persian Conquest." *Biblical World* 9, no. 6 (June 1897): 414–28.

————. "A Sketch of Egyptian History with Special Reference to Palestine Down to about 950 B.C." *Biblical World* 7, no. 6 (June 1896): 438–58.

————. *Some Experiences in the Tomb of Tutenkhamon*. Alumni Pamphlets, no. 2. Chicago: University of Chicago, 1924.

————. *The Story of the Nile-Dwellers: A Syllabus of a Course of Six Illustrated Lecture-Studies*. University Extension, Lecture-Study Department Syllabus no. 214. Chicago: University of Chicago Press, 1908.

Breasted, James Henry, and Carl F. Huth Jr. *A Teacher's Manual Accompanying the Breasted-Huth Ancient History Maps*. Chicago: Denoyer-Geppert, 1918.

Breasted, James Henry, Carl F. Huth Jr., and Samuel Bannister Harding, eds. *Ancient and European History Atlas, Reductions from Large Wall Maps*. Chicago: Denoyer-Geppert, [1920].

Breasted, James Henry, and James Harvey Robinson. *Outlines of European History, Part I*. Boston: Ginn, 1914.

Erman, Adolf. *Egyptian Grammar, with Table of Signs, Bibliography, Exercises for Reading, and Glossary*. Translated by James Henry Breasted. London: Williams and Norgate, 1894.

General Works

Abt, Jeffrey. "The Breasted-Rockefeller Egyptian Museum Project: Philanthropy, Cultural Imperialism, and National Resistance." *Art History* 19, no. 4 (December 1996): 551–72.

————. "Drawing over Photographs: James H. Breasted and the Scientizing of Egyptian Epigraphy, 1895–1928." *Visual Resources* 14, no. 1 (1998): 19–69.

————. "Toward a Historian's Laboratory: The Breasted-Rockefeller Museum Projects in Egypt, Palestine, and America." *Journal of the American Research Center in Egypt* 33 (1996): 173–94.

Abt, Jeffrey, and Richard A. Born. "A History of the Collection." In *A Guide to the Collection: The David and Alfred Smart Museum of Art, University of Chicago*, 13–19. New York: Hudson Hills, 1990.

Adams, Walter S. "George Ellery Hale, 1868–1938." *Biographical Memoirs* (National Academy of Sciences) 21, no. 5 (1940): 181–241.

Akin, William E. *Technocracy and the American Dream: The Technocrat Movement, 1900–1941*. Berkeley: University of California Press, 1977.

Albright, William Foxwell. "How Well Can We Know the Ancient Near East?" In *History, Archaeology, and Christian Humanism*, 103–29. New York: McGraw-Hill, 1963.

————. "James Henry Breasted, Humanist." *American Scholar* 5, no. 3 (Summer 1936): 287–99. Reprinted with revisions in *History, Archaeology, and Christian Humanism*, 217–28. New York: McGraw-Hill, 1963.

————. "Toward a Theistic Humanism." In *History, Archaeology, and Christian Humanism*, 3–61. New York: McGraw-Hill, 1963.

Allen, James P. "The American Discovery of Middle Kingdom Texts." In *The American Discov-*

ery of Ancient Egypt: Essays, edited by Nancy Thomas, 44–55. Los Angeles: Los Angeles County Museum of Art and American Research Center in Egypt, 1996.

Allen, Leslie H., ed. *Bryan and Darrow at Dayton: The Record and Documents of the "Bible-Evolution Trial."* 1925; reprint, New York: Russell and Russell, 1967.

[Arago, M. Dominique François Jean]. *Rapport de M. Arago sur le daguerréotype*. Paris: Bachelier, 1839.

Arnove, Robert F., ed. *Philanthropy and Cultural Imperialism: The Foundations at Home and Abroad*. Boston: G. K. Hall, 1980.

Assmann, Jan. *Moses the Egyptian: The Memory of Egypt in Western Monotheism*. Cambridge, MA: Harvard University Press, 1997.

Atkins, Gaius Glenn, and Frederick L. Fagley. *History of American Congregationalism*. Boston: Pilgrim, 1942.

Baines, John, and Jaromir Malek. *Cultural Atlas of Ancient Egypt*. Rev. ed. Abingdon, UK: Checkmark Books, 2000.

Ballerini, Julia. "The In Visibility of Hadji-Ishmael: Maxime Du Camp's 1850 Photographs of Egypt." In *The Body Imaged: The Human Form and Visual Culture since the Renaissance*, edited by Kathleen Adler and Marcia Pointon, 147–60. Cambridge: Cambridge University Press, 1993.

Banks, Edgar James. *Bismya; or, the Lost City of Adab*. New York: G. P. Putnam's Sons, 1912.

———. *A Plan for the Excavation of Mugheir, or Ur of the Chaldees, a Buried Babylonian City, the Birth-Place of the Biblical Abraham and Sarah*. Cambridgeport, MA: Louis F. Weston, [ca. 1889–1900].

Bashkin, Orit. "The Arab Revival, Archaeology, and Ancient Middle Eastern History." In *Pioneers to the Past: American Archaeologists in the Middle East, 1919–1920*, edited by Geoff Emberling, 91–100. Oriental Institute Museum Publications, no. 30. Chicago: Oriental Institute, University of Chicago, 2010.

Bell, Lanny. "The Epigraphic Survey and the Rescue of the Monuments of Ancient Egypt." In *The Ancient Eastern Mediterranean*, edited by Eleanor Guralnick, 7–15. Chicago: Archaeological Institute of America, 1990.

———. "The Epigraphic Survey: The Philosophy of Egyptian Epigraphy after Sixty Years' Practical Experience." In *Problems and Priorities in Egyptian Archaeology*, edited by Jan Assmann, Gunter Burkard, and Vivian Davies, 43–55. London: KPI, 1987.

———. "New Kingdom Epigraphy." In *The American Discovery of Ancient Egypt: Essays*, edited by Nancy Thomas, 96–109. Los Angeles: Los Angeles County Museum of Art and American Research Center in Egypt, 1996.

Bell, Lanny, William Murnane, and Bernard Fishman. "The Epigraphic Survey (Chicago House)." *NARCE (Newsletter of the American Research Center in Egypt)* 118 (1982): 3–18.

Bernhardsson, Magnus T. *Reclaiming a Plundered Past: Archaeology and Nation Building in Modern Iraq*. Austin: University of Texas Press, 2005.

Berque, Jacques. *Egypt: Imperialism and Revolution*. Translated by Jean Stewart. London: Faber and Faber, 1972.

Block, Jean F. *The Uses of Gothic: Planning and Building the Campus of the University of Chicago, 1892–1932*. Chicago: University of Chicago Library, 1983.

Bowler, Peter J. *Evolution: The History of an Idea*. Berkeley: University of California Press, 1984.

Boyer, John W. "'Broad and Christian in the Fullest Sense': William Rainey Harper and the University of Chicago." *University of Chicago Record* 40, no. 2 (5 January 2006): 2–26.

Breasted, Charles. *Pioneer to the Past: The Story of James H. Breasted, Archaeologist*. New York: Charles Scribner's Sons, 1943.

Breisach, Ernst A. *American Progressive History: An Experiment in Modernization*. Chicago: University of Chicago Press, 1993.

Bremner, Robert H. *American Philanthropy*. 2nd ed. Chicago: University of Chicago Press, 1988.

Brovarski, Edward. "Epigraphic and Archaeological Documentation of Old Kingdom Tombs and Monuments at Giza and Saqqara." In *The American Discovery of Ancient Egypt: Essays*, edited by Nancy Thomas, 24–43. Los Angeles: Los Angeles County Museum of Art and American Research Center in Egypt, 1996.

Brown, Ira V. "The Higher Criticism Comes to America, 1880–1900." *Journal of the Presbyterian Historical Society* 38, no. 4 (December 1960): 193–212.

Bryant, Marsha, and Mary Ann Eaverly. "Egypto-Modernism: James Henry Breasted, H.D., and the New Past." *Modernism/Modernity* 14, no. 3 (September 2007): 435–53.

Bull, Deborah, and Donald Lorimer. *Up the Nile: A Photographic Excursion, Egypt 1839–1898*. New York: Clarkson N. Potter, 1979.

Bull, Ludlow, Ephraim A. Speiser, and Albert T. E. Olmstead. "James Henry Breasted, 1865–1935." *Journal of the American Oriental Society* 56 (1936): 113–20.

Caminos, Ricardo A. "The Recording of Inscriptions and Scenes in Tombs and Temples." In *Ancient Egyptian Epigraphy and Palaeography*, 2nd ed., 3–25. New York: Metropolitan Museum of Art, 1979.

———. "The Talbotype Applied to Hieroglyphics." *Journal of Egyptian Archaeology* 52 (1966): 65–70.

[Carswell, John]. *Artists in Egypt: An Exhibition of Paintings and Drawings by Artists Employed by the Oriental Institute in Egypt, 1920–1935*. Chicago: Oriental Institute, University of Chicago, 1977.

Carter, Howard, and A. C. Mace. *The Tomb of Tut-Ankh-Amen: Discovered by the Late Earl of Carnarvon and Howard Carter*. London: Cassell, 1923.

Carter, Robert Lee. "The 'Message of the Higher Criticism': The Bible Renaissance and Popular Education in America, 1880–1925." Ph.D. diss., University of North Carolina at Chapel Hill, 1995.

[Champollion, Jean-François]. "Note remise au vice-roi pour la conservation des monuments de l'Égypte." In *Lettres écrites d'Égypte et de Nubie en 1828 et 1829*, 454–61. Paris: Didot Frères, 1829, 1833.

[Chicago Theological Seminary Board of Directors Committee]. *Chicago Theological Seminary: Quarter Centennial Historical Sketch*. Chicago: Jameson & Morse, 1879.

Clark, William. *Academic Charisma and the Origins of the Research University*. Chicago: University of Chicago Press, 2006.

Clifford, James. "On Orientalism." In *The Predicament of Culture: Twentieth-Century Ethnography, Literature, and Art*, 255–76. Cambridge, MA: Harvard University Press, 1988.

Cochrane, Rexmond C. *The National Academy of Sciences: The First Hundred Years, 1863–1963*. Washington, DC: National Academy of Sciences, 1978.

Colla, Elliott. *Conflicted Antiquities: Egyptology, Egyptomania, Egyptian Modernity*. Durham, NC: Duke University Press, 2007.

Collini, Stefan. Introduction to *The Two Cultures: And a Second Look*, by C. P. Snow, vii–lxxiii. Cambridge: Cambridge University Press, 1998.

Crawford, O. G. S. "A Century of Air-Photography." *Antiquity: A Quarterly Review of Archaeology* 28, no. 112 (December 1954): 206–10.

———. "History and Bibliography of Archaeology from the Air." In *Wessex from the Air*, edited by O. G. S. Crawford and Alexander Keiller, 3–7. Oxford: Clarendon, 1928.

Cremer, Robert Dale. "An Analysis of the Development of High School World History Textbooks and Enrollments from 1900 to 1959." Ph.D. diss., State University of South Dakota, 1963.

Crinson, Mark. *Empire Building: Orientalism and Victorian Architecture*. London: Routledge, 1996.

Crunden, Robert M. *Ministers of Reform: The Progressives' Achievement in American Civilization, 1889–1920*. New York: Basic Books, 1982.

Curl, James Stevens. *The Egyptian Revival: Ancient Egypt as the Inspiration for Design Motifs in the West*. London: Routledge, 2005.

———. *Egyptomania, the Egyptian Revival: A Recurring Theme in the History of Taste*. Manchester: Manchester University Press, 1994.

Curti, Merle. "Scholarship and Popularization of Learning." In *The Growth of American Thought*, 564–87. New York: Harper and Row, 1943.

Curtiss, Samuel Ives. *Franz Delitzsch: A Memorial Tribute*. Edinburgh: T. & T. Clark, 1891.

———. "Twenty-Five Years as a Seminary Professor, 1878–1903." *Chicago Seminary Quarterly* 37 (July 1903): 5–22.

Darrah, William C. *The World of Stereographs*. Gettysburg, PA: W. C. Darrah, 1977.

Davies, J. Keith, and Gerhard Fichtner. *Freud's Library: A Comprehensive Catalogue*. London: Freud Museum and Edition Diskord, 2006.

Davis, Thomas W. *Shifting Sands: The Rise and Fall of Biblical Archaeology*. Oxford: Oxford University Press, 2004.

Dawson, Warren R., Eric P. Uphill, and M. L. Bierbrier. *Who Was Who in Egyptology*. 3rd ed. London: Egypt Exploration Society, 1995.

De Buck, Adriaan. *The Egyptian Coffin Texts*. 7 vols. Oriental Institute Publications, nos. 34, 49, 64, 67, 73, 81, 87. Chicago: University of Chicago Press, 1935–61.

Degler, Carl N. *In Search of Human Nature: The Decline and Revival of Darwinism in American Social Thought*. Oxford: Oxford University Press, 1991.

DeNovo, John A. *American Interests and Policies in the Middle East, 1900–1939*. Minneapolis: University of Minnesota Press, 1963.

Description de l'Égypte. 19 vols. Paris: Imprimerie Impériale, 1809–28.

Deuel, Leo. *Flights into Yesterday: The Story of Aerial Archaeology*. New York: St. Martin's, 1969.

Dorman, Peter F. "Epigraphy and Recording." In *Egyptology Today*, edited by Richard H. Wilkinson, 77–97. Cambridge: Cambridge University Press, 2008.

Dorrell, Peter G. "The Early Days of Archaeological Photography." In *Photography in Archaeology and Conservation*, 1–7. Cambridge: Cambridge University Press, 1989.

Driver, G. R. "Oriental Studies and the Oriental Institute." *Oxford* 17, no. 2 (May 1961): 56–67.

Dupree, A. Hunter. "The National Academy of Sciences and the American Definition of Science." In *The Organization of Knowledge in Modern America, 1860–1920*, edited by Alexandra Oleson and John Voss, 342–63. Baltimore: Johns Hopkins University Press, 1979.

Dyson, Stephen L. "An American Pioneer." *Archaeology* 51, no. 1 (January–February 1998): 8.

Edwards, John Carver. *Patriots in Pinstripe: Men of the National Security League*. Washington, DC: University Press of America, 1982.

Emberling, Geoff. "Archaeology in the Middle East before 1920: Political Contexts, Historical Results." In *Pioneers to the Past: American Archaeologists in the Middle East, 1919–1920*, edited by Geoff Emberling, 15–20. Oriental Institute Museum Publications, no. 30. Chicago: Oriental Institute, University of Chicago, 2010.

———, ed. *Pioneers to the Past: American Archaeologists in the Middle East, 1919–1920*. Oriental Institute Museum Publications, no. 30. Chicago: Oriental Institute, University of Chicago, 2010.

Emberling, Geoff, and Emily Teeter. "The First Expedition of the Oriental Institute, 1919–1920." In *Pioneers to the Past: American Archaeologists in the Middle East, 1919–1920*, edited by Geoff Emberling, 31–84. Oriental Institute Museum Publications, no. 30. Chicago: Oriental Institute, University of Chicago, 2010.

Endesfelder, Erika. *Die Ägyptologie an der Berliner Universität—Zur Geschichte eines Fachgebietes*. Berlin: Humboldt-Universität zu Berlin, 1988.

The Epigraphic Survey. *Reliefs and Inscriptions at Karnak*. Vol. 4, *The Battle Reliefs of King Sety I*. Oriental Institute Publications, no. 107. Chicago: Oriental Institute, University of Chicago, 1986.

Fagan, Brian M. *The Rape of the Nile: Tomb Robbers, Tourists, and Archaeologists in Egypt*. London: MacDonald and Jane's, 1977.

Fischer, Henry G. "Archaeological Aspects of Epigraphy and Palaeography." In *Ancient Egyptian Epigraphy and Palaeography*, 27–50. New York: Metropolitan Museum of Art, 1976.

Flexner, Abraham. *Funds and Foundations: Their Policies Past and Present*. New York: Harper and Brothers, 1952.

Fosdick, Raymond B. *Adventures in Giving: The Story of the General Education Board*. New York: Harper and Row, 1962.

———. *Chronicle of a Generation: An Autobiography*. New York: Harper and Brothers, 1959.

———. *John D. Rockefeller, Jr.: A Portrait*. New York: Harper and Brothers, 1956.

———. *The Story of the Rockefeller Foundation*. Reprint of 1952 edition with introduction by Steven C. Wheatley. New Brunswick, NJ: Transaction Publishers, 1989.

Freud, Sigmund. *Moses and Monotheism*. Translated by Katherine Jones. New York: Alfred A. Knopf, 1939; reprint, New York: Vintage Books, 1967.

Fromkin, David. *A Peace to End All Peace: Creating the Modern Middle East, 1914–1922*. New York: Henry Holt, 1989.

Funk, Robert W. "The Watershed of the American Biblical Tradition: The Chicago School, First Phase, 1892–1920." *Journal of Biblical Literature* 95, no. 1 (March 1976): 4–22.

Gamwell, Lynn, and Peter Gay. *Sigmund Freud and Art: His Personal Collection of Antiquities*. Binghamton: State University of New York, 1989.

Gardiner, Alan. *My Working Years*. London: Coronet, 1962.

Gardiner, Margaret. "Tut'ankhamun and My Long-Lived Father." In *A Scatter of Memories*, 97–108. London: Free Association Books, 1988.

Gates, Frederick T. *Chapters in My Life*. New York: Free Press, 1977.

Gatewood, Willard B., Jr. *Controversy in the Twenties: Fundamentalism, Modernism, and Evolution*. Nashville: Vanderbilt University Press, 1969.

Gay, Peter. *Freud: A Life for Our Time*. New York: W. W. Norton, 1988.

Gelvin, James L. "The Middle East Breasted Encountered, 1919–1920." In *Pioneers to the Past: American Archaeologists in the Middle East, 1919–1920*, edited by Geoff Emberling, 21–29. Oriental Institute Museum Publications, no. 30. Chicago: Oriental Institute, University of Chicago, 2010.

Gibson, Shimon. "British Archaeological Institutions in Mandatory Palestine, 1917–1948." *Palestine Exploration Quarterly* 131 (July–December 1999): 115–43.

Gliddon, George R. *An Appeal to the Antiquaries of Europe on the Destruction of the Monuments of Egypt*. London: James Madden, 1841.

Goldman, Shalom. *God's Sacred Tongue: Hebrew and the American Imagination*. Chapel Hill: University of North Carolina Press, 2004.

Goode, James F. *Negotiating for the Past: Archaeology, Nationalism, and Diplomacy in the Middle East, 1919–1941*. Austin: University of Texas Press, 2007.

Goodspeed, George Stephen. *A History of the Ancient World*. New York: Charles Scribner's Sons, 1904.

———. *A History of the Babylonians and Assyrians*. New York: Charles Scribner's Sons, 1902.

Goodspeed, Thomas Wakefield. *A History of the University of Chicago: The First Quarter-Century*. 3rd ed. Chicago: University of Chicago Press, 1972.

———. *William Rainey Harper, First President of the University of Chicago*. Chicago: University of Chicago Press, 1928.

Gray, George W. *Education on an International Scale: A History of the International Education Board*. New York: Harcourt, Brace, 1941.

Greene, J. B. *Fouilles exécutées a Thèbes dans l'année 1855, textes hiéroglyphiques et documents inédits*. 2 vols. Paris: Librarie de Firmin Didot Frères, 1855.

Guilmant, Félix. *Le tombeau de Ramsès IX*. Cairo: Imprimerie de l'Institut Français d'Archéologie Orientale, 1907.

Guy, P. L. O. "Balloon Photography and Archaeological Excavation." *Antiquity: A Quarterly Review of Archaeology* 6, no. 22 (June 1932): 148–55.

Hale, George Ellery. *National Academies and the Progress of Research*. Lancaster, PA: New Era, 1915.

———. "The New Heavens." *Scribner's Magazine* 68, no. 4 (October 1920): 387–402.

———. *The New Heavens*. New York: Charles Scribner's Sons, 1922.

———. "Recent Discoveries in Egypt." *Scribner's Magazine* 74 (July 1923): 34–49.

———. *Ten Years' Work of a Mountain Observatory*. Washington, DC: Carnegie Institution, 1915.

———. "The Work of an American Orientalist." *Scribner's Magazine* 74 (October 1923): 392–404.

Hendricks, Luther V. *James Harvey Robinson, Teacher of History*. Morningside Heights, NY: King's Crown, 1946.

Hight, Eleanor M., and Gary D. Sampson, eds. *Colonialist Photography: Imag(in)ing Race and Place*. London: Routledge, 2002.

Hilton, Henry Hoyt. *Observations and Memories with Ginn and Company from Eighteen Ninety to Nineteen Forty-Six*. Boston: Ginn, 1947.

A History of the National Research Council. Reprint and Circular Series of the National Research Council. Washington, DC: National Research Council, 1933.

Holland, Thomas A., ed. *Publications of the Oriental Institute, 1906–1991*. Oriental Institute Communications, no. 26. Chicago: Oriental Institute, University of Chicago, 1991.

Hollis, Ernest Victor. *Philanthropic Foundations and Higher Education*. New York: Columbia University Press, 1938.

Hopkins, Clark. *The Discovery of Dura-Europos*. Edited by Bernard Goldman. New Haven, CT: Yale University Press, 1979.

Hornung, Erik. *Akhenaten and the Religion of Light*. Translated by David Lorton. Ithaca, NY: Cornell University Press, 1999.

Horowitz, Helen Lefkowitz. *Culture and the City: Cultural Philanthropy in Chicago from the 1880s to 1917*. Lexington: University Press of Kentucky, 1976.

Hourani, Albert. *Islam in European Thought*. Cambridge: Cambridge University Press, 1991.

Howe, Barbara. "The Emergence of Scientific Philanthropy, 1900–1920: Origins, Issues, and Outcomes." In *Philanthropy and Cultural Imperialism: The Foundations at Home and Abroad*, edited by Robert F. Arnove, 25–54. Boston: G. K. Hall, 1980.

Howe, Kathleen Stewart. *Excursions along the Nile: The Photographic Discovery of Ancient Egypt*. Santa Barbara, CA: Santa Barbara Museum of Art, 1993.

Howes, Chris. *To Photograph Darkness: The History of Underground and Flash Photography*. Gloucester: Alan Sutton, 1989.

Hughes, George R. "The Epigraphic Survey—the Early Years." In *The Ancient Eastern Mediterranean*, edited by Eleanor Guralnick, 17–21. Chicago: Archaeological Institute of America, 1990.

Humbert, Jean-Marcel, Michael Pantazzi, and Christiane Ziegler. *Egyptomania: Egypt in Western Art, 1730–1930*. Ottawa: National Gallery of Canada, 1994.

Iliffe, J. H. "The Palestine Archaeological Museum, Jerusalem." *Museums Journal* 38, no. 1 (April 1938): 1–22.

Iversen, Erik. *The Myth of Egypt and Its Hieroglyphs in European Tradition*. 2nd ed. Princeton, NJ: Princeton University Press, 1993.

Jacobs, Quentin Snowden. "William Welles Bosworth: Major Works." MA thesis, Columbia University, 1988.

Jacobsen, Thorkild, and John A. Wilson. "The Oriental Institute: Thirty Years and the Present." *Journal of Near Eastern Studies* 8 (January–October 1949): 236–47.

James, T. G. H., ed. *Excavating in Egypt: The Egypt Exploration Society, 1882–1982*. Chicago: University of Chicago Press, 1982.

———. *Howard Carter: The Path to Tutankhamun*. Rev. pbk. ed. London: Tauris Parke, 2001.

Jammes, Andre, and Eugenia Parry Janis. *The Art of the French Calotype*. Princeton, NJ: Princeton University Press, 1983.

Jammes, Bruno. "John B. Greene, an American Calotypist." *History of Photography* 5, no. 4 (October 1981): 305–24.

Karl, Barry D., and Stanley N. Katz. "Donors, Trustees, Staffs: An Historical View, 1890–1930." In *The Art of Giving: Four Views on American Philanthropy*, 3–13. North Tarrytown, NY: Rockefeller Archive Center, 1979.

Karsh, Efraim, and Inari Karsh. *Empires of the Sand: The Struggle for Mastery of the Middle East, 1789–1923*. Cambridge, MA: Harvard University Press, 1999.

Kasdan, Lawrence, and George Lucas. *Raiders of the Lost Ark*. Revised third draft. University City, CA: Medway Productions, 1979.

Kendall, Timothy. "The American Discovery of Meroitic Nubia and the Sudan." In *The American Discovery of Ancient Egypt: Essays*, edited by Nancy Thomas, 150–67. Los Angeles: Los Angeles County Museum of Art and American Research Center in Egypt, 1996.

Keppel, Frederick Paul. "Philanthropy and Learning." In *Philanthropy and Learning, with Other Papers*, 3–30. New York: Columbia University Press, 1936.

Kersel, Morag M. "The Changing Legal Landscape for Middle Eastern Archeology in the Colonial Era, 1800–1930." In *Pioneers to the Past: American Archaeologists in the Middle East, 1919–1920*, edited by Geoff Emberling, 85–90. Oriental Institute Museum Publications, no. 30. Chicago: Oriental Institute, University of Chicago, 2010.

King, Philip J. *American Archaeology in the Mideast: A History of the American Schools of Oriental Research*. Philadelphia: American Schools of Oriental Research, 1983.

Kohler, Robert E. "A Policy for the Advancement of Science: The Rockefeller Foundation, 1924–29." *Minerva* 16, no. 4 (Winter 1978): 480–515.

Kohlstedt, Sally Gregory. "Museums on Campus: A Tradition of Inquiry and Teaching." In *The American Development of Biology*, edited by Ronald Rainger, Keith R. Benson, and Jane Maienschein, 15–47. Philadelphia: University of Pennsylvania Press, 1988.

Kuklick, Bruce. *Puritans in Babylon: The Ancient Near East and American Intellectual Life, 1880–1930*. Princeton, NJ: Princeton University Press, 1996.

Kuspit, Donald. "A Mighty Metaphor: The Analogy of Archaeology and Psychoanalysis." In *Sigmund Freud and Art: His Personal Collection of Antiquities*, edited by Lynn Gamwell and Peter Gay, 133–51. New York: State University of New York, 1989.

LaFollette, Marcel C. *Making Science Our Own: Public Images of Science, 1910–1955*. Chicago: University of Chicago Press, 1990.

The Land of the Pharaohs through the Perfecscope, Describing a Series of One Hundred Original Stereoscopic Photographs. New York: Underwood & Underwood, 1897.

Larson, John A. *Lost Nubia: A Centennial Exhibit of Photographs from the 1905–1907 Egyptian Expedition of the University of Chicago*. Oriental Institute Museum Publications, no. 24. Chicago: Oriental Institute, University of Chicago, 2006.

Lawler, Thomas B. *Seventy Years of Textbook Publishing: A History of Ginn and Company, 1867–1937*. Boston: Ginn, 1938.

Layard, Austen H. *Discoveries in the Ruins of Nineveh and Babylon; with Travels in Armenia, Kurdistan and the Desert: Being the Result of a Second Expedition*. New York: Harper and Brothers, 1859.

Laylander, O[range] J[udd]. *The Ginn Sketchbook*. Boston: Athenaeum, 1933.

Livingstone, David N. *Darwin's Forgotten Defenders: The Encounter between Evangelical Theology and Evolutionary Thought*. Grand Rapids, MI: Wm. B. Eerdmans, 1987.

Lund, Jon W. *Rockford: An Illustrated History*. Chatsworth, CA: Windsor Publications, 1989.

Lundgreen, Peter. "Differentiation in German Higher Education." In *The Transformation of the Higher Learning, 1860–1930: Expansion, Diversification, Social Opening, and Professionalization in England, Germany, Russia, and the United States*, edited by Konrad H. Jarausch, 149–79. Chicago: University of Chicago Press, 1983.

MacDonald, Sally, and Michael Rice. *Consuming Ancient Egypt*. London: Institute of Archaeology, UCL Press, 2003.

Madeira, Percy C., Jr. *Men in Search of Man: The First Seventy-Five Years of the University Museum of the University of Pennsylvania*. Philadelphia: University of Pennsylvania Press, 1964.

Marcanti, Ruth, comp. *The 1919/20 Breasted Expedition to the Near East: A Photographic Study*. Chicago: University of Chicago Press, 1977.

Marsden, George M. *Fundamentalism and American Culture: The Shaping of Twentieth-Century Evangelicalism, 1870–1925*. Oxford: Oxford University Press, 1980.

———. *The Soul of the American University: From Protestant Establishment to Established Nonbelief*. Oxford: Oxford University Press, 1994.

McCarthy, Kathleen D. "The Short and Simple Annals of the Poor: Foundation Funding for the Humanities, 1900–1983." *Proceedings of the American Philosophical Society* 129, no. 1 (March 1985): 3–8.

McGiffert, Arthur Cushman, Jr. *No Ivory Tower: The Story of the Chicago Theological Seminary*. Chicago: Chicago Theological Seminary, 1965.

Meade, C. Wade. *Road to Babylon: Development of U.S. Assyriology*. Leiden: E. J. Brill, 1974.

Meyer, Daniel Lee. "The Chicago Faculty and the University Ideal, 1891–1929." Ph.D. diss., University of Chicago, 1994.

Mitchell, Timothy. *Colonising Egypt*. Cambridge: Cambridge University Press, 1988; reprint, Berkeley: University of California Press, 1991.

Morgan, Lewis H. *Ancient Society; or, Researches in the Lines of Human Progress, from Savagery through Barbarism to Civilization*. New York: Henry Holt, 1877.

Morrison, Theodore. *Chautauqua: A Center for Education, Religion, and the Arts in America*. Chicago: University of Chicago Press, 1974.

Moss, Rosalind. "Some Rubbings of Egyptian Monuments Made a Hundred Years Ago." *Journal of Egyptian Archaeology* 27 (1941): 7–11.

Nelson, Harold H. "Biography of Prof. Breasted: One of Our Greatest Scholars." *Chicago Daily Tribune*, 11 April 1943.

———. "The Epigraphic Survey." In *Medinet Habu, 1924–1928*, 1–36. Oriental Institute Communications, no. 5. Chicago: University of Chicago Press, 1929.

———. "Introduction." In *Medinet Habu*, vol. 1, *Earlier Historical Records of Ramses III*, 1–10. Oriental Institute Publications, no. 8. Chicago: University of Chicago Press, 1930.

Newberry, Percy E., and F. L. Griffith. *El Bersheh*. Archaeological Survey of Egypt, nos. 3–4. London: Egypt Exploration Fund, [1893–1894?].

The 1905–1907 Breasted Expeditions to Egypt and the Sudan: A Photographic Study. 2 vols. Chicago: University of Chicago Press, 1975.

Olmstead, Albert T. E. "Breasted the Historian." *Open Court* 50, no. 936 (January 1936): 1–4.

"The Oriental Institute: The New Building Dedicated." *The University* [of Chicago] *Record*, new ser., 18, no. 1 (January 1932): 1–16.

O'Toole, Patricia. *When Trumpets Call: Theodore Roosevelt after the White House*. New York: Simon and Schuster, 2004.

Perez, Nissan N. *Focus East: Early Photography in the Near East, 1839–1885*. New York: Harry N. Abrams, 1988.

Phillips, C. H. *The School of Oriental and African Studies, University of London, 1917–1967: An Introduction*. London: School of Oriental and African Studies, University of London, 1967.

Pierce, Bessie Louise. *Public Opinion and the Teaching of History in the United States*. New York: Alfred A. Knopf, 1926.

Reeves, Nicholas. *The Complete Tutankhamun: The King, the Tomb, the Royal Treasure*. London: Thames and Hudson, 1990.

Reid, Donald Malcolm. "French Egyptology and the Architecture of Orientalism: Deciphering the Facade of Cairo's Egyptian Museum." In *Franco-Arab Encounters: Studies in Memory of David C. Gordon*, edited by L. Carl Brown and Matthew S. Gordon, 35–69. Beirut: American University of Beirut Press, 1996.

———. "Indigenous Egyptology: The Decolonization of a Profession?" *Journal of the American Oriental Society* 105, no. 2 (1985): 233–46.

———. "Nationalizing the Pharaonic Past: Egyptology, Imperialism, and Egyptian Nationalism, 1922–1952." In *Rethinking Nationalism in the Arab Middle East*, edited by James Jankowski and Israel Gershoni, 127–45. New York: Columbia University Press, 1997.

———. *Whose Pharaohs? Archaeology, Museums, and Egyptian National Identity from Napoleon to World War I.* Berkeley: University of California Press, 2002.

Reiner, Erica. *An Adventure of Great Dimension: The Launching of the Chicago Assyrian Dictionary.* Transactions of the American Philosophical Society, vol. 92, pt. 3. Philadelphia: American Philosophical Society, 2002.

Reingold, Nathan. "National Science Policy in a Private Foundation: The Carnegie Institution of Washington." In *The Organization of Knowledge in Modern America, 1860–1920*, edited by Alexandra Oleson and John Voss, 313–41. Baltimore: Johns Hopkins University Press, 1979.

[Reisner, George A.]. "George Andrew Reisner on Archeological Photography." Edited by Peter Der Manuelian. *JARCE* (*Journal of the American Research Center in Egypt*) 29 (1992): 1–34.

———. "James Henry Breasted: An Appreciation." *Egyptian Gazette*, 14 December 1935.

Revoldt, Daryl L. "Raymond B. Fosdick: Reform, Internationalism, and the Rockefeller Foundation." Ph.D. diss., University of Akron, 1982.

Rinsch, Albert E. "An Analysis of World History Textbooks for High Schools to Determine Modern Trends." MS thesis, Indiana State Teachers College, 1936.

Roberts, Clarence N. *A Clear and Steady Light: A Brief History of North Central College.* Naperville, IL: North Central College, 1981.

Robinson, James Harvey. *The New History: Essays Illustrating the Modern Historical Outlook.* 1912; reprint, Springfield, MA: Walden, 1958.

"Rockefeller Museum." In *Encyclopaedia Judaica.* Jerusalem: Keter, 1972.

Rogge, Allen E. "Little Archaeology, Big Archaeology: The Changing Context of Archaeological Research." Ph.D. diss., University of Arizona, 1983.

Roosevelt, Theodore. "The Dawn and Sunrise of History." *Outlook* 115, no. 7 (14 February 1917): 272–75.

———. "History as Literature." *American Historical Review* 18, no. 3 (April 1913): 473–89.

Rosenthal, Robert. "The Berlin Collection: A History." In *The Berlin Collection: Being a History and Exhibition . . . ,* 3–20. Chicago: University of Chicago Library, 1979.

Saettler, Paul. *The Evolution of American Educational Technology.* Rev. ed. Englewood, CO: Libraries Unlimited, 1990.

Said, Edward W. *Orientalism.* New York: Random House, 1978.

Sakr, Tarek Mohamed Refaat. *Early Twentieth-Century Islamic Architecture in Cairo.* Cairo: American University in Cairo Press, 1993.

Sarton, George. *The History of Science and the New Humanism.* New York: Henry Holt, 1931.

———. "James Henry Breasted (1865–1935): The Father of American Egyptology." *Isis* 34, no. 4 (Spring 1943): 289–91.

Savage, G. S. F. "A Chapter of the Early History of the Chicago Theological Seminary." *Illinois Society of Church History* 1 (1895): 11–23.

Sayyid-Marsot, Afaf Lutfi al-. *Egypt's Liberal Experiment: 1922–1936.* Berkeley: University of California Press, 1977.

Schenk, William P. "James Henry Breasted." *The Red and White of the Lake View High School of Chicago* (December 1932): 13, 26–27.

Schenkel, Albert F. *The Rich Man and the Kingdom: John D. Rockefeller, Jr., and the Protestant Establishment.* Harvard Theological Studies. Minneapolis: Fortress, 1995.

Scott, Donald M. "The Popular Lecture and the Creation of a Public in Mid-Nineteenth-Century America." *Journal of American History* 66, no. 4 (March 1980): 791–809.

Scott, Gerry D., III. "Go Down into Egypt: The Dawn of American Egyptology." In *The Ameri-*

can Discovery of Ancient Egypt, edited by Nancy Thomas, 37–47. Los Angeles: Los Angeles County Museum of Art, 1995.

Seares, Frederick H. "George Ellery Hale: The Scientist Afield." Isis 30, no. 2 (May 1939): 241–67.

Sellin, Ernst. Mose und seine Bedeutung für die israelitisch-jüdische Religionsgeschichte. Leipzig: A. Deichert, 1922.

Sethe, Kurt. Die altägyptischen Pyramidentexte: Nach den Papierabdrücken und Photographien des Berliner Museums. 4 vols. Leipzig: J. C. Hinrichs, 1908–22.

———. Die Thronwirren unter den Nachfolgern Königs Thutmosis' I., Ihr Verlauf und ihre Bedeutung. Untersuchungen zur Geschichte und Altertumskunde Aegyptens, vol. 1. Edited by Kurt Sethe. Leipzig: J. C. Hinrichs, 1896.

Silberman, Neil Asher. Between Past and Present: Archaeology, Ideology, and Nationalism in the Modern Middle East. New York: Henry Holt, 1989.

———. "Desolation and Restoration: The Impact of a Biblical Concept on Near Eastern Archaeology." Biblical Archaeologist 54, no. 2 (June 1991): 76–87.

———. Digging for God and Country: Exploration, Archeology, and the Secret Struggle for the Holy Land. New York: Alfred A. Knopf, 1982.

Snow, C. P. The Two Cultures: And a Second Look. Cambridge: Cambridge University Press, 1964.

Stolper, Matthew W. "The Chicago Assyrian Dictionary at Seventy." Oriental Institute News and Notes 129 (May–June 1991): 1–2, 10.

Storr, Richard J. Harper's University: The Beginnings. Chicago: University of Chicago Press, 1966.

Teeter, Emily, and Leslie Schramer. "Some Decorative Motifs of the Oriental Institute Building." Oriental Institute News and Notes 199 (Fall 2008): 14–19.

Terras, Karen. "James Henry Breasted and the Iraq Expedition: The People and Politics of the 1935 Division." Oriental Institute News and Notes 202 (Summer 2009): 3–6.

Thomas, Nancy. "American Institutional Fieldwork in Egypt, 1899–1960." In The American Discovery of Ancient Egypt, edited by Nancy Thomas, 49–75. Los Angeles: Los Angeles County Museum of Art and American Research Center in Egypt, 1995.

Trigger, Bruce G. "Egyptology, Ancient Egypt, and the American Imagination." In The American Discovery of Ancient Egypt, edited by Nancy Thomas, 21–35. Los Angeles: Los Angeles County Museum of Art and American Research Center in Egypt, 1995.

———. A History of Archaeological Thought. Cambridge: Cambridge University Press, 1989.

A Trip around the World. New York: Underwood & Underwood, 1899.

Underwood & Underwood's 1890 Stereoview Catalog and Other Documents. Edited by T. K. Treadwell. N.p.: Institute for Photographic Research, 1995.

Van Zanten, David. "Formulating Art History at Princeton and the 'Humanistic Laboratory.'" In The Early Years of Art History in the United States, edited by Craig Hugh Smyth and Peter M. Lukehart, 175–82. Princeton, NJ: Department of Art and Archaeology, Princeton University, 1993.

Veysey, Laurence R. The Emergence of the American University. Chicago: University of Chicago Press, 1965.

———. "The Plural Organized Worlds of the Humanities." In The Organization of Knowledge in Modern America, 1860–1920, edited by Alexandra Oleson and John Voss, 51–106. Baltimore: Johns Hopkins University Press, 1979.

Wainer, Howard. Graphic Discovery: A Trout in the Milk and Other Visual Adventures. Princeton, NJ: Princeton University Press, 2005.

Ward, Robert D. "The Origin and Activities of the National Security League, 1914–1919." Mississippi Valley Historical Review 47, no. 1 (June 1960): 51–65.

Washington, Peter. Madame Blavatsky's Baboon: A History of the Mystics, Mediums, and Misfits Who Brought Spiritualism to America. New York: Schocken Books, 1995.

Waterfield, Gordon. Layard of Nineveh. New York: Frederick A. Praeger, 1968.

Webster, Hutton. *Ancient History*. Boston: D.C. Heath, 1913.

Whitehouse, Helen. "Towards a Kind of Egyptology: The Graphic Documentation of Ancient Egypt, 1587–1666." In *Documentary Culture: Florence and Rome from Grand-Duke Ferdinand I to Pope Alexander VII*, edited by Elizabeth Cropper, Giovanna Perini, and Francesco Solinas, 63–79. Bologna: Nuova Elfa Editoriale, 1992.

Whitehouse, Helen, and Jaromir Malek. "A Home for Egyptology in Oxford." *Ashmolean* 16 (Summer–Autumn 1989): 8–9.

Wilson, John A. "James Henry Breasted—the Idea of an Oriental Institute." In *Near Eastern Archaeology in the Twentieth Century: Essays in Honor of Nelson Glueck*, edited by James A. Sanders, 41–56. New York: Doubleday, 1970.

———. "James Henry Breasted, 1865–1935." *Biographical Memoirs* (National Academy of Sciences) 18, no. 5 (1937): 93–121.

———. *Signs and Wonders upon Pharaoh: A History of American Egyptology*. Chicago: University of Chicago Press, 1964.

———. *Thousands of Years: An Archaeologist's Search for Ancient Egypt*. New York: Charles Scribner's Sons, 1972.

Wilson, Karen. *Bismaya: Recovering the Lost City of Adab*. Oriental Institute Publications, no. 137. Chicago: Oriental Institute, University of Chicago, 2010.

Wind, James P. *The Bible and the University: The Messianic Vision of William Rainey Harper*. Atlanta: Scholars Press, 1987.

Wissler, Clark. *The American Indian: An Introduction to the Anthropology of the New World*. New York: D. C. McMurtrie, 1917.

The World's Most Famous Court Trial: Tennessee Evolution Case. Cincinnati: National Book, 1925.

Wörterbuch der aegyptischen Sprache. Edited by Adolf Erman and Hermann Grapow. 7 vols. Leipzig: J. C. Hinrichs, 1926–63.

Wright, G. Ernest. "The Phenomenon of American Archaeology in the Near East." In *Near Eastern Archaeology in the Twentieth Century: Essays in Honor of Nelson Glueck*, edited by James A. Sanders, 3–40. New York: Doubleday, 1970.

Wright, Helen. *Explorer of the Universe: A Biography of George Ellery Hale*. New York: E. P. Dutton, 1966.

Yerushalmi, Yosef Hayim. *Freud's Moses: Judaism Terminable and Interminable*. New Haven, CT: Yale University Press, 1991.

Yurco, Frank J. "The Egyptian Collection and the Legacy of Edward E. Ayer." *Bulletin of the Field Museum of Natural History* 59, no. 10 (November 1988): 20–21.

Zeller, Eduard. *Die Philosophie der Griechen in ihrer geschichtlichen Entwicklung*. 3 vols. Leipzig: O. R. Reisland, 1879–1892.

Index